Rick Steves'

SPAIN

2005

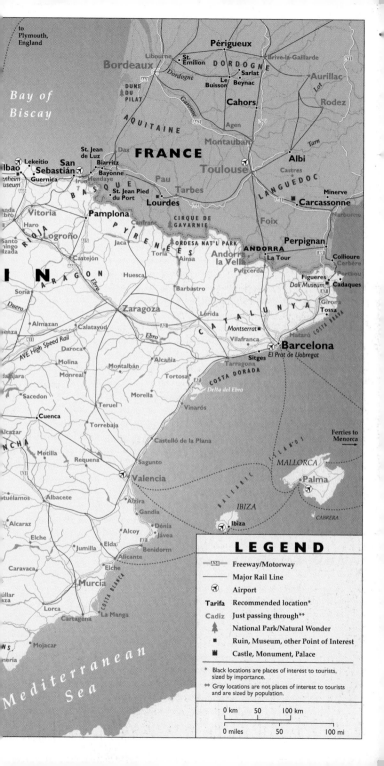

to
Plymouth,
England

Bay of
Biscay

Bilbao · Lekeitio
Blenheim Museum
San Sebastián
Vitoria · Guernica
Haro
Santo Domingo de la Calzada
RIOJA · Logroño
N · ARAGON
Soria · Almazan
Sigüenza
Guadalajara · Sacedon
Cuenca
Alcazar
Motilla
MANCHA · Requena
Alcaraz
Caravaca
Guadix · Baza
NS. · Mojacar
Vera

Bordeaux
Libourne · St. Émilion
DORDOGNE
Dordogne · Le Buisson
Sarlat
Beynac
DUNE DU PILAT
Garonne
Cahors
AQUITAINE
Agen
Montauban
Tarn
FRANCE
Dax · Toulouse
Albi
St. Jean de Luz · Biarritz
Bayonne
Hendaye · Irun
St. Jean Pied du Port
Pau
Tarbes
Castres
LANGUÉDOC
Lourdes
CIRQUE DE GAVARNIE
Foix
Narbonne
Minerve
Carcassonne
Pamplona
Canfranc
PYRENEES
Jaca · ORDESA NAT'L PARK
Torla · Ainsa
Andorra la Vella
ANDORRA
La Tour
Perpignan
Collioure
Cerbère
Portbou
Castejón · Huesca
Puigcerda
Figueres
Dali Museum
Cadaqués
Zaragoza · Barbastro
Lérida
CATALUNYA
Girona
Tossa
Calatayud · Ebro
Montserrat
COSTA BRAVA
Daroca
Molina · Alcañiz
Vilafranca
Mataró
Montalbán
Barcelona
Monreal · Tortosa
Sitges
El Prat de Llobregat
Teruel · Morella
Tarragona
COSTA DORADA
Torrebaja
Delta del Ebro
Vinarós
Castelló de la Plana
Ferries to Menorca
Sagunto
BALEARIC ISLANDS
MALLORCA
Valencia
Palma
Atzira
Gandia
BALEARIC
IBIZA
Albacete
Alcoy
Dénia
Jávea
Ibiza
CABRERA
Jumilla · Elda
Benidorm
Alicante
Elche
COSTA BLANCA
Murcia
Lorca
La Manga
Cartagena

Mediterranean Sea

LEGEND

═══ A24 ═══	Freeway/Motorway
────────	Major Rail Line
✈	Airport
Tarifa	Recommended location*
Cadiz	Just passing through**
🌲	National Park/Natural Wonder
■	Ruin, Museum, other Point of Interest
♜	Castle, Monument, Palace

* Black locations are places of interest to tourists,
sized by importance.

** Gray locations are not places of interest to tourists
and are sized by population.

0 km	50	100 km

0 miles	50	100 mi

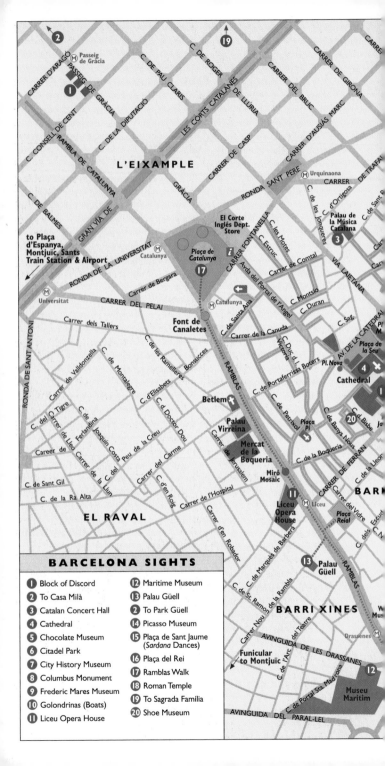

BARCELONA SIGHTS

1. Block of Discord
2. To Casa Milà
3. Catalan Concert Hall
4. Cathedral
5. Chocolate Museum
6. Citadel Park
7. City History Museum
8. Columbus Monument
9. Frederic Mares Museum
10. Golondrinas (Boats)
11. Liceu Opera House
12. Maritime Museum
13. Palau Güell
2. To Park Güell
14. Picasso Museum
15. Plaça de Sant Jaume (Sardana Dances)
16. Plaça del Rei
17. Ramblas Walk
18. Roman Temple
19. To Sagrada Família
20. Shoe Museum

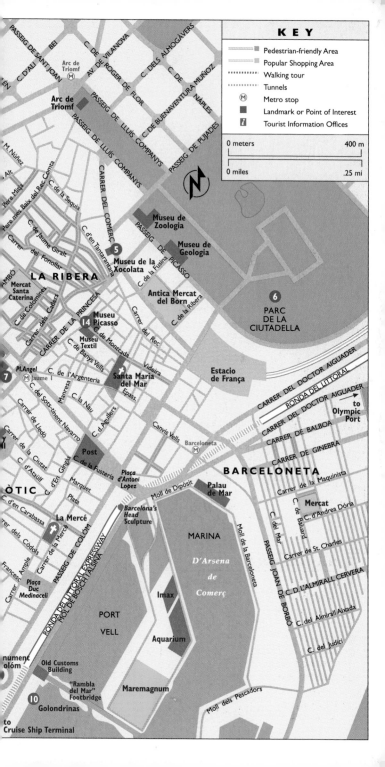

KEY

- Pedestrian-friendly Area
- Popular Shopping Area
- Walking tour
- Tunnels
- Ⓜ Metro stop
- Landmark or Point of Interest
- 𝒊 Tourist Information Offices

0 meters   400 m

0 miles   .25 mi

PASSEIG DE SANT JOAN
BEI
C. D'ALI
C. DE VILANOVA
AV. DE ROGER DE FLOR
C. DELS ALMOGÀVERS
C. DE BUENAVENTURA MUÑOZ

Arc de Triomf Ⓜ
Arc de Triomf
PASSEIG DE LLUÍS COMPANYS
C. DE NAPLES
PASSEIG DE PUJADES

M. Núñez
Alt
Pere Mitja
Baix del Rec Comta
Pere mes
C. de la Sequia
C. de Jaume Giralt
C. del Fonollar
PASSEIG DE LLUÍS COMPANYS
CARRER DEL COMERÇ
C. d'en Tamarantana
5
PASSEIG DE PICASSO

Museu de Zoologia

Museu de Geologia

Museu de la Xocolata
C. de la Fusina

ÀMBÒ
Mercat Santa Caterina
C. de Colomines
C. de les Caders
LA RIBERA

Antica Mercat del Born
C. de la Ribera

6
PARC DE LA CIUTADELLA

CARRER DE LA PRINCESA
14 **Museu Picasso**
C. de Montcada
Carrer del Rec

Museu Tèxtil
C. de Banys Vells

7
Pl. Angel
Ⓜ Jaume I
C. de l'Argenteria
Videira
★ **Santa Maria del Mar**
Epass.

Carrer del Sots-tinent Navarro
C. la Nau
Manresa
C. d'Aguilers
Canvis Vells
Barceloneta
Ⓜ

Estacio de França

CARRER DEL DOCTOR AIGUADER
RONDA DEL LITTORAL
CARRER DEL DOCTOR AIGUADER
→ to Olympic Port
CARRER DE BALBOA
CARRER DE GINEBRA

Carrer de Lledó
C. de la Ciutat
C. d'Arаüif
Gingst
C. del En
Marquet
Plata

Post
C. de la Fustería

Plaça d'Antoni López

BARCELONETA
Carrer de la Maquinista
Mercat
C. de Bаluard
C. d'Andrea Dória
PASSEIG JOAN DE BORBÓ
C. del Mar
Carrer de St. Charles
C. D. L'ALMIRALL CERVERA
C. del Almirall Aixada
C. del Judici

ÒTIC
C. d'en Carabassa
C. dels Codols
Francesc
Ample
Plaça Duc Medinaceli
Carrer

La Mercé ✝
Carrer de la Mercé
PASSEIG DE COLOM
MOLL DE BOSCH I ALSINA
RONDA DEL LITTORAL EXPRESSWAY

Palau de Mar

Moll de Dipòsit
Barcelona's Head Sculpture

MARINA

D'Arsena de Comerç

Moll de la Barceloneta

numenc olóm

Old Customs Building
"Rambla del Mar" Footbridge

10
Golondrinas

to Cruise Ship Terminal

PORT VELL

Imax

Aquarium

Maremagnum

Moll dels Pescadors

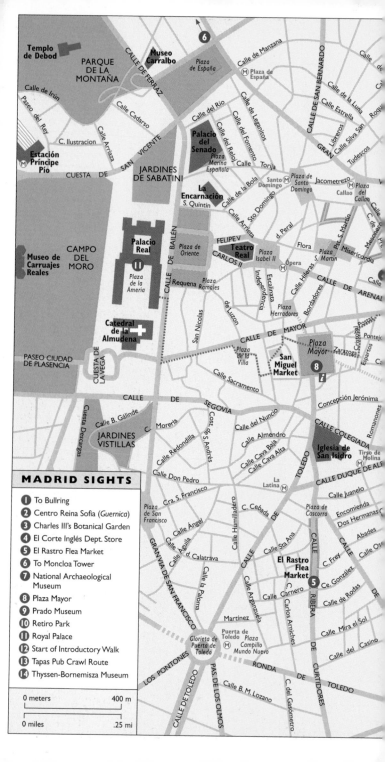

Templo de Debod

PARQUE DE LA MONTAÑA

Museo Carralbo

Plaza de España

Calle de Manzana

Plaza de España

Calle de la Luna

CALLE DE SAN BERNARDO

Calle Estrella

Calle de

Calle

Calle de Irún

Calle Cadarso

Calle del Rio

Calle de Leganitos

GRAN VÍA

Libreros

Calle Silva San Roqu

Tudescos

Paseo del Rey

C. Ilustracion

Calle Arriaza

SAN VICENTE

Calle del Fomento

Palacio del Senado

Calle del Reloj

Calle Torija

Plaza Marina Española

Santo Domingo

Plaza de Santo Domingo

Jacometrezo

Plaza del Callao

Callao

C. de

Estación Príncipe Pío

CUESTA DE

JARDINES DE SABATINI

La Encarnación

S. Quintin

Calle de la Bola

Calle Arrieta

Sto Domingo

d. Peral

St. Martín

Mesone

Pre

Museo de Carruajes Reales

CAMPO DEL MORO

CALLE DE BAILÉN

Palacio Real

Plaza de Oriente

FELIPE V

Teatro Real

CARLOS II

Flora

Plaza Isabel II

Plaza S. Martin

Plaza S. Martin

Plaza de la America

Requena

Plaza Ramales

Ópera

Independencia

Calle Hileras

CALLE DE ARENAL

Calle

Catedral de la Almudena

San Nicolas

de Luzon

Escalinata

Bordadores

Plaza Herradores

Postas

Pontejo

Zarazoga

PASEO CIUDAD DE PLASENCIA

CUESTA DE LA VEGA

Plaza de la Villa

CALLE DE MAYOR

Plaza Mayor **8**

Esparto

Calle Sacramento

San Miguel Market

i

CALLE DE SEGOVIA

Concepción Jerónima

JARDINES VISTILLAS

C. Morera

Cost. de S. Andrés

Calle del Nuncio

Calle Almendro

CALLE COLEGIADA

Romanones

Tirso de Molina

Cuesta Descargas

Calle B. Gálinde

Calle Redondilla

Calle Cava Baja

Calle Cava Alta

Iglesia de San Isidro

Calle Don Pedro

La Latina

TOLEDO

CALLE DUQUE DE ALF

Cra. S. Francisco

Calle Juanelo

Plaza de San Francisco

C. Cebada

DE

Plaza de Cascorro

Encomienda

Dos Hermanas

GRAN VÍA DE SAN FRANCISCO

Calle Angel

Calle S. Aguila

Calle de Calatrava

Calle Humilladero

CALLE

Calle Sta Ana

El Rastro Flea Market **5**

Abades

C. Frey

Calle Ose

Calle la Paloma

Calle Arganzuela

Calle Carnero

RIBERA

Ce. Gonzalez

Calle de Rodas

Martinez

Carlos Arniches

Calle Mira el Sol

Puerta de Toledo

Plaza Campillo Mundo Nuevo

DE

Calle del Casino

LOS PONTONES

Glorieta de Puerta de Toledo

CURTIDORES

PAS. DE LOS OLMOS

CALLE DE TOLEDO

RONDA

Calle B. M. Lozano

C. del Gasometro

DE

TOLEDO

MADRID SIGHTS

1 To Bullring
2 Centro Reina Sofía (*Guernica*)
3 Charles III's Botanical Garden
4 El Corte Inglés Dept. Store
5 El Rastro Flea Market
6 To Moncloa Tower
7 National Archaeological Museum
8 Plaza Mayor
9 Prado Museum
10 Retiro Park
11 Royal Palace
12 Start of Introductory Walk
13 Tapas Pub Crawl Route
14 Thyssen-Bornemisza Museum

0 meters	400 m
0 miles	.25 mi

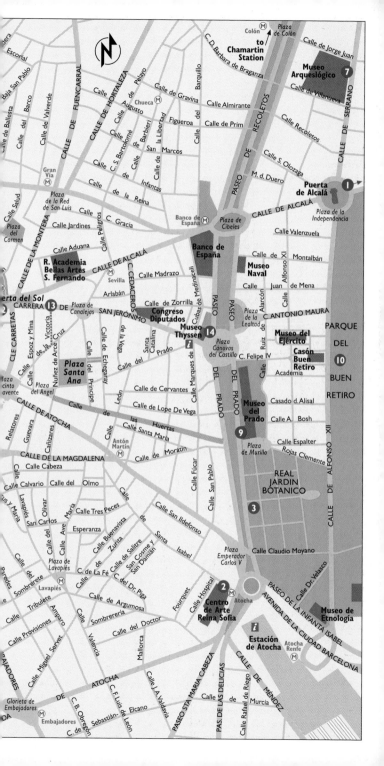

Rick Steves'
SPAIN
2005

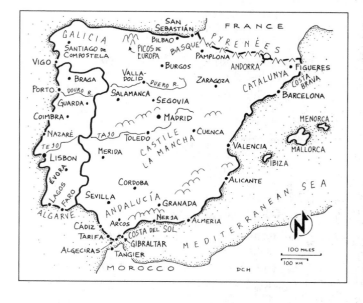

AVALON
TRAVEL

CONTENTS

Top Destinations in Spain

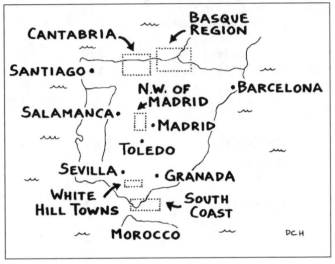

INTRODUCTION

Like a grandpa bouncing a baby on his knee, Spain is a mix of old and new, modern and traditional. Spain can fill your travel days with world-class art, folk life, exotic foods, friendly people, sunshine, and flamenco. And, in spite of its recent economic boom, Spain remains Europe's bargain basement. Tourism is huge here. With 40 million inhabitants, Spain entertains 50 million visitors annually. Spain is very popular—and on your trip, you'll learn why.

This book gives you all the information and opinions necessary to wring the maximum value out of your limited time and money. If you plan a month or less in Spain, this lean and mean little book is all you need.

Experiencing Spain's culture, people, and natural wonders economically and hassle-free has been my goal for more than two decades of traveling, tour guiding, and writing. With this book, I pass on to you the lessons I've learned, updated for 2005.

Rick Steves' Spain is a tour guide in your pocket, with a balanced, comfortable mix of exciting cities and cozy towns, topped off with an exotic dollop of Morocco. It covers the predictable biggies and stirs in a healthy dose of Back Door intimacy. Along with seeing a bullfight, the Prado, and flamenco, you'll buy cookies from cloistered nuns in a sun-parched Andalusian town. I've been selective, including only the most exciting sights and experiences. Rather than listing Spain's countless whitewashed Andalusian hill towns, I recommend the best two—Arcos de la Frontera and Ronda.

The best is, of course, only my opinion. But after spending half my life researching Europe, I've developed a sixth sense for what travelers enjoy.

This Information is Accurate and Up-to-Date

This book is updated every year. Most publishers of guidebooks that cover a region from top to bottom can afford an update only every two or three years, and then the research is often by letter. Since this book is selective, covering only the places I think make the best vacation, my research partner and I update it personally each summer. The telephone numbers, prices, and hours of sights listed in this book are accurate as of mid-2004. Even with annual updates, things change. But if you're traveling with the current edition of this book, I guarantee you're using the most up-to-date information in print (for the latest, see www.ricksteves.com/update). Also at our Web site, check our Graffiti Wall (select "Rick Steves' Guidebooks," then "Spain") for a huge, valuable list of reports and experiences—good and bad—from fellow travelers.

Trust me, you'll regret trying to save a few bucks by traveling with old information. If you're packing an old book, you'll quickly learn the seriousness of your mistake...in Europe. Your trip costs about $10 per waking hour. Your time is valuable. This guidebook saves lots of time.

About This Book

This book is organized by destinations. Each destination is covered as a mini-vacation on its own, filled with exciting sights and homey, affordable places to stay. In each chapter, you'll find the following:

Planning Your Time, a suggested schedule with thoughts on how best to use your limited time.

Orientation, including tourist information, city transportation, and an easy-to-read map designed to make the text clear and your arrival smooth.

Sights with ratings: ▲▲▲—Don't miss; ▲▲—Try hard to see; ▲—Worthwhile if you can make it; no rating—Worth knowing about.

Sleeping and **Eating,** with addresses and phone numbers of my favorite budget hotels and restaurants.

Transportation Connections to nearby destinations by train, bus, or car, with recommended roadside attractions for drivers.

The **appendix** is a traveler's tool kit, with telephone tips, a climate chart, a list of festivals, and cultural background.

Browse through this book, choose your favorite destinations, and link them up. Then have a great trip! You'll travel as a temporary local, getting the absolute most out of every mile, minute, and dollar. You won't waste time on mediocre sights because, unlike other guidebooks, this one covers only the best. Since your major financial pitfall is lousy, expensive hotels, I've worked hard to assemble the best accommodations values for each stop. And, as you travel the route I know and love, I'm happy you'll be meeting some of my favorite Spanish people.

PLANNING

Trip Costs

Five components make up your trip cost: airfare, surface transportation, room and board, sightseeing/entertainment, and shopping/miscellany.

Airfare: Don't try to sort through the mess yourself. Get and use a good travel agent. A basic round-trip flight from the United States to Madrid should cost $700 to $1,000 (less in winter), depending on where you fly from and when you go. Always consider saving time and money by flying "open-jaw" (into one city and out of another, e.g., into Barcelona and out of Sevilla).

Surface Transportation: For a three-week whirlwind trip linking all of my recommended destinations, allow $350 per person for second-class trains and buses ($500 for first-class trains) or $600 per person (based on 2 people sharing) for a three-week car lease, tolls, gas, and insurance. A car rental or lease is cheapest to arrange from home in the United States. While train passes (generally designed to be purchased in your home country—before arriving in Spain) are a convenience, you may save money by simply buying tickets as you go (see "Transportation," page 14).

Room and Board: Although most travelers will spend more (because they've got it and it's fun), you can thrive in Spain on $80 a day per person for room and board. An $80-a-day budget allows $10 for lunch, $20 for dinner, and $50 for lodging (based on 2 people splitting the cost of a $100 double room that includes breakfast). That's doable. Students and tightwads will do it on $30 ($15 per bed, $15 for meals and snacks). But budget sleeping and eating require the skills and information covered below (or more extensively in *Rick Steves' Europe Through the Back Door*).

Sightseeing and Entertainment: In big cities, figure $6 to $10 per major sight (Picasso Museum, Prado), $2 for minor ones (climbing church towers), and about $30 for splurge experiences (flamenco, bullfights). An overall average of $10 a day works for most. Don't skimp here. After all, this category directly powers most of the experiences all the other expenses are designed to make possible.

Shopping and Miscellany: Figure $1 per coffee, beer, ice-cream cone, and postcard. Shopping can vary in cost from nearly nothing to a small fortune. Good budget travelers find that this category has little to do with assembling a trip full of lifelong and wonderful memories.

When to Go

Spring and fall offer the best combination of good weather, light crowds, long days, and plenty of tourist and cultural activities.

July and August are most crowded and expensive in coastal

Whirlwind Three-Week Trip of Spain

Day	Plan	Sleep in
1	Arrive in Barcelona	Barcelona
2	Barcelona	Barcelona
3	Fly or rail (night train) to Sevilla	Sevilla
4	Sevilla	Sevilla
5	To Andalucía's Route of White Hill Towns to Arcos	Arcos
6	To Tarifa	Tarifa
7	Tarifa (day-trip to Morocco)	Tarifa
8	To Nerja via Gibraltar and Costa del Sol	Nerja
9	To Granada	Granada
10	Granada	Granada
11	To Toledo via Consuegra	Toledo
12	Toledo	Toledo
13	To Madrid via El Escorial and Valley of the Fallen	Madrid
14	Madrid	Madrid
15	To Salamanca via Segovia and Ávila	Salamanca
16	Salamanca	Salamanca
17	To Santiago	Santiago
18	Santiago	Santiago
19	To Cantabria	Cantabria (Santillana or Comillas)
20	To San Sebastián via Bilbao	San Sebastián
21	San Sebastián	San Sebastián
22	Fly home	

This itinerary is designed to be done by car, except for the long boring trip from Barcelona to Sevilla, which is best done by a one-hour flight or night train. Spain's long distances make the option of flying or going by rail for at least a portion of the trip worth considering.

The route can also be done by public transportation (5–6 bus days and 6–7 train days) with a few modifications: From Barcelona, fly or take the night train to Granada; take the bus along the Costa del Sol to Tarifa (day-trip to Morocco); take the bus to Arcos and Sevilla; and then take the AVE high-speed train to Madrid. Visit Toledo, Segovia, and El Escorial as side-trips from Madrid. Take the train to Salamanca and Santiago de Compostela, and finish in San Sebastián.

areas, less crowded but uncomfortably hot and dusty in the interior. Air-conditioning is worth the splurge. During these steamy months, lunch breaks can be long, especially in Andalucía.

Off-season, roughly October through April, expect shorter hours, lunchtime breaks, and fewer activities. Confirm your sight-seeing plans locally, especially when traveling off-season.

For weather specifics, see the climate chart in the appendix.

Consider skipping Cantabria, which is a little tricky by public transportation, and then add the extra days to Barcelona or Madrid area.

Both plans assume you'll fly open-jaw into Barcelona and out of San Sebastián. If you're returning to Madrid from San Sebastián, it's an eight-hour train ride (night train possible) or a one-hour flight. Or you can cross into France and take the six-hour TGV train to Paris for more adventures!

Two-Week Options: You can end the three-week route (described above) a week early by returning to Madrid from Salamanca and saving northern Spain for another trip. Another two-week possibility: Start in Barcelona (stay 2 days); fly or take an overnight train to Madrid (stay 5 days total, with 2 days in Madrid and 3 for side-trips to Toledo, El Escorial, and Segovia or Ávila); Granada (2 days); Nerja (1 day); both Ronda and Arcos for drivers, or just Ronda for train-ers (2 days); Sevilla (2 days); and then fly home from Madrid.

Sightseeing Priorities

Depending on the length of your trip, here are my recommended priorities, listed in order:

3 days:	Madrid and Toledo
6 days:	Sevilla, Granada
10 days:	Barcelona, Andalucía (White Hill Towns)
13 days:	Costa del Sol, Morocco

15 days:	Salamanca, Segovia
17 days:	Santiago de Compostela
21 days:	Basque Region (San Sebastián and Bilbao), Cantabria (northern Spain)

This includes everything on the map on page 5.

Itinerary Specifics

Design an itinerary that enables you to hit the festivals, bullfights, and museums on the right days. As you read this book, note the problem days: Mondays, when many museums are closed, and Sundays, when public transportation is meager. Treat Saturday as a weekday (though transportation connections can be less frequent than on Mon–Fri).

Plan ahead for banking, laundry, post-office chores, and picnics. Maximize rootedness by minimizing one-night stands. Mix intense and relaxed periods. Every trip (and every traveler) needs at least a few slack days. Pace yourself. Assume you will return.

Reservations for Granada's Alhambra: The only sight you might want to reserve tickets for in advance is this remarkable Moorish hilltop stronghold that consists of palaces, gardens, a fortress, and a rich history. You can make reservations for the Alhambra upon arrival in Spain (ideally before you reach Granada), but I mention it here for those who like to have things nailed down before they leave home. For more information, check the Granada chapter (page 245).

RESOURCES

Tourist Offices in the United States

National tourist offices are a wealth of information. Before your trip, get their free general information packet and request any specific information you want, such as city maps and schedules of upcoming festivals.

Tourist Offices of Spain: Check their Web sites (www.okspain .org and www.spain.info) and contact their nearest office...

In New York: 666 Fifth Ave., 35th Floor, New York, NY 10103, tel. 212/265-8822, fax 212/265-8864, oetny@tourspain.es.

In Illinois: 845 N. Michigan Ave. #915E, Chicago, IL 60611, tel. 312/642-1992, fax 312/642-9817, chicago@tourspain.es.

In Florida: 1395 Brickell Ave. #1130, Miami, FL 33131, tel. 305/358- 1992, fax 305/358-8223, oetmiami@tourspain.es.

In California: 8383 Wilshire Blvd. #956, Beverly Hills, CA 90211, tel. 323/658-7188, fax 323/658-1061, losangeles@tourspain.es.

Moroccan National Tourist Office: 20 E. 46th St. #1201, New York, NY 10017, tel. 212/557-2520, fax 212/949-8148, www .tourism-in-morocco.com, visitmorocco@onmt.org.ma.

Gibraltar Information Bureau: 1156 15th St. N.W., Suite 1100, Washington, D.C. 20005, tel. 202/452-1108, fax 202/452-1109.

Rick Steves' Books and Public Television Shows

Rick Steves' Europe Through the Back Door 2005 gives you budget travel skills, such as packing light, planning your itinerary, traveling by car or train, avoiding rip-offs, staying healthy, taking great photographs, using mobile phones, and much more. The book also includes chapters on 38 of Rick's favorite "Back Doors," including one in Spain's Andalusian hill towns.

Rick Steves' Guidebooks

Rick Steves' Europe Through the Back Door
Rick Steves' Best European City Walks & Museums
Rick Steves' Easy Access Europe

Country Guides
Rick Steves' Best of Europe
Rick Steves' Best of Eastern Europe
Rick Steves' France
Rick Steves' Germany & Austria
Rick Steves' Great Britain
Rick Steves' Greece*
Rick Steves' Ireland
Rick Steves' Italy
Rick Steves' Portugal
Rick Steves' Scandinavia
Rick Steves' Spain
Rick Steves' Switzerland

City and Regional Guides
Rick Steves' Amsterdam, Bruges & Brussels
Rick Steves' Florence & Tuscany
Rick Steves' London
Rick Steves' Paris
Rick Steves' Prague & the Czech Republic*
Rick Steves' Provence & the French Riviera
Rick Steves' Rome
Rick Steves' Venice

*Coming in 2005

(Avalon Travel Publishing)

Rick Steves' Country Guides, an annually updated series that covers Europe, offer you the latest on the top sights and destinations, with tips on how to make your trip efficient and fun.

My **City and Regional Guides,** freshly updated every year, focus on Europe's most compelling destinations. Along with specifics on sights, restaurants, hotels, and nightlife, you'll get self-guided, illustrated tours of the outstanding museums and most characteristic neighborhoods.

Rick Steves' Easy Access Europe, written for travelers with limited mobility, focuses on London, Paris, Bruges, Amsterdam, and the Rhine.

Rick Steves' Europe 101: History and Art for the Traveler (with Gene Openshaw) gives you the story of Europe's people, history, and art.

Rick Steves' Best European City Walks & Museums (with Gene Openshaw) provides fun, easy-to-follow, self-guided tours in London, Amsterdam, Paris, Rome, Venice, Florence, and Madrid. Madrid's Prado is the thickest chapter in the book.

Rick Steves' Spanish Phrase Book has the survival phrases necessary to communicate your way through a smooth and inexpensive trip. You'll be able to make hotel reservations over the phone, joke with your cabbie, and bargain at a street market.

My public television series, *Rick Steves' Europe,* keeps churning out shows. Of the latest batch of episodes, which began airing in fall of 2004, three feature Spain.

Rick Steves' Postcards from Europe, my autobiographical book, packs 25 years of travel anecdotes and insights into the ultimate 2,000-mile European adventure.

Other Guidebooks

You may want some supplemental travel guidebooks, especially if you are traveling beyond my recommended destinations. When you consider the improvement it will make in your $3,000 vacation, $25 or $35 for extra maps and books is money well spent. For several people traveling by car, the extra weight and expense of a small trip library are negligible.

Lonely Planet's guides to Spain are thorough, well-researched, and packed with good maps and hotel recommendations for low- to moderate-budget travelers (but they're not updated annually—check to see when it was published).

Students and vagabonds will like the hip *Rough Guide: Spain* (written by insightful British researchers—also not updated annually) and the highly opinionated *Let's Go: Spain & Portugal* (by Harvard students, thorough hostel listings, updated annually, includes Morocco). *Let's Go* is best for backpackers who have train passes and are interested in the youth and night scene.

Begin Your Trip at www.ricksteves.com

At ricksteves.com you'll find a wealth of **free information** on destinations covered in this book, including fresh European travel and tour news every month and helpful "Graffiti Wall" tips from thousands of fellow travelers.

While you're there, Rick Steves' **online Travel Store** is a great place to save money on travel bags and accessories specially designed by Rick Steves to help you travel smarter and lighter. These include Rick's popular carry-on bags (wheeled and rucksack versions), money belts, day bags, totes, toiletries kits, packing cubes, clotheslines, locks, clocks, sleep sacks, adapters, and a wide selection of guidebooks, planning maps, and *Rick Steves' Europe* DVDs.

Traveling through Europe by rail is a breeze, but choosing the right railpass for your trip (amidst hundreds of options) can drive you nutty. At ricksteves.com you'll find **Rick Steves' Annual Guide to European Railpasses**—your best way to convert chaos into pure travel energy. Buy your railpass from Rick, and you'll get a bunch of free extras to boot.

Travel agents will tell you about mainstream tours of Europe, but they won't tell you about **Rick Steves' tours.** Rick Steves' Europe Through the Back Door travel company offers more than two dozen itineraries and 250-plus departures reaching the best destinations in this book…and beyond. You'll enjoy the services of a great guide, a fun bunch of travel partners (with group sizes in the mid-20s), and plenty of room to spread out in a big, comfy bus. You'll find tours to fit every vacation size, from weeklong city getaways (Barcelona, Paris, London, Venice, Florence, Rome), to 12–18 day country tours, to three-week "Best of Europe" adventures. For details, visit www.ricksteves.com or call 425/771-8303 ext 217.

Older travelers enjoy Frommer's Spain guides even though they, like the Fodors guides, ignore alternatives that enable travelers to save money by dirtying their fingers in the local culture.

The popular, skinny Michelin Green Guides to Spain are excellent, especially if you're driving. They're known for their city and sightseeing maps, dry but concise and helpful information on all major sights, and good cultural and historical background. English editions are sold in Spain. The well-written and thoughtful Cadogan guide to Spain is excellent for A students on the road. The encyclopedic Blue Guides to Spain are dry as the plains in Spain but just right for some.

The Eyewitness series has editions covering Spain, Barcelona, Madrid, and Sevilla/Andalucía (published by Dorling Kindersley, sold in the United States or Spain). They're extremely popular for their fine graphics, 3-D cutaways of buildings, aerial-view maps of historic neighborhoods, and cultural background. The downside: They're heavy, and if you pull out the art, the print that's left is pretty skimpy. *Time Out* travel guides provide good, detailed coverage of Madrid and Barcelona, particularly on arts and entertainment.

Juan Lalaguna's *A Traveller's History of Spain* provides a readable background on this country's tumultuous history. John Hooper's *The New Spaniards* provides an interesting look at Spain today.

Maps

The black-and-white maps in this book are drawn by Dave Hoerlein, one of our veteran tour guides who is well-traveled in Spain. His concise and simple maps are designed to help you get oriented and find places listed in the text quickly and painlessly. In Spain, any tourist information office and some hotels will have free maps. Better maps are sold at newsstands—take a look before you buy to be sure the map has the level of detail you want.

My *Rick Steves' Spain & Portugal Planning Map* is geared for the traveler and shows sightseeing destinations prominently. Michelin maps are available—and cheaper than in the United States—throughout Spain in bookstores, newsstands, and gas stations. Train travelers can do fine with a simple rail map (such as the one that comes with a train pass) and city maps from the tourist information offices. Drivers should invest in good 1:400,000 maps and learn the keys to maximize the sightseeing value.

PRACTICALITIES

Red Tape: You currently need a passport but no visa and no shots to travel in Spain or Morocco.

Time: In Europe—and in this book—you'll be using the 24-hour clock. After 12:00 noon, keep going—13:00, 14:00, and so on. For anything over 12, subtract 12 and add p.m. (14:00 is 2:00 p.m.).

Morocco, which is in an earlier time zone than Spain, can run up to two hours earlier than Spanish time. Portugal is always one hour earlier than Spain.

Business Hours: For visitors, Spain is a land of strange and frustrating schedules. Many businesses respect the afternoon siesta. When it's 100 degrees in the shade, you'll understand why.

The biggest museums stay open all day. Smaller ones often close for a siesta. Shops are generally open from 9:00 to 13:00 and from 16:00 to 20:00, longer in touristy places. Small shops are often open on Saturday only in the morning and are closed all day Sunday.

Discounts: Discounts for sights are not listed in this book because they are generally limited to European residents and countries that offer reciprocal deals (the U.S. doesn't).

Metric: Get used to metric. A liter is about a quart, four to a gallon. A kilometer is six-tenths of a mile. I figure kilometers to miles by cutting them in half and adding back 10 percent of the original (120 km: 60 + 12 = 72 miles, 300 km: 150 + 30 = 180 miles).

Watt's up? If you're bringing electrical gear, you'll need a two-prong adapter plug (sold cheap at travel stores) and a converter. Travel appliances often have convenient, built-in converters; look for a voltage switch marked 120V (U.S.) and 240V (Europe).

Language Barrier: Spain presents the English-speaking traveler with the one of the most formidable language barriers in Western Europe. Learn the key phrases. Travel with a phrase book, particularly if you want to interact with local people. You'll find that doors open quicker and with more smiles when you can speak a few words of the language. Use the Survival Phrases in the appendix of this book. Considering the fun of eating Spanish tapas, the tapas phrase list (in this book's introduction) is particularly helpful. Use this and you'll eat much better than the average tourist.

MONEY

Exchange Rate

I list prices in euros throughout the book.

> 1 euro (€) = about $1.20

One euro is broken down into 100 cents. You'll find coins ranging from 1 cent to 2 euros, and bills from €5 to €500. To roughly convert prices in euros to dollars, add 20 percent: €20 is about $24, €45 is about $55, and so on.

While traveling, keep spare change and small euro bills on hand for the mom-and-pop shops that don't have enough cash to break big bills.

Banking

ATMs are the way to go. Bring an ATM or debit card (with a PIN code) to withdraw funds from cash machines as you travel, and carry a couple hundred dollars in American cash as a backup. Spain has readily available, easy-to-use, 24-hour ATMs with English instructions. They'll save you time and money (on commission fees). I traveled painlessly throughout Spain in 2004 with my Visa debit card. Before you go, verify with your bank that your card will work, inquire about fees, and alert them that you'll be making withdrawals in Europe; otherwise, the bank may not approve transactions if it perceives unusual spending patterns. Bring an extra copy of your card (or another of your cards) just in case one gets demagnetized or gobbled up by a machine.

Damage Control for Lost or Stolen Cards

You can stop thieves from using your ATM, debit, or credit card by reporting the loss immediately to the proper company. Call these 24-hour U.S. numbers collect: Visa (tel. 410/581-9994), MasterCard (tel. 636/722-7111), and American Express (tel. 336/393-1111).

Providing the following information will help expedite the process: the name of the financial institution that issued you the card, full card number, the cardholder's name as printed on the card, billing address, home phone number, circumstances of the loss or theft, and identification verification: Social Security number or birthdate and your mother's maiden name. (Packing along a photocopy of the front and back of your cards helps you answer the harder questions.) If you are the secondary cardholder, you'll also need to provide the primary cardholder's identification verification details. You can generally receive a temporary card within two or three business days in Europe.

If you promptly report your card lost or stolen, you typically won't be responsible for any unauthorized transactions on your account, although many banks charge a liability fee of $50.

Banks are generally open Monday through Friday nonstop from 9:00 to 14:00. Spanish banks charge acceptable commissions for changing traveler's checks (though if they get wet in your money belt, they will be refused). American Express offices (found only in big cities) offer mediocre rates but change any type of traveler's check without a commission. Better yet, use a cash machine. I've changed my last traveler's check.

VAT Refunds and Customs Regulations

VAT Refunds for Shoppers: Wrapped into the purchase price of your souvenirs is a Value Added Tax (VAT), which is generally about 14 percent. If you make a purchase of more than €90 in Spain at a store that participates in the VAT refund scheme, you're entitled to get most of that tax back. Personally, I've never felt that VAT refunds are worth the hassle, but if you do, here's the scoop.

If you're lucky, the merchant will subtract the tax when you make your purchase (this is more likely to occur if the store ships the goods to your home). Otherwise, here's what you'll need to do:

Get the paperwork. Have the merchant completely fill out the necessary refund document, called a "cheque." You'll have to present your passport at the store.

Have your cheque(s) stamped at the border at your last stop in the European Union by the customs agent who deals with VAT refunds. It's best to keep your purchases in your carry-on for viewing, but if they're too large or dangerous (such as knives) to carry on, then track down the proper customs agent to inspect them before you check your bag. You're not supposed to use your purchased goods before you leave. If you show up at customs wearing your new flamenco get-up, officials might look the other way—or deny you a refund.

To collect your refund, you'll need to return your stamped documents to the retailer or its representative. Many merchants work with a service, such as Global Refund (www.globalrefund.com) or Premier Tax Free (www.premiertaxfree.com), which have offices at major airports, ports, or border crossings. These services, which extract a 4 percent fee, can refund your money immediately in your currency of choice or credit your card (within two billing cycles). If you have to deal directly with the retailer, mail the store your stamped documents and then wait. It could take months.

Customs Regulations: You can take home $800 in souvenirs per person duty-free. The next $1,000 is taxed at a flat 3 percent. After that, you pay the individual item's duty rate. You can also bring in duty-free a liter of alcohol (slightly more than a standard-size bottle of wine), a carton of cigarettes, and up to 100 cigars. To check customs rules and duty rates, visit www.customs.gov.

TRAVEL SMART

Your trip to Spain is like a complex play—easier to follow and really appreciate on a second viewing. While no one does the same trip twice to gain that advantage, reading this book in its entirety before your trip accomplishes much the same thing. This book is filled with practical history and cultural tips, so read even the chapters on destinations you don't plan to visit, or you may miss some fun and helpful factoids.

Reread entire chapters of this book as you arrive in a new destination, and visit local tourist information offices. Buy a phone card or mobile phone and use it for reservations and confirmations. Use taxis in the big cities, bring along a water bottle, and linger in the shade. Connect with the cultures. Set up your own quest for the best main square, paella, cloister, tapas bar, or whatever.

Enjoy the friendliness of the local people. Ask questions. Most locals are eager to point you in their idea of the right direction. Wear your money belt, pack a pocket-size notepad to organize your thoughts, and practice the virtue of simplicity. Those who expect to travel smart, do.

Theft Alert: Thieves target tourists throughout Spain, especially in Barcelona, Madrid, and Sevilla. While hotel rooms are generally safe, cars are commonly broken into, purses are snatched, and pockets are picked. Thieves zipping by on motorbikes grab handbags from pedestrians. A fight or commotion is created to enable pickpockets to work unnoticed. Be on guard, use a money belt, and treat any disturbance around you as a smoke screen for theft. Don't believe any "police officers" looking for counterfeit bills. Drivers should read the tips on page 21. When traveling by train, keep your backpack in sight and get a *couchette* (bed in an attendant-monitored sleeping car) for safety on overnight trips.

Tourist Information

Your best first stop in a new city is the Turismo (tourist information office—abbreviated as **TI** in this book). Get a city map and advice on public transportation (including bus and train schedules), special events, and recommendations for nightlife. Many Turismos have information on the entire country. When you visit a Turismo (TI), try to pick up maps for towns you'll be visiting later in your trip.

While the TI has listings of all lodgings and is eager to book you a room, use its room-finding service only as a last resort (bloated prices, fees, no opinions, and they take a cut from your host). You'll get a far better value by using the listings in this book and going direct.

TRANSPORTATION

By Car or Train?

Cars are best for three or more traveling together (especially families with small kids), those packing heavy, and those scouring the countryside. Trains and buses are best for solo travelers, blitz tourists, and city-to-city travelers.

Overview of Trains and Buses

Public transportation in Spain is becoming as slick, modern, and efficient as in northern Europe. The best public-transportation option is to mix bus and train travel. Always verify bus or train schedules before your departure. Never leave a station without your next day's schedule options in hand. Ask for a schedule at an information window, say, *"Horario para _____–_____* (fill in names of cities), *por favor."* (The local TI will sometimes have schedules available for you to take or copy.) To study train schedules in advance, see www.renfe.es (Spain) or http://bahn.hafas.de/bin/query.exe/en (for international connections).

Trains

While you could save money by purchasing tickets as you go, you may find the convenience of a railpass worth the extra cost, especially if you will take some local trains that do not require reservations. You can buy a "flexi" railpass that allows travel for a given number of days over a longer period of time. If your trip also includes neighboring France, consider the France 'n Spain Pass (see chart on page 15).

Railpasses

Prices listed are for 2004. My free Rick Steves' Guide to European Railpasses has the latest prices and details (and easy online ordering) at www.ricksteves.com/rail.

Saverpass prices are per person for 2 or more people traveling together. Kids 4-11 pay half adult or saver fare on all rail-only passes. Youth prices are only for those under 26.

SPAIN FLEXIPASS

	1st class	2nd class
Any 3 days in 2 months	$225	$175
Extra rail days (max 7)	35	30

IBERIC FLEXIPASS

	1st class Individual	1st class Saverpass
Any 3 days in 2 months	$249	$219
Extra rail days (max 7)	35	30

Covers Spain and Portugal. Saverpass prices are per person based on two or more traveling together. Kids 4-11 half of individual or saver fare, under 4 free.

PORTUGUESE FLEXIPASS

1st class: Any 4 days out of 15 for $105. Kids 4-11 half fare, under 4 free. Not valid on Hotel Train to Madrid.

Iberia:

Map shows approximate point-to-point one-way 2nd class rail fares in $US. 1st class costs 50% more. Add up fares for your itinerary to see whether a railpass will save you money.

SPAIN RAIL & DRIVE PASS

Any 3 rail days and 2 car days in 2 months.

	1st class	extra car day
Economy car	$239	$39
Compact car	249	49
Intermediate car	259	59
Compact automatic	265	59

Prices are per person for 2 traveling together. Solo travelers pay $50-$75 extra. 3rd and 4th persons sharing car buy only the railpass. Extra rail days (2 max) cost $36. To order Rail & Drive passes, call Rail Europe at 800/438-7245.

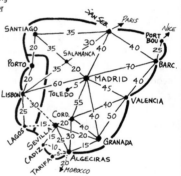

FRANCE 'N SPAIN PASS

	1st class Individual	1st class Saver	2nd class Individual	2nd class Saver	2nd class Youth
Any 4 days in 2 months	$299	$259	$259	$229	$199
Extra rail days (max 6)	33	29	29	25	22

EURAIL SELECTPASS

This pass covers travel in three adjacent countries.

	1st class Selectpass	1st class Saverpass	2nd class Youthpass
5 days in 2 months	$356	$304	$249
6 days in 2 months	394	336	276
8 days in 2 months	470	400	329
10 days in 2 months	542	460	379

Please go to www.ricksteves.com/rail for four- and five-country options.

A Eurail Selectpass lets you travel even farther. Spain also offers a rail-and-drive pass, which gives you the ease of big-city train hops and the flexibility of a car for rural areas such as the Andalusian hill towns. These passes are sold outside of Europe only. For specifics, contact your travel agent or see my Guide to European Railpasses at www.ricksteves.com. Even if you have a train pass, use buses when they're more convenient and direct than the trains. And whenever possible, book ahead for overnight and AVE trains to insure you get a berth and/or seat.

The long second-class train rides from Madrid to either Barcelona or Lisbon cost $60–70 each; from Madrid to either Sevilla or Granada costs about $40–70 each. First class costs 50 percent more—often as much as a domestic flight. Using a railpass to cover these trips can be a good value.

If you're buying point-to-point tickets, note that round-trip tickets are 20 percent cheaper than two one-way tickets. You can get a round-trip discount even if you start with a one-way ticket—as long as you save the ticket and make a return trip. For example, if you buy a one-way ticket from Barcelona to Madrid, visit Madrid, then decide to return to Barcelona, you can bring your one-way Barcelona–Madrid ticket to the train station and get a 40 percent discount on your return trip (this equals a total 20 percent discount for the round trip).

RENFE (the acronym for the Spanish national train system) used to mean "Really Exasperating, and Not For Everyone," but it is getting better. To save time, consider buying tickets or reservations at the RENFE offices located in more than 100 city centers. These are more central—also less crowded and confusing—than the train station. Or, for information and reservations, dial RENFE's national number (tel. 902-240-202) from anywhere in Spain.

Spain categorizes trains this way:

The high-speed train called the **AVE** (AH-vay, stands for Alta Velocidad Española) whisks travelers between Madrid and Sevilla in less than three hours. Franco left Spain a train system that didn't fit Europe's gauge. AVE trains run on European-gauge tracks. AVE trains can be priced differently according to their time of departure. Peak hours *(punta)* are most expensive, followed by *llano* and *valle* (quietest and cheapest times). AVE is almost entirely covered by the Eurailpass (book ahead, a seat reservation fee from Madrid to Sevilla costs Eurailers about $14 in second class; $29 for first class, includes meal). A Madrid–Barcelona link was just completed.

The **TALGO** is fast, air-conditioned, and expensive, and runs on AVE rails. **Intercity** and **Electro** trains fall just behind TALGO in speed, comfort, and expense. **Rápido, Tranvía, Semidirecto,** and **Expreso** trains are generally slower. **Cercanías** are commuter trains for big-city workers and small-town tourists. **Regional** and **Correo** trains are slow, small-town milk runs. Trains get more expensive as they pick up speed, but all are cheaper per mile than their northern European counterparts.

Salidas means "departures" and *llegadas* is "arrivals." On train schedules, "LMXJVSD" are the days of the week, starting with Monday. A train that runs "LMXJV-D" doesn't run on Saturdays. *Laborables* can mean Monday through Friday or Monday through Saturday. Most train stations have handy luggage lockers.

Overnight Trains: For long trips, I go overnight on the train or I fly (domestic shuttle flights are generally less than $100). Overnight trains (and buses) are usually less expensive and slower than the daytime rides. Most overnight trains have berths and beds that you can rent (not included in the cost of your train ticket or rail-pass). A sleeping berth *(litera)* costs $15. A *coche cama,* or bed in a classy quad compartment, costs $20; and a bed in a double costs $25. Night trains are popular, so try to book ahead. Travelers with first-class reservations are entitled to use comfortable "Intercity" lounges in train stations in Spain's major cities.

The overnight train between Madrid and Lisbon is a pricey Hotel Train called the "Lusitania" (first class-$85, second class-$65; sleeper prices with railpass are slightly higher than domestic night trains—about $34 per person for a quad, $58 per person for a double, more for singles or a shower in your compartment; for info on other Hotel Trains, see below). No cheaper rail option exists between these two capital cities. You can save money by taking a bus, or save time by taking a plane.

Overnight Trains to/from Europe: Expensive Hotel Trains connect France, Italy, and Switzerland with Spain. All of these fancy overnight trains (known collectively as TALGO Night) have fancy names: Francisco de Goya (Madrid–Paris), Joan Miró (Barcelona–Paris), Pau Casals (Barcelona–Zürich), and Salvador Dalí (Barcelona–Milan). Full fares range from $145 in a quad to $425 for a Gran Clase single compartment. These trains are not covered by railpasses, but railpass holders (of Eurail, Eurail Select, Spain, Iberic, France, France 'n Spain, France 'n Italy, Italy, and consecutive-day Swiss passes) can get discounted fares on routes within their pass boundaries; you'll give up a flexi-day and pay about half the full fare. If you can easily afford to take a Hotel Train, consider flying instead to save time.

To avoid the expensive luxury of a Hotel Train, you can take a cheaper train trip that involves a transfer at the Spanish border (at Irún on Madrid–Paris runs, at Cerbère on the eastern side). You'll connect to a normal night train with $20 *literas* (*couchettes* in French) on one leg of the trip. This plan is more time-consuming, and may take two days of a flexipass.

Public Transportation Routes

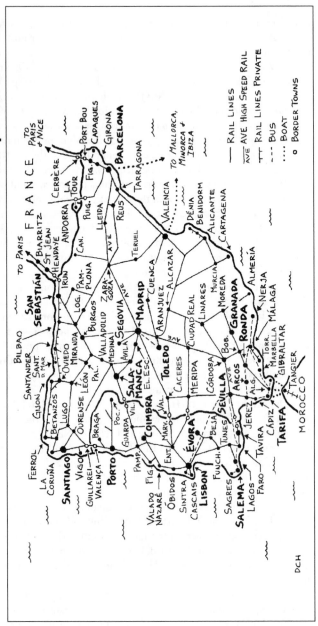

Buses

Spain's bus system is confusing. There are a number of different bus companies (though usually clustered within one building), sometimes running buses to the same destinations and using the same transfer points. If you have to transfer, make sure to look for a bus with the same name/logo as the company you bought the ticket from. The larger stations have an information desk with all of the schedules. In smaller stations, check the destinations and schedules posted on each office window. Bus service on holidays, Saturdays, and especially Sundays can be dismal.

If you arrive in a city by bus and plan to leave by bus, upon your arrival at the bus station check your departure options and buy a ticket in advance if necessary (and possible). If you're downtown, need a ticket, and the bus station isn't central, save time by asking at the tourist office about travel agencies that sell bus tickets.

A few buses are entirely non-smoking; others are non-smoking only in the front. When you buy your ticket for a long-distance bus (8 hours or more), ask for non-smoking *(no fumadores)*. It's usually pointless, since passengers ignore the signs, but it's a statement.

You can (and most likely will be required to) stow your luggage under the bus. For longer rides, give some thought to which side of the bus will get the most sun, and sit on the opposite side, even if the bus is air-conditioned and has curtains. Your ride will likely come with a soundtrack: taped Spanish pop music, a radio, or sometimes videos. If you prefer silence, bring earplugs.

Drivers and station personnel rarely speak English. Buses generally lack WCs, but they stop every two hours or so for a break (usually 15 min, but can be up to 30). Ask the driver "How many minutes here?" *("¿Cuántos minutos aquí?")* so you know if you have time to get out. Bus stations have WCs (rarely with toilet paper) and cafés that offer quick and cheap food.

Taxis

Most taxis are reliable and cheap. Drivers generally respond kindly to the request, "How much is it to ____, more or less?" *("¿Cuánto cuesta a ____, más o menos?")* If there's a long line-up of taxis, ask this question of one of the taxi drivers stuck farther back in line who has time (rather than ask at the head of the line, where you might feel pressured to get in the cab and go). Spanish taxis have extra supplements (for luggage, nighttime, Sundays, train-station or airport pickup, and so on). Rounding the fare up to the nearest large coin (maximum of 10 percent) is adequate for a tip. City rides cost $4 to $6. Keep a map in your hand so the cabbie knows (or thinks) you know where you're going. Big cities have plenty of taxis. In many cases, couples travel by cab for little more than two bus or subway tickets.

AND LEARN THESE ROAD SIGNS

Speed Limit (km/hr)

Yield

No Passing

End of No Passing Zone

One Way

Intersection

Main Road

Freeway

Danger

No Entry

No Entry for Cars

All Vehicles Prohibited

Parking

No Parking

Customs

Peace

Car Rental

It's cheapest to rent a car through your travel agent well before your departure. You'll want a weekly rate with unlimited mileage. Figure about $250 a week. For three weeks or longer, it's cheaper to lease; you'll save money on taxes and insurance. Comparison shop through your agent. Remember that rental offices usually close from midday Saturday until Monday.

I normally rent a small economy model. For peace of mind, I splurge for the CDW insurance (Collision Damage Waiver, about $15 a day), which covers virtually the full value of the car in case of an accident. "Gold" credit cards include CDW insurance if you rent the car using the card; quiz your credit-card company on the worst-case scenario. Travel Guard offers CDW for $7 a day (U.S. tel. 800/826-1300, www.travelguard.com). With the luxury of CDW,

Driving in Spain: Distance and Time

you'll enjoy Spain's highways, knowing you can bring back the car in an unrecognizable shambles and just say, "S-s-s-sorry."

Driving

Driving in Spain is great—sparse traffic and generally good roads. While the International Driver's License is officially required (cheap and easy to obtain from the nearest AAA office; bring 2 photos and $10), I drive in Spain with only my U.S. driver's license. (The Spanish version of AAA is the Real Automóvil Club.)

Good maps are available and inexpensive throughout Spain. Freeways come with tolls (about $4 per hour) but save huge amounts of time. Always pick up a ticket as you enter a toll freeway. On freeways, navigate by direction *(norte, oeste, sur, este)*. Also, since road numbers can be puzzling and inconsistent, navigate by city names. Mileage signs are in kilometers (see page 412 for conversion formula into miles).

Drive defensively. If you're involved in an accident, you will be blamed and will be in for a monumental headache. Seat belts are required by law. Expect to be stopped for a routine check by the police (be sure your car-insurance form is up-to-date). Small towns come with speed traps and corruption. Tickets, especially for foreigners, are issued and paid for on the spot. Insist on a receipt, so the money is less likely to end up in the cop's pocket.

Gas and diesel prices are controlled and the same everywhere—about $4 a gallon for gas, less for diesel. *Gasolina* is either *normal* or *super;* unleaded *(sin plomo)* is now widely available. Note that diesel is called *diesel* or *gasóleo.*

Choose parking places carefully. Leave valuables in the trunk during the day and leave nothing worth stealing in the car overnight. While you should avoid parking lots with twinkly asphalt, thieves break car windows anywhere, even at stoplights. If your car's a hatchback, take the trunk cover off at night so thieves can look in without breaking in. Parking attendants all over Spain holler, *"Nada en el coche"* ("Nothing in the car"). And they mean it. Ask your hotelier for advice on parking. In cities you can park safely but expensively in guarded lots.

COMMUNICATING

Telephones

You cannot travel smartly in Spain without using the telephone—to reserve and confirm hotel rooms, check sightseeing plans, and call home. A few tips will minimize frustration.

Phone Cards: At a phone booth, make calls by using a phone card rather than feeding in a bunch of coins. There are two types of phone cards you can buy:

1) An **insertable phone card,** called a *tarjeta telefónica,* that you stick into a phone. These cards are sold at post offices and many newsstand kiosks. To use an insertable card, simply slide it into the slot on the phone, wait for a dial tone and digital readout to show how much value remains on your card, and dial your local, long-distance, or international call. The cost of the call is automatically deducted from your card.

Spanish pay phones refuse to be rushed. After you *"inserta"* your *"tarjeta"* into the phone, wait until the digital display says *"Marque número"* and then dial. Dial slowly and deliberately. Push the square R button to get a dial tone for a new call. The phone doesn't beep to remind you that you've left the card in, so don't forget to remove it when you're done.

2) An **international phone card,** called a *tarjeta telefónica con código,* that can be used from virtually any phone, even from your hotel room (unless it has an older touch-tone model—try switching it from "pulse" to "tone"). This type of card is not inserted into the phone. Instead, you dial the toll-free access number listed on the card, then follow the prompts, dialing your scratch-to-reveal personal identification number (PIN) and finally the number you want to call.

International phone cards are made by numerous different (sometimes fly-by-night) companies. While you can buy them at most kiosks and newsstands, the best selection is usually at hole-in-the-wall shops catering to immigrants, who are the leading experts on calling home cheaply. These cards can be used to make local and international calls. They offer cheaper per-minute rates for international calls than insertable cards, but they don't consistently work as well. Try to confirm that the card can be used for calls to America (the salesclerk may not know), and buy a lower-denomination card in case the card is defective. Either type of phone card works only in the country where it's purchased.

Dialing Direct: All phone numbers in Spain are nine digits (without area codes) that can be dialed direct throughout the country; for example, in Madrid you dial a nine-digit number whether you're calling across the street or calling Barcelona.

To dial international calls direct, you'll need the international access codes and country codes (see the appendix). Spanish time is generally six/nine hours ahead of the East/West Coast of the United States.

U.S.A. Direct Services: Since direct-dialing rates have dropped, calling cards (offered by AT&T, MCI, and Sprint) are no longer the good value they used to be. It's much cheaper to purchase a phone card in Spain and dial direct.

Mobile Phones: Many travelers now buy inexpensive mobile phones in Europe to make both local and international calls. (Typical American mobile phones don't work in Europe, and those that do have horrendous per-minute costs.) For about $75 you can get a phone with $20-worth of calls that will work in the country where you purchased it. You can buy more time at newsstands or mobile-phone shops. For about $100 you can get a phone that will work in most countries (these phones are called *liberados*—"liberated") if you pick up the necessary chip per country (about $25). If you're interested, stop by any European shop that sells mobile phones, where you'll see prominent store window displays. Find an English-speaking clerk to help you. Confirm with the clerk whether the phone works only in Spain or throughout Europe. You'll need to pick out a policy; different policies have different advantages (like better rates on calls to fixed phones than to mobile phones). Receiving calls is generally free. If you're on a tight budget, skip mobile phones and buy international phone cards instead.

E-mail and Mail

E-mail: Cybercafés and little hole-in-the-wall Internet-access shops (offering a few computers, no food, and cheap prices) are popular in most cities. E-mail use among Spanish hoteliers is increasing. I've listed e-mail addresses when possible. Some family-run pensions can become overwhelmed by the volume of e-mail they receive, so be patient if you don't get an immediate response.

Mail: To arrange for mail delivery, reserve a few hotels along your route in advance and give their addresses to friends, or use the mail services of American Express if you're an AmEx cardholder. Allow 10 days for a letter to arrive. Phoning and e-mail are so easy that I've dispensed with mail stops altogether.

SLEEPING

In the interest of smart use of your time, I favor hotels (and restaurants) handy to your sightseeing activities. Rather than list hotels scattered throughout a city, I describe my favorite couple of neighborhoods and recommend the best accommodations values in each, from $10 bunks to $180 doubles.

Spain offers some of the best accommodation values in Western Europe. Most places are government-regulated, with posted prices. While prices are low, street noise is high (Spaniards are notorious night owls). Always ask to see your room first. Check the price posted on the door, consider potential night-noise problems, ask for another room, or bargain down the price. You can request *con vista* (with a view), or *tranquilo* or *calado* (quiet). In most cases, the view comes with street noise. Breakfast may or may not be included in your room cost. It is often used as a bargaining chip. Ask before accepting a room. Most of the year, prices are soft.

All rooms have sinks with hot and cold water. Rooms with private bathrooms are often bigger and renovated, while the cheaper rooms without bathrooms often will be dingier and/or on the top floor. Any room without a bathroom has access to a bathroom on the corridor. Towels aren't routinely replaced every day, so you should drip-dry and conserve.

You can usually save time by paying your bill the evening before you leave, instead of paying in the busy morning, when the reception desk is crowded with tourists who want to pay up, ask questions, or check in.

Types of Accommodations

Hotels: Don't judge hotels by their bleak and dirty entryways. Landlords, stuck with rent control, often stand firmly in the way of hardworking hoteliers who'd like to brighten up their buildings.

Any regulated place will have a complaint book *(libro de reclamaciones)*. A request for this book will generally solve any problem you have in a jiffy.

Hotels are officially prohibited from using central heat before November 1 and after April 1 (unless it's unusually cold); prepare for cool evenings if you travel in spring and fall. Summer can be extremely hot. Consider air-conditioning, fans, and noise (since you'll want your window open), and don't be shy about asking for ice at the fancier hotels. Many rooms come with mini-refrigerators (if it's noisy at night, unplug it). Conveniently, expensive business-class hotels

Sleep Code

To give maximum information in a minimum of space, I use this code to describe accommodations listed in this book. Prices listed are per room, not per person. When there is a range of prices in one category, the price will fluctuate with the season; these seasons are posted at the hotel desk. Especially in resort areas, prices go way up in July and August. In Spain, some hotels include the 7 percent I.V.A. tax in the room price, others tack it onto your bill. Hotel breakfasts are rarely included in Spain.

S = Single room (or price for one person in a double).
D = Double or twin. Double beds are usually big enough for nonromantic couples.
T = Triple (often a double bed with a single bed moved in).
Q = Quad (an extra child's bed is usually cheaper).
b = Private bathroom with toilet and shower or tub.
s = Private shower or tub only (the toilet is down the hall).
no CC = Does not accept credit cards; pay in local cash.
SE = Speaks English. This code is used only when it seems predictable that you'll encounter English-speaking staff.
NSE = Does not speak English. Used only when it's unlikely you'll encounter English-speaking staff.

You can assume credit cards are accepted unless otherwise noted. According to this code, a couple staying at a "Db-€90, SE" hotel would pay a total of €90 (about $110) for a double room with a private bathroom. The hotel accepts credit cards or cash in payment, and the staff speaks English.

often drop their prices in July and August, just when the air-conditioned comfort they offer is most important.

Most hotel rooms with air-conditioners come with control sticks (like a TV remote, sometimes requires a deposit) that generally have the same symbols and features: fan icon (click to toggle through wind power from light to gale); louver icon (choose steady air flow or waves); snowflake and sunshine icons (heat or cold, depending on season); clock ("O" setting: run x hours before turning off; "I" setting: wait x hours to start); and the temperature control (20° or 21° Celsius is the normal sleeping temperature).

Historic Inns: Spain also has luxurious, government-sponsored, historic inns called paradores. These are often renovated castles, palaces, or monasteries, many with great views and stately atmospheres. While full of Old World character, they are usually run in a sterile, bureaucratic way. They can be a very good value (doubles $80–200), especially for younger people (30 and under) and seniors

(60 and over), who often get discounted rates; for details, bonus packages, and family deals, see www.parador.es. If you're not eligible for any deals, you'll get a better value by sleeping in what I call (and list as) "poor-man's paradors"—elegant, normal places that offer double the warmth and Old World intimacy for half the price.

Rooms in Private Homes: Often located in touristy areas, where locals decide to open up a spare room and make a little money on the side, these rooms are usually as private as hotel rooms, often with separate entries. Especially in resort towns, the rooms might be in small apartment-type buildings. Ask for a *cama, habitación,* or *casa particular.* They're cheap ($10–25 per bed without breakfast) and usually a good experience.

Hostels and Campgrounds: Spain has plenty of youth hostels and campgrounds, but considering the great bargains on other accommodations, I don't think they're worth the trouble and don't cover them in this book. *Hostales* and *pensiones* are easy to find, inexpensive, and, when chosen properly, a fun part of the Spanish cultural experience. If you're on a starvation budget or just prefer camping or hosteling, plenty of information is available in the backpacker guidebooks, through the national tourist offices, and at local tourist information offices.

Making Reservations

Even though Easter, July, and August are often crowded, you can travel at any time of year without reservations. But given the high stakes and the quality of the gems I've found for this book, I'd recommend calling ahead for rooms, especially for Barcelona. In peak times or for big cities, you can reserve long in advance. Otherwise, simply call several days ahead as you travel

For maximum flexibility—especially off-season—you might make a habit of calling between 9:00 and 10:00 on the day you plan to arrive, when the hotel knows who'll be checking out and just which rooms will be available.

Use the telephone and the convenient phone cards. Most hotels listed are accustomed to English-only speakers. But if the language barrier intimidates you, ask the fluent-in-Spanish hotelier of your current hotel to reserve a room for you at your upcoming destination (offer to pay for the call).

A hotel receptionist will trust you and hold a room until 16:00 without a deposit, though some will ask for a credit-card number. Honor (or cancel by phone) your reservations. Long distance is cheap and easy from public phone booths. Don't let these people down—I promised you'd call and cancel if for some reason you won't show up. There's no need to confirm rooms through the tourist office; they'll take a commission.

Those on a tight budget save pocketfuls of euros by traveling off-season with no reservations and taking advantage of the discounted prices that hotels offer when it's clear they'll have empty rooms that day. Some of the hotels I recommend offer discounted prices if you have this book; mention this book—and claim the discount—when you call to reserve.

If you know exactly which dates you need and want a particular place, reserve a room well in advance before you leave home. To reserve from home, e-mail, call, or fax the hotel. Simple English usually works. To fax, use the handy form in the appendix (online at www.ricksteves.com/reservation). Confirm the need and method for a deposit. A two-night stay in August would be "2 nights, 16/8/05 to 18/8/05." (Europeans write the date day/month/year, and hotel jargon uses your day of departure.) You'll often receive a response back requesting one night's deposit. If they accept your credit card number as the deposit, you can pay with your card or cash when you arrive; if you don't show up, you'll be billed for one night. Reconfirm your reservations a day or two in advance for safety. If you have hotel confirmations in writing, bring them along.

EATING

Spaniards eat to live, not vice versa. Their cuisine is hearty and served in big, inexpensive portions. You can eat well in restaurants for $10.

The Spanish eating schedule—lunch from 13:00–16:00, dinner after 21:00—frustrates many visitors. Most Spaniards eat one major meal of the day—lunch *(almuerzo)* at 14:00, when stores close, schools let out, and people gather with their friends and family for the so-called "siesta." Because most Spaniards work until 19:30, supper *(cena)* is usually served at about 21:00 or 22:00. And, since few people want a heavy meal that late, many Spaniards build a light dinner out of appetizer portions called tapas.

Don't buck this system. Generally, no self-respecting *casa de comidas* (house of eating—when you see this label, you can bet it's a good traditional eatery) serves meals at American hours.

In addition, the Spanish diet—heavy on ham, deep-fried foods, more ham, weird seafood, and ham again—can be brutal on Americans more accustomed to salads, fruit, and grains.

To get by in Spain, either adapt yourself to the Spanish schedule and diet, or scramble to get edible food in between. You might consider having a small *pincho* (bar snack) with a coffee in the late morning, relaxing over your main meal at 15:00, and eating a light tapas snack for dinner later.

Some tips on surviving Spanish food: Eat brunch. Many Spaniards have a *bocadillo* (sandwich) at about 11:00 to bridge the gap between their coffee-and-roll breakfast and lunch at 14:00 (hence the popularity of fast-food sandwich chains like Pans & Company).

Tips on Tipping

Tipping in Spain isn't as automatic and generous as it is in the United States, but for special service, tips are appreciated, if not expected. As in the United States, the proper amount depends on your resources, tipping philosophy, and the circumstance, but some general guidelines apply.

Restaurants: In most restaurants, service is included—your menu typically will indicate this by noting *servicio incluido*. Still, if you like to tip and you're pleased with the service, it's customary to leave up to 5 percent. If service is not included *(servicio no incluido)*, tip up to 10 percent. Leave the tip on the table. It's best to tip in cash even if you pay with your credit card. Otherwise the tip may never reach your server.

Taxis: To tip the cabbie, round up. For a typical ride, round up to the next euro on the fare (to pay a €13 fare, give €14); for a long ride, to the nearest €10 (for a €75 fare, give €80). If the cabbie hauls your bags and zips you to the airport to help you catch your flight, you might want to toss in a little more. But if you feel like you're being driven in circles or otherwise ripped off, skip the tip.

Services: Tour guides at public sites sometimes hold out their hands for tips after they give their spiel. If I've already paid for the tour, I don't tip extra, though some tourists do give a euro or two, particularly for a job well done. I don't tip at hotels, but if you do, give the porter a euro for carrying bags and leave a couple of euros in your room at the end of your stay for the maid if the room was kept clean. In general, if someone in the service industry does a super job for you, a tip of a couple of euros is appropriate...but not required.

When in doubt, ask. If you're not sure whether (or how much) to tip for a service, ask your hotelier or the TI; they'll fill you in on how it's done on their turf.

Besides *bocadillos,* you can grab a slice of *tortilla* (potato omelet) or fresh-squeezed orange juice in a bar. For the hunger gap between lunch and late dinner, tapas in bars are the key (see below). And for just a fresh green salad, I have even—yes, I confess—patronized fast-food joints like McDonald's.

Breakfast

Hotel breakfasts are generally €5 and optional. While they are handy and not expensive, it's easy to start your day with a Spanish flair at the corner bar or at a colorful café near the town market hall. If you like a Danish and coffee in American greasy-spoon joints, you must try the Spanish equivalent: Greasy, cigar-shaped fritters called *churros* (or the thicker *porras*) that you dip in warm chocolate pudding.

Here are some key words for breakfast:

café solo	shot of espresso
café con leche	espresso with hot milk
te	tea
zumo de fruta	fruit juice
zumo de naranja (natural)	orange juice (freshly squeezed)
pan	bread
tortilla española	potato omelet (standard dish cooked fresh each morning, served in cheap slices)
sandwich (toast)	Wonder bread (toasted)
...con jamón/queso/mixto	...with ham/cheese/both
...mixto con huevo	...with ham and cheese topped with an over-easy egg

Restaurants

In restaurants, don't expect "My name is Carlos and I'll be your waiter tonight" cheery service. Service is often *serio*—it's not friendly or unfriendly...just white-shirt-and-bowtie proficient.

Although not fancy, Spanish cuisine comes with an endless variety of regional specialties. Two famous Spanish dishes are paella and gazpacho. Paella features saffron-flavored rice as a background for whatever the chef wants to mix in—seafood, sausage, chicken, peppers, and so on. While paella is pretty heavy for your evening meal, jump (like everyone else in the bar) at the opportunity to snare a small plate of paella when it appears hot out of the kitchen in a tapas bar. Gazpacho, an Andalusian specialty, is a chilled soup of tomatoes, bread chunks, and spices—refreshing on a hot day and commonly available in the summer. Spanish cooks love garlic and olive oil. The cheapest meal is simply a *bocadillo de jamón* (ham-on-French-bread sandwich), sold virtually anywhere.

For a budget meal in a restaurant, try a *plato combinado* (combination plate), which usually includes portions of one or two main dishes, a vegetable, and bread for a reasonable price; or the *menu del día* (menu of the day), a substantial three- to four-course meal that usually comes with a carafe of house wine.

Tapas Bars

You can eat well any time of day in tapas bars. Tapas are small portions, like appetizers, of seafood, salads, meat-filled pastries, deep-fried tasties, and on and on—normally displayed under glass at the bar.

Tapas typically cost about €1, up to €10 for seafood. Establish the price before you order, especially if you're on a tight budget or at a possible tourist trap. Most bars push larger portions called *raciones* (dinner-plate-sized) rather than smaller tapas (saucer-sized). Ask

Ordering Tapas

You can often just point to what you want, say *por favor*, and get your food, but these words will help you learn the options and fine-tune your request.

Tapas Terms

pincho	bite-size portion (not always available)
pinchito	tiny *pincho*
tapas	snack-size portions (not always available)
ración	larger portions—half a meal, occasionally available in a smaller version called a "1/2 *ración*" (*media ración*)
frito	fried
...la plancha	sautéed
¿Cuánto cuesta una tapa?	How much per tapa?

Sandwich Words

canapé	tiny open-faced sandwich
pulguitas	small closed baguette sandwich
montadito	tiny *bocadillo* (*montadito de...* means "little sandwich of...")
bocadillos	baguette sandwiches, cheap and basic, a tapa on bread
flautas	sandwich made with flute-thin baguette
pepito	yet one more word for a little sandwich

Typical Tapas

aceitunas	olives
almendras	almonds
atún	tuna
bacalao	cod
banderilla	a mini skewer of spicy, pickled veggies— eat all at once for the real punch (it's named after the spear matadors use to spike the bull)
bombas	fried meat and potatoes ball
boquerones	fresh anchovies
calamares fritos	fried squid rings
caracoles	snails (May–Sept)
cazón en adobo	marinated white fish
champiñones	mushrooms
croquetas de...	greasy, breaded balls of milky flour paste with...

empanadillas	pastries stuffed with meat or seafood
ensaladas (rusa)	salads (Russian)
espinacas	spinach
(con garbanzos)	(with garbanzo beans)
gambas (a la plancha,	shrimp (sautéed,
al ajillo)	with garlic)
gazpacho	cold garlic-and-tomato soup
guiso	stew
mejillones	mussels
pan	bread
paella	saffron rice dish with fish (when it appears fresh out of the kitchen, grab a little plate)
patatas bravas	fried chunks of potato with creamy tomato sauce
pescaditos fritos	assortment of fried little fish
picos	little breadsticks (free)
pimiento (relleno)	peppers (stuffed)
pisto	mixed sautéed vegetables
pulpo	octopus
queso	cheese (or a beautiful woman)
queso manchego	sheep cheese
rabas	squid tentacles
rabo de toro	bull-tail stew
revuelto de...	scrambled eggs with...
...setas	...wild mushrooms
tabla serrana	hearty plate of mountain meat and cheese
tortilla española	potato omelet
tortilla de jamón/queso	potato omelet with ham/cheese
variado fritos	typical Andalusian mix of various fried fish

Cured Meats (Charcutería)

salchichón	sausage
jamón ibérico	best ham, from acorn-fed baby pigs
jamón serrano	cured ham
chorizo	spicy sausage
lomo	pork loin

Typical Desserts

flan de huevo	crème caramel
arroz con leche	rice pudding
helados (variados)	ice cream (various flavors)
fruta del tiempo	fruit in season
un queso	cheese

for the smaller tapas portions, though some bars (especially in the north) simply don't serve anything smaller than a *ración*.

Eating and drinking at a bar is usually cheapest if you eat or drink at the counter *(barra)*. You may pay a little more to eat sitting at a table *(mesa)* and still more for an outdoor table *(terraza)*. Locate the price list (often posted in fine type on a wall somewhere) to know the menu options and price tiers. In the right place, a quiet snack and drink on a terrace on the town square is well worth the extra charge. But the cheapest seats sometimes get the best show. Sit at the bar and study your bartender—he's an artist.

Be assertive or you'll never be served. *Por favor* (please) grabs the guy's attention. Don't worry about paying until you're ready to leave (he's keeping track of your tab). To get the bill ask: "*¿La cuenta?*" (or *la dolorosa*—meaning literally "the sadness"—always draws a confused laugh). Bars come with a formidable language barrier. A small working vocabulary is essential for tapas proficiency (see previous page).

Chasing down a particular bar for tapas nearly defeats the purpose and spirit of tapas—they are impromptu. Just drop in at any lively place. I look for the noisy spots with piles of napkins and food debris on the floor (go local and toss your trash, too), lots of locals, and the TV blaring. Popular television-viewing includes bullfights and soccer games, American sitcoms, and Spanish interpretations of soaps and silly game shows (you'll see Vanna Blanco). While tapas are served all day, the real action begins late—21:00 at the earliest. But for beginners, an earlier start is easier and comes with less commotion.

Get a fun, inexpensive sampler plate. Ask for *un ración de canapés variados* to get a plate of various little open-face sandwiches. Or ask for a *surtido de* (an assortment of...) *charcutería* (a mixed plate of meat) or *queso* (cheese). *Un surtido de jamón y queso* means a plate of different hams and cheeses. Order bread, and two glasses of red wine on the right square—and you've got a romantic (and $10) dinner for two.

Spanish Drinks

Spain is one of the world's leading producers of grapes and that means lots of excellent wine: both red *(tinto)* and white *(blanco)*. Major wine regions include Valdepeñas, Penedès (Cabernet-style wines from near Barcelona), Rioja (spicy reds from the *tempranillo* grape, from the high plains of northern Spain), and Ribera del Duero (north of Madrid). For quality wine, ask for *crianza* (old), *reserva* (older), or *gran reserva* (oldest).

Sherry, a fortified wine from the Jerez region, ranges from dry *(fino)* to sweet *(dulce)*—Spaniards drink the *fino* and export the *dulce*. *Cava* is Spain's answer to champagne. Sangria (red wine mixed with fruit juice) is popular and refreshing.

To get a small draft beer, ask for a *caña* (KAHN-yah). Spain's bars often serve fresh-squeezed orange juice *(zumo de naranja natural)*. For something completely different, try *horchata de chufas,* a sweet, milky beverage made from earth almonds. If ordering mineral water in a restaurant, request a *botella grande de agua* (big bottle). They push the more profitable small bottles.

Here are some words to help you quench your thirst:

agua con/sin gas	water with/without bubbles
un vaso de agua del grifo	glass of tap water
una jarra de agua	pitcher of tap water
refresco	soft drink (common brands are Coca-Cola; Fanta—*limón* or *naranja*; and Schweppes—*limón* or *tónica*)
vino tinto/blanco de la casa	house red/white wine
un tinto	a small glass of house red wine
chato	small glass of house wine
tinto de verano	a lighter sangria
vermú	vermouth
mucho cuerpo	full-bodied
afrutado	fruity
seco	dry
dulce	sweet
cerveza	beer
caña	small glass of draft beer
doble, tubo	tall glass of beer
¡Salud!	Cheers!

TRAVELING AS A TEMPORARY LOCAL

We travel all the way to Europe to enjoy differences—to become temporary locals. You'll experience frustrations. Certain truths that we find "God-given" or "self-evident," such as cold beer, ice in drinks, bottomless cups of coffee, hot showers, and bigger being better, are suddenly not so true. One of the benefits of travel is the eye-opening realization that there are logical, civil, and even better alternatives. A willingness to go local ensures that you'll enjoy a full dose of Spanish hospitality.

While Europeans look bemusedly at some of our Yankee excesses—and worriedly at others—they nearly always afford us individual travelers all the warmth we deserve.

When updating this book, I hear over and over again that my readers are considerate and fun to have as guests. Thank you for traveling as temporary locals who are sensitive to the culture. It's fun to follow you in my travels.

Send Me a Postcard, Drop Me a Line

If you enjoy a successful trip with the help of this book and would like to share your discoveries, please fill out the survey at www.ricksteves .com/feedback, or e-mail me at rick@ricksteves.com. I personally read and value all feedback.

Judging from the happy postcards I receive from travelers, it's safe to assume you're on your way to a great, affordable vacation—with the finesse of an independent, experienced traveler. Thanks, and *buen viaje!*

BACK DOOR TRAVEL PHILOSOPHY
From *Rick Steves' Europe Through the Back Door*

Travel is intensified living—maximum thrills per minute and one of the last great sources of legal adventure. Travel is freedom. It's recess, and we need it.

Experiencing the real Europe requires catching it by surprise, going casual..."through the Back Door."

Affording travel is a matter of priorities. (Make do with the old car.) You can travel—simply, safely, and comfortably—anywhere in Europe for $100 a day plus transportation costs. In many ways, spending more money only builds a thicker wall between you and what you came to see. Europe is a cultural carnival, and, time after time, you'll find that its best acts are free and the best seats are the cheap ones.

A tight budget forces you to travel close to the ground, meeting and communicating with the people, not relying on service with a purchased smile. Never sacrifice sleep, nutrition, safety, or cleanliness in the name of budget. Simply enjoy the local-style alternatives to expensive hotels and restaurants.

Extroverts have more fun. If your trip is low on magic moments, kick yourself and make things happen. If you don't enjoy a place, maybe you don't know enough about it. Seek the truth. Recognize tourist traps. Give a culture the benefit of your open mind. See things as different but not better or worse. Any culture has much to share.

Of course, travel, like the world, is a series of hills and valleys. Be fanatically positive and militantly optimistic. If something's not to your liking, change your liking. Travel is addictive. It can make you a happier American, as well as a citizen of the world. Our Earth is home to six billion equally important people. It's humbling to travel and find that people don't envy Americans. They like us, but, with all due respect, they wouldn't trade passports.

Globe-trotting destroys ethnocentricity. It helps you understand and appreciate different cultures. Travel changes people. It broadens perspectives and teaches new ways to measure quality of life. Many travelers toss aside their hometown blinders. Their prized souvenirs are the strands of different cultures they decide to knit into their own character. The world is a cultural yarn shop. And Back Door travelers are weaving the ultimate tapestry. Come on, join in!

SPAIN
(España)

Spain may seem poor compared to Sweden, but it has a richness—of history, of culture, of people—that has little to do with per capita income. From the stirring *sardana* dance in Barcelona to the sizzling rat-a-tat-tat of flamenco in Sevilla, this country creates its own beat despite the heat. Spaniards are proud and stoic. They can be hard to get to know—but once you've made a connection, you've got a friend for life.

If you fly over Spain, you'll see that parts of the country are parched as red-orange as a desert. But the country thrives, especially in the cool of the evening. Spaniards are notorious night owls. Many clubs and restaurants don't even open until after midnight. The antidote for late nights is a midday nap. Locals—and most businesses—take a siesta (about 13:00–16:00).

Spain is in Europe, but not *of* Europe—it has a unique identity and history, divided from the rest of the Continent by the Pyrenees. For 700 years (711–1492), its dominant culture was Muslim, not Christian. And after a brief Golden Age financed by New World gold (1500–1600), Spain retreated into three centuries of isolation (1600–1900). This continued into the 20th century, as the fascist dictator Francisco Franco virtually sealed the country off from the rest of Europe's democracies. But since Franco's death, Spaniards have almost swung to the opposite extreme, becoming extremely open to new trends and technologies.

Spain's relative isolation created a unique country with odd customs—bullfights, flamenco dancing, and a national obsession with ham. It's a land of world-class art (El Greco, Diego Velázquez, Francisco Goya, Pablo Picasso) and a vibrant contemporary scene in the arts and cinema. The cuisine is hearty and unrefined, ranging from tapas and dry sherry, to paella and sangria, to a full meal of roast suckling pig washed down with spicy Rioja wine.

Spain's topography resembles a giant upside-down cereal bowl, with a coastal lip and a high central plateau. The north is mountainous and rainy; the south is hilly and hot. The large central plain, with Madrid in the center, is flat and dry. Along the Mediterranean coast, Spain has an almost Italian feel. Spain has cosmopolitan cities, but at night, when whole families stream out of their apartments to wander the streets, even the biggest city feels like a rural village.

The country hosts several different languages. "Castilian"— what we call "Spanish"—is spoken throughout the country. But in the far north, Basque is the second language, and Barcelona's natives speak their own Romance language, Catalan. You've heard of

How Big, How Many, How Much

- Spain is 195,000 square miles (three-fourths the size of Texas), 85 percent of the Iberian Peninsula
- 40 million people (200 people per square mile, 80 percent in towns and cities)
- 1 euro (€1) = about $1.20

Basque nationalists, but every other region of Spain also has its own dialect, customs, and (often half-hearted) separatist movement. Basques, Catalonians, Andalusians, Galicians—even Castilians and Leonese—they're all Spanish second.

The Spanish people are proud and straightforward. They own one car, one TV, and look down on status symbols and social climbers. People work to live, not vice versa. Their focus is on friends and family. In fact, the siesta is not so much naptime as it is the opportunity for everyone to shut down their harried public life and enjoy good food and the comfort of loved ones. Nighttime is for socializing, whether it's cruising the streets or watching the soccer game (Real Madrid or F.C. Barcelona) on TV in a crowded bar.

While you can see some European countries by just passing through, Spain is a destination. Learn its history and accept it on its own terms. Gain (or just fake) an appreciation for sliced ham, dry sherry, and bull's-tail soup, and the Spanish will love you for it. If you go, go all the way. Immerse yourself in Spain.

BARCELONA

Barcelona is Spain's second city and the capital of the proud and distinct region of Catalunya. With Franco's fascism now ancient history, Catalan flags wave once again. Language and culture are on a roll in Spain's most cosmopolitan and European corner.

Barcelona bubbles with life in its narrow Gothic Quarter alleys, along the grand boulevards, and throughout the chic, grid-planned, new part of town called Eixample. While Barcelona had an illustrious past as a Roman colony, Visigothic capital, 14th-century maritime power, and—in more modern times—a top Mediterranean trading and manufacturing center, it's most enjoyable to throw out the history books and just drift through the city. If you're in the mood to surrender to a city's charms, let it be in Barcelona.

Planning Your Time

Sandwich Barcelona between flights or overnight train rides. There's little of earthshaking importance within eight hours by train. It's as easy to fly into Barcelona as it is to fly into Madrid, Lisbon, or Paris for most travelers from the United States. Those renting a car can cleverly start here, fly to Madrid, see Madrid and Toledo, and pick up the car as they leave Madrid.

On the shortest visit, Barcelona is worth one night, one day, and an overnight train or evening flight out. The Ramblas is two different streets by day and by night. Stroll it from top to bottom in the evening and again the next morning, grabbing breakfast on a stool in a market café. Wander the Gothic Quarter, see the cathedral, and have lunch in the Eixample (eye-SHAM-plah). The top two sights in town, Antoni Gaudí's Sagrada Família Church and the Picasso Museum, are usually open until 20:00 during the summer (Picasso closes at 15:00 on Sun and all day Mon). The illuminated fountains on Montjuïc make a good finale for your day.

Barcelona

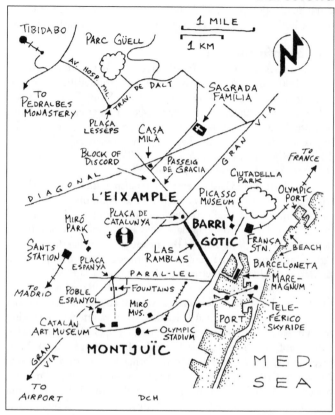

Of course, Barcelona in a day is insane. To better appreciate the city's ample charm, spread your visit over two or three days.

ORIENTATION

The large square, Plaça de Catalunya, sits at the center of Barcelona, dividing the older and newer parts of town. Sloping downhill from the Plaça is the old town (Barri Gòtic, or Gothic Quarter), with the boulevard called the Ramblas running down to the harbor. Above Plaça de Catalunya is the modern residential area called the Eixample. A hill called Montjuïc overlooks the harbor.

The soul of Barcelona is in its compact core—the old town and the Ramblas. This is your strolling, shopping, and people-watching nucleus. The city's sights are widely scattered, but with a map and a willingness to figure out the sleek subway system (or a few euros for taxis), all is manageable.

Mentally, you'll need to orient yourself to a different language—Catalan. While Spanish ("Castilian") is widely spoken, the native tongue in this region is Catalan, as different from Spanish as Italian.

Tourist Information

There are several useful **TI**s in Barcelona: at the **airport** (daily 9:00–21:00, offices in both terminal A and terminal B, free room-finding service, tel. 934-784-704); at the **Sants Train Station** (Mon–Fri 8:00–20:00, Sat–Sun 8:00–14:00, near track 6); and **Plaça de Catalunya** (daily 9:00–21:00; on main square near recommended hotels, look for red sign; also has room-finding service). Most of the TIs sell phone cards and tickets for the Tourist Bus (described in "Getting Around Barcelona," below).

The **Barcelona Card** covers public transportation (buses, Metro, Montjuïc funicular, and *golondrina* harbor tours). It offers free admission to minor sights and discounts on major sights (available from 1–5 days, €17/1 day, up to €27/5 days, sold at TIs and El Corte Inglés department store). The **Tourist Bus ticket** offers smaller discounts on sights, but is more convenient since it provides direct transportation right to the sights (see "Getting Around Barcelona," below).

Note that the two-day version of either the Barcelona Card or the Tourist Bus ticket offers a better value than the one-day version.

On weekends, the TI at Plaça de Catalunya offers two **walking tours** in English. One tour concentrates on the Gothic Quarter (€8, April–Sept Fri–Mon at 10:00, Oct–March Sat–Sun at 10:00, 2 hrs, meet at TI, call to reserve) and the other focuses on the Picasso Museum (€10 includes museum fee, €8 on first Sun of month, Sat–Sun at 10:30). To reserve a spot on either tour, call the TI's toll number (tel. 906-301-282, €0.40/min), or book online at www.barcelonaturisme.com. The same TI also has a half-price ticket booth—"Tiquet 3"—where you can drop by in the early evening (3 hours before showtime) to see what tickets are available.

The all-Catalunya TI offices are at **Passeig de Gràcia** (Mon–Sat 10:00–19:00, Sun 10:00–14:00, #107, tel. 932-384-000) and on **Plaça de Sant Jaume** (Mon–Fri 9:00–20:00, Sat 10:00–20:00, Sun 10:00–14:00; in the City Hall Ajuntament building, last-minute room-finding service, less crowded than other TIs). If you are driving from the north into Barcelona, the TI at **Montseny** is handy (Mon–Sat 10:00–18:00, Sun 10:00–15:00, at kilometer #117 of A7 toll freeway).

At any TI, pick up the free small map or the large city map (€1), the brochure on public transport, and the free quarterly *See Barcelona* guide with practical information on museum hours, restaurants, transportation, history, festivals, and so on.

Throughout the summer, you'll see young red-jacketed tourist-info helpers on the streets in the touristed areas of town.

Palau de la Virreina, an arts-and-culture TI, offers information on Barcelona cultural events—music, opera, and theater (Mon–Sat 10:00–20:00, Sun 10:00–15:00, Ramblas 99).

Arrival in Barcelona

By Train: Although many international trains use the França Station, all domestic (and some international) trains use Sants Station. Both França and Sants have baggage lockers and subway stations: França's subway is Barceloneta (2 blocks away), and Sants' is Sants Estació (under the station). Sants Station has a good TI, a world of handy shops and eateries, and a classy, quiet Sala Euromed lounge for travelers with first-class reservations (TV, free drinks, study tables, and coffee bar). Take the Metro or a taxi to your hotel. Most trains to or from France stop at the subway station Passeig de Gràcia, just a short walk from the center (Plaça de Catalunya, TI, hotels).

By Plane: Barcelona's **El Prat de Llobregat Airport,** eight miles southwest of town, is connected cheaply and quickly by **Aerobus** (immediately in front of arrivals lobby, 4/hr until 24:00, 30 min to Plaça de Catalunya, buy €3.45 ticket from driver) or by the RENFE **train** (at airport, walk through overpass to train station, 2/hr at :13 and :43 after the hour, 20 min to Sants Station and Plaça de Catalunya; €2.30 or buy a T10 card at the airport and use it for this trip—see below). A **taxi** to or from the airport costs less than €20. The airport has a post office, pharmacy, left-luggage office, and ATMs (avoid the gimmicky machines before the baggage carousels; instead use the bank-affiliated ATMs at the far-left end of arrival hall as you face the street). Airport info: tel. 932-983-467 or 932-983-465.

By Car: Barcelona's parking fees are outrageously expensive (the one behind Boquería market charges €23/day). You won't need a car in Barcelona because the public transportation is so good. Rent your car when you're leaving.

Getting Around Barcelona

By Subway: Barcelona's Metro, among Europe's best, connects just about every place you'll visit. It has five color-coded lines. Rides cost €1.10. The T10 Card for €6 gives you 10 tickets, good for all local bus and Metro lines as well as the separate FGC line and RENFE train lines (including the airport). Pick up the TI's guide to public transport. One-, two-, and three-day passes are available (for €4.80, €7.20, and €9.15).

By Tourist Bus: The handy Tourist Bus (Bus Turistic) offers two multi-stop circuits in colorful double-decker buses (red route covers north Barcelona—most Gaudí sights; blue route covers south—Gothic Quarter, Montjuïc) with live multilingual guides (28 stops, 2 hrs per route, 9:00–22:00 in summer, 9:00–21:00 in winter, buses run every 6–30 min, most frequent in summer, buy tickets on bus or at

Barcelona at a Glance

▲▲▲Ramblas Barcelona's colorful, gritty pedestrian thoroughfare. **Hours:** Always open.

▲▲▲Picasso Museum Extensive collection offering insight into the brilliant Spanish artist's early years. **Hours:** Tue–Sat 10:00–20:00, Sun 10:00–15:00, closed Mon.

▲▲▲Sagrada Família Gaudí's remarkable, unfinished cathedral. **Hours:** Daily April–Oct 9:00–20:00, Nov–March 9:00–18:00.

▲▲Casa Milà Barcelona's quintessential modernist building, the famous melting-ice-cream Gaudí creation. **Hours:** daily 10:00–20:00.

▲▲Catalan Art Museum World-class collection of this region's art, including a substantial Romanesque collection. **Hours:** Tue–Sat 10:00–19:00, Sun 10:00–14:30, closed Mon.

▲▲Catalan Concert Hall Best modernist interior in Barcelona. **Hours:** 50-minute English tours daily every 30 minutes 10:00–15:30.

▲Cathedral Colossal Gothic cathedral. **Hours:** Daily 8:00–13:30 & 16:30–19:30.

TI). Ask for a brochure (which has a good city map) at the TI or at a pick-up point. One-day (€16) and two-day (€20) tickets include 10–20 percent discounts on the city's major sights and walking tours (leaving from TI at Plaça de Catalunya), which will likely reimburse you for half the Tourist Bus cost over the course of your visit.

By Taxi: Barcelona is one of Europe's best taxi towns. Taxis are plentiful and honest (€1.40 drop charge, €0.88/km, luggage-€0.85/piece, these "*Tarif* 2" rates are in effect 6:00–22:00, pay higher "*Tarif* 1" rates off-hours, other fees posted in window). Save time by hopping a cab (figure €4 from Ramblas to Sants Station).

Helpful Hints

Theft Alert: You're more likely to be pickpocketed here—especially on the Ramblas—than about anywhere else in Europe. Most of the crime is nonviolent, but muggings do occur. Be on guard. Leave valuables in your hotel and wear a money belt.

Here are a few common street scams, easy to avoid if you recognize them. Most common is the too-friendly local who tries to engage you in conversation by asking for the time, whether you speak English, and so on. If you suspect the person is more interested in your money than your time, ignore him

▲**City History Museum** Tracing Barcelona's history, from Roman times through the Middle Ages to today. **Hours:** June–Sept Tue–Sat 10:00–20:00, Sun 10:00–14:00, closed Mon; Oct–May Tue–Sat 10:00–14:00 & 16:00–20:00, Sun 10:00–14:00, closed Mon.

▲*Sardana* **Dances** Patriotic dance where proud Catalans join hands in a circle (usually Sat at 18:00, Sun at 12:00).

▲**Palau Güell** Exquisitely curvy Gaudí interior. **Hours:** Mon–Sat 10:00–20:00, closed Sun, closes at 18:00 Nov–April.

▲**Block of Discord** Noisy block of competing modernist facades by Gaudí and his rivals. **Hours:** Always open.

▲**Parc Güell** Colorful park at the center of the unfinished Gaudí-designed housing project. **Hours:** Daily 9:00–20:00.

▲**Fundació Joan Miró** World's best collection of art by Catalan native Joan Miró. **Hours:** July–Sept Tue–Sat 10:00–20:00, Thu until 21:30, Sun 10:00–14:30, closed Mon, Oct–June Tue–Sat closes at 19:00.

and move on. A common street gambling scam is the pea-and-carrot game, a variation on the shell game. The people winning are all ringers and you can be sure that you'll lose if you play. Also beware of groups of women aggressively selling carnations, people offering to clean off a stain from your shirt, and people picking things up in front of you on escalators. If you stop for any commotion or show on the Ramblas, put your hands in your pockets before someone else does. Assume any scuffle is simply a distraction by a team of thieves.

U.S. Consulate: Passeig Reina Elisenda 23 (tel. 932-802-227).

Emergency Phone Numbers: Police—092, Emergency—061, directory assistance—010.

24-hour Pharmacy: Near the Boquería Market at #98 on the Ramblas.

American Express: AmEx offices are at Passeig de Gràcia 101 (Mon–Fri 9:30–18:00, Sat 10:00–12:00, closed Sun, includes all travel-agency services, Metro: Diagonal, tel. 932-170-070) and at Las Ramblas 74 (daily 9:00–24:00, banking services only, opposite Liceu Metro station, tel. 933-011-166, toll-free tel. 900-994-426).

"You're not in Spain, You're in Catalunya!"

This is a popular pro-nationalist refrain you might see on T-shirts or stickers around town. Catalunya is *not* the land of bullfighting and flamenco that many visitors envision when they think of Spain (best to wait until you're in Madrid or Sevilla for those).

The region of Catalunya—with Barcelona as its capital—has its own language, history, and culture, and the people have a proud, independent spirit. Historically, Catalunya has often been at odds with the central Spanish government in Madrid. The Catalan language and culture have been repressed or outlawed at various times in Spanish history, as Catalunya often chose the wrong side in wars and rebellions against the kings in Madrid. In the Spanish Civil War (1936–1939), Catalunya was one of the last pockets of democratic resistance against the military coup of the fascist dictator Francisco Franco, who punished the region with four decades of repression. Three of Barcelona's monuments are reminders of that suppression: The Parc de la Ciutadella was originally a much-despised military citadel, constructed in the 18th century to keep locals in line. The Castle of Montjuïc, built for similar reasons, has been the site of numerous political executions, including hundreds during the Franco era. The Sacred Heart Church atop Tibidabo, completed under Franco, was meant to atone for the sins of Barcelonians during the Spanish Civil War—the main sin being opposition to Franco. Although rivalry between Barcelona and Madrid has calmed down in recent times, it rages any time the two cities' football clubs meet.

To see real Catalan culture, look for the *sardana* dance (described on page 54) or an exhibition of castellers. These teams of human-castle builders come together for festivals throughout the year

Internet Access: When **easyInternetcafé** arrived, prices for Internet access fell all over town. Europe's favorite Internet-access venue—with piles of computers, drinks, and munchies—is open daily 8:00–24:00 and offers zippy access (€1.50/hr) at two central locations: One is half a block west of Plaça de Catalunya on Ronda Universitat, and another is near the seedy bottom of the Ramblas at #31. The rival **BBiGG** is at Carrer Comtal 9, near Plaça de Catalunya (Mon–Sat 9:00–23:00, Sun 10:00–23:00, 300 terminals, tel. 933-014-020).

Local Guides: The Barcelona Guide Bureau is a co-op with plenty of excellent local guides who give personalized four-hour tours for €150; Joanna Wilhelm is good (Via Laietana 54, tel. 932-682-422 or 933-107-778, www.bgb.es). Also see the TI's walking tours, described above.

to build towers of flesh that can reach more than 50 feet high, topped off by the bravest member of the team—a child! The Gràcia festival in August and the Mercè festival in September are good times to catch the castellers.

The Catalan language is irrevocably tied to the history and spirit of the people here. Since the end of the Franco era in the mid-1970s, the language has made a huge resurgence. Now most school-age children learn Catalan first and Spanish second. Although Spanish is understood here (and the basic survival words are the same), Barcelona speaks Catalan. Here are the essential Catalan phrases:

Hello	**Hola**	(OH-lah)
Please	**Si us plau**	(see oos plow)
Thank you	**Gracies**	(GRAH-see-es)
Goodbye	**Adéu**	(ah-DAY-oo)
Exit	**Sortida**	(sor-TEE-dah)
Long live Catalunya!	**¡Visca Catalunya!**	(BEE-skah...)

Most place-names in this chapter are listed in Catalan. Here is a pronunciation guide:

Plaça de Catalunya	PLAS-sah duh cat-ah-LOON-yah
Eixample	eye-SHAM-plah
Passeig de Gràcia	PAH-sage duh grass-EE-ah
Catedral	CAH-tah-dral
Barri Gòtic	BAH-rrree GAH-teek
Montjuïc	MOHN-jew-eek

Introductory Walk:
From Plaça de Catalunya down the Ramblas

A ▲▲▲ sight, Barcelona's central square and main boulevard exert a powerful pull. Many visitors spend a major part of their time here, doing laps on the Ramblas. Here's a top-to-bottom orientation walk:
Plaça de Catalunya—This vast central square divides old and new Barcelona. It's also the hub for the Metro, bus, airport shuttle, and both Tourist Bus routes (red northern route leaves from El Corte Inglés, blue southern route from west side of Plaça). The grass around its fountain is the best public place in town for serious necking. Overlooking the square, the huge **El Corte Inglés** department store offers everything from bonsai trees to a travel agency, plus one-hour photo developing, haircuts, and cheap souvenirs (Mon–Sat 10:00–22:00, closed Sun, pick up English directory flier, supermarket in basement, 9th-floor terrace cafeteria/restaurant with great city view—take elevator from entrance nearest the TI, tel. 933-063-800).

Four great boulevards start from Plaça de Catalunya: the Ramblas, the fashionable Passeig de Gràcia, the cozier, but still fashionable, Rambla Catalunya, and the stubby, shop-filled, pedestrian-only Portal de l'Angel. Homesick Americans can even find a Hard Rock Café. Locals traditionally start or end a downtown rendezvous at the venerable Café Zürich.

Cross the street from the café to...

❶ The Top of the Ramblas—Begin your ramble 20 yards down at the ornate fountain (near #129).

More than a Champs-Élysées, this grand boulevard takes you from rich (at the top) to rough (at the port) in a one-mile, 20-minute walk. You'll raft the river of Barcelonian life past a grand opera house, elegant cafés, retread prostitutes, pickpockets, power-dressing con men, artists, street mimes, an outdoor bird market, great shopping, and people looking to charge more for a shoeshine than what you paid for the shoes.

Grab a bench and watch the scene. Open up your map and read some history into it: You're about to walk right across medieval Barcelona from Plaça de Catalunya to the harbor. Notice how the higgledy-piggledy street plan of the medieval town was contained within the old town walls—now gone, but traced by a series of roads named Ronda (meaning "to go around"). Find the Roman town, occupying about 10 percent of what became the medieval town—with tighter roads yet around the cathedral. The sprawling, modern grid plan beyond the Ronda roads is from the 19th century. Breaks in this urban waffle show where a little town was consumed by the growing city. The popular Passeig de Gràcia was literally the road to Gràcia (once a town, now a characteristic Barcelona neighborhood).

Rambla means "stream" in Arabic. The Ramblas used to be a drainage ditch along the medieval wall that once defined what's now called the Gothic Quarter. "Las Ramblas" is plural, a succession of five separately named segments, but address numbers treat it as a single long street.

You're at Rambla Canaletes, named for the fountain. The black-and-gold Fountain of Canaletes is the starting point for celebrations and demonstrations. Legend says that a drink from the fountain ensures that you'll return to Barcelona one day. All along the Ramblas, you'll see newspaper stands (open 24 hrs, selling phone cards) and ONCE booths (selling lottery tickets that support Spain's organization of the blind, a powerful advocate for the needs of people with disabilities).

Got some change? As you wander downhill, drop coins into the cans of the human statues (the money often kicks them into entertaining gear). Warning: Wherever people stop to gawk, pickpockets are at work.

From Plaça de Catalunya
down the Ramblas

NOT TO SCALE-
PLAÇA DE CATALUNYA TO COLUMBUS
MONUMENT IS A 20 MIN. WALK

TO "BLOCK OF DISCORD"

PASSEIG DE GRACIA

PLAÇA DE CATALUNYA

EL CORTE INGLES

CAFE ZÜRICH

CANALETES FOUNTAIN

SANTA ANA

AEROBUS, BUS TURISTIC & TAXIS

ACADEMY OF SCIENCE

BIRDS

CANUDA

CAFE GRANJA VIADER

BAROQUE CHURCH

CARME

PORTAFERRISSA

CULTURAL INFO PALAU VIRREINA

FLOWERS

CIGAR SHOP & EROTIC MUSEUM

LA BOQUERIA MARKET

CARDENAL

"UMBRELLA" BLDG.

HOSPITAL

BARRIO

S. PAU

FERRAN

TO PLAÇA S. JAUME

MIRÓ MOSAIC

XINES

LICEU THEATER

PLAÇA REIAL

NOU RAMBLA

PALAU GÜELL

ESCUDELLERS

MARITIME MUSEUM

COLUMBUS MONUMENT

PASSEIG COLOM

GOLONDRINAS

DCH

HARBOR

RAMBLA DE MAR

Ⓜ - METRO STATIONS

TO MAREMAGNUM

Walk 100 yards downhill to #115 and the...

❷ Rambla of the Little Birds—Traditionally, kids bring their parents here to buy pets, especially on Sundays. Apartment-dwellers find birds, turtles, and fish easier to handle than dogs and cats. Buildings with balconies that have flowers are generally living spaces; balconies with air-conditioners generally indicate offices. The Academy of Science's clock (at #115) marks official Barcelona time—synchronize. The Champion supermarket (at #113) has cheap groceries and a handy deli with cooked food to go.

A recently-discovered Roman necropolis is in a park across the street, 50 yards behind the big, modern Citadines Hotel (go through the passageway at #122). Local apartment-dwellers blew the whistle on contractors, who hoped they could finish their building before anyone noticed the antiquities they had unearthed. Imagine the tomb-lined road leading into the Roman city of Barcino 2,000 years ago.

Another 100 yards takes you to Carrer del Carme (at #2), and...

❸ Baroque Church—The big, plain Betlem church fronting the boulevard is Baroque, unusual in Barcelona. While Barcelona's Gothic age was rich (with buildings to prove it), the Baroque age hardly left a mark. (The city's importance dropped when New World discoveries shifted lucrative trade to ports on the Atlantic.) The Bagues jewelry shop, across Carrer del Carme from the church, is known for its Art Nouveau jewelry (exactingly duplicated from the c. 1898 molds of Masriera displayed in the window, buzz to get inside). At the shop's side entrance, step on the old-fashioned scales (free, in kilos) and head down the narrow lane opposite (behind the church, 30 yards) to a place expert in making you heavier. Café Granja Viader (see "Eating," page 76) has specialized in baked and dairy delights since 1870. (For more sweets, follow "A Short, Sweet Walk," listed in "Eating"—page 82, which begins at the intersection in front of the church.)

Stroll through the Ramblas of Flowers to the subway stop marked by the red M (near #100), and...

❹ La Boquería—This lively produce market is an explosion of chicken legs, bags of live snails, stiff fish, delicious oranges, and sleeping dogs (#91, Mon–Sat 8:00–20:00, best mornings after 9:00, closed Sun). The Conserves shop sells 25 kinds of olives (straight in, near back on right, 100-gram minimum, €0.20–0.40). Full legs of ham *(jamón serrano)* abound; *Paleta Ibérica de Bellota* are the best, and cost about €120 each (see "Sampling Serrano Ham," page 155). Beware:

Huevos del toro are bull testicles—surprisingly inexpensive...and oh so good. Drop by a cafe for an *espresso con leche* or breakfast (*tortilla española*—potato omelet). For lunch and dinner options, consider La Gardunya, located at the back of the market (see "Eating," page 76), Kiosko Universal (also listed under "Eating"), or any bar at the market.

The **Museum of Erotica** is your standard European sex museum—neat if you like nudes and a chance to hear phone sex in four languages (€7.50, daily June–Sept 10:00–24:00, shorter hours Oct–May, across from market at #96).

At #100, Gimeno sells cigars (appreciate the dying art of cigar boxes). Go ahead, do something forbidden in America but perfectly legal here...buy a Cuban (singles from €1). Tobacco shops sell stamps and phone cards.

Farther down the Ramblas at #83, the **Art Nouveau Escriba Café** is an ornate world of pastries, little sandwiches, locally popular chocolates, and fine coffee. Opened in 1820 as shown on the facade, it was remodeled in the modernist style (daily 8:30–21:00, indoor/outdoor seating, tel. 933-016-027).

Fifty yards farther, find the much-trod-upon anchor mosaic, a reminder of the city's attachment to the sea. Created by noted abstract artist Joan Miró, it marks the midpoint of the Ramblas. (The towering statue of Columbus in the distance is at the end of this hike.) From here, walk down to the **Liceu Opera House** (tickets on sale Mon–Fri 14:00–20:30, tel. 902-332-211; 45-minute €5 tour in English daily at 10:00; 20-min €2.50 version from upper balcony—sometimes with no light—daily at 11:00, 12:00, 13:00; reserve in advance, tel. 934-859-914, www.liceubarcelona.com). From the Opera House, cross the Ramblas to Café de l'Opera for a beverage (#74, tel. 933-177-585). This bustling café, with modernist (that is, old-timey) decor and a historic atmosphere, boasts that it's been open since 1929, even during the Spanish Civil War.

Continue to #46; turn left down an arcaded lane to a square filled with palm trees...

❺ **Plaça Reial**—This elegant, neoclassical square comes complete with old-fashioned taverns, modern bars with patio seating, a Sunday coin and stamp market (10:00–14:00), Gaudí's first public works (the two colorful helmeted lampposts), and characters who don't need the palm trees to be shady. **Herbolari Ferran** is a fine and aromatic shop of herbs, with fun souvenirs such as top-quality saffron, or *safra* (Mon–Sat 9:30–14:00 & 16:30–20:00, closed Sun, downstairs at Plaça Reial 18). The small streets stretching toward the water from the square are intriguing, but less safe.

Back across the Ramblas, **Palau Güell** offers an enjoyable look at a Gaudí interior (€3 for 60-min English/Spanish tour, usually open Mon–Sat 10:00–20:00, closed Sun, last tickets sold at 15:00, closes at 18:00 Nov–April, Carrer Nou de la Rambla 3–5, tel. 933-173-974).

This apartment was the first (1886) of Gaudí's innovative buildings, with a parabolic front doorway that signaled his emerging, non-rectangular style. If you plan to see Casa Milà, skip the climb to this less-interesting rooftop.

Farther downhill, on the right-hand side, is...

❻ **Bottom of the Ramblas**—The neighborhood to your right, Barri Xines, is the world's only Chinatown with nothing even remotely Chinese in or near it. Named for the prejudiced notion that Chinese immigrants go hand in hand with poverty, prostitution, and drug dealing, the actual inhabitants are poor Spanish, Arab, and Gypsy people. At night, the Barri Xines is frequented by prostitutes, many of them transvestites, who cater to sailors wandering up from the port. A nighttime visit gets you a street-corner massage—look out. Better yet—stay out.

The bottom of the Ramblas is marked by the Columbus Monument (see next listing). And just beyond that, **La Rambla del Mar** ("Rambla of the Sea") is a modern extension of the boulevard into the harbor. A popular wooden pedestrian bridge—with waves like the sea—leads to Maremagnum, a soulless Spanish mall with a cinema, huge aquarium, restaurants (including the recommended Tapasbar Maremagnum; see "Eating," page 76), and piles of people. Late at night, it's a rollicking youth hangout. It's a worthwhile stroll.

SIGHTS

Ramblas Sights at the Harbor

Columbus Monument (Monument a Colóm)—Marking the point where the Ramblas hits the harbor, this 200-foot-tall monument built for an 1888 exposition offers an elevator-assisted view from its top (€2, April–May daily 9:00–19:30, June–Sept daily 9:00–20:30, Oct–March Mon–Fri 10:00–13:30 & 15:30–18:30, Sat–Sun 10:00–18:30, the harbor cable car offers a better—if less handy—view). It's interesting that Barcelona would so honor the man whose discoveries ultimately led to its downfall as a great trading power. It was here in Barcelona that Ferdinand and Isabel welcomed Columbus home after his first trip to America.

Maritime Museum (Museu Marítim)—Housed in the old royal shipyards, this museum covers the salty history of ships and navigation from the 13th to the 20th century, showing off the Catalan role in the development of maritime technology (for example, the first submarine is claimed to be Catalan). With fleets of seemingly unimportant replicas of old boats explained in Catalan and Spanish, landlubbers may find it dull—but the free audioguide livens it up for sailors (€5.40, daily 10:00–19:00, closed Mon off-season, www.diba.es/mmaritim). For just €0.60 more, visit the old-fashioned sailing ship *Santa Eulàlia*, docked in the harbor across the street.

Cruises—At the foot of the Columbus Monument, tourist boats called *golondrinas* offer 30-minute harbor tours (€3.70, daily 11:45–19:00, until 17:00 Dec–Feb). A glass-bottom catamaran takes longer tours up the coast (€8.80 for 75 min, 6/day, daily 11:30–17:30). For a picnic place, consider one of these rides or the harbor steps.

Cable Car to Montjuïc—You'll see the *teleférico* carrying tourists up to the hill of Montjuïc, which offers views, a castle, and several museums (military, Catalan art, and Joan Miró's art); see "Barcelona's Montjuïc," page 65.

Gothic Quarter (Barri Gòtic): The Cathedral and Nearby

The Barri Gòtic is a bustling world of shops, bars, and nightlife packed between hard-to-be-thrilled-about 14th- and 15th-century buildings. The area around the port is seedy. But the area around the cathedral is a tangled yet inviting grab bag of undiscovered court-yards, grand squares, schoolyards, Art Nouveau storefronts, baby flea markets (Thursdays), musty junk shops, classy antique shops (on Carrer de la Palla), street musicians strumming Catalan folk songs, and balconies with domestic jungles behind wrought-iron bars. Go on a cultural scavenger hunt. Write a poem.

▲**Cathedral (Catedral de Barcelona)**—As you stand in the square looking at the cathedral, you're facing what was Roman Barcelona. On the ground to your right, letters spell out BARCINO—the city's Roman name. The three towers on the building to the right are mostly Roman.

The colossal **cathedral,** started in 1298, took 600 years to complete. Rather than stretching toward heaven, it makes a point of being simply massive (similar to the Gothic churches of Italy). The west front, though built according to the original plan, is only 100 years old (note the fancy, undulating rose window). The cathedral welcomes visitors daily (8:00–13:30 & 16:30–19:30; cloisters open daily 9:00–13:00 & 17:00–19:00; tel. 933-151-554).

The spacious interior—characteristic of Catalan Gothic build-ings—is supported by buttresses. These provide walls for 28 richly ornamented **chapels.** While the main part of the church is fairly plain, the chapels, sponsored by local guilds, show great wealth. Located in the community's most high-profile space, they provided a kind of advertising to illiterate worshipers. Find the logos and sym-bols of the various trades represented. The Native Americans that Columbus brought to town were supposedly baptized in the first chapel on the left.

The chapels ring a finely carved 15th-century **choir** *(coro)*. Pay €1 for a close-up look (with the lights on) at the ornately carved stalls and the emblems representing the various Knights of the Golden Fleece who once sat here. The chairs were folded up, giving

Barcelona's Cathedral

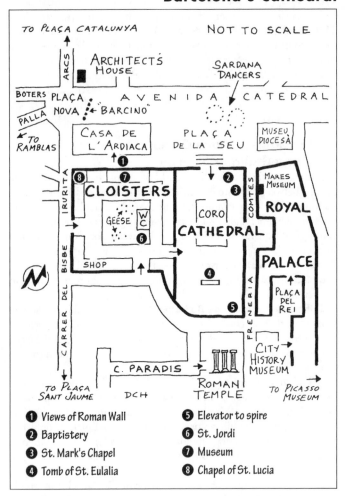

TO PLAÇA CATALUNYA   NOT TO SCALE

ARCS

ARCHITECT'S HOUSE

SARDANA DANCERS

BOTERS

PALLA

PLAÇA NOVA "BARCINO"

AVENIDA CATEDRAL

TO RAMBLAS

CASA DE L'ARDIACA

PLAÇA DE LA SEU

MUSEU DIOCESÀ

IRURITA

❶

❽ ❼

CLOISTERS

❷

❸

COMTES

MARES MUSEUM

ROYAL

GEESE

WC

❻

CORO

CATHEDRAL

PALACE

CARRER DEL BISBE

SHOP

❹

❺

FRENERIA

PLAÇA DEL REI

C. PARADIS

ROMAN TEMPLE

CITY HISTORY MUSEUM

TO PLAÇA SANT JAUME

DCH

TO PICASSO MUSEUM

❶ Views of Roman Wall
❷ Baptistery
❸ St. Mark's Chapel
❹ Tomb of St. Eulalia
❺ Elevator to spire
❻ St. Jordi
❼ Museum
❽ Chapel of St. Lucia

VIPs stools to lean on during the standing parts of the Mass. Each was creatively carved and—since you couldn't sit on sacred things—the artists were free to enjoy some secular fun here. Study the upper tier of carvings.

The **high altar** sits upon the tomb of Barcelona's patron saint, Eulàlia. She was a 13-year-old local girl tortured 13 times by Romans for her faith and finally crucified on an X-shaped cross. Her X symbol is carved on the pews. Climb down the stairs for a close look at her exquisite marble sarcophagus.

Ride the **elevator** to the roof and climb a tight spiral staircase up the spire for a commanding view (€1.40, Mon–Fri 10:30–12:30

& 16:30–18:00, closed Sat–Sun, start from chapel left of high altar).

Enter the **cloister** (through arch, right of high altar). From there, look back at the arch, an impressive mix of Romanesque and Gothic. A tiny statue of St. George slaying the dragon stands in the garden. Jordi (George) is one of the patron saints of Catalunya and by far the most popular boy's name here. Though cloisters are generally found in monasteries, this church added one to accommodate more chapels—good for business. Again, notice the symbols of the trades or guilds. Even the pavement is filled with symbols—similar to Americans getting their name on a brick for helping to pay for something.

Long ago the resident geese—there are always 13, in memory of Eulàlia—functioned as an alarm system. Any commotion would get them honking, alerting the monk in charge.

From the statue of St. Jordi, circle to the right (past a WC hidden on the left). The skippable little €0.60 **museum** (far corner) is one plush room with a dozen old religious paintings. In the corner, built into the cloister, is the dark, barrel-vaulted, Romanesque Chapel of Santa Lucía, a small church that predates the cathedral. People hoping for good eyesight (Santa Lucía's specialty) leave candles outside. Farther along, the Chapel of Santa Rita (her forte: impossible causes) usually has the most candles. Complete the circle and exit at the door just before the place you entered.

Walk uphill, following the church. From the end of the apse, turn right 50 yards up Carrer del Paradis to the **Roman Temple** (Temple Roma d'August). In the corner, a sign above a millstone in the pavement marks "Mont Tabor, 16.9 meters." Step into the courtyard for a peek at a surviving corner of the imposing temple, which once stood here on the city's highest hill, keeping a protective watch over Barcino (free, daily 10:00–14:00 & 16:00–20:00).

To locate the next three sights, see the map on page 53.

Plaça del Rei—The Royal Palace sat on King's Square (a block from the cathedral) until Catalunya became part of Spain in the 15th century. Then it was the headquarters of the local Inquisition. In 1493, a triumphant Christopher Columbus, accompanied by six New World natives (which he called "Indians") and several pure-gold statues, entered the Royal Palace. King Ferdinand and Queen Isabel rose to welcome him home, and honored him with the title "Admiral of the Oceans."

▲**City History Museum**—For a walk through the history of the city, take an elevator down 65 feet (and 2,000 years) to stroll the streets of Roman Barcelona. You'll see sewers, models of domestic life, and bits of an early Christian church. Then, an exhibit in the 11th-century count's palace shows you Barcelona through the Middle Ages (€4 includes museum, presentation, and visits to Pedralbes Monastery, Parc Güell's Center for Interpretation, and

Verdaguer House Museum—see museum pamphlet for details; June–Sept Tue–Sat 10:00–20:00, Sun 10:00–14:00, closed Mon; Oct–May Tue–Sat 10:00–14:00 & 16:00–20:00, Sun 10:00–14:00, closed Mon, Plaça del Rei, tel. 933-151-111).

Frederic Marès Museum—This classy collection combines medieval religious art with a quirky bundle of more modern artifacts—old pipes, pinups, toys, and so on (Tue–Sat 10:00–15:00, Sun 10:00–14:00, closed Mon, Carrer del Comtes, off Plaça de la Seu, next to cathedral, tel. 933-105-800).

▲**Sardana Dances**—The patriotic *sardana* dances are held at the cathedral (usually Sat at 18:00, Sun at 12:00) and at Plaça de Sant Jaume (often on Sun at 18:00 in spring and summer, 18:30 in fall and winter, none in Aug). Locals of all ages seem to spontaneously appear. For some, it's a highly symbolic, politically charged action representing Catalan unity—for most, it's just a fun chance to kick up their heels. Participants gather in circles after putting their things  in the center—symbolic of community and sharing (and the ever-present risk of theft). All are welcome, even tourists cursed with two left feet. Holding hands, they raise their arms Zorba-the-Greek-style as they hop and sway gracefully to the band. The band *(cobla)* consists of a long flute, tenor and soprano oboes, strange-looking brass instruments, and a tiny bongo-like drum *(tambori)*. The rest of Spain mocks this lazy circle dance, but, considering what it takes for a culture to survive within another culture's country, it is a stirring display of local pride and patriotism.

Shoe Museum (Museu del Calçat)—Shoe-lovers enjoy this two-room shoe museum (with a we-try-harder attendant) on the delightful Plaça de Sant Felip Neri (€1.20, Tue–Sun 11:00–14:00, closed Mon, 1 block beyond outside door of cathedral cloister, behind Plaça de G. Bachs, tel. 933-014-533). The huge shoe at the entry is designed to fit the foot of the Columbus Monument at the bottom of the Ramblas.

Plaça de Sant Jaume—On this stately central square (pronounced jow-mah) of the Gothic Quarter, two of the top governmental buildings in Catalunya face each other: The Barcelona city hall (Ajuntament; free, Sun 10:00–13:30), and the seat of the autonomous government of Catalunya (Palau de la Generalitat). *Sardana* dances take place here many Sundays (see "*Sardana* Dances," above).

Barcelona's Gothic Quarter Sights

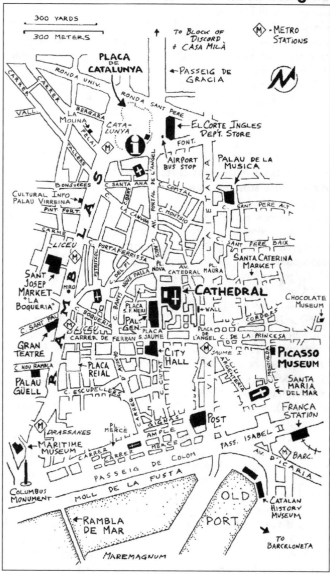

▲▲**Catalan Concert Hall (Palau de la Música Catalana)**—This concert hall, finished in 1908, features the best modernist interior in town. Inviting arches lead you into the 2,000-seat hall. A kaleidoscopic skylight features a choir singing around the sun, while playful carvings and mosaics celebrate music and Catalan culture. Admission is by tour only and starts with a relaxing 20-minute video (€7, 50-min tours in English, daily every 30 min 10:00–15:30, maybe later, about 6 blocks northeast of cathedral, tel. 932-957-200). Ask about concerts (300 per year, inexpensive tickets, www.palaumusica.org).

Gothic Quarter:
The Picasso Museum and Nearby
▲▲▲**Picasso Museum (Museu Picasso)**—This is the best collection in the country of the work of Spaniard Pablo Picasso (1881–1973), and—since he spent his formative years (age 14–21) in Barcelona—it's the best collection of his early works anywhere. By seeing his youthful, realistic art, you can more fully appreciate the artist's genius and better understand his later, more challenging art. It's scattered through two Gothic palaces, six blocks from the cathedral.

Cost, Hours, and Location: €5, or €8 including temporary exhibit on Picasso or his contemporaries, free on first Sun of month, Tue–Sat 10:00–20:00, Sun 10:00–15:00, closed Mon, last entry 30 min before closing, free and required bag check, Montcada 15–23, ticket office at #21, Metro: Jaume I, tel. 933-196-310, www.museupicasso.bcn.es. The ground floor offers a handy array of services (bookshop, WC, bag check, and cafeteria). This generally crowded museum is quieter on sunny days Wed–Sat at about 14:00 and 18:00. For a good lunch, see "Eating—Near the Picasso Museum," page 79.

Background: Picasso's personal secretary amassed a huge collection of his work and bequeathed it to the city. Picasso, happy to have a fine museum showing off his work in the city of his youth, added to the collection throughout his life. (Sadly, since Picasso vowed never to set foot in a fascist, Franco-ruled Spain, and died two years before Franco, the artist never saw the museum.)

Self-Guided Tour: While the rooms are constantly rearranged, the collection (291 paintings) is always presented chronologically. With the help of thoughtful English descriptions for each stage, it's easy to follow the evolution of Picasso's work. The room numbers in parentheses—though not exact—can help you get oriented in the museum. You'll see his art evolve in these 12 stages:

Rooms 1, 2, 3—Boy wonder, age 12–14, 1895–1897: Pablo's earliest art is realistic and serious. A budding genius emerges at age 12 as Pablo moves to Barcelona and gets serious about art. Even this young, his portraits of grizzled peasants show great psychological insight and flawless technique. You'll see portraits of Pablo's first teacher, his father *(Padre del Artista)*. Displays show his art-school work. Every time Pablo starts breaking rules, he's sent back to the standard classic style. The assignment: Sketch nude models to capture human anatomy accurately. Three self-portraits (1896) show the self-awareness of a blossoming intellect. When Pablo was 13, his father quit painting to nurture his young prodigy. Look closely at the portrait of his mother *(Retrato de la Madre del Artista)*. Pablo, then age 15, is working on the fine details and gradients of white in her blouse and the expression in her cameo-like face. Notice the signature. Spaniards keep both parents' surnames, with the father's first, followed by the mother's: Pablo Ruiz Picasso. Pablo was closer to his mom than his dad. Eventually he kept just her name.

Rooms 4, 5, 6—Málaga, exploration of nature: During a short trip to Málaga, Picasso dabbles in Impressionism (unknown in Spain at the time).

Rooms 7, 8—A sponge, influenced by local painters: As a 15-year-old, Pablo dutifully enters art-school competitions. His first big work—while forced to show a religious subject *(Primera Comunión,* or *First Communion,* Room 7)—is more an excuse to paint his family. Notice his sister Lola's exquisitely painted veil. This painting was heavily influenced by local painters.

In Room 8, *Cienca y Caridad (Science and Charity)*, which won second prize at a fine-arts exhibition, got Picasso the chance to study in Madrid. Now Picasso conveys real feeling. The doctor (Pablo's father) represents science. The nun represents charity and religion. But nothing can help, as the woman is clearly dead (notice her face and lifeless hand). Pablo painted a little perspective trick: Walk back and forth across the room to see the bed stretch and shrink. Four small studies for this painting, hanging in the back of the room, show how this was an exploratory work. The frontier: light.

Picasso travels to Madrid for further study. Finding the stuffy fine-arts school in Madrid stifling, Pablo hangs out in the Prado museum and learns by copying the masters. Notice his nearly perfect copy of Felipe IV by Diego Velázquez.

Rooms 4, 8—Independence: Having absorbed the wisdom of the ages, in 1898, Pablo visits Horta, a rural Catalan village, and finds his artistic independence.

Rooms 9, 10—Sadness, 1899–1900: Pablo—poor and without love—returns to Barcelona. It's 1900, and Art Nouveau is the rage. Upsetting his dad, Pablo quits art school and falls in with the avant-garde crowd. These bohemians congregate daily at Els Quatre Gats ("the Four Cats," slang for "a few crazy people"—see "Eating," page 76). Further establishing his artistic freedom, he paints portraits—no longer of his family...but of his new friends. Still a teenager, Pablo puts on his first one-man show.

Room 10—Paris, 1900–1901: Nineteen-year-old Picasso arrives in Paris, a city bursting with life, light, and love. Dropping the paternal surname Ruiz, Pablo establishes his commercial brand name: "Picasso." Here the explorer Picasso goes bohemian and befriends poets, prostitutes, and artists. He paints Impressionist landscapes like Claude Monet, posters like Henri de Toulouse-Lautrec, still lifes like Paul Cézanne, and bright-colored Fauvist works like Henri Matisse. (*La Espera*—with her bold outline and strong gaze—pops out from the Impressionistic background.) It was Cézanne's technique of "building" a figure with "cubes" of paint that inspired Picasso to soon invent Cubism.

Room 11—Blue Period, 1901–1904: The bleak Paris weather, the suicide of his best friend, and his own poverty lead Picasso to his "Blue Period." He cranks out piles of blue art just to stay housed and fed. With blue backgrounds (the coldest color) and depressing subjects, this period was revolutionary in art history. Now the artist is painting not what he sees but what he feels. The touching portrait of a mother and child, *Desamparados* (*Despair*, 1903), captures the period well. Painting misfits and street people, Picasso, like Velázquez and Toulouse-Lautrec, sees "the beauty in ugliness." Back home in Barcelona, Picasso paints his hometown at night from rooftops *(Terrats de Barcelona)*. Still blue, here we see proto-Cubism...five years before the first real Cubist painting.

Room 11—Rose: The woman in pink *(Retrato de la Sra. Canals)*, painted with classic "Spanish melancholy," finally lifts Picasso out of his funk, moving him out of the blue and into a happier "Rose Period" (of which this museum has only the one painting).

Rooms 12, 13, 14—Cubism, 1907–1920: Pablo's invention in Paris of the shocking Cubist style is well-known—at least I hope so, since this museum has no true Cubist paintings. In the age of the camera, the Cubist gives just the basics (a man with a bowl of fruit) and lets you finish it.

Rooms 12, 13, 14—Eclectic, 1920–1950: Picasso is a painter of many styles. We see a little post-Impressionistic Pointillism in a portrait that looks like a classical statue. After a trip to Rome, he paints beefy women, inspired by the three-dimensional sturdiness of ancient statues. To Spaniards, the expressionist horse symbolizes the innocent victim. In bullfights, the horse—clad with blinders and pummeled by the bull—has nothing to do with the fight. To Picasso, the horse symbolized the feminine and the bull, the masculine. Picasso would mix all these styles and symbols—including this image of the horse—in his masterpiece *Guernica* (in Madrid) to show the horror and chaos of modern war.

Rooms 15, 16, 17—Picasso and Velázquez, 1957: Notice the print of Velázquez's *Las Meninas* (in Madrid's Prado) that introduces this section. Picasso, who had great respect for Velázquez, painted more than 50 interpretations of this painting that many consider the greatest painting by anyone, ever. These two Spanish geniuses were artistic equals. Picasso seems to enjoy a relationship with Velázquez. Like artistic soulmates, they spar and tease. He dissects Velázquez, and then injects playful uses of light, color, and perspective to horse around with the earlier masterpiece. In the big black-and-white canvas, the king and queen (reflected in the mirror in the back of the room) are hardly seen, while the self-portrait of the painter towers above everyone. The two women of the court on the right look like they're in a tomb—but they're wearing party shoes. In these rooms, see the fun Picasso had playing paddleball with Velázquez's masterpiece—filtering Velázquez's realism through the kaleidoscope of Cubism.

Room 17—Windows, 1957: All his life, Picasso said, "Paintings are like windows open to the world." Here we see the French Riviera—with simple black outlines and Crayola colors, he paints sun-splashed nature and the joys of the beach. He died with brush in hand, still growing. To the end, through his art Picasso continued exploring and loving life. As a child, he was taught to paint as an adult. Now, as an old man (with little kids of his own and an also-childlike artist Marc Chagall for a friend), he paints like a child.

As a wrap-up, notice 41 works in Rooms 18 and 19, representing Picasso's ceramics made during his later years (1947).

Textile and Garment Museum (Museu Tèxtil i d'Indumentària)— If fabrics from the 12th to 20th centuries leave you cold, have a *café con leche* on the museum's beautiful patio (€3.50, Tue–Sat 10:00–18:00, Sun 10:00–15:00, closed Mon, free entrance to patio— an inviting courtyard with a WC and coffeeshop, which is outside museum but within the walls, 30 yards from Picasso Museum at Montcada 12–14, www.museutextil.bcn.es).

Chocolate Museum (Museu de la Xocolata)—This museum, only a couple of blocks from the Picasso Museum, is a delight for chocolate lovers. It tells the story of chocolate from Aztecs to Europeans via the port of Barcelona, where it was first unloaded and processed. Even if you're into architecture more than calories, don't miss this opportunity to see the Sagrada Família church finished—and ready to eat (€3.80, Mon and Wed–Sat 10:00–19:00, Sun 10:00–15:00, closed Tue, Carrer Comerç 36, tel. 932-687-878, www.museuxocolata.com).

Eixample

Wide sidewalks, hardy shade trees, chic shops, and plenty of Art Nouveau fun make the Eixample a refreshing break from the old town. Uptown Barcelona is a unique variation on the common grid-plan city. Barcelona snipped off the building corners to create light and spacious eight-sided squares at every intersection. For the best Eixample example, ramble Rambla Catalunya (unrelated to the more famous Ramblas) and pass through Passeig de Gràcia (described below, Metro: Passeig de Gràcia for Block of Discord, or Diagonal for Casa Milà).

The 19th century was a boom time for Barcelona. By 1850, the city was busting out of its medieval walls. A new town was planned to follow a gridlike layout. The intersection of three major thoroughfares—Gran Vía, Diagonal, and Meridiana—would shift the city's focus uptown.

The Eixample, or "Expansion," was a progressive plan in which everything was made accessible to everyone. Each 20-block-square district would have its own hospital and large park, each 10-block-square area would have its own market and general services, and each five-block-square grid would house its own schools and day-care centers. The hollow space found inside each "block" of apartments would form a neighborhood park.

While much of that vision never quite panned out, the Eixample was an urban success. Rich and artsy big shots bought plots along the grid. The richest landowners built as close to the center as possible. For this reason, the best buildings are near the Passeig de Gràcia. While adhering to the height, width, and depth limitations, they built as they pleased—often in the trendy new modernist style.

Gaudí's Art and Architecture

Barcelona is an architectural scrapbook of the galloping gables and organic curves of hometown boy Antoni Gaudí (1852–1926). A devoted Catalan and Catholic, he immersed himself in each project, often living on-site. At various times, he called Parc Güell, Casa Milà, and the Sagrada Família home.

▲▲▲Sagrada Família (Holy Family) Church—Gaudí's most famous and persistent work is this unfinished landmark. He worked on the church from 1883 to 1926. Since then, construction has moved forward in fits and starts. (But over 30 years of visits, I've seen considerable progress.) Even today, the half-finished church is not expected to be completed for another 50 years. One reason it's taking so long is that the temple is funded exclusively by private donations and entry fees. Your admission helps pay for the ongoing construction (€8, €6 with Tourist Bus ticket, daily April–Oct 9:00–20:00, Nov–March 9:00–18:00; €3 extra for English tours: 6/day April–Oct, Nov–March usually Fri–Mon only; audioguide-€3; Metro: Sagrada Família, tel. 932-073-031, www.sagradafamilia.org).

Modernist Sights

When the church is finished, a dozen 330-foot spires (representing the apostles) will stand in groups of four and mark the three entry facades of the building. The center tower (honoring Jesus) will reach 580 feet up and be flanked by 400-foot-tall towers of Mary and the four Evangelists. A unique exterior ambulatory will circle the building, like a cloister turned inside out.

1. Passion Facade (on the western side where you enter): It's full of symbolism from the Bible. Find the stylized Alpha and Omega over the door, Jesus—hanging on the cross—with an open book for hair, and the grid of numbers adding up to 33 (Jesus' age at the time of his death). The distinct face of the man on the lower left is a memorial to Gaudí.

The facade and sculpture are inspired by Gaudí's vision but designed and executed by others. Gaudí knew he wouldn't live to complete the church and recognized that later architects and artists would rely on their own muses for inspiration. This artistic freedom was amplified in 1936 when Civil War shelling burned many of Gaudí's blueprints. Judge for yourself how the recently completed and controversial Passion facade by Josep María Subirachs (b. 1927) fits with Gaudí's original formulation.

Now look high above: The colorful ceramic caps of the columns symbolize the mitres (formal hats) of bishops. This is only a side entrance. The nine-story apartment flat to the right will be torn down to accommodate the grand front entry of this church. The three facades—Passion, Nativity, and Glory—will chronicle Christ's life from birth to death to resurrection.

Now walk down to your right to the...

2. Museum (in church basement, or crypt): The museum displays physical models used for the church's construction. As you wander, you'll notice that they don't always match the finished product—these are ideas, not blueprints set in stone. See how the church's design is a fusion of nature, architecture, and religion. The columns seem light, with branches springing forth and capitals that look like palm trees. The U-shaped choir hovers above the nave, tethered halfway up the columns. Find the hanging model showing how Gaudí used gravity to calculate the perfect parabolas incorporated into the church design (the mirror above this model shows how the right-side-up church is derived from this).

Gaudí lived on the site for more than a decade and is buried in the crypt. When he died in 1926, only the stubs of four spires stood above the building site. A window allows you to look down into the neo-Gothic 19th-century crypt (which is how the church began) to see the tomb of Gaudí. There's a move afoot to make Gaudí a saint. Perhaps some day, this tomb will be a place of pilgrimage. Gaudí—a faithful Catholic whose medieval-style mysticism belied his modernist architecture career—was certainly driven to greatness by his passion for God. When undertaking a lengthy project, he said, "My client"—meaning God—"is not in a hurry." You'll peek into a busy workshop where the slow and steady building pace is maintained.

Outside, just after leaving the building, you'll encounter the...

3. Nativity Facade (east side): This, the only part of the church finished in his lifetime, shows Gaudí's original vision. Mixing Gothic-style symbolism, images from nature, and modernist asymmetry, it is the best example of Gaudí's unmistakable cake-in-the-rain style. The sculpture shows scenes from the birth and childhood of Jesus, along with angels playing musical instruments. You can love it, hate it, or adopt a love/hate attitude to it, but you can't deny that it's unique.

Finally you walk through the actual...

4. Construction Zone: The cranking cranes, rusty forests of rebar, and scaffolding require a powerful faith, but the Sagrada Família church offers a fun look at a living, growing, bigger-than-life building. It's estimated that the proposed central tower (550 feet tall) will require four underground pylons of support, each consisting of

Modernisme

The Renaixensa (Catalan cultural revival) gave birth to Modernisme (Catalan Art Nouveau) at the end of the 19th century. Barcelona is its capital. Its Eixample neighborhood shimmers with the colorful, leafy, flowing, blooming shapes of Modernisme in doorways, entrances, facades, and ceilings.

Meaning "a taste for what is modern"—things like streetcars, electric lights, and big-wheeled bicycles—this free-flowing organic style lasted from 1888 to 1906. Breaking with tradition, artists experimented with glass, tile, iron, and brick. The structure was fully modern, using rebar and concrete, but the decoration was a clip-art collage of nature images, exotic Moorish or Chinese themes, and fanciful Gothic crosses and knights to celebrate Catalunya's medieval glory days. It's Barcelona's unique contribution to the Europe-wide Art Nouveau movement. Modernisme was a way of life as Barcelona burst into the 20th century.

Antoni Gaudí (1852–1926), Barcelona's most famous modernist artist, was descended from four generations of metalworkers, a lineage of which he was quite proud. He incorporated ironwork into his architecture and came up with novel approaches to architectural structure and space.

Two more modernist architects famous for their unique style are Lluís Domènech i Muntaner and Josep Puig i Cadafalch. You'll see their work on the Block of Discord.

8,000 tons of cement. Take the elevator on the Passion side (€2) or the stairs on the Nativity side (free but often miserably congested) up to the dizzy lookout that bridges two spires. You'll get a great view of the city and a gargoyle's-eye perspective of the loopy church. If there's any building on earth I'd like to see, it's the Sagrada Família...finished.

▲**Palau Güell**—This is a good chance to enjoy a Gaudí interior (see "Introductory Walk: From Plaça de Catalunya down the Ramblas," page 45). Curvy.

▲▲**Casa Milà (La Pedrera)**—This Gaudí exterior laughs down on the crowds filling Passeig de Gràcia. Casa Milà, also called La Pedrera ("The Quarry"), has a much-photographed roller coaster of melting-ice-cream eaves. This is Barcelona's quintessential modernist building and Gaudí's last major work (1906–1910) before dedicating his final years to the Sagrada Família.

You can visit three sections: the apartment, attic, and rooftop. Buy the €7 ticket to see all three. Starting with the apartment, an elevator whisks you to the *Life in Barcelona 1905–1929* exhibit (good English descriptions). Then, walk through a sumptuously furnished Art Nouveau apartment. Upstairs in the attic, wander under parabola-shaped brick arches and enjoy a multimedia exhibit of models, photos, and videos of Gaudí's works. A stairway leads to the fanciful rooftop, where chimneys play volleyball with the clouds. From here, you can see Gaudí's other principal works, the Sagrada Família to the west, Casa Batlló to the south, and Parc Güell to the north (daily 10:00–20:00; free tour in English Mon–Fri at 16:00, or rent the €3 audioguide; Passeig de Gràcia 92, Metro: Diagonal, tel. 934-845-530).

At the ground level of Casa Milà, poke into the dreamily-painted original entrance courtyard (free). The first floor hosts free art exhibits. During the summer, a concert series called "Pedrera by Night" features live music—jazz, flamenco, tango—a glass of champagne, and the chance to see the rooftop illuminated (€10, July–Sept Fri–Sat at 22:00, tel. 934-845-900).

▲Block of Discord—Four blocks from Casa Milà, you can survey a noisy block of competing, late-19th-century facades. Several of Barcelona's top modernist mansions line Passeig de Gràcia (Metro: Passeig de Gràcia). Because the structures look as though they are trying to outdo each other in creative twists, locals nicknamed the block between Consell de Cent and Arago the "Block of Discord." First (at #43) and most famous is Gaudí's Casa Batlló, with skull-like balconies and a tile roof that suggests a cresting dragon's back; Gaudí based the work on the popular St. Jordi/George-slays-the-dragon legend (€16 includes main floor, roof, and decent audioguide). By the way, if you're tempted to snap your photos from the middle of the street, be careful—Gaudí died under a streetcar.

Next door, at Casa Amatller (#41), check out architect Josep Puig i Cadafalch's creative mix of Moorish- and Gothic-inspired architecture and iron grillwork, which decorates a step-gable like those in the Netherlands.

On the corner (at #35) Casa Lleó Morera has a wonderful interior highlighted by the dining room's fabulous stained glass. The architect, Lluís Domènech i Muntaner, also did the Catalan Concert Hall (you'll see similarities).

The perfume shop halfway down the street has a free and interesting little perfume museum in the back. The Hostal de Rita restaurant, just around the corner on Carrer Arago, serves a fine three-course lunch for a great price at 13:00 (see "Eating," page 76).

▲Parc Güell—Gaudí fans enjoy the artist's magic in this colorful park (free, daily 9:00–20:00). The Center for Interpretation of Parc Güell (Centre d'Interpretació) at the park entrance is a new visitors center, showing Gaudí's building methods plus maps, photos, and models of the park (€2, or €4 combo-ticket including City History Museum, daily 11:00–15:00, red Tourist Bus or bus #24 from Plaça de Catalunya, €8 by taxi, tel. 933-190-222, www.museuhistoria.bcn.es). The small Gaudí Museum is the middle of the park is less interesting than the Center (€4, daily 10:00–20:00, closes at 18:00 Oct–March;

red Tourist Bus or bus #24 from Plaça de Catalunya; €6 by taxi, tel. 932-130-488).

Gaudí intended this 30-acre garden to be a 60-residence housing project—a kind of gated community—rather than a park. As a high-income housing development, it flopped. As a park, it's a delight, offering another peek into the eccentric genius of Gaudí. From the bus stop, you'll hike uphill three blocks to the main (lower) entry to the park. (Taxis take you right there.) Notice the mosaic medallions that say "park" in English, reminding folks that this is modeled on an English garden.

Imagine living here 100 years ago, when this gated community was filled with Barcelona's wealthy. Stepping past fancy gate houses (which now hold a good bookshop and an audiovisual intro), you walk by Gaudí's wrought-iron gas lamps (1900–1914)—his dad was a blacksmith, and he always enjoyed this medium. Climb the grand stairway past the ceramic dragon fountain. At the top, drop by the Hall of 100 Columns, a produce market for the neighborhood's 60 (never-completed) mansions. The fun columns—each different, made from concrete and rebar, topped with colorful ceramic, and studded with broken bottles and bric-a-brac—add to the market's vitality. After shopping, continue up. Look left, down the playful "pathway of columns" that support a long arcade. Gaudí drew his inspiration from nature, and this arcade is like a surfer's perfect "tube." From here, continue up to the terrace. Sit on a colorful bench—designed to fit your body ergonomically—and enjoy one of Barcelona's best views. Look for the Sagrada Família church in the distance.

When considering the failure of Parc Güell, also consider that it was an idea just a hundred years ahead of its time. Back then, high-society ladies didn't want to live so far from the cultural action. Today, the surrounding neighborhoods are some of the wealthiest in town, and a gated community here would be a big hit.

Barcelona's Montjuïc

The Montjuïc ("Mount of the Jews"), overlooking Barcelona's hazy port, has always been a show-off. Ages ago it had an impressive fortress. In 1929, it hosted an international fair, from which most of today's sights originated. And in 1992, the Summer Olympics directed the world's attention to this pincushion of attractions.

Getting to Montjuïc: You have several options—the simplest is to take a taxi directly to your destination (about €7). From the port, the fastest and most scenic way to Montjuïc is via the gondola, called the 1929 Transbordador Aereo (€9 round-trip, daily June–mid-Sept 11:00–20:00, mid-Sept–May 10:45–19:00, 4/hr; at tower in port next to World Trade Center, ride elevator up to catch dangling gondola; tel. 934-430-859).

Otherwise, there are three options, all of which drop you off at

Montjuïc

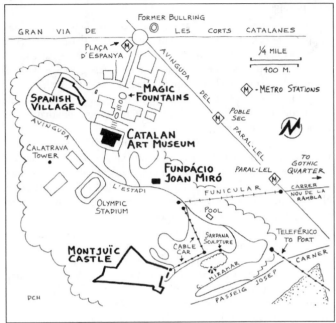

the base of a funicular/cable car below the Castle of Montjuïc: on the blue Tourist Bus route (see "Getting around Barcelona," page 41); by bus #50 from the corner of Gran Vía and Passeig de Gràcia (€1, every 10 min), #55 from Plaça de Catalunya (next to Caja de Madrid building); or by Metro to the Parallel stop (funicular covered by T10 transit pass and Barcelona Card). The cable car *(teleférico)* takes you the last stretch up to the Castle of Montjuïc (€3.40 one-way, €4.80 round-trip, daily 11:15–21:00, fewer trips Nov–March, tel. 934-430-859). Alternately, from the same spot you can walk uphill 20 minutes through the pleasant park.

Castle of Montjuïc—The castle offers great city views and a military museum (€2.50, €1 for views from fortress only, daily 9:30–20:00). The seemingly endless museum houses a dull collection of guns, swords, and toy soldiers. An interesting section on the Spanish-American War of 1898 covers Spain's valiant fight against American aggression (from its perspective). Unfortunately, there are no English descriptions. Those interested in Jewish history will find a fascinating collection of ninth-century Jewish tombstones. The castle itself has a fascist past. It was built in the 18th century by the central Spanish government to keep an eye on Barcelona and stifle citizen revolt. When Franco was in power, the castle was the site of hundreds of political executions.

▲**Fountains (Font Màgica)**—Music, colored lights, and huge amounts of water make an artistic and coordinated splash on summer nights at Plaça Espanya (20-min shows start on the half hour Fri–Sat 19:00–21:00, Thu and Sat in summer until 23:00; from the Plaça Espanya Metro station, walk toward the towering National Palace).

Spanish Village (Poble Espanyol)—This tacky five-acre model village uses fake traditional architecture from all over Spain as a shell to contain gift shops. Craftspeople do their clichéd thing only in the morning (not worth your time or €7, www.poble-espanyol.com). After hours, it's a popular local nightspot.

▲▲**Catalan Art Museum (Museu Nacional d'Art de Catalunya)**—In 2005, this museum, often called "the Prado of Romanesque art," inaugurates new sections, presenting art from the 10th to the mid-20th centuries. The museum has long featured Romanesque, Renaissance, and Baroque works; the Cambo and Thyssen collections; and, on the second floor, 19th- and 20th-century works including lesser-known modernist art (furniture, paintings, and sculpture by artists such as Gaudí, Casas, and Llimona).

This rare, world-class collection of art came mostly from remote Catalan village churches in the Pyrenees (saved from unscrupulous art dealers—many American).

The Romanesque wing features frescoes, painted wooden altar fronts, and ornate statuary. This classic Romanesque art—with flat 2-D scenes, each saint holding his symbol, and Jesus (easy to identify by the cross in his halo)—is impressively displayed on replicas of the original church ceilings.

In the Gothic wing, fresco murals give way to vivid 14th-century wood-panel paintings of Bible stories. A roomful of paintings by the Catalan master Jaume Huguet (1412–1492) deserves a look, particularly his altarpiece of Barcelona's patron saint, George.

Before you leave, ice-skate under the huge dome over to the air-conditioned cafeteria. This was the prime ceremony room and dance hall for the 1929 International Exposition. You can also have a chic lunch, with views over Barcelona, in the second-floor restaurant.

The museum is in the massive National Palace building above the fountains, near Plaça Espanya (museum entry-€6, free first Thu of month, Tue–Sat 10:00–19:00, Sun 10:00–14:30, closed Mon, audioguide, on Tourist Bus ticket, take escalators up, tel. 936-622-0376, www.mnac.es).

▲**Fundació Joan Miró**—For something more up-to-date, this museum—showcasing the modern-art talents of yet another Catalan artist—has the best collection of Joan Miró art anywhere. You'll also see works by other modern artists (such as the American Alexander Calder's *Mercury Fountain*). If you don't like abstract art, you'll leave here scratching your head, but those who love this place are not faking it...they understand the genius of Miró and the fun of abstract art.

As you wander, consider this: Miró believed that everything in the cosmos is linked—colors, sky, stars, love, time, music, dogs, men, women, dirt, and the void. He mixed childlike symbols of these things creatively, as a poet uses words. It's as liberating for the visual artist to be abstract as it is for the poet: Both can use metaphors rather than being confined to concrete explanations. Miró would listen to music and paint. It's interactive, free interpretation. He said, "For me, simplicity is freedom."

To enjoy Miró's art: 1) meditate on it; 2) read the title (for example, *The Smile of a Tear*); 3) meditate on it again. Repeat until epiphany. There's no correct answer—it's pure poetry. Devotees of Miró say they fly with him and don't even need drugs. Take advantage of the wonderful audioguide, included with admission (€7.20, July–Sept Tue–Sat 10:00–20:00, Thu until 21:30, Sun 10:00–14:30, closed Mon; Oct–June Tue–Sat closes at 19:00, Parc de Montjuïc, tel. 934-439-470, www.bcn.fjmiro.es).

More Sights in Barcelona

Citadel Park (Parc de la Ciutadella)—Barcelona's biggest, greenest park, originally the site of a much-hated military citadel, was transformed in 1888 for a World's Fair (Universal Exhibition). The stately Triumphal Arch at the top of the park was built as the main entrance. Inside, you'll find wide pathways, plenty of trees and grass, the zoo, and the geology and zoology museums. In Barcelona, which suffers from a lack of real green space, this park is a haven. Enjoy the ornamental fountain that the young Antoni Gaudí helped design, and consider a jaunt in a rowboat on the lake in the center of the park (€1.20/person for 30 min). Check out the tropical Umbracle greenhouse and the Hivernacle winter garden, which has a pleasant café-bar (daily 8:00–20:00, Metro: Arc de Triomf, east of França train station).

Barcelona's Beach—Take the trek through the charming Barceloneta neighborhood to the tip of this man-made peninsula. The beaches begin here and stretch for 2.5 miles up the coast to the Olympic Port and beyond. Everything you see here—palm trees, cement walkways, and tons of sand—was installed in the mid-1980s in an effort to shape up the city for the 1992 Summer Olympic Games. The beaches are fine for sunbathing (beach chair rental-€3/day), but the water quality is questionable for swimming. Take a lazy stroll down the seafront promenade to the Olympic Port, where you'll find bars, restaurants, and, at night, dance clubs.

Away from the Center

Monastery of Pedralbes—The museum shows off the monastery's six centuries of history (with a peaceful cloister and cells set up for worship, giving a peek into the everyday life of the cloistered nuns).

Unfortunately, it's far from the center (€4, Tue–Sun 10:00–14:00, closed Mon, buses: #22, #63, #64, #75, tel. 932-801-434).

Tibidabo—Tibidabo comes from the Latin for "to thee I shall give," the words the devil used when he was tempting Christ. It's still an enticing offer: At the top of Barcelona's highest peak, you're offered the city's oldest fun-fair (erratic hours, tel. 932-117-942), the neo-Gothic Sacred Heart Church, and—if the weather and air quality are good—an almost limitless view of the city and the Mediterranean.

Getting there is part of the fun: Start by taking the FGC line—similar to, but separate from, the Metro (also covered by the T10 ticket)—from the Plaça de Catalunya station (under Café Zürich) to the Tibidabo stop. The red Tourist Bus stops here, too. Then take Barcelona's only remaining tram—the Tramvía Blau—from Plaça John F. Kennedy to Plaça Dr. Andreu (€2.90, 2–4/hr). From there, take the funicular to the top (€3, tel. 906-427-017).

NIGHTLIFE

Refer to the *See Barcelona* guide (free from TI) and find out the latest at a TI. Sights open daily until 20:00 include the Picasso Museum (closes at 15:00 on Sun), Casa Milà, Gaudí's Sagrada Família, and Parc Güell. On Thursday, the Joan Miró museum stays open until 21:30. On Montjuïc, the fountains on Plaça Espanya make a splash on weekend evenings (Fri–Sat, plus Thu in summer).

For music, consider a performance at Casa Milà ("Pedrera by Night" summer concert series, see page 63), the Liceu Opera House (page 49), or the Catalan Concert Hall (page 56). Two decent music clubs are La Boite (477 Diagonal, near El Corte Inglés) and Jamboree (on Plaça Reial).

SLEEPING

Book ahead. If necessary, the TI at Plaça de Catalunya has a room-finding service. Barcelona is Spain's most expensive city. Still, it has reasonable rooms. Cheap places are more crowded in summer; fancier business-class places fill up in winter and offer discounts on weekends and in summer. Prices listed do not include the 7 percent tax or breakfast (ranging from simple €3 spreads to €13.25 buffets) unless otherwise noted. While many recommended places are on pedestrian streets, night noise is a problem almost everywhere (especially in cheap places, which have single-pane windows). For a quiet night, ask for "*tranquilo*" rather than "*con vista.*"

Eixample

For an uptown, boulevard-like neighborhood, sleep in the Eixample, a 10-minute walk from the Ramblas action.

$$ Hotel Gran Vía, filling a palatial mansion built in the 1870s, offers Botticelli and chandeliers in the public rooms; a sprawling, peaceful sun garden; and 54 spacious, comfy, air-conditioned rooms. While borderline ramshackle, it's charming and an excellent value (Sb-€75, Db-€125, Tb-€150, elevator, Internet access, quiet, Gran Vía de les Corts Catalanes 642, tel. 933-181-900, fax 933-189-997, www.nnhotels.es, hgranvia@nnhotels.es, Juan Gomez SE).

$$ Hotel Continental Palacete fills a 100-year-old chandeliered mansion. With flowery wallpaper and cheap but fancy furniture under ornately gilded stucco, it's gaudy in the city of Gaudí. But it's friendly, clean, quiet, and well-located, and the beds are good. Owner Señora Vallet (whose son, José, runs the recommended Hotel Continental—see "Hotels with 'Personality' on or near the Ramblas," below) has a creative vision for this 19-room hotel (Sb-€90–150, Db-€110–150, Tb-€150–180, includes breakfast and free fruit-and-drink buffet all day, air-con, 2 blocks north of Plaça de Catalunya at corner of Carrer Diputació, Rambla Catalunya 30, tel. 934-457-657, fax 934-450-050, www.hotelcontinental.com, palacete @hotelcontinental.com).

$ Hostal Residencia Neutral, with a classic Eixample address and 28 very basic rooms, is a family-run time warp (tiny Ss-€30, Ds-€46, Db-€52, extra bed-€9.50, €5 breakfast in pleasant breakfast room, elevator, fans, thin walls and some street noise, elegantly located 2 blocks north of Gran Vía at Rambla Catalunya 42, tel. 934-876-390, fax 934-876-848, hostalneutral@arrakis.es, owner Ramón SE). Its sister hotel, **Hotel Universal,** with 18 noisy rooms, lacks the friendly feel and is stark but well-located (Sb-€45, Db-€60, Tb-€70, no breakfast, 4 quieter rooms in interior, Arago 281, tel. 934-879-762, fax 934-874-028, hoteluniversal@arrakis.es).

Sleep Code

(€1 = about $1.20, country code: 34)
S = Single, **D** = Double/Twin, **T** = Triple, **Q** = Quad, **b** = bathroom, **s** = shower only, **no CC** = Credit Cards not accepted, **SE** = Speaks English, **NSE** = No English. Unless otherwise noted, credit cards are accepted.

To help you easily sort through these listings, I've divided the rooms into three categories, based on the price for a standard double room with bath (during high season):

$$$ **Higher Priced**—Most rooms €150 or more.
$$ **Moderately Priced**—Most rooms between €100–150.
$ **Lower Priced**—Most rooms €100 or less.

Business-Class Comfort near Plaça de Catalunya and the Top of the Ramblas

These nine places have sliding glass doors leading to plush reception areas, air-conditioning, and renovated modern rooms. Most are on big streets within two blocks of Barcelona's exuberant central square. As business hotels, they have hard-to-pin-down prices fluctuating wildly with demand.

$$$ **Hotel Catalonia Albinoni,** the best located of all these places, elegantly fills a renovated old palace with wide halls, hardwood floors, and 74 modern rooms with all the comforts. It overlooks a thriving pedestrian boulevard. Front rooms have views; balcony rooms on the back are quiet and come with sun terraces (Db-€170, extra bed-€35 family rooms, great buffet breakfast free when you book direct and show this book, elevator, air-con, a block down from Plaça de Catalunya at Portal de l'Angel 17, tel. 933-184-141, fax 933-012-631, www.hoteles-catalonia.com, albinoni.reservas@hoteles-catalonia.es).

$$$ **Hotel Duques de Bergara** boasts four stars. It has splashy public spaces, slick marble and hardwood floors, 150 comfortable rooms, and a garden courtyard with a pool a world away from the big-city noise (Sb-€143, Db-€171, Tb-€201, air-con, elevator, a half block off Plaça de Catalunya at Bergara 11, tel. 933-015-151, fax 933-173-442, www.hoteles-catalonia.es, duques@hoteles-catalonia.es).

$$$ **Hotel Occidental Reding,** on a quiet street and a five-minute walk west of the Ramblas and Plaça de Catalunya action, rents 44 modern business-class rooms (Db-€118 in low season, €170 in high, extra bed-€51, air-con, elevator, near Metro: Universitat at Gravina 5-7, tel. 934-121-097, fax 932-683-482, www.occidental-hoteles.com, reding@occidentalhoteles.com).

$$$ **Hotel Barcelona** is another big, American-style hotel with 72 bright, prefab, comfy rooms (Sb-€150, Db-€170, Db with terrace-€215, air-con, elevator, a block from Plaça de Catalunya at Caspe 1–13, tel. 933-025-858, fax 933-018-674, www.husa.es, hotelbarcelona@husa.es).

$$$ **Hotel Duc de la Victoria,** with 156 rooms, is a professional-yet-friendly business-class hotel, buried in the Gothic Quarter but only three blocks off the Ramblas (Sb/Db-€175 Mon–Thu or €132 Fri–Sun, Aug rate: Db-€100, superior rooms—bigger and on a corner with windows on 2 sides—are worth €15 extra, air-con, elevator, groups get weekend rate, Duc de la Victoria 15, tel. 932-703-410, fax 934-127-747, www.nh-hotels.com, nhducdelavictoria@nh-hotels.com).

$$$ **H10 Catalunya Plaza,** a business hotel right on the square, was redone in 2003 and has 47 tight, mod rooms with all the air-conditioning and minibar comforts (Sb-€126–180, Db-€150–210 in busy times, elevator, Plaça de Catalunya 7, tel. 933-177-171, fax 933-177-855, www.h10.es, catalunya.plaza@h10.es).

Hotels near the Ramblas

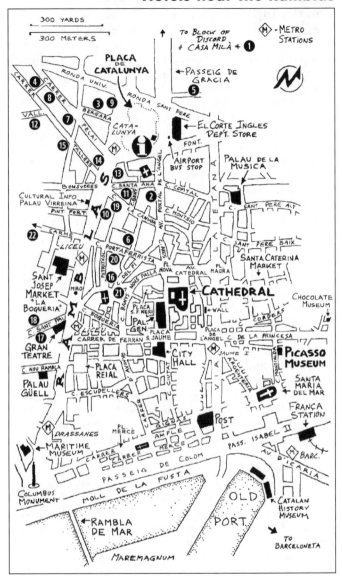

Hotel Key

1 To Hotel Gran Vía, Hotel Continental Palacete, Hotel Residencia Neutral & Hotel Universal

2 Hotel Catalonia Albinoni

3 Hotel Duques de Bergara

4 Hotel Occidental Reding

5 Hotel Barcelona

6 Hotel Duc de la Victoria

7 Hotel Lleó

8 Hotel Atlantis

9 Hotel H1O Catalunya Plaza

10 Citadines Ramblas Aparthotel

11 Nouvel Hotel

12 Meson Castilla

13 Hotel Toledano, Hostal Residencia Capitol & Hotel Continental

14 Hotel Lloret

15 Hostería Grau

16 Hotel Jardi

17 Hotel España

18 Hotel Peninsular & Hostal Opera

19 Hostal Campi

20 Pension Fina

21 Pension Vitoria

22 To Hotel Aneto

$$ **Hotel Lleó** is a well-run business hotel with 90 big, bright, and comfortable rooms and a great lounge (Db-€130–160, on week-ends-€144, summer Db special-€100, add about €25 for extra person, air-con, elevator, 2 blocks west of Plaça de Catalunya at Pelai 22, tel. 933-181-312, fax 934-122-657, www.hotel-lleo.es, reservas @hotel-lleo.es).

$$ **Hotel Atlantis** is a solid business-class hotel with 50 rooms and great prices for the area (Sb-€85, Db-€105, Tb-€125, air-con, elevator, Pelayo 20, tel. 933-189-012, fax 934-120-914, www.hotelatlantis-bcn.com, inf@hotelatlantis-bcn.com).

$$ **Citadines Ramblas Aparthotel** is a clever concept, offering daily rentals of 131 apartments in a bright, modern building right on the Ramblas. Prices range with seasonal demand and rooms come in two categories (studio apartment for 2 with sofa bed or twin and kitchenette-€131–160, apartment with real bed and sofa bed for up to 4 people-€195–240, includes tax, laundry-€9, Ramblas 122, tel. 932-701-111, fax 934-127-421, www.citadines.com, barcelona @citadines.com).

Hotels with "Personality" on or near the Ramblas

The first two listings are hoteleque and comfortable. Hotels Toledano, Residencia Capitol, Continental, and Lloret overlook the Ramblas (at the top, very near Plaça de Catalunya) and offer classic tiny view-bal-cony opportunities if you don't mind the noise. The last five (Jardi, España, Peninsular, Opera, and Aneto) are a few blocks away from the boulevard at about its midpoint. These places are generally family-run with ad-lib furnishings, more character, and much lower prices.

$$$ **Nouvel Hotel,** an elegant, Victorian-style building on a handy pedestrian street, has royal lounges and 78 comfy rooms (Sb-€93–105, Db-€152–199, includes breakfast, manager Gabriel promises 10 percent discount on these prices when booking direct with this book, air-con, Carrer de Santa Ana 18, tel. 933-018-274, fax 933-018-370, www.hotelnouvel.com, info@hotelnouvel.com).

$$ **Meson Castilla** is well-located, with 57 clean rooms, but also pricey, a bit sterile (less quirky), and in all the American guidebooks. It's three blocks off the Ramblas in an appealing university neighborhood (Sb-€95, Db-€122, Tb-€160, Qb apartment-€190, includes buffet breakfast, elevator, air-con, Valldoncella 5, tel. 933-182-182, fax 934-124-020, www.mesoncastilla.com, hmesoncastilla @teleline.es).

$ **Hotel Toledano,** overlooking the Ramblas, is suitable for backpackers and is popular with dust-bunnies. Small, folksy, and with new furniture, it's warmly run by Albert Sanz, his father Juan, Juanma, and trusty Daniel on the night shift (Sb-€34, Db-€56, Tb-€71, Qb-€80, some with air-con, front rooms have Ramblas-view terraces, back rooms have no noise—request your choice when you call; Internet access; Rambla de Canaletas 138, tel. 933-010-872, fax 934-123-142, www.hoteltoledano.com, reservas@hoteltoledano .com). The Sanz family also runs **Hostal Residencia Capitol** one floor above—quiet, plain, cheaper, and also appropriate for backpackers (S-€26, D-€38, Ds-€44, Q-€58, 5-bed room-€63).

$ **Hotel Continental Barcelona** has comfortable rooms, double-thick mattresses, and wildly clashing carpets and wallpaper. To celebrate 100 years in the family, José includes a free breakfast and an all-day complimentary coffee bar. Choose a Ramblas-view balcony or quiet back room (Db with double bed-€75, with twin-€85, with balcony-€95, extra bed-€20, includes tax, special family room, air-con, elevator, Internet access, Ramblas 138, tel. 933-012-570, fax 933-027-360, www.hotelcontinental.com, barcelona@hotelcontinental.com).

$ **Hotel Lloret** is a big, dark, Old World place on the Ramblas with plain, neon-lit rooms. A dark, dusty elevator cage fills the stairwell like Darth Vader—but on a hot day, you're glad it's there (Sb-€48, Db-€85, Tb-€95, Qb-€110, choose a noisy Ramblas balcony or *tranquilo* in the back, air-con in summer, Rambla de Canaletas 125, tel. 933-173-366, fax 933-019-283, www.hlloret.com, info@lloret.com).

$ **Hostería Grau** is a homey, almost alpine place, family-run with 27 clean and woody rooms just far enough off the Ramblas (S-€29, D-€50, Ds-€55, Db-€66, family suites with 2 bedrooms-€120, €6 extra charged July–Sept, fans, Internet, 200 yards up Carrer dels Tallers from Ramblas at Ramelleres 27, tel. 933-018-135, fax 933-176-825, www.hostalgrau.com, reservas@hostalgrau.com, Monica SE).

$ **Hotel Jardi** offers 40 clean and remodeled rooms on a breezy square in the Gothic Quarter. Rooms with tight, little balconies (€15 extra) enjoy an almost Parisian ambience and minimal noise (Sb-€68, Db-€78, Sb/Db with square view-€83, breakfast-€5, air-con, elevator, halfway between Ramblas and cathedral on Plaça Sant Josep Oriol #1, tel. 933-015-900, fax 933-425-733, hoteljardi@retemail.es).

$ **Hotel España** is a big, creaky, circa-1900 place with lavish public spaces still sweet with Art Nouveau decor by locally popular modernist architect Domènech i Muntaner. While it's 50 yards off the Ramblas on a borderline seedy street, it feels safe (84 rooms, Sb-€50, Db-€98, Tb-€130, includes tax and breakfast, air-con, elevator, near Metro: Liceu at Sant Pau 9, tel. 933-181-758, fax 933-171-134, www.hotelespanya.com, hotelespanya@hotelespanya.com).

$ **Hotel Peninsular,** farther down the same street, is a unique and thoughtfully-run value in the old center. A former convent, the 80 still-basic and thinly-furnished rooms—once nuns' cells—gather prayerfully around a bright, peaceful courtyard (S-€30, Sb-€50, D-€50, Db-€70, Tb-€80, prices include tax and breakfast and are the same year-round, air-con, elevator, Carrer Sant Pau 34, tel. 933-023-138, fax 934-123-699, Alex and Augustin SE).

$ **Hostal Opera,** with 70 rooms 20 yards off the Ramblas is simple but modern, clean and comfortable (Sb-€40, Db-€60, Tb-€90, air-con only in summer, elevator, no breakfast, Internet, at Carrer San Pau 20, Tel 933188201, info@hostalopera.com)

$ **Hotel Aneto** offers 18 clean, functional, and a little over-priced rooms, some with balconies 100 yards off the Ramblas (Sb-€60, Db-€80, air-con, elevator after a few steps, next to a little park behind Boqueria market, Carmen 38, tel. 933-019-989, fax 933-019-862, aneto@hotelaneto.com).

Humble Cheaper Places
Buried in the Gothic Quarter

$ **Hostal Campi**—big, quiet, and ramshackle—is a few doors off the top of the Ramblas. The streets can be noisy, so request a quiet room in the back (24 rooms, D-€44, Db-€52, T-€60, Tb-€70 no CC, Canuda 4, tel. & fax 933-013-545, hcampi@terra.es, friendly Sonia and Margarita SE).

$ **Pension Fina** offers more cheap sleeps (24 rooms, S-€32, D-€54, Db-€60, Portaferrissa 11, tel. & fax 933-179-787, hostalfina@hotmail.com).

$ **Pension Vitoria** has loose tile floors and 12 basic rooms, each with a tiny balcony. It's more dumpy than homey, but consider the price (D-€30, Db-€35, T-€40, cheaper off-season, a block off day-dreamy Plaça del Pi at Carrer de la Palla 8, tel. & fax 933-020-834, Mary Cruz SE).

EATING

Barcelona, the capital of Catalan cuisine—featuring seafood and Basque tapas—offers a tremendous variety of colorful places to eat. Many restaurants close in August (or July), when the owners vacation.

Eating Simply yet Memorably near the Ramblas and in the Gothic Quarter

Taverna Basca Irati serves 40 kinds of hot and cold Basque *pintxos* for €1.10 each. These are open-faced sandwiches—like Basque sushi but on bread. Muscle in through the hungry local crowd. Get an empty plate from the waiter, and then help yourself. It's a Basque honor system: You'll be charged by the number of toothpicks left on your plate when you're done. Wash it down with a €1.40 glass of Rioja (full-bodied red wine), €1.40 Txakoli (sprightly Basque white wine), or €1.20 *sidra* (apple wine) poured from on high to add oxygen and bring out the flavor (daily 12:00–24:00, a block off the Ramblas, behind arcade at Carrer Cardenal Casanyes 17, near Metro: Liceu, tel. 933-023-084).

Juicy Jones, next door, is a tutti-frutti vegan/vegetarian place with garish colors, a hip veggie menu (served downstairs), and a stunning array of fresh-squeezed juices served at the bar (lunch and dinner *menu*-€8.75, daily 12:00–24:30, Carrer Cardenal Casanyes 7). Pop in for a quick €3 "juice of the day."

Restaurant Elisabets is a happy little neighborhood eatery packed with antique radios and popular with locals for its "home-cooked" three-course €7.60 lunch special. Stop by for lunch, survey what those around you are enjoying, and order what looks best (Mon–Sat 13:00–16:00, Fri also 21:00–1:00, closed Sun, €12 tapas *menu* only in the evening, 2 blocks west of Ramblas on far corner of Plaça Bonsucces at Carrer Elisabets 2, tel. 933-175-826, run by Pilar).

Café Granja Viader is a quaint time warp, family-run since 1870. They boast to be the first dairy business to bottle and distribute milk in Spain. This feminine place—specializing in baked and dairy delights, toasted sandwiches, and light meals—is ideal for a traditional breakfast (note the "Esmorzars" specials posted). Try a glass of *orxata* (*horchata*—almond milk, summer only), *llet mallorquina* (Majorca-style milk with cinnamon, lemon, and sugar), *crema catalana* (crème brûlée, their specialty) or *suis* (literally, "Switzerland"—hot chocolate with a snowcap of whipped cream). Mentioned on the Ramblas walk on page 48, it's a block off the boulevard behind El Carme church (Mon 17:00–20:45, Tue–Sat 9:00–13:45 & 17:00–20:45, closed Sun, Xucla 4, tel. 933-183-486).

Try eating at **La Boquería market** at least once. Locals fill the market's bars, munching at the counter. The best—and worth the wait—is **Kiosko Universal** (€9 *menus* with different fresh-fish options, better before 12:30 but always packed, tel. 933-178-286). As you enter market from the Ramblas, it's all the way to the left on the first alley—if you see people waiting, ask who's the last in line *(El último?)*. **La Gardunya,** located at the back of La Boquería market, offers tasty meat and seafood meals made with fresh ingredients bought directly from the market (€9.50 lunch *menus* include wine and bread, €13.50 dinner *menus* don't include wine, Mon–Sat 13:00–16:00 & 20:00–24:00, closed Sun, Carrer Jerusalem 18, tel. 933-024-323).

Tired tourists like **La Poma** for a good pizza, pasta, and salads in a bright modern setting at the top of the Ramblas with comfortable views of all the street action (daily 9:00–24:00, Ramblas 117, tel. 933-019-400).

Homesick tourists flock to **The Bagel Shop** for fresh bagels and brownies (Mon–Sat 9:30–21:30, Sun 11:00–16:00, Carrer Canuda 25, tel. 933-024-161).

Shoestring tourists buy **groceries** at El Corte Inglés (Mon–Sat 10:00–22:00, closed Sun, supermarket in basement, Plaça de Catalunya) and Champion Supermarket (Mon–Sat 9:00–22:00, closed Sun, Ramblas 113).

Dining in the Gothic Quarter

A chain of five bright, modern restaurants with traditional cuisine in classy bistro settings with great prices has stormed Barcelona. Because of their three-course €7.30 lunches and €15–20 dinners (both with wine), all are crowded with locals and tourists in the know. They take no reservations and are marked by long lines at the door. Arrive 30 minutes before opening or be prepared to wait. The first three are within a block of the Plaça Reial, the fourth is near the Catalan Concert Hall, and the fifth **(Hostal de Rita)** is described in the Eixample section below: **La Fonda** (daily 13:00–15:30 & 20:30–23:30, a block from Plaça Reial at Escudellers 10, tel. 933-017-515); **Les Quinze Nits** (daily 13:00–15:45 & 20:30–23:30, on Plaça Reial at #6—you'll see the line, tel. 933-173-075); **La Crema Canela** (feels cozier than the others in this chain, daily 13:30–15:45 & 20:00–23:30, Ptge. Madoz 6, 30 yards north of Plaça Reial, tel. 933-182-744); and **La Dolça Herminia** (2 blocks toward Ramblas from Catalan Concert Hall at Magdalenes 27, tel. 933-170-676).

Els Quatre Gats, Picasso's hangout (and the place he first showed off his paintings), still has a bohemian feel in spite of its tourist crowds. Before the place was founded in 1897, the idea of a café for artists was mocked as a place where only *quatre gats*—"four cats," meaning "crazies"—would go (€10 3-course lunch, daily 8:30–24:00, live piano from 21:00, Montsio 3, tel. 933-024-140).

El Pintor Restaurante serves perhaps the best €30 dinner in town. Under medieval arches and rough brick, with candles and friendly service, you'll enjoy Catalan and Mediterranean cuisine

Barcelona's Gothic Quarter Restaurants

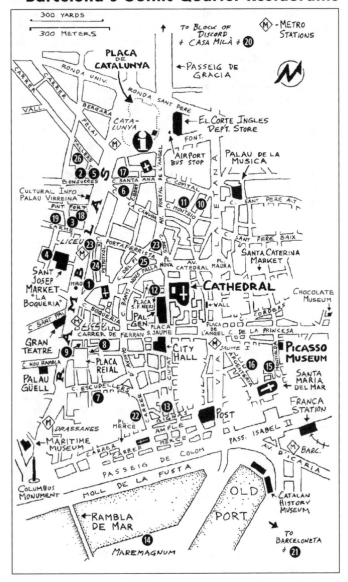

Restaurant Key

1. Taverna Basca Irati & Juicy Jones
2. Restaurant Elisabets
3. Café Granja Viader
4. La Gardunya
5. La Poma Rest. & Champion Supermarket
6. The Bagel Shop
7. La Fonda
8. Les Quinze Nits
9. La Crema Canela
10. La Dolca Herminia
11. Els Quatre Gats
12. El Pintor Restaurante
13. Restaurante Agut
14. Tapasbar Maremagnum
15. El Xampanyet Tapas Bar
16. Celestial Restaurant
17. Self Naturista Veggie Buffet
18. Bio Center Veggie Café
19. Fresc Co Veggie Cafeteria
20. To La Bodegueta, Hostal de Rita & Quasi Queviures
21. To Cova Fumada & Bar Electricitat
22. Carrer Merce tapas bars
23. Casa Colomina Sweet Shops (2)
24. La Pallaresa Granja-Xocolateria
25. Fargas Chocolate Shop
26. Ganpatti

(daily 13:30–16:30 & 20:00–24:00, from Plaça de Sant Jaume walk north on Carrer Sant Honorat to #7, reserve for evening, tel. 933-014-065).

Restaurante Agut, buried deep in the Gothic Quarter four blocks off the harbor, is a fine place with an enticing menu (in English) for local-style food in a local-style setting. It's almost dressy, with white tablecloths and candles (Tue–Sun 13:30–16:00 & 21:00–24:00, closed Mon and Aug, reservations smart for dinner, Carrer Gignas 16, tel. 933-151-709).

At the intersection of **Carrer de Banys Nous** and **Carrer de la Palla,** several places offer great coffee, local cheeses, ham, sausage, and *cava* (sparkling wine).

Out at Sea—Maremagnum

Tapasbar Maremagnum is a big, rollicking, sports-bar kind of tapas restaurant, great for large groups. It's a fun way to end your Ramblas walk, a 10-minute stroll past the Columbus Monument straight out the dock, with breezy harbor views and good local food with emphasis on the sea (daily 11:00–24:00, Moll d'Espanya, tel. 932-258-180).

Near the Picasso Museum

El Xampanyet, a fun and characteristic bar, specializes in tapas and anchovies. A *sortido* (assorted plate) of *carne* (meat) or *pescado* (fish) costs about €6 with *pa amb tomaquet* (pah ahm too-MAH-kaht), bread topped with a mix of crushed tomato and olive oil (Mon–Sat 12:00–15:30 & 19:00–24:00, closed Sun, half a block beyond Picasso Museum at Montcada 22, tel. 933-197-003).

Celestial, close to Santa María church, is an easy option with a lunch and dinner buffet (lunch-€7.60, dinner-€9.65, weekends-€11.60, daily 12:30–16:00 & 20:00–24:00, Argentaria 53, tel. 933-104-294).

Vegetarian Places near Plaça de Catalunya and off the Ramblas

Self Naturista is a quick, no-stress buffet that makes vegetarians and health-food lovers feel right at home. Others may find a few unidentifiable plates and drinks. The food seems tired—pick what you like and microwave it—but the place is very handy (Mon–Sat 11:30–22:00, closed Sun, near several recommended hotels, just off the top of Ramblas at Carrer de Santa Ana 11–17).

Bio Center, a Catalan soup-and-salad place popular with local vegetarians, is better but not as handy (€7.75 lunches, Mon–Sat 13:00–17:00, closed Sun, Pintor Fortuny 25, Metro: Catalunya, tel. 933-014-583). This street has several other good vegetarian places.

Fresc Co is a healthy and hearty buffet in a sleek and efficient cafeteria. For one cheap price (€7 for lunch, €9.70 for dinner and on weekends), you get a drink and all the salad, pasta, soup, pizza, and dessert you want. Choose from two locations: west of Plaça de Catalunya at Ronda Universitat 29, or a block off the Ramblas (near La Boquería market) at Carme 16 (daily 12:45–24:00, tel. 914-474-388).

Juicy Jones is a juice bar with a modern, fun veggie restaurant in back (just off the Ramblas at midpoint, described above).

Ganpatti welcomes those who miss their local organic co-op. Run by Natalia and Alex, this environmentally friendly, fair-commerce place dishes up veggie moussaka, basmati rice, good desserts, and more (Tue–Sat 12:00–21:00, Thu–Sat until 24:00, near the top of the Ramblas at Tallers 29, tel. 933-022-501, SE).

In the Eixample

The people-packed boulevards of the Eixample (Passeig de Gràcia and Rambla Catalunya) are lined with appetizing places with breezy outdoor seating. Many trendy and touristic tapas bars offer a cheery welcome and slam out the appetizers.

La Bodegueta is an unbelievably atmospheric below-street-level bodega serving hearty wines, homemade vermouth, *anchoas* (anchovies), tapas, and *flautas*—sandwiches made with flute-thin baguettes. Its daily €8.50 lunch special (3 courses with wine) is served from 13:00 to 16:00 (Mon–Sat 8:00–24:00, Sun 19:00–24:00, Rambla Catalunya 100, at intersection with Provenza, Metro: Diagonal, tel. 932-154-894). A long block from Gaudí's Casa Milà, this makes a fine sightseeing break.

Hostal de Rita is a fresh and dressy little place serving Catalan cuisine near the Block of Discord. Their lunches (3 courses with wine-€7, Mon–Fri from 13:00) and dinners (€15, à la carte, daily from 20:30) are a great value (a block from the Passeig de Gràcia

Metro stop, near corner of Carrer de Pau Claris and Carrer Arago at Arago 279, tel. 934-872-376). Like its four sister restaurants described above, its prices attract long lines, so arrive just before the doors open...or wait.

Quasi Queviures serves upscale tapas, sandwiches, or the whole nine yards—classic food served fast from a fun menu with modern decor and a sports-bar ambience (daily 7:00–24:00, between Gran Vía and Vía Diputació at Passeig de Gràcia 24, tel. 933-174-512).

Sandwich Shops

Bright, clean, and inexpensive sandwich shops are proudly holding the cultural line against the fast-food invasion hamburgerizing the rest of Europe. You'll find great sandwiches at **Pans & Company** and **Bocatta,** two chains with outlets all over town. Catalan sandwiches are made to order with crunchy French bread. Rather than butter, locals prefer *pa amb tomaquet*—tomato sauce on bread. Study the instructive multilingual menu fliers to understand your options.

Near the Harbor in Barceloneta

Barceloneta is a charming beach suburb of the big city with a village ambience. A grid plan of long, narrow, laundry-strewn streets surrounds the central Plaça Poeta Boscan. For an entertaining evening, wander around the perimeter of this slice-of-life square. Plenty of bakeries, pastry shops, and tapas bars ring a colorful covered produce market. Drop by the two places listed here or find your own restaurant (an unpleasant 15-min walk from the Columbus Monument, Metro: Barceloneta, or taxi). During the day, a lively produce market fills one end of the square. At night, kids play soccer and Ping-Pong.

Cova Fumada, with unmarked wooden doors at #56, is the neighborhood eatery. Josep María and his family serve famously fresh fish (Mon–Fri 9:00–15:00 & 18:30–20:30, closed Sat–Sun and Aug, Carrer del Baluarte 56, on corner at Carrer Sant Carles, tel. 932-214-061). Their *sardinas a la plancha* (grilled sardines-€3) are fresh and tasty. *Calamar a la plancha* (sautéed whole calamari-€4.50) and *bombas* (potato croquets with pork-€1.10) are the house specialty. It's macho to eat your *bombas picante* (spicy with chili sauce); gentler taste buds prefer it *alioli* (with garlic cream). Catalan *bruschetta* is *pa amb tomaquet* (tomato-ey bread, €1). Wash it down with *vino tinto* (house red wine, €0.60).

At **Bar Electricitat,** Lozano is the neighborhood source for cheap wine. Drop in. It's €1.05 per liter; the empty plastic water bottles are for take-away. Try a €0.70 glass of Torroja Tinto, the best local red; Priorato Dulce, a wonderfully sweet red; or the homemade candy-in-heaven vermouth. Owner Agapito can fix a plate of sheep cheese and almonds for €3.50 (Tue–Sun 8:00–15:00 & 18:00–21:00, closed Mon, across square from Cova Fumada, Plaça del Poeta Boscà 61, tel. 932-215-017, NSE).

The Olympic Port, a swank marina district, is lined with harborside restaurants and people enjoying what locals claim is the freshest fish in town (a short taxi ride past Barceloneta from the center).

Tapas on Carrer Mercè in the Gothic Quarter

Tapas aren't as popular in Catalunya as they are in the rest of Spain, but Barcelona boasts great *tascas*—colorful local tapas bars. Get small plates (for maximum sampling) by asking for "*tapas,*" not the bigger "*raciones.*" Glasses of *vino tinto* go for about €0.50.

While trendy uptown places are safer, better lit, and come with English menus and less grease, these places will stain your journal.

From the bottom of the Ramblas (near the Columbus Monument), hike east along Carrer Clave. Then follow the small street that runs along the right side of the church (Carrer Mercè), stopping at the *tascas* that look fun. For restaurant dining in the area, Restaurante Agut (described above) comes with tablecloths and polite service. But for a montage of edible memories, wander Carrer Mercè west to east and consider these places, stopping wherever looks most inviting:

La Pulpería serves up fried fish, octopus, and *patatas bravas,* all with Galician Ribeiro wine. A block down the street, at **Casa del Molinero,** you can sauté your chorizo *al diablo* (sausage from hell). It's great with the regional specialty, *pa amb tomaquet* (tomato bread). Across the street, **La Plata** keeps things wonderfully simple, serving extremely cheap plates of sardines (€1.25), little salads (€1.10), and small glasses of keg wine (€0.50). **Tasca el Corral** serves mountain favorites from northern Spain, such as *queso de cabrales* (very moldy cheese) and chorizo (spicy sausage) with *sidra* (apple wine sold by the €4 bottle). **Sidrería Tasca La Socarrena** (at #21), is the only place that serves hard cider by the glass. At the end of Carrer Mercè, **Bar Vendimia** serves up tasty clams and mussels (hearty *raciones* for €3 a plate—they don't do smaller portions, so order sparingly). Their *pulpo* (octopus) is more expensive and is the house specialty. Carrer Ample and Carrer Gignas, the streets parallel to Carrer Mercè inland, have more refined barhopping possibilities.

A Short, Sweet Walk

To sample three Barcelona sweets, follow this quick walk. Start at the corner of Carrer Portaferrissa midway down the Ramblas. For the best atmosphere, begin your walk at about 18:00.

Walk down Carrer Portaferrissa to #8. **Casa Colomina,** founded in 1908, sells ice cream and the refreshing *orxata* (almond drink) in summer. In winter they sell homemade *turrón*—a variation of nougat made of almond, honey, and sugar, brought to Spain by the Moors 1,200 years ago. Show them this book in winter for a sample *(muestra)* of *blando, duro,* and *yema* (soft, hard, and yolk). They sell sizable slabs for €6 (Mon–Sat 10:00–20:30, Sun 12:30–20:30, tel. 933-122-511; in summer you can sample *turrón* at their other shop at nearby Cucurulla 2).

Continue down Carrer Portaferrissa, taking a right at Carrer Petrixol to **La Pallaresa Granja-Xocolatería,** dating from 1800. Older, elegant ladies gather here for the Spanish equivalent of tea time: *chocolate con churros* (€3.30 for 5 *churros*—sweet thick french fries—and a small chocolate, Mon–Sat 9:00–13:00 & 16:00–21:00, Sun 9:00–13:00 & 17:00–21:00, Petritxol 11, tel. 933-022-036).

For your last stop, head for the ornate **Fargas** chocolate shop (daily 9:30–13:30 & 16:00–20:00, a couple blocks farther toward cathedral at Carrer del Pi 16, tel. 933-020-342). Founded in 1827, this is one of the oldest and most traditional chocolate places in Barcelona. Ask if you can see the old chocolate mill ("*¿Puedo ver el molino?*").

TRANSPORTATION CONNECTIONS

By train to: Lisbon (1/day, 17 hrs with change in Madrid, €113), **Madrid** (6/day, 4.5–5.5 hrs, €59, plus 2 night trains, 9 hrs, €33.50–41.50 plus berth cost; new high-speed AVE connection may be complete in 2005, will reduce time but increase cost), **Paris** (1/day, 12 hrs, €127, night train, reservation required), **Sevilla** (3/day, 11 hrs, €49), **Granada** (2/day, 12 hrs, €48), **Málaga** (2/day, 14 hrs, €50), **Nice** (1/day, 12 hrs, €58, change in Cerbère), **Avignon** (5/day, 6–9 hrs, €38). Train info: tel. 902-240-202.

By bus to: Madrid (12/day, 8 hrs, half the price of a train ticket, departs from station Barcelona Nord at Metro: Marina), Sarfa buses serve all the coastal resorts (tel. 902-302-025).

By plane: To avoid 10-hour train trips, check the reasonable flights from Barcelona to Sevilla or Madrid. Iberia (tel. 902-400-500) and Air Europa (tel. 902-401-501 or 932-983-907) offer $80 flights to Madrid. Airport info: tel. 932-983-467.

Near Barcelona:
Figueres, Cadaques, Sitgues, and Montserrat

Four fine sights are day-trip temptations from Barcelona. For the ultimate in Surrealism and a classy but sleepy port-town getaway, consider a day or two in Cadaques, with a stop at the Dalí Museum in Figueres. Figueres is an hour from Cadaques and two hours from Barcelona. For the consummate day at the beach, head 45 minutes south to the charming and gay-friendly resort town Sitges. Pilgrims with hiking boots head an hour into the mountains for the most sacred spot in Catalunya—Montserrat.

Figueres

▲▲▲**Dalí Museum**—This is the essential Dalí sight. Inaugurated in 1974, the museum is a work of art in itself. Dalí personally conceptualized, designed, decorated, and painted it, intending to showcase his life's work. Highlights include the epic Palace of the Wind ceiling, the larger-than-life Mae West room (complete with fireplaces for nostrils), fun mechanical interactive art (Dalí was into action—bring lots of coins), and the famous squint-to-see Abraham Lincoln. Other major and fantastic works include the tiny *Spectre du Sex-Appeal, Soft Self-Portrait,* and the red-shoe riddle of *Zapato y Vaso de Leche.* Dalí, who was born in Figueres in 1905, is buried in the museum. The only real historical context provided is on the easy-to-miss and unlabeled earphone info boxes in the Mae West room. While not in English, it's plenty entertaining (€9, daily July–Sept 9:00–19:45, Oct–June 10:30–17:45, but closed Mon Jan–March, last entry 45 min before closing, free bag check has your bag waiting for you at the exit; to get to the museum from the train station, simply follow *Museu Dalí* signs; tel. 972-677-500). *A Beating Heart,* part of an extensive collection of bizarre yet original jewelry is nicely displayed in an area accessed by the side of the building, marked as *Joyas* (included with museum ticket).

Connections: Figueres is an easy day trip from Barcelona or a stopover (trains from France stop in Figueres; lockers at station). Trains from Barcelona depart Sants Station or the RENFE station at Metro: Passeig de Gràcia (hrly, 2 hrs, €15 round-trip).

Cadaques

Since the late 1800s, Cadaques has served as a haven for intellectuals and artists alike. Salvador Dalí, raised in nearby Figueres, brought international fame to this sleepy Catalan port in the 1920s. He and his wife, Gala, set up home and studio at the adjacent Port Lligat. Cadaques inspired Surrealists such as Paul Eluard, René Magritte, Marcel Duchamp, Man Ray, Luís Buñuel, and Federico García Lorca. Even Picasso was drawn to this enchanting coastal *cala* (cove), and he

Sights near Barcelona

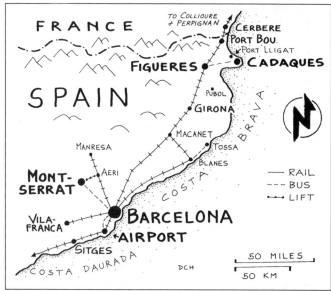

painted some of his Cubist works here.

In spite of its fame, Cadaques is laid-back and feels off the beaten path. If you want a peaceful beach-town escape near Barcelona, there's no better place. From the moment you descend into the town, taking in whitewashed buildings and deep blue waters, you'll be struck by the port's tranquility and beauty. Have a glass of *vino tinto* or *cremat* (a traditional brandy-and-coffee drink served flambé-style) at one of the seaside cafés and savor the lapping waves, brilliant sun, and gentle breeze.

The **Casa Museu Salvador Dalí,** once Dalí's home, gives fans a chance to explore his labyrinthine compound (€8, Tue–Sun 10:30–21:00, closes spring and fall at 18:00, closed Mon and winter, 20-min walk over hill from Cadaques to Port Lligat, limited visits, reservations mandatory, call to book a time, tel. 972-251-015).

The **TI** is at Carrer Cotxe 2 (Mon–Sat 9:00–14:00 & 16:00–21:00, Sun 10:30–13:00, shorter hours and closed Sun off-season, tel. 972-258-315).

Sleeping and Eating: These affordable options are conveniently located in the main square, around the corner from the TI and across from the beach—**Hostal Marina** (D-€27, Ds-€33, Db-€48, breakfast-€3, Riera 3, tel. & fax 972-258-199) and **Hostal Cristina** (24 rooms, D-€36, Ds-€46, Db-€48, La Riera, tel. & fax 972-258-138, Oct–June 10 percent less, David and Rebecca SE). **Hotel Llane Petit,** with 37 spacious rooms, many with view balconies, is on the harbor, a 10-minute walk south of the city center (Db-€60–110, air-con, elevator, Dr. Bartomeus 37, tel. 972-251-020, fax 972-258-778, info@llanetpetit.com, SE).

For a fine dinner, try **Casa Anita,** down a narrow street from La Residencia. Sitting with others around a big table, you'll enjoy house specialties such as *calamares a la plancha* (grilled squid) and homemade *helado* (ice cream). Muscatel from a glass *porrón* finishes off the tasty meal (Juan and family, tel. 972-258-471).

Connections: Cadaques is reached by Sarfa buses from Figueres (3/day, 75 min, €3) or from Barcelona (5/day, 2.5 hrs, €10.50, 2/day off-season, tel. 932-656-508).

Sitges

Sitges is one of Catalunya's most popular resort towns and a world-renowned vacation desti-nation among the gay commu-nity. Despite its jet-set status, the old town has managed to retain its charm. Nine beaches extend about a mile southward from town. Stroll down the sea-side promenade, which stretches from the town to the end of the  beaches. About halfway, the crowds thin out, and the beaches become more intimate and cove-like. Along the way, restaurants and *chiringuitos* (beachfront bars) serve tapas, paella, and drinks. Take time to explore the old town's streets and shops. On the waterfront, you'll see the 17th-century Sant Bartomeu i Santa Tecla Church. It's a quick hike up for a view of town, sea, and beaches.

Connections: Southbound trains depart Barcelona from Sants Station and from the RENFE station at Plaça de Catalunya (hrly, €4.20 round-trip).

Montserrat

Montserrat, with its unique rock formations and mountain monastery, is a popular day trip from Barcelona (30 miles away). This has been Catalunya's most important pilgrimage site for a thousand years. Hymns ascribe this "serrated mountain" to little angels who carved the rocks with golden saws. Geologists blame 10 million years of nature at work.

Montserrat's top attraction is **La Moreneta,** the statue of the

Black Virgin, which you'll find within the basilica (daily 8:00–10:30 & 12:00–18:30). The Moreneta, one of the patron saints of Catalunya, honored on April 27th, is the most revered religious symbol in the province.

Inside the basilica, be sure to see the Virgin close-up (behind the altar). Pilgrims touch her orb; the rest is protected behind glass. Then descend into the prayer room for a view of the Moreneta from behind. Pilgrims dip a memento of their journey into the holy water or even leave a personal belonging (such as a motorcycle helmet for safety) here to soak up more blessings.

Stop by the audiovisual center for some cultural and historical perspective. The interactive exhibition, which includes computer touch-screens and a short video, covers the mountain's history and gives a glimpse into the daily lives of the monastery's resident monks (€2, daily 9:00–18:00, tel. 938-777-701).

The first hermit monks built huts at Montserrat around A.D. 900. By 1025 a monastery was founded. The **Montserrat Escolania,** or choir school, soon followed and is considered to be the oldest music school in Europe. Fifty young boys, who live and study in the monastery itself, make up the choir, which offers performances (Mon–Sat at 13:00 & 18:45, Sun at 12:00, choir on vacation in July). Note: Catch the early show. If you attend the evening performance, you'll miss the last funicular down the mountain.

The **Museu de Montserrat** offers prehistoric tools, religious art, ancient artifacts, and a few paintings by masters such as El Greco, Michelangelo Caravaggio, Claude Monet, Picasso, and Dalí (€5.50, July–Sept daily 9:30–19:00, Oct–June Mon–Fri 10:00–18:00, Sat–Sun 9:30–18:30).

The Moreneta was originally located in the **Santa Cova** (holy cave), a 40-minute hike down from the monastery. The path is lined with statues depicting scenes from the life of Christ. While the original Black Virgin statue is now in the basilica, a replica sits in the cave. A three-minute funicular ride cuts 20 minutes off the hike (€1.60 one-way, €2.50 round-trip).

The **Sant Joan funicular** (see below) continues another 820 feet above the monastery (€3.80 one-way, €6.10 round-trip). At the top of the funicular, a 20-minute walk takes you to the Sant Joan chapel and the starting point of numerous hikes, described in the TI's "Six Itineraries from the Monastery" brochure.

Sleeping: You can sleep in the old **monks' cloister**—now equipped with hotel and apartment facilities—far more comfortably than did its original inhabitants (D-€77, fine restaurant attached, tel. 938-777-701).

Connections: Ferrocarriles Catalanes trains leave hourly for Montserrat from Barcelona's Plaça Espanya (€12 round-trip, cash only, Eurailpass not valid, tel. 932-051-515). The Trans-Montserrat ticket includes the train trip, cable-car ride, or Cremallera mountain train (www.cremallerademontserrat.com), and unlimited funicular rides (€20). The Tot Montserrat ticket includes all of this, plus the museum and a self-serve lunch (€34). If you plan to do it all, you'll save a little money (roughly €1.80) with either ticket (buy at Plaça Espanya TI, or without crowds or rush at the FGC La Molina office next to Plaça de Catalunya—located on map on page 55, Tue–Sat 11:00–14:00 & 16:30–20:30, Mon 16:30–20:30, Pelai 17–39 Triangle, tel. 933-664-553, helpful Rosa). If you don't plan on taking either funicular, it's cheaper to buy just the train ticket (includes cable car).

To get from Barcelona to Montserrat, enter the Plaça Espanya Metro station next to the Plaza Hotel. Follow signs to the "FF de la Generalitat" underground station, then look for train line R5 (direction Manresa, departures at :36 past each hour, 45 min). You have two options: (1) Get off at the Aeri de Montserrat stop at the base of the mountain, where the cable car awaits (the round-trip from Barcelona includes cable-car ride, 4/hr). To be efficient, note that departures at :15 past the hour make the trains leaving at :36 past the hour. The last efficient departure is at 18:15. The last cable-car departs the monastery at 18:45 (17:45 off-season), entailing a 45-minute wait for the train. Or (2) Get off at Monistrol de Montserrat train station one stop after Aeri and catch the Cremallera mountain train. Departures at :06 past the hour from the monastery make the best connections to the train back to Barcelona.

BASQUE REGION

If you're traveling between Spain and France, the coastal resort of **San Sebastián** and the **Guggenheim Bilbao** modern art museum merit a quick visit, if only to see what all the fuss is about.

They're in Basque country, or in Spanish, *País Vasco*. The Basque region stretches 100 miles from Bilbao north to Bayonne, France. And in some ways, *País Vasco* has more in common with the neighboring *Pays Basque* in France than it does with Spain. The Spanish and French Basque regions share a flag (white, red, and green), cuisine, and common language (Euskera), spoken by about a half million Spaniards and French.

Insulated from mainstream Europe for centuries, the plucky Basques have just wanted to be left alone for more than 7,000 years.

For 40 years, Generalissimo Franco did his best to tame the separatist-minded Basques. The bombed city of Guernica (Gernika), halfway between San Sebastián and Bilbao, survives as a tragic example of his efforts to suppress Basque independence.

Today the Basque terrorist organization, ETA (which stands in Spanish for Basque, country, and freedom), is supported by a tiny minority of the population. Although the group periodically is in the news for attacks on the Spanish government (and has been blamed for 800 deaths since 1968), members focus their anger on political targets and go largely unnoticed by tourists.

Because Franco so effectively blunted Basque expression for years, the language was primarily Spanish by default, even though the region was technically bilingual—Euskera and Spanish. But after several Franco-free decades, there's a renewed awareness of the importance of the Basque language (absolutely unrelated to any other). Look for street signs, menus, and signs in shops.

Similarly, today's Basque lands are undergoing a 21st-century renaissance, as the dazzling new architecture of the Guggenheim

Basque Region

Bilbao modern art museum and the glittering resort of San Sebastián are drawing enthusiastic crowds. For small-town fun, drop by the fishing village of **Lekeitio** (near Bilbao) and little **Hondarribia** near the border, providing a good first (or last) stop in Spain.

San Sebastián

Shimmering above the breathtaking bay of La Concha, elegant and prosperous San Sebastián (Donostia) has a favored location with

golden beaches, capped by twin peaks at either end and a cute little island in the center. A delightful beach-front promenade runs the length of the bay, with an intriguing old town at one end and a smart shopping district in the center. It has 180,000 residents and almost that many tourists in high

season (July–Sept). With a romantic setting, the soaring statue of Christ gazing over the city, and the late-night lively old town, San Sebastián has a Rio de Janeiro aura. While there's no compelling museum to visit, the scenic city provides a pleasant Basque-flavored introduction to Spain.

In 1845, Queen Isabel II's doctor recommended she treat her skin problems by bathing here in the sea. Her visit attracted Spain's aristocracy, and soon the city was on the map as a seaside resort. By the turn of the century, Donostia was the toast of the belle époque, and a leading resort for Europe's beautiful people. Before World War I, Queen María Cristina summered here and held court in her Miramar Palace overlooking the crescent beach. Hotels, casinos, and theaters flourished. Even Franco enjoyed 35 summers in a place he was sure to call San Sebastián, not its Basque name, Donostia.

ORIENTATION

The San Sebastián we're interested in surrounds the Bay of Concha (Bahía de la Concha), and can be divided into three areas: Playa de la Concha (best beaches), the shopping district (called *centro román-tico*), and the skinny streets of the grid-planned old town (called *parte vieja*, to the north of the shopping district). *Centro romántico*, just east of Playa de la Concha, has beautiful turn-of-the-century architecture, but no real sights.

It's all bookended by mini-mountains: Monte Urgull to the north and east, Monte Igueldo to the south and west. The River *(Río)* Urumea divides central San Sebastián from the district called Gros (with a lively night scene and surfing beach).

Tourist Information: The TI, which lies on the boulevard between the shopping area and old city, a block from the river, has complete information on city and regional sights. Pick up the excellent town booklet, which has English descriptions of the three walking tours—the Old Quarter/Monte Urgull walk is best. Skip the San Sebastián Card (€10 for 2 days of free bus transport plus minor sightseeing discounts). The TI also has bus and train schedules (June–Sept Mon–Sat 8:00–20:00, Sun 10:00–14:00 & 15:30–19:00; Oct–May Mon–Sat 9:00–13:30 & 15:30–19:00, Sun 10:00–14:00, just off Zurriola bridge at Calle Reina Regente 3, tel. 943-481-166).

Getting Around San Sebastián

You'll do better finding a taxi stand rather than trying to hail one (€3 drop charge, €0.50 per kilometer, you can call a cab at tel. 943-464-646 or tel. 943-404-040).

At Alameda del Boulevard, along the bottom edge of the old town, you'll find a handy taxi stand and a line of public buses ready to take you anywhere in town; tell any driver your destination and he'll tell you the number of the bus to catch (€1, pay driver).

Some handy bus routes: #26 or #28 connects the bus and EuskoTren stations to the TI (get off at "Boulevard"); #16 takes you from the Boulevard/TI, along Playa de la Concha, to the base of the Monte Igueldo funicular.

San Sebastián

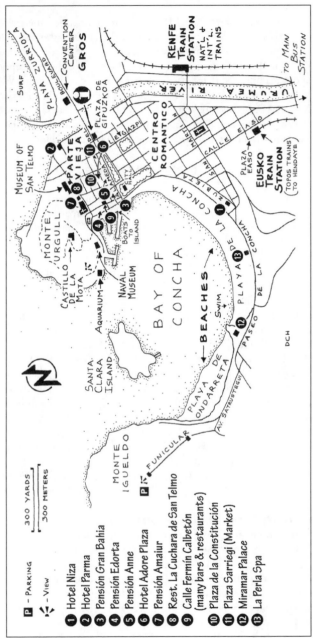

P – PARKING
↘ – VIEW

1. Hotel Niza
2. Hotel Parma
3. Pensión Gran Bahía
4. Pensión Edorta
5. Pensión Anne
6. Hotel Adore Plaza
7. Pensión Amaiur
8. Rest. La Cuchara de San Telmo
9. Calle Fermín Calbetón (many bars & restaurants)
10. Plaza de la Constitución
11. Plaza Sarriegi (Market)
12. Miramar Palace
13. La Perla Spa

A "txu-txu" tourist train and a hop-on, hop-off bus tour are also available, but they're not necessary in this little and lazy city.

Helpful Hints

Useful Phone Numbers: For the police, dial 943-481-320. For flight information, call San Sebastián's airport (in Hondarribia, 12 miles away) at tel. 943-668-500.

Internet: There are several places in the old town; the handiest is Donosti-NET (daily 9:00–23:00, 2 locations a block apart—Calle Embeltrán 2 and Calle San Jerónimo 8, tel. 943-429-497). They also sell cheap phone cards for calling home.

Bookstore: Bilintx, near several recommended restaurants in the old town, has a wide selection, including some guidebooks in English (daily, but closed for 14:00–16:00 siesta, Fermín Calbetón 21, tel. 943-420-080).

Planning Your Time

San Sebastián is worth a day. Stroll the two-mile long promenade and scout the place you'll grab to work on a tan. The promenade leads to a funicular that lifts you to the Monte Igueldo viewpoint (described below). After exploring the old town and port, head up to the hill of Monte Urgull. A big part of any visit to San Sebastián is enjoying the tapas in bars in the old town.

Arrival in San Sebastián

By Train: If you're coming on a regional Topo train from Hendaye on the French border, get off at the EuskoTren station (end of the line, called Amara). It's a level 15-minute walk to the center. Exit the station and walk across the long plaza, then walk eight blocks down Calle Easo to reach the beach. The old town will be ahead to your right, Playa de la Concha to your left. To speed things up, catch bus #26 or #28 along Calle Easo—headed in the same direction you are—and take it to the Boulevard stop, near the TI at the bottom of the old town.

If you're arriving by train from elsewhere in Spain, you'll get off at the RENFE station. It's just across the bridge (Puente María Cristina) from the shopping district. To reach the beach, cross the bridge, take your first right along the river, then first left on Calle San Martín, then right on Calle Easo.

By Bus: If you're arriving by bus from Hondarribia, hop off at pretty Plaza de Gipuzkoa (first stop after crossing the river, in shopping area, near TI). To reach the TI, walk down Legazpi, cross Alameda del Boulevard, and turn right.

By Car: Take the Amara freeway exit, follow *Centro Ciudad* signs into the city center, and park in a pay lot (many are well-signed). If turning in or picking up a rental car, Hertz (Zubieta 5, tel. 943-461-084) and Avis (Triunfo 2, tel. 943-461-556) are near Hotel Niza, and Europcar is at the main train station (tel. 943-322-304).

SIGHTS

The Beach

▲▲La Concha Beach and Promenade—The shell-shaped Playa de La Concha, the pride of San Sebastián, has one of Europe's most appealing stretches of sand. Lined with a two-mile-long promenade,

it allows even backpackers to feel aristocratic. While pretty empty off season, in summer sun-bathers pack its shores. But year-round, it's surprisingly devoid of eateries and money-grubbing businesses. *Cabinas* provide lockers, showers, and shade for a fee. There are free showers, too. The Miramar palace and park, which divides the cres-

cent in the middle, was where Queen María Cristina held court when she summered here. Her royal changing rooms are used today as inviting cafés, restaurants, and a fancy spa (La Perla, see below). For a century, the characteristic and lovingly painted wrought-iron balustrade that stretches the length of the promenade has been a symbol of the city; it shows up on everything from jewelry to headboards.

La Perla Spa—The spa attracts a less royal crowd today and appeals mostly to visitors interested in sampling "the curative properties of the sea." For €17.50, you can enjoy its Thalasso Fitness Circuit—105 minutes of intensive relaxation, featuring a hydrotherapy pool, relaxation pool, panoramic Jacuzzi, cold water pools, seawater steam sauna, dry sauna, and a relaxation area. For those seriously into spas, they offer much more, from Dead Sea mud wraps to massages to day-long "personalized programs" (daily 8:00–22:00, caps and towels rented/sold, bring or buy a swimsuit, on the beach at the center of the crescent, Paseo de La Concha, tel. 943-458-856).

Old Town (Parte Vieja)

Huddling securely in the shadow of its once-protective Monte Urgull, the old town (worth ▲▲) is where San Sebastián was born about 1,000 years ago. This grid plan of streets hides heavy Baroque and Gothic churches, surprise plazas, and fun little shops (venerable pastry shops, rugged produce markets, Basque independence souvenir shops, seafood-to-go delis, and even "THC shops" for the latest from the decriminalized marijuana scene in Spain—adults are allowed to grow two plants). Be sure to wander out to the port to see the fishing industry in action. The old town's main square, Plaza de la Constitución (where bullfights used to be held—notice the seat numbering on the balconies) features inviting café tables spilling from all corners. The highlight of the old town is its incredibly lively tapas (*pintxos*, PEEN-chohs) bars. (See "Eating," page 98.)

Museum of San Telmo—Displayed in rooms around the peaceful cloister of a former Dominican monastery, this humble museum has a few exhibits on Basque folk life and a small collection of 19th- and 20th-century paintings by Basque artists that offer an interesting peek into the spirit, faces, and natural beauty of this fiercely independent region (free, other featured artists include El Greco and Rubens, minimal English information, Tue–Sat 10:30–13:30 & 16:00–19:30, Sun 10:30–14:00, closed Mon, Plaza Zuloaga 1, tel. 943-481-580).

The Port

At the west end of the old town, protected by Monte Urgull, is the port. To reach the first three sights, take the passage through the wall at the appropriately-named Calle Puerto, and jog right along the level, port-side Paseo del Muelle. You'll pass fishing boats unloading the catch of the day (while hungry locals look on), salty sailors' pubs, and fisherfolk mending nets. The trails to Monte Urgull are just above

this scene, near Santa María Church (or climb up the stairs next to the aquarium).

Cruise—Small boats cruise from the old town's port to the island in the bay (Isla Santa Clara), where you can hike the trails and have lunch at the lone café (€2.60 round-trip, every 30 min 10:00–20:00, June–Sept only).

▲Aquarium—San Sebastián's impressive aquarium exhibits include a history of the sea, fascinating models showing various drift-netting techniques, a petting tank filled with nervous fish, a huge whale skeleton, and a 45-foot-long tunnel that allows you to look up at floppy rays and menacing sharks (€9, €5 for kids under 13, April–June daily 10:00–20:00, July–Aug daily 10:00–21:00, Sept–March Mon–Fri 10:00–19:00, Sat–Sun 10:00–20:00, ongoing renovations may close some exhibits, Paseo del Muelle 34, tel. 943-440-099).

Naval Museum (Museo Naval)—Located at the port, the museum shows two floors of the seafaring city's history and provides a link between the Basque culture and the sea (borrow the English translation booklet, €1.20, Tue–Sat 10:00–13:30 & 16:00–19:30, Sun 11:00–14:00, closed Mon, just before aquarium at Paseo del Muelle 24, tel. 943-430-051).

▲**Monte Urgull**—The once-mighty castle (Castillo de la Mota) atop the hill deterred most attackers, allowing the city to prosper in the Middle Ages. The museum of San Sebastián history located within the castle is mildly interesting. The best views from the hill are not from the statue of Christ, but from the ramparts on the left side as you face the hill, just above the port's aquarium. Café El Polvorín, nestled in the park, is a friendly place with salads, sandwiches, and good sangria. The path is technically open only during daytime (daily May–Sept 8:00–21:00, Oct–April 8:00–19:00). Why are some of the directional signs defaced? Because you're in *El País Vasco*, not Spain—and to remind you, some proud Basque has spray-painted over the Spanish.

Other Sights

Monte Igueldo—For commanding city views (if you ignore the tacky amusements on top), ride the funicular up Monte Igueldo, a mirror image of Monte Urgull. The views into the distant green mountains, along the coast, and over San Sebastián are sensational day or night. The entrance to the funicular is behind the tennis club on the far western end of Playa de Ondarreta, which extends from Playa de la Concha to the west (€1.60, July–mid-Sept daily 10:00–22:00, April–June and mid-Sept–Oct daily 11:00–20:00, Nov–March Mon–Fri 11:00–16:00, Sat–Sun 11:00–20:00, closed Wed). If you drive here, you'll pay €1.30 to enter.

Kursaal Conference Center—These two Lego-like boxes (just east and across the river from the old town) mark the spot of what was once a grand casino, torn down by Franco to discourage gambling. While many locals wanted to rebuild it as it once was—in a similar style to the turn-of-the-20th-century buildings in the *centro romántico*—this design, by Rafael Moneo, won instead. The complex is supposed to resemble the angular rocks that make up the town's breakwater. Though the Kursaal has a similarly stark, postmodern style, it's no match for Frank Gehry's Guggenheim in Bilbao (despite what some competitive and deliriously proud San Sebastián residents would have you believe). The Kursaal houses a theater, conference facilities, some gift shops and travel agencies, and a good restaurant (with tapas and a fine €13 lunch *menu*).

SLEEPING

$$$ Hotel Niza, set on the western edge of Playa de la Concha, is understandably often booked long in advance. Half of its 40 rooms (some with balconies) overlook the bay. From its chandeliered and plush lounge, a classic elevator takes you to its comfortable, pastel rooms with wedding-cake molding (Db-€103–118, view rooms cost the same—requests with reservation considered...but no promises, only street-side rooms have air-con, extra bed-€19, buffet breakfast with sea view-€8, elevator, parking-€12/day, Zubieta 56, tel. 943-426-663, fax 943-441-251, www.hotelniza.com, reservas@hotelniza.com, SE). The cheap and cheery restaurant downstairs serves good pizzas and salads.

$$$ Hotel Parma, a business-class place with 27 fine rooms and a family-run attention to detail and service, stands on the edge of the old town, away from the bar-scene noise, overlooking the river and a surfing beach (Sb-€54–72, very quiet internal Db-€79–109, view Db-€97–120, breakfast-€6 or €7 in high season, modern lounge, air-con, Paseo de Salamanca 10, tel. 943-428-893, fax 943-424-082, www.hotelparma.com, hotelparma@hotelparma.com, Iñaki Azurza SE).

$$ Pensión Gran Bahía offers 10 classy rooms a cut above other old-town *pensiones*. You'll enjoy the rich, dark wood floors polished to a slippery shine. Teresa (NSE) has a big personality and lots of rules, but is justifiably proud of her fine *pensión* (June–Sept Db-€85, Tb-€118; off-season Db-€49, Tb-€73; prices soft off-season, 7 percent tax not included, air-con, tries to be non-smoking, Embeltrán 16, tel. 943-420-216, fax 943-428-276, www.paisvasco.com/granbahia in Spanish, granbahia@mixmail.com).

$$ Pensión Edorta elegantly mixes wood, brick, and color into 12 stylish rooms (S-€30–50, D-€40–60, Sb/Db-€60–80, extra bed-€20–25, elevator, Calle Puerto 15, tel. 943-423-773, fax 943-433-570, www.pensionedorta.com, info@pensionedorta.com).

$ Pensión Anne is a tiny, well-run place on a relatively quiet lane in the old town, with six rooms sharing two bathrooms. Its simple rooms are bright and clean but have no sinks (S-€24–38, D-€30–48, Db-€45–60, Esterlines 15, tel. 943-421-438, www.pensionanne.com, pensionanne@yahoo.es, Anne SE).

$ Adore Plaza, run by the same folks, offers similar good-value rooms overlooking the old town's centerpiece, Plaza de la Constitución. Seven rooms—including four with views of the plaza—share four bathrooms (D-€45–60, higher prices are for plaza-view rooms, Db has similar prices but without views, beds in 4-bed room with lockers-€15–25 per person, Plaza de la Constitución 6, tel. & fax 943-422-270, www.adoreplaza.com, adoreplaza@yahoo.es, Miren SE).

Sleep Code

(€1 = about $1.20, country code: 34)
S = Single, **D** = Double/Twin, **T** = Triple, **Q** = Quad,
b = bathroom, **s** = shower only, **no CC** = Credit Cards not accepted,
SE = Speaks English, **NSE** = No English. You can assume a hotel
takes credit cards unless you see "no CC" in the listing. Unless
otherwise noted, assume breakfast is not included; you'll have plenty
of *churrerías* and cafeterias to choose from in the old town.

To help you sort easily through these listings, I've divided
the rooms into three categories based on the price for a standard
double room with bath:

$$$ **Higher Priced**—Most rooms €85 or more.
$$ **Moderately Priced**—Most rooms between €65–85.
$ **Lower Priced**—Most rooms €65 or less.

$ Pensión Amaiur, a popular hangout with the *Let's Go* crowd,
is a cheap and inviting option buried deep in the old town. Flowery
Virginia (SE) gives the place a homey warmth and provides backpackers with a clean and colorful home. Her 13 rooms share seven
bathrooms (S-€24–35, D-€38–50, quiet windowless D-€33–45, T-
€51–72, Q-€66–85, kitchen facilities, Internet access, family room,
next to Santa María church, Calle 31 de Agosto 44, tel. 943-429-
654, www.pensionamaiur.com, amaiur@telefonica.net).

EATING

On menus, you'll see *bacalao* (salted cod), best when cooked *à la
bizkaina* (with tomatoes, onions, and roasted peppers); *merluza*
(hake, a light white fish prepared in a variety of ways); and *chipirones
en su tinta* (squid served in their own black ink). Carnivores will find
plenty of lamb (try *chuletas,* massive lamb chops). Local brews
include *sidra* (hard apple cider), *txacoli* (tax-oh-lee, a local, light,
sparkling white wine—often theatrically poured from high above the
glass for aeration), and *izarra* (herbal-flavored brandy). Spanish wine
is generally served by the glass; *crianza* spends two years in oak kegs
and is *con cuerpo* (full-bodied).

Bar-Hopping

Txiquiteo is the word for hopping from bar to bar, enjoying charac-
teristically small sandwiches and tiny snacks *(pintxos)* and glasses of
local wine. Local competition drives small bars to lay out the most
appealing array of *pintxos*. San Sebastián's old town provides the ideal
backdrop for tapas-hopping. The selection is amazing. Later in the
evening, the best spreads get picked over (20:00 is prime time). I'd

poke into a dozen or so bars to survey the scene and go back to the ones with the liveliest crowds. Places most serious about their food don't have the TV on. Calle Fermín Calbetón has the best concentration of bars (don't miss Bar Goiz Argi, see below). San Jerónimo and 31 de Agosto are also good. For a little grander ambience, consider the bars on Plaza de la Constitución.

Bar Goiz Argi serves its tiny dishes with pride and attitude. Advertising *pintxos calientes,* they cook each treat for you, allowing you a montage of petite gourmet snacks; try their *tartaleta de txangurro* (spider-crab spread on bread). Wash it all down with a glass of whichever wine you like. Open bottles are clearly priced and displayed on the shelf. While it's not on their menu, they can whip up a good salad *(ensalada)* by request so you can call this an entire meal. You stand at the bar since there are no chairs (closed Mon–Tue, Fermín Calbetón 4, tel. 943-425-204).

For top-end tapas, seek out two more bars—each packed with locals rather than tourists: **Ganbara Bar** serves the typical little sandwich *pintxos* but also heaps piles of peppers and mushrooms—whatever's in season—on its bar and sautées tasty *raciones* for a steep price (see the dry-erase board, San Jerónimo 21, tel. 943-422-575, closed Mon). **La Cuchara de San Telmo**—with cooks taught by a big-name Basque chef—is a cramped place that devotes as much space to its thriving kitchen as its bar. It has nothing pre-cooked and on the bar. You order your mini-gourmet plates with a spirit of adventure from the constantly-changing blackboard (*pintxos* go for €2–3, closed Mon, tucked away on a lonely alley behind Museo San Telmo at 31 de Agosto 28, tel. 943-420-840).

Restaurants, Picnics, and *Churros*

For modern Basque cuisine in a dark and traditional setting, try **Bodégon Alejandro** (three-course *menu*-€28, from 13:00 and 21:00, closed Sun–Mon, no dinner Tue, in the thick of the old town on Calle Fermín Calbetón 4, tel. 943-427-158). **Casa Urola,** a block away, is *the* place in the old town for a good traditional sit-down Basque meal (more expensive, reservations smart from 13:00 and 20:00, Calle Fermín Calbetón 20, tel. 943-423-424).

For seafood with a view, check out the half-dozen hardworking, local-feeling restaurants that line the harbor on the way to the aquarium.

For **picnics,** drop by one of the countless tiny grocery stores or the Bretxa public market at Plaza Sarriegi (down the modern escalator) near the TI. Then head for the beach or up Monte Urgull.

Santa Lucía, a '50s-style Basque diner, is ideal for a cheap old-town breakfast or *churros* break. Photos of 20 different breakfasts decorate the walls, and plates of fresh *churros* with sugar keep patrons happy (daily 8:00–22:00, Calle Puerto 6, tel. 943-425-019). Grease is liberally applied to the grill...from a squeeze bottle. To counteract this place's heart-attack potential, get a glass of O.J., fresh-squeezed by the clever machine.

TRANSPORTATION CONNECTIONS

All Barcelona, Madrid, and Paris trains require reservations. If you're connecting with the SNCF French rail system, you'll save time by using San Sebastián's smaller EuskoTren station (tel. 902-543-210).

By train to: Bilbao (hrly, 2.75 hrs—bus is much better option), **Barcelona** (1/day, 8.5 hrs; 1/night except Sat, 10 hrs), **Madrid** (3/day, 6–8.5 hrs; 1/night, 10.5 hr), **Hendaye/French border** (2/hr, 30 min, departs EuskoTren station at :15 and :45 after the hour 7:15–21:45), **Paris** (get to Hendaye via the Eusko station—see above, then 4/day, 5.5 hrs, or 8.5-hr night train).

By bus to: Bilbao (2/hr, 1/hr on weekends, 6:30–22:00, 70 min, get €8 ticket from office, departs San Sebastián's main bus station on Plaza Pío XII, on the river 3 blocks below Eusko Tren station, bus tel. 902-101-210; once in Bilbao, buses leave you a 30-minute walk to the museum), **Hondarribia** (3/hr, 1 hr, buy ticket from driver, many bus stops, most central is on Plaza de Gipuzkoa in shopping area), **Saint-Jean-de-Luz,** France (2 direct 45-min buses daily, 9:00 and 14:30, €4, runs only 1/week off-season, from Plaza Pío XII, tel. 902-101-210).

Hondarribia

For a taste of small-town *País Vasco,* dip into this enchanting, seldom-visited town. Much smaller and easier to manage than San Sebastián, and also closer to France (across the Bay of Txingudi from Hendaye), Hondarribia allows travelers a stress-free opportunity to enjoy Basque culture. While it's easy to think of this as a border town (between France and Spain), culturally it's in the middle of Basque country.

The town comes in two parts: the lower port town and the historic, balcony-lined streets of the hilly and walled upper town. The **TI** is located between the two parts, two blocks up from the port on Jabier Ugarte 6 (Mon–Fri 9:00–13:30 & 16:00–18:30, Sat 10:00–14:00, closed Sun, tel. 943-645-458). You can follow their self-guided tour of the old town (English brochure available) or just lose yourself within the walls. Explore the plazas of the upper city. Today, Charles V's odd, squat castle is a parador inn (Db-€170, Plaza de Armas 14, tel. 943-645-500, fax 943-642-153, hondarribia @parador.es). Tourists are allowed to have sangria in the *muy* cool bar, though the terraces are for guests only. In the modern lower town, straight shopping streets serve a local clientele and a pleasant walkway takes strollers along the beach.

TRANSPORTATION CONNECTIONS

By bus to: San Sebastián (3/hr, 45 min to go 12 miles), **Hendaye/ French border** (2/hr, 20 min, June–Sept only). A bus stop in Hondarribia is across from the post office, one block below the TI.

By boat to: Hendaye (4/hr, 15 min, €1.40, runs about 11:00– 19:00 or until dark).

Bilbao
and the Guggenheim Museum

In the last five years, the cultural and economic capital of the *País Vasco*, Bilbao (pop. 500,000), has seen a transformation like no other Spanish city. Entire sectors of the industrial city's long-depressed port have been cleared away to allow construction of a new opera house, convention center, and the stunning Guggenheim Museum. Still, the city will always be a Marseille-like port; for most, it's worth a visit only for its incredible modern-art museum.

Tourist Information: Bilbao's handiest TI is across from the Guggenheim (July–Aug Mon–Sat 10:00–15:00 & 16:00–19:00, Sun 10:00–15:00; Sept–June Tue–Fri 11:00–14:30 & 15:30–18:00, Sat 11:00–15:00 & 16:00–19:00, Sun 11:00–14:00, closed Mon; Avenida Abandoibarra 2, central TI tel. 944-795-760, www.bilbao .net). If you're interested in anything besides the Guggenheim, pick up a map, the bimonthly *Bilbao Guide* newsletter, and the museum's brochure (describing museums dedicated to everything from Basques and bullfighting to Holy Week processionals).

Bilbao

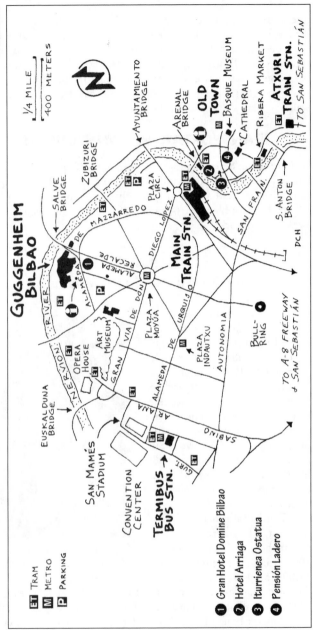

¼ MILE
400 METERS

GUGGENHEIM BILBAO

AYUNTAMIENTO BRIDGE

ARENAL BRIDGE

OLD TOWN

BASQUE MUSEUM

RIBERA MARKET

ATXURI TRAIN STN.

TO SAN SEBASTIÁN

CATHEDRAL

ZUBIZURI BRIDGE

PLAZA CIRC.

SALVE BRIDGE

DE MAZZARREDO

S. ANTON BRIDGE

SAN FRAN.

PCH

DIEGO LOPEZ

ALAMEDA DE RECALDE

ALAMEDA DE DON

MAIN TRAIN STN.

DE URQUIJO

AUTONOMIA

BULL-RING

TO A-8 FREEWAY & SAN SEBASTIÁN

PLAZA MOYÚA

PLAZA INDAUTXU

VIA DE DON

GRAN VIA

ART MUSEUM

OPERA HOUSE

NERVION RIVER

EUSKALDUNA BRIDGE

SAN MAMÉS STADIUM

CONVENTION CENTER

TERMIBUS BUS STN.

SABINO

ARANA

ALAMEDA

GURT.

ET TRAM
M METRO
P PARKING

1 Gran Hotel Domine Bilbao
2 Hotel Arriaga
3 Iturrienea Ostatua
4 Pensión Ladero

Arrival in Bilbao

Thanks to a perfectly planned new tram system (EuskoTran), getting to the museum is a snap. From any point of entry, simply buy a €1 single-ride ticket at a user-friendly green machine, hop on a tram, and head for the Guggenheim stop (only 1 line so you can't get lost, trams come every 10–15 min, www.euskotran.es). When you buy your ticket, validate it at the machine (follow the red arrow), since you can't do it once on board.

The new Metro system, designed by prominent architect Lord Norman Foster, is a work of art...but not practical for most visitors.

If you get lost, ask: "*¿Dónde está el museo Guggenheim?*" (dohn-day ay-stah el moo-say-oo "Guggenheim").

By Train: Bilbao's **RENFE station** (trains from most parts of Spain) is on the river in central Bilbao. Ask for a city map at the train information office. To reach the tram to the Guggenheim, use the exit marked *Hurtado de Amézaga,* and go right to find the BBK bank. Go inside, find the *Automatikoa* door on the right, and buy your ticket at the green machine marked *Abando.* Leave the bank, continuing right around the corner, and take a tram marked *San Mamés* (headed in the direction you just came from).

Trains coming from San Sebastián arrive at the riverside **Atxuri station,** southeast of the museum. Buy and validate your ticket, hop on a tram, and follow the river to the Guggenheim stop.

By Bus: Buses stop at the **Termibus station** on the western edge of downtown, about a mile southwest of the museum. Take a tram (direction: Atxuri) to Guggenheim.

By Car: Parking at the museum itself is a hassle; the closest option is the garage two blocks in front (Calle Iparraguirre 18). But to avoid stressful city traffic and frustrating one-ways, the best plan is this: Use the expressway exit marked *Centro,* following signs to Guggenheim. You'll pass the long train station on your right; continue straight through the traffic circle, veer left at the river, and park at the big garage (called Pío Baroja). Walk 10 minutes to the museum, or hop on the tram (direction: San Mamés).

Guggenheim Bilbao

While the collection of art in this ▲▲▲ museum is no better than that in Europe's other great modern art museums, the building itself—designed by Frank Gehry and opened in 1997—is the reason why so many travelers happily splice Bilbao into their itineraries.

Gehry's triumph offers a fascinating look at 21st-century architecture. Using cutting-edge technologies, unusual materials, and daring forms, he created a piece of sculpture that smoothly integrates with its environment and serves as the perfect stage for some of today's best art.

This limestone and titanium-tile-clad building looks like a huge, silvery fish, and connects the city with its river. Gehry meshed many visions. To him, the building's multiple forms jostle like a loose crate of bottles. They also evoke sails heading out to sea. Gehry keeps returning to his fish motif, reminding visitors that, as a boy, he was inspired by carp...even taking them into the bathtub with him. The building's skin—shiny  metallic fish-like scales—is made of thin titanium, carefully created to give just the desired color and reflective quality.

A great way to really enjoy the exterior is to take a circular stroll up and down each side of the river along the handsome promenade and over the two modern pedestrian bridges.

Guarding the **main entrance** is artist Jeff Koons' 42-foot-tall West Highland Terrier. Its 60,000 plants and flowers, chosen to blossom in concert, grow through steel mesh. A joyful structure, it brings viewers back to their childhood...perhaps evoking humankind's relationship to God...or maybe it's just another notorious Koons hoax. One thing is clear: It answers to "Puppy."

Inside, just beyond the turnstile, you come upon the **atrium**. This is clearly the heart of the building, pumping visitors from various rooms on three levels out and back, always returning to this central area before moving on to the next. Only the floor is straight. The architect invites you to caress the sensual curves of the walls. Notice the sheets of glass that make up the elevator shaft: They overlap like scales on a fish. The various glass and limestone panels are each unique, designed and shaped by a computer—as will likely be standard in constructing the great buildings of the future.

From the atrium, step out onto the riverside **terrace**. The shallow pool lets the river lick at the foundations of the building. Notice the museum's commitment to public spaces: On the right, a grand and public staircase leads under a big green bridge to a tower designed to wrap the bridge into the museum's grand scheme.

As you enter, pick up the English brochure explaining the architecture and the monthly bulletin detailing the art currently on display. Because this museum is part of the Guggenheim "family" of museums, the collection perpetually rotates among the sister Guggenheim galleries in New York, Venice, and Berlin. The best approach to your visit is simply to immerse yourself in a modern-art happening, rather than to count on seeing a particular piece or a specific artist's works. Gehry designed the vast **ground floor** mainly to show off the often huge modern-art installations. Computer-controlled lighting adjusts for different exhibits. Surfaces are clean and bare, so you can focus on the art.

The museum offers excellent audioguides (sometimes included with admission, sometimes a few euros extra), which give descriptions of current exhibits and fascinating information about the building's architecture. For guided tours in English, call 944-359-080 for the schedule (entry price varies depending on exhibit, generally €8–10, July–Aug daily 10:00–20:00, Sept–June Tue–Sun 10:00–20:00, closed Mon, café, no photos, tram stop: Guggenheim, Avenida Abandoibarra 2, tel. 944-359-080, www.guggenheim-bilbao.es).

SLEEPING

(€1 = about $1.20, country code: 34)

Bilbao merits an overnight stay. Even those who are only interested in the Guggenheim find that there's much more to this historic yet quickly changing city. Here are a few options. The first one is across from the Guggenheim, the others are in the Old Town (Casco Viejo), which offers a bustling, pedestrians-only Old World ambience and lots of dining options. To reach this district, turn right out of the train station and follow the tram tracks across the river. The seven percent tax is not included in the prices listed below.

$$$ Gran Hotel Domine Bilbao is *the* place for wealthy modern art fans looking for a handy splurge. It's right across the street from the Guggenheim, with decor clearly inspired by Gehry's masterpiece. Its 135 plush rooms are all postmodern class (standard Db-€200–230, super-swanky "executive" Db-€230–260, but prices very soft; ask about promotional rates, especially on weekends, when you'll pay closer to €155/€170; elevator, Alameda Mazarredo 61, tel. 944-253-300, fax 944-253-301, www.granhoteldominebilbao.com, recepcion@granhoteldominebilbao.com, SE).

$ Hotel Arriaga offers 21 old-fashioned but well-maintained rooms (Sb-€48, Db-€60–64, extra bed-€11, some rooms overlook a busy street—request a quiet back room, Calle Ribera 3, tel. 944-790-001, fax 944-790-516). As you cross the bridge from the station, it's just behind the big theater of the same name.

$ Iturrienea Ostatua, on a quiet pedestrian street in the old town, has 21 rooms packed with brick, stone, and antiques (Sb-€46, Db-€55–60, Tb-€73, breakfast-€4, Santa María Kalea 14, tel. 944-161-500, fax 944-158-929). From the station, cross the bridge and go past the big theater. Turn left, up quaint Santa María Kalea, when the river bends.

$ Pensión Ladero is a fine budget option in the old town. They don't accept reservations, but you can call when you arrive to check availability (S-€20, D-€32, T-€40–45, up 4 flights of stairs; 7 rooms share 1 bathroom up a very tight spiral staircase, but 14 rooms use the other 3 bathrooms on the main floor; no CC, Lotería 1, tel. 944-150-932, SE). You'll find the *pensión* just before the big church at the center of the old town. This is a better value than the more prominent Pensión Roquefer across the street.

TRANSPORTATION CONNECTIONS

By bus to: San Sebastián (2/hr, 6:00–22:30, 70 min, departs Bilbao's Termibus station, arrives in San Sebastián at Plaza Pío XII), **Santander** (hrly, 90 min, transfer there to bus to **Santillana del Mar** or **Comillas,** see Cantabria chapter).

Lekeitio

A small fishing port with an idyllic harbor and a fine beach, Lekeitio is an hour by bus from Bilbao and an easy stop for drivers. It's protected from the Bay of Biscay by a sand spit that leads to the lush and rugged little San Nicolás Island. Hake boats fly their Basque flags and proud Basque locals black out the Spanish translations on street signs.

Lekeitio is a teeming resort during July and August (when its population of 7,000 triples as big-city Basque folks move in to their vacation condos), and it's a sleepy backwater the rest of the year. It's isolated from the modern rat race by its location down a long, windy little road.

While sights are humble here, the 15th-century St. Mary's Parish Church is a good example of Basque Gothic with an impressive altarpiece. The town's back lanes are reminiscent of old days when fishing was the only industry. Fisherwomen sell their husbands' catches each morning from about 10:30 at the tiny Plaza Arranegi market (a block off the harbor). The golden crescent beach is as inviting as the sandbar, which—at low tide—challenges you to join the seagulls out on San Nicolás Island.

The **TI** faces the fish market next to the harbor (mid-June–mid-Sept daily 10:00–14:00 & 16:00–20:00; off-season Tue–Sat 10:30–13:30 & 16:00–19:00, Sun 10:00–14:00, closed Mon; tel. 946-844-017). While buses connect Lekeitio with Bilbao hourly (and San Sebastián 4/day), this stop is most logical for those with a car.

The TI recommends Lekeitio as a base for car explorations of the area (coastal and medieval hill villages). The nearby town of **Guernica** (Gernika in Basque, 9 miles toward Bilbao) is near and dear to Basques and pacifists alike for good reason. This is the site of the Gernikako Arbola (oak tree of Gernika), which marked the ancient assembly point where the Lords of Bizkaia (Basque leaders) met through the ages to assert their people's freedom. Long the symbolic heart of Basque separatism, this was a natural target for Franco in the Spanish Civil War. His buddy Hitler agreed to use Guernica as a kind of target practice in 1937. This historic "first air raid"—a prelude to the horrific aerial bombings of World War II—was made famous by Picasso's epic work, *Guernica* (now in Madrid).

Sleeping: **$ Emperatriz Zita Hotel** is the obvious best bet for your beach-town break. It's named for Empress Zita (who lived here in exile after her Hapsburg family lost World War I and was booted from Vienna). While Zita's mansion burned down, this 1930s rebuild still has a belle époque aristocratic charm, solid classy furniture in 42 spacious rooms, real hardwood floors, and an elegant spa in the basement. Located on the beach a few steps from the harbor, with handy parking and a view restaurant, it's a fine value (Sb-€40–50, Db-€55–68, Db suite-€85–100, views—ask for *vistas del mar*—are worth the extra euros, high prices are for July–Aug, third bed-€19, breakfast-€7, elevator, Santa Elena Etorbidea, tel. 946-842-655, fax 946-243-500, www.aisiahoteles.com in Spanish, ezita@saviat.net). Room prices include a thermal seawater pool and Jacuzzi; the full-service spa is available at reasonable prices.

Eating: Although it's sleepy in the off-season, the harbor promenade is made-to-order in summer for a slow meal or a tapas crawl. For fancy seafood, the local favorite is **Restaurante Zapirain** (€20 plates, Igualdegi 3, tel. 946-840-255). *Txangurro* (baked and stuffed crabs) is a specialty worth asking for.

CANTABRIA

If you're connecting the Basque Country and Galicia, you'll go through Cantabria and Asturias. Both are interesting, but Cantabria (kahn-TAH-bree-ah) has a few villages and sights in particular that are especially worth a visit. The quaint town of **Santillana del Mar** makes a fine home base for visiting the prehistoric **Altamira Caves** replica. **Comillas** is a pleasant beach town.

The dramatic peaks of the **Picos de Europa** and their rolling foothills define this region, giving it a more rugged feel than the "Northern Riviera" ambience of the Basque region. A drive through the Cantabrian countryside is rewarded with glimpses of endless charming stone homes. Though it's largely undiscovered by Americans, Cantabria is heavily touristed by Europeans in July and August, when it can get very crowded.

Planning Your Time

Cantabria doesn't rank high on the list of sightseeing priorities in Spain. Don't go out of your way to get here. However, if you're passing through on the way between the Basque region and Santiago de Compostela, there are some charming diversions along the way. A night or two in this region breaks up the long drive from Bilbao to Santiago (figure 6.5 hours straight through).

Assuming you're coming from San Sebastián, this is a good plan:

Day 1: Leave San Sebastián early for the Guggenheim in Bilbao (trip takes about an hour by expressway, longer along the coast). After seeing the museum, continue on to explore (and sleep in) Santillana del Mar or Comillas.

Day 2: Troglodytes will want to visit the Altamira Caves replica when it opens (9:30). Hikers and high-mountain fans will make a beeline for Fuente Dé in the Picos de Europa. If you get an early

Cantabria

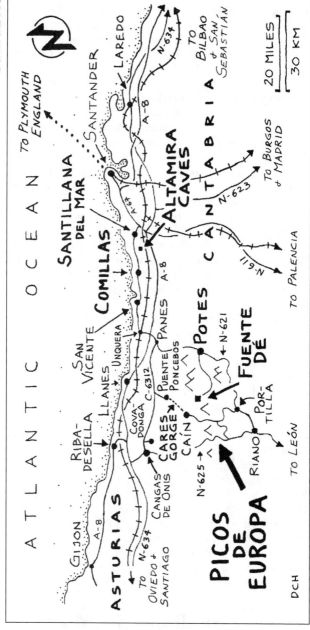

start on either of these attractions, you can still make it to Santiago de Compostela by the end of a very long day (figure 6 hours from this region to Santiago). It's saner to sleep a second night in this region, in which case it's conceivably possible to do both the caves and the mountains on Day 2.

Getting Around Cantabria

This region is best by car; public transportation is complicated, and the payoffs are not so great. Unless you have a special interest in pre-historic art, non-drivers will want to skip Cantabria.

By Car: Cantabria is wonderful by car. The A8 expressway runs roughly along the coast from San Sebastián to Gijón, where it becomes an express two-lane highway the rest of the way to A Coruña in Galicia. To reach Santillana del Mar and Comillas, follow signs to A67 (a jog of the expressway towards Santander), then take the exit for CA131 (signed for Santillana del Mar). This highway takes you through Santillana, Comillas, and San Vicente de la Barquera. In Unquera, it intersects with N621, which leads south through La Hermida Gorge into the Picos de Europa (follow signs for Potes). If you want to go directly to the Picos, there's an exit for N621 directly off the A-8 expressway.

By Bus: Without a car, you'll rely on the bus from the port city of Santander—Cantabria's capital and transportation hub. Buses run from Santander to Santillana del Mar, Comillas, and San Vicente de la Barquera (Mon–Fri 4 buses/day in each direction, Sat–Sun 3/day, about 45 min from Santander to Santillana, then 15 min to Comillas, then 15 more min to San Vicente, tel. 942-720-822).

A different bus goes from Santander to Potes in the Picos de Europa (3/day Mon–Fri, 2/day Sat, 1/day Sun, trip takes 2.25 hrs, tel. 942-880-611). There's also a bus from León, but only in summer (1/day, 3 hrs). Because public transportation is so difficult to and within the Picos de Europa, I'd avoid it without a car.

By Train: There is a scenic train line called the FEVE that runs from Bilbao to Santander and to Ovideo, but it's not particularly helpful for visiting the destinations in this chapter. The train can make sense for getting you to or from Cantabria. Santander, the region's public transportation hub, is connected by train with **Madrid** (3/day, 5–8 hrs, overnight option, Chamartín station), **Bilbao** (3/day, 2.75 hrs on FEVE, www.feve.es), **Santiago de Compostela** (1/day, 13 hrs, transfer in Palencia).

Santillana del Mar

Every guidebook imparts the same two tidbits about Santillana del Mar. One is that it's known as the "town of three lies," as it's nei-

ther holy *(santi)*, nor flat *(llana)*, nor on the
ocean *(del Mar)*. The other is that the exis-
tentialist philosopher Jean-Paul Sartre once
called it the "prettiest village in Spain."

The town is worth the fuss. Santillana is
a proud little stone village, with charming
time-warp qualities that have (barely) survived the stampede of multinational tour
groups here to visit the nearby Altamira Caves.
Despite it all, the town is what Spaniards
would call *preciosa.*

Santillana is three cobbled streets and a
collection of squares, climbing up over mild
hills from where the village meets the main
road. While Santillana has several sights that
cater to the tourist throngs (including a much-promoted zoo), the only
sight that makes a visit worthwhile—aside from the town itself—are
the cave paintings of Altamira in the nearby countryside (see
"Altamira Caves," below).

Tourist Information: The new, modern **TI** is right at the
entrance to the town (daily July–mid-Sept 9:00–21:00, off-season
9:30–13:30 & 16:00–19:00, Jesús Otero 20, tel. 942-818-251). Only
residents (and guests of hotels that offer parking) are allowed to drive
in the center—leave your car in the big lot by the TI (pay in-season,
free off-season).

SLEEPING

Santillana makes a good home base for the region and the caves. My
listings are right in town. You'll find the first three places on Santillana's
main square, Plaza Ramón Pelayo. The fourth is farther up, just around
the corner (to the right) from the big Collegiate Church.

$$$ Two swanky, arrogant paradores hold court on the main
square: **Parador de Santillana** (Sb-€78–91, Db-€97–114, Plaza
Ramón Pelayo 11, tel. 942-818-000, fax 942-818-391, santillana
@parador.es) and **Parador de Santillana Gil Blas** (Sb-€99–112,
Db-€123–140, same address, tel. 942-028-028, fax 942-818-391,
santillanagb@parador.es).

$$ **Hotel Altamira** offers 32 well-priced rooms in an atmospheric
16th-century palace on the main square (Sb-€42–52, standard Db-
€60–90, big Db with sitting room a great value at €63–97, extra bed-
€15–23, top prices are for Aug only, breakfast-€6, Calle Cantón 1,
tel. 942-818-025, fax 942-840-136, www.hotelaltamira.com, info
@hotelaltamira.com).

$ **Hospedaje Octavio** is a fine budget option with 11 comfort-
able, wood-beamed rooms (Db-€30–36, €3 less without bathroom,

Sleep Code

(€1 = about $1.20, country code: 34)
S = Single, **D** = Double/Twin, **T** = Triple, **Q** = Quad,
b = bathroom, **s** = shower only, **no CC** = Credit Cards not
accepted, **SE** = Speaks English, **NSE** = No English. You can
assume a hotel takes credit cards unless you see "no CC" in the
listing. Prices include tax and vary with season (highest
July–Aug). I've listed shoulder- and peak-season rates.

To help you sort easily through these listings, I've divided
the rooms into three categories based on the price for a standard
double room with bath:

$$$ **Higher Priced**—Most rooms €90 or more.
$$ **Moderately Priced**—Most rooms between €60–90.
$ **Lower Priced**—Most rooms €60 or less.

Plaza Las Arenas 4, tel. & fax 942-818-199, Octavio and Milagros
NSE but their sons do).

Altamira Caves

Not far from Santillana del Mar is a replica of a cave containing some
of the best examples of prehistoric art anywhere. In 1879, the daughter of a local archaeologist discovered several 14,000-year-old paintings in a limestone cave. By the 1960s and 1970s, it became a
tremendously popular tourist destination. All of the visitors got to be
too much for the delicate paintings, and the cave was closed in 1979.
But now a replica cave and museum have opened near the original
site, allowing visitors to once again experience these pieces of prehistoric artwork, in something approximating their original setting.

Cost, Hours, Location: €2.40, June–Sept Tue–Sat 9:30–
19:30, Sun 9:30–17:00, Oct–May Tue–Sun 9:30–17:00, always
closed Mon, last tour leaves 30 min before closing. The caves are on
a ridge in the countryside a little over a mile southwest of Santillana
del Mar (no bus; walk 30 min, hitch a ride with a friendly tour bus,
or call a taxi at mobile 608-483-441). Info: tel. 942-818-815,
http://museodealtamira.mcu.es.

Visiting the Caves: While you can't actually visit the original
caves, prehistoric-art fans will still find Altamira worth the trip. Your
visit has two parts: First, a fine museum with good English descriptions, featuring models and reproductions of the cave dwellers who
made these drawings (and their clothes, tools, and remains), as well as
videos and illuminated pictures to bring these people to life. Second is
a 30-minute guided tour of the highly detailed replica cave.

While it's theoretically possible to take an English tour, English speakers get little respect here. Assume you'll tour with a Spanish-speaking guide (and follow along with the self-guided tour below, which is better than the measly posted English info). English tours are scheduled twice a day in summer (June–Sept generally around 11:00 and 16:25, confirm time in advance by calling tel. 942-818-815). From October through May, English tours are unlikely.

Note that if all you're really interested in is the art itself, other replicas are on display in the National Archaeological Museum in Madrid (just the paintings, not the cave experience); see page 179. Remember that what you'll see at Altamira are replicas, too.

Reservations: Only 240 people are allowed to enter the caves each hour (20 people per tour, tours leave every 5 min—or when enough people gather, never more than a 30-min wait). This means that in the busy summer season, spaces fill up fast. In July and August, they recommend getting to the museum when it opens (9:30) to claim your tour appointment.

Better yet, make an advance reservation (no extra charge) through the Banco de Santander. To reserve, drop by a bank branch in the region, or even easier, call them (from Spain: tel. 902-242-424; from abroad: tel. 917-098-520; wait through recording and ask for English speaker). Request a specific date and time (1-hr window) for your tour. To improve your odds of joining a scheduled English tour (but no guarantees), first call the caves to ask for the schedule (tel. 942-818-815), then reserve your time slot through the bank accordingly. At the caves, pass any wait time by exploring the museum.

Self-Guided Tour

You'll begin the tour by watching a four-minute film about the various inhabitants of the cave, the discovery of the paintings in 1879, and the era of over-visitation. The guide leads you into the first part of the caves, where (unless you manage to join an English tour) you're on your own for information. The English descriptions that the guide eagerly points out are marginally helpful. Even better, here's what your guide is talking about:

1. In the Cave: Remember that this isn't the actual cave. It's a painstaking replica (called *Neocueva,* or "Neo-cave"), achieved with special computers. The Neo-cave recreates the caves exactly, so that the art can still be enjoyed without endangering it. It also simulates the original cave's temperature, sound, and humidity.

About 14,000 years ago, hunters, gatherers, and fishermen lived in these caves. They huddled around a fire, protected from the elements. They liked the location because of its proximity to the ocean and a river.

2. Excavation Site: See the tools used by modern scientists to dig up relics from various periods. We're talking about the Upper Paleolithic era here—the time of Cro-Magnon cave people, with big hands and high foreheads. The Upper Paleolithic is divided into three periods, and this cave was inhabited, on two separate occasions, during two of those periods: the Solutrean (about 18,500 years ago) and the Magdalenian (14,000 years ago). You'll see that there are three layers to the excavation: On the bottom are artifacts from Solutrean cavemen (hunting tools and chips of flint); above that is mostly clay, with the remains of a cave bear you'll see in a few minutes; and the top layer is from the Magdalenian period (hearths and other tools).

As you continue on to the next stop, you'll pass a cave bear that once lived in Altamira. Nearby, also look for his paw prints.

3. Artists' Workshop: See the tools used by the prehistoric artists, as well as a video showing how the paintings were created. The most dramatic paintings—all the red buffaloes—were made with reddish ochre dissolved in water, with the outlines in black charcoal. Marrow-burning stone lamps provided light. Many of the images were engraved into the surface of the cave (using flint) before being painted. The reproductions in this Neo-cave were done using the same techniques.

4. Art! Finally we reach the paintings themselves. While most tourists gasp, some hum the *Flintstones* theme.

This part of the cave has various names, including the "Great Hall," the "Polychrome Room," or even "the Sistine Chapel of Prehistoric Art." The ledge with the lights shows where the original floor level of the cave was. This didn't give the cavemen much room to paint, making their creations even more remarkable. Among the fauna in this room are 16 bison, a couple of running boars, some horses, and a giant deer—plus a few handprints and several mysterious symbols.

Unfortunately, the posted English information ends here. These are some of the things to look for (your guide is pointing them out to the ooh-ing and ahh-ing Spaniards in your group):

Bumps and Cracks: Notice that the artists incorporated the ceiling's many topographical features into their creations (see the bison with the big, swollen back, or the one with the big head).

Overlap: Some paintings actually overlap onto each other. These were painted during two different eras, though the most impressive batch—including all those bison—is thought to be by the same artist.

Detail: While a few paintings are incomplete, others are finished. Check out the bison with the highly-detailed hooves and beard.

The "Old Horse": The horse with its back against the wall is probably among the oldest in the cave.

The "Great Deer": The biggest painting of all (more than 7 feet across) is the deer with the little black bison under his chin. Notice it's not quite in proportion; due to the tight quarters, the artist couldn't take a step back to survey his work.

Symbols: The strange hieroglyphic-like symbols scattered around the cave, called tectiforms, are difficult to interpret. Scientists have found very similar symbols in caves far apart, making them wonder if it was some sort of primitive written language (for example, an outline of a horse with a particular symbol might be how to set traps for hunting).

Behavior: The artists captured not only the form, but also the behavior of the animals he depicted. Notice the lowing bison; the curled-up bison; the bison turning its head; and the running boars (with the extra legs).

What's amazing about these paintings is to think they were made by Cro-Magnon cave people. And yet, the artists had an amazing grasp on delicate composition, depicting these animals with such true-to-life simplicity. Some of them are mere outlines, a couple of curvy lines—masterful abstraction that could make Picasso jealous.

So why did they make these paintings? Nobody can know for sure. General agreement is that it's not simply for decoration, and that it must have served some religious or shamanistic purpose.

5. Final Cave: The most impressive paintings were in a single room (whose replica you just visited). However, there are another several hundred feet to the cave that were not reproduced. As you leave this replica cave, you'll see a few more replicas—mostly carvings—that came from other parts of the original cave. Most of them are those mysterious symbols, but at the very end you'll also see three masks carved into the rock.

And with that, your cave visit is over. Yabba dabba doo!

Comillas

Just 15 minutes beyond Santillana del Mar, perched on a hill overlooking the Atlantic, you'll find quirky Comillas. The town presides over a sandy beach, but feels more like a hill town—with twisty lanes clambering away from the sea. Comillas is not as undeniably charming as Santillana—it would do well to go traffic-free, as its neighbor has. But it makes for a fine home base if you prefer beach access and a more lived-in feel to touristy quaintness.

Most notably, Comillas also enjoys a surprising abundance of striking modernist architecture. Three buildings line up along a ridge at the west end of town (just beyond the town center and parking lot, over the big park). Antoni Gaudí, Barcelona's favorite son, designed a villa here called El Capricho—now a restaurant (see below). Next door is the pointy spire of a 17th-century church, and at the end of the row is the Palace of Sobrellano, by Gaudí's mentor Joan Martorell, which hints at early Barcelona-style Modernisme. Peering back at these buildings from a parallel ridge is the huge Pontifical University building, decorated by yet another turn-of-the-20th-century Catalan architect, Lluís Domènech i Muntaner. These modernist masterpieces are compliments of Don Antonio López y López, who left Spain to find fortune in America. He returned to Barcelona (where he acquired a taste for Gaudí and company) and eventually become the Marquis of Comillas.

While the beachside road below is lined with tacky tourist hotels, the town center, up on the hill, is much more pleasant—with an odd jumble of squares surrounding the big Parochial Church.

The westernmost square, Plaza Joaquín de Piélagos, is where you'll find the **TI** (Sept–June Mon–Sat 10:30–13:30 & 16:30–19:30, Sun 10:30–13:30, July–Aug daily 9:00–21:00, Calle Aldea 6, tel. 942-720-768).

SLEEPING

($1 = about €1.20, country code: 34)
Both of these listings are in the town center, south of the big Parochial Church, near the long, skinny, restaurant-lined Plaza de Primo de Rivera (also known as El Corro). The first one is the big, red building a block off the south end of the square; the other is a few blocks above the square, on the uphill street with the blue-trimmed railing.

$$$ Hotel Marina de Campíos offers 20 modern, colorful rooms, each one named for a different opera (standard Sb-€51–81, deluxe Sb-€63–95, standard Db-€64–101, deluxe Db-€78–118, breakfast-€5, elevator, Calle General Piélagos 14, tel. 942-722-754, fax 942-722-749, www.marinadecampios.com, reservas@marinadecampios.com).

$ Pasaje San Jorge, with 11 basic but comfortable rooms in a hundred-year-old house, hovers just over the town center (Db-€42–52, includes breakfast, Calle Carlos Díaz de la Campa 16, tel. & fax 942-720-915, www.pasajesanjorge.com, pasaje.sanjorge@wanadoo.es).

EATING

El Capricho is a surprising piece of Gaudí architecture hiding on a ridge above Comillas' center. The sunflower-dappled exterior alludes to Gaudí's plan for the building: His "sunflower design" attempted to maximize exposure to sunshine by arranging rooms so that they would get sun during the part of the day that they were most used. Today the building is a restaurant, very exclusive-feeling despite its reasonable prices (traditional Spanish entrees for €15–20, €24 *menu*). Look around the back for the sculpture of the architect admiring his work. Don't even try to get inside if you're not eating here. Reservations are smart, especially in season (daily 13:00–15:30 & 21:00–23:00, closed Sun dinner, tel. 942-720-365). There are two roads to this hard-to-find restaurant, both at the west end of town, and both sometimes closed—ask locally for directions.

Near Comillas: San Vicente de la Barquera

As you continue west from Comillas, the road becomes bumpy and follows the coast, soon crossing a wide bay over a long, dramatic bridge to San Vicente de la Barquera. This salty seaside resort overlooks a boat-filled harbor, with glimpses of the dramatic Picos de Europa in the distance.

Picos de Europa

The Picos de Europa—one of Spain's most popular national parks—is a relatively small stretch of cut-glass high-mountain peaks (the steepest in Spain, some taller than 8,500 feet) just 15 miles inland from the ocean. These dramatic mountains are home to goats, brown bears, eagles, vultures, wallcreepers (rare birds), and happy hikers. Outdoorsy types could spend days exploring this dramatic patch of Spain, which is packed with visitors in the summer. For our purposes, we'll focus on the two most important excursions: taking the Fuente Dé funicular up to a mountaintop, and hiking the yawning chasm of the Cares Gorge.

ORIENTATION

The Picos de Europa is a patch of mountains covering an area of about 25 miles by 25 miles. It's located where three of Spain's regions converge: Cantabria, Asturias, and León. (Frustratingly, each region's tourist office pretends that the parts of the park in the other regions don't exist—so it's very hard to get information, say, about Asturias' Cares Gorge in Potes, Cantabria.) In addition to three regions, the park comprises three different limestone massifs, with rivers separating them.

As you venture into the Picos de Europa, pick up a good map (and, for serious hikers, a guide to the region's best walks). The green 1:80,000-scale map you'll see is handy, featuring roads, trails, and topographical features. For hikes, I like the Sunflower guide to the region (published by a British company, www.sunflowerbooks .co.uk). These resources, along with a wide variety of maps and books, are available locally.

Our focus is on the Cantabrian part of the Picos, which contains the region's most accessible and enjoyable bits: the scenic drive through La Hermida Gorge; the charming mountain town of Potes; and the sky-high views from the top of the Fuente Dé cable car. This part of the Picos is doable as a long day trip from Santillana del Mar or Comillas (but easier if you stay in Potes). The next best activity (in León and Asturias, not Cantabria) is the Cares Gorge hike—deeper in the park and requiring another full day.

The Picos de Europa are best with a car. If you don't have wheels, skip it—bus connections are sparse, time-consuming, and frustrating (see "Getting around Cantabria," page 110).

Getting Around the Picos de Europa

The A8 expressway squeezes between the Picos and the north coast of Spain; roads branch into and around the Picos, but beware: Many of them traverse high-mountain passes—often on bad roads—and can take longer to drive through than you expect. *Puerto* means "pass" (slow going) and *desfiladero* means "gorge" (quicker but often still twisty).

Assuming you're most interested in Potes and Fuente Dé, you'll focus on the east part of the park, approaching from the A8 expressway (or from Santillana del Mar and Comillas). You'll go through Unquera and catch the N621 into the park (follow signs for Potes). Wind your way through La Hermida Gorge (Desfiladero de la Hermida) en route to Potes.

The Cares Gorge can be approached from the south (the village of Caín, deep in the mountains beyond Potes) or the north (Puente Poncebos, with easier access).

If you're really serious about tackling the region, and want to do both Fuente Dé and the Cares Gorge, the most sensible plan is this: On Day 1, drive to Potes from Comillas/Santillana del Mar and do the Fuente Dé cable car and hike (sleep in Potes); on Day 2, day-trip to the Cares Gorge hike via Caín (sleep in Potes); and on Day 3, move on to your next destination.

SIGHTS

I've arranged these sights as you'll come to them if you approach from the northeast (that is, from the expressway, Santillana del Mar, or Comillas).

Potes—This quaint mountain village, at the intersection of four valleys, is the hub of Cantabria's Picos de Europa tourist facilities. It's got an impressive old convent and a picturesque stone bridge spanning the Río Deva. It's a good place to buy maps and books. Check in at the TI with any travel questions (July–Sept daily 10:00–14:00 & 16:00–20:00, less off-season—often closed Sun–Mon afternoon and all day Tue, Independencia 12, tel. 942-730-787).

Sleeping in Potes: **$ Casa Cayo** has 17 cozy rooms and a fine restaurant that overlooks the river (Sb-€30, Db-€45, Tb-€52, closed Christmas–Feb, Calle Cántabra 6, tel. 942-730-150, fax 942-730-119, www.casacayo.com, hotel@casacayo.com, SE).

▲▲**Fuente Dé Cable Car (Teleférico Fuente Dé)**—Perhaps the single most thrilling activity in Picos de Europa is to ascend the cable car at Fuente Dé. The longest single-span cable car in Europe

zips you up 2,600 feet in just four ear-popping minutes. Once at the top (altitude 6,000 feet), you're rewarded with a breathtaking panorama of the Picos de Europa. The huge, pointy, Matterhorn-like peak on your right is Peña Remoña (7,350 feet). The cable car station up top has WCs, a cafeteria (commanding views, miserable food), and a gift shop (limited hiking guides—equip yourself before you ascend).

Once you're up there, those with enough time and strong knees should consider **hiking** back down. From the cable-car station at the top, follow the yellow-and-white signs to Espinama, always bearing to the right. You'll hike gradually uphill (gain about 300 feet), then down (3,500 feet) the back side of the mountain, with totally different views than the cable-car ride up: green, rolling hills instead of sharp, white peaks. Once in Espinama, you'll continue down along the main road back to the parking lot at the base of the cable car (signs to Fuente Dé). Figure about four hours total from the top back to the bottom (9 miles). Note that the trails are covered by snow into April, and sometimes even May; ask at the ranger station near Potes about conditions before you hike (see "Information," below).

Cost, Hours, Location: €10 round-trip, €6 one-way (if you're hiking down), goes every 30 min (or with demand), daily in summer

9:00–20:00, in winter 10:00–18:00, closed Jan. When it's busy, there are constant departures. Note that this is a very popular destination in summer, and you may have to wait in long lines to ascend and to descend (up to 2.5 hrs in early Aug, 1 hr in late July; quieter in June, early July, and Sept—if you're concerned, call ahead to find out how long the wait is before you make the trip from Potes). The cable car is a 14-mile drive from Potes. The road dead-ends at Fuente Dé, so you'll have to backtrack to return to Potes. If you're relying on public transportation, you can take the bus from Potes to Fuente Dé (2/day)—but it runs only in summer.

Information: Cable car tel. 942-736-610. The Picos de Europa National Park (not affiliated with the cable car company) runs a helpful information kiosk in the parking lot during peak season (July–Aug), with handouts and advice for different hikes in the area (including the one described above). Even better, stop at the main branch of the National Park office on the way to Fuente Dé from Potes (on the right about a mile after you leave Potes, look for green *Picos de Europa* signs, July–late Sept Mon–Sat 9:00–14:30 & 16:00–18:30, Sun 9:00–13:00, closed Sat–Sun off-season, tel. 942-730-555).

▲**Cares Gorge (Garganta del Cares)**—This impressive gorge hike—surrounded on both sides by sheer cliff walls, with a long-distance drop running parallel to (and sometimes under) the trail—is ideal for hardy hikers. The trail was built in the 1940s to maintain the hydroelectric canal that runs through the mountains, but today it has become an extremely popular summer hiking destination. The trail follows the Río Cares 7 miles between the towns of Caín (in the south) and Camarmeña (near Puente Poncebos, in the north). Along the way, you'll cross harrowing bridges and take trails burrowed into the rock face. Because it's deeper in the mountains and requires a good six hours (13 miles round-trip, with some ups and downs), it's best left to those who are really up for a hike and not simply passing through the Picos. Visitors who just want a glimpse will hike only partway in before heading back.

Getting There: To reach Caín from Potes, you'll drive on rough, twisty roads (N621) over the stunning Puerto de San Gloria pass (5,250 feet, watched over by a sweet bronze deer), into a green, moss-covered gorge. Just past the village of Portilla de la Reina, turn right (following signs for Santa Marina de Valdeón) to reach Caín. Note that this is a very long day trip from Potes, and almost brutal if home-basing in Comillas or Santillana del Mar.

The approach to the gorge from the north (Puente Poncebos) is easier, but won't take you near Potes and Fuente Dé. You can reach Puente Poncebos via the AS114 to Las Arenas, then follow the Cares River on the AS264 to Puente Poncebos.

SANTIAGO DE COMPOSTELA

The best destination in the northwestern province of Galicia, Santiago de Compostela might well be the most magical city in Spain. The place has long had a powerful and mysterious draw on travelers—as more than a thousand years' worth of pilgrims have trod the desolate trail across the north of Spain to just peer up at the facade of its glorious cathedral.

But there's more to this city than pilgrims and the remains of Saint James. Contrary to what you've heard, the rain in Spain does *not* fall mainly on the plain—but in Galicia. This Atlantic Northwest of Spain is like the Pacific Northwest of the United States: hilly, lush terrain that enjoys far more precipitation than in the interior, plus dramatic coastal scenery, delicious seafood, fine local wines, and an easygoing ambience. (The only thing missing is Starbucks.) The Spanish interior might be arid, but bring rain gear for your days in the northwest. Even the tourists here have a grungy vibe; packs of happy hippie pilgrims seek to find themselves while hiking the ancient Camino de Santiago from France. Santiago has a generally festive atmosphere, as travelers from every corner of the globe celebrate the end of a long journey.

There's something vaguely Irish about Galicia—and it's not just the green, rolling hills. The region actually shares a strain of Celtic heritage with their cousins across the Cantabrian Sea. People here are friendly, everything is covered with a layer of warm, glowing moss, and if you listen hard enough, you might just hear the sound of bagpipes.

Planning Your Time

Santiago's biggest downside is its location: a very long car, train, or bus trip from any other notable stop in Spain. But if you decide to visit, you—like a millennium's worth of pilgrims before you—will

Galego

Like Catalunya and the Basque Country, Galicia has its own distinctive language. Galego (called *gallego* in Spanish, and sometimes called "Galician" in English) is a mix between Spanish and Portuguese. Historically, Galego was closer to Portuguese. But Queen Isabella imported Spanish to the region in the 15th century, and ever since, it's gradually come to sound more and more like Spanish. In an attempt at national unity, Franco banned Galego in the mid-20th century (along with Catalan and Euskera). During these trying times, Galicians spoke Spanish in public—and Galego at home. Since the end of the Franco era, Galego is a proud part of this region's cultural heritage. Street signs and sight names are posted in Galego, and I've followed suit in this chapter.

If you don't speak Spanish, you'll hardly notice a difference. Most apparent is the change in articles: *el* and *la* become *o* and *a*—so the big Galician city La Coruña is known as A Coruña around here. You'll also see a lot more *x*'s, which are pronounced "sh" (like "Xacobeo," shah-koh-BAY-oh, the local word for Saint James' pilgrimage route). The Spanish greeting *buenos días* becomes *bos días* in Galego. The familiar *plaza* becomes *praza*. And if you want to impress a local, say *graciñas* (grah-THEEN-yahs)—a super-polite thank you.

find it's worth the trek. You can get a good feel for Santiago in a day, but a second day relaxing on the squares makes the long trip here more worthwhile.

The city has one real sight: the cathedral, with its museum and the surrounding squares. The rest of your visit is for munching seafood, pilgrim-watching, and killing time in small museums.

ORIENTATION

Santiago is built on hilly terrain, with lots of ups and downs. The tourist's Santiago is small: You can walk across the historic center, or Zona Monumental, in about 15 minutes. There you'll find the city's centerpiece—the awe-inspiring cathedral—as well as several other churches, a maze of pretty squares, a smattering of small museums, a bustling restaurant scene, and all of my recommended hotels.

Next to the Zona Monumental is the commercial city center, which is a modern, urban district called Céntrico; on the far side of that is the train station.

Tourist Information

There are several different tourist information facilities in Santiago. First, the **city TI** has three branches, with the main one a few blocks from the cathedral on **Rúa do Vilar** (at #63, daily June–Sept 9:00–21:00, Oct–May 10:00–15:00 & 17:00–20:00, tel. 981-555-129, www.santiagoturismo.com). There is another one very nearby on the edge of the Céntrico district at **Praza Galicia** (similar hours), and a third at the **tour bus parking lot** on the north edge of town (Easter–Sept only).

The **Turgalicia TI** at Rúa do Vilar 43 has information on the entire region (Mon–Fri 10:00–14:00 & 16:00–19:00, Sat 11:00–14:00 & 17:00–19:00, Sun 11:00–14:00, tel. 981-584-081, www.turgalicia.es). The **Center of Information for Pilgrims** nearby has tons of tips and maps for those planning to do the Camino by foot, bike, or horse (Rúa do Vilar #30–32, marked *Xacobeo*, tel. 981-572-004, www.xacobeo.es).

There are no regularly scheduled English-language walking tours, but there is a hop-on, hop-off double-decker **bus tour** with English headphone commentary (€8.50, lasts 1 hr, 7 stops, buses every 30–60 min, meet at the College of Medicine, on Rúa San Francisco a block off Praza do Obradoiro) and a silly **tourist train** (€3.40, or €9 includes both bus and train, 30 min, meet at same place).

In this compact city, skip the bus tours and visit the cathedral on your own with the information in this book. Better yet, hire a good **local guide** (for 3.5 hrs: €70 Mon–Fri, €80 Sat–Sun). Patricia Furelos is great (mobile 630-781-795, pfben@latinmail.com), or contact the Association of Professional Guides of Galicia (tel. 981-589-890, fax 981-553-329, guiasgalicia@ctv.es).

Arrival in Santiago de Compostela

By Train: Santiago's small train station is on the southern edge of the modern Céntrico district. You'll find ATMs, a cafeteria, and a helpful train information office. Computer screens show upcoming departures. To reach the center, leave the station and walk up the grand granite staircase, jog right, cross the busy Avenida de Lugo, and walk uphill for 10 minutes on the Rúa do Hórreo to Praza Galicia. A taxi to your hotel will cost about €5.

By Bus: The bus station is about a 15-minute walk northeast of the historical center. Hop on local bus #10 (€0.70) and take it to the Praza Galicia, a few steps from the historical center.

Helpful Hints

Important Days: Many museums are closed on Mondays. The market is closed on Sunday, slow on Monday, and crowded on Saturday.

Church Hours: Most churches in Santiago are open 9:00–21:00 without a siesta. On Sundays at 12:00 and at 18:00, there's a special pilgrims' Mass in the cathedral.

The Symbols of Santiago

This city—and the pilgrim route leading to it—is rife with symbolism. Here are a few of the key items you'll see adorning Santiago's facades.

• *The Scallop Shell* **(Vieira):** Since scallops are so abundant on the Galician coast, their shells are associated with Santiago throughout Europe. While medieval pilgrims only carried shells with them on the return home—to prove they'd been here, and to scoop water from wells—today's pilgrims also carry them on the way *to* Santiago. The yellow sideways shell that looks like a starburst is used to mark the route for bikers.

• *The Gourd:* Gourds were used by pilgrims to drink water and wine.

• *The Tomb and Star:* Saint James' tomb (usually depicted as a simple coffin or box), and the stars that led to its discovery, appear throughout the city, either together or separately.

• *The Yellow Arrow:* These arrows direct pilgrims (on foot) at every intersection from here to France.

• *The Red Cross:* This long, skinny cross represents the Knights of Santiago, once affiliated with the Knights of Malta—Holy Land crusaders who went on to guard pilgrims along the Camino de Santiago.

• *Shield with Five Stars:* This represents Alonso de Fonseca, a wealthy 15th-century nobleman who founded Santiago's university (and many buildings that still bear his seal).

• **"Nunca Máis":** Galego for "never again," this message of protest captures the anger of local residents towards the tragic oil tanker accident in November of 2002 that spilled black crude all along the Galician coast—their main source of both tourist and fishing income. Locals blame governmental bungling for the accident, and have put great pressure on Spain to improve safety measures to ensure it will never happen again. These words usually appear on a black field with a light-blue diagonal sash—a somber, oil-stained variation on the Galician flag, which is normally white and blue.

Holy Year: On years that the Feast of Saint James (July 25) falls on a Sunday, it's a special Compostela Holy Year (Ano Xacobeo in Galego)—with 25 percent more pilgrims than usual coming to Santiago, and more special services in the cathedral. But cooleth thy jets: The next one isn't until 2010.

Special Exhibits: The several exhibition halls scattered around Santiago have temporary exhibits that change all the time. Ask the TI what's going on when you're in town, or look for fliers and posters.

Internet: You'll see signs around the historic center. Perhaps handiest is Cyber Nova 50 (daily 9:00–24:00, Sun from 10:00, also copies, faxing, phones, Rúa Nova 50, tel. 981-575-188).

Laundry: You'll find a self-service *lavandería* a 20-minute walk from the historic center (Mon–Fri 10:00–14:00 & 17:00–22:00, Sat 10:00–14:00, closed Sun, €4/load, €6.50 for full service, tel. 981-942-110; go down Rúa do Franco until you reach the big Alameda park, walk along Avenida de Xoán Carlos I with park on your right, continue on the avenue as it becomes Avenida de Rosalía de Castro, to #116 on the right).

Music: You'll likely hear bagpipes *(gaitas)* being played in the streets of Santiago. Nobody knows for certain how this unlikely instrument caught on in Galicia, but it has supposedly been passed down since the Celts lived here. Some popular groups use bagpipes, too, including Milladoiro (a favorite of Galicians in their 40s and 50s) and Carlos Nuñez (trendy with younger people today).

Shopping: Jet, the black gemstone (called *azabache* in Spanish) similar to onyx, is believed to keep away evil spirits—and to bring in tourist euros. Along with jet, the silver trade has long been important in Santiago...and continues to be a popular item for tourists. Although the Galicians are a superstitious people and have beliefs about good and bad witches, the made-in-Taiwan witches you see in souvenir shops around the city are a recent innovation.

Best Views: There are beautiful views back towards the cathedral from the Santa Susana park (follow Rúa do Franco to the end and swing right into the grand Alameda park).

SIGHTS

The Cathedral

Santiago's cathedral isn't the biggest in Spain, nor is it the most impressive. Yet it's certainly the most mystical, exerting a spiritual magnetism that attracts people from all walks of life and from all corners of the globe.

Exploring one of the most important churches in Christendom, you'll do some time travel, putting yourselves in the well-worn shoes of the millions of pilgrims who have trekked many miles to this powerful place.

Begin facing the cathedral's main facade, in the big square called...

Praza do Obradoiro: Find the tile with the scallop shell right in the middle of this square. For more than a thousand years, this spot has been

Santiago de Compostela

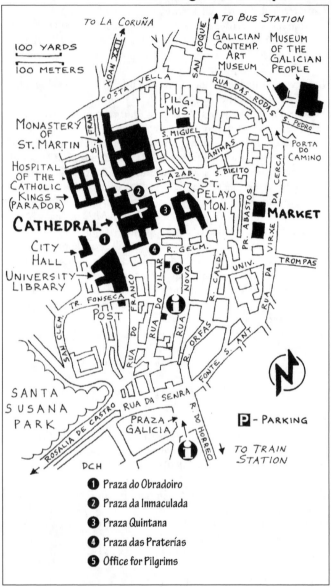

1. Praza do Obradoiro
2. Praza da Inmaculada
3. Praza Quintana
4. Praza das Praterías
5. Office for Pilgrims

where millions of tired pilgrims have taken a deep breath and thought to themselves: "I made it!" To maximize your chance of seeing pilgrims, be here in the late morning—the last stop on the Camino is two miles away, and pilgrims try to get to the cathedral in time for the 12:00 Mass.

Before heading into the cathedral, take a spin around the square.

To your left is the **Hospital of the Catholic Kings** (Hostal dos Reis Católicos). Isabel and Ferdinand came to Santiago in 1501 to give thanks for successfully forcing the Moors out of Granada. When they arrived, they found many sick pilgrims at the square. (Pilgrims often came to Santiago to ask for help in overcoming an illness, and the long walk here only made their condition worse.) Isabel and Ferdinand decided to build this hospital to give pilgrims a place to recover on arrival (you'll see their medallions flanking the intricately carved entryway). It was free, and remained open until 1952 (many locals were actually born here)—when it was converted into a fancy parador and restaurant (see "Sleeping" and "Eating" sections). The modern white windows with the old granite facade might seem jarring—but this contrast is very common in Galicia, maximizing sunlight exposure in this rainy region.

Another 90 degrees to the left is the neoclassical **City Hall** (Concello). Up top, notice the equestrian statue. That's Saint James, riding in from heaven to help the Spaniards defeat the Moors. See any police on the square? Security here has been on high alert since September 11, 2001—and even more so since March 11, 2004, when Madrid's commuter trains were bombed. Santiago's cathedral, as the third most important Christian pilgrimage site in the world (after Jerusalem and Rome), is a high-profile target for Islamic fundamentalists—and it doesn't help that Saint James is butchering Muslims right across the square.

Completing the square is the original **University** building, now just the library. Santiago has Spain's third-oldest university, with more than 30,000 students (medicine and law are especially popular).

You'll likely see Spanish school groups on the square, field-tripping from all over the country. Teachers love to use this spot for an architecture lesson, since it features four different architectural styles (starting with the cathedral and spinning left): 18th-century Baroque; 16th-century Plateresque; 18th-century neoclassical; and 15th-century Romanesque. Now take a look at the...

Cathedral Facade: Twelve hundred years ago, a monk followed a field of stars (probably the Milky Way) to the little Galician village of San Fiz de Solovio and discovered what appeared to be the long-lost tomb of Saint James. On July 25, 813, the local bishop declared that Saint James' relics had been found. They set to building a church there, and named the place Santiago (Saint James) de Compostela

El Camino de Santiago
(The Way of Saint James)

In 951, Godescalco, the Bishop of Le Puy in France, walked to Santiago de Compostela to pay homage to the relics of Saint James. More than a thousand years later, people are still following in his footsteps.

The Camino de Santiago began informally. But in the 12th century, Pope Callistus II decreed that any person who walked to Santiago in a Holy Year, confessed their sins, and took communion here would have all their sins forgiven. This opportunity for a cheap indulgence made the Camino de Santiago one of the most important pilgrimages in the world.

In the Middle Ages, pilgrims came to Santiago from all over Europe—mostly from France, but also from Portugal, Italy, Britain, Holland, Germany, Scandinavia, Eastern Europe, and all across the continent. Many prominent figures embarked on the journey, including Saint Francis of Assisi, Dutch painter Jan van Eyck, and the nun in Chaucer's *Canterbury Tales.*

The trek was so popular by 1130 that it prompted a French monk named Aimery Picaud to write a chronicle of his journey, including tips on where to eat, where to stay, the best way to get from place to place, and how to pack light. This *Codex Calixtinus* was the world's first guidebook—the great-great-granddaddy of the one you're holding right now.

As Europe emerged from the Middle Ages, and the Black Death swept across the continent, the Camino de Santiago was virtually forgotten. As recently as the 1980s, only a few hardy souls still followed the route.

But following the success of the 1992 Expo in Sevilla, the Spanish government decided to pour funds into reviving the tradition for the Holy Year in 1993. They made Santiago a high-profile destination, and shelled out big pesetas for concerts by stars like the Rolling Stones, Bruce Springsteen, and Julio Iglesias (whose father was born in Galicia).

(*campo de estrellas,* or "field of stars," for the celestial bodies that led the monk to the site).

For the last 12 centuries, the cathedral you see today has gradually been added on to that simple chapel. By the 11th century, the church was overwhelmed by the crowds. Construction of a larger cathedral began in 1075, and the work took 150 years. (The granite workers who built it set up shop on this very square—still called Praza do Obradoiro, or "workshop square.") Much of the design is attributed to a palace artist named Maestro Mateo, whom you'll meet a little later.

The exterior of the cathedral you see today is *not* the one that

The plan worked, and now—aided by European Union funding—the route has enjoyed a huge renaissance of interest, with 100,000 pilgrims each year trekking to Santiago.

Even Shirley MacLaine has made the journey (her book *The Camino: A Journey of the Spirit* is popular among pilgrims). Bikers and horse riders are now joining hikers on the journey, and these days it's "in" to follow the seashells to Santiago.

While there are many ways to approach Santiago—including one from Portugal—the most popular has always been the French Road. This 500-mile-long route begins in the rugged Pyrenees, in the town of Saint-Jean-Pied-de-Port. After crossing the mountains to Pamplona, the route wanders through the rough, arid plains of northern Spain—to Burgos, then León. The path crosses into Galicia in the stony mountain village of O Cebreiro, where the terrain changes, becoming lush and green. This last leg of the journey is the most popular—pilgrims pass simple farms, Romanesque churches, apple orchards, flocks of sheep, eucalyptus forests...and plenty of other pilgrims.

The procedure for walking the Camino has remained the same throughout history. The gear includes a cloak; a pointy, floppy hat; a walking stick; and a gourd (for drinking from wells). The route of the Camino is marked with yellow arrows (for hikers) or seashells (for bikers) at every intersection.

Doing the entire French Road of the Camino takes about three weeks (averaging 12–15 miles per day). The walk itself is a type of hut-hopping—at regular intervals along the route, you'll encounter humble little hostels called *albergues,* where pilgrims can get a bunk for the night (free, €2–3 donation requested outside of Galicia, subsidized by the government). Pilgrims carry a sort of a passport, which they get stamped at various *albergues* along the way, to prove that they walked the whole Camino. Those who complete the walk get a special certificate (called a *compostela*) when they reach the cathedral.

medieval pilgrims saw (though the interior is much the same). In the mid-18th century, Santiago's bishop—all fired up from a trip to Baroque-slathered Rome, and wanting to protect the original, now-deteriorating facade—decided to spruce up the building with a new Baroque facade. He also replaced the simple stonework in the interior with gaudy gold.

Scrutinize the facade. Atop the middle steeple is Saint James. Beneath him is his tomb, marked by a star—one of the many symbols you'll see all over the place (see "Santiago's Symbols" on page 124). On either side of the tomb are Theodorus and Athanasius, James' disciples who brought his body back to Santiago. On the side pillars are, to the left, his father Zebedee, and to the right, his mother Salomé.

What a beautiful facade! Don't you wish you had a miniature replica to carry around with you? Actually, you probably do. Check your pocket for a copper-colored euro coin worth €0.01, €0.02, or €0.05. There it is! Of all the churches in Spain, they chose this one as their representative in Euroland.

The cathedral also houses a fine museum with three parts; as you face this facade, the door to the main museum is to the right, the entry to the crypt is dead ahead (under the staircase), and visitors to the Gelmírez Palace use the door on the left (see "Cathedral Museum," page 133).

But that's for later. Head up the stairs to the cathedral and go inside. As you enter, you're face-to-face with the...

Portico of Glory: Take a step back in time (remember, this used to be the main facade of the cathedral). You're a medieval pilgrim, and you've just walked 500 miles from the Frankish lands to reach this cathedral. You're here to request the help of Saint James in recovering from an illness or to give thanks for a success. Maybe you've come to honor the wish of a dying relative or to be forgiven for sins you've committed. But your sore feet have finally brought you to Santiago.

You can't read, but you can tell from the carved images that this magnificent door represents the Final Judgment. There's Jesus, front and center, surrounded by Matthew, Mark, Luke, and John. Beside them are angels carrying tools for the Crucifixion—the cross, the crown of thorns, the spear, and a jug of vinegar. Arching above them are 24 musicians playing celestial music—each one with a different medieval instrument. Under Jesus sits Saint James, and below him, a column with the genealogy of Jesus (with Mary near the top, and above her, the Holy Trinity: Father, Son, and a dove representing the Holy Spirit). Atop the columns to the left are prophets of the Old Testament, and to the right, the apostles of the New Testament—all barefoot in the presence of God. The gang's all here. And at the bases of the columns are monsters—being crushed by the glory of God.

You walk to the column in the middle of the entryway. You squint down the nave and there, at the end, you see a stone statue of Saint James that marks his tomb. You place your hand on the column and bow your head, giving thanks to Saint James for safe passage. (You may see other pilgrims doing the same, but regrettably this post may be covered by protective glass.) Then you go around to the other side of the post and, at knee level, you see Maestro Mateo, who carved this fine facade. What a smart guy! You kneel again and tap your head against his three times—to help improve your intelligence.

Now wander down the...

Nave: Look up, noticing the barrel vault and the heavy, dark Romanesque design of the church. Up near the top, notice the gallery. This is where sweaty, smelly pilgrims sleep (and their animals, too). Man, it stinks in here. Continue up the nave until you reach the high altar, where you'll see a thick rope hanging, which is sometimes attached to the...

Botafumeiro: This huge, silver incense burner (120 pounds and about the size of a small child) is suspended from the ceiling during special Masses (occurring about 25 times a year; ask the TI if one is scheduled during your visit) or when a pilgrim pays to see it (200 medieval shekels...or about 200 21st-century euros). Supposedly the custom began in order to counteract the stench of the pilgrims. And to enhance the good mood of the congregation—already giddy for having completed the Camino de Santiago—priests were once said to add a pinch of cannabis to the mixture. After communion, eight priests (called *tiraboleiros*) pull on the rope, and this huge contraption swings in a wide arc up and down the transept, spewing sweet-smelling smoke. A replica is on display in the cathedral library (see Cathedral Museum, below).

Behind the *botafumeiro*, check out the...

Altar: You'll have to cheat with time travel for this section, since the original medieval choir and altar were replaced with this gilded Baroque piece in the 18th century (though fragments of the original stone choir can be seen in the Cathedral Museum). Look all the way back, at the big, gold altar, to see all three representations of Saint James in one place (see "The Three Santiagos" on page 134): up top on a white horse; below that as a pilgrim; and below that is the original stone Apostle James by Maestro Mateo—still marking his tomb after all these centuries.

The dome over the altar was added in the 16th century to bring some light into this dark Romanesque church.

On the columns up and down the nave and transept, notice the symbols carved into the granite. These are the markings of the masons who made the columns—to keep track of how many they'd be paid for.

Now head back to the Middle Ages. Your long pilgrimage is almost over. Go down the ambulatory on the left side of the altar—

Saint James

Santiago is Spanish for "Saint James." James and his brother John, sons of Zebedee and Salomé, were well-off fishermen on the Sea of Galilee. One fateful day, a charismatic visionary came and said to them, "Come with me, and I will make you fishers of men." They threw down their nets and became apostles.

Along with Peter, James and John were supposedly Jesus' favorites—he called them the "sons of thunder." Some historians even think Jesus and James might have been related. (This close relationship makes James an even more appealing object of worship.)

After Jesus' death, the apostles spread out and brought his message to other lands. Saint James spent a decade as a missionary in Spain, then part of the Roman Empire. The legend goes that as soon as he returned home to the Holy Land in 44 A.D., James was beheaded by Herod Agrippa. Before his body and head could be thrown to the lions—as was the custom in those days—they were rescued by two of his disciples, Theodorus and Athanasius.

These two brought his body back to Spain in a small boat and entombed it in the hills of Galicia—hiding it carefully so it would not be found by the Roman authorities. There it lay hidden for almost eight centuries. In 813, a monk—supposedly directed by the stars—discovered the tomb, and the local bishop proudly exclaimed that Saint James was in Galicia. Santiago de Compostela was born.

But is this the *real* story? Historians are skeptical, for a number of reasons. Why would James return to his homeland after so long in Spain? How could his two disciples have brought his body all the way back here, in a simple boat, through the endless Mediterranean and the rough Atlantic Ocean? And isn't it a little too convenient that the tomb was "discovered" at about the same time that Spain needed to be united behind a Christian cause, as it was fighting Moors in the south?

There are plenty of reasons why it could be a hoax. But yesterday's and today's pilgrims may not care whether the body of Saint James actually lies in this church. That's the whole point of faith.

passing where the *botafumeiro* rope is moored to the pillar—and walk down the little stairway (on your right) to the...

Tomb of Saint James: There he is, in the little silver chest, marked by a star—Santiago de Compostela. You kneel in front of the tomb and make your request or say your thanks. Then you continue through the little passage and trudge up the stairs. You turn left and wander around the ambulatory, noticing the various chapels (built by noblemen who wanted to be buried close to Saint James).

At the very back of the church is the Holy Door, depicting scenes from the life of Saint James—open only during Holy Years.

But there's one more pilgrim ritual to complete. Go to the little door near where you came out from the tomb (perhaps lining up with other pilgrims). Climb the stairs, find Maestro Mateo's stone statue of Saint James, and embrace him from behind.

Congratulations, pilgrim! You have completed the Camino de Santiago. Now go in peace.

Cathedral Museum (Museo da Catedral)

The museum, rated ▲, has three parts: The heart of the collection, the Museum-Cloister (enter through door on the right, as you face main facade); the crypt (under the main staircase in front); and the Gelmírez Palace, where the archbishop traditionally resides (door on the left, as you face main facade). All three parts are covered by the same €5 ticket and have the same hours (daily June–Sept 10:00–13:30 & 16:00–20:00, Oct–May 10:00–13:30 & 16:00–18:30, tel. 981-560-527). Some parts of the museum may be closed during services.

The **Museum-Cloister** is the most interesting part. On the main floor, you'll find the remaining pieces of Maestro Mateo's original stone choir (held together with a new, detailed replica). You'll also see fragments from Roman settlements, before the tomb of St. James was discovered here. Notice the illustration of the pre-Baroque cathedral—with a much plainer facade.

On the first floor up, look for two statues of a pregnant Mary. While this theme is unusual in most of Europe, it's very typical in Galicia. Also visit the coin collection, with examples of money that pilgrims have brought with them from all over Europe (see the displayed map).

On the second floor up, you'll come to the cloister. The crypts around the cloister hold the remains of priests from the cathedral. In the courtyard, you'll see a fountain (which once stood in front of the cathedral and was used by pilgrims to cleanse themselves) and the original church bells (replaced with new models in 1989). As you walk around the cloister, the first door leads to the Royal Chapel—with a beautiful-smelling cedar altar that houses dozens and dozens of relics. The centerpiece holds the remains of Saint James the Lesser (the *other* Apostle James). Note that you can also go directly between the Royal Chapel wing and the cathedral interior.

Continue to the treasury, with fine vestments and a fancy solid-gold monstrance used for carrying the communion wafer around the cathedral on Corpus Christi (it sits in the little round window in the middle). The library is where they store old books, a funky rack for reading (and spinning around) those huge tomes, and the *bota-fumeiro* (gigantic incense burner). Nearby are rooms of tapestries.

The Three Santiagos

You'll see three different depictions of Saint James in the cathedral and throughout the city:

1. Apostle James: James dressed in typical apostle robes, often indiscernible from the other apostles (sometimes with a stick or shell).

2. Pilgrim James: James wearing some or all of the traditional garb of the Camino de Santiago pilgrim: a brown cloak, floppy hat, walking stick, shell, gourd, and sandals.

3. Crusader James: Centuries after his death, the Spaniards called on Saint James for aid in various battles against the Moors (including the Battle of Clavijo in 859 and the reconquest of Coimbra in 1064). According to legend, Saint James appeared from the heavens on a white horse and massacred the Muslim foes. Locals don't particularly care for this depiction—especially these days, when the rising tide of Islamic fundamentalists could justifiably find it provocative.

Up one more floor (passing a shrine to St. Salomé along the way—Saint James' mother), you'll find more tapestries—including some from cartoons by Rubens and Goya. Look for the altar depicting the tale of Saint James—including his beheading, and his body being brought back to Galicia. From here, if the doors are open, you also get a fine view down onto Praza do Obradoiro.

The **crypt,** under a Maestro Mateo–decorated Romanesque vault, is as about as dead as its residents. The **Gelmírez Palace** (Pazo de Xelmírez) gives you the chance to check out a medieval home, including a kitchen. Every day at 12:00, the bishop comes out this door, and walks next door to conduct the pilgrims' Mass.

Cathedral Squares

There is a square on each side of the cathedral, each one lined with interesting sights and other tidbits. You've already visited Praza do Obradoiro, in the front. Here are the other three, working clockwise (to reach the first one, go up the passage to the left as you're facing the main cathedral facade).

Praza da Inmaculada—This was the way that most medieval pilgrims using the French Road actually approached the cathedral. Across the square is **St. Martin's Monastery** (Mosteiro de San Martiño Pinario)—one of two monasteries that sprang up around the church to care for pilgrims, today housing a museum of ecclesiastical artifacts. To the left of the monastery's main door is a fun multimedia exhibit called "Galicia Dixital" (see page 136). The monastery often hosts special exhibits.

Walk to the corner of the square with the arcade, and go to the post with the sign for Rúa Acibechería (next to the garbage can, under the streetlight). If you look to the roof of the cathedral, between the big dome and the tall tower, you can make out a small green cross. This is where the clothes of medieval pilgrims were ritually burned when they finally arrived at Santiago.

Continue along the arcade and around the corner, and you'll enter...

Praza Quintana—The door of the cathedral facing this square is the Holy Door—only open during Holy Years (next in 2010). There's Saint James, flanked by the disciples who brought his body back to Galicia. Below them, to the left of the door, are the 12 apostles; on the right are 12 prophets.

Across the square from the cathedral, you'll see the huge **Saint Pelayo Monastery** (Mosteiro San Paio). The church at the north end of this monastery is worth a peek. It has a frilly Baroque altar and a statue with a typical Galician theme: a pregnant Mary (to the left as you face main altar). Just off this sanctuary is the entrance to the monastery's **Sacred Art Museum** (Museo de Arte Sacra), with a small but interesting collection (€1.50, Mon–Fri 10:30–13:30 & 16:00–19:00, Sat 11:00–14:00 & 16:00–19:00, closed Sun; some posted English-language information, pick up translations of labels as you enter).

Continue around to the...

Praza das Praterías—This "Silversmiths' Square" is where Santiago's silver workers used to have their shops (and some still do). Overlooking the square is a tall tower that was once a fortress for keeping locals—fed up with high taxes—at bay, and for fending off invading enemies over the years, including Normans, Moors, English pirates, and Napoleon's army. An 18th-century bishop added the Baroque top and the bells. At the very top of the tower is a powerful light (most noticeable at night), serving as a beacon to pilgrims.

The cathedral door facing this square actually combines elements of two different stone doors by various artists (including, some say, Maestro Mateo), which were damaged over the centuries. That's why it's a hodgepodge of religious figures and motifs.

Take a look at the **fountain.** Notice the woman sitting on Saint James' tomb, holding aloft a star—a typical city symbol. Under her are animals that seem to be half-horse, half-fish. This is the way that Portuguese pilgrims approached Santiago—some by land, others by sea.

Walk a block down the street beyond to the fountain (Rúa do Vilar). On the left, you'll see the **Office for Pilgrims** (Oficina do Peregrino)—notice the banner with "Welcome" in several languages. At the gift shop next door, look for the *compostela*—the certificate issued by the office to those who can prove they finished the entire

Camino—with the pilgrim's name in Latin, the date, and the priest's signature. In the shop's window is a life-size replica of the *bota-fumeiro*, the giant incense burner.

Other Sights

▲▲**Market (Praza de Abastos)**—This wonderful market, housed in Old World stone buildings, offers a fine opportunity to do some serious people-watching (Mon–Sat 9:00–14:00, closed Sun). Monday's the least interesting day, since the fishermen don't go out

on Sunday. It's most crowded on Saturday.

This is a great chance to get up close and personal with some still-twitching seafood. Keep an eye out for the specialties you'll want to try later—octopus, shrimp, crabs, lobsters, and expensive-as-gold *percebes* (barnacles; see "Eating," below). You'll also see the local spicy sausage.

Grelos is a type of lettuce with a thick stalk and long, narrow leaves—grown only here, and often used in the *caldo galego* soup. The little green *pimientos de Padrón* (in season June–Oct) look like jalapeños, but lack the kick.

In the cheese cases, you'll see what look like giant, yellow Hershey's Kisses. Among typical Galician cheeses are *tetilla* (white, creamy) and *San Simón* (yellow, smoked)—if you linger long enough, they'll offer you a taste.

▲**Museum of Pilgrimages (Museo das Peregrinacións)**—This fine museum examines various aspects of the pilgrimage phenomenon. You'll see a map of pilgrimage sites around the world, then learn more about the pilgrimage that brings people to Santiago. There are models of earlier versions of the cathedral; explanations of the differing depictions of Saint James throughout history (apostle, pilgrim, and crusader); and coverage of the various routes to Santiago and stories of some prominent pilgrims. This well-presented place lends historical context to all of those backpackers you see in the streets. There's no English posted, but pick up the free translation of all the labels as you enter (€2.40, free during special exhibitions, also free Sat afternoon and Sun morning, open Tue–Fri 10:00–20:00, Sat 10:30–13:30 & 17:00–20:00, Sun 10:30–13:30, closed Mon, Rúa de San Miguel 4, tel. 981-581-558).

Galicia Dixital—Housed in the Monastery of St. Martin, this futuristic, kid-friendly exhibit uses various kinds of technology to explore Galicia and Santiago in virtual reality. You'll visit several exhibits, accompanied by a Spanish guide (English groups unlikely, but call ahead to see if an English-speaking group is coming that you can tag along with). First you'll take a 3-D, surround-sound tour of the squares around the cathedral (including a surprise thunderstorm). Then you go on *A Vertixe*—which means "the vertigo," as you'll soon learn. A motion-simulator 3-D "roller coaster" ride zips you around the top of the cathedral, then underground (keep hands inside your chair, which jerks around wildly). You can don a *casco* (helmet) *virtual* and wander through the cathedral. Other 3-D movies include a submarine trip though Galicia's waterways for a look at sea life, as well as an animated tour of the cathedral with a strange little pilgrim creature. While enjoyable, you can't shake the feeling that you could step outside and see most of this stuff in person. Still, it's an enjoyable enough way to get out of the sun for an hour. It ain't Disney World, but it's not bad (free daily, 10:30–14:00 & 16:00–20:30; must go on 1-hr guided visits, which leave regularly—may have to wait a few minutes for more people to show up; last visits begin at 13:00 and 19:30, tel. 981-554-048, www.galiciadixital.xunta.es).

Museum of the Galician People (Museo do Pobo Galego)— If you're intrigued by this very traditional part of Spain, this museum will give you more insight into rural Galician life. The collection, beautifully displayed around a cloister, shows off boat-building and fishing techniques; farming implements and simple horse-drawn carts; tools of trade and handicrafts (including carpentry, pottery, looms, and baskets); traditional costumes; and musical instruments, starring the bagpipes *(gaitas)*. If the farm tools seem old-fashioned, there's a reason: Old inheritance laws mean that plots are increasingly smaller, so modern farming machinery is impractical— keeping traditional equipment alive. There's virtually no English, except for a helpful €1.50 guidebook (free entry, Tue–Sat 10:00–14:00 & 16:00–20:00, Sun 11:00–14:00, closed Mon, at the northeast edge of the historical center in the monastery of San Domingos de Bonaval, just beyond the Porta do Camiño, tel. 981-583-620, www.museodopobo.es in Spanish).

Next door is the **Galician Contemporary Art Museum** (Centro Galego de Arte Contemporánea), with continually rotating exhibits, mostly by local artists (free, Tue–Sun 11:00–20:00, closed Mon, tel. 981-546-619, www.cgac.org).

SLEEPING

Thanks to all those pilgrims, Santiago has a glut of cheap, excellent accommodation. Since the Camino was resurrected in 1993, new hotels are popping up all the time—many of them subsidized by the EU. There aren't many affordable big hotels in town for tour groups, so they tend to stay along the Rías Baixas (fjord-like estuaries) about an hour to the south, where beds are cheap. That means many of Santiago's visitors are day-trippers, arriving around 10:30 and leaving

Sleep Code

(€1 = about $1.20, country code: 34)

S = Single, **D** = Double/Twin, **T** = Triple, **Q** = Quad, **b** = bathroom, **s** = shower only, **no CC** = Credit Cards not accepted, **SE** = Speaks English, **NSE** = No English. You can assume credit cards are accepted unless noted otherwise.

To help you easily sort through these listings, I've divided the rooms into three categories, based on the price for a standard double room with bath during high season:

$$$ **Higher Priced**—Most rooms €80 or more.
$$ **Moderately Priced**—Most room between €50–80.
$ **Lower Priced**—Most rooms €50 or less.

High season is roughly Easter through September; most places charge more during this time. The ranges I've listed represent low season to high season. The *hostales* speak enough English to make a reservation by phone (though sometimes not much more). IVA tax (7 percent) is not included, and there is no breakfast, unless I've noted otherwise.

in the afternoon. After dark, it's just you, the locals, the pilgrims, and Saint James.

$$$ Hotel Virxe da Cerca is a wonderful splurge just on the edge of the historical center, across the street from the market. Its standard rooms are in a modern building, but some of its "superior" and all of its "special" historic rooms—with classy old stone and hardwoods—are in a restored 18th-century monastery. All 43 rooms surround a lush garden oasis (standard Sb-€65–75, superior Sb-€75–85, "special" Sb-€85–95, standard Db-€75–85, superior Db-€85–95, "special" Db-€95–105, extra bed-€15–20, delicious breakfast buffet-€8, beautiful glassed-in breakfast room overlooks garden, elevator, Internet, Rúa Virxe da Cerca 27, tel. 981-569-350, fax 981-586-925, www.pousadasdecompostela.com, SE).

$$$ Hostal dos Reis Católicos brags that it's the oldest hotel in the world. Founded by the Catholic Kings at the beginning of the 16th century to care for pilgrims arriving from the Camino, it was converted into an upscale parador 50 years ago. This grand place is built around a series of four courtyards packed with Santiago history (but not tourists—only guests are allowed to wander). It has the best address in Santiago...and prices to match (Db start at €203, includes breakfast, Praza do Obradoiro 1, tel. 981-582-200, fax 981-563-094, santiago@parador.es, SE). But this place still remembers its roots, offering a free breakfast to pilgrims who've hiked the Camino.

$$ Hotel Residencia Costa Vella, run by the Liñares family, is my favorite spot in Santiago, with 14 comfortable rooms combining classic charm and modern comforts. The glassed-in breakfast room and lounge terrace overlook a peaceful garden, with lovely views of a nearby church and monastery and into the countryside beyond (Sb-€39–44, standard Db-€56–62, Db with balcony-€72–78, breakfast-€5, Calle Puerta de la Peña 17, tel. 981-569-530, fax 981-569-531, www.costavella.com, hotelcostavella@costavella .com, friendly José SE).

$$ Hotel Airas Nunes and **Hotel San Clemente** are both affiliated with Hotel Virxe da Cerca, above. They're equally good; both have 10 rooms in restored old buildings with classy touches, and both can be reserved through the same office (tel. 981-569-350, fax 981-586-925, www.pousadasdecompostela.com). Hotel Airas Nunes is in the busy heart of town (Sb-€50–70, Db-€60–80, extra bed-€15–20, breakfast-€6, Rúa do Vilar 17, reception tel. 981-554-706, SE); Hotel San Clemente is on a peaceful street a few blocks in front of the cathedral (Sb-€50–65, Db-€60–75, extra bed-€15–20, breakfast-€5, Rúa San Clemente 28, reception tel. 981-569-260, SE).

$$ Hotel Sino offers 15 rooms with slick, mod, contemporary design that incorporate some Old World elements. The public spaces are sleek and hip (standard Sb-€53–63, deluxe Sb-€60–70, standard Db-€60–70, deluxe Db-€67–77, Tb-€74–84, prices include tax and breakfast, elevator, Praciña da Algalia de Arriba 5, tel. 981-554-436, fax 981-552-455, www.sino-compostela.com in Spanish, info@sino-compostela.com, SE).

$ Hostal Suso, run by the Quintela family, offers 10 ridiculously cheap, new-feeling rooms around an airy atrium over a bar in the heart of Santiago (Sb-€15–17, Db-€30–36, Rúa do Vilar 65, tel. 981-586-611, fax 981-581-159, NSE).

$ Hostal Residencia Libredon Barbantes consists of two *hostales* that face each other across a square a block from the cathedral. They share a reception desk (at the Libredon), as well as clean, modern, Scandinavian-design rooms that are an excellent value for the near-perfect location. Barbantes' 18 rooms (Sb-€36–40, Db with 1 big bed-€40–45, twin Db-€54–60, Rúa do Franco 3) are newer and a little nicer than Libredon's 19 rooms (Ss-€27–30, Sb-€36–40, Db-€40–45, Praza do Fonseca 5; reception for both at Libredon, generally open 9:00–21:00, closed Sun afternoon, tel. 981-576-520, www.libredonbarbantes.com, SE).

$ Hostal Residencia Mapoula offers 13 fine rooms on a little lane on the edge of the historical center (Sb-€25–30, Db-€30–37, elevator plus a few stairs, Entremurallas 10, tel. 981-580-124, fax 981-584-089, SE).

$ Hospedaje Ramos is a good bet for rock-bottom-budget, basic rooms with lots of stairs right in the center of town (10 rooms, Sb-€16, Db-€28, prices include tax, Raíña 18, tel. 981-581-859, NSE).

Santiago Hotels and Restaurants

1 Hotel Virxe da Cerca
2 Hostal dos Reis Católicos
3 Hotel Residencia Costa Vella & Café
4 Hotel Airas Nunes
5 Hotel San Clemente
6 Hotel Sino
7 Hostal Suso
8 Hostal Residencia Libredon Barbantes (2 bldgs)
9 Hostal Residencia Mapoula
10 Hospedaje Ramos
11 Rúa do Franco Eateries
12 Rúa do Villar Eateries
13 O Dezaseis Restaurant
14 Tránsito dos Gramáticos
15 Restaurante Don Gaiferos
16 Café Restaurante Casa Manolo
17 Café Casino

EATING

One word: seafood. Strolling through the streets of Santiago is like visiting a well-stocked aquarium. Windows proudly display every form of edible sea life, including giant toothy fish, scallops and clams

of every shape and size, monstrous shrimp, and *pulpo* (octopus). Tasting octopus is obligatory in Galicia; it's most often prepared *a la gallega* (tentacles sliced up and boiled in a copper pot, topped with olive oil, garlic, and paprika, and served on a round wooden plate). Eat your *pulpo a la gallega* with toothpicks, never a fork. If you can get beyond those little suckers sticking to the roof of your mouth, it's actually not bad. If you're more adventurous (and have deep pock-

ets), splurge for *percebes*. These barnacles are a delicacy; since they grow only on rocks that see a lot of dangerous waves, it takes a team of two fishermen to collect them—one with a rope tied to his waist, the other spotting him from above. The danger factor raises the price.

Not a fan of seafood? If there's any hope, you'll find it in *caldo galego* soup, a traditional broth that originally came from the left-over stock used to prepare an elaborate Sunday feast. Look for *pimientos de Padrón*—miniature green peppers sautéed in salt.

For a quick meal on the go, grab a traditional meat pie, or *empanada*, which comes *de carne* (with beef), *de bonito* or *de atún* (tuna), *de bacalao* (cod)—and these days, even *de pulpo* (octopus).

For dessert: Locals enjoy cheese with honey at the end of a meal. In the tourist zones, bakeries push samples of *tarta de Santiago*, the local almond cake.

Seafood Spots

The easiest place to get your Santiago seafood fix is on two streets just south of the cathedral: **Rúa do Franco** and **Rúa do Vilar.** These lanes are lined with literally dozens of touristy seafood places. Even the places that seem "local" probably aren't—the Spanish-speaking clientele are mostly tourists from other parts of the country. Go for a stroll, examine the window display cases, and pop into the place that looks best. You've got a wide range of options: atmospheric mid-range spots; high-end, white-tablecloth splurges; and grumpy, simple, stripped-down joints actually frequented by locals (including O Gato Negro and O 42). Generally, these places feel inter-changeable; follow your nose. I enjoyed **Casa Elisa** (Rúa do Franco 36-68, Wed–Mon 11:00–17:00 & 20:00–23:00, closed Tue, tel. 981-583-112).

To get away from the tourist scene, venture a few blocks off the main drag to find these fine places, with good seafood and menus that go beyond the basics:

O Dezaseis ("The Sixteen") is every local's favorite: a friendly, laid-back cellar with stone walls, heavy beams, and interesting art, strewn with old farm implements (*raciones* €4–9, meat and fish dishes €10–12, Mon–Sat 12:00–14:00 & 20:30–24:00, closed Sun, near Galician culture and contemporary art museums at Rúa de San Pedro 16, tel. 981-564-880).

Tránsito dos Gramáticos features inventive, reasonable Galician and international cuisine in an easygoing, smartly decorated place a few steps from the tourist crowds. Their €6 salads are generous and tasty (€10.50 *menu,* daily 7:00–23:00, Calle Tránsito dos Gramáticos 1, tel. 981-572-640). Across the street, look for the "Hemingway slept here" plaque at the former site of Papa's favorite Santiago hotel.

Hostal dos Reis Católicos—the fancy old hospital sharing the square with the cathedral—has two fine restaurants, both downstairs. The main restaurant, **Libredón,** sits under a dramatic stone vault, offering Galician dishes for €12–30. It's as atmospheric as it gets, with stiff tuxedoed service, white tablecloths, and not a hint of fun (daily 13:00–15:30 & 20:30–23:00, reservations smart, Praza do Obradoiro 1, tel. 981-582-200). A few steps away, **Caxebre** offers a livelier, easygoing-tavern vibe, good food, and lower prices (€5–12 dishes, daily 13:00–16:00 & 20:00–23:30, tel. 981-050-527).

Restaurante Don Gaiferos is a classy, highly-regarded splurge, under a stone vault with tubular ceilings (main dishes €15–20, Tue–Sat 13:15–15:45 & 20:15–23:15, Sun–Mon 13:15–15:45 only, Rúa Nova 23, tel. 981-583-894).

For Less Adventurous Souls

Okay, so octopus and barnacles aren't for everybody. Here are a few tamer options for those with more timid palates.

Café Restaurante Casa Manolo is where students on a tight budget go for a classy meal out. This smart little place combines sleek contemporary design, good Galician and Spanish food, and excellent prices (€6 *menu* gives you two generous courses, plus water, bread, and dessert; Mon–Sat 13:00–16:00 & 20:30–23:30, Sun 13:00–16:00, at the bottom of Plaza de Cervantes, tel. 981-582-950).

Costa Vella is tops for a coffee break away from the crowds. This charming hotel—only a few blocks from the cathedral—has a lazy garden in back with dramatic views of San Francisco church and monastery (coffee and sandwiches, daily 8:00–23:00, Calle Puerta de la Peña 17, tel. 981-569-530).

Café Casino is a taste of turn-of-the-20th-century Vienna in Santiago. Local tour guides recommend this smoky place to their timid British groups, who wouldn't touch an octopus with a 10-foot pole (€4 salads, €6 pizzas, daily 9:00–23:00, Rúa do Vilar 35).

TRANSPORTATION CONNECTIONS

By train to: Madrid (3/day, 7.5 hrs by day, 9.25 hrs by night), **Salamanca** (2/day, take Madrid-bound train to Ávila to transfer, 9 hrs), **León** (1/day, 6 hrs), **Bilbao** (1/day, 10 hrs, no night train), **San Sebastián** (1/day, 11 hrs, no night train), **Santander** (1/day, 13 hrs, transfer in Palencia), **Porto,** Portugal (2/day, 5.5 hrs, transfer in Vigo).

By bus to: Madrid (6/day, 7–9 hrs, includes handy night bus 21:30–6:30), **Salamanca** (2/day, 6.5 hrs), **León** (1/day, 6.5 hrs), **Bilbao** (3/day, includes 1 night bus, 11 hrs), **Porto,** Portugal (3–4/week, 4 hrs). Bus info: tel. 981-542-416.

SALAMANCA

This sunny sandstone city boasts Spain's grandest plaza, its oldest university, and a fascinating history, all swaddled in a strolling, college-town ambience. Salamanca—a youthful and untouristy Toledo—is a series of monuments and clusters of cloisters. The many students help keep prices down.

Take a *paseo* with the local crowd down Rúa Mayor and through Plaza Mayor. The young people congregate until late in the night, chanting and cheering, talking and singing. When I asked a local woman why young men all alone on the Plaza Mayor suddenly break into song, she said, "Doesn't it happen where you live?"

Planning Your Time

Salamanca, with its art, university, and atmospheric Plaza Mayor, is worth a day and a night, but is stuck out in the boonies. It's feasible as a side-trip, though not a day trip, from Madrid (it's 2.5 hours one-way from Madrid by car, bus, or train). If you're bound for Santiago de Compostela or Portugal, Salamanca is a natural stop.

ORIENTATION

Tourist Information

The main TI is on Plaza Mayor (daily 9:00–14:00 & 16:00–20:00, closes 18:30 in winter, Plaza Mayor 19, tel. 923-218-342). Pick up the free map, city brochure, and current list of museum hours. Another TI at Casa de Las Conchas on Rúa Mayor serves the region

Salamanca Area

and province, as well as the city (daily 9:00–20:00, Oct–May closed 14:00–17:00, tel. 923-268-571). Summertime-only TIs spring up at the train and bus stations. There's little in the way of organized tourism for the English-speaking visitor.

Arrival in Salamanca

From Salamanca's train and bus stations to Plaza Mayor, it's a 25-minute walk, an easy bus ride (€0.65, pay driver), or a €5 trip by taxi. Day-trippers can store bags in either station's lockers (*consignas,* bus station-€1–2, at bay level facing main building on your left; train station-€3–4.50).

From the train station: To walk to the center, exit left and walk down to the ring road, cross it at Plaza España, then angle slightly left up Calle Azafranal. Or you can take bus #1 from the train station, which lets you off at Plaza Mercado (the market), next to Plaza Mayor.

From the bus station: To walk to the center, exit right and walk down Avenida Filiberto Villalobos; take a left on the ring road and the first right on Ramón y Cajal. Or take bus #4 (exit station right, catch bus on same side of the street as the station) to the city center; the closest stop is on Gran Vía, about four blocks east of Plaza Mayor (ask the driver or a fellow passenger, "*¿Para Plaza Mayor?*").

Drivers will find a handy underground parking lot at Plaza Santa Eulalia (€0.75/hr, €9.40/day, open 24/7); some hotels, including Gran Vía, Ceylan, and Condal, give you a discount stamp on your parking receipt. Two other convenient lots are Parking Plaza Campillo (€7.90/day) and Lemans (€11/day).

Helpful Hints

Internet Access: BBiGG is at Plaza de España 1 (daily 9:00–2:00, 150 terminals, tel. 923-250-063). **Cyberplace Internet** is at Plaza Mayor 10 (Mon–Fri 10:30–2:00, Sat–Sun 11:00–2:00, 1st floor, tel. 923-264-281). **Over The Game,** with 40 computers and a starry galaxy theme, is at Varillas 24 (daily 10:00–24:00, tel. 923-216-991, info-salamanca@overthegame.com). Perhaps your most efficient Internet access is at the laundry (see below).

Self-Service Laundry: It's a five-minute walk from Plaza Mayor (Mon–Fri 9:30–14:00 & 16:00–20:00, Sat 10:00–14:00, closed Sun & Aug 15–30, €6.50 for wash and dry, helpful attendant, Pasaje Azafranal 18, located in passageway a half-block north of Plaza Santa Eulalia). Cleverly, it has about a dozen online computers (€2/hr, Juan Carlos SE).

Travel Agency: Viajes Salamanca, which books flights, trains, and some buses, including buses to Coimbra, Portugal, has two branches on Plaza Mayor at #11 and #24 (tel. 923-211-414 or 923-215-215).

Local Guide: Ines Criado Velasco, a good English-speaking guide, is happy to tailor a town walk to your interests (€60/2 hrs—a special rate for readers of this book, €75/3–5 hrs, €140/all day, for groups of 1–50, tel. 923-207-404, mobile 609-557-528, icriado@interbook.net).

SIGHTS

▲▲**Plaza Mayor**—Built from 1729 to 1755, this ultimate Spanish plaza is a fine place to nurse a cup of coffee (try the venerable Art Nouveau Café Novelty) and watch the world go by. There will probably be events and celebrations to commemorate the square's 250th anniversary (ask at TI).

The town hall, with the clock, grandly overlooks the square. The Arco del Toro (built into the eastern wall) leads to the covered market. While most European squares honor a king or saint, this golden-toned square—ringed by famous Castilians—is for all the people. The square niches above the colonnade surrounding the square depict writers such as Miguel de Cervantes, heroes and conquistadors such as Christopher Columbus and Hernán Cortés, and kings and dictators such as Franco.

Plaza Mayor has long been Salamanca's community living room. Imagine the excitement of the days (until 1893), when bullfights were held in the square. Now old-timers gather here each day, remembering an earlier time when the girls would promenade clockwise around

Salamanca

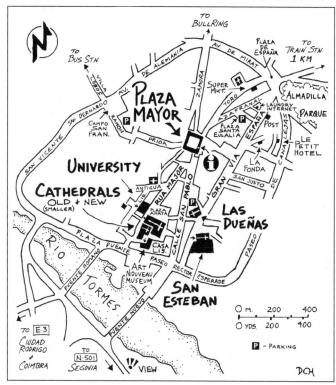

the colonnade while the boys cruised counterclockwise, looking for the perfect *queso* (cheese), as they'd call a cute dish. Perhaps the best time of all for people-watching is Sunday after Mass (13:00–15:00) when the grandmothers gather here in their Sunday best.

▲▲**Cathedrals, Old and New**—These cool-on-a-hot-day cathe-

drals share buttresses and are both richly ornamented. You get to the old through the new. Before entering the new church, check out its ornate front door (west portal). The facade is decorated Plateresque—masonry so intricate it looks like silverwork. It's Spain's version of Flamboyant Gothic. At the side door (on the next facade, around the corner to the left as you face the main entrance), look for the astronaut added by a capricious restorer in 1993. This caused an outrage in town, but now locals shrug their shoulders and say, "He's the person closest to God." I'll give you a chance to find him on your own. Otherwise, look at the end of this listing for help.

The "new" cathedral, built from 1513 to 1733, is a mix of Gothic, Renaissance, and Baroque (free and lackluster). The music (sometimes live) helps. The *coro*, or choir, blocks up half of the church, but its wood carving is sumptuous; look up to see the elaborate organ.

The entrance to the old cathedral (12th-century Romanesque) is near the rear of the new one (€3, free English leaflet, daily 10:00–13:30 & 16:00–19:30, closes at 12:30 and 17:30 in off-season; during Mass the old cathedral is free, but the cloister isn't). Sit in a front pew to study the altarpiece's 53 scenes from the lives of Mary and Jesus (by the Italian Florentino, 1445) surrounding a precious 12th-century statue of the Virgin of the Valley—Salamanca's patron virgin. High above, notice the dramatic Last Judgment fresco with Jesus sending condemned souls into the literal jaws of hell.

Then head into the cloister (off the right transept) and explore the chapels, notable for their unusual tombs, ornate altarpieces, and ceilings with leering faces. In the Capilla de Santa Barbara (second on the left as you enter) you can sit like students did when they were quizzed by a stern circle of professors for their final exam—feet nervously pressed against the well-worn feet of the tomb of the Salamanca bishop who founded the University around 1230. (The University of Salamanca originated with a group of teacher/priests who met in this room.) As you continue through the cloister, you'll see the museum, contained in three rooms on your left *(salas capitulares)*, with a gallery of 15th-century Castilian paintings. Capilla de San Bartólome de Los Anayas, the farthest from the cloister entrance, has a gorgeously carved 16th-century alabaster tomb (with the dog and lion at its foot making peace—or negotiating who gets to eat the worried-looking rabbit) and a wooden 16th-century Mudejar organ. (Mudejar is the Romanesque-Islamic style of the Moors in Spain after the Christian conquest.) For a fantastic view of the old cathedral's dome and a look at the inside passages of the tower, visit the *Torres de la Catedral*, sealed after Lisbon's 1755 earthquake to create structural support and reopened in 2003. A small wooden door at the south end of the cathedral lets you in (€2, daily April–Oct 10:00–20:00, Nov–March 10:00–17:50).

Find that astronaut: He's just a little guy, about the size of a Ken-does-Mars doll, entwined in the stone trim to the left of the door, roughly 10 feet up. If you like that, check out the dragon (an arm's length below). Historians debate whether he's eating an ice cream cone or singing karaoke.

Tourist Tram—The small tram you might see waiting at the cathedral does 20-minute loops throughout the town with a Spanish narration (€3, daily 10:00–14:00 & 16:00–20:00, departs every 20 min from cathedral, mobile 09-466-396).

▲▲**University**—The University of Salamanca, the oldest in Spain (est. 1230), was one of Europe's leading centers of learning for 400 years. Columbus came here for travel tips. Today, while no longer so prestigious, it's laden with history and popular with Americans, who enjoy its excellent summer program. The old lecture halls around the cloister, where many of Spain's Golden Age heroes studied, are open to the public (€4, free Mon mornings, Mon–Sat 9:30–13:30 & 16:00–19:30, Sun 10:00–13:30, last entry 30 min before closing, enter from Calle Libreros, tel. 923-294-400, ext. 1150).

The ornately decorated grand entrance of the university is a great example of Spain's Plateresque style. The people studying the facade aren't art fans. They're trying to find a tiny frog on a skull that students looked to for good luck.

But forget the frog. Follow the facade's symbolic meaning. It was made in three sections by Charles V. The bottom celebrates the Catholic Monarchs. Ferdinand and Isabel saw that the university had no buildings befitting its prestige, and granted the money for this building. The Greek script says something like "From the monarchs, this university. From the university, this tribute as a thanks."

The immodest middle section celebrates the grandson of Ferdinand and Isabel, Charles V. He appears with his queen, the Hapsburg double-headed eagle, and the complex coat of arms of the mighty Hapsburg empire. Since this is a Renaissance structure, it features Greek and Roman figures in the shells. And, as a statement of educational independence from medieval Church control, the top shows the pope flanked by Hercules and Venus.

After paying admission, you get a free English-language leaflet full of details; to follow it, go left (clockwise around the courtyard) upon entering.

In the Hall of Fray Luís de León, the narrow wooden beam tables and benches—whittled down by centuries of studious doodling—are originals. Professors spoke from the Church-threatening *cátedra*, or pulpit. It was here that free-thinking brother Luís de León returned, after the Inquisition jailed and tortured him for five years for challenging the Church's control of the word of God by translating part of the Bible into Castilian. He started his first post-imprisonment lecture with, "As we were saying..." Such courageous men of truth believed the forces of the Inquisition were not even worth acknowledging.

The altarpiece in the nearby chapel depicts professors swearing to Mary's virginity. (How did they know?) Climb upstairs for a peek into the oldest library in Spain. Outside the library, look into the courtyard at the American sequoia, brought here 150 years ago and standing all alone. Notice also the big nests in the bell tower. Storks stop here from February through August on their annual journey from northern Europe to Morocco. There are hundreds of such stork nests in Salamanca.

As you leave the university, you'll see the statue of Fray Luís de León. Behind him, to your left, is the entrance to a peaceful courtyard containing the Museum of the University, notable for Gallego's fanciful 15th-century *Sky of Salamanca* (included in university admission, no photos allowed in museum).

Still looking for the frog? It's on the right pillar of the facade, nearly halfway up, on the left-most of three skulls.

▲**Museo Art Nouveau y Art Deco**—Located in the Casa Lis, this museum—with its beautifully displayed collection of stained glass, jewelry, cancan statuettes, and toy dolls—is a refreshing change of pace. Nowhere else in Spain will you enjoy a modernist (or Art Nouveau) building filled with art and furnishings from that same age. The €0.30 English leaflet thoughtfully describes each part of the collection (€2.50, open weekends only, April–mid-Oct Sat–Sun 11:00–21:00, mid-Oct–March Sat–Sun 11:00–20:00, no photos, Calle Gibraltar 14, between the new/old cathedrals and the river, tel. 923-121-425, www.museocasalis.org).

Church of San Esteban—Dedicated to St. Stephen (Esteban) the martyr, this complex contains a recently-restored cloister, tombs, museum, sacristy, and church. Tour it in this order: fancy facade outside, altarpiece in main nave, upstairs to sit in the choir, and finally a browse through the museum.

Before you enter, notice the Plateresque facade and its bas-relief of the stoning of St. Stephen. The crucifixion above is by Benvenuto Cellini. Once inside, follow the free English pamphlet. The nave is overwhelmed by a 100-foot, 4,000-piece wood altarpiece by José Benito Churriguera (1665–1725) that replaced the original Gothic one in 1693. You'll see St. Francis on the left, St. Dominic on the right, and a grand monstrance holding the Communion wafers in the middle, all below a painting of St. Stephen being stoned. This is a textbook example of the intricately detailed Churrigueresco style that influenced many South American mission buildings. Quietly ponder the dusty, gold-plated cottage cheese, as tourists shake their heads and say "too much" in their mother tongue.

Upstairs step into the balcony choir loft for a fine overview of the nave and a rare opportunity to actually sit in the old wooden choir stalls. Go ahead, flip up the misericord, which allows old and tired Mass-goers to almost sit while they "stand." The big spinnable book holder in the middle of the room held big music books—large enough for all to chant from in an age when there weren't enough books for everyone.

The museum next door has temperature-controlled glass cases preserving illustrated 16th-century Bibles and choir books. Notice also how the curved ivory Filipino saints all look like they're carved out of an elephant's tusk. And don't miss the fascinating "chocolate box reliquaries" on the wall from 1580. Survey whose bones are collected between all the inlaid ivory and precious woods (€1.50, daily 10:00–13:00 & 16:00–20:00, closed at 18:00 in winter).

Convento de las Dueñas—Next door, the much simpler *convento* is a joy. It consists of a double-decker cloister with a small museum of religious art. Check out the stone meanies exuberantly decorating the capitals on the cloister's upper deck (€1.50, daily 10:30–13:00 & 16:30–19:00, closes 17:30 in winter, no English info). The nuns sell sweets daily except Sunday (€3/small box of specialty *Amarillos*— almond, egg white, and sugar; €1/small bag of cookies, no assortments possible even though their display box raises hopes).

Honorable Mention—Historians enjoy the low-slung Roman Bridge *(Puente Romano)*, much of it original, spanning the Río Tormes. The *ibérico* (ancient pre-Roman) headless bull blindly guarding the entrance to the bridge is a symbol of the city. Nearby, at Parque Fluvial, you can rent rowboats (June–Sept only).

▲Tuna Music—Traditionally, Salamanca's poorer students earned money to fund their education by singing in the streets. This 15th- to 18th-century tradition survives today as musical groups of students (representing the various faculties), dressed in the traditional black capes and leggings, play mandolins, guitars, and sing, serenading the public in the bars on and around the Plaza Mayor. The name tuna, which has nothing to do with fish, refers to a vagabond student lifestyle and later was applied to the music these students sing. They're out on summer weeknights (singing for tips from 22:00 until after midnight) because they make more serious money performing for weddings on weekends.

SLEEPING

Salamanca, being a student town, has plenty of good eating and sleeping values. All but one of my listings (Le Petit Hotel) are on or within a three-minute walk of the Plaza Mayor. Directions are given from the Plaza Mayor, assuming you are facing the building with the clock (e.g., 3 o'clock is 90 degrees to your right as you face the clock).

$$$ **Petit Palace Las Torres,** on Plaza Mayor, is a newly-remodeled place with 44 modern, spacious rooms and all the amenities. Its rooms with Plaza Mayor views cost the same as viewless rooms (Sb-€67, Db-€80, Tb-€105, Qb-€115, 30 percent more Sept 1–Oct 12, air-con, elevator, parking-€10/day at nearby Lemans lot, hotel entry just off square at Consejo 4 or from the square at Plaza Mayor 26, exit the plaza at 11 o'clock, tel. 923-212-100, fax 923-212-101, www.hthotels.com, tor@hthotels.com, SE).

$$$ **Hotel Don Juan,** a block off Plaza Mayor, has 16 classy, newly-carpeted, comfy rooms and an attached restaurant (Sb-€53, Db-€72, Tb-€97, 20 percent cheaper in Jan–Feb, air-con, elevator, valet parking-€10/day—give them 10 min to bring your car, exit

Sleep Code

(€1 = about $1.20, country code: 34)
S = Single, **D** = Double/Twin, **T** = Triple, **Q** = Quad,
b = bathroom, **s** = shower only, **no CC** = Credit Cards not
accepted, **SE** = Speaks English, **NSE** = No English. You can
assume credit cards are accepted unless noted otherwise.

To help you easily sort through these listings, I've divided
the rooms into three categories, based on the price for a standard
double room with bath during high season (breakfast and 7 percent IVA tax not included):

$$$ **Higher Priced**—Most rooms €70 or more.
$$ **Moderately Priced**—Most rooms between €40–70.
$ **Lower Priced**—Most rooms €40 or less.

Plaza Mayor at about 5 o'clock and turn right to Quintana 6, tel.
923-261-473, fax 923-262-475, www.hoteldonjuan-salamanca.com,
info@hoteldonjuan-salamanca.com, David or Livia SE).

$$$ **Hotel Salamanca Plaza Mercado** is a business-class hotel
that rents 38 bright, shiny modern rooms across the street from the
covered market (Sb-€49, Db-€88, Tb/Qb-€125, air-con, elevator,
parking-€9/day, Plaza del Mercado 16, tel. 923-272-250, fax 923-270-
932, www.salamancaplaza.com, reservas@salamancaplaza.com, SE).

$$ **Hostal Plaza Mayor,** with 19 finely decorated but small
rooms, has a good location a block southwest of Plaza Mayor (Sb-
€36, Db-€60, Tb-€90, air-con, most rooms served by elevator, exit
Plaza Mayor at 7 o'clock, Plaza del Corrillo 20, attached restaurant,
tel. 923-262-020, fax 923-217-548, hostalplazamayor@hotmail.com).

$$ **Le Petit Hotel,** while away from the characteristic core, is
well located, facing a peaceful, well-tended park and a grand church
two blocks east of Gran Vía. It rents 23 homey yet modern rooms.
The rooms with views of the church are particularly bright; ask for a
vista de iglesia (Sb-€34, Db-€42, Tb/Qb-€55, breakfast-€3.15, no
CC, air-con, elevator, Ronda Sancti Spiritus 39, about 6 blocks east of
Plaza Mayor; exit Plaza Mayor at 3 o'clock and continue east, turn left
on Gran Vía, right on Sancti Spiritus—at Banco Simeon, and left
after the church; tel. 923-600-773 or 923-600-774, no fax, www
.lepetithotel.net, reserve by simply calling and leaving your name and
time of arrival—no more than a month in advance, Hortensia NSE).

$ **Hostal Los Angeles,** at about three o'clock, rents 15 simple
but cared-for rooms, four of which overlook the square. Stand on
the balcony and inhale the essence of Spain (S-€13, D-€25, Db-€32,
T-€35, Tb-€42, Qb-€52, view rooms have full bathrooms, includes
tax, Plaza Mayor 10, tel. & fax 923-218-166, Inma or Juan). To try
for a view, request, *"Con vista, por favor."*

Central Salamanca

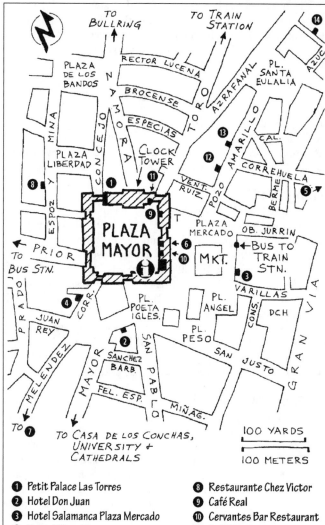

1. Petit Palace Las Torres
2. Hotel Don Juan
3. Hotel Salamanca Plaza Mercado
4. Hostal Plaza Mayor
5. To La Petit Hotel & Rest.
   La Fonda Casa de Comidas
6. Hostal Los Angeles & Internet Café
7. To Hostal Las Vegas Centro
8. Restaurante Chez Victor
9. Café Real
10. Cervantes Bar Restaurant
11. Café Novelty
12. Restaurante Isidro
13. Restaurante Comercio
14. To Launderette

$ Hostal Las Vegas Centro is clean, bright, quiet, and cheap. This cozy 17-room place is owned by the same family that runs Hostal Los Angeles (S-€18, Db-€24–€36, Tb-€45, Qb-€60, 2 blocks off Plaza Mayor, toward cathedral at Meléndez 13, first floor, tel. & fax 923-218-749, www.lasvegascentro.com, lasvegas@usarios .retecal.es, José Antonio, SE).

EATING

Local specialties include *serrano* ham (see sidebar, page 155), roast suckling pig (called *tostón* around here), and *sopa de ajo,* the local garlic soup. *Patatas meneadas* (potatoes with Spanish paprika and bacon) is a simple but tasty local tapa.

Dining Well
Restaurante Chez Victor is the result of the marriage of a Castilian chef (Victor) and a French food-lover (Margarite). This family-run place, elegantly decorated with a feminine French touch and bouquets on the tables, serves modern and creative Franco/Castilian fare—perhaps your best €35–40 meal in town (Tue–Sat 14:00–16:00 & 21:00–23:30, Sun 14:00–15:30, closed Mon and Sun eve, air-con, Espoz y Mina 26, tel. 923-213-123).

La Fonda Casa de Comidas is a dark, woody place with solid traditional cuisine, catering to locals, where you'll happily spend €22 for three courses (daily 13:45–16:30 & 21:00–23:30, a bit smoky, reserve on weekends, 15 yards down the arcade from corner of Gran Vía and Cuesta de Sancti Spiritus at La Reja 2, tel. 923-215-712).

On Plaza Mayor
Here you can enjoy a meal sitting on the finest square in Spain and savor some of Europe's best people-watching. The bars, with little tables spilling onto the square, serve *raciones* and €2 glasses of wine. A *ración de la casa* (house specialty of hams, sausages, and cheese), a *ración* of *patatas bravas* (chunks of potatoes with tomato sauce), and two glasses of wine makes a nice dinner for two for about €25—one of the best eating values in all of Europe. For dessert, stroll with an ice cream cone from Café Novelty.

Café Real serves bar snacks in a tapas style (open daily).

Cervantes Bar is more of a restaurant, with a wide selection of meals, €7 salads, and sandwiches. They also have an indoors section, overlooking Plaza Mayor from one floor up; it's a popular student hangout (tapas daily 10:00–21:00, meals only after 13:30 and 19:30).

Café Novelty is Plaza Mayor's Art Nouveau cafe—dating from 1905, filled with character and literary memories. The metal sculpture depicts a famous local writer, Torrente Ballester (daily 8:00–24:00). Their ice cream sweetens a stroll around the plaza.

Sampling Serrano Ham

Jamón serrano is cured in the *sierras* (mountains) of Spain. While there are many variations of this cured ham from different regions of Spain, Spanish people have a special appreciation for *jamón ibérico,* made with the back legs of black pigs fed mainly on acorns. Originating in Spain, these black pigs are fatter and happier (slaughtered much later than regular pigs). Spaniards treasure memories of grandpa thinly carving a *jamón,* supported in a *jamonero* (ham holder) during Christmas just as we savor the turkey-carving at Thanksgiving. To sample this delicacy without the high price tag you'll find in bars and restaurants, go to the local market, ask for 100 grams (*cien gramos de jamón ibérico extra;* about €70/kilo) and enjoy it as a picnic with red wine and bread.

Eating Simple or Tapas

There are plenty of good, inexpensive restaurants between Plaza Mayor and Gran Vía, and as you leave the Plaza Mayor toward Rúa Mayor. The tapas places along and around Rúa Mayor are abundant and often overrun with students.

Restaurante Isidro is a thriving local favorite—a straightforward, hard-working eatery run by Alberto—offering a good assortment of fish and specialty meat dishes (menu of the day-€8.50, also à la carte €15–20 dinners, good roasts, Mon–Sat 13:00–16:00 & 20:00–24:00, Sun 13:00–16:00, has seating in its *comedor,* quick service, Pozo Amarillo 19, about a block north of covered market, near Plaza Mayor, tel. 923-262-848).

Restaurante Comercio, next door, has tasty food and is warmly decorated with old photos of the square. Their specialities include *sopa castellana* (Castilian soup) and oxtail stew. The €9.50 menu works also for dinner, or consider their €20 à la carte meals (daily 12:30–16:00 & 19:30–24:00, Pozo Amarillo 23, tel. 923-260-280).

The **Pans & Company** sandwich chain is always fast and affordable, with a branch on Calle Prior across from Burger King and another on Rúa Mayor (daily 10:00–24:00).

Picnics: The covered *mercado* (market) on Plaza Mercado has fresh fruits and veggies (Mon–Sat 8:00–14:30, closed Sun, on east side of Plaza Mayor). A small Consum grocery, three blocks east of Plaza Mayor, has just the basics (Mon–Sat 9:30–21:00, closed Sun). For variety, the big Champion Supermercado is your best bet, but it's a six-block walk north of Plaza Mayor on Toro (Mon–Sat 9:15–21:15, closed Sun, across from Plaza San Juan de Sahagun and its church).

If you always wanted seconds at Communion, buy a bag of giant Communion wafers, a local specialty called *obleas.*

TRANSPORTATION CONNECTIONS

By train to: Madrid (6/day, 2.5 hrs, Chamartín station), **Ávila** (6/day, 1 hr), **Barcelona** (1/day, 8:00 departure, 10 hrs), **Santiago** (2/day, 9 hrs, transfer in Ávila), **Coimbra,** Portugal (1/day, 5 hrs, departs Salamanca station at about 4:50 in the morning, no kidding; you can catch a taxi to the train station at any hour from Plaza Mercado—a few steps east of Plaza Mayor—and from Plaza Poeta Iglesias, which is across from the Gran Hotel, immediately south of Plaza Mayor, taxi ride costs €4 during day, €5 at night; for the better bus option to Coimbra, see below). Train info: tel. 902-240-202.

By bus to: Madrid (hrly, 2.5 hrs, Auto-Res buses, www .auto-res.com), **Segovia** (2/day, 4 hrs; 1 direct/day on weekends, otherwise transfer in Labajos or Ávila; consider a brief visit to Ávila en route, Auto-Res buses), **Ávila** (4/day, 1.5 hrs Auto-Res buses), **Ciudad Rodrigo** (nearly hrly, 1 hr, El Pilar buses), **Santiago** (2/day, 6.5 hrs), **Barcelona** (2/day, 11 hrs, Alsa buses), **Coimbra,** Portugal (1/day, departs at 14:00, 5.25 hrs, €24, Alsa buses, tel. 902-422-242, www.alsa.es). Bus info: tel. 923-236-717.

Ciudad Rodrigo

Ciudad Rodrigo is worth a visit only if you're driving from Salamanca to Coimbra, Portugal (although buses connect Salamanca and Ciudad Rodrigo with surprising efficiency in about an hour).

This rough-and-tumble old town of 16,000 people caps a hill overlooking the Río Agueda. Spend an hour wandering among the Renaissance mansions that line its streets and exploring its cathedral and Plaza Mayor. Have lunch or a snack at El Sanatorio (Plaza Mayor 14). The tapas are cheap, the crowd is local, and the walls are a Ciudad Rodrigo scrapbook, including some bullfighting that makes the Three Stooges look demure.

Ciudad Rodrigo's cathedral—pockmarked with scars from Napoleonic cannon balls—has some entertaining carvings in the choir and some pretty racy work in its cloisters. Who says, "When you've seen one Gothic church, you've seen 'em all"?

The **TI** is two blocks from Plaza Mayor, just inside the old wall near the cathedral (Mon–Fri 9:00–14:00 & 17:00–19:00, Sat–Sun until 20:00, Plaza Ameyuelas 5, tel. 923-460-561). They can recommend a good hotel, such as **Hotel Conde Rodrigo** (34 rooms, Sb-€42, Db-€48, Tb-€64, less Nov–April, air-con, elevator, Plaza San Salvador 9, tel. 923-461-404, info@conderodrigo.com).

MADRID

Today's Madrid is upbeat and vibrant, still enjoying a post-Franco renaissance. You'll feel it. Even the living-statue beggars have a twinkle in their eyes.

Madrid is the hub of Spain. This modern capital—Europe's highest, at more than 2,000 feet—has a population of more than four million and is young by European standards. As recently as 1561, King Philip II decided to move the capital of his empire from Toledo to Madrid. One hundred years ago, Madrid had only 400,000 people—so 90 percent of the city is modern sprawl surrounding an intact, easy-to-navigate historic core.

Dive headlong into the grandeur and intimate charm of Madrid. The lavish Royal Palace, with its gilded rooms and frescoed ceilings, rivals Versailles. The Prado has Europe's top collection of paintings. The city's huge Retiro Park invites you for a shady siesta and a hopscotch through a mosaic of lovers, families, skateboarders, pets walking their masters, and expert bench-sitters. Save time for Madrid's elegant shops and people-friendly pedestrian zones.

The city's latest plans include the creation of a pedestrian street crossing the city from the Prado to the Royal Palace (the section from the Prado along Huertas street to Plaza Ángel, near Plaza Santa Ana, has been completed) and a new macro-train station in Puerta del Sol (which will keep that subway station under construction until 2008).

By installing posts to keep cars off sidewalks, making the streets safer after dark, and restoring old buildings, Madrid is working hard to make the city more livable...and fun to visit.

On Sundays, cheer for the bull at a bullfight or bargain like mad at a mega-size flea market. Lively Madrid has enough street-singing, barhopping, and people-watching vitality to give any visitor a boost of youth.

Planning Your Time

Madrid's top two sights, the Prado and the palace, are each worth a half day. On a Sunday (Easter–Oct), consider allotting extra time for a bullfight. Ideally, give Madrid two days and spend them this way:

Day 1: Breakfast of *churros* (see "Eating," page 189) before a brisk, 20-minute good-morning-Madrid walk from Puerta del Sol to the Prado (from Puerta del Sol, walk three blocks south to Plaza Ángel, then take the pedestrian walkway to the Prado along Huertas street); spend the rest of the morning at the Prado; take an afternoon siesta in Retiro Park, or tackle modern art at Centro Arte de Reina Sofía *(Guernica)* and/or Thyssen-Bornemisza Museum; dinner at 20:00, with tapas around Plaza Santa Ana.

Day 2: Follow this book's "Puerta del Sol to Royal Palace Walk"; tour the Royal Palace, lunch near Plaza Mayor; afternoon free for other sights, shopping, or side trip to El Escorial (open until 19:00). Be out at the magic hour—before sunset—when beautifully-lit people fill Madrid.

Note that the Prado, Thyssen-Bornemisza Museum, and El Escorial all close on Monday. For good day-trip possibilities from Madrid, see the next two chapters (Sights Northwest of Madrid and Toledo).

ORIENTATION

The Puerta del Sol marks the center of Madrid. The Royal Palace (to the west) and the Prado Museum and Retiro Park (to the east) frame Madrid's historic center. Southwest of Puerta del Sol is a 17th-century district with the slow-down-and-smell-the-cobbles Plaza Mayor and memories of pre-industrial Spain. North of Puerta del Sol runs Gran Vía, and between the two are lively pedestrian shopping streets. Gran Vía, bubbling with expensive shops and cinemas, leads to the modern Plaza de España. North of Gran Vía is the gritty Malasaña quarter (sleazy-looking *hombres*).

The historic center can be covered on foot. No major sight is more than a 20-minute walk or a €3.50 taxi ride from Puerta del Sol, Madrid's central square. Divide your time between the city's top three attractions: the Royal Palace, the Prado, and its bar-hopping contemporary scene.

Tourist Information

Madrid has five TIs: **Plaza Mayor** at #3 (it may move to the opposite side, Mon–Sat 10:00–20:00, Sun 10:00–15:00, tel. 915-881-636); **near the Prado Museum** (Mon–Sat 9:00–19:00, Sun 9:00–15:00, Duque de Medinaceli 2, behind Palace Hotel, tel. 914-293-705); **Chamartín** train station (Mon–Sat 8:00–20:00, Sun 8:00–15:00, tel. 913-159-976); **Atocha** train station (daily 9:00–21:00); and at the

Madrid

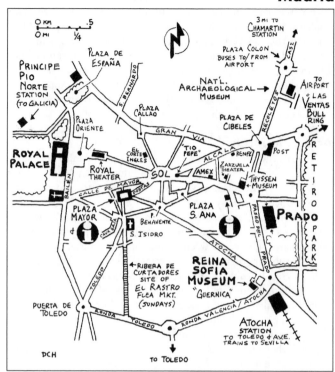

airport (daily 8:00–20:00, tel. 913-058-656). During the summer, small temporary stands with yellow umbrellas pop up at touristed places such as Puerta del Sol, and their yellow-shirted student guides are happy to help out lost tourists.

The general tourist information number is 915-881-636 (or pricier toll call—902-100-007, www.munimadrid.es).

At any TI, pick up a map and confirm your sightseeing plans. Only the most hyperactive travelers could save money buying the TIs' **Madrid Card,** which covers 40 museums, unlimited public transportation, and the Madrid Vision bus tour mentioned in "Tours" below (€28/1 day, €42/2 days, €55/3 days). The free bus map has the most detailed map of the center. Get the three-part brochure on taxi, bus, and Metro costs. TIs have the latest on bull-fights and zarzuela, the local light opera.

For entertainment listings, the TI's free *En Madrid/What's On* is not as good as the easy-to-decipher Spanish-language weekly entertainment guide *Guía del Ocio* (€1, sold at newsstands), which lists events, restaurants, and movies ("v.o." means a movie is in its original language, rather than dubbed).

If you're heading to other destinations in Spain, ask any Madrid TI for free maps and brochures (ideally in English). Since many small-town TIs keep erratic hours and run out of these pamphlets, get what you can here. You can get schedules for buses and some trains, and thus avoid unnecessary trips to the various stations. The TI's free and amazingly informative *Mapa de Comunicaciones España* lists all the Turismos and highway SOS numbers with a road map of Spain. (If they're out, ask for the route map sponsored by the Paradores hotel chain, the camping map, or the golf map.)

Arrival in Madrid

By Train: Madrid's two train stations, Chamartín and Atocha, are both on subway lines with easy access to downtown Madrid. Each station has all the services. Chamartín handles most international trains. Atocha generally covers southern Spain including the AVE trains to Sevilla. Both stations offer long-distance trains *(largo recorrido)* as well as smaller, local trains *(regionales* and *cercanías)* to nearby destinations. To travel between Chamartín and Atocha, don't bother with the subway (which involves a transfer)—the *cercanías* trains are faster (6/hr, 12 min, €1.20, free with railpass, show it at ticket window in the middle of the turnstiles, departs from Atocha's track 2 and generally Chamartín's track 2 or 3—but check the *Salidas Inmediatas* board to be sure).

At the **Chamartín Station,** the TI is opposite track 19. The impressively large Centro de Viajes/Travel Center customer-service office is in the middle of the building. You can relax in the Sala VIP Club if you have a first-class railpass and first-class seat or sleeper reservations (near track 12, next to Centro de Viajes). The *cercanías* platforms cluster around track 5. The station's Metro stop is Chamartín. (If you arrive by Metro at Chamartín, follow signs to *Información* to get to the lobby rather than signs to *Vías*, which send you directly to the platforms.)

The **Atocha Station** is split into two halves—it's easiest to think of the station as having an AVE side (mostly long-distance trains) and a *cercanías* side (mostly local trains), connected by a corridor of shops. Each side of the station has separate schedules and customer-service offices; this can be confusing if you're in the wrong end of the building. The **TI,** located in the AVE side, handles tourist info only—not train info (daily 9:00–21:00, near the interior botanical garden).

Atocha's AVE side, which is in the towering old-station building, has the slick AVE trains, other fast trains, a pharmacy (daily 8:00–23:00), a cafeteria, and the good Samarcanda restaurant (Mon–Fri 13:00–20:00, Sat–Sun 11:00–20:00).

On the AVE side, the long-distance trains—AVE and Grandes Líneas (grand lines)—depart from the upper floor only.

Greater Madrid

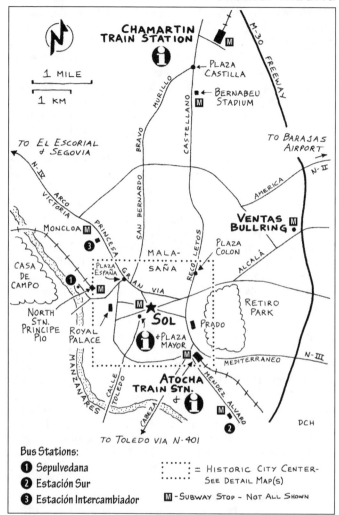

N

1 MILE
1 KM

CHAMARTIN TRAIN STATION

PLAZA CASTILLA

BERNABEU STADIUM

M-30 FREEWAY

TO EL ESCORIAL & SEGOVIA

TO BARAJAS AIRPORT

N-II

N-IV

ARCO VICTORIA

MURILLO

BRAVO

CASTELLANO

SAN BERNARDO

AMERICA

MONCLOA

PRINCESA

MALA-SAÑA

RECO LETOS

PLAZA COLON

VENTAS BULLRING

ALCALÁ

CASA DE CAMPO

PLAZA ESPAÑA

GRAN VIA

SOL

RETIRO PARK

NORTH STN. PRINCIPE PIO

ROYAL PALACE

PLAZA MAYOR

PRADO

MEDITERRANEO

N-III

MANZANARES

CALLE TOLEDO

CABEZA

ATOCHA TRAIN STN.

MENDEZ ALVARO

DCH

TO TOLEDO VIA N·401

Bus Stations:
❶ Sepulvedana
❷ Estación Sur
❸ Estación Intercambiador

⋯⋯ = HISTORIC CITY CENTER— SEE DETAIL MAP(S)

M - SUBWAY STOP - NOT ALL SHOWN

For information on these, try the *Información* counter (daily 6:30–23:30), next to Centro Servicios AVE (this office handles only AVE changes and problems). Both offices are opposite the *Atención al Cliente* office, which deals with problems on Grandes Líneas (daily 6:30–23:30). Also on the AVE side is Atocha's Club AVE, a lounge reserved solely for AVE business-class travelers and for first-class ticket-holders or Eurailers with a first-class reservation (upstairs, past the security check on right, free drinks, newspapers, showers, and info service).

On the *cercanías* side of Atocha Station, you'll find the local *cercanías* trains, *regionales* trains, some eastbound faster trains, and the Metro stop named "Atocha RENFE." (Note that the stop named simply "Atocha" is a different Metro stop in Madrid—not at the train station.) The *Atención al Cliente* office in the *cercanías* section has information only on trains for destinations bordering Madrid.

To buy tickets at Atocha for the local *cercanías* trains (for example, to Toledo), go to the middle of the *cercanías* side and get your ticket from ticket windows in the small rectangular offices (marked *Venta de Billetes sin reserva*). You can buy AVE and other long-distance train tickets in the bigger ticket offices in either half of the building; the airier *Taquillas* office on the AVE side is more pleasant. Since station ticket offices can get really crowded, it's often quicker to buy your ticket at an English-speaking travel agency, such as the El Corte Inglés Travel Agency at Atocha (Mon–Fri 7:00–22:00, weekends only for urgent arrangements, on ground floor of AVE side at the far end) or at the branch within the El Corte Inglés department store at Puerta del Sol (see "Helpful Hints," below). You could also try the downtown RENFE office, which offers train information, reservations, tickets, and minimal English (Mon–Fri 9:30–20:00, closed Sat–Sun, accepts credit cards, go in person, 2 blocks north of the Prado at Calle Alcalá 44, tel. 902-240-202, www.renfe.es). For train travel to points onward, see "Transportation Connections," at the end of this chapter.

By Bus: Madrid's three key bus stations, all connected by Metro, are Sepulvedana (for Segovia, Metro: Príncipe Pío, garage next to Florida Norte Hotel), Estación Sur Autobuses (for Toledo, Ávila, and Granada, on top of Metro: Méndez Álvaro, cash machines, TI open during summer, fast food for sale, tel. 914-684-200), and Estación Intercambiador (for El Escorial, in Metro: Moncloa). For details, see "Transportation Connections" at the end of this chapter.

By Plane: For information on Madrid's Barajas Airport, see "Transportation Connections" page 196.

Getting Around Madrid

By Subway: Madrid's subway is simple, speedy, and cheap (€1.15/ride, runs from 6:00 to 1:30 in the morning, www.metromadrid.es or www.ctm-madrid.es). The 10-ride Metrobus ticket can be shared by several travelers and works on both the Metro and buses (€5.35, sold at kiosks, tobacco shops, and in Metro). The city's broad streets can be hot and exhausting. A subway trip of even a stop or two saves time and energy. Most stations offer free maps *(navegamadrid)*—navigate by subway stops (shown on city maps). To transfer, follow signs to the next subway line (numbered and color-coded). The names of the end stops are used to indicate directions. Insert your ticket in the turnstile, then retrieve it as you pass through. Green

Salida signs point to the exit. Using neighborhood maps and street signs to exit smartly can save lots of walking.

By Bus: City buses, while not as easy as the Metro, can be useful (bus maps at TI or info booth on Puerta del Sol, €1.15 tickets sold on bus, or €5.35 for a 10-ride Metrobus ticket—see "By Subway," above; buses run 6:00–24:00). For an easy hop-on, hop-off bus tour, see "Tours," below.

By Taxi: Madrid's 15,000 taxis are reasonably priced and easy to hail (€1.55 drop, €0.70 *Tarifa 1* rates per kilometer on weekdays, €0.88 *Tarifa 2* rates on weekday nights and weekends, more outside of Madrid, €4.20 supplement for airport, €2.20 supplement for train/bus stations, €13.30/hour waiting). If your cabbie uses anything rather than *Tarifa 1* (shown as an isolated "1" on the meter) during Mon–Fri 6:00–22:00, you're being cheated. Threesomes travel as cheaply by taxi as by subway. A ride from the Royal Palace to the Prado costs about €3.50.

Helpful Hints

Theft Alert: Be wary of pickpockets, anywhere, anytime, but particularly on Puerta del Sol (main square), the subway, and crowded streets. Assume a fight or any commotion is a scam to distract people about to become victims of a pickpocket. Wear your money belt. The small streets north of Gran Vía are particularly dangerous, even before nightfall. Muggings occur, but are rare. Victims of theft can call 902-102-112 for help (English spoken, once you get connected to a person).

Embassies: The U.S. Embassy is at Serrano 75 (tel. 915-872-200); the Canadian Embassy is at Nuñez de Balboa 35 (tel. 914-233-250).

Travel Agencies and Free Maps: The grand department store, El Corte Inglés, has two travel agencies (on first and seventh floors, Mon–Sat 10:00–22:00, just off Puerta del Sol) and gives out free Madrid maps (at information desk, immediately inside door, just off Puerta del Sol at intersection of Preciados and Tetuán; has post office and supermarket in basement). El Corte Inglés is taking over the entire intersection; the main store is the tallest building, with the biggest sign.

American Express: The AmEx office at Plaza Cortes 2 sells train and plane tickets, and even accepts Visa and MasterCard (Mon–Fri 9:00–19:30, Sat 9:00–14:00, closed Sun, 2 blocks from Metro: Banco de España, opposite Palace Hotel, tel. 913-225-445).

Books: For books in English, try **Fnac Callao** (Calle Preciados 8, tel. 915-956-190), **Casa del Libro** (English on ground floor in back, Gran Vía 29, tel. 915-212-219), and **El Corte Inglés** (guidebooks and some fiction, in its Librería branch kitty-corner from main store, see listing within "Travel Agencies and Free Maps," above).

Madrid at a Glance

▲▲▲Prado Museum One of the world's great museums, loaded with masterpieces by Diego Velázquez, Francisco Goya, El Greco, and Hieronymus Bosch. **Hours:** Tue–Sun 9:00–19:00, closed Mon.

▲▲▲Bullfight Spain's controversial pastime. **Hours:** Sundays and holidays March–mid-Oct, plus daily May–mid-June.

▲▲Thyssen-Bornemisza Museum A great complement to the Prado, with lesser-known yet still impressive works (especially good Impressionist collection). **Hours:** Tue–Sun 10:00–19:00, closed Mon.

▲▲Centro Arte de Reina Sofía Modern-art museum featuring Picasso's epic masterpiece *Guernica*. **Hours:** Mon and Wed–Sat 10:00–21:00, Sun 10:00–14:30, closed Tue.

▲▲Royal Palace Spain's sumptuous national palace, lavishly furnished. **Hours:** April–Sept Mon–Sat 9:00–19:00, Sun 9:00–16:00; Oct–March Mon–Sat 9:30–18:00, Sun 9:00–15:00.

▲▲Zarzuela Madrid's delightful light opera. **Hours:** Evenings.

▲Retiro Park Festive green escape from the city, with rental rowboats and great people-watching. **Hours:** Always open.

Laundry: The impeccable **Onda Blue** will wash, dry, and fold your laundry for €8 plus soap (daily 9:00–22:30, self-service available, change machine, 4 Internet terminals, León 3, south of Plaza Santa Ana, tel. 913-695-071). The mostly self-service **Lavamatique,** across the street and half a block up, is a less attractive option—older, fewer machines, no Internet—but it'll do in a pinch (full-service Mon–Fri 9:00–14:00, self-service Mon–Sat 9:00–20:00, closed Sun, León 6).

Internet Access: The popular **easyInternetcafé** offers 250 fast, cheap terminals at Calle de la Montera, a block above Puerta del Sol and a block below piles of tattoo shops and prostitutes (daily 8:00–24:00). **NavegaWeb,** centrally located at Gran Vía 30, is also good (daily 9:00–24:00). **BBiGG** is next to a Starbucks at Calle Alcalá 21 (daily 9:00–2:00, 300 terminals, near Puerta del Sol, tel. 916-647-700). **Zahara**'s Internet café is at the corner of Gran Vía and Mesoneros (Mon–Fri 9:00–24:00, Sat–Sun 9:00–24:00).

▲**El Rastro** Europe's biggest flea market. **Hours:** Sun and holidays 9:00–15:00, best before 11:00.

Charles III's Botanical Garden A relaxing museum of plants, with specimens from around the world. **Hours:** Daily 10:00–21:00, until 18:00 in winter.

Naval Museum Seafaring history of a country famous for its Armada. **Hours:** Tue–Sun 10:00–14:00, closed Mon.

Chapel San Antonio de la Florida Church with Goya's tomb, plus frescoes by the artist. **Hours:** Tue–Fri 10:00–14:00 & 16:00–20:00, Sat–Sun 10:00–14:00, closed Mon, July and Aug only 10:00–14:00.

Royal Tapestry Factory Where you can see traditional tapestries being made. **Hours:** Mon–Fri 10:00–14:40, closed Sat–Sun and Aug.

Moncloa Tower Elevator whisks you up to the best view in town. **Hours:** Tue–Fri 10:00–14:00 & 17:00–19:00, Sat–Sun 10:30–18:00, closed Mon.

Teleférico Cable car dangling over Madrid's city park. **Hours:** Daily July–Aug from 11:00, Sept–June from 12:00.

TOURS

Madrid Vision Hop-On, Hop-Off Bus Tours—Madrid Vision offers three different hop-on, hop-off circuits of the city (historic, modern, and monuments). Buy a ticket (€10.60/1 day, €13.60/2 days) and you can hop from sight to sight and route to route as you like, listening to a recorded English commentary along the way. Each route has about 15 stops and takes about 90 minutes, with buses departing every 10 or 15 minutes. The three routes intersect at the south side of Puerta del Sol (daily 10:00–21:00, shorter in winter, tel. 917-791-888).

Walking Tours—British expatriate Stephen Drake-Jones gives entertaining, informative walks of historic old Madrid almost nightly (along with more specialized walks, such as Hemingway, Civil War, and Bloody Madrid). A historian with a passion for the memory of the Duke of Wellington (the man who stopped Napoleon), Stephen is the founder and chairman of the Wellington Society. For €25, you become a member of the society for one year and get a free two-hour tour that includes stops at two bars for local drinks and tapas. Eccentric Stephen takes you back in time to sort out Madrid's Hapsburg and Bourbon history. Chairman Stephen likes his wine. If that's a problem, skip the tour. Tours start at the statue on Puerta del Sol (maximum 10 people, tel. 609-143-203 to confirm tour and reserve a spot, www.wellsoc.org, chairman@wellsoc.org). Members of the Wellington Society can take advantage of Stephen's helpline (if you're in a Spanish jam, call him to translate and intervene) and assistance by e-mail (for questions on Spain, your itinerary, and so on). Stephen also does private tours and day trips to great spots in the countryside for small groups (about €350 per group per day, explained on his Web site).

LeTango Tourist Services—Carlos Galvin, a Spaniard who speaks flawless English (and has led tours for me since 1998), offers private tours when he's in Madrid. If he's out, his American wife, Jennifer, also works as a guide. Carlos mixes a city drive (for the big Madrid picture) with a historic walk (to get intimate with the old center and its ways). This gives a fine three-hour orientation and introduction to Madrid (€79 for individuals and groups up to 3...4 if you'll squeeze). Carlos and Jennifer can also arrange longer tours of both the city and the region (tel. 914-293-790, mobile 661-752-458, www.letango.com, info@letango.com).

Typical Big Bus City Sightseeing Tours—Juliatours offers standard, inexpensive guided bus tours departing from Gran Vía 68 (no reservations required—just show up 15 min before departure, tel. 915-599-605). Consider these tours: a three-hour city tour (€19, daily at 9:45 and 15:00); Madrid by Night (€12.50, a 2-hour floodlit overview, nightly at 20:30); Valley of the Fallen and El Escorial (€43, makes the day trip easy, covering both sights adequately with commentary en route, Tue–Sun at 8:45 and 15:00); and a marathon tour of El Escorial, Valley of the Fallen, and Toledo (€87, Tue–Sun at 8:30). If you want to pick up a rental car in Toledo, you could take this tour, stow your luggage under the bus, and then leave the tour at Toledo.

Introductory Walk:
From Madrid's Puerta del Sol to the Royal Palace
Connect the sights with the following walking tour. Allow an hour for this half-mile walk, not including your palace visit.

▲▲**Puerta del Sol**—Named for a long-gone medieval gate with the sun carved onto it, Puerta del Sol is ground zero for Madrid. It's a hub for the Metro, buses, political demonstrations, and pickpockets.

Stand by the statue of King Charles III and survey the square. Because of his enlightened urban policies, Charles III (who ruled until 1788) is affectionately called the "best mayor of Madrid." He

Heart of Madrid

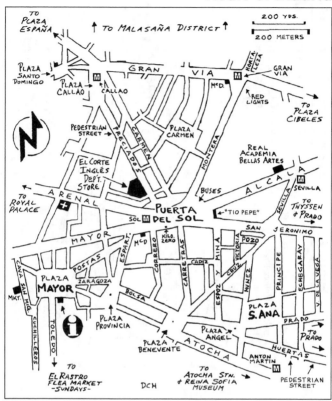

decorated the city squares with fine fountains, got those meddlesome Jesuits out of city government, established the public school system, made the Retiro a public park rather than a royal retreat, and generally cleaned up Madrid.

Look behind the king. The statue of the bear pawing the strawberry bush and the madroño trees in the big planter boxes are symbols of the city. Bears used to live in the royal hunting grounds outside Madrid. And the madroño trees produce a berry that makes the traditional *madroño* liqueur.

The king faces a red-and-white building with a bell tower. This was Madrid's first post office, established by Charles III in the 1760s. Today it's the governor's office, though it's notorious for having been Franco's police headquarters. An amazing number of those detained and interrogated by the Franco police "tried to escape" by jumping out the windows to their deaths. Notice the hats of the civil guardsmen at the entry. It's said the hats have square backsides so the men can lean against the wall while enjoying a cigarette.

From Plaza Mayor to the Royal Palace

1 Puerta del Sol
2 Governor's Office
3 Salon la Mallorquina Pastry Shop
4 Calle de Postas
5 Plaza Mayor
6 Torre del Oro Bar Andalu
7 Mesones
8 Mercado de San Miguel
9 Convent Candy
10 Former City Hall
11 Calle Mayor
12 Royal Palace

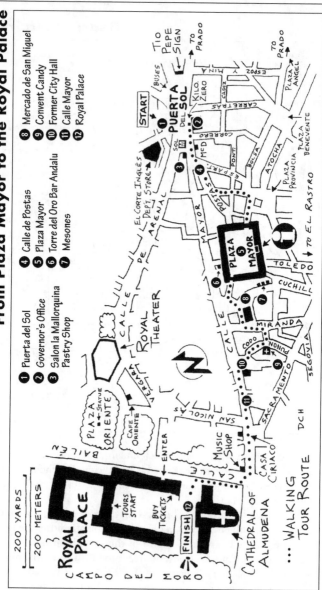

····· WALKING TOUR ROUTE

Crowds fill the square on New Year's Eve as the rest of Madrid watches the action on TV. As Spain's "Big Ben" atop the governor's office chimes 12 times, Madrileños eat one grape for each ring to bring good luck through the coming year.

Cross Calle Mayor. Look at the curb directly in front of the entrance of the governor's office. The scuffed-up marker is "kilometer zero," marking the center of Spain. To the right of the entrance, the plaque on the wall marks the spot where the war against Napoleon started. Napoleon wanted his brother to be king of Spain. Trying to finagle this, he brought nearly the entire Spanish royal family to France for negotiations. An anxious crowd gathered outside this building awaiting word of the fate of their royal family. This was just after the French Revolution, and there was a general nervousness between France and Spain. When locals heard that Napoleon had appointed his brother as the new king of Spain, they gathered angrily in the streets. The French guard simply massacred the mob. Goya, who worked just up the street, observed the event and captured the tragedy in his paintings *2nd of May, 1808* and *3rd of May, 1808*, now in the Prado.

Walking from Puerta del Sol to Plaza Mayor: On the corner of Calle Mayor and Puerta del Sol, across from McDonald's, is the busy *confitería* Salon la Mallorquina (daily 9:00–21:15). Cross Calle Mayor

to go inside. The shop is famous for its sweet Napolitana cream-filled pastry (€1) and savory, beef-filled *agujas* pastries (€1.50). See the racks with goodies hot out of the oven. Look back toward the entrance and notice the tile above the door with the 18th-century view of the Puerta del Sol. Compare this with today's view out the door. This was before the square was widened, when a church stood where the *Tío Pepe* sign stands today. The French used this church to detain local patriots awaiting execution. (The venerable *Tío Pepe* sign, advertising a famous sherry for more than 100 years, was Madrid's first billboard.)

Cross busy Calle Mayor (again), round McDonald's, and veer left up the pedestrian alley called Calle de Postas. The street sign shows the post coach heading for that famous first post office. Medieval street signs included pictures so the illiterate could "read" them. Fifty yards up the street, at Calle San Cristóbal, drop into Pans & Company, a popular sandwich chain. Pick up their translated flier illustrating that Spain is a country of four languages: Catalan (spoken in and around Barcelona), Euskera (Basque), Galego (a Portugese-like language spoken in northwestern Spain—Galicia), and Castilian (what we call

Spanish). From here, hike up Calle San Cristóbal. Within two blocks, you'll pass the local feminist bookshop (Librería Mujeres) and reach a small square. At the square, notice the big, brick 17th-century Ministry of Foreign Affairs building (with the pointed spire)—originally a jail for rich prisoners who could afford the cushy cells. Turn right and walk down Calle de Zaragoza under the arcade into...

▲**Plaza Mayor**—This square, built in 1619, is a vast, cobbled, traffic-free chunk of 17th-century Spain. Each side of the square is uni-

form, as if a grand palace were turned inside out. The statue is of Philip III, who ordered the square's construction. Upon this stage, much Spanish history was played out: bullfights, fires, royal pageantry, and events of the gruesome Inquisition. Reliefs serving as seatbacks under the lampposts tell the story. During the Inquisition, many were tried here—suspected heretics, Protestants, Jews, and Muslims whose "conversion" to Christianity was dubious. The guilty were paraded around the square (bleachers were built for bigger audiences, while the wealthy rented balconies) with billboards listing their many sins. They were then burned. The fortunate were slowly strangled as they held a crucifix, hearing the reassuring words of a priest as this life was squeezed out of them.

The square is painted a democratic shade of burgundy—the result of a citywide vote. Since Franco's death in 1975, there's been a passion for voting here. Three different colors were painted as samples on the walls of this square, and the city voted for its favorite.

A stamp-and-coin market bustles here on Sundays from 10:00 to 14:00, and on any day it's a colorful and affordable place to enjoy a cup of coffee. Throughout Spain, lesser *plazas mayores* provide peaceful pools in the river of Spanish life. The TI is at #3, on the south side of the square. The building decorated with painted figures, on the north side of the square, is the Casa de la Panadería, which used to house the Bakers' Guild (interior closed to public).

The Torre del Oro Bar Andalu is a good place for a drink to finish off your Plaza Mayor visit (northwest corner of square, to the left of the Bakers' Guild, daily 8:00–15:00 & 18:00–24:00). This bar is a temple to bullfighting. Warning: They push expensive tapas on tourists. A *caña* (small beer) shouldn't cost more than €1.50. The bar's ambience is *Andalu* (Andalusian). Look under the stuffed head of Barbero the bull. At eye level, you'll see a *puntilla,* the knife used to put a bull out of his misery at the arena. This was the knife used to kill Barbero.

Notice the breathtaking action captured in the bar's many

Teatro Real Cinema

Empresa: Actividades Cinematográficas, S.L.   Dirección: Enrique Cornejo

patrocina:

AirMadrid

www.airmadrid.com

Ballet Flamenco de Madrid

El gran espectáculo español para el mundo

España

The power of the feeling!

Temporada
a partir
del 14 de Junio

Dirección Artística
Paco Romero

Dirección General
Luciano Ruiz

baila

Flamenco

★★★★
★★★

Comunidad de Madrid
CONSEJERÍA DE CULTURA Y DEPORTES
Dirección General de promoción cultural

Ayuntamiento de Madrid
Concejalía de las Artes

Gira 2005

28 Artistas en escena

www.espanabailaflamenco.com

VENTA DE ENTRADAS
ServiCaixa
902 33 22 11
servicaixa.com

Teatro Real Cinema

Pza.de Isabel II, 7   (Metro / Underground / 地鐵站：**OPERA**)   Tel . Taquilla: 91 547 457

● **INFORMACIÓN / INFORMATION /** 一般訊息

ServiCaixa: 902 332 211 .   **www.servicaixa.com**

● **VENTA DE ENTRADAS / TICKET SALE /** 售票時間

Taquillas del teatro de martes a domingo 11:00 – 13:00. Diario de 16:30 – 22:00 /
Teatre box offices open 11:00 – 13:00 Tuesday to Sunday/ Diary 16:30 – 22:00 /
當場售票：每天上午 11:00 -13:00，週二到週日每天下午四點到晚十時

● **HORARIOS Y PRECIOS / PERFORMANCE TIMES AND PRICES /**
演出時間及票價

Lun	Mon	週一	Descanso personal / Company take a Rest / 劇團休息	
Mat	Tues	週二	20:30 h	30 Euros. 歐元
Mie.	Weds	週三	20:30 h	20 Euros. 歐元
Juv	Thurs	週四	20:30 h	20 Euros. 歐元
Vien	Fri.	週五	20:30 h	30 Euros. 歐元
Sab	Sat	週六	19: 00 h, 22:30 h	30 Euros. 歐元
Dom.	Sun	週日	19:30 h	30 Euros. 歐元

● **PRECIOS ESPECIALES PARA GRUPOS / SPECIAL PRICES GROUPS /** 團體優價票

Tel / 請電: 91 547 4742

photographs. At the end of the bar in a glass case is the "suit of lights" the great El Cordobes wore in his ill-fated 1967 fight. With Franco in attendance, El Cordobes—a working-class hero, the Elvis of bullfighters—went on and on, long after he could have ended the fight, until finally the bull gored him. El Cordobes survived; the bull didn't. Find Franco with El Cordobes at the far end, to the left of Segador the bull. Under the bull is a photo of El Cordobes' illegitimate son, El Cordobes, kissing a bull. Disowned by El Cordobes and using his dad's famous name after a court battle, El Cordobes is one of this generation's top fighters.

Walking from Plaza Mayor to the Royal Palace: Leave Plaza Mayor on Calle Ciudad Rodrigo (far right corner from where you entered the square, and to your right as you exit Torre del Oro). You'll pass a series of fine turn-of-the-20th-century storefronts and shops, such as the recommended Casa Rúa, famous for its cheap *bocadillos de calamares*—fried squid-ring sandwiches.

From the archway you'll see the covered Mercado de San Miguel (green iron posts, on left). Before you enter the market, look left down the street Cava de San Miguel. If you like sangria and singing, come back at about 22:00 and visit one of the *mesones* that line the street. These cave-like bars stretch way back and get packed with locals who—emboldened by sangria, the setting, and Spain—might suddenly just start singing. It's a lowbrow, electric-keyboard, karaoke-type ambience, best on Friday and Saturday nights.

Wander through the produce market and consider buying some fruit (Mon–Fri 9:00–14:30 & 17:15–20:15, Sat 9:00–14:30, closed Sun). Leave the market on the opposite (downhill) side and follow the pedestrian lane left. At the first corner, turn right, and cross the small plaza to the modern brick convent. The door on the right says *venta de dulces;* to buy inexpensive sweets from the cloistered nuns, buzz the *monjas* button, then wait patiently for the sister to respond over the intercom. Say *"dulces"* (DOOL-thays) and she'll let you in (Mon–Sat 9:30–13:00 & 16:00–18:30, closed Sun). When the lock buzzes, push open the door and follow the sign to *torno,* the lazy Susan that lets the sisters sell their baked goods without being seen (smallest quantities: half, or *medio,* kilo). Of the many choices (all good), consider *pastas de almendra* (crumbly) or *mantecados de yema* (moist and eggy).

Follow Calle del Codo (where those in need of bits of armor shopped—see the street sign) uphill around the convent to Plaza de la Villa, the square where City Hall was located until 2004 (when it moved to Plaza de Cibeles). The statue in the garden is of Don Bazán—mastermind of the Christian victory over the Muslims at the naval battle of Lepanto in 1571. This pivotal battle, fought off the coast of Greece, ended the Muslim threat to Christian Europe.

From here, busy Calle Mayor leads downhill for a couple more blocks to the Royal Palace. Halfway down (on the left), there's a tiny square opposite the recommended Casa Ciriaco restaurant (#84). The statue memorializes the 1906 anarchist bombing that killed 23 people as the royal couple paraded by on their wedding day. While the crowd was throwing flowers, an anarchist threw a bouquet lashed to a bomb from a balcony of #84 (the building was a hotel at the time). Photos of the event hang just inside the door of the restaurant.

Continue down Calle Mayor. Within a couple of blocks you'll come to a busy street, Calle de Bailen. (The Garrido-Bailen music store is *the* place to stock up on castanets, unusual flutes, and Galician bagpipes.) Across the busy street is the **Cathedral of Almudena,** Madrid's cathedral. Built between 1883 and 1993, its exterior is a contemporary mix and its interior is neo-Gothic, with a colorful ceiling, glittering 5,000-pipe organ, and the 12th-century coffin (empty, painted leather on wood, in a chapel behind the altar) of Madrid's patron saint, Isidro. Isidro, a humble peasant, loved the handicapped and performed miracles. Forty years after he died, this coffin was opened and his body was found unrotted, which convinced the pope to canonize him as the patron saint of Madrid and of farmers, with May 15 as his feast day. Next to the cathedral is the...

▲▲**Royal Palace (Palacio Real)**—Europe's third-greatest palace (after Versailles and Vienna's Schönbrunn), with arguably the most sumptuous original interior, is packed with tourists and royal antiques.

After a fortress burned down on this site, King Phillip V commissioned this huge 18th-century palace as a replacement. Though he ruled Spain for 40 years, Phillip V was very French. (The grandson of Louis XIV, he was born in Versailles, and spoke French most of the time.) He ordered this palace to be built as his own Versailles (although his wife's Italian origin had a tremendous impact in the style). It's big—more than 2,000 rooms, with tons of luxurious tapestries, a king's ransom of chandeliers, priceless porcelain, and bronze decor covered in gold leaf. While these days the royal family lives in a mansion a few miles away, this place still functions as a royal palace and is used for formal state receptions and tourists' daydreams.

Cost, Hours, and Information: €8 without a tour, €9 with a tour, April–Sept Mon–Sat 9:00–19:00, Sun 9:00–16:00; Oct–March Mon–Sat 9:30–18:00, Sun 9:00–15:00, last tickets sold one hour before closing, palace can close without warning if needed for a royal function (you can call a day ahead to check, tel. 915-475-350). The palace is most crowded on Wednesdays, when it's free for locals. Metro: Opera. (Notice the beer-stein urinals—the rage in Madrid—in the WC just past the ticket booth.)

Touring the Palace: A simple one-floor, 24-room, one-way circuit is open to the public. You can wander on your own or join an English-language tour (check time of next tour and decide as you buy your ticket; tours depart about every 20 min). The tour guides, like the museum guidebook, show a passion for meaningless data. Your ticket includes the armory and the pharmacy, both on the courtyard and worth a quick look. The €2.30 audioguides cover only marginally more of interest than what I describe below (and would never mention beer-stein urinals).

Self-Guided Tour: If you tour the palace on your own, here are a few details beyond what you'll find on the little English descriptions posted in each room:

1. The Palace Lobby: In the old days, horse-drawn carriages would drop you off here. Today, a sign divides the visitors waiting for a tour and those going in alone.

2. The Grand Stairs: Fancy carpets are rolled down (notice the little metal bar-holding hooks) for formal occasions. At the top of the first landing, the blue-and-red coat of arms is of the current—and popular—constitutional monarch, Juan Carlos. While Franco chose him to be his successor, J.C. knew Spain was ripe for democracy. Rather than become "Juan the Brief" (as some were nicknaming him), he turned real power over to the parliament. You'll see his (figure) head on the back of the Spanish euro coin. At the top of the stairs (before entering first room, right of door) is a white marble bust of J.C.'s great-great-g-g-g-great-grandfather Phillip V, who began the Bourbon dynasty in Spain in 1700. That dynasty survives today with Juan Carlos.

3. Guard Room: The guards hung out here. Notice the clocks. Charles IV, a great collector, amassed more than 700—the 150 displayed in this palace are all in working order.

4. Hall of Columns: Originally a ballroom and dining room, today this room is used for formal ceremonies. (For example, this is where Spain formally joined the European Union in 1985—see plaque on far wall.) The tapestries (like most you'll see in the palace) are 17th-century Belgian.

5. Throne Room: Red velvet walls, lions, and frescoes of Spanish scenes symbolize the monarchy in this rococo riot. The chandeliers are the best in the house. The throne is only from 1977. This is where the king's guests salute the king prior to dinner. He receives them relatively informally...standing rather than seated on the throne.

The ceiling fresco (1764), the last great work by Venetian painter Giambattista Tiepolo, celebrates the days of the vast Spanish empire—upon which the sun also never set. Find the Native American (hint: follow the rainbow to the macho, red-caped conquistador). Two rooms later you'll find the...

6. Antechamber: The four paintings are of King Charles IV (looking a bit like a dim-witted George Washington) and his wife, María Luisa (who wore the pants in the palace)—all originals by

Goya. The clock—showing Cronus, god of time, in marble, bronze, and wood—sits on a music box. The gilded decor you see throughout the palace is bronze with gold leaf.

7. Gasparini Room: This room was meant to be Charles III's bedroom, but was unfinished when he died. Instead, with its painted stucco ceiling and inlaid Spanish marble floor (restored in 1992), it was the royal dressing room. The Asian influence was trendy at the time. Dressing, for a divine monarch, was a public affair. The court bigwigs would assemble here as the king, standing on a platform—notice the height of the mirrors—would pull on his leotards. In the next room, the silk wallpaper is new; notice the *J.C.S.* initials of King Juan Carlos and Queen Sofía. Passing through the silk room, you reach the...

8. Charles III Bedroom: Decorated in 19th-century neoclassical style, a chandelier in the shape of the fleur-de-lis (symbol of the Bourbon family) dominates the room. The thick walls separating each room hide service corridors for servants who scurried about generally unseen.

9. Porcelain Room: The 300 separate plates that line this room were disassembled for safety during the Spanish Civil War. (Find the little screws in the greenery that hide the seams.) The Yellow Room leads to the...

10. Gala Dining Room: Up to 12 times a year, the king entertains up to 150 guests at this bowling-lane-size table—which can be extended to the length of the room. Find the two royal chairs. (Hint: With the modesty necessary for 21st-century monarchs, they are just a tad higher than the rest.) The parquet floor was the preferred dancing surface when balls were held in this fabulous room, decorated with vases from China and a fresco depicting the arrival of Christopher Columbus in Barcelona. The table in the next room would be lined with an exorbitantly caloric dessert buffet.

11. Cinema Room (Sala de Monedas y Medallas): In the early 20th century, the royal family enjoyed "Sunday afternoons at the movies" here. Today, it stores glass cases filled with coins and medals.

12. Silver Room: A collection of silver tableware from different periods is presented in this room.

13. Stradivarius Room: The queen likes classical music. When you perform for her, do it with these precious 350-year-old violins. About 300 Antonius Stradivarius–made instruments survive. This is the only matching quartet: two violins, a viola, and a cello. The next room was the children's room—with kid-size musical instruments.

14. China Rooms: Several collections of China from different kings (some from China, others from Sèvres and Meissen) are displayed in this room.

15. Royal Chapel: The Royal Chapel is used for private concerts and funerals. The royal coffin sits here before making the sad trip to El Escorial to join the rest of Spain's past royalty.

16. Queen's Boudoir: This room was for the ladies, unlike the next...

17. Billiards and Smoking Rooms: The billiards room and the smoking room were for men only. The porcelain and silk of the smoking room imitates a Chinese opium den, which, in its day, was furnished only with pillows.

18. Charles IV Bedroom: Small for a king's room, the neoclassical decoration stands out.

19. Fine Woods Room: Fine 18th- and 19th-century French inlaid-wood pieces decorate this room.

You'll exit down the same grand stairway you climbed 24 rooms ago.

Across the courtyard is the **armory,** which displays the armor and swords of El Cid (Christian warrior fighting the Moors), Ferdinand (husband of Isabel), Charles V (ruler of Spain at its peak of power), and Phillip II (Charles' son who watched Spain start its long slide downward). Near the exit is a cafeteria and a bookstore, which has a variety of books on Spanish history.

As you leave the palace, walk around the corner to the left, along the palace exterior, to the grand yet people-friendly Plaza de Oriente. Throughout Europe, energetic governments are turning formerly car-congested wastelands into public spaces like this. Madrid's latest mayor is nicknamed "The Mole" for all the digging he's doing. Where's all the traffic? Under your feet.

To return to Puerta del Sol: With your back to the palace, face the equestrian statue of Philip IV and (behind the statue) the Royal Theater (*Teatro Real,* neoclassical, rebuilt in 1997, open for 30-minute, €4 visits in English Mon and Wed–Fri 10:30–11:00, Sat–Sun at 11:00–13:30, closed Tue, tel. 915-160-660). Walk behind the Royal Theater (on the right, passing Café de Oriente—a favorite with theatergoers) to another square, where you'll find the Opera Metro stop and Calle Arenal—which leads back to Puerta del Sol.

SIGHTS

Madrid's Museum Neighborhood

Three great museums are in east Madrid. A five-minute walk connects the Prado to the Thyssen-Bornemisza Museum; from the Prado to Centro Arte de Reina Sofía is a 10-minute walk. All three will have brand-new modern extensions by well-known architects in 2005.

Museum Pass: If you plan to visit all three museums, you'll save 25 percent by buying the Paseo del Arte combo-ticket (€7.66, sold at each museum, valid for 1 year). Note that the Prado and Centro Arte de Reina Sofía museums are free on Sunday (and anytime for those under 18 and over 65); the Prado and Thyssen-Bornemisza are closed Monday; and the Reina Sofía is closed Tuesday.

Madrid's Museum Neighborhood

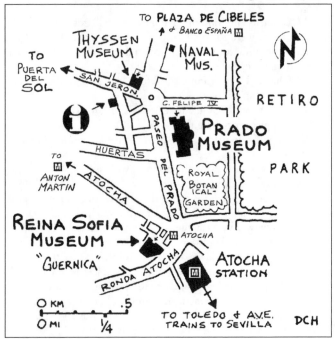

▲▲▲Prado Museum—The Prado holds my favorite collection of paintings anywhere. With more than 3,000 canvases, including entire rooms of masterpieces by Velázquez, Goya, El Greco, and Bosch, it's overwhelming. Pick up the English-language floor plan as you enter. Take a tour or buy a guidebook (or bring along the Prado chapter from *Rick Steves' Best European City Walks & Museums*—available without maps and photos for free at www.ricksteves.com/prado). Focus on the Flemish and northern (Bosch, Albrecht Dürer, Peter Paul Rubens), the Italian (Fra Angelico, Raphael, Titian), and the Spanish art (El Greco, Velázquez, Goya).

Follow Goya through his stages, from cheery *(The Parasol)* to political (*2nd of May, 1808* and *3rd of May, 1808*) to dark ("Negras de Goya": e.g., *Saturn Devouring His Children*). In each stage, Goya asserted his independence from artistic conventions. Even the standard court portraits from his "first" stage

Prado Museum Overview

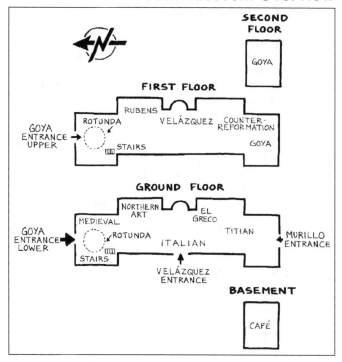

SECOND
FLOOR

GOYA

FIRST FLOOR

RUBENS   VELÁZQUEZ   COUNTER-
ROTUNDA   REFORMATION

GOYA
ENTRANCE
UPPER   GOYA

STAIRS

GROUND FLOOR

NORTHERN
ART   EL
GRECO
MEDIEVAL
GOYA   TITIAN
ENTRANCE   ROTUNDA   MURILLO
LOWER   ITALIAN   ENTRANCE

STAIRS

VELÁZQUEZ
ENTRANCE

BASEMENT

CAFÉ

reflect his politically liberal viewpoint, subtly showing the vanity and stupidity of his royal patrons by the looks in their goony eyes. His political stage makes him one of the first artists with a social conscience. His highly-charged painting of the *3rd of May, 1808* depicts a massacre of Spaniards by Napoleon's troops. Finally, in his gloomy "dark stage," Goya probed the inner world of fears and nightmares, anticipating our modern-day preoccupation with dreams.

Don't miss Velázquez's famous *Las Meninas,* a behind-the-scenes glimpse at royal life, showing Princess Margarita, her two attendants *(meninas)*, a jester, a female dwarf, the family dog, and the painter himself—with King Phillip and his wife looking on as they're being painted.

Seek out Bosch's *The Garden of Earthly Delights*—a three-paneled altarpiece showing creation, the "transparency of earthly pleasures," and the resulting hell. Bosch's self-portrait looks out from hell (with the birds leading naked people around the brim of his hat), surrounded by people suffering eternal punishments appropriate to their primary earthly excesses.

The art is constantly rearranged by the Prado's management, so even the museum's own maps and guidebooks are out of date.

Regardless of the latest location, most art is grouped by painter, and better guards can point you in the right direction if you say, *"¿Dónde está...?"* and the painter's name as Españoled as you can (e.g., Titian is "Ticiano," and Bosch is "El Bosco"). The Murillo (south) entrance—at the end closest to the Atocha train station—often has shorter lines. Lunchtime, from 14:00 to 16:00, is least crowded.

Cost, Hours, Location: €3; free all day Sun and to anyone under 18 and over 65; covered by €7.66 Paseo del Arte combo-ticket; Tue–Sun 9:00–19:00, closed Mon, last entry 30 min before closing (€3 audioguide; free and mandatory baggage check after your things are scanned, just like at the airport; no water bottles inside, photos allowed but no flash, cafeteria in basement at Murillo end); Paseo del Prado, Metro: Banco de España or Atocha—each a 5-min walk from the museum, tel. 913-302-800, http://museoprado .mcu.es. Cabs picking you up at the Prado are likely to overcharge. Insist on the fare meter.

While you're in the neighborhood, consider a visit to the Charles III Botanical Garden (listed under "Near the Prado," on the next page).

▲▲**Thyssen-Bornemisza Museum**—Locals call this stunning museum simply the Thyssen (TEE-sun). It displays the impressive collection that Baron Thyssen (a wealthy German married to a former Miss Spain) sold to Spain for $350 million. It's basically minor works by major artists and major works by minor artists (major works by major artists are in the Prado). But art lovers appreciate how the good baron's art complements the Prado's collection by filling in where the Prado is weak (such as Impressionism). For a delightful walk through art history, ride the elevator to the top floor and do the rooms in numerical order from Primitive Italian (room 1) to Surrealism and Pop Art (room 48). The museum is kitty-corner from the Prado at Paseo del Prado 8 in Palacio de Villahermosa (€4.80, or €6.60 to add current exhibition; covered by €7.66 Paseo del Arte combo-ticket, children under 12 enter free, Tue–Sun 10:00–19:00, closed Mon, ticket office closes at 18:30, audioguide-€3, free baggage check, café, shop, no photos, Metro: Banco de España or Atocha, tel. 914-203-944, www.museothyssen.org). If you're heading to Centro Arte de Reina Sofía and you're tired, hail a cab at the gate to zip straight there.

▲▲**Centro Arte de Reina Sofía**—In this exceptional modern-art museum, ride the fancy glass elevator to the second floor and follow the room numbers for art from 1900 to 1950. The fourth floor continues the collection, from 1950 to 1980. The museum is most famous for Pablo Picasso's *Guernica* (second floor, room 6), an epic painting showing the horror of modern war. Guernica, a village in northern Spain, was the target of the world's first saturation-bombing raid (1937), approved by Franco and carried out by Hitler. Picasso, a Spaniard living in Paris at the time, heard news reports of the event and immediately set to work on this stark black-and-white painting that alerted the world to the growing peril of fascism. Notice the two rooms of studies Picasso did for *Guernica,* filled with iron-nail tears and screaming mouths. *Guernica* was exiled to America until Franco's death, and now it reigns as Spain's national piece of art.

The museum also houses an easy-to-enjoy collection by other modern artists, including more of Picasso (3 rooms divide his art into pre–Civil War, *Guernica,* and post–Civil War) and a mind-bending room of Dalís (room 10). Enjoy a break in the shady courtyard before leaving (€3, free Sat afternoon after 14:30 and all day Sun, always free to those under 18 and over 65; covered by €7.66 Paseo del Arte combo-ticket; Mon and Wed–Sat 10:00–21:00, Sun 10:00–14:30, closed Tue, good brochure, hardworking audioguide-€2.50, no photos, no tours in English, free baggage check, Santa Isabel 52, Metro: Atocha, across from Atocha train station, look for exterior glass elevators, tel. 914-675-062, http://museoreinasofia.mcu.es).

Near the Prado
▲**Retiro Park**—Siesta in this 300-acre green and breezy escape from the city. At midday on Saturday and Sunday, the area around the lake becomes a street carnival, with jugglers, puppeteers, and lots of local color. These peaceful gardens offer great picnicking and people-watching. From the Retiro Metro stop, walk to the big lake (El Estanque), where you can cheaply rent a rowboat. Past the lake, a grand boulevard of statues leads to the Prado.

Charles III's Botanical Garden (Real Jardín Botánico)—After your Prado visit, you can take a lush and fragrant break in this sculpted park, wandering among trees from around the world. The flier in English explains that this is actually more than a park—it's a museum of plants (€1.50, daily 10:00–21:00, until 18:00 in winter, entry opposite Prado's Murillo entry, Plaza de Murillo 2).

Naval Museum—This tells the story of Spain's navy from the Armada to today (free, Tue–Sun 10:00–14:00, closed Mon, a block north of the Prado across boulevard from Thyssen-Bornemisza Museum, Paseo del Prado 5, entrance at Calle de Montalbán 2, 913-795-299).

More Sights in Madrid
National Archaeological Museum (Museo Arqueológico Nacional)—If you're intrigued by prehistoric cave paintings, you'll dig this place. Located underground in the museum's garden, the paintings are replicas from northern Spain's Altamira Caves (for more on the paintings, see page 113). The ancient art, big on bison, gives you a thrill at the skill of the cave artists who created the originals 14,000 years ago. This museum, displaying Iberian art from

prehistory to the 19th century, also boasts the marble bust of a woman with an elaborate headress—*Dama de Elche,* dating from the 4th century B.C. (€3, free Sat afternoon and Sun, Tue–Sat 10:00–21:00, Sun 10:00–14:30, closed Mon, Calle Serrano 13, Metro: Serrano or Colón, tel. 915-777-912, www.man.es). The National Library, which shares the same building, has a first-edition copy of *Don Quixote* by Cervantes.

Chapel San Antonio de la Florida—Goya's tomb stares up at a splendid cupola filled with his own frescoes. On June 13, local ladies line up here to ask St. Anthony for a boyfriend, while outside a festival rages, with street musicians, food, and fun (free entry, Tue–Fri 10:00–14:00 & 16:00–20:00, Sat–Sun 10:00–14:00, closed Mon, July and Aug only 10:00–14:00, Glorieta de San Antonio de la Florida, Metro: Príncipe Pío, tel. 915-420-722). This chapel is near the Sepulvedana bus station with service to Segovia. If you're day-tripping to Segovia, it's easy to stop by before or after your trip.

Hungry? Next door to the chapel is **Restaurante Casa Mingo**, popular for its cheap chicken, chorizo, and *cabrales* cheese served with cider. Ask the waiter to pour the cider for you. For dessert, try the *tarta de Santiago* almond cake (daily 11:00–24:00, Paseo de la Florida 34, tel. 915-477-918).

Royal Tapestry Factory (Real Fábrica de Tapices)—Have a look at traditional tapestry-making (€3, Mon–Fri 10:00–14:00, closed Sat–Sun and Aug, some English tours, Calle Fuenterrabia 2, Metro: Menendez Pelayo, take Gutenberg exit, tel. 914-340-551). You can actually order a tailor-made tapestry (starting at $10,000).

Moncloa Tower (Faro de Moncloa)—This tower's elevator zips you up 300 feet to the best skyscraper view in town (€1, Tue–Fri 10:00–14:00 & 17:00–19:00, Sat–Sun 10:30–18:00, closed Mon, Metro: Moncloa, tel. 915-448-104). If you're going to El Escorial by bus, this is a convenient sight near the bus station.

Teleférico—For city views, ride this cable car from downtown over Madrid's sprawling city park to Casa de Campo (€2.90 one-way, €4.20 round-trip, daily July–Aug from 11:00, Sept–June from 12:00, departs from Paseo del Pintor Rosales, Metro: Arguelles, tel. 915-417-450, www.teleferico.com). Do an immediate round-trip to skip Casa de Campo's strange mix of rental rowboats, prostitutes, addicts, a zoo, and an amusement park.

SHOPPING

Shoppers focus on the colorful pedestrian area between Gran Vía and Puerta del Sol. The giant Spanish department store El Corte Inglés, a block off Puerta del Sol, is a handy place to pick up just about anything you need (Mon–Sat 10:00–21:30, closed Sun, free maps at info desk, supermarket in basement).

▲**El Rastro**—Europe's biggest flea market, held on Sundays and holidays, is a field day for shoppers, people-watchers, and thieves (9:00–15:00, best before 11:00). Thousands of stalls titillate more than a million browsers with mostly new junk. If you brake for garage sales, you'll pull a U-turn for El Rastro. Start at the Plaza Mayor, with its gentle coin-collectors market, and head south or take the subway to Tirso de Molina. Hang on to your wallet. Spin the wheel to try for two cookies for the price of one. Munch on a *pepito* (meat-filled pastry). Europe's biggest stamp market thrives simultaneously on Plaza Mayor.

NIGHTLIFE

Just walking the streets of Madrid seems to be the way the locals spend their evenings. Even past midnight on a hot summer night, whole families with little kids are strolling, licking ice cream, and greeting their neighbors. Start at Puerta del Sol and explore. (See "Tapas: the Madrid Pub-Crawl Dinner," page 194.)

Disco dancers may have to wait until after midnight for the most popular clubs to even open, much less start hopping. Spain has a reputation for partying very late, not ending until offices open in the morning.

▲▲▲**Bullfight**—Madrid's Plaza de Toros hosts Spain's top bull-fights on Sundays and holidays from March through mid-October and nearly every day during the San Isidro festival (May through mid-June—generally sold out long in advance). Fights start between 17:00 and 19:00 (early in spring and fall, late in summer). Tickets range from €3.50 to €100. There are no bad seats at the Plaza de Toros; paying more gets you in the shade and/or closer to the gore. (The action often intentionally occurs in the shade to reward the expensive-ticket holders.) To be close to the bullring, choose areas 8, 9, or 10; for shade: 1, 2, 9, or 10; for shade/sun: 3 or 8; for the sun and cheapest seats: 4, 5, 6, or 7. (Note that fights advertised as *Gran Novillada con Picadores* feature younger bulls and rookie matadors.)

Hotels and booking offices are convenient, but they add 20 per-cent or more and don't sell the cheap seats. Call both offices before you buy (Plaza Carmen 1—daily 9:30–13:30 & 16:00–19:00, tel. 915-312-732; and Calle Victoria 3—daily 10:00–14:00 & 17:00–19:00, tel. 915-211-213). To save money, stand in the bull-ring ticket line, except for important bullfights or during the San Isidro festival. About a thousand tickets are held back to be sold on the five days leading up to a fight, including the day of the fight. The bullring is at Calle Alcalá 237 (Metro: Ventas, tel. 913-562-200, www.las-ventas.com in Spanish). See the appendix for more on the "art" of bullfighting.

Madrid's **bullfighting museum** (Museo Taurino) is not as good as

Sevilla's or Ronda's (free, Tue–Fri and Sun 9:30–14:30, closed Sat and Mon and early on fight days, at the back of bullring, tel. 917-251-857).

▲▲**Zarzuela**—For a delightful look at Spanish light opera that even English speakers can enjoy, try zarzuela. Guitar-strumming Napoleons in red capes; buxom women with masks, fans, and castanets; Spanish-speaking pharaohs; melodramatic spotlights; and aficionados clapping and singing along from the cheap seats, where the acoustics are best—this is zarzuela...the people's opera. Originating in Madrid, zarzuela is known for its satiric humor and surprisingly good music. You can buy tickets at Theater Zarzuela, which alternates between zarzuela, ballet, and opera throughout the year (€10–30, box office open 12:00–18:00 for advance tickets or until showtime for that day, Jovellanos 4, near the Prado, Metro: Banco de España, tel. 915-245-400, http://teatrodelazarzuela.mcu.es). The TI's monthly guide has a special zarzuela listing.

▲**Flamenco**—While Sevilla is the capital of flamenco, Madrid has two easy and affordable options.

Taberna Casa Patas attracts big-name flamenco artists. You'll quickly understand why this intimate (30-table) and smoky venue is named, literally, "the house of legs." Since this is for locals as well as tour groups, the flamenco is contemporary and may be jazzier than your notion—it depends on who's performing (€25 for Mon–Thu at 22:30, €30 for Fri–Sat at 21:00 and 24:00, closed Sun, 75–90 min, price includes cover and first drink, reservations smart, no flash cameras, Cañizares 10, tel. 914-298-471 or 913-690-496, www.casapatas.com). Its restaurant is a logical place for dinner before the show (€20 dinners, Mon–Sat from 20:00). Or, since this place is three blocks south of the recommended Plaza Santa Ana tapas bars, this could be your post-tapas-crawl entertainment.

Las Carboneras is more downscale—an easygoing, folksy little place a few steps from Plaza Mayor with a nightly 60-minute flamenco show (€22 includes a entry and a drink, €45 gets you a table up-front with dinner and unlimited cheap drinks if you reserve ahead, Mon–Thu at 22:30, Fri–Sat at 21:00 and 23:00, closed Sun, earlier shows possible if a group books, reservations recommended, Plaza del Conde de Miranda 1, tel. 915-428-677, Ronan SE).

Regardless of what your hotel receptionist may want to sell you, other flamenco places like Arco de Cuchilleros (Calle de los Cuchilleros 7), Café de Chinitas (Calle Torija 7, just off Plaza Mayor), Corral de la Morería (Calle de Morería 17) and Torres Bermejas (off Gran Vía) are filled with tourists and pushy waiters.

Mesones—Just west of Plaza Mayor, the lane called Cava de San Miguel is lined with *mesones:* long, skinny, cave-like bars famous for drinking and singing late into the night. Toss lowbrow locals, Spanish karaoke, electric keyboards, crass tourists, cheap sangria, and greasy calamari into a late-night blender and turn it on. Probably lively only on Friday and Saturday, but you're welcome to pop in to several places (such as Guitarra, Tortilla, or Boquerón) and see what you can find.

SLEEPING

Madrid has plenty of centrally located budget hotels and *pensiones*. You'll have no trouble finding a sleepable double for €30, a good double for €60, and a modern air-conditioned double with all the comforts for €100. Prices are the same throughout the year, and it's almost always easy to find a place. Anticipate full hotels from May 15 to May 25 (the festival of Madrid's patron saint, Isidro) and the last week in September (conventions). In July and August prices can be softer—ask about promotional deals. All of the accommodations I've listed are within a few minutes' walk of Puerta del Sol.

The Pedestrian Zone between Puerta del Sol and Gran Vía

Reliable and away from the seediness, these hotels are good values for those wanting to spend a little more. Their formal prices may be inflated, and some offer weekend and summer discounts whenever it's slow. Use Metro: Sol for all but Hotel Opera (Metro: Opera). See the map on page 185 for location.

$$$ **Hotel Regente** is a big and traditional place with 154 tastefully decorated and comfortable air-conditioned rooms, a great location, and a great value (Sb-€63, Db-€105, Tb-€128, tax not included, breakfast-€4.50, parking-€13, midway between Puerta del Sol and Plaza del Callao at Mesonero Romanos 9, tel. 915-212-941, fax 915-323-014, www.hotelregente.com, info@hotelregente.com).

$$$ **Hotel Arosa** charges the same for all of its 134 rooms, whether they're sleekly remodeled Art Deco or just aging gracefully. Ask for a remodeled room with a terrace (Sb-€116, Db-€178, Tb-€240, 20 percent cheaper July–Aug, tax not included, breakfast-€13, air-con, memorably tiny triangular elevator, a block off Plaza del Carmen, Calle Salud 21, tel. 915-321-600, fax 915-313-127, arosa @hotelarosa.com).

$$$ The huge, business-class **Hotel Liabeny** has 220 plush, spacious rooms and all the comforts (Sb-€100, Db-€135, Tb-€155, 10 percent cheaper July–Aug, tax not included, breakfast-€14, air-con, if one room is smoky ask for another, sauna, gym, off Plaza del Carmen at Salud 3, tel. 915-319-000, fax 915-327-421, www.liabeny .es, reservas@hotelliabeny.es).

$$$ **Hotel Opera,** a serious and modern hotel with 79 classy rooms, is located just off Plaza Isabel II, a four-block walk from Puerta del Sol toward the Royal Palace (Sb-€99, Db-€132, Db with big view terrace-€145, Tb-€170, tax not included, buffet breakfast-€10, air-con, elevator, free Internet access, ask for a higher floor—there

Sleep Code

(€1 = about $1.20, country code: 34)

S = Single, **D** = Double/Twin, **T** = Triple, **Q** = Quad, **b** = bathroom, **s** = shower only, **no CC** = Credit Cards not accepted, **SE** = Speaks English, **NSE** = No English. Breakfast is not included unless noted; credit cards are accepted unless noted. In Madrid, the 7 percent IVA tax is sometimes included in the price.

To help you easily sort through these listings, I've divided the rooms into three categories, based on the price for a standard double room with bath during high season:

$$$ **Higher Priced**—Most rooms €100 or more.
  $$ **Moderately Priced**—Most between €60–100.
    $ **Lower Priced**—Most rooms €60 or less.

are 8—to avoid street noise; consider their "singing dinners" offered nightly at 21:30—average price €55, reservations wise; Cuesta de Santo Domingo 2, Metro: Opera, tel. 915-412-800, fax 915-416-923, www.hotelopera.com, reservas@hotelopera.com). Hotel Opera's cafeteria is understandably popular.

$$$ Hotel Santo Domingo has artsy paintings, an inviting lounge, and 121 rooms, each decorated differently (Sb-€127, Db-€184, tax not included, pricier superior rooms are not necessary, air-con, elevator, non-smoking floor, facing Metro: Santo Domingo, Plaza de Santo Domingo 13, tel. 915-479-800, fax 915-475-995, www.hotelsantodomingo.net, reserva@hotelsantodomingo.net). Prices drop €30—and breakfast is included—on weekends (Fri–Sun) and July–Aug.

$$ Hotel Europa has red-carpet charm: a royal salon, plush halls with happy Muzak, polished wood floors, an attentive staff, and 80 squeaky-clean rooms with balconies overlooking the pedestrian zone or an inner courtyard (Sb-€59, Db-€75–95, Tb-€105, Qb-€120, Quint/b-€135, tax not included, breakfast-€5.50, easy phone reservations with credit card, fans or air-con, elevator, fine lounge on 2nd floor, Calle del Carmen 4, tel. 915-212-900, fax 915-214-696, www.hoteleuropa.net, info@hoteleuropa.net, Antonio and Fernando Garaban and their helpful and jovial staff, Javi and Jim, SE). The convenient Europa cafeteria/restaurant next door is a great scene, fun for breakfast, and a fine value any time of day.

$$ Hotel Carlos V, a Best Western place with 67 classy high-ceiling rooms and an elegant breakfast and lounge, is a fair value. Its central location off Preciados pedestrian street makes it convenient (Sb-€94, Db-€124, Tb-€167, air-con, elevator, Maestro Victoria 5, tel. 915-314-100, fax 915-313-761, www.hotelcarlosv.com, recepcion @hotelcarlosv.com).

Madrid's Center—Hotels & Restaurants

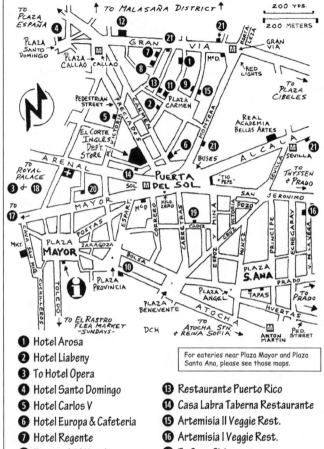

1. Hotel Arosa
2. Hotel Liabeny
3. To Hotel Opera
4. Hotel Santo Domingo
5. Hotel Carlos V
6. Hotel Europa & Cafeteria
7. Hotel Regente
8. Euromadrid Hotel
9. Hotel Anaco
10. Hotel Plaza Mayor
11. Hostales Acapulco & Triana
12. Hostales at Gran Vía 44

For eateries near Plaza Mayor and Plaza Santa Ana, please see those maps.

13. Restaurante Puerto Rico
14. Casa Labra Taberna Restaurante
15. Artemisia II Veggie Rest.
16. Artemisia I Veggie Rest.
17. To Casa Ciriaco
18. To La Bola Taberna & Café Ricordi
19. Bar Majaderitos
20. Chocolatería San Ginés
21. Internet Cafés (multiple locations)

$$ Euromadrid Hotel—like a cross between a Motel 6 and an old hospital—rents 35 white rooms in a modern but well-worn shell (big Sb-€60, Db-€80, tight Tb-€96, includes continental breakfast but not tax, air-con, discounted rate for parking-€13/day, Mesonero Romanos 7, tel. 915-217-200, fax 915-214-582, clasit @infonegocio.com).

$$ The basic **Hotel Anaco** has a drab color scheme and a dreary lobby, but offers 39 quiet, comfortable rooms in a central location (Sb-€78, Db-€97, Tb-€131, bed extra €34, tax not included, breakfast-€5, air-con, elevator, non-smoking floor, Tres Cruces 3, a few steps off Plaza del Carmen and its underground parking lot-€13.80/day, tel. 915-224-604, fax 915-316-484, www.anacohotel .com, info@anacohotel.com).

$$ Hotel Plaza Mayor, with 32 solidly outfitted rooms, is beautifully situated a block off Plaza Mayor (Sb-€48, Db-€70–80, corner "suite" Db-€85, Tb-€85, air-con, elevator, buffet breakfast-€7, Calle Atocha 2, tel. 913-600-606, fax 913-600-610, www .h-plazamayor.com, info@h-plazamayor.com, Fedra SE).

$ Hostal Acapulco, overlooking the fine little Plaza del Carmen, rents 16 bright rooms with air-conditioning and all the big hotel gear. The neighborhood is quiet enough that it's smart to request a room with a balcony (Sb-€43, Db-€53, Tb-€67, elevator, Salud 13, 4th floor, tel. 915-311-945, fax 915-322-329, hostal _acapulco@yahoo.es, Marco SE).

$ Hostal Triana, at the same address as Acapulco and also a fine deal, is bigger—with 40 rooms—and offers a little less charm for a little less money (Sb-€37, Db-€50, Tb-€65, €3 extra for air-con, taxes included, half the rooms have only fans, elevator, Calle de la Salud 13, 1st floor, tel. 915-326-812, fax 915-229-729, www .hostaltriana.com, triana@hostaltriana.com, Victor González SE).

$ *Hostales at Gran Vía 44:* The next three are in the same building at Gran Vía 44, overlooking the busy street. All are cheap and work in a jam. **Hostal Helena,** on the ninth floor, is a homey burgundy-under-heavy-drapes kind of place, renting 10 fine rooms. Enjoy the great little roof garden (S-€30, Ds-€42, Db-€45, Tb-€60, elevator, fans, Internet access, Gran Vía 44, tel. & fax 915-217-585, www .geocities.com/hostalhelena, hostalhelena@yahoo.es, José Luis, SE). The next two are well-worn with stark rooms and traffic noise: **Hostal Residencia Valencia** with 30 rooms (Sb-€40, Ds-€50, Db-€53, Tb-€68, includes tax, 5th floor, tel. 915-221-115, fax 915-221-113, www.hostal-valencia.com, info@hostal-valencia.com, Antonio SE) and **Hostal Residencia Continental** with 34 rooms (Sb-€37, Db-€48, Tb-€66, includes tax, fans, 3rd floor, tel. 915-214-640, fax 915-214-649, www.hostalcontinental.com, continental@mundivia.es, Andres SE).

Plaza Santa Ana Area

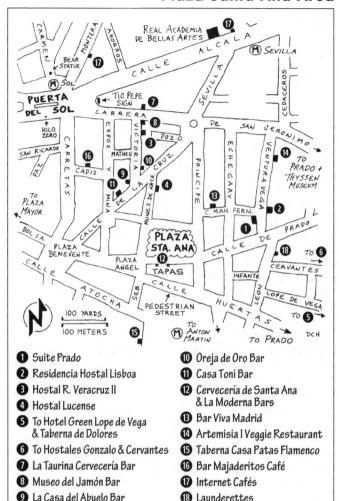

1. Suite Prado
2. Residencia Hostal Lisboa
3. Hostal R. Veracruz II
4. Hostal Lucense
5. To Hotel Green Lope de Vega & Taberna de Dolores
6. To Hostales Gonzalo & Cervantes
7. La Taurina Cervecería Bar
8. Museo del Jamón Bar
9. La Casa del Abuelo Bar
10. Oreja de Oro Bar
11. Casa Toni Bar
12. Cervecería de Santa Ana & La Moderna Bars
13. Bar Viva Madrid
14. Artemisia I Veggie Restaurant
15. Taberna Casa Patas Flamenco
16. Bar Majaderitos Café
17. Internet Cafés
18. Launderettes

On or near Plaza Santa Ana

The Plaza Santa Ana area has small, cheap places mixed in with fancy hotels. While the neighborhood is noisy at night, it has a rough but charming ambience, with colorful bars and a central location (3 min from Puerta del Sol's *Tío Pepe* sign; walk down Calle San Jerónimo and turn right on Príncipe; Metro: Sol). To locate hotels, see map above.

$$$ **Suite Prado,** two blocks toward the Prado from Plaza Santa Ana, is a good value, offering 18 sprawling, elegant, air-conditioned

suites with a modern yet homey feel (suites are all the same size, charging €122 for single, €153 double, and €176 triple occupancy; sitting rooms, refrigerators, kitchens, 2nd kid free, breakfast at café next door-€4, elevator, Manuel Fernández y González 10, at intersection with Venture de la Vega, tel. 914-202-318, fax 914-200-559, www.suiteprado.com, hotel@suiteprado.com, Paula and Elena SE).

$ **Residencia Hostal Lisboa,** across the street from Suite Prado (above), is a good budget place (25 rooms, Sb-€44, Db-€54, Tb-€75, interior rooms quieter on weekends, air-con, elevator, Ventura de la Vega 17, tel. 914-294-676, fax 914-299-894, www.hostallisboa.com, hostallisboa@inves.es, SE).

$ **Hostal R. Veracruz II,** between Plaza Santa Ana and Puerta del Sol, rents 22 decent, quiet rooms (Sb-€36, Db-€50, Tb-€63, no breakfast, elevator, air-con, Victoria 1, 3rd floor, tel. 915-227-635, fax 915-226-749, hostalveracruz@yahoo.es, NSE).

$ *Cheap Hostel Alternative:* Because of the following place, I don't list a youth hostel for Madrid. For supercheap beds in a dingy time warp, consider **Hostal Lucense.** Bathrooms are down the hall and there's no heat during winter (13 rooms, S-€15–18, D-€18–25, Db-€28–36, T-€38, €1.20 per shower, no CC, Nuñez de Arce 15, 1st floor, tel. 915-224-888, run by not-so-friendly Sr. and Sra. Michaela García, both interesting characters, Señor SE).

Near the Prado

$$$ **Hotel Green Lope de Vega** is your best business-class hotel value near the Prado. A four-star place that opened in 2000, it's a "cultural-themed" hotel inspired by the 17th-century writer Lope de Vega. It feels cozy and friendly for a formal business-class hotel (60 rooms, Sb-€108, Db-€135, Tb-€182, 1 child sleeps free, prices about 20 percent lower on weekends and during most of the summer, elevator, air-con, Internet access, parking-€18/day, Calle Lope de Vega 49, tel. 913-600-011, fax 914-292-391, www.hotellopedevega.com, lopedevega@hotellopedevega.com, SE).

$ *At Cervantes 34:* Two fine budget places are at Cervantes 34 (Metro: Anton Martín). **Hostal Gonzalo**—with 15 spotless, comfortable rooms, well run by friendly and helpful Javier—is deservedly in all the guidebooks. Reserve in advance (Sb-€45, Db-€52, Tb-€63, elevator, 3rd floor, tel. 914-292-714, fax 914-202-007, www.hostalgonzalo.com). Downstairs, the nearly as polished **Hostal Cervantes,** also with 15 fine rooms, is likewise good (Sb-€45, Db-€55, Tb-€65; cheaper on weekdays, in low season, and for longer stays; 2nd floor, tel. 914-298-365, fax 914-292-745, www.hostal-cervantes.com, correo@hostal-cervantes.com, Fabio SE).

EATING

In Spain, only Barcelona rivals Madrid for tastebud thrills. You have three dining choices: an atmospheric sit-down meal in a well-chosen restaurant, an unmemorable basic sit-down meal, or a stand-up meal of tapas in a bar or four. Many restaurants are closed in August (especially through the last half).

Eating Cheaply North of Puerta del Sol

Restaurante Puerto Rico has good meals, great prices, and few tourists (€7.50 3-course *menu*, Mon–Sat 3:00–16:30 & 20:30–24:00, closed Sun, Chinchilla 2, between Puerta del Sol and Gran Vía, tel. 915-322-040).

Hotel Europa Cafetería is a fun, high-energy scene with a mile-long bar, traditionally-clad waiters, great people-watching, local cuisine, and a fine €8 lunch *menu* (daily 7:30–24:00, next to Hotel Europa, 50 yards off Puerta del Sol at Calle del Carmen 4, tel. 915-212-900).

El Corte Inglés' seventh-floor cafeteria is popular with locals (Mon–Sat 10:00–11:30 & 13:00–16:15 & 17:30–20:00, closed Sun, has non-smoking section, just off Puerta del Sol at intersection of Preciados and Tetuán).

Casa Labra Taberna Restaurante is famous among locals as the place where the Spanish Socialist Party was founded in 1879...and where you can get great cod. Packed with locals, it's a wonderful scene with three distinct sections: the stand-up bar (cheapest, 2 different lines for munchies and drinks), a peaceful little sit-down area in back (a little more expensive but still cheap; good €4 salads), and a fancy restaurant (€15 lunches). Their tasty little €1 *bacalao* (cod) dishes put it on the map. The waiters are fun to joke around with (daily 11:00–15:30 & 18:00–23:00, a block off Puerta del Sol at Calle Tetuán 12, tel. 915-310-081).

Vegetarian: **Artemisia II** is a hit with vegetarians who like good, healthy food in a smoke-free room (great €9.50 three-course lunch *menu* Mon–Fri only, daily 13:30–16:00 & 21:00–24:00, 2 blocks north of Puerta del Sol at Tres Cruces 4, a few steps off Plaza Carmen, tel. 915-218-721). **Artemisia I,** II's older sister, is located two blocks east of Plaza Santa Ana at Ventura de la Vega 4, off San Jerónimo (same hours, tel. 914-295-092).

On or near Plaza Mayor

Many Americans are drawn to Ernest Hemingway's favorite, **Sobrino del Botín** (daily 13:00–16:00 & 20:00–24:00, Cuchilleros 17, a block downhill from Plaza Mayor, tel. 913-664-217). It's touristy, pricey (€24–30 average), and the last place he'd go now...but still, people love it and the food is excellent. If phoning to make a reservation, choose between the downstairs (for dark, medieval-cellar ambience) or upstairs (for a still-traditional but airier and lighter elegance). While this restaurant boasts that it's the oldest in the world (dating from 1725), a nearby restaurant teases, "Hemingway never ate here."

Restaurante los Galayos is less touristy and plenty *típico*, with good local cuisine (daily 8:00–24:00, lunch specials, lunch from 12:00, dinner anytime, arrive early or make a reservation, 30 yards off Plaza Mayor at Botoneras 5, tel. 913-663-028). For many, dinner right on the square at a sidewalk café is worth the premium (consider Cervecería Pulpito, southwest corner of the square at #10).

La Torre del Oro Bar Andalu on Plaza Mayor has soul. Die-hard bullfight aficionados hate the gimmicky bull bar (La Taurina) listed under "Tapas" on page 194. Here the walls are lined with grisly bullfight photos from annual photo competitions (read the gory description in "Introductory Walk," page 166). Have a drink, but establish all prices first. Don't let the aggressive staff bully you into high-priced tapas you don't want (daily 8:00–15:00 & 18:00–24:00, closed Jan, Plaza Mayor 26, tel. 913-665-016).

Plaza Mayor is famous for its *bocadillos de calamares*. For a cheap and tasty squid-ring sandwich, line up at **Casa Rúa** at Plaza Mayor's northwest corner, a few steps up Calle Ciudad Rodrigo (daily 9:00–23:00). Hanging up behind the bar is a photo/ad of Plaza Mayor from the 1950s, when the square contained a park.

Calle Cava Baja, South of Plaza Mayor

Few tourists frequent this traditional neighborhood—Barrio de los Austrias, named for the Hapsburgs. It's three minutes south of Plaza Mayor, or a 10-minute walk from Puerta del Sol. Lined with a diverse array of restaurants and tapas bars, the street called Cava Baja is clogged with locals out in search of a special meal. For a good, authentic Madrileño dinner experience, take time to survey the many places along this street—between the first and last listings described below—and choose your favorite. A key wine-drinking phrase is *mucho cuerpo* (full-bodied).

Posada de la Villa serves Castilian cuisine in a 17th-century posada. Peek into the big oven to see what's cooking (€30 meals, Mon–Sat 13:00–16:00 & 20:00–24:00, closed Sun and Aug, Calle Cava Baja 9, tel. 913-661-860).

El Schotis is less expensive and specializes in meat and fish dishes. Named after a popular local dance, the restaurant retains the traditional character of old Madrid (daily 12:00–17:00 & 20:00–24:00, Calle Cava Baja 11, tel. 913-653-230).

Julian de Tolosa, a classy, pricey, elegantly simple place popular with locals who know good food, offers a small, quality menu of Navarra's regional cuisine from T-bone steak *(chuletón)* to red *tolosa*

Eating near Plaza Mayor

1 Sobrino del Botín
2 Rest. los Galayos
3 La Torre del Oro Bar Andalu
4 Casa Rua
5 Posada de la Villa
6 El Schotis
7 Julian de Tolosa
8 Taberna los Lucio

9 Casa Lucio
10 Taberna Tempranillo
11 El Madroño
12 Taberna los Austrias
13 Taberna de los 100 Vinos
14 Flamenco--Las Carboneras
15 Mesones (cave bars)

beans (Mon–Sat 13:30–16:00 & 21:00–24:00, Sun 13:30–16:00; when having lunch, claim your free apéritif with this book; Calle Cava Baja 18, tel. 913-658-210).

Taberna los Lucio has good tapas, salads, *huevos estrellados* (scrambled eggs with potatoes), and wine (Wed–Mon 13:00–16:00 & 20:30–24:00, closed Tue, Calle Cava Baja 30, tel. 913-662-984).

For a splurge, dine with power-dressing locals at **Casa Lucio.** While the king and queen of Spain eat here, it's more stuffy than expensive (daily 13:00–17:00 & 21:00–24:00, Calle Cava Baja 35; unless you're the king or queen, reserve several days in advance, tel. 913-653-252).

Taberna Tempranillo, ideal for hungry wine-lovers, offers tapas and 250 kinds of wine. Use their fascinating English menu to assemble your dream meal. Arrive by 20:00 or wait (daily 13:00–15:30 & 20:00–24:00, closed Aug, Cava Baja 38, tel. 913-641-532).

Tapa-Hopping on Calle del Nuncio (near Calle Cava Baja)

El Madroño ("The Strawberry Tree," a symbol of Madrid) is a fun tapas bar that preserves chunks of old Madrid. A tile copy of Velázquez's famous *Drinkers* grins from its facade. Inside, look above the stairs for photos of 1902 Madrid. Study the coats of arms of Madrid through the centuries as you try a *vermut* on tap and a €2 sandwich, or ask to try the *licor de madroño* (€7.80 lunch *menu* also available, Tue–Sun 9:00–17:00 & 20:00–24:00, closed Mon, Plaza Puerta Cerrada 7, tel. 913-645-629).

Taberna los Austrias, two blocks away, serves tapas, salads, and light meals on wood-barrel tables (daily 12:00–16:00 & 20:00–24:00, Calle Nuncio 17).

Next door is the very hip and popular **Taberna de los 100 Vinos** ("Tavern of 100 Wines"), a classy wine bar serving top-end tapas and fine wine by the glass—see the chalkboard. Eat delicious €3.25 *pinchos* standing up, or sit down for excellent €10 *raciones* (Tue–Sat 13:00–16:00 & 20:00–24:00, closed Sun–Mon, Calle Nuncio 17).

Near the Royal Palace

Casa Ciriaco is popular with locals who appreciate good traditional cooking (€30 meals, Thu–Tue 13:30–16:00 & 20:30–24:00, closed Wed and Aug, halfway between Puerta del Sol and the Royal Palace at Calle Mayor 84, tel. 915-480-620). It was from this building in 1906 that an anarchist bombed the royal couple on their wedding day (for details, see "Introductory Walk," page 166). A photo of the carnage is inside the front door.

La Bola Taberna, touristy but friendly and tastefully elegant, specializes in *cocido Madrileño*—Madrid stew. The €15 stew consists of various meats, carrots, and garbanzo beans in earthen jugs. It's big enough to split and is served as two courses; first you enjoy the broth as a soup (weekdays 13:00–16:00 & 20:30–23:00, often closed Sat–Sun, cash only, midway between the Royal Palace and Gran Vía at Calle Bola 5, tel. 915-476-930).

Café Ricordi, just a block from the Royal Theater, is a delightfully romantic little spot, perfect for theatergoers. You can enjoy tiny sandwiches with a glass of wine, coffee, and an elegant sweet, or a full meal in this café/bar/restaurant (Tue–Sat 12:00–24:00, closed Sun-Mon, Calle Arrieta 5, tel. 915-479-200).

Near the Prado

Each of the big-three art museums has a decent cafeteria. Or choose from these three places, all within a block of the Prado:

La Platería Bar Museo is a hardworking little café/wine bar with a good menu for tapas, light meals, and hearty salads (listed as *raciones* and ½ *raciones* on the chalkboard). Its tables spill onto the leafy little Plaza de Platerías de Martínez (daily 7:30–24:00, directly across busy boulevard Paseo del Prado from Atocha end of Prado, tel. 914-291-722).

Taberna de Dolores, a winning formula since 1908, is a commotion of locals enjoying €2 *canapés* (open-face sandwiches), tasty *almejas* (clams), and *cañas* (small beers) at the bar or at a few tables in the back (daily 13:00–24:00, Plaza de Jesús 4, tel. 914-292-243).

VIPS is where good-looking young tour guides eat cheap and filling salads. This bright, popular chain restaurant is engulfed in a big bookstore (daily 9:00–3:00 in morning, across Paseo del Prado boulevard from northern end of Prado in Galería del Prado under Palace Hotel facing Plaza Canovas). Spain's first Starbucks opened in April 2001, just next door.

Fast Food and Picnics

Fast Food: For an easy, light, cheap meal, try **Rodilla**—a popular sandwich chain with a shop on the northeast corner of Puerta del Sol at #13 (Mon–Fri 9:30–23:00, Sat 10:00–23:00, Sun 11:00–23:00). **Pans & Company,** with shops throughout Madrid and Spain, offers healthy, tasty sandwiches and chef's salads (daily 9:00–24:00, on Puerta del Sol, Plaza Callao, Gran Vía 30, and many more).

Picnics: The department store **El Corte Inglés** has a well-stocked **deli** downstairs (Mon–Sat 10:00–22:00, closed Sun). A perfect place to assemble a cheap picnic is downtown Madrid's neighborhood market, **Mercado de San Miguel.** How about breakfast surrounded by early-morning shoppers in the market's café? (Mon–Fri 9:00–14:30 & 17:15–20:15, Sat 9:00–14:30, closed Sun; to reach the market from Plaza Mayor, face the colorfully painted building and exit from the upper left-hand corner.) The

Museo del Jamón (Museum of Ham) sells cheap picnics to go (see "Tapas: The Madrid Pub-Crawl Dinner," below).

Churros con Chocolate

Those not watching their cholesterol will want to try the deep-fried doughy treats called *churros* (or the thicker *porras*), best enjoyed by dipping them in pudding-like hot chocolate. **Bar Majaderitos** is a good bet (daily 7:00–24:00, Sun from 9:00, best in morning, 2 blocks off Tío Pepe end of Puerta del Sol, south on Espoz y Mina, turn right on Calle de Cádiz). Their tasty grilled cheese sandwich (with ham and/or egg) rounds out your breakfast. With luck, the *churros* machine in the back will be cooking. Notice the expressive WC signs.

The classy **Chocolatería San Ginés** is much loved by locals for its *churros* and chocolate (Tue–Sun 18:00–7:00, closed Mon). While empty before midnight, it's packed with the disco crowd in the wee hours; the popular dance club Joy Eslava is next door. Dunk your *churros* into the chocolate pudding, as locals have done here for more than 100 years (from Puerta del Sol, take Calle Arenal 2 blocks west, turn left on book-lined Pasadizo de San Ginés, you'll see the café—it's at #5, tel. 933-656-546).

Tapas: The Madrid Pub-Crawl Dinner

For maximum fun, people, and atmosphere, go mobile and do the "tapa tango," a local tradition of going from one bar to the next, munching, drinking, and socializing. Tapas are the toothpick appetizers, salads, and deep-fried foods served in most bars. Madrid is Spain's tapas capital—tapas just don't get any better than here. Grab a toothpick and stab something strange, but establish the prices first, especially if you're on a tight budget or at a possible tourist trap. Some items are very pricey, and most bars push larger *raciones*, rather than smaller tapas. The real action begins late (around 20:00). But for beginners, an earlier start, with less commotion, can be easier. The litter on the floor is normal; that's where people traditionally toss their trash and shells. Don't worry about paying until you're ready to go. Then ask for *la cuenta* (the bill).

If done properly, a pub crawl can be a highlight of your trip. Before embarking upon this culinary adventure, study and use the "Tapas Tips" section on page 30.

Prowl the area between Puerta del Sol and Plaza Santa Ana. There's no ideal route, but the little streets (in this book's map) between Puerta del Sol, San Jerónimo, and Plaza Santa Ana hold tasty surprises. Nearby, the street Jesús de Medinaceli is also lined with popular tapas bars. Below is a five-stop tapa crawl. These places are good, but don't be afraid to make some discoveries of your own.

1. From Puerta del Sol, walk east a block down Carrera de San Jerónimo to the corner of Calle Victoria. Across from the Museo del

Jamón, you'll find **La Taurina Cervecería,** a bullfighters' Planet Hollywood (daily 8:00–24:00). Wander among trophies and historic photographs. Each stuffed bull's head is named, along with its farm, awards, and who killed him. Among the many gory photos, study the first post: It's Che Guevara, Orson Welles, and Salvador Dalí, all enjoying a good fight. Around the corner, the Babe Ruth of bull-fighters, El Cordobes, lies wounded in bed. The photo below shows him in action. Kick off your pub crawl with a drink here. Inspired, I went for the *rabo de toro* (bull-tail stew, €10.50)—and regretted it. If a fight's on, the place will be packed with aficionados gathered around the TV. Across the street at San Jerónimo 5 is the...

2. Museo del Jamón (Museum of Ham), tastefully decorated—unless you're a pig (or a vegetarian). This frenetic, cheap, stand-up bar is an assembly line of fast and simple *bocadillos* and *raciones*. Photos show various dishes and their prices. For a small sandwich, ask for a *chiquito* (€0.60, unadvertised). The best ham is the pricey *jamón ibérico*—from pigs who led stress-free lives in acorn-strewn valleys. Just point and eat, but be specific: A *jamón blanco* portion costs only €5, while *jamón ibérico* costs €12 (daily 9:00–24:00, sit-down restaurant upstairs). Next, forage halfway up Calle Victoria to the tiny...

3. La Casa del Abuelo, for seafood-lovers who savor sizzling plates of tasty little *gambas* (shrimp) and *langostinos* (prawns). Try *gambas a la plancha* (grilled shrimp, €4.15) or *gambas al ajillo* (ahh-HHEEE-yoh, shrimp version of escargot, cooked in oil and garlic and ideal for bread dipping, €5.80), and a €1.20 glass of red wine (daily 11:30–15:30 & 18:30–23:30, Calle Victoria 12). Across the street is...

4. Oreja de Oro ("Golden Ear"), named for what it sells—sautéed pigs' ears (*oreja*, €2.50). While pigs' ears are a Madrid specialty, this place is Galician, so people also come here for *pulpo* (octopus, €8.50), *pimientos de Padrón* (green peppers...some sweet and a few hot surprises, €3), and the distinctive *ribeiro* (ree-BAY-roh) wine, served Galician-style, in characteristic little ceramic bowls (to disguise its lack of clarity). Jaime is a frantic one-man show who somehow gets everything just right. Have fun at this place. For a perfect finale, continue uphill and around the corner to...

5. Casa Toni, for refreshing bowls of gazpacho—the cold tomato-and-garlic soup (€1.50, available all year but only popular when temperatures soar). Their specialties are *berenjena* (deep-fried slices of eggplant, €3.60) and *champiñones* (sautéed mushrooms, €3.70; open daily 11:30–16:00 & 18:00–23:30, closed July, Calle Cruz 14).

More Options: If you're hungry for more, and want a trendy, up-to-date tapas scene, head for Plaza Santa Ana. The south side of the square is lined with lively bars offering good tapas, drinks, and a classic setting right on the square. Consider **Cervecería de Santa Ana** (tasty tapas with two zones: rowdy beer-hall and classier sit-down) and **La Moderna** (wine, pâté, and cheese plates).

If you're picking up speed and looking for a place filled with old tiles and young people, power into **Bar Viva Madrid** (daily 13:00–3:00, Calle Manuel Fernández y González, tel. 914-293-640). The same street has other late-night bars filled with music.

TRANSPORTATION CONNECTIONS

By train to: Toledo (5/day on weekdays, 3/day on weekends, 1.25 hr, change to bus in Algodor; from Madrid's Atocha station leave from *cercanías* [theyr-kah-NEE-ahz] section, not the AVE section, though an AVE link is being built between Madrid and Toledo—ask if it's been completed), **Segovia** (9/day, 2 hrs, both Chamartín and Atocha stations), **Ávila** (hrly, 90–120 min, from Chamartín, and Atocha), **Salamanca** (6/day, 2.5 hrs, from Chamartín), **Santiago** (3/day, 8–9 hrs, includes night train), **Barcelona** (6/day, 4.5-5.5 hrs, mostly from Chamartín, plus 2 night trains, 9 hrs; new high-speed AVE connection may be complete in 2005, will reduce time but increase cost), **Granada** (2/day, 6 hrs), **Sevilla** (18/day, 2.5 hrs by AVE; 2 slower TALGO trains/day, 3.5 hrs; both from Atocha), **Córdoba** (18 AVE trains/day, 2 hrs, from Atocha, 12 TALGO trains/day, 2 hrs), **Málaga** (7/day, 4 hrs, from Atocha), **Lisbon** (1/day departing at 22:45, 10 hrs, pricey overnight Hotel Train from Chamartín), **Paris** (1/day, 13.5 hrs, 1 direct overnight—a €130 Hotel Train, €119 in winter, from Chamartín).

Spain's AVE (AH-vay) bullet train opens up some good itinerary options. Pick up the brochure at the station. Prices vary with times and class. The basic Madrid–Sevilla second-class fare is €59 (€12 less on the almost-as-fast TALGO). AVE is heavily discounted for Eurail passholders (the Madrid–Sevilla second-class trip costs Eurailers about €9). Consider this exciting day trip to Sevilla from Madrid: 7:00 depart Madrid, 8:45–12:40 in Córdoba, 13:30–21:00 in Sevilla, 23:30 back in Madrid. Reserve each AVE segment (tel. 902-240-202 for Atocha AVE info). AVE is also planned to run between Madrid and Barcelona. General train info: tel. 902-240-202.

By bus to: Segovia (€8.82 return, 2/hr, 1.25 hrs, first departure 6:30, last return at 21:30, La Sepulvedana buses, Paseo de la Florida 11, from Metro: Príncipe Pío, go past Hotel Florida Norte and look for yellow mailbox—near it is the Sepulvedana bus station, tel. 915-304-800).

Reach the following destinations by bus from Estación sur Autobuses: **Ávila** (€10.02 return, 2/hr, 90 min), **Toledo** (€3.89 one-way, 2/hr, 60–75 min, Continental Auto bus company at office #45, tel. 917-456-300), **Santiago** (6/day, 7–9 hrs, includes hourly 24:00–8:30 night bus), and **Granada** (11/day, 5.25 hrs, Continental Auto, tel. 915-272-961). The bus station sits squarely atop Metro: Méndez Álvaro and has eateries and a small TI open daily 9:00–20:45 (Avenida de Méndez Álvaro, tel. 914-684-200):

Buses for **Salamanca** (€14.70, hrly, 2.5 hrs) leave from the Conde de Casal station (Calle Fernández Shaw 1, Metro: Conde de Casal, Auto-Res, tel. 902-020-999, www.auto-res.net, tel. 902-020-999).

By bus, train, and car to El Escorial: Buses leave from the basement of Madrid's Moncloa Metro stop Intercambiador de Moncloa and drop you in the El Escorial center (€2.85/one way, 4/hr, 45 min, in Madrid take bus #664 or slower #661 from Intercambiador's bay #3, Herranz Bus, tel. 918-969-028). One bus a day (€7.90 return ticket including entrance, except for Mon, when sights are closed) is designed to let travelers do the Valley of the Fallen as a side trip from El Escorial; the bus leaves El Escorial at 15:15 (15-min trip) and leaves the Valley of the Fallen at 17:30. Trains run hourly to El Escorial but let you off a 20-minute walk (or a shuttle-bus ride, 2/hr) from the monastery and city center. By car, it's easy to visit El Escorial and the Valley of the Fallen on the way to Segovia (note sights closed Mon).

Driver's Note: Avoid driving in Madrid. Rent your car when you depart. To leave Madrid from Gran Vía, simply follow signs for A6 (direction Villalba or Coruña) for Segovia, El Escorial, or Valley of the Fallen (see next chapter for details). It's cheapest to make car-rental arrangements before you leave home. In Madrid, consider **Europcar** (central reservations tel. 902-105-030, San Leonardo 8 office tel. 915-418-892, Chamartín station tel. 913-231-721, airport tel. 913-937-235), **Hertz** (central reservations tel. 902-402-405, Gran Vía 88 tel. 915-425-803, Chamartín station tel. 917-330-400, airport tel. 913-937-228), **Avis** (Gran Vía 60 tel. 915-472-048, airport tel. 913-937-222), **Alamo** (central reservations tel. 902-100-515), and **Budget** (central reservations tel. 901-201-212, www.budget.es). Ask about free delivery to your hotel. At the airport, most rental cars are returned at Terminal 1.

Madrid's Barajas Airport

Ten miles east of downtown, Madrid's modern airport has three terminals, connected by long indoor walkways (an 8-minute walk apart). The Metro is in Terminal 2.

If you are flying internationally, you'll likely land at Terminal 1, which has the following: a helpful English-speaking **TI** (marked *Oficina de Información Turística*, daily 8:00–20:00, tel. 913-058-656); an **ATM** (part of the BBVA bank where you can also buy Alhambra tickets) that's far busier than the lonely American Express window; a 24-hour **exchange office** (plus shorter-hour exchange offices); a **flight info office** (marked simply *Information* in airport lobby, open 24 hrs/day, tel. 902-353-570); a **post-office** window; a **pharmacy;** lots of **phones** (buy a phone card from the machine near the phones); a few scattered **Internet** terminals (small fee); **eateries;** a **RENFE office** (where you can get train info and buy train tickets; daily 8:00–21:00, tel. 913-058-544); and on-the-spot **car-rental agencies** (see above).

Iberia, Spanair, and Air Europa are Spain's airlines, connecting a reasonable number of cities in Spain, as well as international destinations (ask for best rates at travel agencies).

Getting between the Airport and Downtown: By public transport, consider an affordable, efficient **airport bus/taxi combination.** Take the airport bus #89 (no number on bus, but sign *Plaza de Colón-Aeropuerto*, usually blue, ignore bus #101 that goes to the outskirts) from the airport to Madrid's Plaza Colón (€2.50, 4/hr, 20–30 min, leaves Madrid 4:45–1:30 in morning, leaves airport 4:45–2:00 in morning, stops at both Terminals 1 and 2; at the airport, the bus stop is outside Terminal 1's arrivals door, all the way to the right; at Plaza Colón, the stop is underground—marked at top of stairs on square as *Terminal Bus Aeropuerto*). Then, to reach your hotel from Plaza Colón, catch a taxi (insist on meter, ride to hotel should be less than €6; to avoid €2.20 supplement charge for rides from a bus station, it's a little cheaper to go upstairs and flag down a taxi). Or from Plaza Colón, take the subway (from the underground bus stop, walk up the stairs and face the blue *URBIS* sign high on a building—the subway stop, M. Serrano, is 50 yards to your right; it takes one transfer at Bilbao to reach Puerta del Sol).

Consider the simpler **AeroCity shuttle bus service,** which provides door-to-door transport. The fee of €17 covers up to three people per trip; extra passengers pay more (runs 24 hrs, price includes one piece of luggage and one carry-on per person, can book at one of their desks at the airport: Terminal 1—near arrival gate 2; Terminal 2—between arrival gates 5 and 6; or reserve in advance online or by phone or fax; credit card holds reservation but payment required in cash; tel. 917-477-570, fax 917-481-114, www.aerocity.com).

The **Metro** is the cheapest way to get downtown, but involves two transfers (€1.15, or get a shareable 10-pack—10 *viajes*—for €5.35). The airport's futuristic Aeropuerto Metro stop (notice the cash machines, subway info booth, and huge lighted map of Madrid) is in Terminal 2. Access the Metro at the check-in level; to reach the Metro from Terminal 1's arrivals level, stand with your back to the baggage claim, then go to your far right, up the stairs, and follow red-and-blue Metro diamond signs to the station (8-min walk). To get to Puerta del Sol, take line #8 for 12 minutes to Nuevos Ministerios, then continue on line #10 to Tribunal, then line #1 to Puerto del Sol (30 min more total); or exit at Nuevos Ministerios and take a €5 taxi or bus #150 straight to Puerto del Sol.

For a **taxi** to or from the airport, allow €20 during the day or €30 at night and on weekends. Insist on the meter. The €4.20 airport supplement is legal.

NORTHWEST OF MADRID

Before slipping out of Madrid, consider several fine side-trips northwest of Spain's capital city, all conveniently reached by car, bus, or train.

Spain's lavish, brutal, and complicated history is revealed throughout Old Castile. This region, where the Spanish language Castilian originated, is named for its many castles—battle scars from the long-fought Reconquista.

An hour from Madrid, tour the imposing and fascinating palace at **El Escorial,** headquarters of the Spanish Inquisition. Nearby at the awe-inspiring **Valley of the Fallen,** pay tribute to the countless victims of Spain's bloody civil war.

Segovia, with its remarkable Roman aqueduct and romantic castle, is another worthwhile side trip. At **Ávila,** you can walk the perfectly preserved medieval walls.

Planning Your Time

See El Escorial and the Valley of the Fallen together in less than a day (but not on Monday, when sights are closed). By car, do them en route to Segovia; by bus, make it a day trip from Madrid.

Segovia is worth a half day of sightseeing and is a joy at night. Ávila, while it has its charm, merits only a quick stop (if you're driving and in the area, 1.5 hrs from Madrid) to marvel at its medieval walls and, perhaps, check out St. Teresa's finger.

In total, these sights are worth two days if you're in Spain for less than a month. If you're in Spain for just a week, I'd still squeeze in a quick side-trip from Madrid to El Escorial and the Valley of the Fallen.

Northwest of Madrid

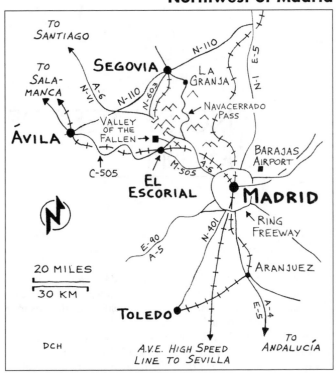

El Escorial

The Monasterio de San Lorenzo de El Escorial is a symbol of power rather than elegance. This 16th-century palace, 30 miles northwest of Madrid, gives us a better feel for the Counter-Reformation and the Inquisition than any other building. Built at a time when Catholic Spain felt threatened by Protestant "heretics," its construction dominated the Spanish economy for a generation (1563–1584). Because of this bully in the national budget, Spain has almost nothing else to show from this most powerful period of her history.

The giant, gloomy building made of gray-black stone looks more like a prison than a palace. About 650 feet long and 500 feet wide, it has 2,600 windows, 1,200 doors, more than 100 miles of passages, and 1,600 overwhelmed tourists.

El Escorial

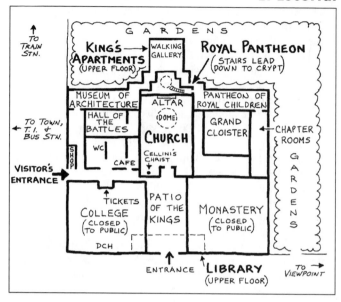

Four hundred years ago, the enigmatic, introverted, and extremely Catholic King Philip II (1527–1598) ruled his bulky empire and directed the Inquisition from here. To Philip, the building embodied the wonders of Catholic learning, spirituality, and arts. To 16th-century followers of Martin Luther, it epitomized the evil of closed-minded Catholicism. To architects, the building—built on the cusp between styles—exudes both Counter-Reformation grandeur and understated Renaissance simplicity. Today, it's a time capsule of Spain's "Golden Age," packed with history, art, and Inquisition ghosts. (And at an elevation of nearly 3,500 feet, it can be friggin' cold.)

The building was conceived by Philip II to serve several purposes: as a grand mausoleum for Spain's royal family, starting with his father, Charles V (known as Carlos I in Spain); as a monastery to pray (a lot) for the royal souls; as a small palace to use as a Camp David of sorts for Spain's royalty; and as a school to embrace humanism in a way that promoted the Catholic faith.

The Monasterio looks confusing at first, but you simply follow the *visita* arrows and signs in one continuous walk-through. This is the general order you'll follow (though some rooms may be closed for renovation):

The **Chamber of the Honor Guards** is hung with 16th-century tapestries including fascinating copies of Hieronymus Bosch's most famous and preachy paintings (which Philip II fancied). Don't miss El Greco's towering painting of the *Martyrdom of St. Maurice*. This was the artist's first commission after arriving in Spain from Venice. It was too subtle and complex for the king, so El Greco moved on to Toledo to find work.

Downstairs (Sala 1) is the fascinating **Museum of Architecture** (Museo de Arquitectura), with long parallel corridors of easy-to-appreciate models of the palace and some of the actual machinery and tools used to construct it. Huge stone-pinching winches, fat ropes, and rusty old mortar spades help convey the immensity of this 21-year project involving 1,500 workers. At the big model, notice how the complex is shaped like a grill, and recall how San Lorenzo—St. Lawrence, a Christian Spaniard martyred by pagan Romans (A.D. 258)—was killed by being barbecued on a grill. Throughout the palace, you'll see this symbol associated with the saint. The grill's "handle" was the palace, or actual living quarters of the royal family. The rest—the monastery and school—gathered around the huge basilica.

Detouring upstairs, you'll find the **Hall of Battles** (Sala de Batallas), lined with frescoes celebrating Spain's great military victories—including the Battle of San Quentin over France (1557) on St. Lawrence's feast day that inspired the construction of El Escorial. The sprawling series, painted in 1590, helped teach the new king all the elements of warfare. Stroll the length for a primer on army skills.

From here, a corridor lined with various family trees (some scrawny, others lush and fecund) leads into the royal living quarters (the building's grill handle). Immediately inside the first door, find the small portrait of Philip II flanked by two large portraits of his daughters. The palace was like Philip: austere. Notice the simple floors, plain white walls, and bare-bones chandelier. This was the bedroom of one of his daughters. Notice the sheet warmer beside her bed—often necessary during the winter. Bend down to see the view from her bed...of the high altar in the basilica next door. The entire complex of palace and monastery buildings was built around that altar.

In the next room, notice the reclinable sedan chair that Phillip II, thick with gout, was carried in (for 7 days) on his last trip from Madrid to El Escorial. He wanted to be here when he died.

The **Audience Chamber** is now a portrait gallery filled with Hapsburg royals painted by popular local artists. The portraits of unattractive people that line the walls provide an instructive peek at the consequences of inbreeding among royals—a common problem throughout Europe in those days.

The Spanish emperor Charles V, Philip II's dad (1500–1558), was the most powerful man in Europe, having inherited not just the Spanish crown, but also Germany, Austria, the Low Countries (Belgium and the Netherlands), and much of Italy. When he announced his abdication in 1555, his son Philip II inherited much of this territory...plus the responsibility of managing it. Philip's draining wars with France, Portugal, Holland, and England—including the disastrous defeat of Spain's navy, the Spanish Armada, by England's Queen Elizabeth I (1588)—knocked Spain from its peak of power and began centuries of decline.

The guy with the good-looking legs next to Charles was his illegitimate son—famous for his handsome looks, thanks to a little fresh blood. Many other portraits show the unhappy effects of mixing blue blood with more of the same blue blood. When one king married his niece, the result was Charles II (1665–1700). His severe underbite (an inbred royal family trait) was the least of his problems. An epileptic before that disease was understood, poor "Charles the Mad" would be the last of the Spanish Hapsburgs. He died without an heir in 1700, ushering in the Continent-wide War of the Spanish Succession and the dismantling of Spain's empire.

In the **Walking Gallery,** the royals got their exercise privately, with no risk of darkening their high-class skins with a tan. Study the 16th-century maps that line the walls. The slate strip on the floor is a sundial. It lined up with a (now plugged) hole in the wall so that at noon a tiny beam hit the middle of the three lines. Palace clocks were set by this. Where the ray crossed the strip indicated the date and sign of the zodiac.

As you enter the King's Antechamber, look back to study the fine inlaid-wood door (a gift from the German emperor that celebrates the exciting humanism of the age).

Philip II's bedroom is austere, like his daughter's. Look at the king's humble bed...barely queen-size. He too could view Mass at the basilica's high altar without leaving his bed. The red box next to his pillow holds the royal bedpan. But don't laugh—the king's looking down from the wall behind you. At age 71, Philip II, the gout-ridden king of a dying empire, died in this bed (1598).

From here, his body was taken to the **Royal Pantheon** (Panteón Real), the gilded resting place of 26 kings and queens...four centuries' worth of Spanish monarchy. All the kings are included—but only those queens who became mothers of kings.

There is a post-mortem filing system at work in the Pantheon. The first and greatest, Charles V and his Queen Isabel, flank the altar on the top shelf. Her son, Philip II, rests below Charles and opposite (only) one of Philip's four wives, and so on. There is a waiting process, too. Before a royal corpse can rest in this room, it needs to decompose for several decades. The three empty niches are already booked. The bones of the current king Juan Carlos' grandmother, Victoria Eugenia (who died in 1964), are just about ready to be moved in. Juan Carlos' father, Don Juan (who died in 1993), is also on the waiting list. But where does that leave Juan Carlos? This hotel is *todo completo.*

The next rooms are filled with the tombs of lesser royals: Each bears that person's name (in Latin), relationship to the king, and slogan or epitaph. They lead to the lazy-Susan-like **Pantheon of Royal Children** (Panteón de los Infantes) that holds the remains of various royal children who died before the age of seven (and their first Communion).

The **Chapter Rooms** (Salas Capitulares), where the monks met to do church business, are lined with big-name paintings: José Ribera, El Greco, Titian, and Velázquez. (More great paintings are in the monastery's Museum of Painting.) The **cloister** glows with bright, newly restored paintings by Pellegrino Tibaldi. Off the cloister are two rooms: the **Antesacristia,** with a liturgical fountain, and the **Old Church** (Iglesia Vieja), which they used from 1571 to 1586, while finishing the basilica. During that time, the bodies of several kings, including Charles V, were interred here. Among the many paintings you'll see, look for the powerful *Martyrdom of Saint Laurence* by Tiziano (Titian).

Follow the signs to the **basilica.** In the center of the altar wall, find the flame-engulfed grill that features San Lorenzo (the same St. Lawrence from the painting) meeting his famous death—and taking "turn the other cheek" to new extremes. Lorenzo was so cool, he reportedly told his Roman executioners: "You can turn me over now—I'm done on this side." With your back to the altar, go to the right corner for the artistic highlight of the basilica: Benvenuto Cellini's marble sculpture *The Crucifixion*. Jesus' features are supposedly modeled after the Shroud of Turin. Cellini carved this from Carrara marble for his own tomb in 1562 (according to the letters under Christ's feet).

Last comes the immense **library** *(biblioteca)*—where it's clear that education was a priority for the Spanish royalty. Savor this room. The ceiling (by Tibaldi, depicting various disciplines labeled in Latin, the lingua franca of the multinational Hapsburg empire) is a burst of color. At the far end of the room, the elaborate model of the solar system looks like a giant gyroscope, revolving  unmistakably around the Earth, with a misshapen, under-explored North America. As you leave, look back above the door. The plaque warns *"Excomunión..."*—you'll be excommunicated if you take a book without checking it out properly. Who needs late fees when you hold the keys to Hell?

Admission to the palace is €8 for the works *(completa)*, or €7 for a *principal* ticket, which skips the Chapter Rooms and Royal Pantheon (April–Sept Tue–Sun 10:00–19:00, closed Mon, Oct–March closes at 18:00, last entry 60 min before closing, tel. 918-905-904). It's worth the extra euro to see it all. But be warned that if you arrive less than 90 minutes before closing, you can get only the cheaper ticket. There's also an €8.50 combo-ticket that includes Valley of the Fallen (buy ticket before 15:00 April–Sept or 14:00 Oct–March), but this makes sense only for drivers, since people taking the bus to the Valley of the Fallen have the site admission included in the cost of transportation.

You'll find scanty captions in English within the palace. For more information, get the *Guide: Monastery of San Lorenzo El Real de El Escorial,* which follows the general route you'll take (€7.50, available at any of several shops in the palace). While you can pay €9 for admission with a guided tour (ask at ticket office for next English tour), I'd rent the €2.30 audioguide instead (for €3, you also get a voucher for the audioguide at Valley of the Fallen).

Eating: To shop for a picnic, stop by the Mercado Público on Calle del Rey 9, a four-minute walk from the palace (Mon–Fri 9:00–14:00 & 17:00–20:00, Sat 10:00–14:00, closed Thu and Sat afternoons and Sun). For a change from Spanish fare, consider pizza at Tavolata Reale (Plaza de las Ánimas, a block from Monasterio entrance, tel. 918-904-591) or Restaurante China Hong Kong (Calle San Antón 6, tel. 918-961-894).

TRANSPORTATION CONNECTIONS

Coming from Madrid: Buses leave from the basement level of Madrid's Moncloa Metro stop and drop you in the town center of San Lorenzo de El Escorial, a 10-minute walk from the Monasterio (4/hr, 45 min, hrly on weekends, none Sun 15:00–17:30, in Madrid take faster bus #664 or #661 from Intercambiador's bay #3).

Once in El Escorial, it's a pleasant 10-minute stroll from the station through the town of San Lorenzo de El Escorial. Exit the bus station from the back ramp that leads over the parked buses, turn left, and follow the newly cobbled pedestrian lane, Calle Juan de Leyra (which veers once to the right). In a few blocks, it dead-ends at Duque de Medinaceli, where you'll turn left and see the palace. Stairs lead past several decent eateries, through a delightful park, past the TI (Mon–Fri 11:00–18:00, Sat–Sun 10:00–19:00, tel. 918-905-313), and directly to the tourist entry of the immense palace/monastery.

Taking the **train** from Madrid is less convenient. Although trains leave twice hourly from Madrid's Atocha and Chamartín stations, you'll have to choose your secondary transportation into town.

From the train station, it's a pleasant 20-minute walk (through Casita del Príncipe park, straight up from the station), a €4 taxi ride, or a €1 shuttle-bus ride (2/hr) to the San Lorenzo de El Escorial town center and Monasterio.

To Valley of the Fallen: Without a car, the easiest way there is to negotiate a deal with a taxi (to take you there, wait for you 30–60 min, and then bring you back to El Escorial, about €30). Otherwise one bus a day connects the Valley of the Fallen with El Escorial (15 min, leaves El Escorial at 15:15, leaves Valley of the Fallen at 17:30, €7.80 round-trip includes admission to the site, no bus on Mon when El Escorial monastery and Valley of the Fallen are closed).

By car: It's quite simple. Taxi to your car-rental office in Madrid (or ask if they'll deliver the car to your hotel). Pick up the car by 8:30 and ask directions to highway A6. From Gran Vía in central Madrid it's easy: Follow signs to A6 (direction *Villalba* or *Coruña*). The freeway leads directly out of town. Stay on the A6 past the first El Escorial exit. At kilometer 37, you'll see the cross marking the Valley of the Fallen ahead on the left. Exit 47 takes you to both the Valley of the Fallen (after a half mile, a granite gate on right marks *Valle de los Caídos* turn-off) and El Escorial (follow signs to San Lorenzo del Escorial).

The nearby **Silla de Felipe** (Philip's Seat) is a rocky viewpoint where the king would come to admire his palace as it was being built. From El Escorial, follow directions to Ávila, then M-505 to Valdemorillo; look for a sign on your right after about a mile.

When you leave El Escorial for Madrid, Toledo, or Segovia, follow signs to *A6 Guadarrama*. After about six miles, you pass the Valley of the Fallen and hit the freeway.

Valley of the Fallen
(Valle de los Caídos)

Six miles from El Escorial, high in the Guadarrama Mountains, a 500-foot-tall granite cross marks an immense and powerful underground monument to the victims of Spain's 20th-century nightmare—its civil war (1936–1939).

Approaching by car or bus, you enter the sprawling park through a granite gate (€5, or €7.80 to include round-trip bus from El Escorial; €8.50 for combo-ticket with El Escorial—best for drivers, see previous page; April–Sept Tue–Sun 10:00–19:00, closed Mon, last entry 60 min before closing, basilica closes 30 min before site

closes, Oct–March closes at 18:00, tel. 918-907-756). The best views of the cross are from the bridge (but note that it's illegal to stop anywhere along this road). Above you, the tiny chapels along the ridge mark the Stations of the Cross, where pilgrims stop on their hike to this memorial.

In 1940, prison workers dug 220,000 tons of granite out of the hill beneath the cross to form an underground basilica, then used the stones to erect the cross (built like a chimney, from the inside). Since it's built directly over the dome of the subterranean basilica, a seismologist keeps a careful eye on things.

The stairs that lead to the imposing monument are grouped in sets of tens, meant to symbolize the Ten Commandments (including "Thou shalt not kill"—hmm). The emotional *pietà* draped over the basilica's entrance is huge—you could sit in the palm of Christ's hand. The statue was sculpted by Juan de Ávalos, the same artist who created the dramatic figures of the four Evangelists at the base of the cross. It must have had a powerful impact on mothers who came here to remember their fallen sons.

A solemn silence and a stony chill fill the basilica—at 870 feet long, larger than St. Peter's. Many Spaniards pass under the huge, foreboding angels of fascism to visit the grave of General Franco—an unusual place of pilgrimage, to say the least.

After walking through the two long vestibules, stop at the iron gates of the actual basilica. The line of torch-like lamps adds to the shrine ambience. Notice the bare rock still showing on the ceiling. Franco's prisoners, the enemies of right, dug this memorial out of solid rock from 1940 to 1959. The sides of the monument are lined with copies of 16th-century Brussels tapestries of the Apocalypse, and side chapels contain alabaster copies of Spain's most famous statues of the Virgin Mary.

Interred behind the high altar and side chapels (marked "RIP, 1936–1939, died for God and country") are the remains of the approximately 50,000 people, both *Republicanos* and Franco's *Nacionalistas,* who lost their lives in the war. Regrettably, the urns are not visible, so it is Franco who takes center stage. His grave, strewn with flowers, lies behind the high altar. In front of the altar is the grave of José Antonio Primo de Rivera (1903–1936), the founder of Spanish fascism, who was killed by Republicans during the Civil War. Between these fascists' graves, the statue of a crucified Christ is

The Spanish Civil War
(1936–1939)

Thirty-three months of warfare killed 200,000 Spaniards. Unlike America's Civil War, which split America roughly north and south, Spain's war was between classes and ideologies, dividing every city and village, and many families. It was especially cruel, with atrocities and reprisals on both sides.

The war began as a military coup to overthrow the democratically-elected Republic, a government too liberal for the army and conservative powers. The rebel forces, called the Nationalists *(Nacionalistas)*, consisted of the army, monarchy, Catholic church, big business, and rural estates, with aid from Germany, Italy, and Portugal. Trying to preserve the liberal government were the Republicans *(Republicanos)*, also called Loyalists: the government, urban areas, secularists, small business, and labor unions, with aid from the United States (minimal help), and the "International Brigades" of communists, socialists, and labor organizers.

In the summer of 1936, the army rebelled and took control of their own garrisons, rejecting the Republic and pledging allegiance to General Francisco Franco (1892–1975). These Nationalists launched a three-year military offensive to take Spain region by region, town by town. The government ("Republicans") cobbled together an army of volunteers, local militias, and international fighters. The war pitted conservative Catholic priests against socialist factory workers, rich businessmen against radical students, sunburned farmers loyal to the old king against upwardly-mobile small businessmen. People suffered. You'll notice that nearly any Spaniard in his or her 70s is very short—a product of trying to grow up during these hungry and very difficult Civil War years.

Spain's civil war attracted international attention. Adolf Hitler of Germany and Benito Mussolini of Italy sent troops and supplies to their fellow fascist, Franco. It was Hitler's Luftwaffe that helped Franco bomb the town of Guernica (April 1937), an event captured on canvas by the artist Picasso. On the Republican side, hundreds of Americans (including Ernest Hemingway) steamed over to Spain to fight for democracy as part of the "Lincoln Brigade."

By 1939, only Barcelona and Madrid held out. But they were no match for Franco's army. On April 1, 1939, the war ended, beginning 37 years of iron-fisted rule by Franco.

lashed to a timber Franco himself is said to have felled. The seeping stones seem to weep for the victims.

As you leave, stare into the eyes of those angels with swords and two right wings and think about all the "heroes" who keep dying "for God and country," at the request of the latter. A Mass closes off the entire front of the basilica (altar and tombs) to the public daily from 11:00 to 12:05. The resident boys' choir (the "White Voices"—Spain's answer to the Vienna Boys' Choir) generally sings during the Mass (you can sit through the service, but not sightsee during this time). The €2 audioguide is heavy on the theological message of the statues and tapestries and ignores Franco.

The expansive view from the monument's terrace includes the peaceful, forested valley and sometimes snow-streaked mountains. For an even better view, consider taking a funicular trip—with a short commentary in English—to the base of the cross (€1.50 one-way, €2.50 round-trip, April–Sept Tue–Sun 11:00–19:00, closed Mon, 3/hr; Oct–March Tue–Sun 11:00–16:30, closed Monday, 2/hr, has restaurant and public WC). You can hike back down in 25 minutes. If you have a car, you can drive up past the monastery and hike from the start of the trail marked *Sendero a la Cruz*.

Near the parking lot and bus stop at Valley of the Fallen is a small snack bar and picnic tables. Basic overnight lodging is available at the monastery behind the cross (100 rooms, Sb-€37, Db-€40, includes meals, tax, and a pass to enter and leave the park after hours, tel. 918-905-494, fax 918-961-542, NSE). A meditative night here is good mostly for monks.

For information on how to reach the Valley of the Fallen from El Escorial by bus, see "Transportation Connections" in El Escorial, page 205.

Segovia

Fifty miles from Madrid, this town of 55,000 boasts a great Roman aqueduct, a cathedral, and a castle. Segovia is a medieval "ship" ready for your inspection. Start at the stern—the aqueduct—and stroll up Calle de Cervantes to the prickly Gothic masts of the cathedral. Explore the tangle of narrow streets around the playful Plaza Mayor and then descend to the Alcázar at the bow. Since the city is more than 3,000 feet above sea level and just northwest of a mountain range exposing it to the north, people from Madrid come here for a break from the summer heat.

ORIENTATION

Tourist Information: Segovia has two tourist offices. The one on Plaza Mayor covers both Segovia and the region (at #10, daily in summer 9:00–20:00, off-season 9:00–14:00 & 17:00–20:00, tel. 921-460-334, segoviaturism@vianwe.com). The other one, at Plaza del Azoguejo at the base of the aqueduct, specializes in Segovia and may still be under renovation in 2005 (daily 10:00–20:00, have a look at the wooden model of Segovia, tel. 921-462-906 or 921-462-914).

Arrival in Segovia: The train station is a 35-minute walk from the center. Take a city bus #2 (marked *Puente de Hierro*) from the station to get to Calle de Colón, about 100 yards from Plaza Mayor (catch bus on the same side of the street as the station—confirm by asking, "*¿Para Plaza Mayor?*"; 2/hr, €0.70, pay driver). Taxis are a reasonable option (€4 to Plaza Mayor). If you arrive by bus, it's a 15-minute walk to the center (turn left out of the bus station and continue straight across the street, jog right and you're on Avenida Fernández Ladreda, which leads to the aqueduct). Day-trippers can store luggage at the train station (buy €3 tokens at ticket window), but not at the bus station. If arriving by car, see "Transportation Connections," page 205.

Helpful Hint: If you buy handicrafts such as tablecloths from street vendors, make sure the item you're buying is the one you actually get; some unscrupulous vendors substitute inferior goods at the last minute.

SIGHTS

▲**Roman Aqueduct**—Segovia was a Roman military base and needed water. So Emperor Trajan's engineers built a nine-mile aqueduct to channel water (eight gallons per second) from the Río Frío to the city. The famous and exposed section of the 2,000-year-old *acueducto romano* is 2,500 feet long and 100 feet high, has 118 arches, was made from 20,000 granite blocks without any mortar, and can still carry a stream of water.

On Plaza del Azoguejo, a grand stairway leads from the base of the aqueduct to the top—offering close-up looks at the imposing work.

Cathedral—Segovia's cathedral—built in Renaissance times (1525–1768, the third on this site)—was Spain's last major Gothic building. Embellished to the hilt with pinnacles and flying but-

Segovia

1. Hostal Plaza
2. Hotel Los Linajes
3. Hotel Infanta Isabel
4. Hotel Sirenas
5. Pensión Ferri
6. Hostal Don Jaime
7. Hospedaje el Gato
8. To Youth Hostel
9. Rest. Mesón de Candido
10. Rest. José Maria & Café Jeyma
11. Rest. Casa Chapete
12. Rest. Narizotas & Rest. Bar San Martin
13. Rodilla
14. Lima y Menta Pastry Shop

tresses, the exterior is a great example of the final, overripe stage of Gothic, called Flamboyant. The dark, spacious, and elegantly simple interior provides a delightful contrast (€2, free only on Sun 9:00–13:30; daily March–Oct 9:00–18:30, Nov–Feb 9:30–17:30). The painting *Tree of Life,* by Ignacio Ries (as you enter, go right, to the last chapel—the painting is on the wall to the left of the altar), shows hedonistic mortals dancing atop the Tree of Life. As a skeletal Grim Reaper prepares to receive them into Hell, Jesus rings a bell imploring them to wake up before it's too late.

The peaceful cloister's museum, housing some Hispano-Flemish painting and 17th-century Flemish tapestries, is opposite the cathedral entrance. In Room 14, notice the dramatic, gilded, wheeled "Carroza de la Custodia." The Holy Communion wafer is placed in the top of this temple-like cart and paraded through town each year during the Corpus Christi festival (museum closed Sun 9:00–14:00).

▲**Alcázar**—Once a favorite summer residence and hunting palace of the monarchs of Castile, this castle burned in 1862. What you see today is rebuilt—a Disneyesque exaggeration of the original. It's still fun to explore the fine Moorish decor, historic furnishings, and grand Segovia view from its tower. After its stint as a palace, the Alcázar was a prison for 200 years and then a Royal Artillery School. Since the fire, it's basically been a museum. As you wander, you'll see a big mural of Queen Isabel the Catholic being proclaimed Queen of Castile and León in Segovia's main square in 1474. The Hall of the Monarchs is lined with statues of all the rulers of Castile and León until Spain was unified. In the chapel, note the painting of St. James the Moorslayer—with Moorish heads literally rolling at his feet. He's the patron saint of Spain, and his name was the rallying cry in the centuries-long Christian crusade to push the Moors back into Africa. The well on the terrace marks the end of the nine-mile-long Roman aqueduct. From here you can enjoy such fine views as the mountain nicknamed *Mujer Muerta*, meaning "dead woman"—can you see why? (€3.50 for palace, €1 for tower, €4.50 for combo-ticket, April–Sept daily 10:00–19:00, Oct–March until 18:00, audioguide-€3, get the free English leaflet; buy tickets at Casa de Chimia, facing palace on your left; tel. 921-460-759.)

Church of San Justo—This church, near the base of the aqueduct in the newer part of town, has well-preserved 12th- and 13th-century frescoes and a storks' nest atop its tower (free, Mon–Sat 12:00–14:00 & 17:00–19:00; in winter 12:00–14:00 & 16:00–18:00; closed Sun and when the volunteer caretaker, Rafael, may need to run an errand; located a couple of blocks from Plaza del Azoguejo). Kind old Rafael may let you risk climbing the (dangerous) bell tower for "the best view of Segovia."

Historic Segovia Walk: From the Main Square to the Aqueduct

This 15-minute walk is all downhill from the city's main square along the pedestrian-only street to the Roman aqueduct. It's most enjoyable just before dinner, when it's cool and filled with strolling locals.

Start on Segovia's inviting **Plaza Mayor,** once the scene of bullfights, with spectators jamming the balconies. In the 19th century, the bullfights were stopped. When locals complained, they were given a more gentle form of entertainment—bands in the music kiosk. The

Romanesque church opposite the city hall is where Isabel was proclaimed Queen of Castile in 1474. The symbol of Segovia is the aqueduct. Find it in the seals on the Theater Juan Bravo and atop the city hall. Head down Calle de Isabel la Católica (downhill, to right of Hotel Infanta Isabel) and tempt yourself with the local pastry in the window display of the corner bakery.

After 100 yards, at the first intersection, on the right you'll see the Corpus Christi Convent. You're welcome to pop in, knock on the window, ask the nun for the key ("*La llave, por favor;*" lah YAH-vay, por fah-vor), and see the church, which was a synagogue, which was a mosque.

After another 100 yards, you come to the complicated Plaza de San Martín, a commotion of history surrounding a striking statue of Juan Bravo. When Charles V, a Hapsburg who didn't even speak Spanish, took power, he imposed his rule over Castile. This threatened the local nobles, who—inspired and led by Juan Bravo—revolted in 1521. While Juan Bravo lost the battle—and his head—he's still a symbol of Castilian pride. This statue was erected on the 400th anniversary of his death.

On the same square, the 12th-century Church of St. Martín is Segovian Romanesque in style (a mix of Christian Romanesque and Moorish styles). The 14th-century Tower of Lozoya, behind the statue, is one of many fortified towers that marked the homes of feuding local noble families. Clashing loyalties led to mini civil wars (as in Italy with the families of Romeo and Juliet during the same age). In the 15th century, as Ferdinand and Isabel centralized authority in Spain, nobles were required to lop their towers. You'll see the stubby towers (once tall) of 15th-century noble mansions all over Segovia,.

At the bottom of the square stands the bold and bulky House of Siglo XV. Its fortified *Isabelino* style was typical of 15th-century Segovian houses. Later, in a more peaceful age, the boldness of these houses was softened with the decorative stucco work—Arabic-style floral and geometrical patterns—that you see today. At Plaza del Platero Oquendo, 50 yards farther downhill, you'll see a similar house with a cropped tower.

At the next corner find the "house of a thousand pyramids" with another truncated tower. This building, maintaining its original Moorish design, has a wall just past the door, which blocks your view from the street. This wall, the architectural equivalent of a veil, hid this home's fine courtyard—Moors didn't flaunt their wealth. Step inside to see art students at work and perhaps an exhibit on display.

From here, stroll 100 yards, and you'll see the Roman aqueduct, which marks the end of this walk.

Near Segovia

Vera Cruz Church—This 12-sided, 13th-century Romanesque church, built by the Knights Templar, once housed a piece of the "true cross" (€1.50, Tue–Sun 10:30–13:30 & 15:30–19:00, closed Mon and Nov, closes at 18:00 in winter, outside of town beyond the castle, a 25-min walk from main square, tel. 921-431-475). There's a postcard view of the city from here, and more views follow as you continue around Segovia on the small road below the castle, labeled *ruta turística panorámica*.

▲**La Granja Palace**—This "little Versailles," six miles south of Segovia, is much smaller and happier than El Escorial. The palace and gardens were built by the homesick French-born King Philip V, grandson of Louis XIV. Today, it's restored to its original 18th-century splendor with its royal collection of clocks and crystal (actually made at the palace's royal crystal factory). It's a must for tapestry lovers, featuring mostly tapestries designed by Albrecht Dürer in the 16th century. Plumbers and gardeners imported from France and Italy made Philip a garden that rivaled Versailles'. The fanciful fountains feature mythological stories (explained in the palace audioguide). The Bourbon Philip chose to be buried here rather than with his Hapsburg predecessors at El Escorial (tombs in the adjacent church included with your ticket). Entry to the palace includes a required 45-minute guided tour, usually in Spanish (€5, April–Sept Tue–Sun 10:00–18:00, closed Mon; Oct–March Tue–Sat 10:00–13:30 & 15:00–17:00, Sun 10:00–14:00; tel. 921-470-019, www.patrimonionacional.es). Fourteen buses a day (fewer on weekends) make the 20-minute trip from Segovia (catch at the bus station) to San Ildefonso–La Granja. The park is free (daily 10:00–19:00, until 18:00 in winter).

SLEEPING

The best places are on or near the central Plaza Mayor. This is where the city action is: the best bars, most touristic and *típico* eateries, and the TI. During busy times—on weekends and in July and August—arrive early or call ahead. Buses from the station go to Plaza Mayor (near most of these recommended hotels).

In the Old Center, near Plaza Mayor

$$$ **Hotel Los Linajes** is ultraclassy, with rusticity mixed into its newly-poured concrete. This poor man's parador is a few blocks beyond the Plaza Mayor, with territorial views and modern, air-conditioned niceties (Sb-€73, Db-€99, big Db-€129, Tb-€118, cheaper off-season, breakfast-€9, elevator, parking-€11, Dr. Velasco 9, tel. 921-460-475,

Sleep Code

(€1 = about $1.20, country code: 34)
S = Single, **D** = Double/Twin, **T** = Triple, **Q** = Quad, **b** = bathroom, **s** = shower only, **no CC** = Credit Cards not accepted, **SE** = Speaks English, **NSE** = No English. You can assume credit cards are accepted unless noted otherwise.

To help you easily sort through these listings, I've divided the rooms into three categories, based on the price for a standard double room with bath during high season (breakfast and 7 percent IVA tax not included):

$$$ **Higher Priced**—Most rooms €85 or more.
$$ **Moderately Priced**—Most rooms between €30–85.
$ **Lower Priced**—Most rooms €30 or less.

fax 921-460-479, www.loslinajes.com, hotelloslinajes@terra.es). From Plaza Mayor, take Escuderos downhill; at the five-way intersection, angle right on Dr. Velasco. Drivers, follow brown hotel signs from the aqueduct to its tight but handy garage.

$$$ Hotel Infanta Isabel, right on Plaza Mayor, is the ritziest hotel in the old town, with 38 elegant rooms (Sb-€66, Db-€86–102 depending on room size, some rooms with plaza views, 20 percent off in winter, elevator, valet parking-€9, tel. 921-461-300, fax 921-462-217, www.hotelinfantaisabel.com, hinfanta@teleline.es, SE).

$$ Hostal Plaza, just off Plaza Mayor, has a *serio* management, snaky corridors, and faded bedspreads. But its 28 rooms are clean and cozy (S-€21, Sb-€32, D-€30, Db-€39, Tb-€53, parking-€9, Cronista Lecea 11, tel. 92-146-0-303, fax 921-460-305, www.hostal-plaza.com in Spanish, informacion@hostal-plaza.com).

$$ Hotel Sirenas is big and hotelesque, with a stuffy entrance. But it's centrally located and rents comfortable rooms with a well-worn elegance (Sb-€53, Db-€70–85, Tb-€90, air-con, elevator, parking-€11, 3 blocks down from Plaza Mayor at Calle Juan Bravo 30, tel. 921-462-663, fax 921-462-657, www.hotelsirenas.com, hotelsirenas@terra.es, NSE).

$ Pensión Ferri, half a block off Plaza Mayor, opposite a Guinness beer sign, is a quiet, dumpy, unmarked, five-room place cheaper than the youth hostel (S-€14, D-€20, shower-€2, no CC, Escuderos 10, tel. 921-460-957, Carmen, NSE).

Outside of the Old Town, near the Aqueduct

$$ Hostal Don Jaime, near the base of the aqueduct, opposite the Church of San Justo, is a family-run place with 31 shiny, clean, well-maintained rooms; seven rooms are in an annex across the street (S-€22, D-€30, Db-€40, Tb-€50, Qb-€55, parking-€6,

Ochoa Ondategui 8; from TI at aqueduct, cross under the aqueduct, go right, angle left, then snake uphill for 2 blocks, tel. & fax 921-444-787, www.viasegovia.com/hostaldonjaime in Spanish, hostaldonjaime@terra.es, SE).

$$ Hospedaje el Gato is another very clean, family-run place on the same quiet nondescript street just outside the old town; its 10 rooms are modern and comfortable (Sb-€20, Db-€32, Tb-€46, air-con, bar serves breakfast and good tapas, uphill from Hostal Don Jaime and aqueduct at Plaza del Salvador 10, tel. 921-423-244, fax 921-438-047, elgato@tottel.com).

$ The **Segovia Youth Hostel** is a great 120-bed hostel—easygoing, comfortable, clean, friendly, very cheap—and open to members only (€9.32 beds, €13.82 for full board, open July–Aug only, Paseo Conde de Sepúlveda 4, between the train and bus stations, tel. 921-441-111, fax 921-438-027).

EATING

Look for Segovia's culinary claim to fame, roast suckling pig (*cochinillo asado:* 21 days of mother's milk, into the oven, and onto your plate—oh, Babe). It's worth a splurge here, or in Toledo or Salamanca.

For lighter fare, try *sopa castellana*—soup mixed with eggs, ham, garlic, and bread—or warm yourself up with the local *judiones de la granja*, a popular soup made with flat white beans from the region.

Ponche segoviano, a dessert made with an almond-and-honey *mazapán* base, is heavenly after an earthy dinner or with a coffee in the afternoon (at the recommended Lima y Menta—see next page).

Roast Suckling Pig

Mesón de Candido, one of the top restaurants in Castile, is famous as *the* place to spend €30 on a memorable dinner. Even though it's filled with tourists, it's a grand experience. Take time to wander around and survey the photos of celebs—from King Juan Carlos to Antonio Banderas and Melanie Griffith—who've suckled here (daily 13:00–16:30 & 20:00–23:00, Plaza del Azoguejo 5, air-con, under aqueduct, tel. 921-428-103 for reservations, www.mesondecandido.es, candido@mesondecandido.es, gracious Candido and family SE).

José María is the place to pig out in the old town (a block off Plaza Mayor). While it doesn't have the history or fanfare of Candido, locals claim it serves the best roast suckling pig in town. Still, it's filled mostly with tourists (€30 à la carte dinner, daily 13:00–16:00 & 20:00–23:30, air-con, Cronista Lecea 11, tel. 921-466-017, reservas@rtejosemaria.com).

Restaurante Casa Chapete, a homey little place filled with smoke, happy locals, and not a tourist in sight, serves the traditional lamb and pig dishes—but only for lunch (€16.25-course meals including wine, daily 12:00–16:00, 2 blocks beyond aqueduct, across from recommended Hostal Don Jaime at Calle Ochoa Ondategui 7, tel. 921-421-096).

The Old Center (No Pig)

Segovia's playful Plaza Mayor provides a great backdrop for a light lunch, dinner, or drink. Grab a table at the place of your choice and savor the scene. For me, **Café Jeyma** has the best setting and cathedral view. Survey their tapas selection at the bar. They'll happily make you an assorted plate of *(surtido de...)* deep-fried savory turnovers *(empanadillas)* and little sandwiches *(canapés)* for €6.

Narizotas serves more imaginative and non-Castilian alternatives to the gamey traditions. You'll dine outside on a delightful square or inside with modern art under medieval timbers. Their "Right Hand Left Hand" sampler menu provides a time-consuming (allow about 75 min) but wonderful eating experience for €26–30 (daily 12:30–16:00 & 20:30–24:00, midway down Calle Juan Bravo at Plaza de Medina del Campo 1, tel. 921-462-679).

Restaurante Bar San Martín is a no-frills place popular with locals, with a lively tapas bar, great outdoor seating on the same square by the fountain, and a smoky restaurant in the back. They can assemble a *surtido de canapés*—assorted plate of small sandwiches for €6, or order à la carte (daily 13:00–16:00 & 20:30–23:00, Plaza de San Martín 3, tel. 921-462-466).

Rodilla, the popular chain, offers a great assortment of cheap and tasty sandwiches and salads (Mon–Fri 9:30–22:00, Sat–Sun 10:00–22:30, on Calle Juan Bravo, at intersection with Calle de la Herrería).

Inexpensive bars and eateries line Calle de Infanta Isabel, just off Plaza Mayor. For nightlife, the bars on Plaza Mayor, Calle de Infanta Isabel, and Calle Isabel la Católica are packed. There are a number of late-night dance clubs along the aqueduct.

Lima y Menta offers a good, rich *ponche segoviano* cake by the slice for €2, or try the lighter almond and honey *crocantinos* (daily 9:30–21:30, seating inside, Isabel la Católica 2, tel. 921-462-141).

An **outdoor produce market** thrives on Plaza Mayor (Thu 8:00–14:00). Nearby, a few stalls are open Monday through Saturday on Calle del Cronista Ildefonso Rodríguez.

TRANSPORTATION CONNECTIONS

By train to: Madrid (9/day, 2 hrs, both Chamartín and Atocha stations). If day-tripping from Madrid, look for the *cercanías* (commuter train) ticket window and departure board in either of Madrid's train stations. Pick up a return schedule here or from the Segovia TI. Train info: tel. 902-240-202.

By bus to: La Granja Palace (14/day, 20 min), **Ávila** (5/day but only 2 on weekends, 1 hr), **Madrid** (2/hr, 1 hr, quicker than train, stops at Madrid's Moncloa Intercambiador, then 10 minutes later at La Sepulvedana at Metro: Príncipe Pío, Paseo de la Florida 11, tel. 915-304-800), and to **Salamanca** (3/day, 3 hrs, transfer in Labajos, it's smart to call ahead to reserve a seat for the Labajos–Salamanca segment—call Madrid's La Sepulvedana office at tel. 915-304-800 to book your seat); consider busing from Segovia to Ávila for a visit, then continuing to Salamanca by bus or train.

By car: Leave Madrid on A6. Exit 39 gets you to Segovia via a slow, winding route over the scenic mountain. Exit at 60 (after a long €2.75 toll tunnel) or get there quicker by staying on the toll freeway all the way to Segovia (add €1.80 weekdays or €2.90 on weekends). At the Segovia aqueduct, follow *casco histórico* signs to the old town (on the side where the aqueduct adjoins the crenellated fortress walls).

Parking in Segovia: Free parking is available in the Alcázar's lot, but you must move your car out by 19:00, when the gates close. Or try the lot northwest of the bus station by the statue of Candido, along the street called Paseo de Ezequiel González. Outside of the old city, there's an Acueducto Parking underground garage cater-corner from the bus station.

If you want to park near Plaza Mayor, be legal or risk an expensive ticket. Buy a ticket from the nearby machine to park in areas marked by blue stripes, and place the ticket on your dashboard (€0.30 for 30 min, 2-hr maximum, 9:00–14:00 & 16:30–20:00; free parking 20:00–9:00, Sat afternoon, and all day Sun).

Segovia to Salamanca (100 miles): Leave Segovia by driving around the town's circular road, which offers good views from below the Alcázar. Then follow signs for Ávila (road N110). Notice the fine Segovia view from the three crosses at the crest of the first hill. The Salamanca road leads around the famous Ávila walls to the right. The best wall view is from the signposted Cuatro Postes, a mile northwest of town. Salamanca (N501) is clearly marked, about an hour's drive away.

About 20 miles before Salamanca, you might want to stop at the huge bull on the left of the road. There's a little dirt lane leading right up to it. As you get closer, it becomes more and more obvious it isn't real. Bad boys climb it for a goofy photo. For a great photo op of Salamanca, complete with river reflection, stop at the edge of the city (at the light before the first bridge).

In Salamanca, the only safe parking is in a garage; try the underground lot at Plaza Santa Eulalia, Plaza Campillo, or Lemans (closer to recommended Petit Palace Las Torres), or even easier, try one of the hotels (such as Hotel Don Juan) with valet parking for comparable fees (see page 151).

Ávila

A popular side-trip from Madrid, Ávila is famous for its perfectly preserved medieval walls, as the birthplace of St. Teresa, and for its yummy *yemas*. For more than 300 years, Ávila was on the battlefront between the Muslims and Christians, changing hands several times. Today, perfectly peaceful Ávila has a charming old town. With several fine churches and monasteries, it makes for an enjoyable quick stop between Segovia and Salamanca (each about an hour away by car).

Tourist Information: The TI has fine free maps and information on walking tours (daily 9:00–14:00 & 17:00–20:00, July–mid-Sept 9:00–20:00, facing the cathedral at Plaza Catedral 4, tel. 920-211-387). Another TI should be open in 2005 outside the wall, opposite the Basilica of San Vicente.

A **tourist train** departs every 30 minutes from outside the wall by St. Vincent's Basilica, with a stop at the Cuatro Postes viewpoint (€3).

Arrival in Ávila: Approaching by bus, train, or car, you'll need to make your way through the nondescript modern part of town to find the walled old town. The bus is 10 minutes away, while the train station is a 15-minute walk of the cathedral and wall. By car, park at public parking east of Puerta del Alcázar, just south of the cathedral, or at Parking Dornier (€0.60/hour).

On a quick stop, everything that matters is within a few blocks of the cathedral (actually part of the east end of the wall).

SIGHTS

▲**The Wall**—Built from around 1100, Ávila's fortified wall is the oldest, most complete, and best preserved in Spain. It has three access

points—two at each side of the cathedral and one by the parador inn—where you can buy tickets. The €3.50 admission comes with a helpful 20-page brochure that makes a walk around the walls more meaningful (April–mid-Oct  Tue–Sun 10:00–20:00, mid-Oct–March 11:00–18:00, closed Mon except July–Aug). A night visit gives you the same walk, with the wall beautifully lit (€3.50, mid-June–mid-Sept Sun–Thu 22:00–24:00).

The best views are actually from street level (especially along the north side, which drivers will see as they circle to the right from Puerta de San Vicente to catch the highway to Salamanca). The best overall view of the walled town is about a mile away on the Salamanca road (N501) at a clearly marked turn-out for the Cuatro Postes (four posts).

Ávila

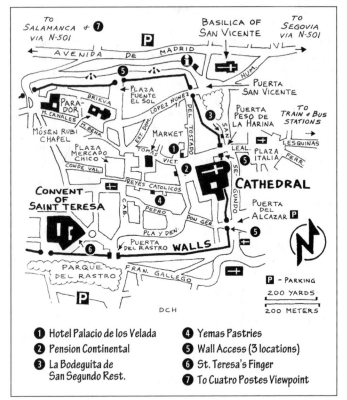

TO
SALAMANCA & ❼
VIA N-501

BASILICA OF
SAN VICENTE

TO
SEGOVIA
VIA N-501

P

AVENIDA DE MADRID

❺

PLAZA
FUENTE
EL SOL

BRIEVA

M. CANALES

PARA-
DOR

M. BENA

MOSEN RUBI
CHAPEL

PLAZA
MERCADO
CHICO

CONDE VAL.

LOPEZ NUNEZ

EST. DOM.

MARKET

TOMAS

❶

VICT.

REYES CATOLICOS

CONVENT
OF
SAINT TERESA

PEPRO

CAB.

❻

PUERTA
DEL RASTRO

PARQUE
DEL RASTRO

P

PLA Y DEN.

DON GER.

DEL TOSTADO

❹

❷

PUERTA
SAN VICENTE

PUERTA
PESO DE
LA HARINA

LEAL.

❸

SAN

SE
GUNDO

PLAZA
ITALIA

❺

HUM.

VL

TO
TRAIN & BUS
STATIONS

LESQUINAS

FERR.

CATHEDRAL

PUERTA
DEL
ALCAZAR

P

❺

N

WALLS

FRAN. GALLEGO

DCH

P — PARKING

200 YARDS

200 METERS

❶ Hotel Palacio de los Velada
❷ Pension Continental
❸ La Bodeguita de
   San Segundo Rest.

❹ Yemas Pastries
❺ Wall Access (3 locations)
❻ St. Teresa's Finger
❼ To Cuatro Postes Viewpoint

Cathedral—While it started as Romanesque, Ávila's cathedral, finished in the 16th century, is considered the first Gothic cathedral in Spain. Its position—with its granite apse actually part of the fortified wall—underlines the "medieval alliance between cross and sword." You can view the nave from near the entry for free or pay €3 to tour its sacristy, cloister, and museum—which includes an El Greco painting (Mon–Sat 10:00–20:00, Sun 12:00–20:00, off-season Mon–Sat 10:00–17:00, Sun 12:00–17:00).

Convent of St. Teresa—Built in the 17th century on the spot where the saint was born, this convent is a big hit with pilgrims (10-min walk from cathedral). A lavishly gilded side chapel marks the actual place of her birth and a room of relics (facing the church on your right, *Sala de Reliquias*). They connect to the shop that shows off Teresa's finger, complete with a fancy ring, along with her sandals and the bones of St. John of the Cross (daily 9:30–13:30 & 15:30–19:30). A museum in the crypt dedicated to the saint is worth a view for devotees (€2, daily April–Oct

10:00–14:00 & 16:00–19:00, Nov–March 10:00–13:30 & 15:30–17:30).

St. Teresa (1515–1582)—reforming nun, mystic, and writer—bought a house in Ávila and converted it into a convent with more stringent rules than the one she belonged to. She faced opposition in her hometown from rival nuns and those convinced her visions of Heaven were the work of the Devil. However, with her mentor and fellow mystic, St. John of the Cross, she established convents of Discalced (shoeless) Carmelites throughout Spain, and her visions and writings led her to sainthood (canonized 1622).

Yemas—These pastries, made by local nuns, are like a soft-boiled egg yolk that has been cooled and sugared. They're sold all over town. The shop Las Delicias del Convento is actually a retail outlet for the cooks of the convent (€4.50/small box, daily 10:00–14:00 & 16:30–20:30 except Sun morning, a block from TI, at Calle Reyes Católicos 12, tel. 920-220-293).

SLEEPING AND EATING

(€1 = about $1.20, country code: 34)

Two hotels—one antique-classy, the other antique-cheap—face the cathedral.

$$$ Hotel Palacio de los Velada is a five-centuries-old palace with 145 elegant rooms surrounding a huge and inviting arcaded courtyard (Sb-€108, Db-€130, Tb-€161, air-con, elevator, Plaza de la Catedral 10, tel. 920-255-100, fax 920-254-900, palaciodelosvelada @veladahoteles.com).

$ Pension Continental reeks of long-gone elegance, with grand, musty public rooms and 57 basic bedrooms (S-€16, D-€28, Db-€35, Plaza de la Catedral 4, tel. 920-211-502, fax 920-211-563).

Eating: For a classy light lunch, **La Bodeguita de San Segundo,** owned by a locally famous wine connoisseur, serves fine wine by the glass with gourmet tapas, including smoked-cod salad and wild-mushroom scrambled eggs (along the outside of wall near cathedral at San Segundo 19, tel. 920-257-309).

TRANSPORTATION CONNECTIONS

While there are no lockers at Ávila's bus station, you can leave bags at the train station—a 15-minute walk away.

By bus to: Segovia (5 buses/day weekdays, 2 on weekends, 75 min), **Madrid** (1 train/hr, 90 min, TALGO trains only 75 min, more frequent connections with Chamartín station than Atocha; 8 buses/day, 4 on weekends; Larrea bus at Estación Sur de Autobuses in Madrid, tel. 915-304-800), **Salamanca** (7 trains/day, 65 min; 4 buses/day, 2 on weekends, 90 min). Train info: tel. 902-240-202.

TOLEDO

An hour south of Madrid, Toledo teems with tourists, souvenirs, and great art by day, delicious roast suckling pig, echoes of El Greco, and medieval magic by night. Incredibly well-preserved and full of cultural wonder, the entire city has been declared a national monument.

Spain's former capital crowds 3,500 years of tangled history—Roman, Jewish, Visigothic, Moorish, and Christian—onto a high, rocky perch protected on three sides by the Tajo (Tagus) River. It's so well-preserved that the Spanish government has forbidden any modern exteriors. The rich mix of Jewish, Moorish, and Christian heritages makes it one of Europe's art capitals.

Perched strategically in the center of Iberia, Toledo was for centuries a Roman transportation hub with a thriving Jewish population. After Rome fell, the city became a Visigothic capital (A.D. 554). In 711, the Moors (Muslims) made it a regional center. In 1085, the city was reconquered by the Christians, but many Moors remained in Toledo, tolerated and respected as scholars and craftsmen. And from Toledo's earliest times, the city was a haven for Sephardic Jews—educated, wealthy, and cosmopolitan—who were commonly persecuted elsewhere in Europe.

During its medieval heyday (c. 1350), Toledo was famous for intellectual tolerance—a city for the humanities, where God was known by many names. It was a *Sesame Street* world of cultural diversity, home to Jews, Muslims, and Christians, living together in harmony.

Toledo

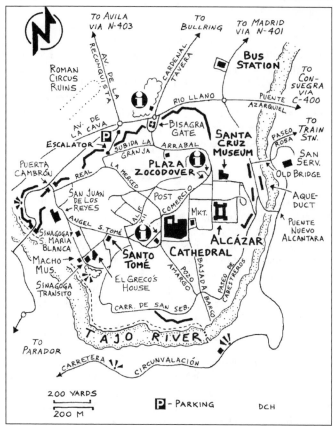

Toledo remained Spain's political capital until 1561, when it reached its natural limits of growth as defined by the Tajo River Gorge. When the king moved to more-spacious Madrid, Toledo was mothballed, only to be rediscovered by 19th-century Romantic travelers who wrote of it as a mystical place.

Today, Toledo thrives as a provincial capital and a busy tourist attraction. It remains the historic, artistic, and spiritual center of Spain. In spite of tremendous tourist crowds, Toledo sits enthroned on its history, much as it was when Europe's most powerful king and El Greco called it home.

Planning Your Time

To properly see Toledo's museums (great El Greco), cathedral (best in Spain), and medieval atmosphere (best after dark), you'll need two nights and a day. Plan carefully for lunch closings, and note that a few sights are closed Monday (including Museo El Greco and Sinagoga del Tránsito).

Toledo is just 60 minutes away from Madrid by bus (2/hr), train (3/day), or taxi (about €65 one-way from Puerta del Sol—negotiate ride without a meter). The new high-speed AVE connection will cut the journey by rail to just 15–20 minutes, when it ever gets finished. A car is useless in Toledo. Ideally, see the town outside of car-rental time; pick up or drop off your car here. **Hertz** is at the train station (tel. 925-253-890) and **Avis** is on Calle Venancio González, below the main square (Mon–Fri 9:30–13:30 & 16:30–20:00, Sat 9:30–14:00, closed Sun, tel. 925-214-535).

ORIENTATION

Toledo sits atop a circular hill, with the cathedral roughly dead center. Lassoed into a tight tangle of streets by the sharp bend of the Tajo River (called the Tejo in Portugal, where it hits the Atlantic at Lisbon), Toledo has Spain's most confusing medieval street plan. But it's a small town of 70,000, the major sights are well-signposted, and most locals will politely point you in the right direction.

Those driving into Toledo can enjoy a scenic big-picture orientation by following the *Ronda de Toledo* signs on a big circular drive around the city. The best time for this is the magic hour before sunset, when the top viewpoints are busy with tired old folks and frisky young lovers.

Look at the map and take a mental orientation walk past Toledo's main sights. Starting in the Plaza Zocódover (zoh-KOH-doh-ver), go southwest along the Calle Comercio. After passing the cathedral on your left, follow the signs to Santo Tomé and the cluster of other sights. The visitor's city lies basically along one small but central street—and most tourists never stray from this axis. Make a point to get lost. The town is small and bounded on three sides by the river. When it's time to get somewhere, I pull out the map or ask, "*¿Dónde está Plaza Zocódover?*"

Tourist Information

Toledo has three TIs. The one that covers Toledo, as well as the region, is in a free-standing brick building just outside the Bisagra Gate (the last surviving gate of the 10th-century fortifications), where those arriving by train or bus enter the old town (Mon–Fri 9:00–18:00, Sat 9:00–19:00, Sun 9:00–15:00, longer hours in summer, tel. 925-220-843).

The second TI is in front of the cathedral on Plaza Ayuntamiento (Mon 10:30–14:30, Tue–Sun 10:30–14:30 & 16:30–19:00, tel. 925-254-030). A handier, third TI, which includes a convenience store and restaurant, is close to Plaza Zocódover at Sillería 14 (daily

10:30–19:00, closes at 18:00 Oct–March, tel. 925-220-300).

Consider the readable local guidebook, *Toledo: Its Art and Its History* (small version for €5, sold all over town). It explains all of the sights (which generally provide no on-site information) and gives you a photo to point at and say, "*¿Dónde está...?*"

Arrival in Toledo

"Arriving" in Toledo means getting uphill to Plaza Zocódover. From the **train station,** that's a 20-minute hike, €3 taxi ride, or easy bus ride (#5 or #6, €0.80, pay on bus, confirm by asking, "*¿Para Plaza Zocódover?*"). You can stow extra baggage at the station. Consider buying a city map at the kiosk; it's better than the free one at the TI. If you're walking, turn right as you leave the station, cross the bridge, pass the bus station, go straight through the roundabout, and continue uphill to the TI and the Bisagra Gate.

If you arrive by **bus,** go upstairs to the station lobby. You'll find the luggage storage and a small bus-information office opposite the cafeteria. Confirm your departure time (probably every half hour on the hour to Madrid). When you buy your return ticket to Madrid—which you can put off until just minutes before you leave—specify you'd like a *directo* bus; the *ruta* trip takes longer (60 min vs. 75 min). From the bus station, Plaza Zocódover is a 15-minute walk (see directions from train station, above), €3 taxi ride, or short bus ride (catch #5 downstairs, underneath the lobby, €0.80, pay on bus).

A series of **escalators** runs near the Bisagra Gate, giving you a free ride up, up, up into town (daily 8:00–22:00). You'll end up near the synagogues and far from Plaza Zocódover, but this doesn't matter. It's great for drivers, who can park free in the streets near the base of the escalator or for a fee (€12.50/day) in the parking lot across from it. Toledo is no fun to drive in. If you don't park near the escalator, drive into town and park in the Garage Alcázar (opposite the Alcázar in the old town—€1.20/hr, €12.50/day).

SIGHTS

▲▲▲**Cathedral**—Holy Toledo! Spain's leading Catholic city has a magnificent cathedral. Shoehorned into the old center, its exterior is hard to appreciate. But the interior is so lofty, rich, and vast that it'll have you wandering around like a Pez dispenser stuck open, whispering "Wow."

Cost and Hours: While the basic cathedral is free, seeing the

Toledo Center

1 Plaza Zocódover
2 Zamorano Knives
3 Tickets & Cathedral Entrance

great art—located in four separate places within the cathedral (the choir, chapter house, sacristy, and treasury)—requires a €5.50 ticket sold in the Tienda la Catedral shop opposite the church entrance (shop open Mon–Sat 10:30–18:00, Sun 14:00–18:00; also rents audioguides for €3). The strict dress-code sign covers even your attitude: no shorts, no tank tops...and no slouching.

The cathedral itself is free and open to the public (daily 8:00–12:00 & 16:00–18:00, no WC in cathedral or cathedral shop). The four sights inside are open 10:30–18:00. Even though the cathedral closes from 12:00 to 16:00, if you have a ticket you can get in and tour the cathedral as well, with fewer crowds. (Note that the cloister is closed to everyone 13:00–15:30.)

Self-Guided Tour: Holy redwood forest, Batman! Wander among the pillars. Sit under one and imagine a time when the light bulbs were candles and the tourists were pilgrims—before the *No Photo* signs, when every window provided spiritual as well as physical light. The cathedral is primarily Gothic, but since it took more than 250 years to build (1226–1495), you'll see a mix of styles—Gothic,

Toledo at a Glance

▲▲▲**Cathedral** One of Europe's best, with a marvelously vast interior and great art. **Hours:** Cathedral—daily 8:00–12:00 & 16:00–18:00; sights inside—daily 10:30–18:00.

▲▲**Santa Cruz Museum** Renaissance building housing wonderful artwork, including 15 El Grecos. **Hours:** Unpredictable.

▲**Alcázar** Imposing former imperial residence that dominates Toledo's skyline. **Hours:** Interior currently closed for renovation.

▲**Santo Tomé** Simple chapel with El Greco's masterpiece, *The Burial of the Count of Orgaz.* **Hours:** Daily 10:00–18:45, until 17:45 mid-Oct–March.

Museo El Greco and "El Greco's House" Replica of El Greco–era home, featuring 20 works by the painter. **Hours:** Tue–Sat 10:00–14:00 & 16:00–21:00 (closes Tue–Sat at 18:00 Dec–Feb), Sun 10:00–13:45, closed Mon.

Sinagoga del Tránsito Museum of Toledo's Jewish past. **Hours:** Tue–Sat 10:00–14:00 & 16:00–17:45, Sun 10:00–13:45, closed Mon.

Sinagoga de Santa María Blanca Harmoniously combines Toledo's three religious influences: Jewish, Christian, and Moorish. **Hours:** Daily April–Sept 10:00–18:45, Oct–March 10:00–17:45.

Museo Victorio Macho Collection of the 20th-century Toledo sculptor's works, with expansive river-gorge view. **Hours:** Mon–Sat 10:00–19:00, Sun 10:00–15:00.

San Juan de los Reyes Monasterio Church/monastery that was to be the final resting place of Isabel and Ferdinand. **Hours:** Daily 10:00–19:00, until 18:00 in winter.

Renaissance, and Baroque. Enjoy the elaborate wrought-iron work, lavish wood carvings, window after colorful window of 500-year-old stained glass, and a sacristy with a collection of paintings that would put any museum on the map.

This confusing collage of great Spanish art deserves a close look. Hire a private guide, freeload on a tour (they come by every few minutes during peak season), or follow this quick tour. Here's a framework for your visit:

Toledo's Cathedral

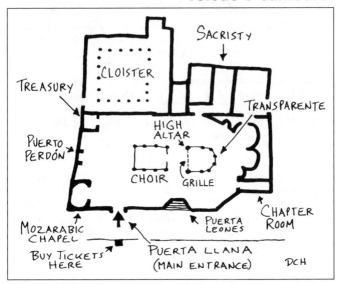

1. High Altar: First, walk to the high altar to marvel through the iron grille at one of the most stunning altars in Spain. Real gold on pine wood, by Flemish, French, and local artists, it's one of the country's best pieces of Gothic art. About-face to the...

2. Choir: Facing the high altar, the choir is famous for its fine carving and requires a piece of your four-part ticket. The

lower wooden stalls are decorated with scenes celebrating the slow one-city-at-a-time Christian victory as the Muslims were pushed back into Africa. Each idealized castle has the reconquered town's name on it, culminating with the final victory at Granada in 1492. The upper stalls (which flank the grand throne of the archbishop) feature Old Testament figures carved out of alabaster. And, as is typical of choir decoration, the carvings on the misericords (the tiny seats allowing tired worshippers to lean while they "stand") feature the frisky, folksy, sexy, profane art of the day. Apparently, since you sat on it, it could never be sacred anyway. There are two fine pipe organs: one 18th-century Baroque and the other 19th-century neoclassical. Note the serene beauty of the 13th-century Madonna and Child at the front, thought to be a gift from the French king to Spain.

The iron grille of the choir is notable for the dedication of the man who built it. Domingo de Céspedes, a Toledo ironworker, accepted the commission to build the grille for 6,000 ducats. The project, which took from 1541 to 1548, was far more costly than he anticipated. The medieval Church didn't accept cost overruns, so to finish it, he sold everything he owned and went into debt. He died a poor—but honorable—man.

3. Chapter House: Face the altar and go around it to your right to the chapter house *(sala capitular)*. Its lavish ceiling celebrates Italian Renaissance humanism with a groundbreaking fresco. You're surrounded by interesting Bible-storytelling frescoes and a pictorial review of 1,900 years of Toledo archbishops. Though the upper row of portraits were not painted from life, the lower portraits were, and therefore are of more historic and artistic interest. Imagine sitting down to church business surrounded by all this tradition and theology. As you leave, notice the iron-pumping cupids carved into the pear-tree panels lining the walls.

The *transparente,* behind the high altar, is a unique feature of the cathedral. In the 1700s, a hole was cut into the ceiling to let a sunbeam brighten the Mass. Melding this big hole into the Gothic church presented a challenge that resulted in a Baroque masterpiece. Gape up at this riot of angels doing flip-flops, babies breathing thin air, bottoms of feet, and gilded sunbursts. Study the altar, which looks chaotic but is actually thoughtfully structured: The good news of salvation springs from baby Jesus, up past the angel (who knows how to hold a big fish correctly) to the Last Supper high above, and beyond into the light-filled dome. I like it, as did, I guess, the long-dead cardinal whose faded red hat hangs from the edge of the hole. (A perk that only cardinals enjoy is choosing the place in the cathedral where their hat will hang until it rots.)

4. Sacristy: The cathedral's sacristy has 20 El Grecos as well as masterpieces by Francisco de Goya, Titian, Peter Paul Rubens, Diego Velázquez, Michelangelo Caravaggio, and Giovanni Bellini. First, notice the fine perspective work on the 18th-century ceiling (frescoed by Lucca Giordano from Naples). Then walk to the end of the room for the most important painting in the collection, El Greco's *The Spoliation* (a.k.a. *The Denuding of Christ*).

Spain's first great painter was Greek, and this is his first masterpiece (1579) after arriving in Toledo. El Greco's painting, which hangs above a marble altar that he may have personally designed, shows Jesus surrounded by a sinister mob and suffering the humiliation of being stripped in public before his execution.

The scarlet robe is about to be yanked off, and the women (lower left) avert their eyes, turning to watch a carpenter at work (lower right) who bores the holes for nailing Jesus to the cross. While the carpenter bears down, Jesus—the other carpenter—looks up to heaven, with a "Why me?" expression. The contrast between the motley crowd gambling for his clothes and Jesus' noble face underscores the quiet dignity with which he endures the humiliation. Jesus' delicate white hand stands out from the flaming red tunic with an odd gesture that's common in El Greco's paintings. Some say this was the way Christians of the day swore they were true believers, not merely Christians-for-convenience, like former Muslims or Jews who converted out of necessity.

On the right is a rare religious painting by Goya, the *Betrayal of Christ*, which shows Judas preparing to kiss Jesus, thus identifying him to the Roman soldiers. Enjoy the many other El Grecos. Find the small but lifelike 17th-century carving of St. Francis by Pedro de Mena (to your right as you entered the door).

5. Treasury: The *tesoro* has plenty to see. The highlight is the 10-foot-high, 430-pound monstrance—the tower designed to hold the Holy Communion bread (the Host) during the festival of Corpus Christi (body of Christ) as it parades through the city. Built in 1517 by Enrique de Arfe, it's made of 5,000 individual pieces held together by 12,500 screws. There are diamonds, emeralds, rubies, and 400 pounds of gold-plated silver. The inner part is 35 pounds of solid gold. Yeow. The base is a later addition from the Baroque period. Traditionally, it's thought that much of this gold and silver arrived in Columbus' first load home.

To the right of the monstrance, find the fancy sword of Franco. To the right of that is a gift from St. Louis, the king of France—a 700-year-old Bible printed and beautifully illustrated by French monks. (It's actually a copy, and the precious original is stored elsewhere.) Imagine the exquisite experience for medieval eyes of reading this, with its lavish illustrations. The finely-painted small crucifix on the opposite side—by the great Gothic Florentine painter Fra Angelico—depicts Jesus alive on the back and dead on the front. This was a gift from Mussolini to Franco. Hmmm. There's even a gift in this room from Toledo's sister city, Toledo, Ohio.

If you're at the cathedral between 9:00 and 9:15, you can peek into the otherwise-locked **Mozarabic Chapel** (Capilla Mozárabe). The Visigothic Mass, the oldest surviving Christian ritual in Western Europe, starts at 9:15 (9:45 on Sun). You're welcome to partake in this stirring example of peaceful coexistence of faiths—but once the door closes, you're a Visigoth for 30 minutes.

▲▲**Santa Cruz Museum**—For years, this museum has been in a confused state of renovation—not really open, not really closed. During renovation, the museum's cloister and a room full of its best art will be open and free. If the core of the building is filled with a temporary exhibit, you can generally wander in for a free look. The building's Plateresque facade is worth seeing anytime.

This great Renaissance building was an orphanage and hospital, built from money left by the humanist and diplomat Cardinal Mendoza when he died in 1495. The cardinal, confirmed as Chancellor of Castile by Queen Isabel, was so influential he was called "the third king." The building is in the form of a Greek cross under a Moorish dome. After renovation, the arms of the building—formerly wards—will be filled with 16th-century art, tapestries, furniture, armor, and documents. It'll be a stately, classical, music-filled setting with a cruel lack of English information (Mon–Sat 10:00–18:30, Sun 10:00–14:00, just off Plaza Zocódover, go through arch, Cervantes 3).

The collection includes 15 El Grecos. The highlight: the impressive *Assumption of Mary,* a spiritual poem on canvas. This altarpiece, finished one year before El Greco's death (in 1614), is the culmination of his unique style, combining all of his techniques to express an other-worldly event.

While on earth, the city of Toledo sleeps, a vision taking place overhead. An angel in a billowing robe spreads his wings and flies up, supporting Mary, the mother of Christ. She floats up through warped space, to be serenaded by angels and wrapped in the radiant light of the Holy Spirit. Mary flickers and ripples, charged from within by her spiritual ecstasy, caught up in a vision that takes her breath away. No painter before or since has captured the supernatural world better than El Greco.

Find the lavish but faded Astrolabe Tapestry (c. 1480, Belgian) which shows a new world view at the dawn of the Renaissance and the age of discovery: God oversees all, as Atlas spins the Cosmos containing the circular Earth, and the wisdom gang (far right) heralds the new age.

An enormous blue banner hangs like a long, skinny tooth opposite the entry. This flew from the flagship of Don Juan of Austria and recalls the pivotal 1571 naval victory over the Muslims at the Battle of Lepanto off the coast of Greece. Lepanto was a key victory in the centuries-long struggle of Christian Europe against the Muslim threat.

▲**Alcázar**—This huge former imperial residence—built on the site of Roman, Visigothic, and Moorish fortresses—dominates the Toledo skyline. Currently closed for renovation, it will be the National Military Museum when it reopens, likely in 2007. The Alcázar became a kind of right-wing Alamo during Spain's civil war, when a force of Franco's Nationalists (and hundreds of hostages) were besieged for two months in 1936. Finally,

El Greco
(1541–1614)

Born on Crete and trained in Venice, Doménikos Theoto-kópoulos (tongue-tied friends just called him "The Greek") came to Spain to get a job decorating El Escorial. He failed there, but succeeded in Toledo, where he spent the last 37 years of his life. He mixed all three regional influences into his palette. From his Greek homeland, he absorbed the solemn, abstract style of icons. In Italy, he learned the bold use of color, elongated figures, twisting poses, and dramatic style of the later Renaissance. These styles were then fused in the fires of fanatic Spanish-Catholic devotion.

Not bound by the realism so important to his 16th-century contemporaries, El Greco painted dramatic visions of striking colors and figures—bodies unnatural and lengthened as though stretched between Heaven and Earth. He painted souls, not faces. His work is on display at nearly every sight in Toledo. Thoroughly modern in his disregard of realism, he didn't impress the austere Spanish king. But his art seems as fresh as contemporary art today.

after many fierce but futile Republican attacks, Franco sent in an army that took Toledo and freed the Alcázar. The place was rebuilt and glorified under Franco.

▲**Tourist Train**—For great city views, hop on the cheesy Tren Imperial Tourist Tram. Crass as it feels, you get a 50-minute putt-putt through Toledo and around the Tajo River Gorge. It's a great way to get a general city overview and for non-drivers to enjoy views of the city from across the Tajo Gorge (€3.60, buy ticket from TI at Sillería 14, daily from 11:00, leaves Plaza Zocódover on the hour, tape-recorded English/Spanish commentary, no photo stops but it goes slow; for the best views of Toledo across the gorge, sit on right side, not behind driver; tel. 925-220-300).

Southwest Toledo

▲**Santo Tomé**—A simple chapel holds El Greco's most-loved painting. *The Burial of the Count of Orgaz* couples Heaven and Earth in a way only The Greek could. It feels so right to see a painting left in situ where the artist put it 400 years ago. Take this slow. Stay a while—let it perform.

The year is 1312. You're at the burial of the good count, who's being laid to rest right here in this chapel. He was so holy, even saints Augustine and Stephen have come down from Heaven to be pallbearers. (The painting's subtitle is "Such is the reward for those who serve God and his saints.")

More than 250 years later, in 1586, a priest hired El Greco to make a painting of the burial to hang over the count's tomb. The funeral is attended by all of Toledo's most distinguished citizens. The painting is divided in two by a serene line of noble faces—Heaven above and Earth below. Above the line of long, somber faces, the count's soul, symbolized by a little baby, rises up through a mystical birth canal to be reborn in Heaven, where he's greeted by Jesus, Mary, and all the saints. A spiritual wind blows through as colors change and shapes stretch. This is Counter-Reformation propaganda—notice Jesus pointing to St. Peter, the symbol of the pope in Rome, who controls the keys to the Pearly Gates. Each face is a detailed portrait. El Greco himself (eyeballing you, 7th figure in from the left) is the only one not involved in the burial. The boy in the foreground—pointing to the two saints as if to say, "One's from the first century, the other's from the fourth...it's a miracle!"—is El Greco's son. On the handkerchief in the boy's pocket is El Greco's signature, written in Greek (€1.50, daily 10:00–18:45, until 17:45 mid-Oct–March, free audioguide, tel. 925-256-098).

Museo El Greco and "El Greco's House"—While many call this El Greco's House, it's actually a traditionally-furnished Renaissance "monument house" built near where he likely lived. You'll see about 20 El Greco paintings, including his masterful *View of Toledo* and portraits of the Apostles. Period pottery and furniture recreate the home and studio of this sophisticated foreigner, who hung out with Spain's writers, bishops, and philosophers (€2.40, free Sat afternoon from 14:30 and all day Sun; Tue–Sat 10:00–14:00 & 16:00–21:00, until 18:00 in winter, Sun 10:00–13:45, closed Mon, Samuel Levi 3).

Sinagoga del Tránsito (Museo Sefardí)—Built in 1361, this is the best surviving slice of Toledo's Jewish past. The museum displays Jewish artifacts, including costumes, menorahs, and books (€2.40, free Sat afternoon from 14:30 and all day Sun, audioguide-€3; Tue–Sat 10:00–14:00 & 16:00–21:00, Sun 10:00–13:45, Dec–Feb closes Tue–Sat at 18:00, closed Mon, near Museo El Greco, with same price and hours, on Calle de los Reyes Católicos).

The synagogue's interior decor looks more Muslim than Jewish. After Christians reconquered the city in 1085, many Moorish workmen stayed on, beautifying the city with their unique style called Mudejar. The synagogue's intricate, geometrical carving (in alabaster) features leaves, vines, and flowers, but no human shapes, since that would violate the Koran's prohibition on making "graven images." In the frieze (running along the upper wall, just below the ceiling), the Arabic-looking script is actually Hebrew, quoting psalms from the Bible. The back-wall balcony is the traditional separate worship area for women.

This 14th-century synagogue was built at the peak of Toledo's enlightened tolerance—built for Jews, with Christian approval, by

Toledo's Muslim Legacy

You can see the Moorish influence in the:
- Sinagoga del Tránsito's Mudejar plasterwork
- Sinagoga de Santa María Blanca's mosque-like horseshoe arches
- Bisagra Gate's horseshoe arch
- Square minaret-like towers (like on the Alcázar, originally built by the Moors)
- The city's labyrinthine, medina-like streets

Moorish craftsmen. Nowhere else in the city does Toledo's three-culture legacy—Christians, Muslims, and Jews—shine brighter than at this synagogue. But in 1391, just a few decades after it was built, Spanish kings began a violent campaign to unite Spain as a Christian nation, forcing Jews and Muslims to convert or leave. In 1492, Ferdinand and Isabel exiled Spain's remaining Jews. It's estimated that, in the 15th century, a third of Spain's Jews were killed, a third survived by converting to Christianity, and a third moved elsewhere.

Sinagoga de Santa María Blanca—This synagogue-turned-church with Moorish horseshoe arches and wall carvings is an eclectic but harmonious gem, and a vivid reminder of the religious cultures that shared this city (€1.50, daily 10:00–18:45, Oct–March until 17:45, no photos allowed, Calle de los Reyes Católicos 2–4).

Museo Victorio Macho—After *mucho* El Greco, try Macho. Overlooking the gorge, this small, attractive museum—once the home and workshop of the early-20th-century sculptor Victorio Macho—offers several rooms of his bold work interspersed with view terraces. The highlight is *La Madre,* Macho's life-size sculpture of an older woman sitting in a chair. But the big draw for many is the air-conditioned theater featuring two fast-moving nine-minute videos. One sweeps through Toledo's history, while the other focuses on Jews in Toledo (€3, half-price for young and old, Mon–Sat 10:00–19:00, Sun 10:00–15:00, request video showing in English, longer 29-minute history video available, Plaza de Victorio Macho 2, between the two *sinagogas* listed above, tel. 925-284-225).

The **river gorge view** from the Museo Vitorio Macho terrace (or free terraces nearby) shows well how the River Tajo served as a formidable moat protecting the city. Imagine trying to attack from this side. The 14th-century bridge on the right and the remains of a bridge on the left connected the town with the region's *cigarrales*—mansions of wealthy families with orchards of figs and apricots that dot the hillside even today.

San Juan de los Reyes Monasterio—St. John of the Monarchs is a grand, generally Flemish-style monastery, church, and cloisters—

Plaza Zocódover

TO BISAGRA GATE

NUNEZ

ALF.

SILLERIA

CADENAS

C. NUEVA

CALLE TOLEDO OHIO

CALLE COMERCIO

PLAZA ZOCÓ-DOVER

ARCH

TO SANTA CRUZ MUSEUM

CAFE TELESFORO

BARRIO REY

Mc DONALDS

TO CATHEDRAL & EL GRECO'S HOUSE

MAGDALENA CHURCH

CUESTA CARLOS IV

ALCÁZAR

JUAN LAB.

❶ Hotel Las Conchas
❷ Hotel Imperio
❸ Hostal Centro
❹ Hostal Nuevo Labrador
❺ Hotel Maravilla
❻ Pensión Castilla
❼ Pensión Lumbreras
❽ Rincón de Eloy Restaurant
❾ Restaurant La Parrilla
❿ Santo Tomé Mazapán Shop

* NOT TO SCALE-
PLAZA ZOC. TO
PENSION LUMBRERAS
IS A 5 MIN. WALK

N

thought-provoking because the Catholic Monarchs (Isabel and Ferdinand) planned to be buried here. But after the Moors were expelled in 1492 from Granada, their royal bodies were planted there to show Spain's commitment to maintaining a Moor-free peninsula. Today the courtyard is a delightful spot where happy critters carved into the columns seem to chirp with the birds in the trees. Notice the arrows and yoke representing the kingdom's unity achieved by the Royal Monarchs (€1.50, daily 10:00–19:00, until 18:00 in winter, San Juan de los Reyes 2, tel. 925-223-802).

SHOPPING

Toledo probably sells as many souvenirs as any city in Spain. This is the place to buy medieval-looking swords, armor, maces, three-legged stools, lethal-looking letter-openers, and other nouveau antiques. It's also Spain's damascene center, where, for centuries, craftspeople have inlaid black steel with gold, silver, and copper wire.

At the workshop of English-speaking **Mariano Zamorano,** you can see swords and knives being made. Judging by what's left of Mariano's hand, his knives are among the sharpest (Mon–Sat 9:00–14:00 & 16:00–19:00, closed Sat afternoon and Sun, Calle Ciudad 19, near cathedral and Plaza Ayuntamiento, tel. 925-222-634, www.marianozamorano.com).

El Martes, Toledo's colorful outdoor flea market, bustles on

Paseo de Marchen, better known to locals as "La Vega" (near TI at Bisagra Gate), on Tuesdays from 9:00 to 14:00.

SLEEPING

Madrid day-trippers darken the sunlit cobbles, but few stay to see Toledo's medieval moonrise. Spend the night. Spring and fall are high season; November through March and July and August are less busy. There are no private rooms for rent.

Near Plaza Zocódover

$$ **Hotel Las Conchas,** a three-star hotel, gleams with marble and sheer pride. It's so sleek and slick it almost feels more like a hospital than a hotel. Its 35 rooms are plenty comfortable (Sb-€55, Db-€75, Db with terrace-€85, breakfast-€5, includes tax, 5 percent discount with this book, air-con, near the Alcázar at Juan Labrador 8, tel. 925-210-760, fax 925-224-271, www.lasconchas.com, lasconchas @ctv.es, Sole SE).

$ **Hotel Imperio** is well run, offering 21 basic air-conditioned rooms with marginal beds in a handy old-town location. Weekends can be noisy; ask for a *tranquilo* room (Sb-€28, Db-€42, Tb-€57, includes tax, 5 percent discount with this book, elevator, cheery café, from Calle Comercio at #38 go a block uphill to Calle Cadenas 5, tel. 925-227-650, fax 925-253-183, www.terra.es/personal/himperio, himperio@teleline.es, friendly Pablo and Esther SE).

$ **Hostal Centro** rents 28 modern, clean, and comfy rooms just around the corner (Sb-€30, Db-€45, Tb-€60, roof garden, 50 yards off Plaza Zocódover, first right off Calle Comercio at Calle Nueva 13, tel. 925-257-091, fax 925-257-848, www.hostalcentro.com, hostalcentro@telefonica.net, Asun or Ángel, SE).

Sleep Code

(€1 = about $1.10, country code: 34)
S = Single, **D** = Double/Twin, **T** = Triple, **Q** = Quad, **b** = bathroom, **s** = shower only, **no CC** = Credit Cards not accepted, **SE** = Speaks English, **NSE** = No English. Breakfast and the 7 percent IVA tax are not included unless noted. Credit cards are accepted unless otherwise noted.

To help you easily sort through these listings, I've divided the rooms into three categories, based on the price for a standard double room with bath during high season:

$$$ **Higher Priced**—Most rooms €90 or more.
$$ **Moderately Priced**—Most rooms between €60–90.
$ **Lower Priced**—Most rooms €60 or less.

$ The quiet, modern **Hostal Nuevo Labrador,** with 14 clean, shiny, and spacious rooms, is another good value (Sb-€28, Db-€42, Tb-€55, Qb-€65, includes tax, no breakfast, elevator, Juan Labrador 10, half-board possible in next-door restaurant Rincón de Eloy, tel. 925-222-620, fax 925-229-399, hostalcentro@telefonica.net, NSE, jointly owned with Hostal Centro, above).

$ **Hotel Maravilla,** wonderfully central and convenient, has gloomy, claustrophobic halls and 18 simple rooms (Sb-€33, Db-€50, Tb-€67, Qb-€80, includes tax, back rooms are quieter, air-con, a block behind Plaza Zocódover at Plaza de Barrio Rey 5, tel. 925-228-317, fax 925-228-155, hostalmaravilla@infonegocio.com, Felisa María SE).

$ **Pensión Castilla,** a family-run cheapie, has seven basic rooms (S-€18, Db-€28, extra bed possible, no CC, fans, Calle Recoletos 6, tel. 925-256-318, Teresa NSE).

$ **Pensión Lumbreras** has a tranquil courtyard and 12 simple rooms, some with views, including rooms 3, 6, and 7 (S-€19, D-€33, reception is at Carlo V Hotel around the corner, air-con, Juan Labrador 9, tel. 925-221-571).

Near the Bisagra Gate

$$$ **Hostal del Cardenal,** a 17th-century cardinal's palace built into Toledo's wall, is quiet and elegant with a cool garden and a stuffy restaurant. This poor-man's parador, at the dusty old gate of Toledo, is closest to the station but below all the old-town action— however, the new escalator takes the sweat out of getting into town (Sb-€63, Db-€102, Tb-€133, 20 percent cheaper mid-Dec through mid-March, breakfast-€7.28, air-con, nearby parking-€12.50/day, *serioso* staff, enter through town wall 100 yards below Bisagra Gate, Paseo de Recaredo 24, tel. 925-224-900, fax 925-222-991, www .hostaldelcardenal.com, cardenal@hostaldelcardenal.com).

$ **Hotel Sol,** with 25 newly-decorated rooms in tasteful colors, is a great value. It's on a quiet street halfway between the Bisagra Gate and Plaza Zocódover (Sb-€40, Db-€55, Tb-€68, includes tax, breakfast-€3.60, 10 percent discount with this book, air-con, parking-€8/day, 50 yards down lane off busy main drag at Hotel Real, Azacanes 8, tel. 925-213-650, fax 925-216-159, www.fedeto.es /hotel-sol, hotel.sol@to.adade.es, José Carlos SE). Their "Hostal Sol" annex across the street is just as comfortable and a bit cheaper. A handy launderette is next door.

$ **Hostal Hospedería de los Reyes,** good for drivers, has 15 colorful and thoughtfully-appointed rooms in a new, attractive, yellow building 100 yards north of the Bisagra Gate, outside the wall (Sb-€38, Db-€50, includes breakfast, air-con, elevator, Perala 37, tel. 925-283-667, fax 925-283-668, www.hospederiadelosreyes.com).

Toledo Hotels and Restaurants

```
200 YARDS
200 METERS
```
← – VIEW

TO MADRID & ❻
TO ❶❽
BUS STATION

BISAGRA GATE
🛈
RIO LLANO

CITY WALLS

TO ❽
SUBIDA LA GRANJA
ALTIBES
ESCALATOR
PLAZA MERCED

CALLE REAL
S. ILD.
S. LEO.
MERCED
DON
❷

CUESTA

RIO
NUNEZ
ARCO

S. ROMAN
❶ ❻
POST
NAV.
CARDENAS
FABIO
BLANCO
❸

TO TRAIN STATION & ❼

SANTA CRUZ MUSEUM
❶❷
GILL
CERVANTES
🛈
TO TRAIN STN.

SAN JUAN LOS REYES

❶❹
LA PLATA
❶❶
COMERCIO
TAXIS

SANTO TOMÉ
ANGEL
❶❺
ALFONSO
TOMÉ
TRINIDAD
SALV.
❶❼

ALCÁZAR
❾
❹
CATHEDRAL

SINAGOGA SANTA MARIA BLANCA
❶❸
SAN JUAN DIO
MORO
S. URSULA
ISABEL
❶❺
❺

MUSEO VICTORIO MACHO
❸
PARK
EL GRECO'S HOUSE
PLAZA AYUNTAMIENTO & CITY HALL
D C H

RIO TAJO
SINAGOGA TRANSITO

NOTE: STREET WIDTH IS EXAGGERATED FOR CLARITY

❶ Hostal & Rest. del Cardenal
❷ Hotel Sol
❸ Hotel Pintor El Greco
❹ La Posada de Manolo
❺ Hotel Santa Isabel
❻ To Hostal Gavilánes II, Hostal Madrid & Hotel Maria Cristina
❼ To Youth Hostel San Servando
❽ To Parador Conde de Orgaz & Hotel Residencia la Almazara

❾ Los Cuatro Tiempos Rest.
❿ Restaurant Casa Aurelio I
⓫ Rest. Casa Aurelio II & III (on Sinagoga St.) & Pizzeria Pastucci
⓬ Rest. Cason Lopez de Toledo
⓭ La Perdiz Restaurant
⓮ Restaurante-Meson Palacios
⓯ Bar Cervecería Gambrinus
⓰ Taverna de Amboades
⓱ Mercado Municipal (Market)
⓲ To Hostal Hospederia de los Reyes

Deep in Toledo

$$$ **Hotel Pintor El Greco,** at the far end of the old town, has 33 plush and rustic-feeling rooms with all the comforts, yet it's in a historic 17th-century building. A block from Santo Tomé in a Jewish Quarter garden, it's very quiet (Sb-€83, Db-€103, Tb-€122, tax not included, elevator, air-con, Alamillos del Tránsito 13, tel. 925-285-191, fax 925-215-819, www.hotelpintorelgreco.com, info@hotelpintorelgreco.com).

$$ La Posada de Manolo rents 14 thoughtfully-furnished rooms across from the downhill corner of the cathedral. Manolo Junior recently opened "The House of Manolo" according to his father's vision: a comfortable place with each of its three floors themed a little differently—Moorish, Jewish, and Christian (Sb-€42, Db-€66, big Db-€72–84, includes buffet breakfast, 10 percent discount when booked directly with this book, no elevator, air-con, 2 nice view terraces, Calle Sixto Ramón Parro 8, tel. 925-282-250, fax 925-282-251, www.laposadademanolo.com, laposadademanolo @wanadoo.es).

$ Hotel Santa Isabel, in a 15th-century building two blocks from the cathedral, has 42 clean, modern, and comfortable rooms and squeaky tile hallways (Sb-€30, Db-€45, Tb-€62, includes tax, breakfast-€4, elevator, air-con, great roof terrace; buried deep in old town so take a taxi instead of the bus; drivers enter from Calle Pozo Amargo, parking-€6; Calle Santa Isabel 24, tel. 925-253-120, fax 925-253-136, www.santa-isabel.com, santa-isabel@arrakis.es, Andres SE).

Outside of Town

$$$ Hotel María Cristina, next to the bullring, is part 15th-century and all modern. This sprawling 74-room hotel has all the comforts under a thin layer of prefab tradition (Sb-€62, Db-€97, Tb-€130, €154 suites available, tax not included, breakfast-€6, elevator, air-con, attached restaurant, parking-€9.35/day, Marqués de Mendigorría 1, tel. 925-213-202, fax 925-212-650, www.hotelmariacristina.com, informacion@hotelmariacristina.com, SE).

$ On the road to Madrid (near bullring): There's a conspiracy of clean, modern, and hardworking little hotels with comfy rooms a five-minute walk beyond the Bisagra Gate near the bus station and bullring (Plaza de Toros, bullfights only on holidays). Drivers enjoy easy parking here. While it's a 15-minute uphill hike to the old-town action, buses #4 and #6 go from just west of Hostal Madrid directly to Plaza de Zocódover. Two good bets are **Hostal Gavilánes II** (18 renovated rooms, Sb-€33, Db-€42, Db suite-€81, Tb-€56, Qb-€65, includes taxes, breakfast-€2.50, parking-€5.50/day, air-con, Marqués de Mendigorría 14, tel. & fax 925-211-628, www.gavilanes.to, hostallosgavilanes2@hotmail.com or javi@acceso0.es, NSE) and **Hostal Madrid** (20 rooms, Sb-€27, Db-€39, Tb-€53, includes tax, café next door, parking-€6/day, air-con, Marqués de Mendigorría 7, tel. 925-221-114, fax 925-228-113, NSE). This *hostal* rents nine lesser rooms in an annex across the street.

$ Hostel: The **Albergue Juvenil San Servando** youth hostel is lavish and newly-renovated but cheap, with small rooms for two, three, or four people; a swimming pool; views; cafeteria; and good management (95 beds, €8.60 per bed if under age 26, €11.30 if age 26 or older, hostel membership required—you can buy it here for

€11, add €2.10 to include breakfast, in 10th-century Arab castle of
San Servando, 10-min walk from train station, 15-min hike from
town center, over Puente Viejo outside town, tel. 925-224-554,
reservations tel. 925-267-729, ralberguesto@jccm.es, NSE).

Outside of Town with the Grand Toledo View

$$$ Toledo's **Parador Nacional Conde de Orgaz** is one of Spain's
best-known inns, enjoying the same Toledo view El Greco made
famous from across the Tajo Gorge (76 rooms, Sb-€58, Db-€120,
Db with view-€136, Tb with view-€179, breakfast-€10, €26 *menus*
in their fine restaurant overlooking Toledo, 2 windy miles from town
at Cerro del Emperador, tel. 925-221-850, fax 925-225-166, www
.parador.es/english/index.jsp, toledo@parador.es, SE).

$ **Hotel Residencia La Almazara** was the summer residence of
a 16th-century archbishop of Toledo. A friend of the cardinal and
fond of this location's classic Toledo view, El Greco hung out here
for inspiration. A lumbering old place with cushy public rooms, 28
simple bedrooms, and a sprawling garden, it's truly in the country but
just 1.5 miles out of Toledo (Sb-€30, Db-€41, Db with view-€57,
Tb-€48, 10 rooms have view, air-con, Ctra. de Arges 47, follow signs
from circular Ronda de Toledo road, tel. 925-223-866, fax 925-250-
562, www.hotelalmazara.com, reservas@hotelalmazara.com).

EATING

Dining in Traditional Elegance

A day full of El Greco and the romance of Toledo after dark puts me
in the mood for game. Typical Toledo dishes include partridge
(perdiz), venison *(venado)*, wild boar *(jabalí)*, roast suckling pig
(cochinillo asado), or baby lamb *(cordero)* similarly roasted after a few
weeks of mother's milk. After dinner, find a *mazapán* place (such as
Santo Tomé) for dessert.

Los Cuatro Tiempos Restaurante specializes in local game and
roasts, proficiently served in a tasteful and elegant setting (€18 set
menu lunches, €25–30 à la carte dinners, daily 13:30–16:00 &
20:30–23:00, at downhill corner of cathedral at Sixto Ramón Parro
5, tel. 925-223-782).

Toledo's three **Casa Aurelio** restaurants all offer traditional
cooking (game, roast suckling pig, traditional soup), with a classy
atmosphere more memorable than the meals (13:00–16:30 &
20:00–23:30, 2 closed Sun night, each closed either Mon, Tue, or
Wed, air-con). All are within three blocks of the cathedral: Plaza
Ayuntamiento 4 is festive (tel. 925-227-716), Sinagoga 6 is most
típico (tel. 925-222-097), and Sinagoga 1 is the newest and dressi-
est, with a wine cellar (popular with Toledo's political class, tel.
925-221-392).

Restaurante Casón López de Toledo, a fancy restaurant located in an old noble palace, specializes in Castilian food, particularly venison and partridge. Its character unfolds upstairs (€18 meals, Mon–Sat 13:30–16:00 & 20:30–23:30, closed Sun, Calle Sillería 3, near Plaza Zocódover, tel. 925-254-774).

Hostal del Cardenal Restaurante, a classic hotel restaurant near the Bisagra Gate at the bottom of town, is understandably popular with tourists for its decent traditional roast dishes (daily 13:00–16:00 & 20:30–23:30, Puerto de Recaredo 24, tel. 925-220-862).

For a splurge near the Santa Tomé sights, consider the classy **La Perdiz,** which offers partridge (as the restaurant's name suggests), venison, suckling pig, fish, and more (Tue–Sat 13:00–16:00 & 20:00–23:00, closes Sun about 16:00, closed Mon and first half of Aug, Calle de los Reyes Católicos 7, tel. 925-214-658).

Eating Simply, but Well

Restaurante-Mesón Palacios serves good regional food at reasonable prices in a warm and friendly atmosphere. Their bean soup with partridge *(judías con perdiz)* and fish-stuffed peppers *(pimientos de piquillo rellenos de pescado)* are the most popular appetizers among locals (Mon–Sat from 13:00 and from 19:30, closed Sun, Alfonso X 3, near Plaza de San Vicente, tel. 925-215-972, Jesús is appropriately friendly).

Rincón de Eloy is bright, modern, and a cool refuge for lunch on a hot day (€9.50 *menu,* Mon–Sat 13:00–16:00 & 20:00–22:30, closed Sun night, air-con, Juan Labrador 10, near Alcázar, tel. 925-229-399).

Bar Cervecería Gambrinus is a good tapas bar (try their local veal stew *carcamusas* in small frying pans). Restaurant seating is available in its leafy courtyard or in the more elegant upstairs area (daily 9:00–24:00, near Santo Tomé at Santo Tomé 10, tel. 925-214-440).

Restaurante La Parrilla is on a tiny square behind Plaza Zocódover (facing the Casa Telesforo on Plaza Zocódover, go left down alley 30 yards to Plaza de Barrio Rey). The bars and cafés on Plaza Zocódover are reasonable, seasoned with some fine people-watching.

At **Taverna de Amboades,** a humble but earnest wine-and-tapas bar near the Bisagra Gate, expert Miguel Ángel enjoys explaining the differences among Spanish wines. To try some really good wines with quality local cheese and meat, drop by and let Miguel impress you (2 quality wines and a plate of cheese and meat for €7, Tue–Sat 19:30–24:00, also Thu–Sun 12:30–16:00, closed Mon, Alfonso VI 5, mobile 678-483-749).

Pizzeria Pastucci is the local favorite for pizza (Tue–Sun 12:00–16:00 & 19:00–24:00, closed Mon, near cathedral at Calle de la Sinagoga 10).

Picnics are best assembled at the **Mercado Municipal** on Plaza Mayor (on the Alcázar side of cathedral, with a supermarket inside open Mon–Sat 9:00–20:00 and stalls open mostly in the mornings until 14:00, closed Sun). This is a fun market to prowl, even if you don't need food. If you feel like munching a paper-plate-size Communion wafer, one of the stalls sells crispy bags of *obleas*—a great gift for your favorite pastor.

And for Dessert: *Mazapán*

Toledo's famous almond-fruity-sweet *mazapán* is sold all over town. Locals say the best is made by **Santo Tomé** (several outlets, including a handy one on Plaza Zocódover, daily 9:00–22:22). Browse their tempting window displays. They sell *mazapán* goodies individually (2 for about €1, *sin relleno*—without filling—is for purists, *de piñon* has pine nuts, *imperiales* is with almonds, others have fruit fillings) or in small mixed boxes. Their *Toledanas* is a crumbly cookie favorite with a subtle thread of pumpkin filling.

For a sweet and romantic evening moment, pick up a few pastries and head down to the cathedral. Sit on the Plaza Ayuntamiento's benches (or stretch out on the stone wall to the right of the TI). The fountain is on your right, Spain's best-looking city hall is behind you, and there before you: her top cathedral, built back when Toledo was Spain's capital, shining brightly against the black night sky.

TRANSPORTATION CONNECTIONS

Far more buses than trains connect Toledo with Madrid—take the bus.

To Madrid: by bus (2/hr, 60–75 min, *directo* is faster than *ruta*, Madrid's Estación sur Autobuses, Metro: Mendez Álvaro, Continental Auto bus company, tel. 925-223-641), **by train** (5/day weekdays, 3/day weekends 1.25 hrs; while new AVE fast train is being completed, you need to bus from Toledo to Algodor, then take the train to Madrid's Atocha station), **by car** (40 miles, 1 hr). Toledo bus info: tel. 925-215-850; train info: tel. 902-240-202.

To Granada: To get to Granada from Toledo, it's best to transfer in Madrid. Ideally, return to Madrid to spend the night, then catch the morning train to Granada (departs Chamartín station at 8:10, confirm time at station, 6 hrs).

La Mancha

(Visit only if you're driving between Toledo and Granada.) Nowhere else is Spain so vast, flat, and radically monotonous. La Mancha, from the Arabic word for "parched earth," makes you feel small—lost in rough seas of olive-green polka dots. Random buildings look like houses and hotels hurled off some heavenly Monopoly board. It's a rough land where roadkill is left to rot, bugs ricochet off the windshield and keep on flying, and hitchhikers wear red dresses and aim to take you for the ride.

This is the setting of Miguel de Cervantes' *Don Quixote,* published in the early 17th century, after England sank the Armada and the Spanish Empire began its decline. Cervantes' star character fights doggedly for good, for justice, and against the fall of Spain and its traditional old-regime empire. Ignoring reality, Don Quixote is a hero fighting a hopeless battle. Stark La Mancha is the perfect stage.

The epitome of Don Quixote country, the town of **Consuegra** (TI tel. 925-475-731) must be the La Mancha Cervantes had in mind. Drive up to the ruined 12th-century castle and joust with a windmill. It's hot and buggy here, but the powerful view overlooking the village, with its sun-bleached, light-red roofs; modern concrete reality; and harsh, windy silence makes for a profound picnic (a 1-hour drive south of Toledo). The castle belonged to the Knights of St. John (12th and 13th centuries) and is associated with their trip to Jerusalem during the Crusades. Originally built from the ruins of a nearby Roman circus, it has been newly restored (€1.50). Sorry, the windmills are post-Cervantes, only 200 to 300 years old.

If you've seen windmills, the next castle north (above Almonacid, 8 miles from Toledo) is free and more interesting than the Consuegra castle. Follow the ruined lane past the ruined church up to the ruined castle. The jovial locals hike up with kids and kites.

Route Tips for Drivers

Granada to Toledo (250 miles, 5 hrs): The Granada–Toledo drive is long, hot, and boring. Start early to minimize the heat and make the best time you can. Follow signs for *Madrid/Jaén/N323* into what some call "the Spanish Nebraska"—La Mancha. After Puerto Lapice, you'll see the Toledo exit.

Arriving in Toledo by car: View the city from many angles along the Circunvalación road across the Tajo Gorge. Stop at the street-side viewpoint or drive to Parador Conde de Orgaz just south of town for the view (from the balcony) that El Greco made famous in his portrait of Toledo.

As people have for centuries, you may enter Toledo via the Bisagra Gate. Or, to take advantage of the new escalator (opposite recommended Hostal del Cardenal, explained above), park across the street at the pay lot or free on the streets beyond. Those driving into town can park across the street from the Alcázar (€1.20/hr, €12/day).

Toledo to Madrid (40 miles, 1 hr): It's a speedy *autovía* north, past one last bullboard to Madrid (on N401). The highways converge into M30, which circles Madrid. Follow it to the left ("*Nor*" or "*Oeste*") and take the Plaza de España exit to get back to Gran

Vía. If you're airport-bound, keep heading into Madrid until you see the airplane symbol (N-II). Turn in your rental car at terminal T-1.

If your Madrid hotel is close to the Prado, return your car at the Atocha train station and walk or take the subway from Atocha RENFE to Sol. To drive to Atocha, take the exit off M-30 for Plaza de Legazpi, then take Delicias (second on your right off the square). Parking for car return is on the north side of the train station.

GRANADA

For a time, Granada was the grandest city in Spain, but in the end, it was left in the historic dust. Today it's a provincial town with more than its share of history and bumper stickers reading, "Life is short. Don't run." We'll keep things fun and simple, settling down in the old center and exploring monuments of the Moorish  civilization and monuments of its conquest. And we'll taste the treats of an African-flavored culture that survives today.

Granada's magnificent Alhambra fortress was the last stronghold of the Moorish kingdom in Spain. The city's exotically tangled Moorish quarter bustles under the grand Alhambra, which glows red in the evening while locals stroll, enjoying the city's cool late-night charms.

There is an old saying: "Give him a coin, woman, for there is nothing worse in this life than to be blind in Granada." This city has much to see, yet it reveals itself in unpredictable ways. It takes a poet to sort through the jigsaw-puzzle pieces of Granada. Peer through the intricate lattice of a Moorish window. Hear water burbling unseen among the labyrinthine hedges of the Generalife garden. Listen to a flute trilling deep in the swirl of alleys around the cathedral. Don't be blind in Granada—open your senses.

Planning Your Time

Granada is worth one day and two nights. Consider the night-train connection with Madrid (or Barcelona), giving the city a night and a day. The Costa del Sol's best beach town, Nerja, is just two hours away (by bus), white hill towns such as Ronda are three hours away (bus or train), and Sevilla is an easy three-hour train ride. To use your time efficiently in Granada, reserve in advance for the Alhambra (see "The Alhambra," page 251).

In the morning, tour the cathedral and Royal Chapel (both closed roughly 13:00–16:00) and stroll the pedestrian-zone shopping scene. Do the Alhambra in the late afternoon. Be at the Albayzín viewpoint in the Moorish Quarter for sunset, and then find the right place for a suitably late dinner.

ORIENTATION

While modern Granada sprawls (300,000 people), its sights are all within a 20-minute walk of Plaza Nueva, where dogs wag their tails to the rhythm of the street musicians. Nearly all of my recommended hotels are within a few blocks of Plaza Nueva. Make this the hub of your Granada visit.

Plaza Nueva was a main square back when kings called Granada home. This historic center is in the Darro River Valley, which separates two hills (the river now flows under the square). On one hill is the great Moorish palace, the Alhambra, and on the other is the best-preserved Moorish quarter in Spain, the Albayzín. To the southeast are the cathedral, Royal Chapel, and Alcaicería (Moorish market), where the city's two main drags, Gran Vía de Colón and Calle Reyes Católicos, lead away into the modern city.

Tourist Information

There are three TIs. The newest and most central is just off Plaza Nueva on Santa Ana street, facing the church. Another TI is at the entrance of the Alhambra (daily 8:00–19:00). Both cover Granada as well as all Andalucía. The TI on Plaza de Mariana Pineda focuses on Granada, but offers free maps of other Andalusian towns, which cost €0.60 apiece at the other TIs (Mon–Fri 9:00–20:00, Sat 10:00–19:00, Sun 10:00–15:00, 3 blocks south of Plaza Carmen and Puerta Real, tel. 958-247-128, www.turismodegranada.org). At any TI, get a free city map, the *Viva Granada* magazine in English, and verify your Alhambra plans. Ask about the new sightseeing bus. During peak season (April–Oct), TI kiosks sometimes pop up in Plaza Nueva and Bib-Rambla.

Arrival in Granada

By Train: Granada's train station is connected to the center by frequent buses, a €4 taxi ride, or a 30-minute walk down Avenida de la Constitución and Gran Vía de Colón. The train station has luggage storage. Reserve your train out upon arrival.

Exiting the train station, walk straight ahead down the tree-lined

Greater Granada

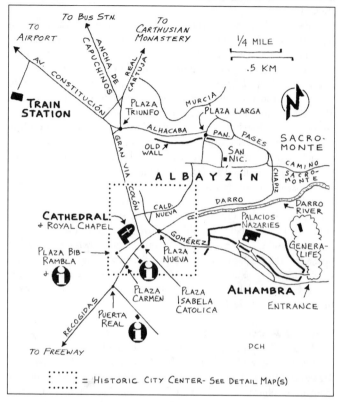

To Bus Stn.
To Airport
To Carthusian Monastery
1/4 MILE
.5 KM
ANCHA DE CAPUCHINOS
REAL CARTUJA
AV. CONSTITUCIÓN
TRAIN STATION
Plaza Triunfo
MURCIA
Plaza Larga
ALHACABA
PAN.
PAGES
SACRO-MONTE
GRAN VÍA
OLD WALL
SAN NIC.
A L B A Y Z Í N
CAMINO SACRO-MONTE
COLÓN
CALD. NUEVA
DARRO
CHAPIZ
DARRO RIVER
CATHEDRAL + ROYAL CHAPEL
PALACIOS NAZARIES
GENERA-LIFE
GOMÉREZ
PLAZA BIB-RAMBLA
PLAZA NUEVA
PLAZA CARMEN
PLAZA ISABELA CATÓLICA
ALHAMBRA
ENTRANCE
RECOGIDAS
PUERTA REAL
TO FREEWAY
DCH
·····: = HISTORIC CITY CENTER- SEE DETAIL MAP(S)

road. At the first major intersection (Avenida de la Constitución), you'll see the bus stop on your right. Take bus #4, #6, #9, or #11 and confirm by asking the driver, "¿Catedral?" (kat-ay-dral; the nearest stop to Plaza Nueva, ticket-€0.90, pay driver). Get off when you see the fountain of Plaza Isabel la Católica in front of the bus at the stop near the cathedral; cross the busy Gran Vía and walk three short blocks to Plaza Nueva.

By Bus: Granada's bus station (with a café, ATMs, luggage storage, and a don't-bother-me-with-questions info office, tel. 958-185-480, or 902-422-242 for Barcelona or east coast destinations) is located on the outskirts of the city. To get to the center, either take a taxi (€4.50) or buses #3 or #33 (€0.85, pay driver). It's about a 20-minute ride by bus; nearing the center, the bus goes up Gran Vía de Colón. For Plaza Nueva, get off at the stop for the cathedral (cathedral not visible from bus), a half block before the grand square Plaza Isabel la Católica—from the bus you'll see the big modern glass building across the square. From this stop, you're a three-block walk from Plaza Nueva (facing the glass building, go left up Calle Reyes Católicos).

By Car: Driving in Granada's historic center is restricted to buses, taxis, and tourists with hotel reservations (tell the police officer). The *autovía* (freeway) circles the city with a *circumvalación* road (Ronda Sur). To reach Plaza Nueva, take exit #129, direction *Centro, Recogidas.* Calle Recogidas leads directly into the heart of town. There will probably be a police block at Puerta Real (Victoria Hotel). You can pull into Plaza Nueva if you have a hotel reservation: There are posts with hotel buzzers on Calle Reyes Católicos and on Calle Elvira on the approach to Plaza Nueva. You press a button on the pillar for your hotel; the hotel buzzes back, releasing the roadblock to allow you through. Of Granada's many parking garages, one is at Puerta Real (€10/day; as you enter the city on Recogidas, turn right on Acera de Darro) and another is Parking San Agustín, near the cathedral, just off Gran Vía (€16/24 hrs; on Gran Vía as you approach Plaza Isabel la Católica, follow blue sign to Parking).

By Plane: To get between the airport and downtown, you can take a taxi (€18–20) or, much cheaper, the airport bus, timed to leave when flights arrive and depart (6/day, 30 min, €3). Hop on (or get off) at Gran Vía del Colón, nearly across from the cathedral. Airport info: tel. 958-245-223.

Getting Around Granada

With such cheap taxis, efficient minibuses, and nearly all points of interest an easy walk from Plaza Nueva, you may not even need the regular city buses. Three handy little red minibuses depart frequently from Plaza Nueva (roughly every 10 min until late in evening): Bus #30 goes up to the Alhambra and back; bus #31 does the Albayzín loop (a few go through Sacromonte); and bus #32 connects the Alhambra and Albayzín (from Plaza Nueva, the bus goes up to the Alhambra, returns to Plaza Nueva, then loops through the Albayzín and ends at Plaza Nueva). The schedule is listed at the bus stop and at the TI. You buy bus tickets (€0.90) from the driver. Sharable Bonobus tickets for nine trips (€5) or 20 trips (€10) save you money if you'll be taking a lot of trips, or if you're part of a group (buy from driver, valid on minibuses and city buses, you don't need to pay for connecting bus if you transfer within 45 min).

Helpful Hints

Theft Alert: If aggressive, obnoxious Gypsy women force sprigs of rosemary on you, avoid them like the plague. They may even grab at you. They're usually waiting in the Alcaicería neighborhood near the cathedral. By accepting the sprig, you start a relationship. This, while free, can lead to palm reading (which isn't) and even thievery. Firmly say no, and walk away.

City Pass: The Bono Turístico city pass covers the Alhambra, cathedral, Royal Chapel, La Cartuja Monastery, new sightseeing bus, and 10 free bus trips, plus other lesser sights and discounts on more (€25, valid for a week). When you buy your pass, the vendor schedules a time for your Alhambra visit. Passes are sold at the Royal Chapel, Alhambra, and Caja General de Ahorros bank on Plaza Isabel la Católica. You can save time by calling ahead to purchase your pass by credit card, and it will be ready for you when you arrive at the vendor (12 percent commission, tel. 902-100-095). During peak season (spring through fall), particularly if you'll be in town for only a day, it's worth ordering the pass in advance to avoid the small risk of not getting into the Alhambra, rather than waiting to buy it in person. Note that some of the fancier hotels provide one free pass per room for stays of two nights or more during peak season.

Long-Distance Buses, Trains, and Flights: To save yourself a trip to the train or bus stations, get information from any TI or a travel agency. All travel agencies book flights, and many also sell long-distance bus and train tickets (generally open Mon–Fri 9:00–13:30 & 17:00–20:00, Sat 10:00–13:30, closed Sun; Viajes Bonanza is convenient at Calle Reyes Católicos 30, tel. 958-223-578).

American Express: It's on Calle Reyes Católicos 31 (Mon–Fri 9:30–13:30 & 16:30–19:30, Sat 10:00–15:00, closed Sun, tel. 958-224-512).

Internet Access: There are many Internet points scattered throughout Granada. Navegaweb, a chain that sells tickets useable in other locations, including Madrid and Barcelona, has 96 computers (daily 10:00–23:00, Calle Reyes Católicos 55, tel. 958-210-528). Madar Internet is in the midst of tea shops at Calderería Nueva 11 (20 computers, Mon–Fri 10:00–24:00, Sat–Sun 12:00–24:00, 2 long blocks off Plaza Nueva).

Post Office: It's on Puerta Real (Mon–Fri 8:30–20:30, Sat 9:30–14:00, closed Sun, tel. 958-221-138).

Festivals: From late June to early July, the International Festival of Music and Dance offers classical music, ballet, flamenco, and zarzuela nightly in the Alhambra at reasonable prices. Ask at any TI for the latest location of the ticket office (open mid-April–Oct). Tickets can also be booked online at www.granadafestival.org from February on (popular shows sell out early in the season). During the festival, flamenco is free every night at midnight; ask the ticket office or any TI for the venue.

Local Guide: Margarita Landazuri, a local English-speaking guide, knows how to teach and has good rates (tel. 958-221-406); if she's busy, her partner, Miguel Ángel, is also good.

Granada at a Glance

▲▲▲**The Alhambra** The last and greatest Moorish palace, highlighting the splendor of Moorish civilization in the 13th and 14th centuries. Reservations recommended. **Hours:** Daily 8:30–20:00, also March–Oct Tue–Sat 22:00–23:30 and Nov–Feb 20:00–21:30.

▲▲**San Nicolás Viewpoint** Vista over the Alhambra and the Albayzín. **Hours:** Always open; best at sunset.

▲▲**Royal Chapel** Lavish 16th-century Plateresque Gothic chapel with the tombs of Queen Isabel and King Ferdinand. **Hours:** April–Oct Mon–Sat 10:30–13:00 & 16:00–19:00, opens Sun at 11:00; Nov–March Mon–Sat 10:30–13:00 & 15:30–18:30, opens Sun at 11:00.

Cathedral One of only two Renaissance churches and the second-largest cathedral in Spain. **Hours:** April–Oct Mon–Sat 10:45–13:30 & 16:00–20:00, Sun 16:00–20:00; Nov–March Mon–Sat 10:45–13:30 & 16:00–19:00, Sun 16:00–19:00.

Alcaicería Tiny shopping lanes filled with a silk and jewelry market. **Hours:** Always open, with shops open long hours.

Plaza Isabel la Católica The square at the intersection of Granada's two grand boulevards, Gran Vía de Colón and Calle Reyes Católicos, featuring a fine Columbus statue. **Hours:** Always open.

Paseo de los Tristes A prime strolling strip with eateries along the Darro River. **Hours:** Always open; best in the evenings.

Arab Baths Tranquil spot for soaks and massages. **Hours:** Daily 10:00–24:00.

Center for the Interpretation of Sacromonte Digs into geology and cave building, as well as Gypsy crafts, food, and music. **Hours:** Thu–Fri 10:00–14:00 & 17:00–21:00 Sat–Sun 10:00-21:00, closed Mon–Wed.

Walking Tours: Cicerone, run by locals, offers daily informative, 2.5-hour bilingual tours that depart at 10:30 from the City Hall, labeled *Ayuntamiento,* on Plaza Carmen (€10, tours also Fri–Sat at 18:00, show up or call mobile 670-541-669 or 600-412-051, www.ciceronegranada.com, info@ciceronegranada.com).

SIGHTS

The Alhambra

A ▲▲▲ sight, this last and greatest Moorish palace is one of Europe's top sights. Attracting up to 8,000 visitors a day, it's the reason most tourists come to Granada. Nowhere else does the splendor of Moorish civilization shine so beautifully.

The last Moorish stronghold in Europe is, with all due respect, really a symbol of retreat. Granada was only a regional capital for cen-

turies. Gradually the Christian Reconquista moved south, taking Córdoba (1237) and Sevilla (1248). The Nazarids, one of the many diverse ethnic groups of Spanish Muslims, held Granada until 1492. As you tour their grand palace, remember that while Europe slumbered through the Dark Ages, Moorish magnificence blossomed—busy stucco, plaster "stalactites," colors galore, scalloped windows framing Granada views, exuberant gardens, and water, water everywhere. Water—so rare and precious in most of the Islamic world—was the purest symbol of life to the Moors. The Alhambra is decorated with water: standing still, cascading, masking secret conversations, and drip-dropping playfully.

The Alhambra—not nearly as confusing as it might seem—consists of four sights clustered together atop a hill:

▲▲▲**Palacios Nazaries**—Exquisite Moorish palace, the one must-see sight.

▲**Generalife Gardens**—Fancy, manicured gardens.

▲**Charles V's Palace**—Christian Renaissance palace plopped on top of the Alhambra after the Reconquista (free entry).

Alcazaba—Empty old fort with tower and views.

These sights are described in more detail in "The Alhambra in Four Parts," below. Note that some rooms or portions of the Alhambra may be closed for restoration.

Cost: The Alcazaba fort, Moorish palace (Palacios Nazaries), and Generalife Gardens require a €10 combo-ticket. If the Palacios Nazaries is booked up during the day, consider getting the new €5 ticket covering only the Generalife and Alcazaba, viewing the

Alhambra

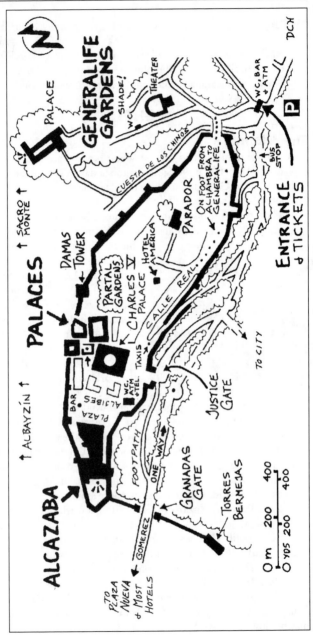

garden and fort during the day, and then visiting the palace at night (see "Alhambra by Moonlight," below). Only Charles V's Palace is free. Audioguides are €3, available at the entrance and in a more limited quantity at Charles V's Palace.

A good map is included with your ticket, but make sure you ask for it when you pick up your ticket at the window. If you forget, the information ladies with green handkerchiefs or shawls that walk around the grounds have free maps too. You can buy a guidebook (see "Guidebooks," page 256) at the bookshop adjacent to the ticket office and at shops throughout the Alhambra.

Hours: The Alhambra is open daily 8:30–20:00 (closes Nov–Feb at 18:00); the ticket office opens at 8:00 and closes an hour earlier (tel. 902-441-221).

Alhambra by Moonlight: Late-night visits include only Palacios Nazaries and not the fort or gardens—but hey, the palace is 80 percent of the Alhambra's thrills (March–Oct Tue–Sat 22:00–23:30, reserve ahead during peak season, ticket office open 21:45–22:45; Nov–Feb only Fri–Sat 20:00–21:30, ticket office open 19:45–20:15).

Getting a Reservation for the Alhambra: Some tourists never get to see the Alhambra, because the tickets can sell out fast. It's smart to make a reservation in advance, especially if you know the dates you'll be in Granada—and if you'll be visiting during peak season (April–Oct, especially Holy Week and July–Aug), on weekends, or on major holidays. Off-season, you might be able to just walk right in. Still, it can be worth the peace of mind and your valuable time to reserve ahead.

The Alhambra's top sight is the Moorish palace—Palacios Nazaries. Only 350 visitors per half hour are allowed inside. Your 30-minute time span is printed on your ticket (you can request a particular half hour). While you must enter Palacios Nazaries within this time, once inside you may linger as long as you like.

The Alhambra is trying out some crowd-control techniques. If your entry time to Palacios Nazaries is before 14:00, you can enter the grounds anytime in the morning, see the palace at your appointed time, and leave the Alhambra by 14:00 (although you can get away with staying longer in the fort, gardens, or palace, you won't be allowed to enter any of these sites after 14:00). If your ticket is stamped for 14:00 or later, you can enter the Alhambra no earlier than 14:00. For instance, if you have a reservation to visit Palacios Nazaries between 16:30 and 17:00, you can enter the Alhambra grounds as early as 14:00 and see the fort and Generalife Gardens before the palace. (Because of the time restriction on afternoon visits, morning times sell out the quickest, but for most travelers, an afternoon allows ample time to see the site.)

Here's the scoop on how to make a reservation for the Alhambra.

Reserving in Advance: There are three possibilities; each is equally good and costs a worthwhile €0.90 surcharge. With any of these options, you might be required to show your passport (as an identity card) when you pick up your ticket at the Alhambra.

1. Order online at www.alhambratickets.com.

2. You can order by phone. If you're calling within Spain, dial 902-224-460. If calling internationally, dial the international access code first (00 from a European country, 011 from the U.S. or Canada), then 34-915-379-178 (daily 8:30–16:00, can reserve between 1 day and a year in advance). Pay with a credit card (Visa or MasterCard only). You'll get a reference number to tell the ticket-window clerk at the Alhambra to get your ticket; you'll be advised to pick up your ticket an hour before your palace entry time.

3. You can drop by any BBVA bank in Spain and make a reservation (Banco Bilbao Vizcaya Argentaria, Mon–Fri 8:30–14:15, closed Sat–Sun). The BBVA bank personnel usually speak just enough English to make this transaction (which takes about 10 min). If you know when you'll be in Granada, it's simple to reserve a ticket soon after you arrive in Spain. BBVA banks are easy to find in virtually every Spanish town. At the bank, you'll pay in advance and get a piece of paper that you take to the ticket window at the Alhambra to exchange for your ticket. To allow yourself enough time to pick up the ticket (the line can be up to 20–30 minutes long) and to walk to the palace from the ticket office (15 min), arrive at the Alhambra an hour before your entry time.

If you're in Granada without a reservation: You have a number of alternatives, the least appealing of which involves getting up unnaturally early.

1. Your hotel (particularly if it's a fancier one) may be willing to book a reservation for you. Ideally request this when you reserve your room, but if you didn't, ask your hotelier upon arrival. The Alhambra sets aside 400 tickets daily except Sunday for hotel guests (Mon–Sat 9:00–19:00). Your hotel may charge a €0.75 fee. Don't let your hotel talk you into a guided tour unless you want it.

2. Make a reservation at a BBVA bank in Granada (possible for a following day, usually not the same day). People wait in line at the most visible BBVA bank in Granada—on Plaza Isabel la Católica—but any of the many BBVA branches in Granada (or anywhere in Spain) can make a reservation for you at a minimal €0.90 surcharge (Mon–Fri 8:30–14:15, closed Sat–Sun). You'll find a branch near Plaza Nueva at Plaza Carmen.

3. Stand in line at the Alhambra. The Alhambra admits 7,800 visitors a day. Six thousand tickets are sold in advance. The rest—1,800—are sold each day at the Alhambra ticket window (near Generalife Gardens and parking lot). On busy days in peak season, tickets can sell out as early as 10:00.

The ticket office opens at 8:00. People start lining up at about 7:30, but generally if you're in line by 8:15, you'll get an entry time. On a slow day, you'll get in right away. During busy times, you'll have an appointment for later that day. However, you're on vacation, and it's a pain to get up this early and miss breakfast to stand in line. It's more efficient to reserve in advance.

4. Consider getting Granada's Bono Turístico city pass if you'll be staying at least two days in the city. It costs €25, covers admission to the Alhambra and the city's other top sights (including the new sightseeing bus), and includes a reservation for the Alhambra (scheduled when you buy the pass). The pass is valid for seven days. Usually you can get into the palace on the second day (possibly even the first). If you have only a day in Granada, this is risky. Even with two days, though it's probable you'll get in, there are no guarantees (especially during April–June and Sept–Oct). This pass is easy to buy at the Royal Chapel and the Alhambra (and can be ordered in advance by phone, see "Helpful Hints," page 249).

5. Take a tour of the Alhambra. The pricier hotels can book you on a €38 GranaVisión tour that includes transportation to the Alhambra and a guided tour of Palacios Nazeries. The same company also offers tours of the city and province (tel. 958-535-875).

Getting to the Alhambra: There are three ways to get to the Alhambra:

1. From Plaza Nueva, hike 30 minutes up the street Cuesta de Gomérez. Keep going straight, with the Alhambra high on your left, and follow the street to the ticket pavilion at the far side of the Alhambra, near the Generalife Gardens.

2. From Plaza Nueva, catch a red minibus #30 or #32, marked *Alhambra* (€0.90, runs every 15 min).

3. Take a taxi (€3, taxi stand on Plaza Nueva).

Don't drive. Parking is convenient, near the entrance of the Alhambra (€6.50/4 hrs), but when you leave, one-way streets will send you into the traffic-clogged center of New Granada.

Planning Your Visit: It's a 15-minute walk from the entry (at one end of the long, narrow hilltop) to Palacios Nazaries at the other end. Be sure to arrive at the Alhambra with enough time to make it to the palace before your allotted half-hour appointment ends. The ticket-checkers at Palacios Nazaries are strict. (Because of crowd-control restrictions, note that if you have an appointment for Palacios Nazaries after 14:00, you can't be admitted to the Alhambra any earlier than 14:00.)

To minimize walking, see Charles V's Palace and the Alcazaba fort before your visit to Palacios Nazaries. When you finish touring Palacios Nazaries, you'll leave through the Partal Gardens. (Don't duck out early to visit the fort; this is your only chance to see these particular gardens and their grand views of the Albayzín.) You'll exit the Partal Gardens near the Alhambra entrance, not far from the Generalife Gardens. Depending on your time, you can visit the Generalife Gardens before or after your visit to Palacios Nazaries. If you have any time to kill before your palace appointment, you can do it luxuriously at the parador bar (actually within the Alhambra walls). While you can find drinks, WCs, and guidebooks near the entrance of Palacios Nazaries, you'll find none inside the actual palace. If you're going to the Albayzín afterwards, take bus #32, which goes direct from the Alhambra to the Albayzín, saving you time.

Cuisine: There are only three eateries within the Alhambra walls: the restaurants at the parador and Hotel América, and a small bar/café kiosk in front of the Alcazaba fort (near entrance of Palacios Nazaries). Snack vending machines are at the entrance and the Charles V Palace (near WCs). You're welcome to bring in a picnic as long as you eat it in a public area.

Guidebooks: Consider getting a guidebook in town and reading it the night before to understand the layout and history of this remarkable sight before entering. The classic is *The Alhambra and the Generalife* (€6, includes great map, available in town and at shops throughout the Alhambra), but even better is the slick *Alhambra and Generalife in Focus*, which combines vibrant color photos and more readable text (€8, sold at many bookstores around town). The guide called the "official guide" is not as good.

The Alhambra in Four Parts

I've listed these sights in the order you're likely to visit them.

Charles V's Palace—It's only natural for a conquering king to build his own palace over his foe's palace, and that's exactly what the Christian King Charles V did. The Alhambra palace wasn't good enough for Charles, so he built this one—destroying the dramatic Alhambra facade and financing his new palace with a salt-in-the-wound tax on Granada's defeated Moorish population. This palace, a unique circle within a square, is Spain's most impressive Renaissance building, designed by Pedro Machuca, a devotee of Michelangelo and Raphael. Stand in the circular courtyard, then climb the stairs. Imagine being here for one of Charles' bullfights. Charles' palace was never finished because his son Philip II abandoned it to build his own palace, El Escorial. Inside the palace are two boring museums: Museo de Bellas Artes (€1.50, Tue 14:00–20:00, Wed–Sat 9:00–20:00, Sun 9:00–14:00, closed Mon, shorter hours off-season, located upstairs) and the better Museo de la Alhambra, showing off some of the Alhambra's best Moorish art (free, Tue–Sat 9:00–14:30, closed Sun–Mon, on ground floor). The palace itself is free; to see only this, you can enter the Alhambra at either of the two gates located midway along the length of the grounds (between the fort and official entrance).

Alcazaba Fort—The fort—the original "red castle," or "Alhambra"—is the oldest and most ruined part of the complex, offering exercise and fine city views. What you see is mid–13th century, but there was probably a fort here in Roman times. Once upon a time this tower defended a town (or medina) of 2,000 Arabs living within the Alhambra walls. From the top (looking north) find Plaza Nueva and the Albayzín viewpoint. To the south are the mountains. Is anybody skiing today?

Think of that day in 1492 when the cross and flags of Aragon and Castile were raised on this tower and the fleeing Moorish King Boabdil looked back from those mountains and wept. His mom chewed him out, saying, "Don't weep like a woman for what you couldn't defend like a man." Much later, Napoleon stationed his troops here, contributing substantially to its ruin when he left.

To get to Palacios Nazaries, follow the signs down and around to the palace (WCs to right of entry). If you're early, duck into the exhibit across from the palace entry. It's in Spanish, but the models of the Alhambra upstairs are easy to appreciate.

Palacios Nazaries—During the 30-minute window of time stamped on your ticket, enter the jewel of the Alhambra: the Moorish royal palace. You'll walk through three basic sections: royal offices, ceremonial rooms, and private quarters. Built mostly in the 14th century, this palace offers your best possible look at the refined, elegant Moorish civilization of Al-Andalus.

You'll visit rooms decorated from top to bottom with carved wood ceilings, stucco "stalactites," ceramic tiles, molded-plaster walls, and filigree windows. Open-air courtyards in the palace feature fountains with bubbling water like a desert oasis, the Koran's symbol of Heaven. The palace is well-preserved, but the original interior decor must have been overwhelming. Imagine sultans with hookah pipes lounging on pillows on Persian carpets, with tapestries on the walls, heavy curtains on the windows, and ivory-studded wooden furniture. The whole place was once painted in bright colors, many suggested by the Koran—red (blood), blue (Heaven), green (oasis), and gold (wealth). And throughout the palace, walls, ceilings, vases, carpets, and tiles were covered with decorative patterns, mostly calligraphy writing out verses from the Koran.

As you tour the palace, keep the palace themes in mind: water, no images, "stalactite" ceilings throughout—and few signs telling

Alhambra's Palacios Nazaries

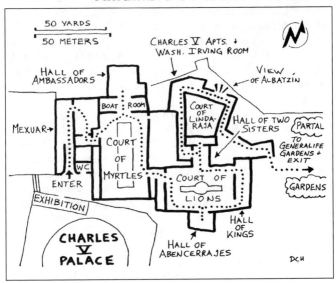

you where you are. Even today, the route constantly changes. Use the map in this chapter to locate these essential stops:

Court of Myrtles (Patio de los Arrayanes): Walk through a few administrative rooms (the *mexuar*) and a small courtyard until you hit the big rectangular courtyard with a fish pond lined by a myrtle-bush hedge—the Court of Myrtles. Moors loved their patios—with a garden and water, and under the sky. Women, who rarely went out, stayed in touch with nature here. The living quarters for the women (harem) were upstairs—the Koran allowed a man "all the women you can maintain with dignity." Notice the wooden "jalousies"—screens (erected by jealous husbands) that allow the cloistered women to look out without being clearly seen.

Boat Room: Head left (north) from the entry into the long, narrow antechamber to the throne room, called the "Boat Room." While it's understandable that many think this is named for the upside-down-hull shape of its fine cedar ceiling, the name is actually a corruption of the Arab word *baraka*, meaning "divine blessing and luck." This was the waiting room for meetings with the sultan, and blessings and luck are exactly what you'd need if you had business in the next room. Oh, it's your turn now...

The Hall of the Ambassadors (Gran Salón de Embajadores): The palace's largest room functioned as the throne room. It was here that the sultan, seated on a throne opposite the entrance, received foreign emissaries. Ogle the room—a perfect cube—from top to bottom. The star-studded, domed ceiling, made of cedar of Lebanon

Islamic Art

Rather than making paintings and statues, Islamic artists expressed themselves with beautiful but functional objects. Ceramics (mostly blue and white, or red and white), carpets, glazed tile, stucco-work ceilings, and glass tableware are covered everywhere with complex patterns. The intricate interweaving, repetition, and unending lines suggest the complex, infinite nature of their God, Allah.

You'll see only a few pictures of humans or animals, since the Islamic religion was wary of any "graven images" or idols forbidden by God. However, secular art by Muslims for their homes and palaces was not bound by this restriction; you'll get an occasional glimpse of realistic art of men and women enjoying a garden paradise, a symbol of the Muslim heaven.

Look for floral patterns (twining vines, flowers, and arabesques) and geometric designs (stars and diamonds). The most common pattern is calligraphy—elaborate lettering of an inscription in Arabic, the language of the Koran (and the lettering used even in non-Arabic languages). A quote from the Koran on a vase or lamp combines the power of the message with the beauty of the calligraphy.

(8,000 inlaid pieces) suggests the complexity of Allah's infinite universe. Plaster "stalactites" form the cornice, made by troweling on layers of plaster several inches thick, then carving into it. The stucco walls, even without their original paint and gilding, are still glorious, decorated with ornamental flowers made by pressing a mold into the wet plaster. The filigree windows once held stained glass, and had heavy drapes to block out the heat. A visitor here would have stepped from the glaring Court of Myrtles into a dim, cool, incense-filled world, forced to meet the silhouetted sultan while still a bit disoriented, waiting for his eyes to adjust.

Note the finely carved Arabic script. Muslims avoided making images of living things—that was God's work. But they could carve decorative religious messages. One phrase—"only Allah is victorious"—is repeated 9,000 times throughout the palace. Find the character for "Allah"—it looks like a cursive W with a nose on its left side. The swoopy toboggan blades underneath are a kind of artistic punctuation marking off one phrase.

In 1492, two historic events took place in this room. Culminating a 700-year-long battle, the Reconquista was completed here as the last Moorish king, Boabdil, signed the terms of his surrender before packing light and fleeing to Africa.

And it was here that Columbus made his pitch to Isabel and Ferdinand to finance a sea voyage to the Orient. Imagine the scene: The king, the queen, and the greatest minds from the University of Salamanca gathered here while Columbus produced maps and pie charts to make his case that he could sail west to reach the East. Ferdinand and the professors laughed and called Columbus mad—not because they thought the world was flat (most educated people knew otherwise), but because they thought Columbus had underestimated the size of the globe, and thus the length and cost of the journey. But Isabel said *"Sí, señor."* Columbus fell to his knees (promising to wear a money belt and to use the most current guidebook available), and she gave him an ATM card with a wad of traveler's checks as a backup.

Continue deeper into the palace to a court where, 600 years ago, only the royal family and their servants could enter. It's the much-photographed...

Court of the Lions: The Patio de los Leones features a fountain with 12 lions. Why 12? Since the fountain was a gift from a Jewish leader celebrating good relations with the sultan (Granada had a big Jewish community), the lions probably represent the 12 tribes of Israel. During Moorish times, the fountain functioned as a clock, with a different lion spouting water each hour. (Conquering Christians disassembled the fountain to see how it worked, and it's never worked since.) From the center, four streams went out—figuratively to the corners of the earth and literally to various apartments of the royal family. Notice how the court resembles, with its 124 columns, the cloister of a Catholic monastery.

Six hundred years ago the Muslim Moors could read the Koranic poetry that ornaments this court, and they could understand the symbolism of this lush, enclosed garden, considered the embodiment of paradise or truth. ("How beautiful is this garden/where the flowers of Earth rival the stars of Heaven./What can compare with this alabaster fountain, gushing crystal-clear water?/Nothing except the fullest moon, pouring light from an unclouded sky.") Imagine—they appreciated this part of the palace even more than we do today.

On the right, off the courtyard, is a square room called the **Hall of the Abencerrajes (Sala de los Abencerrajes).** According to legend, the father of Boabdil took a new wife and wanted to disinherit the children of his first marriage—one of whom was Boabdil. In order to deny power to Boabdil and his siblings, the sultan killed nearly the entire pro-Boabdil Abencerraje family. He thought this would pave the way for the son of his new wife to be the next sultan. Happily, he stacked 36 Abencerraje heads in the pool under this sumptuous honeycombed stucco ceiling. But his scheme failed, and

Boabdil ultimately assumed the throne. Bloody power struggles like this were the norm here in the Alhambra.

The Hall of the Kings (Sala de los Reyes) is at the end of the court opposite where you entered. Notice the ceilings of the three chambers branching off this gallery. Breaking from the tradition of imageless art, paintings on the goat-leather ceiling depict scenes of the sultan and his family. The center room shows a group portrait of the first 10 of the Alhambra's 22 sultans. The scene is a fantasy, since these people lived over a span of many generations. The two end rooms show scenes of princely pastimes, such as hunting and shooting skeet. In a palace otherwise devoid of figures, these offer a rare look at royal life in the palace.

The next room, the **Hall of the Two Sisters,** has another oh-wow stucco ceiling lit from below by clerestory windows. The room features geometric patterns and stylized Arabic script quoting verses from the Koran, but no figures.

Washington Irving Room: That's about it for the palace. From here you wander through a few more rooms including one (marked with a large plaque) where Washington Irving wrote *Tales of the Alhambra*. While serving as the U.S. ambassador to Spain in 1829, Irving lived in the Alhambra. It was a romantic time, when the place was home to Gypsies and donkeys. His "tales" kindled interest in the place, causing it to become recognized as a national treasure. Here's a quote from Irving's "The Alhambra by Moonlight": "On such heavenly nights I would sit for hours at my window inhaling the sweetness of the garden, and musing on the checkered fortunes of those whose history was dimly shadowed out in the elegant memorials around."

Hallway with a view: Stop at the open-air hallway for the best-in-the-palace view of the labyrinthine Albayzín—the old Moorish town on the opposite hillside. Find the famous viewpoint at the base of the white St. Nicolás church tower breaking the horizon. Creeping into the mountains on the right are the Gypsy neighborhoods of Sacromonte. Still circling old Granada is the Moorish wall (built in the 1200s to protect the city's population, swollen by Muslim refugees driven south by the Reconquista).

Leaving the Palacios Nazaries, follow signs to the Partal Gardens, go through the gardens, then follow signs directing you left to the Generalife Gardens or right to the exit.

Generalife Gardens—On the hillside to the east, the garden with carefully pruned hedges is Generalife (hen-ne-raw-LEEF-ay). This most perfect Arabian garden in Andalucía was the summer home of the Moorish kings, the closest thing on earth to the Koran's description of Heaven. If you have a long wait before your entry to the Palacios, tour these gardens first, then the Alcazaba fort and Charles V's Palace.

Central Granada

1 Cathedral Entry   **3** Alcaicería Neighborhood
2 Royal Chapel Entry   **4** Cicerone Walking Tours

Your visit to the Alhambra is complete, and you've earned your reward. "Surely Allah will make those who believe and do good deeds enter gardens beneath which rivers flow; they shall be adorned therein with bracelets of gold and pearls, and their garments therein shall be of silk." (Koran 22.23)

Central Granada

▲▲**Royal Chapel (Capilla Real)**—Without a doubt Granada's top Christian sight, this lavish chapel holds the dreams—and bodies—of Queen Isabel and King Ferdinand (€3, April–Oct Mon–Sat 10:30–13:00 & 16:00–19:00, opens Sun 11:00; Nov–March Mon–Sat 10:30–13:00 & 15:30–18:30, opens Sun at 11:00, no photos, entrance on Calle Oficios, just off Gran Vía de Colón; go through iron gate, tel. 958-227-848).

In the lobby, before you enter the chapel, notice the painting of Boabdil (on the black horse) giving the key of Granada to the conquering King Ferdinand. Boabdil wanted to fall to his knees, but the Spanish king, who had great respect for his Moorish foe, embraced him instead. They fought a long and noble war (for instance, respectfully returning the bodies of dead soldiers). Ferdinand is in red, and Isabel is behind him wearing a crown. Next to her (under a black hood) is their daughter Juana. And next to Juana is her husband, Philip the Fair, wearing a crown. These four people are buried in this chapel. The painting is flanked by two large portraits of Ferdinand and Isabel.

Isabel decided to make Granada the capital of Spain (and burial place for Spanish royalty) for three reasons: 1) With the conquest of Granada, Christianity had overcome Islam in Europe; 2) her marriage with Ferdinand, followed by the conquest of Granada, had marked the beginning of a united Spain; and 3) in Granada, she agreed to sponsor Columbus' fateful voyage.

Step into the **chapel.** It's Plateresque Gothic—light and lacy, named for and inspired by the fine silverwork of the Moors. This was the most lavish interior money could buy 500 years ago. Ferdinand and Isabel spent a fourth of their wealth on it. Because of its speedy completion (1506–1521), the chapel is an unusually harmonious piece of architecture.

The four **royal tombs** are Renaissance-style. Carved in Italy in 1521 out of Carrara marble, they were sent by ship to Spain. The faces—based on death masks—are considered accurate. If you're facing the altar, Ferdinand and Isabel are on the right. (Isabel fans attribute the bigger dent she puts in the pillow to brains.) Isabel's contemporaries described the queen as being of medium height, with auburn hair and blue eyes, with a serious, modest, and gentle personality. (Compare Ferdinand and Isabel's tomb statues with painted wood statues of them kneeling in prayer, flanking the altarpiece.)

Philip the Fair and Juana the Mad are on the left. Philip was so "Fair" it drove the insanely jealous Juana "Mad." Philip died young, and for two years Juana kept his casket at her bedside, kissing his embalmed body good night. Philip and Juana's son, Charles V (known as Carlos I in Spain), was a key figure in European history, as his coronation merged the Holy Roman Empire (Philip the Fair's Hapsburg domain) with Juana's Spanish empire. Europe's top king, he ruled a vast empire stretching from Holland to Sicily, from Bohemia to Bolivia (1519–1556).

When Philip II, the son of Charles V, decided to build El Escorial and establish Madrid as the single capital of a single Spain, Granada lost power and importance. More important, Spain declined. After the reign of Charles V, Spain squandered her awesome wealth trying to maintain this huge and impossible empire. She did it not for material riches, but to defend the romantic, quixotic dream of a Catholic empire—ruled by one divinely ordained

Catholic monarch—against an irrepressible tide of nationalism and Protestantism that was sweeping across the country. Spain's relatively poor modern history can be blamed, in part, on her stubborn unwillingness to accept the end of this old-regime notion.

Look at the fine carving on the tombs (unfortunately vandalized by Napoleon's troops). It's a humanistic statement, with healthy, organic, realistic figures rising above the strict and heavy Gothic past.

From the feet of the marble tombs, step downstairs to see the actual coffins. They are plain. Isabel was originally buried in the Franciscan monastery (in what is today the parador at the Alhambra). The fifth coffin (with *PM* on it) is that of a young Prince Michael, who would have been king of a united Spain and Portugal. A sad—but too long—story...

The **high altar** is one of the finest Renaissance works in Spain. It's dedicated to John the Baptist and John the Evangelist. In the center, you can see the Baptist and the Evangelist chatting as if over tapas—an appropriately humanist scene. ("John" was the name of both Ferdinand's and Isabel's dads.) Scenes from the Baptist's life are on the left: John beheaded after Salome's fine dancing and (below) John baptizing Jesus. Scenes from the Evangelist's life are on the right: John's martyrdom (a failed attempt to boil him alive in oil) and John on Patmos (where he wrote the last book of the Bible, Revelation). John is talking to the eagle that flew him to Heaven, according to legend.

The Plateresque (silver-filigree-style) arch leads to a small glass pyramid in the **treasury.** This holds Queen Isabel's silver crown, ringed with pomegranates (symbolizing Granada), and King Ferdinand's sword. Beside the entry arch you'll see the devout Isabel's prayer book, in which she followed the Mass. The book and its sturdy box date from 1496. The fancy box on the other side of the door is supposedly the one that Isabel (cash-poor because of her military expenses) filled with jewels and gave to Columbus. Columbus sold these to finance his journey. Next, in the corner (and also behind glass), is the cross that Cardinal Mendoza, staunch supporter of Queen Isabel, carried into the Alhambra on that historic day in 1492. Next, the big silk, silver, and gold tapestry is the altar banner for the mobile campaign chapel of Ferdinand and Isabel, who always traveled with their army. In the next case you'll see the original Christian army flags raised over the Alhambra in 1492.

The room holds the first great art collection ever established by a woman. Queen Isabel amassed more than 200 important paintings. After Napoleon's visit, only 30 remained. Even so, this is a fine collection, all on wood, featuring works by Sandro Botticelli, Perugino, the Flemish master Hans Memling, and less-famous Spanish masters.

Finally, at the end of the room, the two carved sculptures of Ferdinand and Isabel were the originals from the high altar. Charles V considered these primitive and replaced them with the ones you saw earlier.

Cathedral—One of only two Renaissance churches in Spain (the other is in Córdoba), Granada's cathedral is the second-largest in Spain after Sevilla's. Its spacious and bright interior is a refreshing break from the dark Gothic and gilded-lily Baroque of so many Spanish churches. In a modern move back in the 18th century, the choir walls were taken out so that people could be involved in the worship. To make matters even better, an 18th-century bishop ordered the interior painted with lime (for hygienic reasons, during a time of disease). The people liked it, and it stayed white. Most of the side chapels are decorated in Baroque style. On the far wall (to the right of the high altar) is St. James the Moorslayer, with his sword raised high and an armored Moor under his horse's hooves. Granada's own Alonso Cano (1601–1667) did the Renaissance facade and paintings of the Virgin in the rotunda (€3, April–Oct Mon–Sat 10:45–13:30 & 16:00–20:00, Sun 16:00–20:00; Nov–March Mon–Sat 10:45–13:30 & 16:00–19:00, Sun 16:00–19:00, audioguide-€2.50, entrance off Gran Vía de Colón through iron gateway, tel. 958-222-959).

Alcaicería—Originally an Arab silk market, this neighborhood (around the cathedral) still functions as a silk and jewelry market. Remember, ignore the women who shove twigs of rosemary at you (see "Helpful Hints," page 248). Explore the mesh of tiny shopping lanes between the cathedral and Calle Reyes Católicos. Go on a photo and sound safari: popcorn machines popping, men selling balloons, leather goods spread out on streets, kids playing soccer, barking dogs, dogged shoeshine boys, and the whirring grind of bicycle-powered knife sharpeners.

The exuberant square behind the cathedral is **Bib-Rambla**. While today it's fine for coffee or a meal amidst the color and fragrance of flower stalls, in Moorish times this was a place of public execution. A block away, the square Pescadería is a smaller, similarly lively version of Bib-Rambla.

Plaza Isabel la Católica—Granada's two grand boulevards, Gran Vía de Colón and Reyes Católicos, meet a block off Plaza Nueva at Plaza Isabel la Católica. Here you'll see a fine statue of Columbus unfurling a long contract with Isabel. It lists the terms of Columbus' MCDXCII voyage: ("Forasmuch as you, Columbus, are going by our command to discover and subdue some Islands and Continents in the ocean....")

Isabel was driven by her desire to spread Catholicism. Columbus was driven by his desire for money. For adding territory to Spain's Catholic empire, Isabel promised Columbus the ranks of Admiral of the Oceans and Governor of the New World. To sweeten the pie, she tossed in one-eighth of all the riches he brought home. Isabel died thinking that Columbus had found India or China. Columbus died poor and disillusioned.

From here, Calle Reyes Católicos leads to Puerta Real. There Acera de Darro takes you through modern Granada to the river via the huge El Corte Inglés department store and lots of modern commerce.

Paseo de los Tristes—In the cool of the evening—with dinner as a popular destination—consider strolling the street called Paseo de los Tristes that runs east from Plaza Nueva along the Darro River. (If you're tired, note that buses #31 and #32 stop here.) This "walk of the sad ones" was once the route of funeral processions to the cemetery at the edge of town.

Start at Plaza Nueva. The Church of Santa Ana, at the far end of the square, was originally a mosque, its tower a minaret. Notice the ceramic brickwork. This is Mudejar art, the technique of the Moors used by Christians. Inside you'll see a fine Alhambra-style cedar ceiling. Follow Carrera del Darro along the River Darro under the Alhambra. (Six miles upstream, part of the Darro is diverted to provide water for the Alhambra's many fountains.) Past the church, on your right is the turn-off for the Arab Baths (described below), and on the left is Santa Catalina de Zafra, a convent of cloistered nuns (they worship behind a screen that divides the church's rich interior in half). Farther ahead, on the right, across from the Archaeological Museum, is the Church of San Pedro, the parish church of Sacromonte's Gypsy community. Within its rich interior is an ornate oxcart used to carry the Host on the annual pilgrimage to Rocio near Portugal. Finally, you reach the Paseo de los Tristes. Covered with happy diners, this is a great spot at night, under the floodlit Alhambra. From here the road arcs up into Sacromonte (past a rank of "burro taxis" for those into adventure sports). And from here a lane (called Cuesta de los Chinos or Carretera del Rey Chico) leads up to the Alhambra "through the back door."

Arab Baths—Consider a visit to the Arab baths at Hammam Baños Arabes Al-Andalus. The 75-minute soak and a 15-minute massage cost €19.50; for a 90-minute bath only, it's €12 (daily 10:00–24:00, appointment times scheduled every hour, co-ed with mandatory swimsuits, quiet atmosphere encouraged, free lockers available, just off Plaza Nueva at Santa Ana 16; from Plaza Nueva, it's the first right—over a bridge—past the church; reservation necessary, especially on weekends—some hoteliers are happy to call for you; tel. 958-229-978).

To recharge after the bath, consider two nearby options—the teahouse on the second floor that offers Moroccan tea and pastries (daily 15:30–12:00) and **Pilar del Toro,** with a tapas menu, peaceful fountain patio, and wrought-iron entrance (daily 13:30–16:00 & 20:30–12:00, Santa Ana 12).

Albayzín Neighborhood

NOTE:
NOT TO SCALE
PLAZA NUEVA TO
SAN NICOLAS IS
A 20 MIN WALK
UPHILL

❶ Calderería Nueva
(tapas bars, tea shops)
❷ Restaurante El Ladrillo I
❸ Restaurante El Ladrillo II
❹ Restaurante Reina Monica
❺ Restaurante Casa Torcuato
❻ Carmen de las Tomasas
❼ Carmen Mirador de Morayma
❽ Restaurante Naturi Albayzín
& Kasbah Tea Shop

❾ Bar Restaurant Las Cuevas
❿ Bodega Castaneda
⓫ Arab Baths
⓬ Bus for Albayzín Loop
⓭ Bus to Alhambra
⓮ To Gypsy Caves & Sacromonte
Interpretation Center

Albayzín

Explore Spain's best old Moorish quarter, with countless colorful corners, flowery patios, and shady lanes to soothe the 21st-century-mangled visitor. Climb high to the San Nicolás church for the best view of the Alhambra. Then wander through the mysterious backstreets. Warning: Thefts have increased after dark in the Albayzín; take the bus or a taxi back to your hotel if you linger here for a late-night dinner.

Getting to the Albayzín: A handy city minibus threads its way around the Albayzín from Plaza Nueva (see Albayzín Circular Bus Tour, below), getting you scenically and sweatlessly to the St. Nicolás viewpoint. You can also taxi to the St. Nicolás church and explore from there. Consider having your cabbie take you on a Sacromonte detour en route.

If walking up, leave the west end of Plaza Nueva on Calle Elvira. After about 200 yards, turn right on Calderería Nueva. Follow this stepped street past tapas bars and *teterías* (see "Eating," page 275) as it goes left around the church, slants, winds, and zigzags up the hill, heading basically straight. Pass the peach-colored building on your left (resisting the temptation to turn left on Muladar Sancha). When you reach a T-intersection, go left on Calle del Almirante. Near the crest, turn right on Camino Nuevo de San Nicolás, then walk several blocks to the street that curves up left (look for brown sign *Mirador de San Nicolás*, where a street sign would normally be). Soon you'll see steps leading up to the church's viewpoint.

▲▲San Nicolás Viewpoint—For one of Europe's most romantic viewpoints, be here at sunset when the Alhambra turns red and the Albayzín widows share the benches with local lovers and tourists. In 1997 President Clinton made a point to bring his family here—a favorite spot from a trip he made as a student.

Exploring the Albayzín: From the San Nicolás viewpoint you're at the edge of a hilltop neighborhood even people of Granada recognize as a world apart. From the viewpoint, turn your back to the Alhambra and walk north (passing the church on your right and the Biblioteca Municipal on your left). A lane leads past a white stone arch (on your right)—now a chapel built into the old Moorish wall. At the end of the lane, step down to the right through the 11th-century "New Gate" (Puerta Nueva—older than the Alhambra) and into **Plaza Larga.** In medieval times, this tiny square (called "long," because back then it was) was the local marketplace. It still is a busy market each morning, with locals blaring their cheap, pirated cassettes as if to prove there is actually music on them. Casa Pasteles, at the near end of the square, serves good coffee and cakes.

Leave Plaza Larga on Calle Agua de Albayzín (as you face Casa Pasteles it's to your right). The street, named for the public baths that used to line it, shows evidence of the Moorish plumbing system: gutters. Back when Europe's streets were filled with muck, Granada actually had Roman Empire–style gutters with drains leading to clay and lead pipes.

This road leads to a T-intersection. You can turn left for the recommended restaurant Casa Torcuato (a block away, see "Eating," page 275) or right for the recommended El Ladrillo (2 blocks away). Or just explore. You're in the heart of the Albayzín. Poke into an old church. They're plain by design—to go easy on the Muslim converts, who weren't used to being surrounded by images as they worshiped. You'll see lots of real Muslim culture living in the streets, including many recent Spanish converts. Those aren't the Spice Girls, just Gypsy teenagers—as influenced by TV as any teenagers these days.

If you got here on foot, an easy way back to the center is bus #7 or #F—go left from Casa Torcuato to the main street, Carretera de Murcia, where you can catch the bus. On a hot day, consider doing this walk in reverse (downhill) by taking bus #7 or #F opposite the cathedral to Casa Torcuato. That way you can enjoy most of your walk downhill and finish at Plaza Nueva.

Albayzín Circular Bus Tour—The handy Albayzín bus #31 makes a 15-minute loop, departing from Plaza Nueva about every 10 minutes (pay driver €0.85, better views on the right, bus #32 does the same loop but—depending on where you catch it—goes to Alhambra first). While good for a lift to the top of the Albayzín, I'd stay on for an entire circle (and return to the Albayzín later for dinner—either on foot or by bus). Although just a few #31 buses detour up Sacromonte (see schedule at bus stop), all pass its entrance. Two stops later the driver announces the San Nicolás *mirador* (viewpoint). The next stop is San Miguel el Bajo (a fun square with several fine little restaurants). Just after that you get a commanding view of modern Granada on the left. Hitting the city's main drag, Gran Vía de Colón, you make a U-turn at the Garden of the Triumph, celebrating the Immaculate Conception of the Virgin Mary (notice her statue atop a column). Behind Mary stands the old Royal Hospital—built in the 16th century for Granada's poor by the Catholic kings after the Reconquista, in hopes of winning the favor of Granada's conquered residents. From here you zip past the cathedral and home to Plaza Nueva.

Sacromonte and Granada's Gypsies

Marking the entrance to Sacromonte is a statue of Chorrohumo ("black as smoke"), a Gypsy from Granada popular in the 1950s for guiding people around the city. Spain's Gypsies, traditionally good with crafts and animals, came from India via Egypt. The Spanish word for Gypsy, *gitano*, comes from the Spanish word for "Egyptian." They settled mostly in the south, where they found people more tolerant. Granada's Gypsies arrived in the 15th century and have stuck together ever since. Today 50,000 Gypsies call Granada home.

In most of Spain, Gypsies are more assimilated into the general community, but Granada's Sacromonte district is a large, distinct Gypsy community. (After the difficult Civil War era, they were joined by many farmers who, like the Gypsies, opted for Sacromonte's affordable, practical cave dwellings—warm in the winter and cool in the summer.)

Spaniards, who consider themselves accepting and not racist, claim that in maintaining such a tight community, the Gypsies segregate themselves. The Gypsies call Spaniards *payos* ("whites"). Recent mixing of Gypsies and *payos* has given birth to the term *gallipavo* (rooster-duck), although who is whom depends upon whom you ask.

Sacromonte has one main street. Camino del Sacromonte is lined with caves primed for tourists and restaurants ready to fight

Duende in Granada

To have *duende* is to have flamenco magic. And most often, it's Gypsies who possess *duende*. At sunset in a setting like the Albayzín or Alhambra, the *duende* forces multiply, producing impromptu flamenco singing. *Peñas* (flamenco clubs), bars, and festivals give you an opportunity to enjoy these. Most programs take place in the summer, but there are also some in the winter. La Chumbera offers free flamenco shows nearly every Saturday at 20:00 (go an hour before to get a free ticket; also serves meals but not in same room as show; on Camino del Sacromonte near Center for the Interpretation of Sacromonte, tel. 958-215-647).

over the bill. (Don't come here expecting to get a deal on anything.) Intriguing lanes run above and below this main drag.

Zambra—A long flamenco tradition exists in Granada. Sacromonte is a good place to see *zambra,* a flamenco variation with a more Oriental feel in which the singer also dances. Two good *zambra* venues are Zambra Cueva del Rocio (€23, includes a drink, 22:00 show, 90 min, your hotel may be able to arrange a hotel pick-up, Camino del Sacromonte 70, tel. 958-227-129) and María la Canastera (€22, includes a drink and transportation from hotel, €15 without transport, May–Oct daily shows at 22:00 and 23:00, fewer off-season, Camino del Sacromonte 89, tel. 958-121-183).

Center for the Interpretation of Sacromonte—The new Centro de Interpretación del Sacromonte offers insight into Sacromonte's geology and environment, cave building, Gypsy crafts, food, and music traditions, as well as views over Granada and the Alhambra. It also features €10 flamenco shows on some Wednesdays and other music, such as classical guitar, on Fridays for €5 (both July–Aug at 22:00, includes drink). If you come at 21:00 on a show day, you can see the museum, have some tapas, and enjoy the show. To see just the museum, come early or late, or be prepared to hike in the heat. Easy to miss, it's located 500 yards up the hill from the Venta el Gallo restaurant on the main Sacromonte lane (€4, Thu–Fri 10:00–14:00 & 17:00–21:00 Sat–Sun 10:00–21:00, closed Mon–Wed, explanations in English, Barranco de los Negros, tel. 958-215-120, www.sacromontegranada.com).

Near Granada

Carthusian Monastery (La Cartuja)—A church with an interior that looks as if it squirted out of a can of whipped cream, La Cartuja is nicknamed the "Christian Alhambra" for its elaborate white Baroque stucco work. In the rooms just off the cloister, notice the gruesome paintings of martyrs placidly meeting their grisly fates. It's located a mile north of town on the way to Madrid. Drive north on Gran Vía de Colón and follow the signs, or take bus #8 from Gran Vía de Colón (entry-€3, April–Oct Mon–Sat 10:00–13:00 & 16:00–20:00, Sun 10:00–12:00 & 16:00–20:00, Nov–March closes at 18:00, tel. 958-161-932).

SLEEPING

In July and August, when the streets are littered with sunstroke victims, rooms are plentiful. Crowded months are April, May, June, September, and October. Except for the hotels near the Alhambra and the train station, all recommended hotels are within a five-minute walk of Plaza Nueva (see map on next page). While few of the hotels have parking facilities, all can direct you to a garage (such as Parking San Agustín, just off Gran Vía de Colón, €16/24 hrs.)

On or near Plaza Nueva
Each of these is big, professional, plenty comfortable, and perfectly located. Prices vary with the demand.

$$$ **Hotel Inglaterra,** a chain hotel, is modern and peaceful, with 36 rooms offering all the comforts (Sb-€76–96, Db-€79–120, extra bed-€31–48, buffet breakfast-€9.80, 20 parking spaces at €12/day, elevator to 3rd floor only, air-con, Cetti Merien 4, tel. 958-221-559, fax 958-227-100, nhinglaterra@nh-hotels.com).

$$ **Hotel Residencia Macia,** right on the colorful Plaza Nueva, is a hotel-esque place with 44 clean, modern, and classy rooms. Choose between an on-the-square view or a quieter interior room (Sb-€48, Db-€70, Tb-€87, 10 percent discount when you show this book at check in—but not if you booked online, good

---

Sleep Code

(€1 = about $1.20, country code: 34)
S = Single, **D** = Double/Twin, **T** = Triple, **Q** = Quad, **b** = bathroom, **s** = shower only, **no CC** = Credit Cards not accepted, **SE** = Speaks English, **NSE** = No English. Breakfast and the 7 percent IVA tax are usually not included. You can assume credit cards are accepted unless noted otherwise.

To help you easily sort through these listings, I've divided the rooms into three categories based on the price for a standard double room with bath during high season:

$$$ **Higher Priced**—Most rooms €100 or more.
$$ **Moderately Priced**—Most rooms between €50–100.
$ **Lower Priced**—Most rooms €50 or less.

Granada Hotels and Restaurants

TO TRAIN STATION

100 YARDS
100 METERS

ALBAYZÍN
MOORISH QUARTER

TO SAN NICOLAS VIEWPOINT + PLAZA LARGA

CATHEDRAL + ROYAL CHAPEL

GRAN VIA DE COLÓN

CALLE ELVIRA

CALD. NUEVA

GREGORIO

CALD. VIEJA

ALMIR.

PLAZA NUEVA

PASTRY

PLAZA BIB RAMBLA

OFICIOS

ZACATIN

CATOLICOS

PLAZA ISABEL CATOLICA

ANIMAS

CUESTA GOMEREZ

REYES

PLAZA CARMEN

TURISMO

TO ALHAMBRA

1 Hotel Inglaterra
2 Hotel Residencia Macia
3 Hotel Anacapri
4 Hotel Gran Vía
5 Casa del Capitan Nazari
6 Hostal Landazuri
7 Hostal Residencia Britz
8 Hostal Navarro Ramos
9 Hostal Viena & Hotel Austria

10 To Hotel Navas & Los Diamantes & Bar Las Copas Fish Bars
11 Hotel Residencia Lisboa
12 Hotel Los Tilos
13 To Hotel Reina Cristina
14 To Paseo de los Tristes

15 Bodega Castaneda
16 Restaurante Naturi Albayzín & Kasbah Tea Shop
17 Los Italianos/La Veneciana Ice Cream
18 Royal Chapel Entry
19 Cathedral Entry
20 Alcaicería Neighborhood

buffet breakfast-€5.30, air-con, elevator, Plaza Nueva 4, tel. 958-227-536, fax 958-227-533, maciaplaza@maciahoteles.com, SE).

$$ **Hotel Anacapri** is a bright, cool, marble oasis with 49 modern rooms and a quiet lounge (Sb-€54–61, Db-€72–90, extra bed-€20, elevator, air-con, 2 blocks toward Gran Vía de Colón from Plaza Nueva at Calle Joaquín Costa 7, just a block from cathedral bus stop, tel. 958-227-477, fax 958-228-909, www.hotelanacapri .com, reservas@hotelanacapri.com, helpful Kathy speaks Iowan).

$$ **Hotel Gran Vía,** right on Granada's main drag, has a stately lobby with Euro-modern business-class rooms (Sb-€60, Db-€90, Tb-€110, show this book for a 10 percent discount on these prices, air-con, elevator, parking-€11/day, 5-min walk from Plaza Nueva,

Gran Vía de Colón 25, tel. 958-285-464, fax 958-285-591, granvia @maciahoteles.com, SE).

$$ **Casa del Capitel Nazarí,** just off the north (church) end of the Plaza Nueva, is a restored 16th-century, Renaissance palace transformed into 17 rather smallish but tastefully decorated rooms facing a courtyard (Sb-€68, Db-€85, extra bed-€30, breakfast-€8, parking-€10/day, air-con, Cuesta Aceituneros 6, tel. 958-215-260, fax 958-215-806, www.hotelcasacapitel.com, info@hotelcasacapitel.com).

Cheaper Places on Cuesta de Gomérez

These are cheap and ramshackle lodgings on the street leading from Plaza Nueva up to the Alhambra.

$ **Hostal Landazuri** is run by friendly, English-speaking Matilda Landazuri and her son, Manolo. While most of its 18 rooms are well-worn, a few are newly renovated with new mattresses and windows. It has a great roof garden with an Alhambra view and hardworking, helpful management. If your room gets too hot, ask for a fan (S-€20, Sb-€28, D-€24, Db-€36–40, Tb-€50, simple €1.80 breakfast or their hearty €2.30 eggs-and-bacon breakfast, includes tax, no CC, 7 parking spaces-€10, ring intercom access to parking lot, Cuesta de Gomérez 24, tel. & fax 958-221-406). The Landazuris also run a good, cheap café.

$ **Hostal Residencia Britz** is a simple, no-nonsense place overlooking Plaza Nueva. All of its 24 basic rooms—with double-paned windows—are streetside. Bring earplugs (S-€18, D-€28, Db-€40, includes tax, no breakfast, coin-op washing machine and dryer, elevator, Plaza Nueva y Gomérez 1, tel. & fax 958-223-652).

$ **Hostal Navarro Ramos** has 15 rooms that are comfortable enough (S-€15, D-€21, Db-€30, Tb-€40.50, no breakfast, no CC, Cuesta de Gomérez 21, 1st floor, tel. 958-250-555, NSE).

$ **Hostal Viena,** run by English-speaking Austrian Irene (ee-RAY-nay), is on a quieter side street, with 32 basic backpacker-type rooms (S-€25, D-€35, Db-€42, Tb-€56, family rooms, includes tax, no breakfast, air-con, next-door bar noisy on weekends, Hospital de Santa Ana 2, 10 yards off Cuesta de Gomérez, tel. & fax 958-221-859, hostalviena@hostelviena.com). Some of these rooms are in nearby and similar **Hotel Austria,** also run by Irene.

$ **Hostal Gomérez** is run by English-speaking Sigfrido Sanchez de León de Torres (who will explain to you how Spanish surnames work if you have the time). This nine-room basic place is listed in nearly every country's student-travel guidebook, as it's another fine cheapie. Quieter rooms are in the back (S-€15, D-€25, T-€35, Q-€40, includes tax, no breakfast, no CC, laundry service-€9, Cuesta de Gomérez 10, 1 floor up, tel. & fax 958-224-437).

Near Plaza Carmen

Two blocks from the TI is the pleasant Plaza Carmen and the beginning of Calle Navas, a pedestrian street offering a couple of good values (and two deep-fried fish bars: **Los Diamantes** and **Bar Las Copas,** both close to Hotel Navas and very popular with locals).

$$$ **Hotel Navas,** a block down Calle Navas, is a modern, well-run, tour-friendly, business-class hotel with 49 spacious rooms (Sb-€77, Db-€101, Tb-€123, breakfast buffet-€7.35, includes tax, air-con, elevator, attached restaurant, Calle Navas 24, tel. 958-225-959, fax 958-227-523, www.hotelesporcel.com, navas@hotelesporcel .com, SE).

$ **Hotel Residencia Lisboa,** which overlooks Plaza Carmen opposite Granada's city hall, offers 28 simple but well-maintained rooms with friendly owners (S-€20, Sb-€32, D-€30, Db-€46, T-€36, Tb-€53, includes tax, no breakfast, elevator, Plaza de Carmen 27, tel. 958-221-413, fax 958-221-487, www.lisboaweb.com, Mary and Juan José).

Near the Cathedral

$$ **Hotel Los Tilos** offers 30 comfortable rooms, some with balconies, on the charming, traffic-free Bib-Rambla square behind the cathedral. All clients are welcome to use the fourth-floor view terrace overlooking the great café, shopping, and people-watching neighborhood (Sb-€41, Db-€65, Tb-€77, includes tax, 20 percent discount with this book and cash, breakfast buffet-€5, air-con, parking-€9/day, Plaza Bib-Rambla 4, tel. 958-266-712, fax 958-266-801, clientes@hotellostilos.com, friendly José-María SE).

$$ **Hotel Reina Cristina** has 43 quiet, elegant rooms a few steps off Plaza Trinidad, a park-like square, near the lively Pescadería and Bib-Rambla squares. Check out the great Mudejar ceiling and the painting at the entrance of this house, where the famous Spanish poet Federico García Lorca hid and was captured before being executed by the Guardia Civil (Sb-€61, Db-€92, Tb-€108, air-con, elevator, Tablas 4, tel. 958-253-211, fax 958-255-728, www.hotelreinacristina.com, clientes@hotelreinacristina.com).

Near the Train Station

$$$ **Hotel Condor,** with 104 modern rooms in a high-rise, has more four-star comfort than character. It's an eight-minute walk from the station, and 15 minutes—or a bus ride—to the center of town (Sb-€80 Db-€118, breakfast-€7.50, laundry service, non-smoking floor, attached restaurant, Avenida de la Constitución 6, tel. 958-283-711, fax 958-283-850, condor@maciahoteles.com).

In or near the Alhambra

If you want to stay on the Alhambra grounds, there are two popular options—famous, overpriced, and often booked up. These are a half mile up the hill from Plaza Nueva.

$$$ **Parador Nacional San Francisco,** offering 36 air-conditioned rooms in a converted 15th-century convent, is called Spain's premier parador (Db-€213, Tb-€288, breakfast-€12, free parking, Real de la Alhambra, tel. 958-221-440, fax 958-222-264, granada @parador.es, SE). You must book six to eight months ahead to spend the night in this lavishly located, stodgy, classy, and historic place. Any peasant, however, can drop in for a coffee, drink, snack, or meal (daily 13:00–16:00 & 20:30–23:00).

$$$ Next to the parador, the elegant and cozy **Hotel América** rents 17 rooms (Ss-€68, Db-€107, includes tax, closed Dec–Feb, tel. 958-227-471, fax 958-227-470, reservas@hotelamericagranada.com, SE). Book three months in advance in high season.

EATING

Traditionally, Granada bars serve a small tapas plate free with any beer or wine ordered. Two well-chosen beers can actually end up being a light meal. In search of an edible memory? A local specialty, *tortilla Sacromonte,* is a spicy omelet with pig's brain and other organs.

These areas are peppered with lively eateries and tapas bars: Paseo de los Tristes, Albayzín, Calle Elvira (near Plaza Nueva), Calle Navas (off Plaza Carmen), and the squares Bib-Rambla and Pescadería (a block apart from each other, just west of the cathedral).

In the Albayzín

The most interesting meals hide out deep in the Albayzín quarter. Two good squares are near the San Nicolás viewpoint. Plaza San Miguel el Bajo has some charming restaurants and kids playing soccer (look for the view over the modern city a block away). Plaza Larga, within two blocks of the first four listings below, also has good eateries (to find the square, ask any local, take bus #31 or #32 from Plaza Nueva, or follow directions and map on page 267). If dining late, take the bus or a taxi back to your hotel rather than wander the backstreets with pickpockets.

For fish, consider **El Ladrillo,** with outdoor tables on a peaceful square (Plaza Fátima, just off Calle Pages), or **El Ladrillo II,** with indoor dining only and a more extensive menu (Calle Panaderos 35, off Plaza Larga, tel. 958-286-123). They both serve a popular *barco* (€8.40 "boatload" of mixed fried fish), a fishy feast that stuffs two to the gills. The smaller *medio-barco,* for €6, fills one adequately. (A *medio-barco* and a salad feed two.) Both restaurants open daily (12:00–24:00). On the same street, just before Ladrillo II, **Restaurante Reina**

Monica, run by friendly Rhi, offers good-value three-course €5.50 *menus,* à la carte options, and free live music—mostly flamenco and Arabic (Tue–Sun 12:00–2:00, music Thu–Sat from 21:30, Nov–April from 20:30, menu includes local and Moroccan specialties, closed Mon, Calle Panaderos 20, tel. 958-203-543).

For fewer tourists, more locals and village atmosphere, and great inexpensive food, try **Casa Torcuato** (Mon–Sat 13:00–16:00 & 20:00–24:00, closed Sun, 2 blocks beyond Plaza Larga on Placeta de Carniceros, Calle Carniceros 4, tel. 958-202-039).

Carmens: For a more memorable but expensive experience, consider fine dining with Alhambra views in a *carmen,* a typical Albayzín house with a garden (notice all the ceramic plates at the front door).

Carmen de las Tomasas has quality food and fine views (Mon–Sat 21:00–24:00, closed Sun, Carril de San Agustín, tel. 958-224-108, Cristina).

Carmen Mirador de Morayma, with an intimate, garden-view mansion ambience, requires reservations (€28 meals, daily 13:30–15:30 & 20:30–23:30, July–Aug closed Sun, Calle Pianista García Carrillo 2, tel. 958-228-290).

Near Plaza Nueva

For people-watching, consider the many restaurants on Plaza Nueva, Bib-Rambla (south of cathedral), or Paseo de los Tristes (by the river Darro, Alhambra-lighted night view, 10 min walk north of Plaza Nueva).

The cheap and easy **Antigua Bodega Castaneda,** a half-block off Plaza Nueva, serves fine *ensaladas,* €3 baked potatoes with a fun variety of toppings, and a €7.90 *surtido de tapas,* an assortment of four tapas (daily 12:30–16:30 & 20:00–12:00, on Calle Elvira, just 20 yards off Plaza Nueva, not the other bodega a block away with the same name—which doesn't serve baked potatoes).

Hippie Options on Calle Calderería Nueva: From Plaza Nueva, walk two long blocks down Calle Elvira and turn right onto the wonderfully hip and Arabic-feeling Calderería Nueva, which leads uphill into the Albayzín. The street is lined with trendy *teterías.* These small tea shops, open all day, are good places to linger, chat, and imagine an America where marijuana was legal. Some are conservative and unmemorable, and others are achingly romantic, filled with incense, beaded cushions, live African music, and effervescent young hippies. They sell light meals and a worldwide range of teas. The plush Kasbah has good (canned) music and Moorish dishes, desserts, and teas. Here's your chance to smoke perfumed tobacco in an opium pipe-like *narguile.*

Naturi Albayzín is a vegetarian place with €7.95 rotating three-course meals, typically featuring classy couscous (daily 13:00–16:00 & 19:00–23:00, Fri 19:00–23:00, reserve for eves and weekends,

Calle Calderería Nueva 10, tel. 958-227-383). Wafting up to the end of the teahouse street you'll find **Bar Restaurante Las Cuevas**— its rickety tables spilling onto the street—serving salads, Moorish dishes, tapas, and wine to a fun family/bohemian crowd (daily 12:30–23:00, tel. 680-235-492, Calle Calderería Nueva 30, next to San Gregorio church).

Dessert: Los Italianos, also known as **La Veneciana,** is popular among locals for its ice cream, *horchata* (almond drink), and shakes (March–mid-Oct daily 8:00–3:00, closed mid-Oct–Feb, Gran Vía de Colón 4, across street from cathedral and Royal Chapel, tel. 958-224-034).

Markets: Though heavy on meat, the Mercado San Agustín also sells fruits and veggies. If nothing else, it's as refreshingly cool as a meat locker (Mon–Sat 8:00–15:30, closed Sun, has small café/bar, Calle Cristo San Agustín, a block north of cathedral, half block off Gran Vía de Colón). The Pescadaría square, a block from Bib-Rambla, usually has some fruit stalls on its northern end, along with inviting restaurants on the square itself.

TRANSPORTATION CONNECTIONS

By train to: Barcelona (1/day, 12 hrs, handy night train), **Madrid** (2/day, 6 hrs, depart Granada at 7:55 and 16:40, confirm time at station), **Toledo** (only 1 train works well, with a transfer in Madrid, leave Granada at 7:55, confirm time at station, allow 10 hours including transfer in Madrid), **Algeciras** (3/day, 4.5 hrs; also 6 buses/day, 3.5–5 hrs), **Ronda** (3/day, 2.5hrs), **Sevilla** (4/day, 3 hrs; also 9 buses/day, 3–4 hrs), **Córdoba** (1/day, 4–6.5 hrs, transfer in Bobadilla; also 9 buses/day, 3 hrs), **Málaga** (3/day, 3–5 hrs, transfer in Bobadilla; also 15 buses/day, 2 hrs). Train info: tel. 902-240-202.

By bus to: Nerja (4/day, 2 hrs, more frequent with transfer in Motril), **Sevilla** (9/day, 3 hrs *directo*, 4 hrs *ruta*; plus trains, above), **Córdoba** (9 buses/day, 3 hrs; plus trains, above), **Málaga** (15/day, 2 hrs; plus trains, above), **Algeciras** (6/day, 3.5–5 hrs, some are *directo*, some are *ruta*), **Línea/Gibraltar** (1/day, 5 hrs). Bus info: tel. 958-185-480.

To better handle the winding roads, some tourists like to reserve a seat at the front of the bus (generally seats 1–30). You (or your hotel or travel agency) can call the station to book a seat— they'll hold it until 40 minutes before departure (tel. 958-185-480, or 902-422-242 for Barcelona or east-coast destinations). Or, if you don't want to show up early to claim your seat, you can buy your ticket in advance with a credit card (tel. 902-330-400).

By car: To drive to Nerja (1.5 hours away), take the exit for the coastal town of Motril. You'll wind through scenic 50 miles south of Granada, then follow signs for Málaga.

SEVILLA

This is the flamboyant city of Carmen and Don Juan, where bullfighting is still politically correct and where little girls still dream of growing up to become flamenco dancers. While Granada has the great Alhambra, and Córdoba the remarkable Mezquita, Sevilla has a soul. It's a wonderful-to-be-alive-in kind of place.

Sevilla, the gateway to the New World in the 16th century, boomed when Spain did. The explorers Amerigo Vespucci and Ferdinand Magellan sailed from its great river harbor. Gold, silver, cocoa, and tobacco arrived on return trips. In the 17th century, Sevilla was Spain's largest and richest city. Local artists Diego Velázquez, Bartolomé Murillo, and Francisco de Zurbarán made it a cultural center. Sevilla's Golden Age, with its New World riches, ended when the harbor silted up and the Spanish empire crumbled.

In the 19th century, Sevilla was a big stop on the Romantic "Grand Tour" of Europe. To build on this tourism and promote trade among Spanish-speaking nations, Sevilla planned a grand exposition in 1929. Bad year. The expo crashed with the stock market. In 1992 Sevilla got a second chance at a World's Fair. This expo was a success, leaving the city with an impressive infrastructure: new airport, train station, sleek bridges, and the super AVE bullet train, making Sevilla a 2.5-hour side-trip from Madrid.

Today, Spain's fourth-largest city (pop. 700,000) is Andalucía's leading city, buzzing with festivals, life, orange and jacaranda trees, sizzling summer heat, color, guitars, and castanets. James Michener

Greater Sevilla

wrote, "Sevilla doesn't *have* ambience, it *is* ambience." Sevilla has its share of impressive sights, but the real magic is the city itself, with its tangled Jewish Quarter, riveting flamenco shows, thriving bars, and teeming evening *paseo*.

Planning Your Time

If ever there were a big Spanish city to linger in, it's Sevilla. On a three-week trip, spend two nights and a day here. On a shorter trip, zip here on the slick AVE train for a day trip from Madrid.

The major sights—the cathedral and the Alcázar (worth about 3 hours) and a wander through the Santa Cruz district (1 hour)—are few and simple for a city of this size. You could spend half a day touring its other sights (listed below). Stroll along the bank of the Guadalquivir River and cross the Bridge of Triana for a view of the tower (Torre del Oro) and cathedral. An evening is essential for the *paseo* and a flamenco show. Bullfights are on most Sundays, April through October. Sevilla's Alcázar is closed on Monday.

Córdoba (described briefly at the end of this chapter) is worth a stop-over if you're taking the AVE.

ORIENTATION

For the tourist, this big city is small. Sevilla's major sights, including the lively Santa Cruz district and the Alcázar, surround the cathedral. The central north-south boulevard, Avenida de la Constitución (with TI, banks, and a post office), zips right past the cathedral to Plaza Nueva (gateway to the shopping district). Nearly everything is within easy walking distance. The bullring is a few blocks west of the cathedral, and Plaza de España is a few blocks south. The area on the west bank of the Guadalquivir River is working-class and colorful, but lacks tourist sights. With taxis so reasonable (€2.50 minimum), friendly, and easy, I rarely bother with the bus.

Tourist Information

Sevilla has several handy tourist offices: The **central** office is a block toward the river from the cathedral (Mon–Fri 9:00–19:00, Sat 10:00–14:00 & 15:00–19:00, Sun and festivals 10:00–14:00, Avenida de la Constitución 21, tel. 954-221-404). The less-crowded **county/city TI** is at Plaza Triunfo, across from the cathedral (Mon–Fri 10:30–20:45, closed Sat–Sun, tel. 954-501-001). There is also a **train station TI** (Mon–Fri 9:00–20:00, Sat–Sun 10:00–14:00, tel. 954-537-626) and an **airport TI** (Mon–Fri 9:00–21:00, Sat–Sun 11:00–15:00, tel. 954-449-128). The TI nearest the Plaza de Armas **bus station** is by the Triana Bridge (Mon–Fri 8:00–20:45, Sat–Sun 9:00–14:00, Calle Arjona 28, tel. 954-221-714).

At any TI, ask for the city map (far better than the one in the promo city magazine); the English-language magazines *Welcome Olé* and *The Tourist*; a current listing of sights, hours, and prices; and a schedule of bullfights. The free monthly events guide, *El Giraldillo*, written in Spanish basic enough to be understood by travelers, covers cultural events in all of Andalucía, with a focus on Sevilla. If heading south, ask for the "Route of the White Towns" brochure and a Jerez map (€0.60 each). Helpful Web sites are www.turismo.sevilla.org and www.andalucia.org.

Arrival in Sevilla

By Train: Trains arrive at the sublime Santa Justa station (banks, ATMs, TI, luggage storage). The town center, marked by the ornate Giralda Cathedral bell tower (visible from the front of the station), is a 30-minute walk, €4 taxi ride, or bus ride away (hike 2 blocks from station to catch bus #21 to cathedral; pay driver €1 as you board). To get near the Santa Cruz quarter from the train station, catch bus #C1 (bus stop in front of station) or #70 (bus stop on Avenida Kansas City); you'll arrive at Jardines de Murillo, just south of the Santa Cruz neighborhood. If you do not have a hotel room reserved, the **Infhor** booth will help you find one for no fee (daily 8:00–22:00, tel. 954-541-952, infhor@yahoo.es).

By Bus: Sevilla's two major bus stations have information offices, cafés, and luggage storage. The Prado de San Sebastián station covers Andalucía, Barcelona, and points east. To get downtown from the station, it's a 10-minute walk—turn right on the major street, San Fernando, then right again on Avenida de la Constitución (Mon–Fri 7:30–22:00 Sat–Sun 9:00–21:00, luggage storage, information tel. 954-417-111, NSE).

The Plaza de Armas station (near the river, opposite Expo '92 site) serves southwest Spain, Madrid, Salamanca, and Portugal. To get downtown from this station, head toward the angled brick apartment building and cross the busy Boulevard Expiración. Go a half block up Calle Arjona to the stop for bus #C4, which goes into town (€1, pay driver; get off at Puerta de Jerez, near main TI), or, even better, continue walking a couple more blocks to the helpful, uncrowded TI at Calle Arjona 28 (see "Tourist Information," previous page). From here you can catch bus #C4 or walk 15 minutes into the center (following map you'll pick up at the TI).

By Car: Driving in Sevilla is difficult, and many cars are broken into. I'd pay to park in a garage. Try the big garage under the bus station at Plaza de Armas (€9/day), the Cristóbal Colón garage (by the bullring and river, €1.15/hr, €12/day), or Avenida Roma (at Puerta de Jerez, €15/24 hr, no CC).

To enter Sevilla, follow signs to *Centro Ciudad* (city center) and drive along the river. For short parking, the riverside Paseo de Cristóbal Colón has two-hour meters and hardworking thieves. Ignore the bogus traffic wardens who direct you to an illegal spot, take a tip, and disappear later when your car gets towed. Consider hiring a taxi to lead you to your hotel, where you can get parking advice.

Getting Around Sevilla

On a hot day, buses in Sevilla can save your life. A single trip costs €1 (pay driver) or you can buy a Bonobus pass, which gives you 10 trips for €4 (sold at kiosks). #C buses make a circular loop that covers

María Luisa Park and Basílica de la Macarena. The #C3 stops in Murillo Gardens, Triana (district south of the river), then Macarena. The #C4 goes the opposite direction without entering Triana.

Helpful Hints

Sevilla Festivals: Sevilla's peak season is April and May. And it has two one-week festival periods when the city is packed. While **Holy Week** (*Semana Santa*—the week between Palm Sunday and Easter Sunday—March 20–27 in 2005) is big all over Spain, it's biggest in Sevilla. Then two weeks after Easter, after taking enough time off to catch its communal breath, Sevilla holds its **April Fair** (described below). This is a celebration of all that's Andalusian, with plenty of eating, drinking, singing, and merrymaking (though most of the revelry takes place in private parties at a large fairground). Book rooms well in advance for festival times. Warning: Prices can go sky-high, and many hotels have four-night minimums.

Train and Plane Tickets: The RENFE offices give out train schedules and sell train tickets. There's a RENFE Travel Center at the train station (daily 8:00–22:00, take a number and wait, call tel. 902-240-202 for reservation and info) and one near Plaza Nueva in the center (Mon–Fri 9:30–14:00 & 17:30–20:00, closed Sat–Sun, Calle Zaragoza 29, tel. 954-211-455, SE). Many travel agencies sell train tickets for the same price as the train station (look for train sticker in agency window).

American Express: AmEx will cash traveler's checks for no fee, change money, or dole out cash to cardholders (Mon–Fri 9:30–13:30 & 16:30–19:30, Sat 10:00–13:00 at Plaza Nueva 7, next to recommended Hotel Inglaterra).

Telephone: A telephone office, Locutorio Público, has metered phone booths. Calls are slightly more expensive than calls made with Spanish phone cards, but you get a quiet setting with a seat (Mon–Fri 10:00–14:00 & 17:00–21:00, Sat 10:00–14:00, closed Sun, in passage at Sierpes 11, near intersection with Calle de Rafael Padura, tel. 954-226-800).

Internet Access: Sevilla has lots of places to get wired, including Internet Workcenter (daily 7:00–23:00, on river side of Alcázar at San Fernando 1, tel. 954-212-074).

Post Office: The post office is at Avenida de la Constitución 32, across from the cathedral (Mon–Fri 8:30–20:30, Sat 9:30–14:00, closed Sun).

Laundry: Lavanderia Roma offers quick and economical drop-off service (€6 per load wash and dry, Mon–Fri 9:30–13:30 & 17:00–20:30, Sat 9:00–14:00, closed Sun, Castelar 2, tel. 954-210-535).

Sevilla

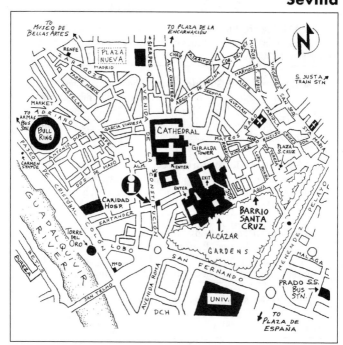

TOURS

Guided City Walks—Concepción Delgado, an enthusiastic teacher and a joy to listen to, takes small groups on English-language-only walks. Using me as her guinea pig, Concepción has designed a fine two-hour introduction to the city, sharing important insights the average visitor misses. Her cultural show-and-tell is worthwhile, even on a one-day visit (€10/person, daily except Sun at 9:30 and 11:30, starting from statue in Plaza Nueva, always call to confirm departure and to reserve a place, tel. 902-158-226, mobile 616-501-100, www.sevillawalkingtours.com, info@sevillawalkingtours.com). For those wanting to really understand the city's two most important sights, she also offers a Cathedral/Alcázar tour daily at 15:15 (€12 plus admissions, 2.5 hours, call first to confirm and meet at statue in Plaza Triunfo).

Hop-on, Hop-off Bus Tours—Two competing city bus tours leave from the curb near the riverside Golden Tower (Torre del Oro). You'll see the buses parked with salespeople handing out fliers. Each does about an hour-long swing through the city with a tape-recorded narration (green route slightly better because it includes María Luisa Park). The tours, which allow hopping on and off at four stops, are

Sevilla at a Glance

▲▲▲**Flamenco** Flamboyant, riveting music-and-dance performances, offered at clubs throughout town. **Hours:** Shows start as
early as 21:00.

▲▲**Cathedral and Giralda Tower** The world's largest Gothic
church, with Columbus' tomb, a treasury, and climbable tower.
Hours: June–mid-Sept Mon–Sat 9:30–15:30, free on Sun
14:30–18:00, mid-Sept–June Mon–Sat 11:00–18:00, free on Sun
14:30–19:00.

▲▲**Basílica de la Macarena** Church and museum with the
much-venerated Weeping Virgin statue and two significant floats
from Sevilla's Holy Week celebrations. **Hours:** Daily 9:30–14:00
& 17:00–20:00.

▲▲**Evening *Paseo*** Locals strolling in the cool of the evening,
mainly through the Barrio Santa Cruz and along the
Guadalquivir River between the San Telmo and Isabel II bridges.
Hours: Spring through fall, until very late in summer.

▲▲**Bullfight Museum** Guided tour of the Plaza de Toros'
arena and its museum. **Hours:** Daily 9:30–19:00, fight days
9:30–15:00.

▲**Bullfights** Some of Spain's best bullfighting, held at Sevilla's
arena. **Hours:** Most Sundays, Easter through October at 18:30
or 19:30.

▲**Alcázar** Palace built by the Moors in the 10th century,
revamped in the 14th century, and still serving as royal digs.
Hours: Tue–Sat 9:30–19:00, Sun 9:30–17:00, off-season
Tue–Sat 9:30–17:00, Sun 10:30–13:00, closed Mon.

▲**Museo de Bellas Artes** Andalucía's top collection of paintings, including Spanish masters such as Murillo and Zurbarán.
Hours: Tue 14:30–20:30, Wed–Sat 9:00–20:30, Sun 9:00–14:30,
closed Mon.

▲**Quickie Town Walk** A jaunt from Plaza Nueva to Calle
Sierpes, sampling the town's lively center. **Hours:** Always open.

▲**Plaza de España** A delightful square with the *azulejo*
tile–decorated Spanish Pavilion, view balconies, and great people-
watching. **Hours:** Always open, best during the 14:00–15:00 and
19:00–20:00 peak *paseo* times.

heavy on Expo '29 and Expo '92 neighborhoods of little interest in '05. While the narration does its best, Sevilla is most interesting where buses can't go (€11, departures daily 10:00–21:00).

Horse and Buggy Tours—A carriage ride is a classic, popular way to survey the city and a relaxing way to enjoy María Luisa Park (about

€30 for a 45-min clip-clop, find English-speaking driver for better narration, if shared by 2 couples the ride is actually quite inexpensive, look for rigs at Plaza América, Plaza Triunfo, Torre del Oro, Alfonso XIII hotel, and Avenida Isabel la Católica).

Boat Cruises—One hour, panoramic tours leave every 30 minutes from the dock behind Torre de Oro (€12, tel. 954-561-692).

More Tours—**Visitours,** a typical big bus-tour company, does €70 all-day trips to Córdoba daily, except Sunday (tel. 954-460-985, www.visitours.es.mn, visitours@terra.es).

American expat **Daniel O'Beirne** organizes and leads tours in Sevilla and throughout Andalucía. Tours include Roman Sevilla, Sephardic Sevilla, and the wine and horses of Jerez (starting at €45/half day, discount for readers with this book, mobile 615-291-736, www.magicalspain.com).

For other guides, contact the **Guides Association of Sevilla** (tel. 954-210-037, apitsevilla@alehop.com).

SIGHTS

Cathedral and Giralda Tower

A ▲▲ sight, this is the third-largest church in Europe (after the

Vatican's St. Peter's and London's St. Paul's) and the largest Gothic church anywhere. When they ripped down a mosque of brick on the site in 1401, the Reconquista Christians bragged, "We'll build a cathedral so huge that anyone who sees it will take us for madmen." They built for 120 years. Even today, the descendants of those madmen proudly display an enlarged photocopy of their *Guinness Book of Records* letter certifying, "The cathedral with the largest area is: Santa María de la Sede in Sevilla, 126 meters long, 82 meters wide, and 30 meters high" (€7, June–mid-Sept Mon–Sat 9:30–15:30, free on Sun 14:30–18:00, mid-Sept–June Mon–Sat

Sevilla's Cathedral

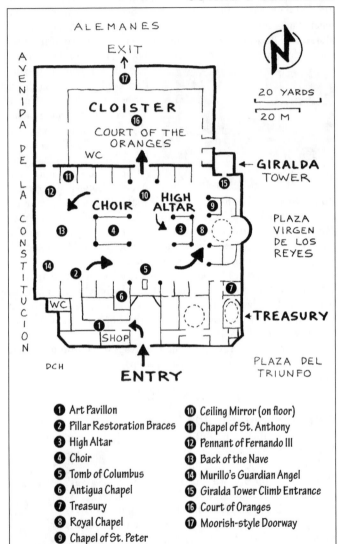

1 Art Pavillon
2 Pillar Restoration Braces
3 High Altar
4 Choir
5 Tomb of Columbus
6 Antigua Chapel
7 Treasury
8 Royal Chapel
9 Chapel of St. Peter
10 Ceiling Mirror (on floor)
11 Chapel of St. Anthony
12 Pennant of Fernando III
13 Back of the Nave
14 Murillo's Guardian Angel
15 Giralda Tower Climb Entrance
16 Court of Oranges
17 Moorish-style Doorway

11:00–18:00, free on Sun 14:30–19:00, last entry 1 hr before closing, WC and drinking fountain inside near entrance and in courtyard near exit, tel. 954-214-971). The €3 audioguides explain each side chapel in a dry manner (consider Concepción Delgado's tour instead, described on page 283).

Enter the cathedral at the south end (closest to the Alcázar). Here's a self-guided tour:

Art Pavilion and Restoration: Just past the turnstile you step into a pavilion of paintings, including works by Sevilla's two 16th-century masters of realism—*St. Ferdinand* by Bartolomé Murillo and *St. John the Baptist in the Desert* by Francisco de Zurbarán. Stepping into the actual church, the first things you'll see are the **restoration braces** supporting huge pillars. These help keep the building from collapsing as people search for an answer to the problem of the pillars' cracking. The likely solution is to empty them (they're hollow, filled with a rubble concrete) and fill them with a modern material that is more flexible.

High Altar: Sit down in front of the high altar in the center of the church. Look through the wrought-iron Renaissance grill at what is called the largest altarpiece *(retablo mayor)* ever made—65 feet tall, with 44 scenes from the life of Jesus carved out of walnut and chestnut and blanketed with a staggering amount of gold leaf (and dust). The main figures were carved by Pierre Dancart, but the whole work took three generations to complete (1481–1564). Dancart used a trick of perspective—its statues get bigger as it gets higher (best seen from the left). The design zigzags from the bottom (birth of Jesus) to the dizzying top (crucifixion).

The Choir: Facing the high altar, the choir features an organ of 7,000 pipes (played at the 10:00 Mass, free for worshipers). A choir area like this (an enclosure within the cathedral for more intimate services) is common in Spain and England, but rare in churches elsewhere. The big spinnable book holder in the middle of the room held giant hymnals—large enough for all to chant from in an age when there weren't enough for everyone. (Facing the huge altarpiece, turn 90 degrees to the right to find Columbus' Tomb.)

Tomb of Columbus: In front of the cathedral's pilgrims' entrance are four kings carrying the tomb of Christopher Columbus. His pallbearers represent Castile, Aragon, León, and Navarre (identify them by their team shirts). Columbus even traveled a lot posthumously. He was buried first in Spain, then in Santo Domingo, then Cuba, and—when Cuba gained independence from Spain, around 1900—he sailed home again to Sevilla. Are the remains actually his? Sevilla likes to think so. (There's a DNA study in the works...stay tuned.) High above on the left is a mural of St. Christopher—patron saint of travelers—from 1584. The clock above dates from 1788.

Immaculate Conception

Throughout Sevilla and Spain, you'll see paintings titled *The Immaculate Conception*, all looking quite similar. Young, lovely, and beaming radiantly, these virgins look pure, untainted…you might even say "immaculate." According to Catholic doctrine, Mary, the future mother of Jesus, entered the world free from the original sin that other mortals share. When she died, her purity allowed her to be taken up directly to Heaven (the "Assumption").

The doctrine of Immaculate Conception can be confusing, even to Catholics. It does not mean that the Virgin Mary herself was born of a virgin. Rather, Mary's mother and father conceived her in the natural way. But at the moment Mary's soul animated her flesh, God granted her a special exemption from original sin. The doctrine of Immaculate Conception had been popular since medieval times, though it was not codified until 1854. It was Sevilla's own Bartolomé Murillo (1617–1682) that pioneered the formula used by so many lesser artists. In Counter-Reformation times (when Murillo lived), paintings of a fresh-faced, ecstatic Mary made abstract doctrines like the Immaculate Conception and the Assumption tangible and accessible to all.

In the next chapel on the right, the **Antigua Chapel,** is the gilded fresco of the Virgin Antigua, the oldest art in the church. It was actually painted onto the horseshoe-shaped prayer niche of the former mosque which, when conquered in 1248, served as a church for about 120 years—until it was torn down to be replaced by this huge church. Rebuilders, captivated by the beauty of the Virgin holding the rose and Christ child holding the bird, decided to save it. From here, we'll tour the cathedral counterclockwise, starting with the Tesoro.

Treasury: The Tesoro fills several rooms in the corner of the church. Start by marveling at the ornate 16th-century Plateresque dome of the main room, a grand souvenir from Sevilla's Golden Age. God is way up in the cupola. The three layers of figures below him show the heavenly host, relatives in Purgatory looking to Heaven and hoping you do them well, and the wretched in Hell, including a topless sinner engulfed in flames and teased cruelly by pitchfork-wielding monsters. The pure gold reliquaries hold hundreds of holy bones. One features "a piece of the true cross."

Wandering deeper into the treasury, you'll find the first oval dome in Europe—in the 16th-century chapter room (Sala Capitular) where monthly meetings take place with the bishop (see his throne). Spain's most valuable crown is in the square, wood-paneled "room of ornaments." The Corona de la Virgen de los Reyes sparkles with 11,000 precious stones and the world's largest pearl—used as the torso of an angel. Above the bishop's throne in the chapter room hangs what is perhaps the finest of Murillo's many paintings of the Virgin Mary, called *The Immaculate Conception* (1668).

Royal Chapel (Capilla Real): Returning to the nave, continue counterclockwise around the church, passing by the lavish Royal Chapel, where several of the kings of Castile are buried. On the main altar sits a silver urn with the mortal remains of *"El Santo,"* Fernando III (1201–1252), who was one of Spain's greatest early kings. He liberated Sevilla from the Muslims in 1248, united the kingdoms of Castile and León, founded the University of Salamanca, and set the country on a course to eventually unite under the Christian religion. When he died, he was acclaimed a saint, an opinion ratified by the pope in 1671.

The next chapel, the **Chapel of St. Peter** (Capilla de San Pedro), is filled with paintings by Francisco de Zurbarán that illustrate scenes from the life of St. Peter. Sevilla's favorite painter in the 1630s, Zurbarán portrays Peter with a gritty realism that brings heavenly events right down to earth. His brutal realism gave way to the softer-edged realism of Sevilla's favorite painter of the 1650s, Murillo.

Continuing on, notice the entry to the Giralda Tower. The glass case just before the entry displays the Guinness certificate declaring that this is indeed the largest church in area.

Continuing counterclockwise, you'll walk over a **mirror on the floor** (near the high altar and choir), providing a neck-friendly way to admire the Plateresque tracery on the ceiling. The intricate masonry resembles lacy silverwork (from *plata*—silver).

The **Chapel of St. Anthony** (Capilla de San Antonio), the last chapel on the right, is used for baptisms. The Renaissance baptismal font has angels carved along its base. In Murillo's *Vision of St. Anthony* (1656), the saint kneels in wonder as a baby Jesus comes down surrounded by a choir of angels. Anthony is one of Spain's most popular saints. As the patron saint of lost things, people come here to pray for Anthony's help in finding jobs, car keys, and life partners. Above that is the *Baptism of Christ*, also by Murillo. The stained glass dates from 1685.

Nearby, a glass case displays the **pennant of Fernando III** raised over the minaret of the mosque on November 23, 1248, as Christian forces finally expelled the Moors from Sevilla. It was long paraded through the city on special days.

Continuing on, stand at the **back of the nave** (behind the choir) and appreciate the ornate immensity of the church. Can you see the angels trumpeting on their Cuban mahogany? Just left of the main door (blocked by a massive candlestick holder from 1560) is a niche with **Murillo's *Guardian Angel*** pointing to the light and showing an astonished child the way.

Christopher Columbus
(1451–1506)

This Italian wool-weaver ran off to sea, was shipwrecked in Portugal, married a captain's daughter, learned Portuguese and Spanish, and convinced Spain's monarchs to finance his bold scheme to trade with the East by sailing west. On August 3, 1492, Columbus set sail from Palos (near Huelva, 60 miles west of Sevilla) with three ships and 90 men, hoping to land in Asia, which Columbus estimated was 3,000 miles away. Three thousand miles later—with the superstitious crew ready to mutiny, having seen evil omens like a falling meteor and a jittery compass—Columbus landed on an island in the Bahamas (October 12, 1492), convinced he'd reached Asia. They traded with the "Indians" and returned home to Palos harbor, where they were received as heroes.

Columbus made three more voyages to the New World and became rich with gold. He gained a bad reputation among the colonists, was arrested, and returned to Spain in chains. Though pardoned, Columbus fell out of favor with the court. On May 20, 1506, he died in Valladolid. His son said he was felled by "gout and by grief at seeing himself fallen from his high estate," but historians speculate that diabetes or syphilis may have contributed. Columbus died thinking he'd visited Asia, unaware he'd opened up Europe to a New World.

Backtrack the length of the church toward the Giralda Tower, and notice the back of the choir's Baroque pipe organ. The exit sign leads to the Orange Patio and the exit, but first, some exercise...

Giralda Tower Climb: Your church admission includes entry to the bell tower. Notice the beautiful Moorish simplicity as you climb to its top, 330 feet up, for a grand city view. The spiraling ramp was designed to accommodate riders on horseback—who galloped up five times a day to give the Muslim call to prayer.

Court of Oranges: Today's cloister was once the mosque's Court of the Oranges *(Naranjas)*. Twelfth-century Muslims stopped at the fountain in the middle to wash their hands, face, and feet before praying. The ankle-breaking lanes between the bricks were once irrigation streams—a reminder that the Moors introduced irrigation to Iberia. The mosque was made of bricks; the church is built of stone. The only remnants of the mosque today are the Court of Oranges, the Giralda Tower, and the site itself.

As you exit the Court of Oranges (and the cathedral), notice the arch over the **Moorish-style doorway.** As with much of the Moorish-looking art in town, it's the work of 16th-century Moorish artists under Christian rule—the two coats of arms are a giveaway. The relief above the door (looking in from outside) shows the Bible story of Jesus ridding the temple of the merchants...a reminder to contemporary merchants that there will be no retail activity in the church. The plaque on the right is one of many scattered throughout town showing a place Miguel de Cervantes—the great 16th-century Spanish writer—mentioned in his books. (In this case, the topic was pickpockets.) The huge green doors are a bit of the surviving pre-1248 mosque—wood covered with bronze. Study the fine workmanship.

Giralda Tower Exterior: Step across the street from the exit gate and look at the bell tower. Formerly a Moorish minaret from which Muslims were called to prayer, it became the cathedral's bell tower after the Reconquista. It's crowned by a 4,500-pound bronze statue symbolizing the Triumph of Faith (specifically the Christian faith over the Muslim one) that caps it and serves as a weathervane (*giralda* in Spanish). In 1356, the original top of the tower fell. You're looking at a 16th-century Christian-built top with a ribbon of letters proclaiming, "The strongest tower is the name of God" (you can see *"Fortísima"*).

Needing more strength than their bricks could provide for the lowest section of the tower, the Moors used Roman-cut stones. Now circle around for a close look at the corner of the tower at ground level; you can actually read the Latin on one of the stones. The tower offers a brief recap of the city's history—sitting on a Roman foundation, a long Moorish period capped by our Christian age. Today, by law, no building can be higher than the statue atop the tower.

Alcázar and Nearby

▲Alcázar—Originally a 10th-century palace built for the governors of the local Moorish state, this still functions as a royal palace...the oldest still in use in Europe. What you see today is an extensive 14th-century rebuild, done by Moorish workmen (Mudejar) for the Christian King Pedro I. Pedro was nicknamed either "the Cruel" or "the Just," depending on which end of his sword you were on (€5, Tue–Sat 9:30–19:00, Sun 9:30–17:00, off-season Tue–Sat 9:30–17:00, Sun 10:30–13:00, closed Mon, tel. 954-502-323). The €3 audioguide is tempting and tries hard. But, sorry, there's no way to make this palace worth a flowery hour of hard-to-follow commentary. (Again, you could consider Concepción's tour—described on page 283.)

The Alcázar is a thought-provoking glimpse of a graceful Al-Andalus (Moorish) world that might have survived its Castilian conquerors—but didn't. But I have a tough time hanging any specific history on it. The floor plan is intentionally confusing, part of the style designed to make experiencing the place more exciting and surprising. While Granada's Alhambra was built by Moors for Moorish rulers, what you see here is essentially a Christian ruler's palace, built in the Moorish style.

Just past the turnstiles, walk through the Patio of the Lions and stop under the arch of the wall to orient yourself. Facing the Patio de la Montería, you see the palace's three wings: Ahead is King Pedro the Cruel's Palace; the wing on the right is the 16th-century Admiral's Apartments; and on the left is the 13th-century Gothic wing.

Admiral's Apartments: When Queen Isabel debriefed Columbus here after his New World discoveries, she realized this could be big business. In 1503, she created this wing to administer Spain's New World ventures.

On the right, you'll find the Santa María de los Buenos Aires Chapel (St. Mary of the Fair Winds—or, as many Spanish boys would say, "of the good farts"). The Virgin of the Fair Winds was the patron saint of navigators and a favorite of Columbus. The fine Virgin of the Navigators altarpiece (painted by Alejo Fernández in the 1530s) is said to have the only portrait of Ferdinand (on left with gold cape) with Columbus (blond guy on right; Columbus' son said of his dad: "In his youth his hair was blond, but when he reached 30, it all turned white"). As it's the earliest known portrait of Columbus, it's considered the most accurate. Notice how the Virgin's cape seems to protect everyone under it—even the Indians in the dark background (the first time Indians were painted in Europe). On the left is a model of Columbus' *Santa María*, his flagship and the only one of his three ships not to survive the 1492 voyage. Columbus complained that the *Santa María*—a big cargo ship, different from the sleek *Niña* and *Pinta* caravels—was too slow. On Christmas Day, it ran aground and tore a hole in its keel. The ship was dismantled to build the first permanent structure in America, a fort for 39 colonists. (After Columbus left, the natives burned the fort and killed the colonists.) Opposite the altarpiece is the family coat of arms of Columbus' descendants, who now live in Spain and Puerto Rico. It reads: "To Castile and to León, Colón (that's "Columbus" in Spanish) gave a new world."

Before leaving, pop into the room just right of the grand, still-used reception room for a look at (mostly foreign) handheld ornate fans and a long painting showing 17th-century Sevilla during Holy Week. Follow the procession, which is much like today's procession of traditional floats, carried by teams of 24 to 48 men and followed by a parade of KKK-looking penitents.

King Pedro the Cruel's Palace: This 14th-century nucleus of the complex, the real Alcázar, is centered around the elegantly proportioned Court of the Maidens (Patio de las Doncellas), decorated in Moorish style below and Renaissance above.

King Pedro (1334–1369) cruelly abandoned his wife and moved into the Alcázar with his mistress. He hired Muslim workers from Granada to recreate the romance of that city's Alhambra in the stark Alcázar. The designers created a microclimate engineered for coolness: water, plants, pottery, thick walls, and darkness. Even with the inevitable hodgepodge of style that comes with 600 years of renovation, it's considered Spain's best example of the Mudejar style. Notice the sumptuous ceilings; you'll see peacocks, castles, and kings that you wouldn't find in religious Muslim decor, which avoids images. The stylized Arabic script (creating a visual chant of Koranic verses in Moorish buildings, such as the Alhambra) survives, but propaganda phrases such as "dedicated to the magnificent Sultan Pedro—thanks to God!" have been added.

A passageway leads to the second courtyard, the smaller and more delicate Dolls' Court (Patio de las Muñecas)—for the king's private and family life. Originally, the center of the courtyard had a pool, cooling the residents and reflecting the decorative patterns once brightly painted on the walls.

Gothic Charles V wing: Next, climb a few steps and enter the Gothic wing of the palace. The tapestries—celebrating Emperor Charles V's 1535 victory in Tunis over the Turks—are from Brussels (1554). The great Emperor Charles picked the Alcázar for his wedding reception with Isabel of Portugal. Study the great map with the unusual perspective—Africa being at the top. It's supposed to be from a Barcelona aerial perspective. Find the big fortified city in the middle (Barcelona), Lisboa (Lisbon), Gibraltar, Italy, Sicily, and the Mediterranean islands. The artist paints himself holding the legend—with a scale in both leagues and miles. This is an 18th-century copy of the original.

The Garden: The best-tended and safest in town, it's full of tropical flowers, wild cats, cool fountains, and hot tourists. The intimate geometric zone nearest the palace is the Moorish garden. The far-flung garden beyond that was the backyard of the Christian ruler.

Archivo de Indias—The building (in Lonja Palace, across street from Alcázar) was designed by the same person who did El Escorial. Originally a market, it's the top building in Sevilla from its 16th-century glory days. Today it houses the archive of documents of the discovery and conquest of the New World. This could be fascinating, but little of importance is on display (old maps of Havana) and there's barely a word of English (likely open in 2005 after renovation, though part of building will be closed off).

Barrio Santa Cruz Walk

1. Plaza del Triunfo
2. Patio de Banderas
3. Callejón del Agua
4. Plaza de Santa Cruz
5. Plaza de Refinadores
6. Casa de Murillo
7. Convent of San José del Carmen
8. Plaza de los Venerables
9. Plaza de Doña Elvira
10. Plaza de la Alianza

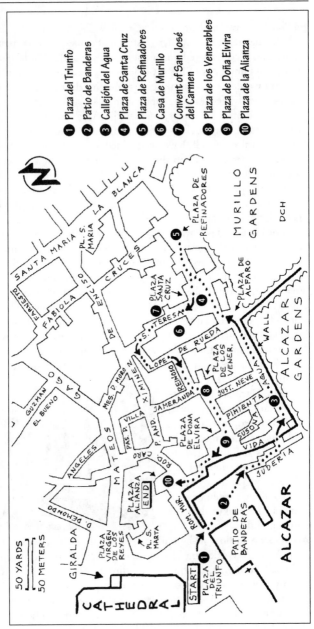

Walk through Barrio Santa Cruz

Only the tangled street plan survives from the days when this was
Sevilla's Jewish Quarter. This classy maze of lanes (too narrow for cars),
small plazas, *azulejo* tile-covered patios, and whitewashed houses with

wrought-iron latticework draped
with flowers is a great refuge
from the summer heat and
bustle of Sevilla. The narrow
streets—some with buildings so
close they're called "kissing
lanes"—were actually designed
to maximize shade. Even today,
locals claim the Barrio Santa
Cruz is three degrees cooler than
the rest of the city.

Orange trees abound. Since they never lose their leaves, they
provide constant shade. But forget about eating any of the oranges.
They're bitter and used only to make vitamins, perfume, cat food,
and that marmalade you can't avoid in England's B&Bs.

The Barrio is made for wandering and just getting lost. Getting
lost is easy, and I recommend doing just that. But to get started,
here's a plaza-to-plaza walk that loops you through the *corazón*
(heart) of the neighborhood and back out again. Ideally, skip the walk
in the morning, when the Barrio's charm is trampled by tour groups.

Start at the cathedral and head toward the Alcázar (both
described above) through **Plaza del Triunfo** with its statue of the
Virgin. Pass through an opening in the Alcázar wall under the arch.
You'll emerge in a courtyard called the **Patio de Banderas.** Named
for "flags," not Antonio, the Banderas courtyard has a postcard view
of the Giralda Tower.

Exit the courtyard at the far corner, through the Judería arch,
walking alongside the Alcázar wall. The street turns left (east), then
right, and soon becomes the narrow alleyway called **Callejón del
Agua,** which follows the wall of the Alcázar gardens. On the left,
peek through iron gates for the occasional glimpse of the flower-
smothered patios of exclusive private residences. The patio of #2 is
especially nice, ringed with columns and colored with glazed tiles.
The tiles are not only decorative, they keep buildings cooler in the
summer heat. At the end of the street is an entrance into the pleasant Murillo Gardens, formerly the fruit-and-vegetable gardens for
the Alcázar.

Continue past the gates to where Callejón del Agua leads into
Plaza de Santa Cruz, arguably the heart of the Barrio. In the center
stands the ornate, wrought-iron iron Cross of the Locksmiths
(Cerrajería, 1692). On the square you'll find the recommended Los
Gallos flamenco bar (described below).

Bartolomé Murillo
(1617-1682)

The son of a barber of Seville, Bartolomé Murillo got his start selling paintings for export to frontier churches in the Americas. In his 20s, he became famous after painting a series of saints for Sevilla's Franciscan monastery. By mid-century, Murillo's accesible style was spreading through Spain and beyond.

He painted street kids with cute smiles and grimy faces, and radiant young Marías with Ivory-soap complexions and rapturous poses (Immaculate Conceptions). Murillo's paintings view the world through a soft-focus lens, wrapping everything in warm colors and soft light, with a touch (too much, for some) of sentimentality.

Murillo became rich, popular, a family man, and the toast of Sevilla's high society. In 1664, his wife died, leaving him heartbroken, but his last 20 years were his most prolific. At age 65, Murillo died painting, falling off a scaffold.

Follow Calle Mezquita further east to the nearby **Plaza de Refinadores.** Sevilla's most famous (if fictional) citizen is honored here with a statue. Don Juan Tenorio was a notorious sex addict and atheist who thumbed his nose at the morals of his day. After heartlessly seducing a general's daughter, he killed the general in a duel, then later mocked the man's statue. In the final act, the statue comes to life and drags Don Juan down to Hell. The legend, set in the wide-open city of Sevilla in the 1600s, inspired plays by Molière and Tirso de Molina, as well as Mozart's opera *Don Giovanni*. In Spain, an 1844 version by José Zorrilla is still performed regularly.

Backtrack to Plaza de Santa Cruz and turn right (north) on Calle Santa Teresa. At #8 is **Casa de Murillo.** One of Sevilla's famous painters lived here, soaking in the ambience of street life and reproducing it in his paintings of cute beggar children.

Directly across from Casa Murillo, the **Convent of San José del Carmen** is where Saint Teresa stayed when she visited from her hometown of Ávila. The convent keeps relics of the mystic nun, such as the manuscript of her treatise *Las Moradas* ("The Interior Castle," where truth dwells) and a portrait of Teresa done by a contemporary.

Continue north on Calle Santa Teresa, then left (west) on Calle Lope de Rueda, then right on Calle Reinoso. Calle Reinoso— so narrow that the buildings almost touch—is one of the Barrio's "kissing lanes."

The street spills into **Plaza de los Venerables,** another candidate for heart of the Barrio. The streets branching off it (Jamerdana and Susona) ooze local ambience. The large, harmonious, Baroque-style Hospital of the Venerables (1675) was once an old priests' home

Sevilla's Jews

In the summer of 1391, smoldering anti-Jewish sentiment flared up in Sevilla. On June 6, the city's Jewish Quarter (Judería) was ransacked by Christian mobs. Four thousand Jews were killed, 5,000 Jewish families driven from their homes, synagogues were stripped and transformed into churches, the Star of David came down, and the former Judería became the neighborhood of the Holy Cross—Barrio Santa Cruz. Sevilla's uprising spread through Spain (and Europe), the first of many nasty pogroms during the next century.

Before the pogrom, Jews had lived in Sevilla for centuries as the city's respected merchants, doctors, and bankers. They flourished under the Muslim Moors. When Sevilla was "liberated" by King Ferdinand (1248), Jews were given protection by Spain's kings and allowed a measure of self-government, though they were confined to the Jewish neighborhood.

But by the 14th century, Jews were increasingly accused of everything from poisoning wells to ritually sacrificing Christian babies. Mobs killed suspected Jews; some of Sevilla's most respected Jewish citizens had their fortunes confiscated; and Jewish kids were mocked and bullied on the playground.

After 1391, Jews faced a choice: be persecuted (even killed), move, or convert to Christianity. Those who converted—called *conversos,* New Christians, or *marranos* ("swine")—were always under suspicion of practicing their old faith in private, undermining true Christianity. Fanning the suspicion was the fact that Old Christians were threatened by this new social class of converted Jews who now had equal status.

To root out the (perceived) problem of underground Judaism, the "Catholic Kings" Ferdinand and Isabel established the Inquisition in Spain (1478). Under the direction of Grand Inquisitor Tomás de Torquemada, these religious courts arrested and interrogated *conversos* suspected of practicing Judaism. Using long solitary confinement and torture, they extracted confessions.

On February 6, 1481, Sevilla hosted Spain's first *auto da fe* ("act of faith"), a public confession and punishment for heresy. Six accused *conversos* were paraded barefoot into the cathedral, made to publicly confess their sins, then were burned at the stake. Over the next three decades, thousands of *conversos* (some historians say hundreds, some say tens of thousands) were tried and killed in Spain.

In 1492, the same year the last Moors were driven from Spain, Ferdinand and Isabel decreed that all remaining Jews convert or be expelled, and Spain emerged as a nation unified under the banner of Christianity.

(the "venerables"). The highlight is the courtyard, featuring a round, sunken fountain. The hospital's church (1698) is decorated with frescoes by Valdes León and his son. The complex now houses temporary art exhibits (€4.75, daily 10:00–14:00 & 16:00–20:00, tel. 954-562-696.)

Also on the plaza is Hostería del Laurel. Act I, Scene 1, of *The Libertine of Seville* begins here: The curtain rises on Don Juan at the inn, trying to write a letter, surrounded by loud, heavy-drinking partyers. Let your imagination (or a pitcher of sangria) bring the scene alive.

Continuing west on Gloria, you soon reach **Plaza de Doña Elvira,** named for the woman who Don Juan passionately loves then heartlessly dumps to pursue the general's daughter. This small square, with orange trees, tile benches, and a stone fountain, sums up our Barrio walk. Shops sell works by local artisans, such as ceramics, embroidery, and fans.

From the Plaza, head north along Calle Rodrigo Caro, passing the recommended La Cueva restaurant (see below), into **Plaza de la Alianza.** Ever consider a career change? Gain inspiration at the John Fulton Studio, an art gallery featuring the work of the American who pursued two dreams. Though born in Philadelphia, Fulton got hooked on bullfighting. He trained in the tacky bullrings of Mexico, then in 1956 he moved to Sevilla, the world capital of the sport. His career as matador was not top-notch, and the Spaniards were slow to warm to the Yankee, but his courage and persistence earned their grudging respect. After retirement, he put down the cape and picked up a brush, making the colorful paintings in this studio.

From Plaza de la Alianza, you can return to the cathedral by turning left (west) on Calle Romero Murube (along the wall). Or head east/northeast on Callejón de Rodrigo Caro, which intersects with Calle Mateos Gago, lined with atmospheric tapas bars.

Between the River and the Cathedral

Hospital de la Caridad—This Charity Hospital was founded by a nobleman in the 17th century. Peek into the fine courtyard. On the left, the chapel has some gruesome art (above both doors) illustrating that death is the great equalizer, and an altar so sweet only a Spaniard could enjoy it. The Dutch tiles depicting scenes of the Old and New Testament are a reminder of the time when the Netherlands were under Spanish rule in the mid-16th century (€3, Mon–Sat 9:00–13:30 & 15:30–19:30, Sun 9:00–18:00, tel. 954-223-232).

Torre del Oro/Naval Museum—Sevilla's historic riverside Golden Tower was the starting point and ending point for all shipping to the New World. It's named for the golden tiles that once covered it—not for all the New World booty that landed here. Since the Moors built it in the 13th century, it has been part of the city's fortifications, with a heavy chain draped across the river to protect the harbor. Today it houses a dreary little naval museum. Looking past the dried fish and charts of knots, find the mural showing the world-spanning journeys of Vasco da Gama and Juan Sebastián Elcano; the model of the *Santa María* (the first ship to have landed in the New World); and an interesting mural of Sevilla in 1740. Enjoy the view from the balconies upstairs. The Guadalquivir River is now just a trickle of its former self, after canals built in the 1920s siphoned off most of its water to feed ports downstream (€1, free Tue, Tue–Fri 10:00–14:00, Sat–Sun 11:00–14:00, closed Mon and Aug, tel. 954-222-419).

Near Plaza Nueva

▲Quickie Town Walk: Plaza Nueva to Calle Sierpes—While many tourists never get beyond the cathedral and the Santa Cruz neighborhood, it's important to wander west into the lively shopping center of town, which also happens to be the oldest part of Sevilla. Plaza Nueva—a 19th-century square facing the ornate city hall—features a statue of Ferdinand III, a local favorite because he freed Sevilla from the Moors in 1248. From here, wander down Calle Tetuán into Sevilla's pedestrian-zone shopping center—a delightful alternative to the suburban mall. This is a hit for Spanish fashions (Zara, shoes, and so on).

Follow Calle Jovellanos (after checking out the frilly fancy ladies' shoes at Pilar Burgos) to the right. At the first kink in the lane is Capilla de San José—Saint Joseph's Chapel, located in the historic carpenters' quarter (daily 8:00–12:30 & 18:30–20:30). I have to say, it's excess like this that gives Baroque a bad name. Check out the votive offerings—requests for help and thanks for miracles—in the rear. Ten steps beyond the church is a glazed-tile scene that shows the 1929 Sevilla fair.

Continue to Calle Sierpes, the best shopping street in town. A commercial center for 500 years, it's the main street of the Holy Week processions, when it's packed and the balconies bulge with spectators.

Near Calle Sierpes and Calle Sagasta, a shop shows off traditional shawls and fans. Andalusian women have various fans to match different dresses. The mantilla (ornate head scarf) comes in black (worn only on Good Friday and by the mother of the groom at weddings) and white (worn at bullfights during the April fair). Cross Calle Sierpes to Calle Sagasta and notice it has two names—the modern version and a medieval one: "Antigua Calle de Gallegos" ("Ancient Street of the Galicians"). With the Christian victory in 1248, the Muslims were given one month to evacuate. To consolidate Christian control, settlers from the north were planted here. This street was home to the Galicians.

The street Calle Sagasta leads to Plaza del Salvador and Sevilla's second-most-important church, El Salvador (closed indefinitely). If it's open, take a good look at the figures carried through town during Holy Week processions. Floats carrying scenes from the Crucifixion are always followed by a float with a statue of a weeping Virgin. Sevilla's many adored Virgins are always portrayed weeping.

The church and surrounding streets are on the high ground where Phoenicians originally established the town. The Romans built their forum here. The Arabs held their market here. Today it's fun to window-shop in the colorful lanes that surround the church. Calle Francos leads past a classy modern mall (Tiendas Peyré Centro at #40, nice air-conditioned café) back to the cathedral. Or, for multiple tapas options, walk two blocks up Alcaicería to Alfalfa square and Pérez Galdos street. Popular spots include Caracoles, Manolo, and La Espuela.

Near Plaza de España

University—Today's university was yesterday's *fábrica de tabacos* (tobacco factory), which employed 10,000 young female *cigareras*—including the saucy femme fatale of Bizet's opera *Carmen*. In the 18th century, it was the second-largest building in Spain, after El Escorial. Wander through its halls as you walk to Plaza de España. The university's bustling café is a good place for cheap tapas, beer, wine, and conversation (Mon–Fri 8:00–21:00, Sat 9:00–13:00, closed Sun).

▲**Plaza de España**—The square, the surrounding buildings, and the nearby María Luisa Park are the remains of the 1929 international fair—where for a year the Spanish-speaking countries of the world enjoyed a mutual admiration fiesta. This delightful area, the epitome of World's Fair–style building, is great for people-watching (especially during 14:00–15:00 and 19:00–20:00 peak *paseo* hours). Stroll through the park and along the canal. The highlight is what was once the Spanish Pavilion. Its *azulejo* tiles (a trademark of Sevilla) show historic scenes and maps from every province of Spain (arranged in alphabetical order from Álava to Zaragoza). Climb to one of the balconies for a fine view. Beware, this is a classic haunt of thieves and con artists. Believe no one here. Thieves, posing as lost tourists, will come at you with a map unfolded to hide their speedy, greedy fingers.

Away from the Center

▲**Museo de Bellas Artes**—Sevilla's passion for religious art is preserved and displayed in its Museum of Fine Art—the Museo de Bellas Artes. While most Americans go for El Greco, Goya, and Velázquez (not a forte of this collection), this museum gives a fine look at the other, less-appreciated Spanish masters—Zurbarán and Murillo. Rather than exhausting, the museum is pleasantly enjoyable (€1.50, Tue 14:30–20:30, Wed–Sat 9:00–20:30, Sun 9:00–14:30, closed Mon, bus #C1, #C2, #C3, or #C4 to Pasarela de la Cartuja, Plaza Museo 9, tel. 954-220-790). If short on time, you can see a representative sampling of Zurbarán and Murillo paintings in the cathedral.

Several of Spain's top artists—Velázquez, Murillo, and Zurbarán—lived in Sevilla. This was Spain's wealthy commercial capital. It was New York City, while Madrid was a newly-built center of government, like Washington D.C. In the early 1800s, Spain's liberal government was disbanding convents and monasteries, and secular fanatics were looting churches. Thankfully, the region's religious art was rescued and hung safely here in this convent-turned-museum.

Spain's economic Golden Age—the 1500s—blossomed into the golden age of Spanish painting—the 1600s. Artists such as Zurbarán combined realism with mysticism. He painted balding saints and monks with wrinkled faces and sunburned hands. The style suited Spain's spiritual climate, as the Catholic Church used this art in its Counter-Reformation battle against the Protestant rebellion. The core of the collection is in Rooms 3 through 10. Most of the major works are displayed in Room 5, the convent's former chapel. Tour the collection.

Francisco de Zurbarán (soor-ber-ON, 1598–1664) paints saints and monks, and the miraculous things they experience, presented with unblinking, crystal-clear, brightly-lit, highly-detailed realism. Monks and nuns could ponder Zurbarán's meticulous paintings (Room 10 and the room leading to 10) for hours, finding God in the details.

Zurbarán shines a harsh spotlight on his subject, creating strong shadows. Like the secluded monks themselves, Zurbarán's people stand starkly isolated against a dark, single-color background. He was the ideal painter of the austere religion of Spain.

In Zurbarán's *St. Hugo visiting the Cartugian Monks at Supper* (Room 10), white-robed monks gather together for their simple meal in the communal dining hall. Above them hangs a painting of Mary, baby Jesus, and John the Baptist. Zurbarán painted paintings for monks' dining halls like this. His audience: celibate men and women who lived in isolation, as in this former convent, devoting their time to quiet meditation, prayer, and Bible study.

The *Apotheosis of St. Thomas Aquinas* (ground level, Room 5) is considered Zurbarán's most beautiful and important work. It was done at the height of his career, when stark realism was all the rage. Here again Zurbarán presents the miraculous in a believable, down-to-earth way.

Bartolomé Murillo (mur-EE-oh, 1617–1682) was the son of a barber of Seville (see page 296). His *Madonna and Child* (*La Servilletta*, 1665, ground floor Room 5) shows the warmth and appeal of his work. By about 1650, Murillo's easy-to-appreciate style had replaced Zurbarán's harsh realism.

The Immaculate Conception (several versions in the museum, ground floor, Room 5) was Murillo's favorite subject. To many Spaniards, Mary is their main connection to Heaven. They pray directly to her, asking her to intercede for them with God. This Mary looks very receptive.

▲▲**Basílica de la Macarena**—Sevilla's Holy Week celebrations are Spain's grandest. During the week leading up to Easter, the city is packed with pilgrims witnessing 50 processions carrying about 100 religious floats. Get a feel for this event by visiting Basílica de la Macarena (built in 1947) to see the two most impressive floats and the darling of Semana Santa, the Weeping Virgin (Virgen de la Macarena or La Esperanza, church free, museum-€3, daily 9:30–14:00 & 17:00–20:00, taxi to Puerta Macarena or bus #C3 or #C4 from Puerta Jerez, tel. 954-901-800).

Grab a pew and study Mary, complete with crystal teardrops. She's like a 17th-century doll with human hair and articulated arms, and even dressed with underclothes. Her beautiful expression—halfway between smiling and crying—is moving, in a Baroque way. Her weeping can be contagious—look around you. Filling a side chapel (on left) is the Christ of the Sentence (from 1654), showing Jesus the day he was condemned.

The two most important floats of the Holy Week parades—the floats that Mary and Jesus ride every Good Friday—are parked behind the altar (through the door left of the altar).

The three-ton float, slathered in gold leaf, shows a commotion of figures acting out the sentencing of Christ (who's placed in the front of this crowd). Pontius Pilate is about to wash his hands. Pilate's wife cries as a man reads the death sentence. While pious Sevillan women wail in the streets, relays of 48 men carry this—only their feet showing under the drapes—as they shuffle through the streets from midnight to 14:00 every Good Friday. Shuffle upstairs for another perspective.

La Esperanza follows the Sentencing of Christ in the procession. Her smaller (1.5-ton) float, in the next room, seems all silver and candles—"strong enough to support the roof but tender enough to quiver in the soft night breeze." Mary has a wardrobe of three huge mantles (each displayed here) worn in successive years. The big green one is from 1900. Her six-pound gold crown/halo (in a glass case in the wall) is from 1913. This float has a mesmerizing effect on the local crowds. They line up for hours, clapping, weeping, and throwing roses as it slowly works its way through the city. My Sevillan friend explained, "She knows all the problems of Sevilla and its people. We've been confiding in her for centuries. To us, she is hope. That's her name—Esperanza."

Before leaving, find the case of matador outfits (also upstairs) given to the church over the years by bullfighters in thanks for the protection they feel they received from La Macarena. Considered the protector of bullfighters, she's big in bullring chapels. In 1912, the bullfighter José Ortega, hoping for protection, gave her the five emerald brooches she wears. It worked for eight years...until he was gored to death in the ring.

Outside, notice the best surviving bit of Sevilla's old walls. Originally Roman, what remains today is 12th-century Moorish, a reminder that for centuries Sevilla was the capital of the Moorish kingdom in Iberia. And yes, it's from this city that a local dance band changed the world by giving us "The Macarena."

Bullfighting

▲Bullfights—Some of Spain's best bullfighting is done in Sevilla's 14,000-seat Plaza de Toros (fights on most Sundays, Easter–Oct, 18:30 or 19:30). Serious fights with adult matadors—called *corrida de toros*—are in April and October (and often sold out in advance). Summer fights are usually *novillada*, with teenage novices doing the killing. (*Corrida de toros* seats range from €20 for high seats looking into the sun to €100 for the first three rows in the shade under the royal box; *novillada* seats are half that—and easy to buy at the arena a few minutes before showtime; get information at TI, your hotel, or call 954-210-315.)

▲▲Bullfight Museum—Follow a two-language (Spanish and English), 20-minute guided tour through the Plaza de Toros' strangely quiet and empty arena, its museum, the first-aid room where injured fighters are rushed, and the chapel where the matador prays before the fight. The two most revered figures of Seville, the Virgin of Macarena and the Christ of Gran Poder (All Power), are represented in the chapel. In the museum you'll see great classic scenes and the heads of a few bulls—awarded the bovine equivalent of an Oscar for a particularly good fight. Also see the mother of the bull that died while killing the famous matador Manolete in 1947. They were so appalled that Manolete was killed that they killed the mother of the bull who gored him (€4, tours 3/hour, daily 9:30–19:00; or 9:30–15:00 on fight days, though the chapel and horse room are closed). Matadors—dressed to kill—are heartthrobs in their "suits of light." Many girls have their bedrooms wallpapered with posters of cute bull fighters. See the appendix for more on the "art" of bullfighting.

The April Fair

For seven days each April (April 12–17 in 2005), much of Sevilla is packed into its vast fairgrounds for a grand party. The fair, seeming to bring all that's Andalusian together, feels friendly, spontaneous,

and very real. The local passion for horses, flamenco, and sherry is clear—riders are ramrod straight, colorfully clad girls ride sidesaddle, and everyone's drinking sherry spritzers. Women sport outlandish dresses that would look clownish all alone but are somehow brilliant here en masse. Horses clog the streets in an endless parade until about 20:00, when they clear out and the street fills with exuberant locals. The party goes for literally 24 hours a day for the entire week.

Countless private party tents, or *casetas*, line the lanes. Each tent is the private party zone of a family, club, or association. You need to know someone in the group—or make friends quickly—to get in. Because of the exclusivity, it has a real family-affair feeling. In each *caseta*, everyone knows everyone in what seems like a thousand wedding parties being celebrated at the same time.

Any tourist can have a fun and memorable evening by simply crashing the party. The city's entire fleet of taxis (who'll try to charge double) and buses seems dedicated to shuttling people from downtown to the fairgrounds. With the traffic jams, you may be better off hiking: From the Golden Tower, cross the San Telmo bridge to Plaza Cuba and hike down Calle Asunción. You'll see the towering gate to the fairgrounds in the distance. Just follow the crowds (there's no admission charge). Get there before 20:00 to see the horses, but stay later, as the ambience improves after they giddy-up on out. Some of the larger tents are sponsored by the city and open to the public, but the best action is in the streets, where party-goers from the livelier *casetas* spill out. While private tents have bouncers, everyone is so happy, it's not tough to strike up an impromptu friendship, become a "special guest," and be invited in. The drink flows freely and the food is fun and cheap.

NIGHTLIFE

▲▲**Evening *Paseo***—Sevilla is meant for strolling. The areas along either side of the river between the San Telmo and Isabel II bridges (Paseo de Cristóbal Colón and Triana district; see "Eating," page 304), around Plaza Nueva, at Plaza de España, and throughout the Barrio Santa Cruz thrive every non-winter

evening. On hot summer nights, even families with toddlers may be out and about past midnight. Spend some time rafting through this sea of humanity. Savor the view of floodlit Sevilla by night from the far side of the river—perhaps over dinner (but the seedy Alameda de Hercules district is best avoided).

▲▲▲Flamenco—This music-and-dance art form has its roots in the Gypsy and Moorish cultures. Even at a packaged "Flamenco Evening," sparks fly. The men do most of the flamboyant machine-gun footwork. The women concentrate on graceful turns and a smooth, shuffling step. Watch the musicians. Flamenco guitarists, with their lightning-fast finger-roll strums, are among the best in the world. The intricate rhythms are set by castanets or the hand-clapping (called *palmas*) of those who aren't dancing at the moment. In the raspy-voiced wails of the singers you'll hear echoes of the Muslim call to prayer.

Like jazz, flamenco thrives on improvisation. Also like jazz, good flamenco is more than just technical proficiency. A singer or dancer with "soul" is said to have *duende*. Flamenco is a happening, with bystanders clapping along and egging on the dancers with whoops and shouts. Get into it. For a tourist-oriented flamenco show, your hotel can get you nightclub show tickets (happily, since they snare a hefty commission for each sale).

Los Gallos gives nightly two-hour shows at 21:00 and 23:30 (€27 ticket includes a drink, manager Nuria promises goosebumps and a €2 per person discount to those who reserve directly with Los Gallos and show this book—maximum 2 per book; arrive 30 min early for better seats without obstructed views, Plaza de la Santa Cruz 11, tel. 954-216-981). **El Arenal** also does a good show (€29 including a drink, shows at 21:00 and 23:00, near bullring at Calle Rodo 7, tel. 954-216-492). **El Patio Sevillano** is more of a variety show (€29, shows at 19:30 and 22:00, next to bullring at Paseo de Cristóbal Colón, tel. 954-214-120). These packaged shows can be a bit sterile, and an audience of tourists doesn't help. But I find both Los Gallos and El Arenal professional and riveting. El Arenal may have a slight edge on talent, but Los Gallos has a cozier setting, with cushy rather than hard chairs—and it's cheaper.

Casa de la Memoria de Al-Andalus (House of the Memory of Al-Andalus), run by devotees of the Andalusian culture Sebastián and Rossana, offers more of an intimate concert with a smaller cast and more classic solos. In an alcohol-free atmosphere, tourists sit on folding chairs circling a small stage for shows featuring flamenco, Sephardic, or other Andalusian music. Their exhibits on Sephardic and Muslim art and musical instruments are a fresh change in a city full of Baroque and Christian icons. It's also a perfect place to prac-tice your Spanish fan *(abanico)* skills on warm nights. Summer con-certs are nightly at 21:00 and 22:30 (off-season at 21:00). Wednesday concerts are Sephardic, rather than flamenco (€11, 60-min shows vary, reservations welcome, be there 45 min before show starts for best seats, Ximénez de Enciso 28, in Barrio Santa Cruz, adjacent to Hotel Alcántara, tel. 954-560-670, memoria@teleline.es).

Impromptu flamenco still erupts spontaneously in bars throughout the old town after midnight. Just follow your ears as you wander down Calle Betis, leading off Plaza de Cuba across the bridge. The **Lo Nuestro** and **Rejoneo** bars are local favorites (at Calle Betis 30 and 32).

For flamenco music without dancing, consider **La Carbonería Bar.** The sangria equivalent of a beer garden, it's a sprawling place with a variety of rooms leading to a big, open, tented area filled with young locals, casual guitar strummers, and nearly nightly flamenco music after midnight. Located just a few blocks from most of my recommended hotels, this is worth finding for anyone not quite ready to end the day (no cover, €2 sangria, 20:00–3:00, near Plaza Santa María find Hotel Fernando III, the side alley Céspedes dead-ends at Levies, head left to Levies 18, unsigned door).

SHOPPING

The popular pedestrian streets Sierpes, Tetuán, and Velázquez, as well as the surrounding lanes near Plaza Nueva, are packed with people and shops (see "Quickie Town Walk: Plaza Nueva to Calle Sierpes," page 299). Nearby is Sevilla's top department store, El Corte Inglés. While small shops close between 13:30 and 16:00 or 17:00, big ones like El Corte Inglés stay open (and air-conditioned) right through the siesta. It has a supermarket downstairs and a good but expensive restaurant (Mon–Sat 10:00–22:00, closed Sun). Popular souvenir items include ladies' fans, ceramics, and items from flamenco (castanets, guitars, costumes) and bullfighting (posters).

Flea markets hop on Sunday: stamps and coins at Cabildo Square near the cathedral and animals at Alfalfa Square. El Jueves, held on Thursday on Feria street, is the oldest market in Sevilla (dating from the Moors), offering an assortment of odds and ends.

SLEEPING

All of my listings are centrally located, within a five-minute walk of the cathedral. The first are near the charming but touristy Santa Cruz neighborhood. The last group is just as central but closer to the river, across the boulevard in a more workaday, less touristy zone.

Room rates as much as double during the two Sevilla fiestas (Holy Week—March 20–27 in 2005, and the weeklong April Fair, held 2 weeks after Easter). In general, the busiest and most expensive months are April, May, September, and October. Hotels put

Sleep Code

(€1 = about $1.20, country code: 34)
S = Single, **D** = Double/Twin, **T** = Triple, **Q** = Quad,
b = bathroom, **s** = shower only, **no CC** = Credit Cards not
accepted, **SE** = Speaks English, **NSE** = No English. You can
assume credit cards are accepted unless otherwise noted.

To help you easily sort through these listings, I've divided
the rooms into three categories, based on the price for a standard
double room with bath during high season:

$$$ **Higher Priced**—Most rooms €100 or more.
$$ **Moderately Priced**—Most rooms between €60–100.
$ **Lower Priced**—Most rooms €60 or less.

rooms on the discounted push list in July and August—when people
with any sense avoid this furnace—and November through
February. Prices rarely include the 7 percent IVA tax. A price range
indicates low- to high-season prices (but I have not listed festival
prices). Hoteliers speak enough English. Ground-floor rooms come
with more noise. Ask for upper floors *(piso alto)*. Many of these
hotels are reportedly unreliable for reservations, particularly the
small, family *pensiones* (as opposed to normal big hotels). Always
telephone to reconfirm what you think is a reservation. If you do
visit in July or August, the best values are central business-class
places. They offer summer discounts and provide a necessary cool,
air-conditioned refuge.

Santa Cruz Neighborhood

These places are off Calle Santa María la Blanca and Plaza Santa
María.

$$$ **Hotel Las Casas de la Judería** has quiet, elegant rooms and
suites tastefully decorated with hardwood floors and a Spanish flair.
The rooms surround a series of peaceful courtyards. This is a roman-
tic splurge and a fine value (Sb-€87–101, Db-€128–156, Db suite-
€147–174, Qb suite-€218–250, extra bed-€30–50; low-season
prices—July, Aug, late-Nov–Feb—are discounted a further 10
percent to those with this book who ask; great buffet breakfast-€15,
air-con, elevator, valet parking-€15/day, on small traffic-free lane off
Plaza Santa María, Callejón de Dos Hermanas 7, tel. 954-415-150,
fax 954-422-170, www.casasypalacios.com, juderia@zoom.es, SE).

$$ **Hotel Amadeus** is a little gem that music-lovers will appreciate (it even has a couple of soundproofed rooms with pianos—
something I've never seen in Europe). It's lovingly decorated with a
music motif around a little courtyard and a modern glass elevator that
takes you to a roof terrace. While small, this 14-room place is classy

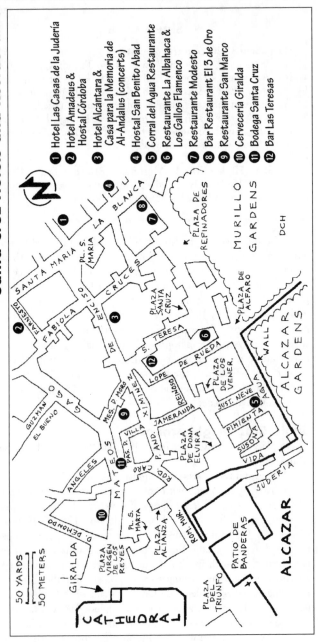

Santa Cruz Hotels and Restaurants

1. Hotel Las Casas de la Judería
2. Hotel Amadeus & Hostal Córdoba
3. Hotel Alcántara & Casa para la Memoria de Al-Andalus (concerts)
4. Hostal San Benito Abad
5. Corral del Agua Restaurante
6. Restaurante La Albahaca & Los Gallos Flamenco
7. Restaurante Modesto
8. Bar Restaurant El 3 de Oro
9. Restaurante San Marco
10. Cervecería Giralda
11. Bodega Santa Cruz
12. Bar Las Teresas

and comfortable, with welcoming public spaces and a charming staff (Db-€76, big Db-€90, 2 suites €105 and €126, air-con, Calle Farnesio 6, elevator, parking-€12, breakfast-€7, lounge or enjoy breakfast on the delightful roof garden, tel. 954-501-443, fax 954-500-019, www.hotelamadeussevilla.com, reservas@hotelamadeussevilla.com, Zaida, Christina, & María Luisa SE).

$$ **Hotel Alcántara** is new, offering more comfort than style or character. Well-located but strangely out of place in the midst of the Santa Cruz jumble, it rents 21 slick rooms at a good price (Sb-€64, small Db-€72, bigger Db twin-€80, fancy Db-€98, breakfast-€5, air-con, elevator, Ximénez de Enciso 28, tel. 954-500-595, fax 954-500-604, www.hotelalcantara.net, info@hotelalcantara.net). The hotel is adjacent to Casa de la Memoria de Al-Andalus, which offers concerts (see "Nightlife," page 304).

$$ **Hostal Córdoba,** a homier and cheaper option, has 12 tidy, quiet, air-conditioned rooms, solid modern furniture, and a showpiece plant-filled courtyard (S-€25–35, Sb-€30–45, D-€45–50, Db-€50–60, Nov–March cheaper, includes tax, no breakfast, no CC, a tiny lane off Calle Santa María la Blanca, Farnesio 12, tel. 954-227-498, hostalcordoba@mixmail.com).

$ **Hostal San Benito Abad,** with eight humble rooms, faces a traditional Sevilla courtyard buried at the end of a dead-end lane just off Plaza Santa María. The rooms are dark, with windows that open onto an inner courtyard. Communication here is very difficult, but the family is hardworking and offers some of the best cheap rooms in town (S-€16–20, D-€34, Db-€36, Tb-€48, no breakfast, a tiny lane next to Cano y Cueto at Calle Canarios 4, tel. 954-415-255, www.hostalsanbenito.com, burlon11@hotmail.com, Tomás Ortíz SE, his family doesn't).

Sleeping Cheap between the Alcázar and Avenida de la Constitución

These small, funky, short-on-service places get mixed reviews from readers, but they're cheap, central, and relatively quiet.

$ **Pensión Alcázar** rents eight basic rooms. The lower rooms have ceiling fans, the three top rooms are air-conditioned and have terraces (Db-€45–54, Qb-€60–75, no CC, Dean Miranda 12, tel. 954-228-457, owners Micky and Liliane SE). Note: Taxi drivers often confuse this with *Hotel* Alcázar.

$ **Hostal Arias** is cool, clean, and no-nonsense. Its 14 basic rooms are air-conditioned and come equipped with medieval disco balls (big Sb-€37, Db-€47, Tb-€63, Qb-€69, Quint/b-€81, nearby parking-€14/day, Calle Mariana de Pineda 9, tel. 954-226-840, fax 954-211-649, www.hostalarias.com, reservas@hostalarias.com, manager Manuel Reina SE, but rest of staff doesn't).

Sevilla Hotels

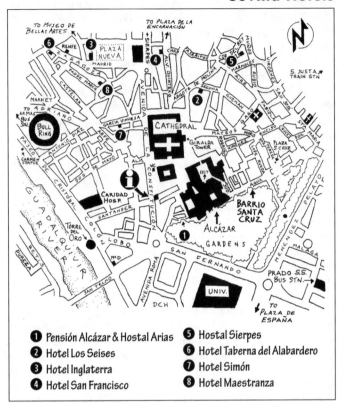

- **1** Pensión Alcázar & Hostal Arias
- **2** Hotel Los Seises
- **3** Hotel Inglaterra
- **4** Hotel San Francisco
- **5** Hostal Sierpes
- **6** Hotel Taberna del Alabardero
- **7** Hotel Simón
- **8** Hotel Maestranza

Near the Cathedral

$$$ **Hotel Los Seises,** a modern business-class place spliced tastefully into the tangled old town, offers a fresh and spacious reprieve for anyone ready for good old contemporary luxury. You'll eat breakfast amid Roman ruins. Its rooftop garden includes a pool and a great cathedral view (42 rooms, Sb-€101–138, Db-€132–189, extra bed-€30, breakfast-€15, lower prices in July–Aug and Dec–Feb, aircon, elevator, valet parking-€17, 2 blocks northwest of cathedral at Segovias 6, tel. 954-229-495, fax 954-224-334, www.hotellosseises .com, info@hotellosseises.com).

$$$ **Hotel Inglaterra,** a big blocky four-star place on the nononsense Plaza Nueva, has 109 rooms and all the professional amenities (high season April–May, low season rest of year, big Sb-€93–104, Db-€118–132, extra bed-€25–37, buffet breakfast-€10, air-con, non-smoking floor, elevator, attached restaurant and Irish pub, American Express office, Plaza Nueva 7, tel. 954-224-970, fax 954-561-336, www.hotelinglaterra.es, hotin@hotelinglaterra.es).

$$ Hotel San Francisco, with a classy facade but little character, offers 16 rooms with metal doors, a central location, and a good value (Sb-€40–55, Db-€50–68, Tb-€62–80, no breakfast, air-con, elevator, rooftop terrace, Álvarez Quintero 38, tel.954-501-541).

$ Hostal Sierpes is sprawling, with 36 small rooms, fine lounges, and a big, airy courtyard. The place annoys some of my readers; reconfirm reservations (Sb-€44, Db-€65, Tb-€85, Qb-€105, breakfast-€6, most rooms have air-con, noisy downstairs, quieter rooms upstairs, popular with backpackers, parking-€14/day, Corral del Rey 22, tapas bar next door, tel. 954-224-948, fax 954-212-107, reservas@hsierpes.com).

West of Avenida de la Constitución

$$$ Hotel Taberna del Alabardero is a unique hotel with only seven rooms, taking the top floor of a poet's mansion (above a classy restaurant, Taberna del Alabardero, listed in "Eating," below). It's well-located and a great value but often booked in advance. The ambience is perfectly 1900 (Db-€152, Db suite-€185, includes breakfast, air-con, elevator, closed in Aug, Zaragoza 20, tel. 954-502-721, fax 954-563-666, www.tabernadelalabardero.com, hotel.alabardero@esh.es).

$$ Hotel Simón is a classic 18th-century mansion with a faded-elegance courtyard. Although room quality varies, many of its 30 rooms are decorated with period furniture under high ceilings. On weekends, avoid rooms on the noisy street (Sb-€45–50, Db-€67–80, extra person-€18, high prices are only for April–May, continental breakfast-€4, air-con, a block west of cathedral at Calle García de Vinuesa 19, tel. 954-226-660, fax 954-562-241, www.hotelsimonsevilla.com, info@hotelsimonsevilla.com). They have a scam charging your credit card in dollars at a poor rate, so it's best to pay cash.

$ Hotel Maestranza has 18 small, clean, simple rooms well-located on a quiet street just off Plaza Nueva (Sb-€47, Db-€65 most of the year, Db-€87 July–Aug, extra bed-€20, no breakfast, elevator, air-con, Gamazo 12, tel. 954-561-070, fax 954-214-404, www.hotel-maestranza.com, sevilla@hotel-maestranza.com).

EATING

A popular Andalusian meal is fried fish, particularly marinated *adobo*. The soups, such as *salmorejo* (Córdoba-style super-thick gazpacho) and *ajo blanco* (almond-based with garlic), are tasty.

If you're hungry for dinner before the Spaniards are, do the tapas tango, using the "Tapas Tips" page 30. Wash down your tapas with *fino* (chilled dry sherry) or the more refreshing *tinto de verano* (literally, "summer" red wine), an Andalusian red wine with soda, like a mild sangria. A good light white wine is *barbadillo*.

Restaurants and Flamenco in Sevilla

1 To Plazuela Santa Ana: Taberna la
   Plazuela, Rest. Bistec
   & Bar Santa Ana

2 Rest. Río Grande
   & La Primera del Puente

3 Horno San Buenaventura Café

4 Bodega Morales & Freiduría la Isla
   (fried fish)

5 El Buzo Restaurant
   & Cafeteria Mesón Serranito

6 Bodega Paco Gongora

7 Mercado del Arenal (market)

8 Taberna del Alabardero

9 El Arenal (flamenco)

10 El Patio Sevillano (flamenco)

11 Lo Nuestro & Rejoneo Bars

12 La Carboneria Bar

13 To Alfalfa Square tapas bars

Eating in Triana, across the River

The colorful Triana District—south of the river, between the San
Telmo and Isabel II bridges—is filled with rustic and fun eateries.

Tapas: The riverside street, Calle Betis ("Betis" is the Roman
name for the Guadalquivir River), is best for tapas bars. Before sitting down, walk to the Santa Ana church (midway between the
bridges, two blocks off the river), where tables spill into the square
in the shadow of the floodlit church spire. It feels like the whole
neighborhood is out celebrating. On Plazuela Santa Ana, two
restaurants feed the neighborhood: **Taberna la Plazuela** is self-
service, doing simpler fare with enticing €9 *tostones*—giant, fancy
Andalusian *bruschetta* (good for 3–4 people) and €1.80 *montaditos*

(little sandwiches). **Restaurante Bistec,** with most of the square's tables, does grilled fish with enthusiasm. I liked *taquitos de merluza* (hake fish), but for a mix of fish, ask for *frito variado* (daily 11:30–16:00 & 20:00–24:00, Plazuela de Santa Ana, tel. 954-274-759.)

For tapas in a rougher bull bar, head a block down the street where **Bar Santa Ana,** draped in bullfighting and Weeping Virgin memorabilia, is busy filling locals from a fun list of tapas like *delicia de solomillo*—tenderloin (long hours, closed Sun, Pureza 82, tel. 954-272-102).

Riverside Dinners: For a restaurant dinner (with properly attired waiters and full menus, as opposed to tapas), consider these neighbors on Calle Betis, next to the San Telmo bridge. **Río Grande** is your candlelight-fancy option (€30 dinners, daily 13:00–16:00 & 20:00–24:00, tel. 954-273-956); its terrace is less expensive, more casual, and a better value. Next door, the simpler **Restaurante La Primera del Puente** serves about the same thing with nearly the same view for half the price (Thu–Tue 11:30–17:00 & 20:00–24:00, closed Wed and the last half of Aug, tel. 954-276-918).

At the Isabel II bridge, in the yellow bridge tower, **El Faro de Triana** offers inexpensive tapas, a €6 lunch *menu*, €15 à la carte dinners, and the best views over the river from the top floor (Thu–Tue 8:00–1:00, closed Wed, tel. 954-336-192). Nearby, in tippy tables lined up along the riverbank, **La Esquina del Puente** (along with a couple other places) serves *pescados fritos* (fried fish) *raciones* for €8 to locals out for maximum romance at a minimum price (Wed–Mon 12:00–16:00 & 20:00–23:00, closed Tue, Puente de Isabel II, tel. 954-330-069).

Tapas in Barrio Santa Cruz

For tapas, the Barrio Santa Cruz is trendy and *romántico.* Plenty of atmospheric-but-touristy restaurants fill the neighborhood near the cathedral and along Calle Santa María la Blanca.

From the cathedral, walk up Mateos Gago, where several classic old bars—with the day's tapas scrawled on chalkboards—keep tourists and locals well fed and watered. (Turn right at Mesón del Moro for several more.)

Cervecería Giralda (at Mateos Gago 1) is a long-established meeting place for locals. It's famous for its fine tapas (confirm prices). A block farther you'll find **Bodega Santa Cruz** (a.k.a. Las Columnas), a popular standby with good cheap tapas. At the next intersection, turn right off Mateos Gago onto Calle Mesón del Moro, which leads past the recommended San Marco pizzeria to **Las Teresas,** a fine and characteristic little bar draped in fun photos. It serves good tapas from a user-friendly menu (daily, Calle Santa Teresa 2, tel. 954-213-069). Just down Calle Santa Teresa is the artist Murillo's house (free when open and a good example of a local courtyard). Calle Santa Teresa continues past a convent of cloistered nuns to the most romantic little square in Santa Cruz (where you'll find the recommended Restaurante La Albahaca, described just below, and the Los Gallos flamenco club, see page 305).

Dining in Barrio Santa Cruz

Corral del Agua Restaurante, a romantic pink-tablecloth place with classy indoor and charming courtyard seating, serves fine Andalusian cuisine deep in the Barrio Santa Cruz (plan on €25 per meal, Mon–Sat 13:00–16:00 & 20:00–24:00, closed Sun, reservations smart, Callejón del Agua 6, tel. 954-224-841).

Restaurante La Albahaca fills a luxurious mansion, with tables spilling onto a quaint Santa Cruz square, offering French Basque and Spanish food in a convenient location next to the Los Gallos flamenco club (daily menu €30, €18 plates, Mon–Sat 13:00–16:00 & 20:30–24:00, closed Sun, air-con, Plaza de Santa Cruz 12, tel. 954-220-714).

Restaurante Modesto is a bustling local favorite serving pricey but top-notch Andalusian fare—especially fish—with atmospheric outdoor seating and forgettable indoor seating. They offer creative, fun meals—look around before ordering—and a good €17 daily menu with energetic, friendly service. Their mixed salad is a meal (daily, just off Santa Cruz near Santa María la Blanca at Cano y Cueto 5, tel. 954-416-811).

Eating Cheap in Barrio Santa Cruz

Bar Restaurante El 3 de Oro is a fried-fish-to-go place, with great outdoor seating and a restaurant across the street that serves fine wine or beer. You can order a cheap cone of your choice of tasty fish and sip a nice drink, almost dining for the cost of a picnic. Stand in line and study the photos of the various kinds of seafood available— *un quarto* (250 grams for about €5) serves one (daily until 24:00, Santa María la Blanca 34, tel. 954-426-820).

Restaurante San Marco offers cheap pizza and fun, basic Italian cuisine under the arches of what was an Arab bath in the Middle Ages (and a disco in the 1990s). The atmosphere is air-conditioned and easygoing (good salads, pizza and pasta for €6, daily 13:15–16:30 & 20:15–24:00, closed much of Aug, Calle Mesón del Moro 6, tel. 954-564-390).

Eating with Atmosphere along Calle García de Vinuesa

I don't like the restaurants surrounding the cathedral. But many good places are just across Avenida de la Constitución. Calle García de Vinuesa leads past several colorful and cheap tapas places to a busy corner surrounded with happy eateries.

Horno San Buenaventura, across from the cathedral, is slick, chrome, spacious, and handy for tapas, coffee, pastries, and ice cream (open daily, light meals are posted on the door, good quiet seating upstairs).

Bodega Morales is farther up Calle García de Vinuesa (#11, Mon–Sat 12:00–16:00 & 20:00–24:00, closed Sun, tel. 954-22-1242). While the front area is more of a drinking bar, go in the back section (around the corner) to munch tiny sandwiches *(montaditos)* and tapas and sip wine among huge kegs. Everything is the same price *(montaditos*-€1.80, tapas-€1.80, half-*raciones* €6—order at the bar) with the selection chalked onto huge kegs.

Freiduría la Isla (next door) has been frying fish since 1938 (they just renovated and changed the oil). Along with *pescado frito,* they also sell wonderful homemade potato chips and fried almonds. Try €4.80 *cazón* (marinated shark) or *frito variado* for a fish sampler. Their €1.20 gazpacho is a great starter (Mon 20:00–23:30, Tue–Sat 13:00–15:30 & 20:00–23:30, closed Sun).

At the end of Calle García de Vinuesa, angle right and you'll find several good places. The **"5J" Bar** on the corner is a mod alternative to all the traditional bars—popular with locals for its ham.

The **El Buzo** restaurant is a busy neighborhood place on a lively street corner, with good outdoor seating and homey indoor seating, frisky service, and great fish and seafood (€15 meals, more with seafood, be careful: appetizers are priced per person and they push pricey options, daily 12:00–24:00, Calle Antonia Díaz 5, tel. 954-210-231). Just down the street, **Cafetería Mesón Serranito** is full of bull lore and locals consuming €6 *platos combinados* (Antonia Díaz 4, tel. 954-211-243).

Bodega Paco Góngora is colorful and a bit classier than a tapas bar, with a tight dining area and a popular tapas counter that specializes in fish. Its sit-down meals are well-presented and reasonable (daily 12:00–16:00 & 20:00–24:00, ask for the English menu, off Plaza Nueva at Calle Padre Marchena 1, tel. 954-214-139).

Picnickers forage at the covered fish-and-produce **Mercado del Arenal** (with a small café/bar for breakfast inside, Mon–Sat 9:00–14:30, closed Sun, not lively on Mon, on Calle Pastor y Landero at Calle Arenal, just beyond bullring). A more bustling market recently opened, just across the Isabel II bridge in Triana.

Dining between Cathedral and Plaza Nueva

Taberna del Alabardero, one of Sevilla's finest restaurants, serves refined Spanish cuisine in chandeliered elegance just a couple of blocks from the cathedral. While the à la carte menu will add up to about €45 a meal, for €47 they offer a fun seven-course sampler menu with lots of little surprises from the chef. Or consider their €15 starter sampler, followed by an entrée (daily 13:00–16:00 & 20:00–24:00, closed Aug, air-con, reservations smart, Zaragoza 20, tel. 954-502-721). The service in the fancy upstairs dining rooms gets mixed reviews (understand the bill)…but the setting is stunning.

Taberna del Alabardero student-served lunch: Their ground-floor dining rooms (elegant but nothing like upstairs) are popular with local office workers for their great-value student-chef sampler menu (€10.10 for 3 delightful courses, Mon–Fri 13:00–16:30, €14.75 for same thing on Sat–Sun). To avoid a wait, arrive before 13:30.

TRANSPORTATION CONNECTIONS

To: Madrid (2.5 hrs by AVE express train, departures 7:00–23:00 on the hour, €10 reservation fee with railpass; 11 buses/day, €17), **Córdoba** (hrly, 1.5 hrs for €6; 50 min by speedy AVE for €18; 10 buses/day, 2 hrs), **Málaga** (5 trains/day, 2.5 hrs; 11 buses/day, 7 direct, 2.5 hrs), **Ronda** (3 trains/day, 3 hrs, change at Bobadilla; 5 buses/day, 3 hrs), **Tarifa** (4 buses/day, 3 hrs), **La Línea/Gibraltar** (4 buses/day, 4 hrs), **Granada** (4 trains/day, 3 hrs; 10 buses/day, 3 hrs), **Arcos** (2 buses/day, 2 hrs), **Jerez** (15/day, 1.25 hrs, 6 buses/day), **Barcelona** (3 trains/day, 10–12 hrs, 2 buses/day), **Algeciras** (3 trains/day, 5 hrs, change at Bobadilla; 10 buses/day, 3.5 hrs), **Lisbon** (fastest option by bus: Mon, Wed, Fri at 9:30, 5 hrs, €29; slower option by bus: Damas SA, 5–6 buses/week, departs Plaza de Armas station Tue–Sun at 15:00, off-season not on Wed, 7 hrs, €29 one-way, buy ticket at station, reservations not necessary, Eurolines, tel. 954-907-844, www.eurolines.es; or slowest, overnight option by train: you can take AVE to Madrid and then the pricey night train to Lisbon). Train info: tel. 902-240-202. Bus info: tel. 954-908-040 but rarely answered, go to TI for latest schedule info.

By bus to Lagos, Portugal: Take the direct bus (€17, 2/day, 4.5 hrs, schedule from Sevilla to Lagos: 7:30–12:00 & 16:30–21:00, runs year-round, confirm schedule, tel. 954-908-040 or 954-901-160). The bus departs from Sevilla's Plaza de Armas bus station and arrives at the Lagos bus station.

Córdoba

Córdoba is one of Spain's three most important Moorish cities. Even though it was the center of Moorish civilization in Spain for 300 years (and an important Roman city before that), Sevilla and Granada are far more interesting. Córdoba has a famous mosque surrounded by the colorful Jewish Quarter, and that's it.

The **Mezquita** (meh-SKEET-ah) was the largest Islamic mosque in its day. Today it's a Christian church, but you can wander past its ramshackle "patio of oranges" and into the cavernous 1,200-year-old building. Grab the English-language pamphlet at the door (which predictably describes the church's history much better than the mosque's). The interior is a moody world of 857 (formerly 1,013) rose- and blue-marble columns and as many Moorish arches. If a guide told me I was in the basement of something important, I'd believe him. The center was gutted to make room for an also-huge Renaissance cathedral (€6.50, Mon–Sat opens at 10:00, Sun opens at 14:00, closes at 19:00 April–June, 18:30 March and July–Oct, 17:30 Feb and Nov, 17:00 Dec–Jan, hours change—call to confirm, tel. 957-470-512). The mosque is near the **TI** (Mon–Fri 9:30–18:30, Sat 10:00–14:00 & 17:00–20:00, Sun 10:00–14:00, closes early in winter, tel. 957-471-235). The TI also has a handy kiosk at the train station (with a room-finding service).

From the station to the mosque, it's a €3 ride or a pleasant 30-minute walk (left on Avenida de América, right on Avenida del Gran Capitán, which becomes a pedestrian zone; when it ends ask someone "*¿Dónde está la mezquita?*" and you'll be directed downhill through the whitewashed old Jewish Quarter).

Sleeping and Eating in Córdoba: Two comfortable, air-conditioned, and expensive hotels are located within a five-minute walk of the station. **Hotel Gran Capitán** is closer (96 rooms, Sb-€85, Db-€135, breakfast-€11, parking-€12, Avenida de América 5, tel. 957-470-250, fax 957-474-643, www.occidental-hoteles.com, cordoba .ogc@oh-es.com). **Hotel Tryp Gallos** is cheaper (115 rooms, Sb-€99, Db-€112, extra bed-€25, cheaper June–Aug and Nov–Feb: Sb-€58, Db-€89; tax included, breakfast-€9, elevator, Avenida de Medina Azahara 7, tel. 957-235-500, fax 957-231-636, www.trypgallos .solmelia.com, tryp.gallos@solmelia.com). For food, consider **Taverna Salinas** (Mon–Sat 12:00–16:00 & 20:00–24:00, closed Sun, Tendidores 3, tel. 957-480-135).

TRANSPORTATION CONNECTIONS

Now that Córdoba is on the slick AVE train line, it's an easy stopover between **Madrid** and **Sevilla** (15 trains/day, about 1.5 hrs from either city, reservations required on all AVE trains).

By bus to: Granada (9/day, 3 hrs), **Málaga** (5/day, 3 hrs), **Algeciras** (4/day, 4.5–5 hrs; 2 direct, 2 with transfers in Bobadilla). The bus station is at Plaza de las Tres Culturas (tel. 957-404-040).

ANDALUCÍA'S WHITE HILL TOWNS
(Pueblos Blancos)

Just as the American image of Germany is Bavaria, the Yankee dream of Spain is Andalucía. This is the home of bullfights, flamenco, gazpacho, pristine-if-dusty whitewashed hill towns, and glamorous Mediterranean resorts. The big cities of Andalucía (Granada, Sevilla, and Córdoba) and the Costa del Sol are covered in separate chapters. This chapter explores its hill-town highlights.

The Route of the White Towns *(Ruta de los Pueblos Blancos)*, Andalucía's charm bracelet of cute towns perched in the sierras, gives you wonderfully untouched Spanish culture. Spend a night in the romantic queen of the white towns, Arcos de la Frontera. Towns with "de la Frontera" in their names were established on the front line of the centuries-long fight to recapture Spain from the Muslims, who were slowly pushed back into Africa. The hill towns—no longer strategic, no longer on any frontier—are now just passing time peacefully. Join them. Nearby, the city of Jerez is worth a peek for its famous horses and a sherry.

To study ahead, visit www.andalucia.com for information on hotels, festivals, museums, nightlife, and sports in the region.

Planning Your Time
On a three-week vacation in Spain, the region is worth two nights and two days sandwiched between Sevilla and Tarifa. Arcos makes the best home base, though the towns can be (and often are) accessed from the Costa del Sol resorts via Ronda. Arcos, near Jerez and close to interesting smaller towns, is conveniently situated halfway between Sevilla and Tarifa.

See Jerez on your way in or out, spend a day hopping from town to town (Grazalema and Zahara, at a minimum) in the more remote interior, and enjoy Arcos early and late in the day.

Without a car you might keep things simple and focus only on

Southern Andalucía

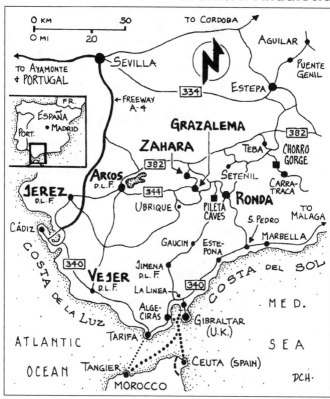

Arcos and Jerez (both well-served by public buses). Spring and fall are high season throughout this area. In summer you'll find heat, empty hotels, and no crowds.

Arcos de la Frontera

Arcos smothers its long, narrow hilltop and tumbles down the back of the ridge like the train of a wedding dress. It's larger than the other Andalusian hill towns, but equally atmospheric. Arcos consists of two towns: The fairy-tale old town on top of the hill, and the fun-loving lower, or new, town. The old center is a labyrinthine wonderland, a photographer's feast. Viewpoint-hop

through town. Feel the wind funnel through the narrow streets as cars inch around tight corners. Join the kids' soccer game on the church-yard patio. Enjoy the moonlit view from the main square.

Though it tries, Arcos doesn't have much to offer other than its basic whitewashed self. The locally-produced English guidebook on Arcos waxes poetic and at length about very little. You can arrive late and leave early and miss little.

ORIENTATION

Tourist Information: The TI, on the main square across from the parador, is helpful and loaded with information, including bus schedules (March–Sept Mon–Sat 10:00–14:00 & 16:00–20:00, Sun 10:30–13:30; Oct–Feb Mon–Sat 10:00–14:00 & 15:30–19:30, Sun 10:30–13:30; Plaza del Cabildo, tel. 956-702-264, www.ayuntamientoarcos.org—mostly in Spanish).

The TI organizes two different one-hour **walking tours:** Old Town and Patios of Arcos. They cost €5, leave from around from the main square, and are given in Spanish and/or English. The Old Town walks describe the church and town's history (Mon–Fri at 10:30 and 17:00, Sat at 10:30 only, 1 hr). The Patios walk gets you into private courtyards and covers lifestyles, Moorish influences, and the two main churches (Mon–Fri at 12:00 and 18:30, Sat at 12:00, 1 hr). Individuals or groups can hire a private guide through the TI for any walk at any time (€46).

Arrival in Arcos

By Bus: The bus station is on Calle Corregidores, at the foot of the hill. To get up to the old town, catch the shuttle bus marked *Centro* (€1, 2/hr, runs 8:15–21:15 but not on Sun), hop a taxi (€4 fixed rate), or take a 15-minute uphill walk: As you leave the station, turn left on Corregidores, angle left uphill, cross the four-way intersection, angle right uphill, and take Muñoz Vázquez up into town. Go up the stairs by the church to the main square and TI.

By Car: You can park in the main square of the old town at the top of the hill (Plaza del Cabildo, ticket from machine €0.70/hr, only necessary Mon–Fri 9:30–14:00 & 17:30–20:30 and Sat 9:00–14:00—confirm times on machine, can get €3 all-day ticket from old-town hotels, free Sat afternoon and all day Sun). If arriving to check in at a hotel, tell the uniformed parking man the name of your hotel. If there's no spot, wait until one opens up (he'll help). Once you grab a spot, tell him you'll be back from your hotel with a ticket.

Plenty of parking is available in the new town, including the underground lot at Plaza España. From this lot, catch a taxi or the shuttle bus up to the old town (2/hr, from traffic circle at garage entrance).

Getting Around Arcos

The old town is easily walkable, but it's fun and relaxing to take a **circular minibus joyride.** The little shuttle bus circles through the town's one-way system and around the valley constantly (€1.30, 2/hr, daily 8:15–21:15 except Sun). For a 30-minute tour, hop on. You can catch it just below the main church in the old town (near mystical stone circle, described below). As you wind through the old town, sit in the front seat for the best view of the tight squeezes and the schoolkids hanging out. Passing under a Moorish gate, you enter a modern residential neighborhood, circle under the eroding cliff, and return to the old town via Plaza España. The bus generally stops for five minutes at Plaza España, where you can get out to enjoy that slice-of-life scene.

Helpful Hints

For **Internet access,** try Café Olé in the new town on Plaza España or Arcomputer on Paseo de Andalucía. The little **post office** is in the old town at Paseo de Boliches 26, a few doors away from Hotel Los Olivos (Mon–Fri 8:30–14:30, Sat 9:30–13:00, closed Sun). For **laundry,** Presto is full-service and reliable (€15, Mon–Fri 9:00–14:00 & 17:30–21:00, Sat 9:00–14:00, closed Sun, in new town, across from recommended Hotel La Fonda on Calle Debajo del Corral 6, tel. 956-700-555).

The best **town view** for those driving into town is from a tiny park just beyond the new bridge on the El Bosque road.

Self-Guided Tour of the Old Town

Start at the top of the hill, in the main square dominated by the church. (Avoid this walk during the hot midday siesta.)

1. Plaza del Cabildo: Stand at the viewpoint opposite the church on the town's main square. Survey the square, which in the old days doubled as a bullring. On your right is the parador, a former palace of the governor. On your left is the city hall (with the TI), below the 11th-century Moorish castle where Ferdinand and Isabel held Reconquista strategy meetings (closed to the public). Directly in front is the Church of Santa María. Notice the church's fine but unfinished bell tower. The old one fell in the earthquake of 1755 (famous for destroying Lisbon). The new replacement was intended to be the tallest in Andalucía after Sevilla's—but money ran out. It looks like someone lives on an upper floor. Someone does. The church guardian lives there in a room strewn with bell-ringing ropes.

Arcos de la Frontera

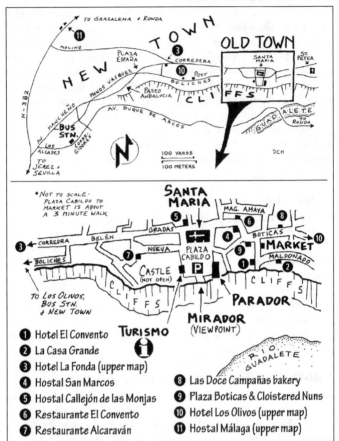

1 Hotel El Convento
2 La Casa Grande
3 Hotel La Fonda (upper map)
4 Hostal San Marcos
5 Hostal Callejón de las Monjas
6 Restaurante El Convento
7 Restaurante Alcaraván

8 Las Doce Campañas bakery
9 Plaza Boticas & Cloistered Nuns
10 Hotel Los Olivos (upper map)
11 Hostal Málaga (upper map)

Enjoy the square's viewpoint. Belly up to the railing and look down. The people of Arcos boast that only they see the backs of the birds as they fly. Ponder the parador's erosion concerns (it lost part of its lounge in the 1990s—dropped right off), orderly orange groves, and fine views toward Morocco. The city council considered building an underground parking lot to clear up the square, but nixed it because of the land's fragility. You're 330 feet above the river. This is the town's suicide departure point for men (women jump from the other side).

2. Inside the Church of Santa María: After Arcos was retaken from the Moors in the 13th century, this church was built—atop a mosque. Buy a ticket (€1.50, Mon–Fri 10:00–13:00 & 16:00–19:00, Sat 10:00–14:00, closed Sun and Jan–Feb) and step into the center, where you can see the finely carved choir. The organ was built in 1789 with that many pipes. The fine Renaissance high altar—carved in wood—covers up a Muslim prayer niche that survived from the older mosque. The altar shows God with a globe in his hand (on top), scenes from the life of Jesus (on the right) and Mary (left). Circle the church counterclockwise and notice the elaborate chapels. While most of the architecture is Gothic, the chapels are decorated in Baroque and Rococo styles. The ornate statues are used in Holy Week processions. Sniff out the "incorruptible body" (miraculously never rotting) of St. Felix— a third-century martyr. Felix may be nicknamed "the incorruptible," but take a close look at his knee. He's no longer skin and bones...just bones and the fine silver mesh that once covered his skin. Rome sent his body in 1764, after recognizing this church as the most important in Arcos. In the back of the church, under a huge fresco of St. Christopher (carrying his staff and baby Jesus), is a gnarly Easter candle from 1767.

3. Church Exterior: Back outside, circle clockwise around the church. Down four steps, find the third-century Roman votive altar with a carving of the palm tree of life. While the Romans didn't build this high in the mountains, they did have a town and temple at the foot of Arcos. This carved stone was found in the foundation of the original Moorish mosque, which stood here before the first church was built.

Head down a few more steps and come to the main entrance (west portal) of the church (open for worship on Sundays and every evening at 20:00, 19:00 in winter). This is a fine example of Plateresque Gothic—Spain's last and most ornate kind of Gothic. In the pavement, notice the 15th-century magic circle: 12 red and 12 white stones—the white ones have various constellations marked. When a child would come to the church to be baptized, the parents would stop here first for a good Christian exorcism. The exorcist would stand inside the protective circle and cleanse the baby of any evil spirits. While locals no longer do this (and a modern rain drain now marks the center), Sufis, a sect of Islam, still come here in a kind of magical pilgrimage. (Down a few more steps and 10 yards to the left, you can catch the public bus for a circular minibus joyride through Arcos; see "Getting Around Arcos," page 321.)

Continue around the church to the intersection below the flying buttresses. These buttresses were built to shore up the church when it was wounded by an earthquake in 1696. Thanks to these supports, the church survived the bigger earthquake of 1755. (Look at the arches that prop up the houses downhill on the left; all over town, arches support earthquake-damaged structures.) The spiky security grille (over the window above) protected cloistered nuns when this building was a convent.

At the corner, Sr. González Oca's tiny barbershop has some

exciting posters of bulls running Pamplona-style through the streets of Arcos during Holy Week—an American from the nearby Navy base at Rota was killed here by a bull in 1994. (Sr. González Oca is happy to show off his posters; drop in and say, *"Hola."* Need a haircut? €7.) Downstairs in Sr. González Oca's bar, you can see a framed collection of all the euro coins of each of the 12 participating nations. Continuing along under the buttresses, notice the scratches of innumerable car mirrors on each wall (and be glad you're walking).

4. From the Church to the Market: Completing your circle around the church, turn left under more earthquake-damaged arches and walk east down the bright, white Calle Escribanos. From now to the end of this walk, you'll go basically straight until you come to the town's second big church (St. Peter's). After a block, you hit Plaza Boticas. At the end of the street on your left is the top restaurant in town, El Convento (see "Eating," page 328). On your right is the last remaining convent in Arcos. Notice the no-nunsense window grilles high above, with tiny peepholes in the latticework for the cloistered nuns to see through. Step into the lobby under the fine portico to find their one-way mirror and a blind spinning cupboard. Push the buzzer, and one of the eight sisters (several are from Kenya and speak English well) will spin out some €5 boxes of excellent, freshly-baked pine-nut cookies for you to consider buying. (Be careful, if you stand big and tall to block out the light, you can actually see the sister through the glass.) If you ask for *magdalenas,* bags of cupcakes will swing around (€1.50). These are traditional goodies made from completely natural ingredients (daily but not reliably 8:30–14:30 & 17:00–19:00). Buy some cupcakes to support their church work, and give them to kids as you complete your walk.

The covered market *(mercado)* at the bottom of the plaza (next to the convent) resides in an unfinished church. At the entry, notice what is half of a church wall. The church was being built for the Jesuits, but construction stopped in 1767 when King Charles III, tired of the Jesuit appetite for politics, expelled the order from Spain. The market is closed on Sunday and on Monday—because they rest on Sunday, there's no produce, fish, or meat ready for Monday. Poke inside. It's tiny but has everything you need. Pop into the *servicio público* (public WC)—no gender bias here.

5. From the Market to the Church of St. Peter: Continue straight (passing the market on your right) down Calle Boticas. Peek discreetly into private patios. These wonderful, cool-tiled courtyards filled with plants, pools, furniture, and happy family activities are typical of Arcos (and featured on the TI's Patios walks). Except in the mansions, these patios are generally shared by several families. Originally, each courtyard served as a catchment system, funneling rainwater to a drain in the middle, which filled the well. You can still see tiny wells in wall niches with now-decorative pulleys for the bucket.

Look for Las Doce Campañas bakery, which sells traditional and delicious *sultana* cookies (€1 each). These big, dry macaroons (named for the wives of sultans) go back to Moorish times. At the next corner, squint back above the bakery to the corner of the tiled rooftop. The tiny and very eroded mask was placed here to scare evil spirits from the house. This is Arcos' last surviving mask from a tradition that lasted until the mid-19th century.

At the next intersection, notice the ancient columns on each corner. All over town, these columns—many actually Roman, appropriated from their ancient settlement at the foot of the hill—were put up to protect buildings from reckless donkey carts.

As you walk down the next block, notice that the walls are scooped out on either side of the windows. These are a reminder of the days when women stayed inside but wanted the best possible view of any people-action in the streets. These "window ears" also enabled boys in a more modest age to lean inconspicuously against the wall to chat up eligible young ladies.

Opposite the old facade ahead, find the Association of San Miguel. Duck right, past a bar, into the oldest courtyard in town—you can still see the graceful Gothic lines of this noble home. The bar is a club for retired men—always busy when a bullfight's on TV or during card-game times. The guys are friendly. Drinks are cheap (a stiff Cuba Libre costs €1.50). You're welcome to flip on the light and explore the old-town photos in the back room.

Just beyond (facing the elegant front door of that noble house) is Arcos' second church, St. Peter's. You know it's St. Peter's because St. Peter, mother of God, is the centerpiece of the facade. Let me explain. It really is the second church, having had an extended battle with Santa María for papal recognition as the leading church in Arcos. When the pope finally favored Santa María, St. Peter's parishioners even changed their prayers. Rather than honoring "María," they wouldn't even say her name. They prayed "St. Peter, mother of God."

In the cool of the evening, the tiny square in front of the church—about the only flat piece of pavement around—serves as the old-town soccer field for neighborhood kids. Until a few years ago, this church also had a resident bellman—notice the cozy balcony halfway up. He was a basket-maker and a colorful character, famous for bringing a donkey into his quarters, which grew too big to get back out. Finally, he had no choice but to kill and eat the donkey (€1 donation, church open Mon–Fri 10:30–14:00, Sat–Sun sporadically).

Twenty yards beyond the church, step into the fine Galería de Arte San Pedro, featuring painting, pottery, and artisans in action. Walk inside. Find the water drain and the well.

Across the street, a sign directs you to *Mirador*—a tiny square

100 yards away that affords a commanding view of the countryside.

From St. Peter's church, circle down and around back to the main square, wandering the tiny neighborhood lanes (the delightful Higinio Capote is particularly picturesque with its many geraniums), peeking into patios, kicking a few soccer balls, and savoring the views.

NIGHTLIFE

New-Town Evening Action—The newer part of Arcos has a modern charm. All the generations enjoy life out in the cool of the evening around Plaza España (10-min walk from the old town). Several fine tapas bars border the square.

The big park (Recinto Ferial) below Plaza España is the late-night fun zone in the summer (June–Sept) when *carpas* (restaurant tents) fill with merrymakers, especially on weekends. The scene includes open-air tapas bars, disco music, and dancing. Throughout the summer there are free live concerts here on Friday evenings and free open-air cinema on Sunday evenings.

Flamenco—On Plaza del Cananeo in the old town and three other venues (check TI), amateur flamenco sizzles on Thursday and Saturday evenings (free, from 22:00 July–Aug).

SLEEPING

In the Old Town

$$$ **Parador de Arcos de la Frontera** is royally located, elegant, recently refurbished, and reasonably priced, with 24 rooms (8 with balconies). If you're going to experience a parador, this is a good one (Sb-€91, Db-€113, breakfast-€10, elevator, air-con, minibars, free parking, Plaza del Cabildo, tel. 956-700-500, fax 956-701-116, www.parador .es, arcos@parador.es, SE). Rooms with a terrace cost €20 extra.

$$ **Hotel El Convento,** deep in the old town just beyond the parador, is the best value in town. Run by a hardworking family, this cozy hotel offers 13 fine rooms—all with great views, half with view balconies. In 1998 I enjoyed a big party with most of Arcos' big shots as they dedicated a fine room with a grand-view balcony to "Rick Steves, Periodista Turístico"—a hint to where I sleep when in Arcos (Sb-€55, Db-€65, Db with terrace-€80, 10 percent discount with cash and this book, third person-€18 extra, includes tax, 20 percent less Nov–Feb, parking on Plaza del Cabildo-€3, Maldonado 2, tel. 956-702-333, fax 956-704-128, www.webdearcos.com/elconvento, elconvento@viautil.com, Estefania and María SE). Over an à la carte breakfast, bird-watch on their view terrace, with all of Andalucía spreading beyond your *café con leche.*

$$ **La Casa Grande** is a lovingly appointed *Better Homes and*

Sleep Code

(€1 = about $1.20, country code: 34)
S = Single, D = Double/Twin, T = Triple, Q = Quad,
b = bathroom, s = shower only, no CC = Credit Cards not
accepted, SE = Speaks English, NSE = No English. You can
assume credit cards are accepted unless otherwise noted. A price
range reflects off-season to peak-season prices. Breakfast is not
included, nor is the 7 percent IVA tax (unless noted below). Note
that some hotels double their rates during the motorbike races in
Jerez (early May) and Holy Week (March 20–27 in 2005); I have
not listed these spikes in the prices below.

To help you easily sort through these listings, I've divided
the rooms into three categories, based on the price for a standard
double room with bath during high season.

$$$ **Higher Priced**—Most rooms €100 or more.
  $$ **Moderately Priced**—Most rooms between €50–100.
    $ **Lower Priced**—Most rooms €50 or less.

Moroccan Tiles kind of place that rents eight rooms with grand-view
windows. Like in a lavish B&B, you're free to enjoy its fine view terrace, homey library, and classy courtyard, where you'll be served a
traditional breakfast (Db-€77, Db suite-€88–94, Tb-€112–121, Qb
suite-€131–138, Maldonado 10, tel. 956-703-930, fax 956-717-095,
www.lacasagrande.net, info@lacasagrande.net, friendly owners Elena
and Ferrán).

$ Hotel La Fonda is a great traditional Spanish inn, with all 19
rooms off one grand hall above a tacky little lobby (Sb-€27, Db-€45,
third person-€12, 10 percent discount with this 2005 book, no breakfast, air-con, request a quiet *tranquilo* room, Calle Corredera 83, tel.
956-700-057, fax 956-703-661, lafonda@pobladores.com, SE).

$ Hostal San Marcos, in the heart of the old town, offers four
air-conditioned rooms and a great sun terrace above a neat little bar
(Sb-€20, Db-€35, Tb-€45, includes tax, complimentary drink,
Marqués de Torresoto 6, tel. 956-700-721, sanmarcosarcos@mixmail
.com, Loli NSE).

$ Hostal Callejón de las Monjas, with a tangled floor plan and
nine simple rooms (7 with air-con), offers the best cheap beds in the
old town. It's on a sometimes-noisy street behind the Church of
Santa María (Sb-€18, D-€27, Db-€33, Db with terrace-€39, Tb-
€44, two big Qb-€66, includes tax, Calle Dean Espinosa 4, tel. &
fax 956-702-302, NSE). Friendly Sr. González Oca runs a tiny barbershop in the foyer and a restaurant in the cellar.

In the New Town

$$ Hotel Los Olivos is a bright, cool, and airy place with a fine courtyard, roof garden, bar, view, friendly English-speaking folks, and easy parking. Unfortunately, this poor-man's parador is located on a motorbike-infested street. Since 12 of its 19 rooms are on the less-noisy back side, it's smart to request a quiet room with no view (Sb-€45, Db-€70, Tb-€82, extra bed-€18, breakfast-€6, includes tax, 10 percent discount for readers of this 2005 book, San Miguel 2, tel. 956-700-811, fax 956-702-018, losolivosdele@terra.es, Raquel, María José or Miguel, SE).

$ Hostal Málaga is surprisingly nice, if for some reason you want to stay on the big, noisy road at the Jerez edge of town. Nestled on a quiet lane between truck stops on A-382, it offers 18 clean, attractive rooms and a breezy two-level roof garden (Sb-€18–21, Db-€33–36, Qb apartment-€48, air-con, easy parking, Ponce de León 5, tel. & fax 956-702-010, hostalmalaga@teleline.es, Josefa speaks German). She also rents two apartments in the center of Arcos overlooking lively Plaza España in the new town (Db-€48).

EATING

Restaurante El Convento is wonderfully atmospheric and graciously run by Señora María Moreno-Moreno and her husband, Señor José Antonio Roldan. It serves quality Andalusian cuisine in a dressy setting (generally daily 13:00–16:00 & 19:00–22:00, closed 1 rotating day a week—call to check, near parador at Marqués de Torresoto 7, reservations recommended, tel. 956-703-222). The hearty €24 menu of the day includes a fine house red wine and a glass of sherry with dessert. This is a good opportunity to dine on game.

The **Parador** has an expensive restaurant with a cliff-edge setting. Its €24 11-course sampler menu is an interesting option. A costly drink on the million-dollar-view terrace can be worth the price (lunch and dinner daily, on main square).

To eat more cheaply in the old town, try **Restaurante San Marco,** which offers a good €8 menu, or prowl the many tapas bars along the main drag (Calle Dean Espinosa). The *típico* **Alcaraván** serves barbecued pork chops *(solomillo)* under medieval vaults in what was the castle's dungeon (closed Mon, Calle Nueva 1).

Plaza España, in the lower new town, is lined with tapas bars and restaurants.

TRANSPORTATION CONNECTIONS

By bus to: Jerez (hrly, 30 min), **Ronda** (4/day, 2 hrs), **Cádiz** (9/day, 1 hr), **Sevilla** (2/day direct, 2 hrs, more departures with a change in Jerez). From Jerez, there are hourly connections to Sevilla. Two bus companies share the Arcos bus station. Their Jerez offices keep longer hours and know the Arcos schedules (Jerez tel. 956-342-174 or 956-341-063—make it clear you're in Arcos).

By car to: Sevilla (just over an hour if you pay €5 for the toll road), **Portugal** (follow freeway to Sevilla, skirt the city by turning west on C-30, direction Huelva, and it's a straight shot).

Ronda

With 40,000 people, Ronda is one of the largest white towns. With its gorge-straddling setting, it's also one of the most spectacular. While day-trippers from the touristy Costa del Sol clog Ronda's streets during the day, locals retake the town in the early evening

and nights are peaceful. Since it's served by train and bus, Ronda makes a relaxing break for nondrivers traveling between Granada, Sevilla, and Córdoba.

Ronda's main attractions are its gorge-spanning bridges, the oldest bullring in Spain, and an interesting old town. Spaniards know it as the cradle of modern bullfighting and the romantic home of old-time *banditos*. Its cliffside setting, dramatic today, was practical back in its day. For the Moors, it provided a tough bastion, taken by the Spaniards only in 1485, seven years before Granada fell. To 19th-century bandits, it was Bolivia without the boat ride.

ORIENTATION

Ronda's breathtaking ravine divides the town's labyrinthine Moorish quarter and its new, noisier, and more sprawling Mercadillo quarter. A massive-yet-graceful 18th-century bridge connects these two neighborhoods. Most things of touristic importance (TI, post office, hotels, bullring) are clustered within a few blocks of the bridge. The *paseo* (early evening stroll) happens in the new town, on Ronda's major pedestrian street, Carrera Espinel.

Tourist Information: The main TI is on the main square, Plaza España, opposite the bridge (Mon–Fri 9:00–19:30, Sat–Sun 10:00–14:00, tel. 952-871-272). Get the free Ronda map, the excellent Andalusian road map, and a listing of the latest museum hours. Consider buying maps of Granada, Sevilla, or the Route of the White Towns (€0.60 each). A second TI is located opposite the bullring, at Paseo Blas Infante (Mon–Fri 9:30–19:00, Sat–Sun 10:00–14:00 & 15:30–18:30, tel. 952-187-119).

Ronda

200 YARDS
200 METERS

TO COSTA DEL SOL, MALAGA

CITY WALL

SANTA MARIA LA MAYOR

BANDOLERO MUSEUM

MONDRAGON PALACE

SOUTH

MOORISH QUARTER

ARAB BRIDGE

OLD BRIDGE

PUENTE NUEVO

GUADALEVIN RIVER

LOS REMEDIOS

PEÑAS
CANTOS

PLAZA C. ABELA

VILLA

PLAZA ESPAÑA

MERCA-DILLO QUARTER

CORTES

PLAZA NUEVA

ENTER

PLAZA DE TOROS

NARANJA

ESPINEL

VIRGEN

RAMON

ALMENDRA

SOUVIRON

Post

ALAMEDA
WC

PLAZA MERCED

MONTERO

POZOR

MOLINO

DR FLEMING

TO SEVILLA, ARCOS & PILETA CAVES & ②

TO TREU

TO TRAIN STATION & ⑭

MADRID

ANDALUCIA

SAN JOSE

BUS STATION

① Parador de Ronda
② To Hotel Reina Victoria
③ Hotel La Casona
④ Hotel La Español & Rest. Tragabuches
⑤ Hotel San Gabriel
⑥ Hotel Rest. Alavera de Los Baños
⑦ Hotel Don Miguel
⑧ Hotel Enfrentearte Ronda
⑨ Hotel Royal
⑩ Hotel San Francisco
⑪ Hostal Ronda Sol
⑫ Hostal Biarritz
⑬ Hotel El Tajo
⑭ To Hostal Andalucía
⑮ Restaurante Pedro Romero
⑯ Restaurante Santa Pola
⑰ Restaurante del Escudero
⑱ To Casa Manolo Restaurante
⑲ Supermarket Mercadona
㉑ Casa del Rey Moro Garden
㉒ Palacio del Marqués de Salvatierra

Arrival in Ronda

The train station is a 15-minute walk from the center. To get to the center, turn right out of the station on Avenida Andalucía, turn left at the roundabout (you will see the bus station is on your right), and then walk four blocks to cross Calle Almendra (where several recommended hotels are located) and Calle Lauría (with recommended restaurant Casa Manolo). At the pedestrian street (Carrera Espinel, a few blocks farther), turn right to reach the TI. From the bus station (lockers inside, buy coin at kiosk by exit), cross the roundabout and follow directions above. A taxi to the center costs about €4.

Drivers coming up from the coast catch A376 at San Pedro de Alcántara and climb about 20 miles into the mountains. A369 offers a much longer, winding, but scenic alternative that takes you through a series of whitewashed villages. The handiest place to park is the underground lot at Plaza del Socorro (1 block from bullring, €12/24 hrs).

TOURS

Ronda Bus Tour—You may see a tiny Tajotur bus parked in front of the TI. Tourists gather for a fun, entertaining multimedia drive outside of town to the most scenic places, viewing the gorge and bridge, as well as other historic points (€9, 60 min, taped English narration, runs erratically up to 5 times/day, Joaquín, mobile 616-909-483, tajotour@ronda.net).

Local Guide—Energetic and knowledgeable Antonio Jesús Naranjo will take you on a two-hour walking tour of the city's sights (€60 on Mon–Sat, €90 on Sun, plus €1 per person, reserve early, tel. 952-879-215, mobile 639-073-763). If Antonio is busy, ask the TI for a list of guides.

SIGHTS

Ronda's New Town

▲▲▲**The Gorge and New Bridge**—The ravine, called El Tajo—360 feet down and 200 feet wide—divides Ronda into the white-washed old Moorish town (La Ciudad) and the new town (El Mercadillo) that was built after the Christian reconquest in 1485. Ronda's main bridge, called Puente Nuevo (New Bridge), mightily spans the gorge. A bridge was built here in 1735 but fell after six years. This one was built from 1751 to 1793. Look down...carefully. Legend has it the architect fell to his death while inspecting it, and hundreds from both sides were thrown off this bridge during Spain's brutal civil war.

You can see the foundations of the original bridge (and a super view of the New Bridge) from the park named Jardines Ciudad de

Cuenca. From Plaza España, walk down Calle Villanueva and turn right on Calle Los Remedios at the sign for the park.

▲▲**Bullfighting Ring**—Ronda is the birthplace of modern bull-fighting, and this ring was the first great Spanish bullring. While Philip II initiated bullfighting as war training for knights in the 16th century, it wasn't until the early 1700s that Francisco Romero established the rules of modern bullfighting and introduced the scarlet cape, held unfurled with a stick. His son Juan further developed the ritual (or art), and his grandson Pedro was one of the first great matadors (killing nearly 6,000 bulls in his career).

To see the bullring, stables, and **museum,** buy tickets from the booth at the main entrance (it's at the back of the bullring, the furthest point from the main drag). The museum is located just before the entry into the arena.

This museum—which has translations in English—is a shrine to bullfighting and the historic Romero family. You'll see stuffed heads (of bulls), photos, artwork, posters, and costumes (€5, daily May–Sept 10:00–20:00, Oct–April 10:00–18:00, on main drag in new town, 2 blocks up and on left from the New Bridge and TI, tel. 952-874-132).

Take advantage of the opportunity to walk in the actual arena, with plenty of time to play *toro,* surrounded by 5,000 empty seats. The arena was built in 1784. Notice the 176 classy Tuscan columns. With your back to the entry, look left and to see the ornamental columns and painted doorway where the dignitaries sit (over the gate where the bull enters). On the right is the place for the band—in the case of a small town like Ronda, a high school band.

Bullfights are scheduled for the first weekend of September and occur only rarely in the spring. For September bullfights, tickets go on sale the preceding July (tel. 952-876-967); *sol* means "sun" (cheap seats) and *sombra* means "shade" (pricier seats).

The Alameda del Tajo park, a block away, is a fine place for people-watching or a snooze in the shade.

Parador National de Ronda—Walk around and through this newest of Spain's fabled paradors. The views from the walkway just below the outdoor terrace are magnificent. Anyone is welcome at the cafés, but you have to be a guest to use the pool.

Ronda's Old Town

Santa María la Mayor Collegiate Church—This 15th-century church shares a fine park-like square with orange trees and the city hall. Its Renaissance bell tower still has parts of the old minaret. It was built on and around the remains of Moorish Ronda's main mosque (which was itself built on the site of a temple to Julius Caesar). Partially destroyed by an earthquake, the reconstruction of the church resulted in the Moorish/Gothic/Renaissance/Baroque fusion (or confusion) you see today. Enjoy the bright frescoes, elaborately carved choir and altar, and the new bronze sculpture depicting the life of the Virgin Mary. The treasury displays vestments that look curiously like matadors' brocaded outfits (€2, daily May–Sept 10:00–20:00, Oct–April 10:00–19:00, closed Sun lunch, Plaza Duquesa de Parcent in old town).

Mondragón Palace (Palacio de Mondragón)—This beautiful Moorish building was built in the 14th century, possibly as the residence of Moorish kings, and was carefully restored in the 16th century. It houses an enjoyable prehistory museum, with exhibits on Neolithic toolmaking and early metallurgy (many captions in English). Even if you have no interest in your ancestors, this is worth it for the architecture alone (€2, May–Sept Mon–Fri 10:00–19:00, Sat–Sun 10:00–15:00, Oct–April closes an hour earlier, on Plaza Mondragón in old town, tel. 952-878-450). Linger in the two small gardens, especially the shady one.

Wander out to the nearby Plaza de María Auxiliadora for more views and a look at the two rare *pinsapo* trees (resembling firs) in the middle of the park; this is the only area of the country where these ancient trees are found.

Museo del Bandolero—This tiny museum, while not as intriguing as it sounds, is an interesting assembly of *bandito* photos, guns, clothing, and knickknacks. The Jesse Jameses and Billy el Niños of Andalucía called this remote area home, and brief but helpful English descriptions make this a fun detour. One brand of romantic bandits were those who fought Napoleon's army—often more effectively than the regular Spanish troops (€2.70, daily May–Sept 10:00–20:00, Oct–April 10:00–18:00, across main street below Church of Santa María la Mayor at Calle Armiñan 65, tel. 952-877-785).

Museo Joaquín Peinado—Housed in an old palace, this fresh new museum features a Cubist collection by Joaquín Peinado, a pal of Picasso's (€3, Mon–Sat 10:00–14:00 & 17:00–20:00, Sun 10:00–14:00, Plaza del Gigante, tel. 952-871-585).

Walk through Old Town—From the New Bridge you can descend into a world of whitewashed houses, tiny grilled balconies, and winding lanes—the old town.

The **Casa del Rey Moro** garden may be in jeopardy if a five-star hotel opens on this site as planned. They may or may not offer access to "the Mine," an exhausting series of 365 stairs (like climbing down and then up a 20-story building) leading to the floor of the gorge. The Moors cut this zigzag staircase into the wall of the gorge in the 14th century. They used Spanish slaves to haul water to the thirsty town.

Fifty yards downhill from the garden is **Palacio del Marqués de Salvatierra** (closed to public). With the "distribution" following the Reconquista here in 1485, the Spanish king gave this fine house to the Salvatierra family. The facade is rich in colonial symbolism from

Spanish America. Note the pre-Columbian–looking characters flanking the balcony above the door and below the family coat of arms.

Continuing downhill you come to **Puente Viejo** (Old Bridge), built in 1616 upon the ruins of an Arab bridge. From here, look down to see the old Puente Romano, originally built by the Romans. Far to the right you can glimpse some of the surviving highly fortified Moorish city walls. Crossing the bridge, you see stairs on the right, leading scenically along the gorge back to the New Bridge via a fine viewpoint. Straight ahead bubbles the welcoming Eight Springs fountain.

Near Ronda: Pileta Caves

The Pileta Caves (Cuevas de la Pileta) are the best look a tourist can get at prehistoric cave painting in Spain. The caves, complete with stalagmites, bones, and 20,000-year-old paintings, are 14 miles from Ronda, past the town of Benaoján, at the end of the road.

Farmer José Bullón and his family live down the hill from the caves. He offers tours on the hour, leading up to 25 people through the caves, which were discovered by his grandfather. Call the night before to make sure no groups are scheduled for the time you want to visit—otherwise you'll have to wait (€6.50, daily 10:00–13:00 & 16:00–18:00, closes off-season at 17:00, closing times indicate last entrance, no reservations taken—just join the line, minimum of 12 people required for tour, bring flashlight, sweater, and good shoes—it's slippery inside, tel. 952-167-343).

Sr. Bullón is a master at hurdling the language barrier. As you walk the cool half mile, he'll spend an hour pointing out lots of black, ochre, and red drawings, which are five times as old as the Egyptian pyramids. Mostly it's just lines or patterns, but there are also crude fish, horses, and buffalo, made from a mixture of clay and fat by finger-painting prehistoric *hombres.* The 200-foot main cavern is impressive, as are some weirdly recognizable natural formations such as the Michelin man and a Christmas tree. The famous caves at Altamira in northern Spain are closed (though a replica cave has opened nearby, see page 112); if you want to see real Neolithic paintings in Spain, this is it.

It's possible to get here without wheels (taking the Ronda–Benaoján bus—2/day, 8:30 & 13:00, 30 min—then a 2-hr, 3-mile, uphill hike), but I wouldn't bother. You can get from Ronda to the caves by taxi (€25) and try to hitch a ride back with another tourist, or hire the taxi for a round-trip (€45). If you're driving, it's easy: Leave Ronda on the highway to Sevilla—formerly C339, now A376, and after a few miles, exit left toward Benaoján. Follow signs, bearing right just before Benaoján, up to the dramatic dead end. Leave nothing of value in your car. Nearby Montejaque has a great outdoor restaurant, La Casita.

SLEEPING

Ronda has plenty of reasonably priced, decent-value accommodations. It's crowded only during Holy Week (the week leading up to Easter, March 20–27 in 2005) and the first week of September. Most of my recommendations are in the new town, a short walk from the New Bridge and a 10-minute walk from the train station. (The exceptions are Hostal Andalucía, across from the train station, and Reina Victoria, at the edge of town—and at the edge of the gorge.) In the cheaper places, ask for a room with a *ventana* (window) to avoid the few interior rooms. Breakfast and the 7 percent IVA tax are usually not included in the price.

$$$ You can't miss the striking **Parador de Ronda** on Plaza España. It's an impressive integration of stone, glass, and marble. All 78 rooms have hardwood floors and most have fantastic view balconies (ask about family-friendly duplexes). There's also a pool overlooking the bridge (Sb-€96, Db-€120–141—depending on views, breakfast-€10, air-con, garage-€10, Plaza España, tel. 952-877-500, fax 952-878-188, ronda@parador.es, SE). Consider at least a drink on the terrace.

$$$ The royal **Reina Victoria,** hanging over the gorge at the edge of town, has a marvelous view—Hemingway loved it—but you'll pay for it (89 rooms, Sb-€74–82, Db-€100–124, extra bed-€20–23, breakfast-€10, air-con, elevator, pool, free parking, 10-min walk from city center and easy to miss, look for intersection of Avenida Victoria and Calle Jerez, Jerez 25, tel. 952-871-240, fax 952-871-075, www.hotelreinavictoriaronda.com, reinavictoriaronda @husa.es, SE).

$$$ **Hotel La Casona,** a beautiful splurge in the old town, is close to the Minarete de San Sebastián mosque tower. The hotel features nine thoughtfully decorated rooms (some are suites), a swimming pool, and a garden (Db-€90, special doubles and suites-€103–150, less in low season, breakfast-€10, air-con, Internet access, elevator, parking-€10, Marqués de Salvatierra 5, tel. 952-879-595, fax 952-161-095, www.lacasonadelaciudad.com, reservas@lacasonadelaciudad.com, Bely and Lourdes).

$$ **Hotel La Española** has 16 comfy rooms with air-conditioning and modern bathrooms (Sb-€41, Db-€82, Tb-€105, includes breakfast buffet but not tax, 15–20 percent less in June–July & Nov–Feb, 10 percent discount if you show this book, José Aparicio 3, tel. 952-871-052, fax 952-878-001, www.ronda.net/usuar/laespanola, laespanola@ronda.net, SE).

$$ Family-run **Hotel San Gabriel** has 16 pleasant rooms, a kind staff, and a fine garden terrace (Sb-€68, Db-€82, Db suite-€102, air-con, Calle Marqués de Moctezuma 19, just off Plaza Poeta Abul-Beca, tel. 952-190-392, fax 952-190-117, www.hotelsangabriel.com,

Sleep Code

(€1 = about $1.20, country code: 34)
To help you easily sort through these listings, I've divided the rooms into three categories, based on the price for a standard double room with bath during high season:

$$$ **Higher Priced**—Most rooms €90 or more.
  $$ **Moderately Priced**—Most rooms between €50–90.
    $ **Lower Priced**—Most rooms €50 or less.

info@hotelsangabriel.com, friendly Ana SE). If you are a cinema-lover, settle into one of the seats from the old Ronda theater that now grace the charming TV room. In the breakfast room, check out photos of big movie stars that have stayed at the hotel.

$$ **Alavera de Los Baños,** located next to ancient Moorish baths at the bottom of the hill, has 10 clean and colorful rooms (Db-€75, Db with terrace-€85, includes tax and breakfast, closed Dec–Jan, Calle San Miguel, tel. & fax 952-879-143, www.andalucia.com/alavera, alavera@telefonica.net, personable Christian and Imma SE). This hotel offers a rural setting within the city, a swimming pool, a peaceful Arabic garden, and a wonderful restaurant that makes a unique combination in Ronda. (see "Eating," page 337).

$$ The gorge-facing **Don Miguel** is just left of the bridge. Of its 30 comfortable rooms, 20 have balconies and/or gorgeous views at no extra cost, but street rooms come with a little noise (Sb-€55, Db-€85, includes buffet breakfast, air-con, elevator, parking garage a block away-€9/day, Plaza España 4, tel. 952-877-722, fax 952-878-377, reservas@dmiguel.com, SE).

$$ Relaxed and friendly **Hotel En Frente Arte Ronda** has 14 spacious rooms with dim lights, a peaceful tropical garden, views, terraces, a small swimming pool, and avant-garde decor (Sb-€45-60, Db-€78-100, extra bed-€38; includes buffet breakfast, lunch, and drinks; elevator, air-con, Internet access, Real 40, tel. 952-879-088, fax 952-877-217, www.enfrentearte.com, reservations@enfrentearte.com).

$$ The 65-room **Hotel El Tajo** has decent, quiet rooms once you get past the tacky Moorish decoration in the foyer (Sb-€32, Db-€53, parking-€6/day, air-con, Calle Cruz Verde 7, a half block off the pedestrian street, tel. 952-874-040, fax 952-875-099, www.hoteleltajo.com, reservas@hoteleltajo.com, SE).

$ **Hotel Royal** has 29 clean, spacious, but boring rooms—many on a busy street. Ask for a *tranquilo* room in the back (Sb-€26, Db-€43, Tb-€54, air-con, Virgen de la Paz 42, 3 blocks off Plaza España, tel. 952-871-141, fax 952-878-132, www.ronda.net/usuar/hotelroyal, hroyal@ronda.net, some English spoken).

$ **Hotel San Francisco** offers 27 small, nicely decorated

rooms a block off the main pedestrian street in the town center (Sb-€25, Db-€45–50, Tb-€65, includes tax, 6 parking spaces-€6, air-con, María Cabrera 20, tel. 952-873-299, fax 952-874-688, www.hotelsanfranciscoronda.com, hotelronda@terra.es).

$ Hostal Ronda Sol has a homey atmosphere with 15 cheap but monkish rooms (S-€11, D-€17, no CC, parking-€10/day, Almendra 11, tel. 952-874-497, friendly María or Rafael NSE). Next door, run by the same owner, **Hostal Biarritz** offers 21 similar rooms, some with private baths (S-€11, D-€17, Db-€25, T-€25, Tb-€36, includes tax, no CC, parking-€10/day, Almendra 7, tel. 952-872-910, NSE).

$ Hostal Andalucía, a plain but clean place with 11 comfortable rooms, is immediately across the street from the train station (Sb-€24, Db-€36, includes tax, air-con, easy street parking, Martínez Astein 19, tel. 952-875-450, NSE).

EATING

Dodge the tourist traps. They say the best meal in Ronda is at the **parador** (*muy elegante,* figure €25). **Plaza del Socorro,** a block in front of the bullring, is a wonderful local scene, where families enjoy the square and its restaurants. Take a *paseo* with the locals down pedestrian-only Carrera Espinel and choose a place with tables spilling out into the action. The best drinks and views in town are enjoyed on the terraces of the **Hotel Don Miguel** or the parador.

Restaurante Pedro Romero—assuming a shrine to bullfighting draped in *el toro* memorabilia doesn't ruin your appetite—gets good reviews but is touristy (€16 menus, or €30 à la carte, daily 12:30–16:00 & 19:00–23:00, air-con, across the street from bullring at Calle Virgen de la Paz 18, tel. 952-871-110). Rub elbows with the local bullfighters or dine with the likes (well, photographic likenesses) of Orson Welles, Ernest Hemingway, and Franco.

Restaurante Santa Pola offers traditional food with friendly service and gorge views (3-course dinners-€24, good foie gras, oxtail stew, roasted lamb or honey-tempura eggplant, lunch from 12:30, dinner 20:00–23:30, crossing New Bridge, take the first left downhill and you'll see the sign, Calle Santo Domingo, tel. 952-879-208).

Alavera de los Baños, located in the hotel of the same name, serves tasty Moorish specialties such as lamb and chicken *tajine,* along with vegetarian dishes, and offers great outdoor dining (daily, open to public only for dinner, Calle San Miguel, tel. 952-879-143).

Restaurante del Escudero serves tasty Spanish cuisine with a modern touch on a terrace over the gorge (worth-it €13.50 and €21.84 gourmet *menus,* also extensive à la carte menu, Mon–Sat 12:00–16:00 & 19:00–23:00, Sun 12:00–16:00, Paseo Blas Infante 1, tel. 952-871-367).

Trendy, spendy **Restaurante Tragabuches** serves "nouvelle cuisine Andalouse," prepared by Spain's renowned chef, Daniel García (multicourse *menu*–€65—drinks not included, à la carte around €45, Tue–Sat 13:30–15:30 & 20:30–22:30, Sun 13:30–15:30, closed Mon, José Aparicio 1, tel. 952-190-291, www.tragabuches.com).

The no-frills **Café & Bar Faustino** offers the cheapest tapas in town (€0.90–1) to a lively crowd of students, blue-collar workers, and tourists (Tue–Sun 12:00–24:00, closed Mon, just off Plaza Carmen Abela, Santa Cecilia 4, tel. 952-190-307).

Simple **Casa Manolo,** a 10-minute walk from the town center, is an affordable option popular with locals, especially at lunchtime. It's a convenient stop on the way to or from the bus or train station (3-course lunch–€6, daily 12:00–16:00 & 20:30–23:00, good oxtail stew, Lauría 54; go up Carrera Espinel, left on Montejeras, then third right; tel. 952-878-050).

Picnic shoppers find supermarket **Mercadona** convenient, at Calle Cruz Verde 18 opposite Hotel El Tajo. (Mon–Sat 9:00–21:30). A good picnic spot is the Alameda park (with WC) north of the bullring.

TRANSPORTATION CONNECTIONS

By bus to: Algeciras (1/day, Mon–Fri only), **Arcos** (4/day, 2 hrs), **Benaoján** (2/day, 30 min), **Jerez** (4/day, 3 hrs), **Grazalema** (2/day, 1 hr), **Zahara** (2/day, Mon–Fri only, 1 hr), **Sevilla** (5/day, 2.5 hrs, less on weekends; also see trains below), **Málaga** (8/day, 1.75 hrs, 2 slower *ruta* buses, 3 hrs; access other Costa del Sol points from Málaga), **Marbella** (5/day, 75 min), **Fuengirola** (5/day, 2 hrs), **Nerja** (4 hrs, transfer in Málaga; can take train or bus from Ronda to Málaga). There's no efficient way to call "the bus company" because there are four sharing the same station; one of them is at tel. 952-187-061. It's best to just drop by and compare schedules (on Plaza Concepción García Redondo, several blocks from train station).

By train to: Algeciras (5/day, 2 hrs), **Bobadilla** (6/day, 1 hr), **Málaga** (6/day, 2.5 hrs, transfer in Bobadilla), **Sevilla** (3/day, 4hrs, transfer in Bobadilla), **Granada** (3/day, 2.5 hrs, transfer in Bobadilla), **Córdoba** (6/day, 2 hrs direct, 3.5 hrs with transfer in Bobadilla), **Madrid** (2/day, 5–7 hrs, 1 direct night train—23:27–8:40). It's a sleepy station serving only 11 trains a day. Transfers are a snap and time-coordinated in Bobadilla; with four trains arriving and departing simultaneously, double-check that you've jumped on the right one. Train info: tel. 902-240-202.

More Andalusian Hill Towns:
Zahara, Grazalema, and Jerez

There are plenty of undiscovered and interesting hill towns to explore. About half of the towns I visited were memorable. Unfortunately, public transportation is frustrating. I'd do these towns only by car. Good information on the area is rare. Fortunately, a good map, the tourist brochure (pick it up in Sevilla or Ronda), and a spirit of adventure work fine. Along with Arcos, Zahara and Grazalema are my favorite white villages.

Zahara

This tiny town in a tingly setting under a Moorish castle (worth the climb) has a spectacular view. While the big church facing the town square is considered one of the richest in the area, the smaller church has the most-loved statue. The Virgin of Dolores is Zahara's answer to Sevilla's Virgin of Macarena (and is similarly paraded through town during Holy Week). Zahara is a fine overnight stop for those who want to hear only the sounds of the wind, birds, and elderly footsteps on ancient cobbles. (**TI** open Mon–Sat 9:00–14:00 & 16:00–19:00, Sun 9:00–14:00, tel. 956-123-114.)

SIGHTS

▲**Zahara Castle**—During Moorish times, Zahara lay within the fortified castle walls above today's town. It was considered the gateway to Granada and a strategic stronghold for the Moors by the Christian forces of the Reconquista. Locals tell of the Spanish conquest of the Moors' castle (in 1402) as if it happened yesterday:

After the Spanish failed several times to seize the castle, a clever Spanish soldier noticed that the Moorish sentinel would check if any attackers were hiding behind a particular section of the wall by tossing a rock and setting the pigeons in flight. If they flew, the sentinel figured there was no danger. One night a Spaniard

Route of the White Hill Towns

hid there with a bag of pigeons and let them fly when the sentinel tossed his rock. Seeing the birds fly, the guard assumed he was clear to enjoy a snooze. The clever Spaniard then scaled the wall and opened the door to let his troops in, and the castle was conquered. That was in 1482. Ten years later Granada fell, the Muslims were back in Africa, and the Reconquista was complete. Today the castle is little more than an evocative ruin (free, always open) offering a commanding view and some newly discovered Roman ruins along the way. The lake is actually a reservoir. Before 1991 the valley had only a tiny stream.

El Vínculo—This family-run olive mill welcomes visitors for a look at its traditional factory, as well as a taste of some homemade sherry and the olive oil that the Urruti family has been producing on this site for centuries. Juan will treat you to a glass of sherry if you show the current edition of this book (€4.50, daily 9:30–20:00, on CA531 just outside Zahara, tel. 956-123-002, mobile 696-404-368, www.zaharadelasierra.info/elvinculo). Juan also rents the houses of his estate, with access to a big swimming pool and great views surrounded by the olives' trees and fragrance (big house, sleeps up to 12-€300/night, small house sleeps up to 7-€271/night).

SLEEPING AND EATING

(€1 = about $1.20, country code: 34)
Also see El Vínculo, above, for accommodations.

$$ **Hotel Arco de la Villa**—long on comfort, short on character—has 17 rooms with views just five minutes from the main square (Sb-€32, Db-€55, extra bed-€12.10, Camino Nazarí, tel. 956-123-230, fax 956-123-244, info@tugasa.com).

$ **Hostal Marqués de Zahara** is the best central hotel and a good value, with 10 comfortable rooms gathered around a cool, quiet courtyard. The hostess cooks traditional specialties in the restaurant (Sb-€30, Db-€40, Db-€45 with view, less Nov–March, breakfast-€5, air-con, San Juan 3, tel. & fax 956-123-061, www.marquesdezahara .com, info@marquesdezahara.com, Santiago SE).

$ Pensión Los Tadeos is a simple, blocky place just outside of town by the municipal swimming pool *(piscina)* offering 10 remodeled rooms with great views (Db-€37–40, Tb-€50, basic breakfast-€1.50, Paseo de la Fuente, tel. 956-123-086, family Ruíz NSE).

Eating: Sr. Manolo Tardio runs **Mesón Los Estribos,** a fine little restaurant with great views across from the church (Tue–Sun 13:00–16:00 & 20:00–23:00, closed Mon), and rents affordable apartments (tel. 956-123-145).

Grazalema

Another postcard-pretty hill town, Grazalema offers a royal balcony for a memorable picnic, a square where you can watch old-timers playing cards, and plenty of quiet, whitewashed streets to explore. Graced with cork, carob, and *pinsapo* pine trees, Grazalema offers lots of scenery with greenery.

Plaza de Andalucía, a block off the view terrace, has several decent little bars and restaurants and a popular candy store. Shops sell the town's beautiful handmade wool blankets.

Situated on a west-facing slope of the mountains, Grazalema catches clouds and is known as the rainiest place in Spain—but I've had only blue skies on every visit (**TI** open March–Sept Tue–Sun 10:00–14:00 & 18:00–20:00, Oct–Feb Tue–Sun 10:00–14:00 & 17:00–19:00, closed Mon, Plaza de España 11, tel. 956-132-225).

For horseback riding, consider Al-Hazán (€15/1–3 hr, €70/full-day with lunch, tel. 956-132-296, www.el-andaluz.com/alhazan .htm, run by Hanna, SE). For other adventures, including canoeing, caving, and hiking, contact Horizon (off Plaza de España at Corrales Terceros 29, tel. & fax 956-132-363, www.horizonaventura.com, info@horizonaventura.com).

SLEEPING AND EATING

$$ Villa Turística de Grazalema is a big, popular, happy place for locals enjoying their national park. It has 38 apartments and 24 regular hotel rooms, with balconies on the first floor or opening onto the swimming-pool garden on the ground floor (Sb-€32, Db-€55, plus tax, extra person-€12.10, apartments-€65–103, includes breakfast, 15 percent more in Aug, restaurant, half mile outside town, tel. 956-132-136, fax 956-132-213).

$ **Casa de las Piedras** has 16 comfortable rooms just a block up from the town center—ask for a room in their newer wing (Sb-€34, Db-€43, Tb-€61, two €45 1-room and €76 2-room apartments with kitchen and fireplace, includes tax, discounts for kids, 10 percent discount with current book for stays of 2 or more nights, buffet breakfast-€6, Calle Las Piedras 32, 11610 Grazalema, tel. & fax 956-132-014, www.casadelaspiedras.net, info@casadelaspiedras.net, Katy and Rafi, SE). Casa de las Piedras also has a good **restaurant** with a pleasant patio and local specialties, such as tasty and tender *solomillo ibérico* (Iberian pig tenderloin with eggplant) and *sopa de tomate* (bread and tomato soup with mint leaves and garlic).

Jerez

With nearly 200,000 people, Jerez is your typical big-city mix of industry, garbage, car bandits, and dusty concrete suburbs, but it has a lively center and two claims to touristic fame: horses and sherry.

Jerez is ideal for a noontime (or midday) visit on a weekday. See the famous horses, sip some sherry, wander through the old quarter, and swagger out.

Tourist Information: The helpful TI on Plaza Alameda Cristina gives out free maps and info on the sights (mid-June–mid-Sept Mon–Fri 10:00–15:00 & 17:00–19:00, Sat–Sun 9:30–14:30; mid-Sept–mid-June Mon–Fri 9:30–14:30 & 16:30–18:30, Sat–Sun 9:30–14:30, tel. 956-331-150).

Arrival in Jerez: The bus station (at Calle Cartuja and Madre de Dios) can't store baggage, but the train station, a block away, has 30 lockers; buy a €3 locker token *(ficha)* at the ticket window (daily 7:00–22:30).

Exit the bus station furthest from the WCs and turn left. The center of town and the Plaza Alameda Cristina TI are a 20-minute walk away. At the five-way intersection angle right on Honda until you reach Plaza Alameda Cristina—the TI is tucked away on your right.

If you're arriving by train, angle right as you leave the station. Cross the intersection at the roundabout. The bus station is on your left. Continue straight, following directions from the bus station, above. Taxis from the station to the horses cost about €4.

SIGHTS

▲▲**Royal Andalusian School of Equestrian Art**—If you're into horses, this is a must. Even if you're not, this is horse art like you've never seen. The school does its Horse Symphony show at noon every Thursday, as well as every Tuesday from March through October, and every Friday from July through October. Prices are €13 for general

Jerez

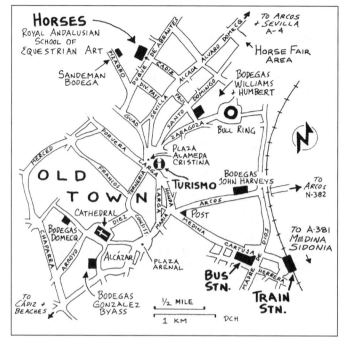

HORSES
ROYAL ANDALUSIAN SCHOOL OF EQUESTRIAN ART

SANDEMAN BODEGA

PIZARRO
DUQUE DE ABRANTES
CADIZ
ALCADA
ALVARO DOMECQ

TO ARCOS & SEVILLA A-4

HORSE FAIR AREA

BODEGAS WILLIAMS & HUMBERT

DIV. PAZ
SEVILLA
PAUL
SANTO DOMINGO
GUAD
ZARAGOZA

BULL RING

PORVERA
MERCED
FRANCOS
TORNERIA
CARDA

PLAZA ALAMEDA CRISTINA

TURISMO

N

OLD TOWN

BODEGAS JOHN HARVEYS

TO ARCOS N-382

CATHEDRAL
DIEZ
CONSIST.
HONDA
ARCOS
POST
MEDINA

BODEGAS DOMECQ
CHAPARRA
ARROYO
ALCÁZAR
PLAZA ARENAL

MARIA
CARTUJA
MAITRE DE DIOS

TO A-381 MEDINA SIDONIA

TO CÁDIZ & BEACHES

BODEGAS GONZALEZ BYASS

BUS STN.
MAITRE HERRERA
TRAIN STN.

½ MILE
1 KM
DCH

For reservations, call tel. 956-318-008 or fax 956-318-015 (show explanations are in Spanish, call for current schedule or check online at www.realescuela.org).

This is an equestrian ballet with choreography, purely Spanish music, and costumes from the 19th century. The stern horsemen and their talented and obedient steeds prance, jump, hop on their hind legs, and do-si-do in time to the music, to the delight of an arena filled with mostly tourists and local horse aficionados.

The riders, trained in dressage (dress-AZH), cue the horses with the slightest of commands (verbal or body movements). You'll see both pure-bred Spanish horses (various colors, long tails, calm personalities, and good jumping ability) and mixed breeds (larger, short tails, walk don't prance). The horses must be three years old before their three-year training begins, and most performing horses are male

Sherry

Spanish sherry is not the sweet dessert wine sold in the States as "sherry." In Spain, sherry is (most commonly) a chilled, white, very dry, fortified wine, often served with appetizers (tapas, seafood, and cured meats).

Sherry is made by blending wines from different grapes and different vintages, all aged together. Start with a strong, acidic wine (from grapes that grow well in the hot, chalky soil around Jerez). Mature it in large vats until a yeast crust *(flor)* forms on the surface, protecting the wine from the air. Then fortify it with distilled wine.

Next comes sherry-making's distinct *solera* process. Pour the young, fortified wine into the top barrel of a unique contraption—a stack of oak barrels called a *criadera.* Every year, one-third of the oldest sherry (in the barrels on the ground level) is bottled. To replace it, one-third of the sherry in the barrel above is poured in, and so on, until the top barrel is one-third empty, waiting to be filled with the new year's vintage.

Fino is the most popular type of sherry (and the most different from Americans' expectations)—white, dry, and chilled. (The best-selling commercial brand of *fino* is Tío Pepe, and *manzanilla* is a regional variation of *fino.*) Darker-colored and sometimes sweeter varieties of sherry include *amontillado* and *oloroso.* And yes, Spain also produces the thick, sweet cream sherries served as dessert wines. A good, raisin-y, syrupy sweet variety is Pedro Ximénez, made from sun-dried grapes of the same name.

British traders invented the sherry-making process as a way of transporting wines that wouldn't go bad on a long sea voyage. Some of the most popular brands (Sandeman, Osbourne) were begun by Brits, and for years it was a foreigners' drink. But today, the drink is typically Spanish.

(stallions or geldings), since mixing the sexes brings problems.

Training sessions offer a €6 sneak preview and are open to the public usually on Monday, Wednesday, and Friday (plus Tues Nov–Feb) from 10:00 to 13:00; schedules vary so it's wise to call ahead. Practice sessions can be exciting or dull, depending on what the trainers are working on.

Amble along (training days only) during a one-hour guided tour of the stables, horses, tack room, and horse health center. Sip sherry in the arena's bar to complete this Jerez experience.

If you're driving, follow signs from the center of Jerez to Real Escuela Andaluza del Arte Ecuestre (street parking).

▲▲**Sherry Bodega Tours**—Spain produces more than 10 million gallons per year of this fortified wine. The name "sherry" comes from English attempts to pronounce "Jerez." While traditionally the drink of England's aristocracy, today it's more popular with Germans. Your tourist map of Jerez is speckled with wine barrels. Each of these barrels is a sherry bodega that offers tours and tasting.

Sandeman Sherry Tour: Just over a fence from the horse school is the venerable Sandeman Bodega, which has been producing sherry since 1790 and is the longtime choice of English royalty. This tour is the aficionado's choice for its knowledgeable guides and their quality explanations of the process (€5, tours Mon–Fri 10:30–17:00, last tour at 16:30, Sat 11:30 and 13:30, bottling finishes at 14:00, closed Sun, finale is a chance to taste 3 varieties, reservations not required, call 956-312-995 for English tour times, fax 956-302-626). It's efficient to see the Horse Symphony (ends at 13:30) and walk to Sandeman's for the English tour at 14:15.

Harvey's Bristol Cream: Their 90-minute English-language tours (Mon–Fri at 10:00 and noon or by arrangement) aren't substantial but include a 15-minute video, a visit of the winery, and all the sherry you like in the tasting room (€5, Calle Pintor Muñoz Cebrian, reservations recommended, tel. 956-346-000, fax 956-349-427, jerez@domecq.es).

González Byass: The makers of the famous Tío Pepe offer a tourist-friendly tour, with more pretense and less actual sherry-making on display (it's done in a new, enormous plant outside of town), but it's the only bodega that offers daily tours (€7, March–Nov 10:15–18:30 on the hour, Manuel María González 12, tel. 956-357-000, fax 956-357-046). González Byass is Disney-ing its tours, and schedules change frequently—call for the latest.

Alcázar—This gutted castle looks tempting, but don't bother. The €1.30 entry fee doesn't even include the Camera Obscura (€3.30 combo-ticket covers both, daily 10:00-18:00). Its underground parking is convenient for those touring González Byass Bodega (€1.10/hr).

TRANSPORTATION CONNECTIONS

Jerez's bus station is shared by six bus companies, each with its own schedules, some specializing in certain destinations, others sharing popular destinations such as Sevilla and Algeciras. Shop around for the best departure time. By car it's a zippy 30 minutes from Jerez to Arcos.

By bus to: Tarifa (3/day, 2 hrs), **Algeciras** (8/day, 2.5 hrs), **Arcos** (hrly, 30 min), **Ronda** (3/day, 2.5 hrs), **Sevilla** (18/day, 90 min), **Málaga** (1/day, 5 hrs), **Córdoba** (1/day, 3 hrs), **Madrid** (6/day, 7 hrs). Bus info: tel. 956-345-202.

By train to: Sevilla (11/day, 1 hr), **Madrid** (2/day, 4 hrs), **Barcelona** (2/day, 12 hrs). Train info: tel. 902-240-202.

Drivers: In Jerez, blue-line zones require prepaid parking tickets on your dashboard on weekdays 9:00–13:30 and 17:00–20:00 and on Saturday 9:00–14:00; Sundays and July and August afternoons are free. Otherwise there's the handy underground parking lot near the Alcázar and at Plaza Alameda Cristina (€1.10/hour).

Easy Stops for Drivers

If you're driving between Arcos and Tarifa, here are several sights to explore.

Yeguada de la Cartuja—This breeding farm, which raises Hispanic Arab horses according to traditions dating back to the 15th century, offers shows on Saturday at 11:00 (€10, Finca Fuente del Suero, Ctra. Medina–El Portal, km 6.5, Jerez de la Frontera, tel. 956-162-809, www.yeguadacartuja.com). From Jerez, take the road to Medina Sidonia, then take a right in the direction of El Portal—you'll see a cement factory on your right. Drive for five minutes until you see the Yeguada de la Cartuja. A taxi from Jerez will charge about €12 one-way.

Medina Sidonia—The town is as whitewashed as can be, surrounding its church and hill, which is topped with castle ruins. Give it a quick look. Signs to Vejer and then *Centro Urbano* route you through the middle to Plaza de España—great for a coffee stop. Or, if it's lunchtime, consider buying a picnic, as all the necessary shops are nearby and the plaza benches afford a fine workaday view of a perfectly untouristy Andalusian town at play. You can drive from here up to Plaza Iglesia Mayor to find the church and **TI** (Tue–Sun 10:00–14:00 & 18:00–20:00 in summer, 10:00–14:00 & 16:00–18:00 in winter, closed Mon, tel. 956-412-404). At the church, a man will show you around for a tip. Even without a tip, you can climb yet another belfry for yet another vast Andalusian view. The castle ruins just aren't worth the trouble.

Vejer de la Frontera—Vejer, south of Jerez and just 20 miles north of Tarifa, will lure all but the very jaded off the highway. Vejer's strong Moorish roots give it a distinct Moroccan (or Greek Island) flavor—you know, black-clad women whitewashing their homes, and lanes that can't decide if they're roads or stairways. Only a few years ago, women wore veils. The town has no real sights (other than its women's faces) and very little tourism, but it makes for a pleasant stop. (**TI** open June–Sept Mon–Fri 8:00–14:30 & 18:00–22:00, Sat–Sun 10:30–14:30 & 18:00–22:00; Oct–May Mon–Fri 8:00–15:00 & 17:00–20:00, closed Sat–Sun, Marqués de Tamarón 10, tel. 956-451-736.)

The coast near Vejer is lonely, with fine but windswept beaches. It's popular with windsurfers and sand flies. The Battle of Trafalgar was fought just off Cabo de Trafalgar (a nondescript lighthouse today). I drove the circle so that you need not do so.

Sleeping in Vejer: A newcomer on Andalucía's tourist map, the old town of Vejer has only two hotels. Both are at the entrance to the old town, at the top of the switchbacks past the town's lone traffic cop.

$$ Convento de San Francisco is a poor-man's parador in a classy refurbished convent (Sb-€45, Db-€63.50, breakfast-€3.70, prices soft off-season, La Plazuela, tel. 956-451-001, fax 956-451-004, convento-san-francisco@tugasa.com, SE). They have the rare but unnecessary Vejer town map.

$ Hostal La Posada, with 10 clean and charming rooms, is a much better value (S-€15–18, Db-€30–36, cheaper off-season, also 6 €72 apartments, Los Remedios 21, tel. & fax 956-450-258, www.hostallaposada.com in Spanish only, NSE).

Route Tips for Drivers

Arcos to Tarifa (80 miles): Drive from Arcos to Jerez in 30 minutes. If you're going to Tarifa, take the tiny C343 road at the Jerez edge of Arcos toward Paterna and Vejer. Later, you'll pick up signs to Medina Sidonia and then to Vejer and Tarifa.

Sevilla to Arcos: The remote hill towns of Andalucía are a joy to tour by car with Michelin map #446 or any other good map. Drivers can zip south on N-IV from Sevilla along the river, following signs to Cádiz. Take the fast toll freeway (blue signs, E5, A4). The toll-free N-IV is curvy and dangerous. About halfway to Jerez, at Las Cabezas, take CA403 to Villamartín. From there, circle scenically (and clockwise) through the thick of the Pueblos Blancos—Zahara and Grazalema—to Arcos.

It's about two hours from Sevilla to Zahara. You'll find decent but winding roads and sparse traffic. It gets worse (but very scenic) if you take the tortuous series of switchbacks over the 4,500-foot summit of Puerto de Las Palomas (Pass of the Pigeons, climb to the viewpoint) on the direct but difficult road from Zahara to Grazalema (several stops closer to Zahara offer hiking trailheads). Remember to refer to your "Ruta de los Pueblos Blancos" pamphlet.

Another scenic road option from Grazalema to Arcos is the road that goes through Puerto del Boyar (Pass of the Boyar), El Bosque, and Benamahoma. The road from Ronda to El Gastor, Setenil (cave houses and great olive oil) and Olvera is another scenic alternative.

Traffic flows through old Arcos only from west to east (coming from the east, circle south under town). The TI, my recommended hotels, and parking (Paseo Andalucía or Plaza del Cabildo) are all in the west. Driving in Arcos is like threading needles. But if your car is small and the town seems quiet enough, follow signs to the parador, where you'll find the only parking lot in the old town.

SPAIN'S SOUTH COAST
(Costa del Sol)

It's so bad, it's interesting. To northern Europeans the sun is a drug, and this is their needle. Anything resembling a quaint fishing village has been bikini-strangled and Nivea-creamed. Oblivious to the concrete, pollution, ridiculous prices, and traffic jams, tourists lie on the beach like game hens on skewers—cooking, rolling, and sweating under the sun.

Where Europe's most popular beach isn't crowded by high-rise hotels, most of it's in a freeway choke hold. Wonderfully undeveloped beaches between Tarifa and Cádiz and east of Almería are ignored, while lemmings make the scene where the coastal waters are so polluted that hotels are required to provide swimming pools. It's a fascinating study in human nature.

Laugh with Ronald McDonald at the car-jammed resorts. But if you want a place to stay and play in the sun, unroll your beach towel at **Nerja**. And you're surprisingly close to jolly olde England. The land of tea and scones, fish and chips, pubs and bobbies awaits you—in **Gibraltar**. And beyond "The Rock" is the whitewashed port of **Tarifa**, the least developed piece of Spain's generally overdeveloped south coast, which provides an enjoyable springboard for a quick trip to Morocco (see next chapter). These three alone—Nerja, Gibraltar, and Tarifa—make the Costa del Sol worth a trip.

Planning Your Time

My opinions on the "Costa del Turismo" are valid for peak season. If you're there during a quieter time and you like the ambience of a

Costa del Sol

DELIGHTFUL
TOLERABLE
AWFUL

0 KM   50   100
0 MI   50

SEVILLA

GRANADA

LANJARÓN

P U E B L O S
B L A N C O S

CAVES

FRIGI-
LIANA   ALM.   MOTRIL
RONDA

ARCOS

MÁLAGA   NERJA   SALO-
BREÑA

TORREMOLINOS

CÁDIZ   VEJER   S.
PEDRO   MARBELLA   FUENGIROLA
D.L.F   ESTEPONA

COSTA
DE LA
LUZ   ALGE-
CIRAS   LA LINEA

C O S T A   D E L   S O L

TARIFA   GIBRALTAR
(U.K.)

ATLANTIC
OCEAN

MEDITERRANEAN
SEA

TANGIER   CEUTA
(SP.)

MOROCCO

DCH

beach resort, it can be a pleasant stop. Off-season it can be neutron-bomb quiet.

The whole 150 miles of coastline takes six hours by bus and four hours to drive (probably less when the new freeway opens between Algeciras and Marbella). You can resort-hop by bus across the entire Costa del Sol and reach Nerja for dinner. If you want to party on the beach, it can take as much time as Mazatlán.

To day-trip to Tangier, Morocco, you can take a tour from Gibraltar, Tarifa (best), and Algeciras.

Nerja

While cashing in on the fun-in-the-sun culture, Nerja has actually kept much of its quiet, Old World charm. It has good beaches, a fun evening *paseo* (strolling scene) that culminates in the proud Balcony of Europe terrace, enough pastry shops and nightlife, and locals who get more excited about their many festivals than the tourists do.

ORIENTATION

The tourist center of Nerja is right along the water, along the bluff with its "Balcony of Europe." Two fine beaches flank the bluff. The old town is just inland from the Balcony, while the more modern section slopes away from the water.

Tourist Information: The helpful, English-speaking TI has bus schedules, tips on beaches and side trips, and brochures for nearby destinations such as Málaga and Gibraltar (Mon–Fri 10:00–14:00 & 17:30–20:30, Sat 10:00–13:00, Nov–March Mon–Sat 10:00–19:00, closed Sun, Puerta del Mar 2, just off Balcony of Europe, tel. 952-521-531, www.nerja.org, turismo@nerja.org). Ask for a free city map (or buy the more detailed version for €0.70) and the *Leisure Guide*, which has a comprehensive listing of activities. Their booklet on hiking is good, and you can reach some of the trailheads by bus.

To get a free flier with the latest theater and musical events, stop by the Villa de Nerja Cultural Center at Granada 45 (shows take place here, too, tel. 952-523-863). In the third week of July, they host the music festival in the Caves of Nerja.

Helpful Hints

Internet Access: The most scenically situated of Nerja's few Internet cafés are Med Web C@fé, at the end of Calle Castilla Pérez, on a square overlooking the beach (daily 10:00–24:00, 10 computers and cold snacks) and next door at Europa@web (10:00–22:00, closes at 24:00 in summer, 10 computers, tel. 952-526-147).

Radio: For a taste of the British expatriate scene, pick up the monthly *Street Wise* magazine or tune in to Coastline Radio at 97.7 FM.

Market: The lively open-air market is colorful and fun (food on Tue 9:30–14:00 and flea market on Sun 9:30–14:00, along Calle Almirante Ferrándiz, in the west end of town).

Getting Around Nerja

You can easily walk anywhere you need to go. A goofy little **tourist train** does a 30-minute loop through town every 45 minutes (€3, daily 10:30–22:00, until 24:00 July–Aug, departs from Plaza Cavana, you can get off and catch a later train by using same ticket, route posted on door of train). Nerja's **taxis** charge set fees (e.g., €6 to Burriana beach, taxi tel. 952-524-519). To clip-clop in a **horse and buggy** through town, it's €20 for about 25 minutes (hop on at Balcony of Europe).

SIGHTS

▲▲**Balcony of Europe (Balcón de Europa)**—This bluff over the beach is the center of the town's *paseo* and a magnet for street performers. The mimes, music, and puppets can draw bigger crowds than the balcony, which overlooks the Mediterranean, miles of coastline, and little coves and caves below.

Nerja

* NOT TO SCALE -
BUS INFO KIOSK TO
BALCON DE EUROPA
IS A 10 MIN WALK

BUS INFO KIOSK

TO CAVES & GRANADA

N-340

ANDUEZ

N-340 AV. DE PESCIA

TO MÁLAGA

PLAZA CANTARERO

SAN MIGUEL

ACE J. BUENO

HERR. ORIA

RUPERTO

SAN PAB

TAPAS

S. JUAN

PLAZA ERMITA

NUÑEZ

USA

MÉNDEZ

PINTADA

COLON

CRISTO

CARRETAS

FERRANDIZ

LA PARRA

TO N-340 & FRIGILIANA

CRUZ

BRONCE

ANGUSTIAS

NUEVA

LOS HUERTOS

LOTS OF CASAS PARTICULARES

PEREZ

ANIMAS

CRUZ

ALMIRANTE

TO MKT.

CASTILLA

DIPUTACIÓN

GRANADA

PROV.

PASEO NUEVO

CRISTO

POST/CORREOS

TO

EL BARRIO

TEL.

CARABEO

PLAZA CAVANA

PASEO DEL MAR

PLAYA CARABEO

PLAYA CALAHONDA

PLAYA BURRIANA

PLAYA DEL SALON (BEST BEACH)

BALCON DE EUROPA

MEDITERRANEAN SEA

← TO PLAYA LA TORRECILLA

❶ Hotel Plaza Cavana
❷ Hotel Puerta del Mar
❸ Hotel Balcón de Europa
❹ Hostal Marissal
❺ Hostal Lorca
❻ Pensión El Patio
❼ Hostal Residencia Mena
❽ Hostal Atembeni
❾ Hostal Residencia Don Peque
❿ Bar El Pulguilla
⓫ Bar El Chispa
⓬ Bar Los Cuñaos
⓭ Bar El Molino
⓮ To Parador & Hotel Paraiso del Mar
⓯ More restaurant options

Promenades—Pleasant seaview promenades lead in opposite directions from the Balcony of Europe, going east to Burriana Beach (promenade may be closed for renovation most of 2005) and west to Torrecilla Beach (10-min walk). Even if you're not a beach person, you're likely to enjoy the views. At Torrecilla Beach, the promenade ends at the delightful Plaza de los Cangrejos, with cascading terraces of cafés (with Internet access) and greenery spilling into an overlook of the beach (at the end of Avenida Castilla Pérez).

Beaches—Nerja has several good beaches. The sandiest—and most crowded—is Playa del Salón, down the walkway to the right of the Restaurante Marissal, just off the Balcony of Europe. The pebblier beach, Playa Calahonda, is full of fun pathways, crags, and crannies (head down through the arch to the right of the TI office) and has a

fine promenade (mentioned above, may be closed in 2005) leading east to a bigger beach, Playa de Burriana. This is Nerja's leading beach, with paddleboats and entertainment options. Another beach, Playa de la Torrecilla, is a 10-minute walk west of the Balcony of Europe. All of the beaches have showers, bars, restaurants, and—in season—beach chairs (about €4/day). Watch out for red flags on the beach, which indicate that the seas are too rough for safe swimming.

▲**Caves of Nerja (Cuevas de Nerja)**—These caves, 2.5 miles east of Nerja (exit 295), have the most impressive array of stalactites and stalagmites I've seen anywhere in Europe, their huge caverns filled with expertly backlit formations and appropriate music. The visit is a 30-minute unguided ramble deep into the mountain, up and down lots of dark stairs congested with Spanish families. At the end, you reach the Hall of the Cataclysm, where you'll circle what is the world's largest stalactite-made column, according to Guinness. Someone figured out that it took one trillion drops to make the column (€5, daily 10:00–14:00 & 16:00–18:30, until 20:00 July–Aug, tel. 952-529-520).

The free exhibit in the Centro de Interpretación (orange house next to bus parking) explains the cave's history and geology—the exhibit is in Spanish, but it includes a free brochure in English.

To get to the caves, catch a bus from the Nerja bus stop on Avenida de Pescia (€0.73, 15/day, 10 min). During the festival held here the third week of July, the caves provide a cool venue for hot flamenco and classical concerts. The restaurant with a view offers set three-course menus for €8, but the picnic spot with pine trees, benches, and a kids' play area just up and behind the ticket office is even better.

Frigiliana—This picture-perfect whitewashed village, only four miles from Nerja, is easy by car or bus (9/day, 15 min, €0.80). It's a worthwhile detour from the beach, particularly if you don't have time for the Pueblos Blancos hill towns (see www.frigiliana.com for more information). To make it more real, listen to the 1,001 stories about village traditions by David Riordan, an American who has lived here for 12 years and now leads two walks a day (at 10:15 for 1.75-hr tour for €7, at 12:30 for 1.25 hr and €5, depart from TI, no tours in Aug, Frigiliana Tours, tel. 952-534-240, vaquerodave@aol.com).

SLEEPING

The entire Costa del Sol is crowded during August and Holy Week, when prices are at their highest. Reserve in advance for peak season, basically mid-July through mid-September, prime time for Spanish workers to hit the beaches. Any other time of year you'll find Nerja has plenty of comfy, low-rise, easygoing, resort-type hotels and rooms. Room rates are three-tiered, from low season (Nov–March) to high season (July–Sept). Compared to the pricier hotels, the better *hostales* (Marissal and Lorca) are an excellent value.

$$$ **Hotel Plaza Cavana** overlooks a plaza lily-padded with cafés. If you like a central location, marble floors, modern furnishings, an elevator, and a small rooftop swimming pool, dive in (39 rooms, Sb-€56, €66, or €76; Db-€77, €92, or €107; Tb-€94, €110, or €125; 10 percent discount with current edition of this book; some view rooms, includes breakfast, tax extra, air-con, a second small pool in basement, your car can ride an elevator down into the garage for €9/day, 2 blocks from Balcony of Europe at Plaza Cavana 10, tel. 952-524-000, fax 952-524-008, www.hotelplazacavana.com, hotelplazacavana@infonegocio.com, SE).

$$$ The most central place in town is **Balcón de Europa,** right on the water and on the square, with the prestigious address Balcón de Europa 1. It has 110 rooms with all the modern comforts, including a pool and an elevator down to the beach. All the suites have a seaview balcony and most regular rooms come with a sea view (Sb-€65, €75 or €95; standard Db-€85, €105, or €125; add about €24 for sea view and balcony; Db suite with Jacuzzi-€160, €185, or €208; breakfast-€9, air-con, elevator, drivers should follow signs to parking garage, parking-€8/day, tel. 952-520-800, fax 952-524-490, www .hotel-balconeuropa.com, balconeuropa@spa.es, SE).

$$$ Nerja's **parador,** housed in a new office-type building rather than a castle, lacks character but has 98 spacious, suite-like rooms and overlooks Burriana Beach (Sb-€78–99; Db-€97–221 depending on view, size and Jacuzzi; less Nov–Feb, air-con, free parking, large-for-Nerja swimming pool, 10-min walk from town center, Almuñecar 8, tel. 952-520-050, fax 952-521-997, nerja@parador.es, SE).

Sleep Code

(€1 = about $1.20, country code: 34)
S = Single, **D** = Double/Twin, **T** = Triple, **Q** = Quad,
b = bathroom, **s** = shower only, **no CC** = Credit Cards not accepted,
SE = Speaks English, **NSE** = No English spoken. You can assume
credit cards are accepted unless otherwise noted. Breakfast and 7
percent IVA tax are not included (unless noted).

To help you easily sort through these listings, I've divided
the rooms into three categories, based on the price for a standard
double room with bath during high season:

$$$ **Higher Priced**—Most rooms €100 or more.
  $$ **Moderately Priced**—Most rooms between €50–100.
    $ **Lower Priced**—Most rooms €50 or less.

$$ Hotel Puerta del Mar, just around the corner from Hotel
Plaza Cavana and run by the same owners, offers 24 new rooms at
a better value (Sb-€36–60, Db-€50–90, Qb-€65–120, 5 apart-
ments €60–150, 10 percent discount with current edition of this
book, includes breakfast next door, air-con, use of Cavana pool,
Calle Gómez, tel. 952-527-304, www.hotelpuertadelmar.com,
hotelpuertademar@telefonica.net).

$$ Hotel Paraíso del Mar, next to the parador listed above, is a
destination place, with 16 attractive rooms, a great setting on the
bluff, and a pool and two terraces en route to a private stairway to
Burriana Beach (150 stairs). You might not feel the need to make
the 10-minute walk to the town center (Sb-€50, €75, or €80; Db-
€60, €88, or €94; about €10 extra for sea view and Jacuzzi, suites
available for 40 percent more, includes buffet breakfast, tax extra,
quiet, air-con, friendly dog Ringo, underground parking, Calle
Prolongación de Carabeo 22, tel. 952-521-621, fax 952-522-309,
info@hispanica-colint.es, Alicia SE).

$$ Hostal Marissal, just next door to the fancy Balcón de
Europa hotel, has an unbeatable location and 23 modern, spacious
rooms, six with small view balconies overlooking the action on the
Balcony of Europe (Db-€40, €50, or €60, double-paned windows,
air-con, elevator, Internet connection, Balcón de Europa 3, recep-
tion at Marissal café, tel. 952-520-199, fax 952-526-654, www
.marissal.net, reservas@marissal.net, María SE).

A quiet residential section five minutes from the center (and 3
blocks from the bus stop), offers the following two good options
(near a small, handy grocery store and free parking lot):

$ Hostal Lorca—run by a friendly young Dutch couple,
Femma and Rick—has nine modern, comfortable rooms and an
inviting, compact backyard that contains a terrace, palm tree, singing

bird, and small pool. You can use the microwave and take drinks—on the honor system—from the well-stocked fridge. This quiet, homey place is a winner (Sb-€29–32, Db-€32–47, extra bed-€12, includes tax, breakfast-€4, no CC, Mendez Nuñez 20, look for yellow house, near bus stop, tel. 952-523-426, www.hostallorca.com, hostallorca@teleline.es, SE).

$ **Pensión El Patio** has four clean, simple rooms. If you want to go local, this is worth the communication struggles (Sb-€18–36, Db-€25–40, Tb-€36–48, no CC, Mendez Nuñez 12, near bus stop, tel. 952-522-930, Angeles NSE). If no one answers, ask at #12.

The following three places are central—within three blocks of the Balcony of Europe—but none will stun you with warmth.

$ **Hostal Residencia Mena** is erratically run but has 11 fine rooms, four with terraces and sea views, and a quiet breezy garden (Sb-€17–23, Db-€25–37, €3.50 more for terrace, includes tax, street noise, El Barrio 15, tel. 952-520-541, fax 952-528-345, hostalmena@hotmail.com, María speaks some English).

$ **Hostal Atembeni** is family run and has 19 basic rooms (Sb-€23, €29, or €33; Db-€28, €36, or €41; includes tax, no breakfast, ceiling fans, closed Oct–April, Diputación 12, tel. 952-521-341, some English spoken).

$ **Hostal Residencia Don Peque,** across from Hostal Atembeni, has 10 simple rooms (with older bathrooms), eight with balconies, and (I hope) friendlier new management in 2005. Front rooms over the noisy street have air-conditioning (Db-€32–42, includes tax, breakfast-€3, Diputación 13, tel. & fax 952-521-318, some English spoken).

Your cheapest and often most interesting bet may be a room in a private home *(casa particular)*. Walk around with your backpack on the residential streets within about a six-block radius of Calle La Parra or Calle Nueva. Ask around.

EATING

There are three Nerjas: the private domain of the giant beachside hotels; the central zone packed with fun-loving expatriates and tourists enjoying great food with trilingual menus; and the back streets, where local life goes on as if there were no tomorrow (or tourists). The whole old town around the Balcony of Europe sizzles with decent restaurants. It makes no sense for me to recommend one over the others. Wander around and see who's eating best. The street, Almirante Ferrándiz, offers lots of tasty options. Consider **El Pulguilla,** which specializes in seafood, with clams so fresh they squirt (€10–15 dinners, Tue–Sun 13:00–16:00 and 19:00–24:00, closed Mon, Almirante Ferrándiz 26, tel. 952-521-384).

Farther inland, prices go down, and locals fill the bars and tables. A 10-minute hike uphill takes you into the residential thick of things, where the sea views come thumbtacked to the walls. The following two restaurants are within a block of each other around Herrera Oria (see map). Each specializes in seafood and is fine for a sit-down meal or a stop on a tapas crawl. Remember that tapas are snack-size portions. To turn tapas into more of a meal, ask for a *ración, media* (half) *ración*—or a menu.

El Chispa is big on seafood, with an informal restaurant terrace on the side (Tue–Sun 11:00–16:00 & 19:30–24:00, closed Mon, San Pedro 12, tel. 952-523-697). **Los Cuñaos** is most fun late in the evening, when families munch tapas, men watch soccer on TV, women chat, and kids wander around like it's home (daily 12:00–16:00 & 19:00–23:00, good seafood and prices, Herrera Oria 19, tel. 952-521-107). These places are generally open all day for tapas and drinks; I've included just their serving hours in case you're hungry for a good meal.

If you're out late, consider **Bar El Molino** for folk singing after 23:00; it's touristy but fun (Calle San José 4).

TRANSPORTATION CONNECTIONS

Nerja

The Nerja bus station is actually just a bus stop on Avenida de Pescia with an info booth (daily 6:00–21:00, helpful schedules posted on booth, tel. 952-521-504).

By bus to: Nerja Caves (15/day, 10 min), **Frigiliana** (9/day, 15 min, none on Sun), **Málaga** (20/day, 70–90 min), **Granada** (4/day, more frequent with Motril transfer, 2.5 hrs), **Córdoba** (3/day, 4.5 hrs, 1 *directo* 3 hrs), **Sevilla** (3/day, 4 hrs).

Málaga

The train station nearest Nerja is an hourly 90-minute bus ride away in Málaga. Málaga's train and bus stations—a block apart from each other—each have pickpockets and lockers (train station lockers are better). You can rent a car at the train station at Atesa or Europcar.

From Málaga by train to: Ronda (4/day, 2 hrs, transfer in Bobadilla), **Madrid** (7/day, 4.25–7 hrs on TALGO train), **Córdoba** (10/day, 2–2.5 hrs, fastest on TALGO), **Granada** (3/day, 3.25 hrs, transfer in Bobadilla), **Sevilla** (5/day, 2.5 hrs), **Barcelona** (2/day, 13.5 hrs). Train info: tel. 902-240-202.

Buses: Málaga's bus station, a block from the train station, has a helpful information office with bus schedules (daily 7:00–22:00) and a TI (daily 11:00–19:00, Internet access, ATM, and lockers, on Paseo de los Tilos, tel. 952-350-061).

By bus to: Algeciras (10/day, 3 hrs, 9 *directo* take 1.75 hrs), **Nerja** (19/day, 70–90 min), **Ronda** (18/day, 2 hrs), **La Línea/Gibraltar**

(4/day, 3 hrs), **Sevilla** (10/day, 2.5 hrs), **Jerez** (1/day, 5 hrs), **Granada** (17/day, 2 hrs), **Córdoba** (7/day, 3 hrs), **Madrid** (10/day, 6 hrs).

SIGHTS

From Nerja to Gibraltar

Buses take five hours to make the Nerja–Gibraltar trip. They leave nearly hourly and stop at each town mentioned.

Fuengirola and Torremolinos—The most built-up part of the region, where those most determined to be envied settle down, is a bizarre world of Scandinavian package tours, flashing lights, pink flamenco, multilingual menus, and all-night happiness. Fuengirola is like a Spanish Mazatlán with a few less-pretentious, older, budget hotels between the main drag and the beach. The water here is clean and the nightlife fun and easy. James Michener's idyllic Torremolinos has been strip-mauled and parking-metered.

Marbella—This is the most polished and posh town on the Costa del Sol. High-priced boutiques, immaculate streets, and beautifully landscaped squares are testimony to Marbella's arrival on the world-class-resort scene. Have a *café con leche* on the beautiful Plaza de Naranjas in the old city's pedestrian section. Wander down to new Marbella and the high-rise beachfront apartment buildings to check out the beach scene. Marbella is an easy stop on the Algeciras–Málaga bus route (as you exit the bus station, take a left to reach the center of town).

San Pedro de Alcántara—This town's relatively undeveloped sandy beach is popular with young travelers. San Pedro's neighbor, Puerto Banús, is "where the world casts anchor." This luxurious jet-set port, complete with casino, is a strange mix of Rolls-Royces, yuppies, boutiques, rich Arabs, and budget browsers.

Gibraltar

One of the last bits of the empire upon which the sun never set, Gibraltar is a fun mix of Anglican propriety, "God Save the Queen" tattoos, English bookstores, military memories, and tourist shops. The few British soldiers you'll see are enjoying this cushy assignment in the Mediterranean sun as a reward for enduring and surviving an assignment in another remnant of the British Empire: Northern Ireland. While things are cheaper in pounds, your euros work here, as well as your English words.

The 30,000 Gibraltarians have a mixed and interesting heritage. The Spanish call them Llanitos (yah-nee-tohs), meaning "flat" in Spanish, though the residents live on a rock. The locals—a fun-loving and tolerant mix of British, Spanish, and Moroccan—speak a Creole-like Spanglish and call the place "Gib."

Gibraltar

300 YARDS

300 METERS

1 Eliott Hotel
2 Bristol Hotel
3 Queen's Hotel
4 Continental Hotel
5 Cannon Hotel
6 Emile Youth Hostel
7 Queensway Quay
   Marina & Eateries

You'll need your passport to cross the border (and you may still be able to charm an official into stamping it—ask, or you'll get just a wave-through).

Planning Your Time

Make Gibraltar a day trip (or just an overnight); rooms are expensive compared to Spain.

For the best day trip to Gibraltar, consider this plan: Walk across the border, catch bus #3 and ride it to the end, following the self-guided tour (see page 362). Ride bus #3 back to the cable-car station, then catch the cable car to the top, and walk down via St. Michael's Cave and the Apes' Den. From there, either walk or take the cable car back into town. Spend your remaining free time in town before returning to Spain.

Tourists who stay overnight find Gibraltar a peaceful place in the evening, when the town can just be itself. No one is in a hurry. Families stroll, kids play, seniors window-shop, and everyone chats.

You can day-trip to Morocco from here (see page 367), but it's easier and cheaper from Tarifa or Algeciras.

ORIENTATION

(tel. code: 9567 from Spain, 350 from other countries)
Gibraltar is a narrow peninsula (3 miles by 1 mile) jutting into the Mediterranean. Virtually the entire peninsula is dominated by the steep-faced Rock itself. Most tourist sights are up on the mountain. The locals live down below in the long, skinny town at the western base of the mountain (much of it on reclaimed land). Everyone must enter Gibraltar from the north. You need to travel through town to get access up the mountain (via cable car or taxi/minibus tour).

Tourist Information: Gibraltar's main TI is at Casemates Square, the grand square at the entrance of town (Mon–Fri 9:00–17:30, Sat 10:00–15:00, Sun 10:00–13:00, tel. 74982, www.gibraltar.gi). Another TI is in the Duke of Kent House on Cathedral Square, nearer the town center (Mon–Fri 9:00–17:30, closed Sat–Sun, bus #3 stops here, just after NatWest House, tel. 74950). More TIs are at Customs where you cross the border and at the Coach Park (bus terminal). The TIs give out free maps and can inform about tours of caves and the WWII tunnels that crisscross the island (€3/£2 per tour, 1.5 hrs).

Arrival in Gibraltar

By Bus: Spain's La Línea bus station is a five-minute walk from the Gibraltar border. You can't store luggage at the bus station, but you can at Gibraltar's airport, a 10-minute walk south of the border (€3–7.50/£2–5 per day depending on size; daily 8:00–21:30, if baggage office looks closed, ask at airport information desk for help).

From the La Línea bus station walk to the border (flash your passport). To get into town from the "frontier" (as the border is called), you can walk (30 min), take a taxi to the cable-car station (pricey at €7.50/£5), or catch a bus (€0.60/40 pence). Catch either the #3 minibus to the TI at Cathedral Square (can stay on to continue self-guided tour, below) or the double-decker bus #9 to Casemates Square—which also has a TI (€0.60/40p, every 15 min). To walk into town, walk straight across the runway (look left, right, and up), then head down Winston Churchill Avenue, angling right at the Shell station on Smith Dorrien Avenue.

By Car: After taking the La Línea-Gibraltar exit off the main Costa del Sol road, continue as the road curves left with the Rock to your right. Do not drive into Gibraltar unless you're prepared for waits of up to 90 minutes in either direction to cross the border—worst between 16:00 and 19:00, when lines are longest. (It's better to park in La Línea, walk five minutes across the border, and catch a bus or taxi into town.)

Enter the left-hand lane at the traffic circle prior to the border and you'll end up in La Línea. A handy place to park is at the Fo Cona underground parking lot (€1/hr, €6/day, on street called 20th of April by the Spanish, Winston Churchill Avenue by Gibraltarians). You'll also find blue-lined parking spots in this area (€1/hr from meter, bring coins, leave ticket on dashboard, Sun free).

If you insist on driving into Gibraltar, get in the righthand lane at the traffic circle before the border. You'll find plenty of parking lots (like the huge one near the cable car).

Helpful Hints

Telephone: To telephone Gibraltar from Spain, dial 9567 followed by the five-digit local number. To call the Rock from European countries other than Spain, dial 00-350-local number. To call from America or Canada, dial 011-350-local number. If you plan to make calls from Gibraltar, note that phone booths take English coins or phone cards bought in Gibraltar (available at kiosks).

Electricity: If you have electrical gadgets, note that Gibraltar, like Britain, uses three-prong plugs. Your hotel may be able to loan you an adapter (which plugs onto a European plug).

Internet Access: Café Cyberworld has pricey Internet access (daily 12:00–24:00, Queensway 14, in Ocean Heights Gallery, near Casemates end of town, tel. 51416).

Hours: This may be the United Kingdom, but Gibraltar follows a siesta schedule, with some businesses closing 13:00–15:00 on weekdays and shutting up at 14:00 on Saturdays until Monday morning.

Spain vs. Gibraltar

Spain has been annoyed about Gibraltar ever since Great Britain snagged this prime 2.5-square-mile territory through the 18th-century Treaty of Utrecht (1713) at the end of the War of the Spanish Succession. Although Spain long ago abandoned efforts to reassert its sovereignty by force, it still tries to make Gibraltarians see the error of their British ways by messing up things like border crossings and the phone system. Still, given the choice—and they got it in referenda in 1967 and 2002—Gibraltar's residents steadfastly remain Queen Elizabeth's loyal subjects, voting overwhelmingly to continue as a self-governing British dependency.

A key British military base in World Wars I and II, Gibraltar is now a banking, shipping, and tourist magnet, connected to Spain by a sandy isthmus. Over the years, Spain has limited air and sea connections and choked traffic at the three-quarter-mile border in efforts to convince Gibraltar to give back the Rock. And then there's the phone issue. Spain refuses to recognize (or dial) a separate country code for Gibraltar, which essentially ends up making Gibraltar's phone system part of Spain's. This means that Spain can decide how many numbers Gibraltar residents get—and it's a lot less than they want. That's why when you call Gibraltar from Spain, you first dial 9567, the area code for the Spanish province of Cádiz, and when you call Gibraltar from anywhere else, you dial the country code, 350. There have been similar problems with mobile phones. Gibraltar, a European Union member, has made its case all the way up to the European Commission, which told Spain and Britain to sort it out. Please hold...

Money: Gibraltar uses the British pound sterling (£1 = $1.70) but also accepts euros. Be aware that if you pay for something in euros, you may get pounds back in change.

TOURS

It's easy to visit the Rock's uppermost sights on your own at your own pace. For example, you can take bus #3 (or walk) to the cable-car lift, take the lift up, and hike down to the sights. Allow about three hours total for the trip.

Those with more money than time take a tour (covers admission to the Upper Rock Nature Reserve sights included on tour). There are two types of tours: by minibus and by taxi. For the minibus tours, book at a travel agency. You can catch a taxi tour at the border (or cheaper at taxi stands at squares in the center).

By Minibus: Travel agencies offer approximately 90-minute tours for a set fee (about €16.50–22/£11–15). Stops include St. Michael's Cave, the Apes' Den, and Siege Tunnels. Consider Thomas Cook Exchange Travel (tours on Mon, Wed, and Fri, 241 Main Street, near Marks & Spencer, tel. 76151), Bland Travel (tours also on Mon, Wed, and Fri, 220 Main Street, tel. 79068), or Parodytur (Mon, Wed, Fri departs 12:45, priciest but offers tours daily, Cathedral Square, tel. 76070). If you call ahead to reserve a seat, you pay when you arrive in Gibraltar. Or just drop by any agency when you're in town (usually open Mon–Fri 9:30–18:00, closed Sat–Sun). Nearly every travel agency in town offers the tour, with only minor variations.

By Taxi: Lots of aggressive cabbies at the border would love to take you for a ride—about €24/£16 per person if the taxi is packed (at least four people). More people in a taxi means a lower cost per person; try to buddy up with other travelers. Cabbies at taxi stands in the center of Gibraltar are more low-key and charge a bit less (though it's harder to gather a group). The basic tour consists of four stops: a Mediterannean viewpoint (called the Pillar of Hercules), St. Michael's Cave (for a 15- to 20-minute visit), near the top of the Rock, and some taxis stop at the Siege Tunnels (for 15–20 minutes). A fifth stop—the ATM at NatWest House—is added for people who mistakenly thought they could pay for this tour with a credit card.

By Foot: One-hour **walking tours** of the town center give you the essentials on the history of the Rock (€7.50/£5, Mon–Fri at 12:00, departs from Let's Go sentry box in Casemates Square, tel. 956-778-434 from Spain, www.letsgogibraltar.com, info@letsgogibraltar.com).

The Quick, Cheap, Bus #3 Self-Guided Orientation Tour

At the border, pick up a map at the customs TI. Then walk straight ahead for 200 yards to the bus stop on the right. Catch minibus #3 and enjoy the ride (4/hr, pay driver €0.60/40p, 15–20 min to Europa Point and the end of the line). To return, you will have to pay again.

You enter Gibraltar by crossing an **airstrip.** Fourteen times a week, the entry road into Gibraltar is closed to allow airplanes to land or take off. (You can fly to London for as little as $180.) The airstrip, originally a horse-racing stadium, was filled in with stones excavated from the 30 miles of military tunnels in the Rock. This airstrip was a vital lifeline in the days when Spain and Britain were quarreling over Gibraltar (especially 1970–1985) and the border was closed.

Just after the airstrip, the bus passes a road leading left (which heads clockwise around the Rock to the town of Catalan Bay, peaceful beaches, and the huge mountainside rainwater-catchment wall).

As you pass apartments on the left, find the **Moorish castle** above (now a prison; only the tower is open to the public).

Over the bridge and on the right after the next stop you'll see **World War memorials.** The first is the American War Memorial (a building-like structure with a gold plaque and arch), built in 1932 to commemorate American sailors based here in World War I. Further along you'll see 18th-century cannons and a memorial to Gibraltarians who died in World War II.

The following sights pass by quickly: Passing the NatWest House office tower on the left, you'll immediately see a **synagogue** (only the top peeks out above a wall; the wooden doors in the wall bear the Star of David). In the 19th century half of Gibraltar was Jewish. The Jewish community now numbers 600.

Just after the synagogue is little **Cathedral Square,** with a playground, TI, and the Moorish-looking Anglican church (behind the playground).

Now you'll pass a lo-o-o-ong wall; most of it is the back of the Governor's Residence (also called the Convent). The bus stops before the old **Charles V wall,** built in response to a 1552 raid in which the pirate Barbarossa captured 70 Gibraltarians into slavery.

Immediately after you pass under the wall, you'll see—on your left—a green park that contains the **Trafalgar cemetery** (free, daily 9:00–19:00). Buried here are some British sailors who died defeating the French off the coast of Portugal's Cape Trafalgar in 1805.

The next stop is at the big parking lot for the **cable car** to the top of the Rock, as well as for the **botanical gardens** (free, daily 8:00–sunset) at the base of the lift. You can get off now or later, on the ride back into town.

Heading uphill out of town you pass the big, ugly casino and the path leading up the Rock (a 2.5-hour hike). Reaching the end of the Rock you pass modern apartments and the mosque. The lighthouse marks the windy Europa Point—end of the line. Buses retrace the route you just traveled, departing about every 15 minutes (check schedule before exploring further).

The **Europa Point,** up the mound from the bus stop and tourist shop (on right), is an observation post. A plaque here identifies the mountains of Morocco 15 miles across the strait. The light of the lighthouse (150 feet tall, from 1841, closed to visitors) can be seen from Morocco.

The **King Fahd Mosque,** a gift from the Saudi sultan, was completed in 1997. Gibraltar's 900 Muslims worship here each Friday. Here—as across the strait in Morocco—five times a day the imam sings the call to prayer. Visitors (without shoes) are welcome except at prayer time.

SIGHTS

Gibraltar's Upper Rock Nature Reserve

The Reserve covering the Rock contains a number of sights—including St. Michael's Cave and the Apes' Den—accessible by car or cable car (or by tour, listed above).

To get to the top of the Rock and the Reserve, take the cable car from the south end of Main Street (€7.50/£5 one-way, €10/£6.50 round-trip for cable car only; or €18/£12 one-way and €20/£13.50 round-trip including all of the Upper Rock Nature Reserve sights; Mon–Sat 9:30–17:15, last cable car down at 17:45, 6/hr, closed Sun and when it's windy, brochure with necessary map included with ticket). The lift, usually closed on Sunday, opens on Sunday during peak season, April through September.

Buying a one-way ticket up saves a little money and gives you a chance to hike down to all of the sites (the hike is mostly downhill but has some uphill). Allow 90 minutes to hike—or as much as 2.5 hours if you stop at the following listed sights in the Upper Rock Nature Reserve, which you'll see in order as you descend from the top of the Rock.

If you get a round-trip ticket and you're in a hurry, your best strategy is to take the cable car up, hike downhill to St. Michael's Cave and the Apes' Den, and then take the cable car down into town from the Apes' Den, skipping the other sights. Why hike at all, you ask? Because you'd miss St. Michael's Cave if you relied solely on the cable car.

Approximate hiking times: From the top of cable-car lift to St. Michael's Cave—25 min; from the Cave to Apes' Den—20 min; from the Apes' Den to Siege Tunnels—30 min; from the Tunnels to *City Under Siege* exhibit—5 min; from exhibit to Moorish Castle—5 min; and down to town—10 min. Total from top to bottom: about 1.5 hours, not including sightseeing.

The entire Upper Rock Nature Reserve is open daily 9:30–19:00. Only the Apes' Den is free with your cable-car ticket. A pass for admission to the other sites is €10/£7.

▲▲▲The Rock—The real highlight of Gibraltar is the spectacular Rock itself. The limestone massif is nearly a mile long and five football fields wide, rising 1,388 feet high with very sheer faces. In ancient legend, this was one of the "Pillars of Hercules" (paired with another mountain across the water in Africa), marking

the edge of the known world. In A.D. 711, the Muslim chieftain Tarik ibn Ziyad crossed over from Africa and landed on the Rock, beginning the Moorish conquest of Spain and naming the Rock after himself—"The Rock of Tarik," or Djebel-Tarik, which became Gibraltar.

The cable car drops you at a slick **restaurant/view terrace** (2nd stop) at the top of the Rock, from which you can explore old ramparts and drool at the 360-degree view of Morocco (including the Rif Mountains and Jebel Musa, the other "Pillar of Hercules"), the Strait of Gibraltar, the bay stretching west toward Algeciras, and the twinkling Costa del Sol arcing eastward. The views are especially crisp on brisk off-season days. Below you (to the east) stretches the giant catchment system that the British built to catch rainwater in the not-so-distant past, when Spain allowed neither water nor tourists to cross its disputed border. Broad sheets catch the rain, sending it through channels to reservoirs located inside the rock.

▲▲O'Hara's Battery—If the Battery is still closed for renovation in 2005, it's not worth the 20-minute hike from the top of the cable-car lift (confirm status at cable-car lift or local TI). At 1,400 feet, this is the highest point on the Rock. A 28-ton, 9-inch gun sits on the summit where a Moorish lookout post once stood. It was built after World War I, and the last test shot was fired in 1974. Locals are glad it's been mothballed. During test firings, if locals didn't open their windows to allow air to move freely after the concussion, the windows would shatter. Thirty miles of tunnels, like the tiny bit you see here, honeycomb this strategic rock.

During World War II an entire garrison could have survived six months with the provisions stored in this underground base. Early in the war, when fascist forces occupied virtually the entire European continent, U.S. General Dwight D. Eisenhower made a damp Gibraltar cave his headquarters (November 1942) to plan the Allied invasion of North Africa, a prelude to the assault on Europe (if renovation is complete, the battery is open Mon–Sat 10:00–17:30, closed Sun; from top of cable-car lift, walk 10 min down and then 10 min up). The iron rings you might see are anchored pulleys used to haul up guns such as the huge one at O'Hara's Battery.

▲St. Michael's Cave—Studded with stalagmites and stalactites, eerily lit and echoing with classical music, this cave is dramatic, corny, and slippery when wet. Considered a one-star sight since Neolithic times, these caves were alluded to in ancient Greek legends—when the caves were believed to be the Gates of Hades (or the entrance of a tunnel to Africa). In the last century, they were prepared (but never used) as a World War II hospital and are now just another tourist site with an auditorium for musical events. Notice the polished cross-section of a stalagmite that shows weirdly beautiful rings similar to a tree's. Spelunkers who'd enjoy a three-hour subterranean hike through the lower cave can make arrangements in advance at the TI

(€7.25/£5 per person). To continue to the Apes' Den, refer to your map (free with lift ticket) and take the left fork.

Apes' Den—This small zoo without bars gives you a chance at a close encounter with some of the famous (and very jaded) apes of  Gibraltar. There are about 200 apes (actually, tailless monkeys) total on the Rock. The males are bigger, females have beards, and newborns are black. They live about 15–20 years. Legend has it that as long as the apes remain here, so will the Brits. Keep your distance from the apes and beware of their kleptomaniac tendencies; they'll ignore the peanut in your hand and claw after the full bag in your pocket. The man at the little booth posts a record of the names of all the apes. If there's no ape action, wait for a banana-toting taxi tour to stop by and stir some up. Note that it's against the law to feed the apes, and offenders—though rarely caught—can get a £500 ticket.

The cable car stops here; you can catch the car down to town from here (if it's too crowded with visitors descending from the top for you to get on, ask the driver to save a spot for you on the next trip down) or continue on foot to see the following sights.

▲Siege Tunnels—Also called the Upper Galleries, these chilly tunnels were blasted out of the rock by the Brits during the Spanish and French siege of 1779 to 1783. The clever British, safe inside the Rock, used hammers and gunpowder to carve these tunnels in order to plant four big guns on the north face and drive the French off. During World War II, 30 more miles of tunnels were blasted out. Hokey but fun dioramas help recapture a time when Brits were known more for conquests than for crumpets. The tunnels are at the northern end of the Rock, about a mile from the Apes' Den.

Gibraltar, A City Under Siege Exhibition—A spin-off of the Siege Tunnels, this excuse for a museum gives you a look at life during the siege. It's worth a stop only if you already have a combo-ticket (just downhill from Siege Tunnels).

Moorish Castle—Actually more tower than castle, this building offers a tiny museum of Moorish remnants and carpets. It was built on top of the original castle built by the Moor Tarik ibn Ziyad in A.D. 711, who gave his name to Gibraltar (see "The Rock" listing, page 364). The tower marks the end of the Upper Rock Nature Reserve. Head downhill to reach the lower town and Main Street.

Lower Gibraltar

The town at the base of the hill (pop. 30,000) survives on banking, tourism, and its port facilities (especially refueling). Most locals speak both English and Spanish. There's not much to the town except souvenir and cheap electronics shops, but here are a few sights:

Gibraltar Museum—Built atop a Moorish bath, this museum in Gibraltar's lower town tells the story of a rock that has been fought over for centuries. Highlights are the history film and the prehistoric remains discovered here.

On the ground floor, you can see the 15-minute film, a "teaser" prehistoric-skull display, and the empty rooms of the 14th-century Moorish baths. The first floor contains military memorabilia, a model of the Rock, paintings by local artists, and, in a cave-like room off the art gallery, a collection of prehistoric remains and artifacts. The famous skull of a Neanderthal woman found in Forbes' Quarry is a copy (original in British Museum in London). This first Neanderthal skull was found in Gibraltar in 1848, though no one realized its significance until a similar skull found years later in Germany's Neanderthal Valley was correctly identified—stealing the name, claim, and fame from Gibraltar (€3/£2, Mon–Fri 10:00–18:00, Sat 10:00–14:00, closed Sun, no photos, on Bomb House Lane off Main Street).

▲**Catalan Bay**—Gibraltar's tiny second town originated as a settlement of Italian shipwrights whose responsibility was keeping the royal ships in good shape. Today it's just a huddle of apartments around a cute little Catholic church and the best beach on the Rock (fully equipped). Catch bus #4 or bus #2 from opposite the Governor's Residence or the roundabout near the airport.

Dolphin-Watching Cruises—Numerous companies take you on two-hour cruises of the bay to look for dolphins (€30–37/£20–25). Nautilus runs boats with glass fronts and sides (€34/£22.50, 3/day, Admirals Walk 4, tel. 73400) and Dolphin World refunds your money if dolphins aren't sighted (€30/£20, 5/day, Admirals Walk, Marina Bay Pier, mobile 677-278-845).

Day Trip to Tangier, Morocco

Virtually any travel agency in Gibraltar offers day trips to Tangier (ask at the TI for their "Tangier Day Trips" list, stop by any travel agency in Gibraltar, or check with Thomas Cook Exchange Travel and Parodytur—both listed in "Tours," page 361). Depending on the company, you'll pay about €50–65/£35–45 for the tour, which covers the ferry crossing, a tour of Tangier, lunch, a shopping stop at the market, and the return by ferry. Some tours leave from Gibraltar, others from Algeciras. But because Gibraltar is pricey compared to Spain, it makes sense to use your time here just to see the Rock, and day-trip to Morocco from a cheaper home base such as Tarifa or Algeciras (see page 371).

SLEEPING

To call Gibraltar from Spain, dial 9567 plus the five-digit local number. To call from Europe, dial 00-350-local number. To call from America or Canada, dial 011-350-local number.

$$$ **Eliott Hotel** is four stars and then some—it has a rooftop pool with a view, a nice restaurant, bar, and terrace; fine sit-a-bit public spaces; and 114 modern, settle-in rooms (Db-€180–260/£120–175, breakfast-€19/£13, air-con, laundry service, elevator, non-smoking floor, free parking, centrally located at Governor's Parade, tel. 70500, fax 70243, www.gib.gi/eliotthotel, eliott@gibnet.gi).

$$$ **Bristol Hotel** offers drab, overpriced rooms in the heart of Gibraltar (Sb-€73–80/£49–53, Db-€95–103/£64–69, Tb-€110–120/£74–81, higher prices for exterior rooms, breakfast-€7.25/£5, air-con, elevator, swimming pool oddly located off breakfast room in the annex, free parking, Cathedral Square 10, tel. 76800, fax 77613, www.gib.gi/bristolhotel, bristhtl@gibnet.gi).

$$ **Queen's Hotel,** near the cable-car lift, has 62 comfortable rooms in a noisy location (S-€39/£26, Sb-€60/£40, D-€54/£36, Db-€75–90/£50–60, Db with sea view-€105/£70, Tb-€112/£75, Qb-€127/£85, includes breakfast, 20 percent discount for students with ISIC cards and paying cash, free parking, elevator, at #3 bus stop, Boyd Street 1, tel. 74000, fax 40030, www.queenshotel.gi, queenshotel@gibnynex.gi).

$$Charming and central **Cannon Hotel** is a good value, with 18 quiet rooms (most without bathroom) and a little patio. It's located between a hotel and a upper-scale youth hostel (S-€37/£24.50, D-€54/£36.50, Db-€67/£45, T-€69/£46.50, Tb-€76/£52, includes full

---

Sleep Code

(€1 = about $1.20, £1 = about $1.70, tel. code: 9567 from Spain, or 350 international)
S = Single, **D** = Double/Twin, **T** = Triple, **Q** = Quad
b = bathroom, **s** = shower only, **no CC** = Credit Cards not accepted. Exterior rooms (with views and traffic noise) often cost more than interior rooms (quiet, without a view). You can assume credit cards are accepted unless otherwise noted.

To help you easily sort through these listings, I've divided the rooms into three categories, based on the price for a standard double room with bath during high season:

$$$ **Higher Priced**—Most rooms €100/£70 or more.
$$ **Moderately Priced**—Most rooms between €50/£35 and €100/£70.
$ **Lower Priced**—Most rooms €50/£35 or less.

English breakfast, Cannon Lane 9, behind cathedral, tel. 51711, fax 51789, www.cannonhotel.gi, cannon@gibnet.gi). The bar downstairs is open all day.

$$ Continental Hotel isn't fancy but has a friendly feel. Its 18 high-ceilinged, air-conditioned rooms border an unusual elliptical atrium (Sb-€63/£42, Db-€82/£55, Tb-€105/£70, Qb-€126/£85, includes continental breakfast, 10 percent discount when you pay cash, elevator, in pedestrian area just off Main Street, a couple of blocks from Casemates TI, Engineer Lane, tel. 76900, fax 41702, contiho@gibnet.gi). The hotel runs an inexpensive café downstairs.

$ The cheapest place in town is **Emile Youth Hostel Gibraltar** (44 beds, D-€45/£30, dorm bed-€22/£15, includes breakfast, lockout 10:30–17:00, just outside Casemates Square entry on Montagu Bastion, tel. & fax 51106).

EATING

Take a break from *jamón* and sample some English pub grub: fish 'n' chips, meat pies, jacket potatoes (baked potatoes with fillings), or a hearty English breakfast of eggs, bacon, and side dishes. English-style beers include chilled lagers and nearly-room-temperature ales, bitters, and stouts.

Casemates Square, the big square at the entrance of Gibraltar, contains a variety of restaurants, ranging from fast food (fish 'n' chips joint, Burger King, and Pizza Hut) to pubs spilling out into the square. Consider the **All's Well** pub, near the TI, with €7.50/£5 meals (burgers, fish 'n' chips, and more) and pleasant tables with umbrellas under leafy trees (daily 9:30–24:00).

Queensway Quay Marina is the place to be when a misty sun sets over the colorful marina and rugged mountains of Spain. The string of restaurants that line the promenade have indoor and outdoor seating, offer seafood and other dishes, and are usually open daily for lunch and dinner. One option is **Claus on the Rock Bistro** (closed Sun, colorful menu from around the world, good cigar and wine selection, tel. 48686). **Waterfront,** farther on, is less expensive, and the **Jolly Parrot** (just tapas and drinks) offers the cheapest seat on the promenade. Queensway Quay is at the cable-car end of town (walk through Ragged Staff Gate toward the water).

For good-value meals, consider **The Little Chef,** an adventure when the one English-speaking guy is off-duty. They have tasty, cheap €5/£3.50 meals but no menu. You just ask—in Spanish if necessary—what's cooking (daily 8:00–15:00, no dinner, Cornwall's Parade 7, a few blocks from Casemates Square). **The Clipper** has filling €7.50/£5 pub meals (English breakfast €5.70/£3.95, daily 9:00–11:00, on Irish Town, at intersection with tiny Irish Place).

Grocery: A Checkout supermarket is on Main Street (Mon–Fri 8:30–20:00, Sat 8:30–18:00), off Cathedral Square and next to Marks & Spencer (Mon–Sat 8:30–20:00, Sun 10:00–15:00, has a take-away window that serves roast chicken). Fruit stands bustle at the Market Place (Mon–Sat 9:00–15:00, closed Sun, outside entry to Casemates Square).

TRANSPORTATION CONNECTIONS

If you're leaving Gibraltar without a car, you must walk five minutes from Gibraltar's border into Spain to reach La Línea, the nearest bus station. The region's main transportation hub is Algeciras, with lots of train and bus connections, and ferries to Tangier and Ceuta. (For Algeciras connections, see the end of "Tarifa," below.) If you're traveling between La Línea and Algeciras, buy tickets on the bus. Otherwise buy tickets inside the station.

La Línea by bus to: Algeciras (2/hr, 45 min), **Tarifa** (7/day, 1 hr), **Málaga** (4/day, 2.5 hrs), **Granada** (2/day, 5 hrs), **Sevilla** (3/day, 4 hrs), **Jerez** (3/day, 3.75 hrs), **Huelva** (1/day, 6.25 hrs), **Madrid** (2/day, 8 hrs). Tel. 956-170-093 or 956-172-396.

Tarifa

Europe's most southerly town is a pleasant alternative to gritty, noisy Algeciras. It's a whitewashed, Arab-looking town with a lovely beach, an old castle, restaurants swimming in fresh seafood, inexpensive places to sleep, and enough windsurfers to sink a ship, and best of all, hassle-free boats to Morocco.

As I stood on Tarifa's town promenade under the castle, looking out at almost-touchable Morocco across the Strait of Gibraltar, I regretted only that I didn't have this book to steer me clear of Algeciras on earlier trips. Tarifa, with usually daily 35-minute trips to Tangier, is the best jumping-off point for a Moroccan side-trip.

Tarifa has no blockbuster sights (and is pretty dead off-season), but it's a town where you just feel good to be on vacation.

ORIENTATION

The old town, surrounded by a wall, slopes gently up from the water's edge, with the modern section farther inland.

Tourist Information: The TI is on Paseo Alameda (June–Sept daily 10:00–14:00 & 16:00–20:00, Oct–May Mon–Sat 11:00–13:00 & 17:00–19:00, closed Sun, tel. 956-680-993).

Arrival in Tarifa: The bus station (really just a ticket office) is at Batalla del Salado 19 (Mon–Fri 7:30–11:00 & 14:30–19:00,

Sat–Sun 15:00–20:00, tel. 956-684-038). When you get off the bus, orient yourself by facing the old-town gate. The recommended hotels in the old town are through the gate; the hotels in the newer part of town are a couple of blocks behind you.

If you arrive by car and plan to stay in the center of town, follow signs for Alameda or Puerto, take a left just before the port, and go around the castle to the free parking lot at the other side of the port.

Internet Access: Try Pandora, in the heart of the old town, across from Café Central and near the church (cheap prices, long hours, 15 computers).

Laundry: Acuario Laundry is small but convenient and central. Leave your load of laundry (8 pounds max), and they will wash and dry it for €8 (Mon–Sat 10:00–13:30 & 19:30–21:00, Calle Colón 14, tel. 956-627-037, Christian SE).

Ferry to Morocco (Marruecos)

Boats to Tangier, Morocco, sail from both Tarifa and nearby Algeciras. As recently as August 2003, the Tarifa–Tangier crossing was open only to people from E.U. countries, but now it's open to anyone of any nationality, whether solo or on a tour. However, the port still might close to non-Europeans at times (most likely at end of June and beginning of July, and end of July and beginning of Aug). E-mail the TI or Marruecotur (see "Tours" below) for details prior to your trip.

Although the only ferry from Tarifa is now a fast Nordic hydrofoil that theoretically takes 35 minutes, it usually leaves 30 minutes late. If you go on your own without a tour, officials will check your passport and stamp your ticket aboard the boat. If you take a tour, you will have to wear a sticker, and upon arrival in Tangier, someone will guide you to your guide. If you already have your ticket, you do not need to be at the terminal more than 15 or 20 minutes in advance. The boat is equipped with WCs, a shop, and a snack bar. The new terminal has a cafeteria and WCs.

Note that the Spanish refer to Morroco as Marruecos (mar-WAY-kohs) and Tangier as Tanger (pronounced with a guttural "g" at the back of the throat, sounding like tahn-hair).

Tours: Ideally get your ticket the day before you sail, when you arrive in Tarifa. Prices are roughly the same at the various travel agencies (€22.50 one-way, €45 round-trip, or only €49.50 for a day-long tour—they make money off commissions if you shop; up to 7 boats run daily).

Marruecotur in Tarifa offers a day trip that takes you from Tarifa to Tangier, then on a panoramic bus tour, a walking tour of old Tangier, a typical lunch in the medina, and a stroll through the bazaar (€49.50, groups of 15–20 people, leaves at 9:00 & 11:30, back at 15:30 & 18:30 respectively, two-day option available for €86 per person).

Tarifa

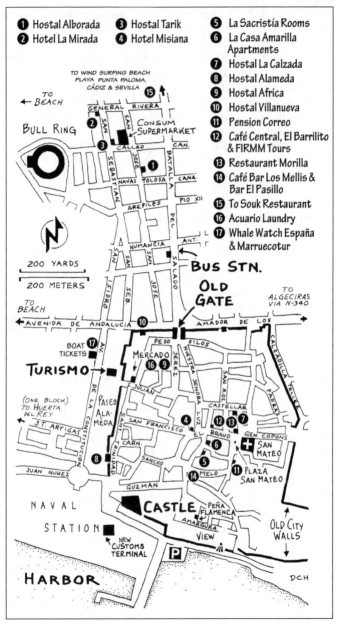

1. Hostal Alborada
2. Hotel La Mirada
3. Hostal Tarik
4. Hotel Misiana
5. La Sacristía Rooms
6. La Casa Amarilla Apartments
7. Hostal La Calzada
8. Hostal Alameda
9. Hostal Africa
10. Hostal Villanueva
11. Pension Correo
12. Café Central, El Barrilito & FIRMM Tours
13. Restaurant Morilla
14. Café Bar Los Mellis & Bar El Pasillo
15. To Souk Restaurant
16. Acuario Laundry
17. Whale Watch España & Marruecotur

Marruecotur's office, across the street from the Tarifa TI, is open long hours (daily June–Sept 7:40–21:00, Oct–May 8:00–20:00, also books flights, trains, and some long-distance buses to destinations in Spain and Portugal, Avenida de la Constitución 5, tel. 956-681-821 or 956-681-242, fax 956-680-256, mcotur1@e-savia.net, helpful Luís and Emma SE).

Speedlines Tours, across from the bus station, books Tangier tours as well as flights, trains, car and bike rentals, and more (Batalla del Salado 10, tel. 956-627-048, www.speedlines-tours.com).

FRS Iberia is yet another travel agency for you to consider, either for tours or ferry tickets (tel. 956-681-830, at the Tarifa terminal).

SIGHTS

Castle of Guzmán el Bueno—This castle was named after a 13th-century Christian general who gained fame in a sad show of courage while fighting the Moors. Holding Guzmán's son hostage, the Moors demanded he surrender the castle or they'd kill the boy. Guzmán refused, even throwing his own knife down from the ramparts. It was used on his son's throat. Ultimately, the Moors withdrew to Africa, and Guzmán was a hero. *Bueno.* The castle itself is a concrete hulk in a vacant lot, interest-

ing only for the harbor views from the ramparts (€1.20, mid-June–Sept Tue–Sat 11:00–14:00 & 18:00–20:00, Sun 11:00–14:00, Oct–mid-June Tue–Sat 11:00–14:00 & 17:00–19:00, Sun 11:00–14:00, closed Mon).

Church of St. Matthew—Tarifa's main church faces its main drag. Most nights it seems life squirts from the church out the front door and into the fun-loving Calle El Bravo. Wander inside (daily 9:00–13:00 & 17:30–21:00, English-language leaflets—unless they're out—are inside on the right).

1. Find the tiny square (about the size of a piece of copier paper) of an **ancient tombstone** in the wall just before the transept on the right side. Probably the most important historic item in town, it proves there was a functioning church here during Visigothic times, before the Moorish conquest. The tombstone reads, in a kind of Latin Spanish, "Flaviano lived as a Christian for 50 years, a little more or less. In death he received forgiveness as a servant of God on March 30, 674. May he rest in peace." If that gets you in the mood to light a candle, switch on an electric "candle" for a coin.

2. Step into the transept beyond the candles. The centerpiece of the **altar** is a boy Jesus. By Andalusian tradition he used to be naked,

but these days he's clothed with outfits that vary with the Church calendar. On the left is a fine 17th-century statue of the "Virgin (protector) of the Fishermen."

3. A statue of **St. James the Moorslayer** (missing his sword) is on the right wall of the main central altar. Since the days of the Reconquista, James has been Spain's patron saint.

4. The chapel to the left of the main altar harbors several **statues** that go on parade through town during Holy Week. The **Captive Christ** (with hands bound) goes back to the days when Christians were held captive by Moors.

5. Circling around to the left side you'll find a side door, the **"door of pardons."** For a long time, Tarifa was a dangerous place— on the edge of the Reconquista. To encourage people to live here, the Church offered a huge amount of forgiveness to anyone who lived in Tarifa for a year. One year and one day after moving to Tarifa, they would have the privilege of passing through this special "door of pardons," and a Mass of thanksgiving would be held in that person's honor.

Bullfighting—Tarifa has a third-rate bullring where novices botch fights on occasional Saturdays through the summer. Professional bullfights take place the first week of September. The ring is a short walk from the town. You'll see posters everywhere.

▲Whale Watching—Daily whale- and dolphin-watching excursions are offered by several companies in Tarifa. In little more than 40 years, people in this area went from eating whales to protecting them and sharing them with 20,000 visitors a year. Talks are underway between Morocco and Spain to protect the Strait of Gibraltar by declaring it a national park.

For any of the tours, it's wise to reserve one to three days in advance, though same-day bookings are possible. You'll get a multilingual tour and a two-hour trip (usually no WC on board). Sightings occur more than 90 percent of the time. Dolphins and pilot whales frolic here any time of year, while sperm whales visit May through July and orcas stay July through August. Depending on the wind and weather, boats may leave from Algeciras instead (drivers follow in a convoy, people without cars usually get rides from staff).

The best company is the Swiss nonprofit **FIRMM** (Foundation for Information and Research on Marine Mammals), which gives a 25-minute educational talk prior to departure—and if you don't see any dolphins or whales, you can go on another trip for free (€27 per person, cash only, runs 1–5 trips/day April–Oct, Pedro Cortés 4, around the corner from Café Central—one door inland, also offers courses, details on their Web site, tel. 956-627-008, fax 956-681-424, mobile 619-459-441, www.firmm.org, SE).

Another good option is the first non-profit to launch these trips, **Whale Watch España,** part of a Whale Protection Association that runs classes and studies dolphins and whales (€27 per person, includes helpful illustrated brochure, also offers a second, free trip if you don't see whales or dolphins, leaves from Algeciras or La Línea when windy, runs 1–4/day April–Oct, across from TI on Avenida de la Constitución 6, tel. 956-627-013, mobile 670-796-508, www.whalewatchtarifa.org, run by Lourdes SE). Yet another company is **Turmares** (tel. 956-680-741, mobile 696-448-349, www.tumares.com).

▲**Windsurfing**—The vast, sandy beach **Playa Punta Paloma** lies about five miles northwest of town. On windy summer days, the sea is

littered with sprinting wind-surfers, while the beach holds a couple hundred vans and fun-mobiles from northern Europe. Under mountain ridges lined with modern energy-generating wind-mills, it's a fascinating scene. Drive down the sandy road and stroll along the beach. You'll find a cabana-type hamlet with rental gear, beachwear shops, a bar, and a hip, healthy restaurant with great lunch salads.

For drivers, it's a cinch to reach. Without a car, you're in luck July through September, when inexpensive buses do a circuit of nearby campgrounds, all on the waterfront (€1.75, Mon–Fri every 2 hours from 8:00–22:00, Sat–Sun 8:00–3:00, the stop Punta Paloma is best, catch bus across from bus station at Batalla del Salado 10, tel. 956-627-048, confirm times with TI).

SLEEPING

Outside the City Wall

These hotels are right off the main drag and close to the beach—Batalla del Salado—with easy parking, in the plain, modern part of town. To get oriented if arriving by bus, face the old-town gate. These hotels are several blocks behind you.

$$ **Hostal Alborada** is a squeaky-clean 37-room place with two attractive courtyards. It's a few blocks from the old town on a plain street (Sb-€25, €35, or €50; Db-€35, €45, or €60; Tb-€55, €65, or €80; get your price and then show this book for a 10 percent discount any time of year *except* high season—mid-June–Sept, includes tax, €10 laundry, 6 Internet posts, Calle San José 52, tel. 956-681-140, fax 956-681-935, www.hotelalborada.com, alborada@cherrytel.com).

$$ **Hotel La Mirada** has 25 modern rooms, some of which come with sea views at no extra cost (Sb-€30, €36, or €42; Db-€54, €60, or €66; extra bed-€9, breakfast-€3.60, extra for American-type breakfast, includes tax, elevator, sea views from large terrace, attached restaurant

Sleep Code

(€1 = about $1.20, country code: 34)
S = Single, **D** = Double/Twin, **T** = Triple, **Q** = Quad,
b = bathroom, **s** = shower only, **no CC** = Credit Cards not
accepted, **SE** = Speaks English, **NSE** = No English spoken. You
can assume credit cards are accepted unless otherwise noted.

To help you easily sort through these listings, I've divided
the rooms into three categories, based on the price for a standard
double room with bath during high season:

$$$ **Higher Priced**—Most rooms €100 or more.
$$ **Moderately Priced**—Most rooms between €50–100.
$ **Lower Priced**—Most rooms €50 or less.

Room rates vary with the season (3 seasonal tiers vary but are,
roughly: high—mid-June–Sept; medium—spring and fall; and
low—winter). Breakfast and the 7 percent IVA tax are not
included (unless noted).

serving dinner, Calle San Sebastián 41, tel. 956-684-427, fax 956-681-162, www.hotel-lamirada.com, hotel-lamirada@cherrytel.com,
Antonio and Salvador speak some English). It's two blocks off the
main drag and about five blocks away from the old town.

$$ The motel-style **Hostal Tarik** is a lesser value. Clean but
noisy, it's a bit tattered, and short on windows on the ground floor;
ask for a room upstairs. Of its 18 rooms, 8 are newly renovated with
balconies and views (Db-€35, €45, or €64; Tb-€42, €60, or €78;
breakfast-€2.30, Calle San Sebastián 34, tel. 956-680-648, Mario
speaks some English). Surrounded by warehouses, it's one block
toward the town center from Hotel La Mirada.

On or inside the City Wall

$$$ **La Sacristía,** formerly a Moorish stable, offers 10 fine rooms,
each decorated differently, fancier on the first floor, Japanese-style
on the second floor (Db-€115–135, extra bed-€30, includes break-fast, music Tue–Sun nights until late in the courtyard, non-smoking
rooms, fans, *hammam* sauna, roof terrace with views, very central at
San Donato 8, tel. 956-681-759, fax 956-685-182, www.lasacristia
.net, tarifa@lasaristia.net, helpful Indra SE).

$$ **Hotel Misiana** has 13 comfortable, newly remodeled, spa-cious rooms. The top-floor suite is grand, with private elevator
access, a Jacuzzi, great views, and a big terrace—worth the splurge.
The management is friendly and casual (Sb-€37, €47, or €74; Db-€58, €79, or €98; top-floor Db suite-€126, €157, or €184; tax extra,
includes breakfast after 9:00, double-paned windows, elevator,

restaurant and trendy bar on ground floor open late in summer weekend nights, a block from Café Central, Sancho IV El Bravo 18, tel. 956-627-083, fax 956-627-055, www.misiana.com, reservas @misiana.com).

$$ La Casa Amarilla (The Yellow House) offers 11 posh apartments with modern decor and tiny kitchens (Db-€44–66, Tb-€58–88, Qb-€73–109, tax extra, 20 percent deposit requested, across street from Café Central, Calle Sancho IV El Bravo 9, entrance on alley, tel. 956-681-993, fax 956-684-029, www.lacasaamarilla.net, info@lacasaamarilla.net).

$$ Hostal La Calzada has eight airy, well-appointed rooms right in the noisy-at-night, old-town thick of things (Db-€42, €48, or €55; Tb-€48, €57, and €64; includes tax, closed Nov–March, Calle Justino Pertinez 3, veer left and down from the old-town gate, tel. 956-680-366 or 956-681-492, NSE).

$$ Hostal Alameda, overlooking a square where the local children play, glistens with pristine marble floors and dark red decor. Its 11 bright rooms, five with a view, are above its restaurant, which serves tasty gazpacho (Db-€40, €50, or €60; Tb-€55, €65, or €75; breakfast-€3.30, includes tax, Paseo Alameda 4, tel. 956-684-029, fax 956-681-181, www.hostalalameda.com, some English spoken).

$ Hostal Africa, with 13 bright new rooms and a roof garden, has a Moorish ambience in a very quiet street in the center of town (S-€15–25, D-€22–35, Sb-€20–30, Db-€30–45, no CC, includes tax, breakfast options in the market next door, laundry-€7, storage for boards and bikes, Calle María Antonia Toledo 12, tel. 956-680-220, mobile 606-914-294, hostal_africa@hotmail.com, Miguel and Eva SE).

$ Hostal Villanueva is your best budget bet. It's simple, clean, and friendly, with 12 remodeled rooms with double-paned windows, and includes an inviting terrace that overlooks the old town. It's on a busy street, and the four quiet rooms in the back come with the best views (Sb-€20–25 Db-€35–45, includes tax, breakfast-€2.50, CC for 2-night minimum, attached restaurant, Avenida de Andalucía 11, just west of the old-town gate, with access outside the wall, tel. & fax 956-684-149, Pepe SE).

$ Pensión Correo rents eight simple rooms at a good value (Db-€30–50, extra bed-€15–17, reservations accepted only within 24 hours of arrival, roof garden, Coronel Moscardo 8, tel. 956-680-206, pensioncorreo@ya.com, María José and Lucca SE).

EATING

You'll find good tapas throughout the old town. **Café Central** is the happening place nearly any time of day. The tapas are priced at €1.20; go to the bar and point. They also offer great, ingenious

€5 salads (study the menu) and impressively therapeutic, healthy fruit drinks (daily 9:00–24:00 off Plaza San Mateo, near church, tel. 956-680-560). Across the street, the popular **El Barrilito** makes interesting sandwiches (€1.80–2.40, daily 8:00–24:00), with a tapas option and indoor/outdoor seating. A few doors down, in front of the church, **Restaurante Morilla** serves good local-style fish—grilled or baked—on the town's prime piece of people-watching real estate (daily 13:00–16:30 & 19:30–23:00, Calle Sancho IV El Bravo, tel. 956-681-757).

From Café Central follow the cars 100 yards to the first corner on the left to reach the simple, untouristy **Bar El Francés** ("The French," after owner Marcial), popular for its fine tapas (generally €0.90), especially oxtail *(rabo del toro)*, snails *(caracoles,* June–mid-July only), pork with tomato sauce *(carne con tomate)*, and pork with spice *(chicharrones)*. Show this book and be treated to a glass of local white wine *(vino de Chiclana)* with your tapas (Oct–March closes Sat–Sun nights, bar has no sign, it's at #21A).

The nearby **Café Bar Los Mellis** is family-friendly and serves a good chorizo sandwich and *patatas bravas*—potatoes with a hot tomato sauce served on a wooden board, as well as stuffed chicken (daily 12:00–16:00 & 20:00–24:00, closed Wed in winter, run by brothers José and Ramón; from Bar El Francés, cross parking lot and take Calle del Legionario Ríos Moya up 1 block). **Bar El Pasillo,** next to Mellis, also serves tapas (closes Mon).

From Mellis, you can circle around toward the church past some very gritty and colorful tapas bars. Just to the sea side of the church, you'll see the mysterious **Casino Tarifeño.** This is an old-boys' social club "for members only," but it offers a big, musty, Andalusian welcome to visiting tourists, including women. Wander through. There's a low-key bar with tapas, a TV room, a card room, and a lounge.

From the town center, walk the narrow Calle San Francisco to survey a number of good restaurants, such as the only place offering outdoor seating on the street, **El Rincón de Juan** (sample the local fish—*hurta* and *voraz*, €15 dinners, Fri–Wed 12:00–15:00 & 20:00–23:00, tel. 956-681-018).

The street Huerta del Rey is a family scene at night. Stop by the produce shop for fruit and veggies, the *heladería* for ice cream, or **El Tuti** for a drink (outside the old city walls, 2 blocks west; a clothing market is held here Tue 9:00–14:00).

Confitería la Tarifeña serves super pastries and flan (at the top of Calle Nuestra Señora de la Luz, near the main old-town gate).

With a car, head to the bars at Camping Torre de la Peña to check out Tarifa's popular windsurfing scene—give **Chozo** or **Spin Out** a try.

For a more romantic dinner with a Moroccan and Thai flavor, **Souk** is a good place to spend €20, if you don't mind a 15-minute walk. Head towards Sevilla; the restaurant is off Batalla del Salado at Mar Tirreno 46 (daily 8:00–24:00, closes Tue Sept–June and Feb, tel. 956-627-065, Patricia is very friendly). It's also a Moroccan-style tea house during the day.

Picnics: Stop by the *mercado municipal* (Mon–Sat 8:00–14:00, closed Sun, in old town, inside gate nearest TI), any grocery, or the **Consum supermarket** (Mon–Sat 9:00–21:00, closed Sun, simple cafeteria, at Callao and San José, near the hotels in the new town).

TRANSPORTATION CONNECTIONS

Tarifa
By bus to: La Línea/Gibraltar (7/day, 1 hr, first departure at 10:40, last return at 20:00), **Algeciras** (12/day, 30 min, first departure from Tarifa weekdays at 6:30, on Sat 8:00, on Sun 10:00; return from Algeciras as late as 21:00), **Jerez** (3/day, 2 hrs), **Sevilla** (4/day, 3 hrs), **Huelva** (1/day, 5 hrs), and **Málaga** (2/day, 3.5 hrs). Bus info: tel. 956-684-038.

Algeciras
Algeciras is only worth leaving. It's useful to the traveler mainly as a transportation hub, offering ferries to Tangier (see Tangier chapter) and trains and buses to destinations in southern and central Spain. The **TI** is on Juan de la Cierva, a block inland from the port, and on the same street as the train station and the Comes bus station, which runs buses to Tarifa (Mon–Fri 9:00–14:00, closed Sat–Sun, tel. 956-572-636). If you need a place to stay, try **Hotel Reina Cristina** (Db-€100, free parking, easy walk to ferry dock, Paseo de la Conferencia, tel. 956-602-622).

Trains: The train station is four blocks inland on the far side of Hotel Octavio (up Juan de la Cierva, lockers on platform for €3— buy token at ticket window, tel. 956-630-202). If arriving by train, head down Juan de la Cierva toward the sea for the TI and port.

By train to: Madrid (2/day, 6 hrs during day, 11 hrs overnight), **Ronda** (6/day, 2 hrs), **Granada** (3/day, 4.5 hrs), **Sevilla** (6/day, 5 hrs, transfer in Bobadilla), **Córdoba** (4/day, 4.5–5 hrs; 2 direct, 2 with transfers in Bobadilla), **Málaga** (4/day, 4 hrs, transfer in Bobadilla). With the exception of the route to Madrid, these are particularly scenic trips; the best is the mountainous journey to Málaga via Bobadilla.

Buses: Algeciras has three bus stations.

The **Comes bus station** (half block away from train station, next to Hotel Octavio, tel. 956-653-456) runs buses to **La Línea** (2/hr, 45 min, from 7:00–21:30), **Tarifa** (10/day, 7/day on Sun), **Sevilla** (4/day, 3.5 hrs), **Jerez** (3/day, 2.5 hrs), **Huelva** (1/day, 6 hrs), and **Madrid** (4/day, 8 hrs).

The **Portillo bus station** (on waterfront, kitty-corner from the port, Calle Virgen Carmen 15, next door to Restaurante Portillo, tel. 956-654-304) offers frequent, direct buses to **Málaga** (11/day, 2 hrs) and **Granada** (4 direct/day, 4 hrs).

The **Linesur bus station** (also on waterfront, 1 long block past Portillo station, Calle Virgen Carmen 31, tel. 956-667-649) offers the most frequent direct buses to **Sevilla** (8/day, 3.25 hrs) and **Jerez** (8/day, 1.25 hrs).

Route Tips for Drivers

Tarifa to Gibraltar (45 min): It's a short drive, passing a silvery-white forest of windmills, from peaceful Tarifa past Algeciras to La Línea (the Spanish town bordering Gibraltar). Passing Algeciras, continue in the direction of Estepona. At San Roque, take the La Línea–Gibraltar exit.

Gibraltar to Nerja (130 miles): Barring traffic problems, the trip along the Costa del Sol is smooth and easy by car—much of it on new highways. Just follow the coastal highway east. After Málaga follow signs to Almería and Motril.

Nerja to Granada (80 miles, 90 min, 100 views): Drive along the coast to Motril, catching N323 north for about 40 miles to Granada. While scenic side trips may beckon, don't arrive late in Granada without a firm reservation.

MOROCCO
(Al Maghrib)

A young country with an old history, Morocco is a photographer's delight and a budget traveler's dream. It's cheap, exotic, and comes with lots of hotels and decent transportation. Along with a rich culture, Morocco offers plenty of contrast—from beach resorts to bustling desert markets, from jagged mountains to sleepy mud-brick oasis towns.

Morocco (*Marruecos* in Spanish; *Al Maghrib* is Arabic) also provides a good dose of culture shock—both bad and good. It makes Spain and Portugal look meek and mild. You'll encounter oppressive friendliness, brutal heat, the Arabic language, the Islamic faith, ancient cities, and aggressive beggars.

Most of the English-speaking Moroccans that the tourist meets are hustlers. Most visitors develop some intestinal problems by the end of their visit. Most women are harassed on the streets by horny but generally harmless men. Things don't work smoothly. In fact, compared to Morocco, Spain resembles Sweden in terms of efficiency.

While Morocco is clearly a place apart from Mediterranean Europe, it doesn't really seem like Africa either. It's a mix, reflecting its strategic position between the two continents. Situated on the Strait of Gibraltar, Morocco has been flooded by waves of invasions over the centuries. The Berbers, the native population, have had to contend with the Phoenicians, Carthaginians, Romans, Vandals, and more.

The Arabs brought Islam to Morocco in the seventh century A.D. and stuck around, battling the Berbers in various civil wars. A series of Berber and Arab dynasties rose and fell; the Berbers won out and still run the country today.

From the 15th century on, European countries carved up much of Africa. By the early 20th century, most of Morocco was under French control. In 1956, France granted Morocco independence.

Arabic Numerals

0	•	SIFR
1	١	WAAHID
2	٢	ITNEEN
3	٣	TALAATA
4	٤	ARBA'A
5	٥	KHAMSA
6	٦	SITTA
7	٧	SAB'A
8	٨	TAMANYA
9	٩	TIS'A
10	١٠	'ASHRA

When you cruise south across the Strait of Gibraltar, leave your busy itineraries and split-second timing behind. Morocco must be taken on its own terms. In Morocco things go smoothly only *"Inshallah"*—if God so wills.

Helpful Hints

Friday: Friday is the Muslim day of rest, when most of the country (except Tangier) closes down.

Money: Euros work here. Bring along lots of €1 and €0.50 coins for tips, small purchases, and camel rides. If you change money into dirhams, go to banks—or even easier, ATMs (available at most major banks), all of which have uniform rates. The black market is dangerous. Change only what you need, and keep the bank receipt to reconvert if necessary. Don't leave the country with Moroccan money. (But if you do, the Bank of Morocco branch in Algeciras may buy it back from you.)

Health: Morocco is much more hazardous to your health than Spain or Portugal. Eat in clean—not cheap—places. Peel fruit, eat only cooked vegetables, and drink reliably bottled water (Sidi Harazem or Sidi Ali). When you do get diarrhea—and you should plan on it—adjust your diet (small and bland meals, no milk or grease) or fast for a day, but make sure you replenish lost fluids. Relax: Most diarrhea is not serious, just an adjustment that will run its course.

Information: For an extended trip, bring travel information from home or Spain. The guides published by Lonely Planet, Rough Guide, and Let's Go (*Let's Go: Spain & Portugal* includes

How Big, How Many, How Much

- About 172,000 square miles (a little bigger than the state of California)
- 31 million people (about 180 people per square mile)
- 9 dirhams = about $1
- Time zone difference: Moroccan time is generally two hours earlier than Spanish time.

Morocco) are good. The green Michelin *Morocco* guidebook is worthwhile (if you read French). Buy the best map you can find locally—names are always changing, and it's helpful to have towns, roads, and place names written in Arabic.

Language: The Arabic squiggle-script, its many difficult sounds, and the fact that French is Morocco's second language make communication tricky for English-speaking travelers. A little French goes a long way, but learn a few words in Arabic. Have your first local friend help you pronounce:

please	**min fadlik**	meen FAD-leek
thank you	**shokran**	SHOW-kron
excuse me	**ismahli**	ees-MAY-lee
yes	**yeh**	EE-yuh
no	**lah**	lah
goodbye	**maa salama**	mah sah-LEM-ah

In markets, I sing "la la la la la" to my opponents. *Lah shokran* means, "No, thank you."

Listen carefully and write new words phonetically. Bring an Arabic phrase book. Make a point of learning the local number symbols; they are not like ours (which we call "Arabic").

Ramadan: On this major month-long religious holiday (Oct 4–Nov 2 in 2005), Muslims focus on prayer and reflection. Following Islamic doctrine, they refrain during daylight hours from eating, drinking (including water), smoking, and having sex. On the final day of Ramadan, Muslims celebrate *Eid* (an all-day feast and gift-giving party, similar to Christmas) and travelers may find some less-touristy stores and restaurants closed.

Keeping your bearings: Navigate the labyrinthine *medinas* (old towns) by altitude, gates, and famous mosques or buildings. Write down what gate you came in, so you can enjoy being lost—temporarily. *Souk* is Arabic for a particular market (such as leather, yarn, or metalwork).

Hustlers: While Moroccans are some of Africa's wealthiest people, you are still incredibly rich to them. This imbalance causes predictable problems. Wear your money belt. Assume con artists are more clever than you. Haggle when appropriate (prices skyrocket for tourists). You'll attract hustlers like flies at every famous tourist sight. They'll lie to you, get you lost, blackmail you, and pester the heck out of you. Never leave your car or baggage where you can't get back to it without your "guide." Anything you buy in their company gets them a 20 percent commission. Normally locals, shopkeepers, and police will come to your rescue when the hustlers' heat becomes unbearable. I usually hire a guide, since it's helpful to have a translator, and once you're "taken," the rest seem to leave you alone.

Marijuana: In Morocco, marijuana *(kif)* is as illegal as it is popular, as many Westerners in local jails would love to remind you. Some dealers who sell it cheap make their profit after you get arrested. Cars and buses are stopped and checked by police routinely throughout Morocco—especially in the north and in the Chefchaouen region, which is Morocco's *kif* capital.

Getting around Morocco: Moroccan trains are quite good. Second class is cheap and comfortable. Buses connect all smaller towns quite well. By car, Morocco is easy, but drive defensively and never rely on the oncoming driver's skill. Night driving is dangerous. Pay a guard to watch your car overnight.

TANGIER

Go to Africa. As you step off the boat, you realize that the crossing (35 min–2.5 hrs, depending on the port you choose) has taken you further culturally than did the trip from the United States to Iberia. Morocco needs no museums; its sights are living in the streets. Offered daily and year-round, the one-day excursions

from Tarifa, Algeciras, and Gibraltar are well-organized and reliable. Given that tours from Spain (rather than pricier Gibraltar) are virtually the cost of the boat passage alone, the tour package is a good value for those who can spare only a day for Morocco. For an extended tour of Morocco, see below.

Morocco in a Day?

There are many ways to experience Morocco, and a day in Tangier is probably the worst. But all you need is a passport (no visa or shots required), and if all you have is a day, this is a real and worthwhile adventure. Tangier is the Tijuana of Morocco, and everyone there seems to be expecting you.

You can use ATMs in Tangier to get Moroccan dirhams, but for a short one-day trip, there's no need to change money. Everyone you meet will be happy to take your euros, dollars, or pounds. (If you're arriving from Tarifa for a longer stay, consider changing money at the port; there's an exchange office near the supermarket.)

Whether on a tour or on your own, carefully confirm the time your return boat departs from Tangier. The time difference between the countries can be up to two hours. (I'd keep my watch on Spanish time and get my departure time clear in Spanish time.) Plan on

Tangier

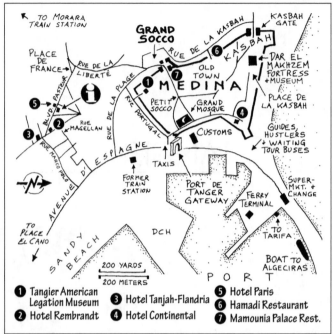

- ❶ Tangier American Legation Museum
- ❷ Hotel Rembrandt
- ❸ Hotel Tanjah-Flandria
- ❹ Hotel Continental
- ❺ Hotel Paris
- ❻ Hamadi Restaurant
- ❼ Mamounia Palace Rest.

spending one hour of your day in lines (passport control and so forth).

On Your Own: Just buy a ferry ticket at the port or from a local travel agency. Both Algeciras and Gibraltar have fine, modern ferry terminals, but Tarifa is by far the best place to cross. It's more pleasant than Algeciras and cheaper than Gibraltar. Coming from Tarifa, you can buy your ticket at the terminal or in any of the travel agencies I suggest (see page 387). If you are traveling without a tour, you will have to show your passport and have it stamped before you board the boat. If you are taking a tour, a stamp is not required.

If you plan to sail from Algeciras, buy your ticket at the port instead of at one of the many divey-looking travel agencies littering the town. To find the right office at the Algeciras port, go to the very furthest building, which is labeled in large letters: *Estación Marítima Terminal de Pasajeros* (luggage storage available here and at train station, easy parking at port-€6). The official offices of the seven boat companies are inside this main port building, directly behind the helpful little info kiosk (daily 6:45–21:45, tel. 956-585-463, SE). Get your ticket here. There are 8–22 crossings daily to Tangier.

Tarifa makes a cheaper home base for a day trip than Gibraltar, but if you're not going to Tarifa, consider day-tripping from the Rock (see page 367).

By Tour: You rarely need to book a tour more than a day in advance, even during peak season. Tours generally cost about €50 from Spain or €50–65 from Gibraltar. This includes a round-trip crossing and a guide who meets you at a prearranged point and hustles you through the hustlers and onto your bus. Excursions vary, but they usually offer a city tour, possibly a trip to the desolate Atlantic Coast for some rugged African scenery and the famous ride-a-camel stop (€1 to ride the camel for less than 5 min), a walk through the medina (old town) with a too-thorough look at a sales-starved carpet shop, and lunch in a palatial Moroccan setting with live music.

Sound cheesy? It is. But no amount of packaging can gloss over how exotic and different this culture really is. This kind of cultural voyeurism is almost embarrassing, but it's nonstop action and more memorable than another day in Spain. The shopping is—Moroccan. Bargain hard!

The day trip is so tightly organized that you'll have hardly any time alone in Tangier. For many people, that's just fine. Some, however, spend a night there and return the next day. If you're interested, ask travel agencies about the two-day tour (sample cost: €49–51 for one-day tour from Tarifa; €86 for two-day tour). The first day of a two-day tour is the same as the one-day tour; you just go to a fancy hotel (with dinner), rather than to the afternoon boat, and then you catch the same boat 24 unstructured hours later.

Tour tips: If you get a voucher when you pay for your tour at a travel agency, exchange it at the boat office to get your ticket prior to boarding. Confirm where you will meet the guide.

Travel Agencies Offering Tours

There are dozens, particularly in Algeciras. Here are several:

In Tarifa: Marruecotur is across from the TI (€51 for one-day tour, daily in summer 7:40–21:00, Avenida de la Constitución 5, tel. 956-681-821 or 956-681-242, fax 956-680-256, mcotur1@e-savia.net). Others are Speedlines Tours, across from Tarifa's bus station (Batalla del Salado 10, tel. 956-627-048) and FRSMaroc at Tarifa's dock (tel. 956-681-830).

In Algeciras: Marruecotur is at the port (€49 for one-day tour, open long hours, Estación Marítima C-6, tel. 956-656-185, fax 956-653-132, mcotur@e-savia.net).

In Gibraltar: Consider Thomas Cook Exchange Travel (241 Main Street, tel. 76151) and Parodytur (Cathedral Square, tel. 76070). Tours cost €50–65. The agencies are open weekdays 9:30–18:00 (closed Sat–Sun).

Ferries to Morocco

Ferries have mediocre cafeteria bars, plenty of WCs, stuffy indoor chairs, and grand views. Boats are most crowded in August, when the Costa del Sol groups come en masse. Only a few crossings a year are canceled because of storms, mostly in winter.

The following information is for people going to Tangier on their own. If you're taking a tour, skip this section.

From Tarifa to Tangier: Only by speed boat, 5–7/day, 35 min (€22.50 one-way, €45 round-trip).

From Algeciras to: Tangier (22/day in summer, 10/day in winter, 2.5 hrs by slow boat; 6 1-hr fast boats; €25.30 one-way, €50.60 round-trip; to bring a car: €78.30 one-way, €155.60 round-trip), **Ceuta** (hrly in summer, 7 ferries/day in winter, 35 min by fast ferry, €21 one-way, €43 round-trip; to bring a car: €62.75 one-way, €125.50 round-trip). Ceuta, an uninteresting Spanish possession in North Africa, is the cheapest car-entry point, but requires more waiting in line once you're in Africa, and it is not for those relying on public transport (for info on the crossing, see "Extended Tour of Morocco," page 393).

From Gibraltar to Tangier: 2/day, 1 hr (€30 one-way, €50 round-trip, the morning boat returns from Tangier later the same day; the afternoon sailing forces an overnight in Tangier, returning the next day).

Tangier

Tangier is split into two. The new town has the TI and fancy hotels. The medina (old town) has the markets, the Kasbah (with its palace), cheap hotels, decrepit homes, and 2,000 wanna-be guides. The twisty, hilly streets of the old town are caged within a wall accessible by keyhole gates. The big square, Grand Socco, is the link between the old and new parts of town.

ORIENTATION

Many assume they'll be lost in Tangier—because it's in Africa. Although the city could use more street signs, it's laid out simply. From the boat dock, you'll see the old town—circled by its medieval wall—on the right (behind Hotel Continental). The new town sprawls past the industrial port zone to the left. Nothing listed under "Sights" (page 390) is more than a 15-minute walk from the port. Petit Taxis are a godsend for the hot and tired tourist. Use them generously, and go ahead and just pay double the meter for any ride.

Tourist Information: Get a free map and advice at the TI (Mon–Sat 8:30–12:00 & 14:30–18:30, Boulevard Pasteur 29, in newer section of town, tel. 94-80-50, fax 94-86-61).

Exchange rate: 9 dirhams = about $1.

Telephone: To call Tangier from Spain, dial 00 (international access code), 212 (Morocco's country code), 39 (Tangier's city code), then the local six-digit number.

Arrival in Tangier

If you're taking a tour, follow the leader.

Independent travelers will take a five-minute walk from the boat, through customs, and out of the port. Consider hiring a guide (see "Guides," below). Taxis at the port are more expensive. Ask the cost before taking one. The big yellow Port de Tanger gateway defines the end of the port area and the start of the city. Leave mental bread crumbs, so you can find your way back to your boat. It will stay put all day. Just outside the port gate on the busy traffic circle, you'll find plenty of fair, metered Petit Taxis, along with a line of decent fish restaurants, the boulevard arcing along the beach into the new town, and stairs leading up into the old town and the market (on the right).

Planning Your Time

Catch a Petit Taxi to the TI. From there you can walk to the Grand Socco and market. Or, to minimize uphill walking, catch a taxi to the Place de la Kasbah at the top of the old town and work your way downhill to the port.

In the old town, start at the Museum of the Kasbah, then wander through the fortress (Dar el-Makhzem) and the Old American Legation Museum. Then shop through the Petit Socco. Walk out of the old town into the noisy Grand Socco. From there, catch a taxi to the beach (Plage el Cano) and sightsee along the beach and then along Avenue d'Espagne back to the port.

Guides

If you're on your own, you'll be fighting off "guides" all day. In order to have your own translator and a shield from less scrupulous touts who hit up tourists constantly throughout the old town, I recommend hiring a guide. Stress your interest in the people and culture

rather than shopping. Guides, hoping to get a huge commission from your purchases, can cleverly turn your Tangier day into the equivalent of the Shopping Channel.

I've had good luck with the private guides who meet the boat. These hardworking, English-speaking, and licensed guides offer their services for the day for €12. To avoid the stress of being mobbed by potential guides at the port, book a guide through an agency like Marruecotur in Tarifa or the Tangier TI before you arrive, and arrange for the guide to meet you at the port.

Aziz Begdouri is great ($13 for 5 hrs, easier to reach him from Spain on his Spanish mobile—tel. 607-897-967—than his Moroccan mobile, tel. 61-63-93-32, aziztour@hotmail.com).

Marco Polo Travel can help you with guides, hotels, and tours in other parts of the country (72 Avenue d'Espagne, tel. 32-22-24, mobile 63-61-40-99, marcopol@iam.net.ma).

The **TI** also has official guides (half day for $13, or 120 dirhams; full day for about $16, or 150 dirhams, including lunch for the guide; tel. 94-80-50, or call guides' association directly at tel. 93-13-72, dttanger@menara.com).

If you don't want a guide, ask directions of people who can't leave what they're doing (such as the only clerk in a shop) or of women who aren't near men. Ask "Kasbah?" or wherever you want to go, and you'll get pointed in the right direction. Fewer hustlers are in the new (but less interesting) part of town.

SIGHTS

Kasbah—This is the fortress atop old Tangier. You'll find a history museum in a former palace on Place de la Kasbah (10 dirhams, Wed–Mon 9:00–12:30 & 15:00–17:00, closed Tue, tel. 93-20-97) and a colorful gauntlet of Kodak moments waiting to ambush tour groups as they wander through: snake charmers, squawky dance troupes, and colorful water vendors. Before descending out of the Kasbah, don't miss the ocean viewpoint, the Mosque de la Kasbah, and Dar el-Makhzen, the fortress of the pasha of Tangier.

The Medina and Petit Socco—From the Kasbah, a maze of winding lanes and tiny alleys weave through the old-town market area. Petit Socco, a little square in the old town, is lined with tea shops. A casual first-time visitor cannot stay oriented. I just wander, knowing that if I keep going downhill I'll eventually pop out at the port; if I veer to the right while going downhill I'll come to a gate leading into the modern town, probably via the Grand Socco, the big and noisy market square. The market is filthy and reportedly dangerous after dark. Plain-clothed tourist police are stationed throughout, making sure you're safe as you wander.

Tangier American Legation Museum—Morocco was one of the first countries to recognize the United States as an independent country. The original building, given to the United States by the sultan of Morocco, became the American government's first foreign acquisition. Our embassy (or consulate) from 1821 to 1956, it's still owned by the United States—our only U.S. national historic landmark overseas. Today this nonprofit museum and research center, housed in a

19th-century mansion, is a strangely peaceful oasis within Tangier's intense old town. It offers a warm welcome, lots of interesting paintings, and a reminder of how long the United States and Morocco have had good relations (requires a guided English tour, free but donations appreciated, Mon–Fri 10:00–13:00 & 15:00–17:00, during Ramadan holiday 10:00–15:00, closed Sat–Sun, Rue America 8, tel. 93-53-17, www.maroc.net/legation, talm@wanadoo.net.ma).

Grand Socco—This big square is a transportation hub. From here, a gate leads into the old-town market; Rue de la Kasbah leads uphill along the old wall to Porte de la Kasbah (a gate leading into the Kasbah); Rue de la Liberté leads to Place de France and Boulevard Pasteur (TI and recommended hotels); and Rue de la Plage leads to the train station, the port, and the beach.

Tangier Beach—Lined by fun eateries, this fine, white-sand crescent beach stretches eastward from the port. It's packed with locals doing what people around the world do at the beach—with a few variations. You'll see lazy camels and people, young and old, covered in hot sand to combat rheumatism.

SLEEPING

These hotels are centrally located, near the TI and American Express (Boulevard Pasteur 54), and within walking distance of the market. The first two are four-star hotels. To reserve from Europe, dial 00 (Europe's international access code), 212 (Morocco's country code), 39 (Tangier's city code), then the local number. July through mid-September is high season, when rooms may be a bit more expensive and a reservation is wise. Most hotels charge an extra tax of 6 dirhams per person per night.

$$$ **Hotel Rembrandt,** with a restaurant, bar, and swimming pool surrounded by a great grassy garden, has 75 clean, comfortable rooms, some with views (Sb-418–539 dirhams, Db-506–627 dirhams, breakfast-52 dirhams, air-con, elevator, Boulevard Mohammed V 1, tel. 93-78-70 or 33-33-14, fax 93-04-43, www.hotel-rembrandt.com in French, rembrandt@menara.net.ma, SE).

$$$ **Hotel Tanjah-Flandria,** across the street with 155 rooms, is more formal, stuffy, and comfortable, but a lesser value (Sb-626 dirhams, Db-725 dirhams, 30 percent discount when you show this book, breakfast-52 dirhams, air-con, elevator, restaurant, rooftop terrace, small pool, Boulevard Mohammed V6, tel. 93-32-79, fax 93-43-47, hotelflandria@hotmail.com, SE).

$$ **Hotel Continental,** the Humphrey Bogart option, is a grand old place sprawling along the old town. It overlooks the port, with lavish, atmospheric public spaces, a chandeliered breakfast room, and 70 spacious bedrooms with rough hardwood floors. Jimmy, who's always around and runs the hotel and the Moroccan

Sleep Code

(9 dirhams = about \$1, country code: 212, area code: 39)
S = Single, **D** = Double/Twin, **T** = Triple, **Q** = Quad,
b = bathroom, **s** = shower only, **no CC** = Credit Cards not
accepted, **SE** = Speaks English, **NSE** = No English. You can
assume credit cards are accepted unless otherwise noted.

To help you easily sort through these listings, I've divided
the rooms into three categories, based on the price for a standard
double room with bath (during high season):

$$$ **Higher Priced**—Most rooms 450 dirhams or more.
$$ **Moderately Priced**—Most rooms between 400–450
                              dirhams.
$ **Lower Priced**—Most rooms 400 dirhams or less.

shop next door, says he offers everything but Viagra. When I said,
"I'm from Seattle," he said, "206." Test him—he knows your area
code (Sb-284–339 dirhams, Db-365–420 dirhams, includes tax and
breakfast, Dar Baroud 36, tel. 93-10-24, fax 93-11-43, hcontinental
@iam.net.ma, SE).

$ **Hotel Paris,** a 27-room place across from the TI, is noisy,
dingy, and friendly. Ask for a room in the back—and a mop (Sb-
271–331 dirhams, Db-318–378 dirhams, price varies according to
size, no CC, Boulevard Pasteur 42, tel. 93-18-77, the helpful and
informative manager Karim SE).

EATING

A few big, ornate places offer menus that include *harira* (Moroccan
chickpea soup), couscous (a plain rice-like side dish), *pastela* (chicken
pastry with cinnamon), dessert, and Moroccan music. Both places I
recommend below are in the medina (market). While the only locals
you'll see here are the waiters, these places offer travelers a safe, comfortable break.

Hamadi is as luxurious a restaurant as a tourist can find in
Morocco, offering a good menu at reasonable prices (Rue Kasbah 2,
tel. 93-45-14). **Mamounia Palace,** a good option right on Petit
Socco, is more in the middle of the action. A meal here will cost you
about €8 for three courses—less if you order from the menu.

TRANSPORTATION CONNECTIONS

In Tangier, all train traffic comes and goes from the new suburban
Gare Tanger Ville train station, one mile from the city center and a
short Petit Taxi ride away (10 dirhams, or \$1.10). Before you leave

the Tanger Ville station, check the information booth at the entrance for schedules for all trains in Morocco. Consider the 150-dirham discount card that gives you a reduction of 50 percent on 16 rides.

From Tangier by train to: Rabat (6/day, 4 hrs), **Casablanca** (6/day, 5 hrs), **Marrakech** (5/day, 8.5 hrs), **Fès** (6/day, 4.5 hrs), **Ceuta** and **Tétouan** (hrly buses, 1 hr).

From Fès to: Casablanca (9/day, 4.5 hrs), **Marrakech** (7/day, 7.5 hrs), **Rabat** (9/day, 3.15 hrs), **Meknès** (9/day, 45 min), **Tangier** (5/day, 5 hrs).

From Rabat to: Casablanca (2/hr, 45 min), **Fès** (9 buses/day, 3.25 hrs), **Tétouan** (2 buses/day, 4.50 hrs).

From Casablanca to: Marrakech (6/day, 5 hrs).

From Marrakech to: Meknès (7/day, 6hrs), **Ouarzazate** (4 buses/day, 4 hrs).

By Plane: Flights within Morocco are convenient and reasonable (about $100 one-way from Tangier to Casablanca).

Extended Tour of Morocco

Morocco gets much better as you go deeper into the interior. The country is incredibly rich in cultural thrills—but you'll pay a price in hassles and headaches. It's a package deal, and if adventure is your business, it's a great option.

To get a fair look at Morocco, you must get past the hustlers and con artists of the north coast (Tangier, Tétouan). It takes a minimum of four or five days to make a worthwhile visit—ideally seven or eight. Plan at least two nights in either Fès or Marrakech. A trip over the Atlas Mountains gives you an exciting look at Saharan Morocco. If you need a vacation from your vacation, check into one of the idyllic Atlantic beach resorts on the south coast. Above all, get past the northern day-trip-from-Spain, take-a-snapshot-on-a-camel fringe. Oops, that's us. Oh, well.

If you're relying on public transportation for your extended tour, sail to Tangier, blast your way through customs, listen to no hustler who tells you there's no way out until tomorrow, and hop into a Petit Taxi for the Morora train station three miles away (24 dirhams, or $2.70). From there, set your sights on Rabat, a dignified, European-type town with fewer hustlers, and make it your get-acquainted stop in Morocco. Trains go farther south from Rabat.

If you're driving a car, sail from Algeciras to Ceuta, a Spanish possession. Crossing the border is a bit unnerving, since you'll be forced to jump through several bureaucratic hoops. You'll go through customs at both borders, buy Moroccan insurance for your car (cheap and easy), and feel at the mercy of a bristly bunch of shady-looking people you'd rather not be at the mercy of. Don't pay anyone on the Spanish side. Consider tipping a guy on the Moroccan side if you feel he'll shepherd you through. Relax and let him grease those customs wheels. He's worth it. As soon as possible, hit the road and drive to Chefchaouen, the best first stop for those with their own wheels.

SIGHTS

Moroccan Towns

▲▲**Chefchaouen**—Just two hours by bus or car from Tétouan, this is the first pleasant town beyond the Tijuana-type north coast. Monday and Thursday are colorful market days. Stay in the classy old Hotel Chaouen on Place el-Makhzen. This former Spanish parador (inn) faces the old town and offers fine meals and a refuge from hustlers. Wander deep into the whitewashed old town from here.

▲▲**Rabat**—Morocco's capital and most European city, Rabat is the most comfortable and least stressful place to start your North African trip. You'll find a colorful market (in the old neighboring town of Salé), bits of Islamic architecture (Mausoleum of Mohammed V), the king's palace, mellow hustlers, and fine hotels.

▲▲▲**Fès**—More than just a funny hat that tipsy Shriners wear, Fès is Morocco's religious and artistic center, bustling with craftsmen, pilgrims, shoppers, and shops. Like most large Moroccan cities, it has a distinct new town from the French colonial period, as well as an exotic (and stressful) old, walled Arabic town (the medina), where you'll find the market.

For twelve centuries, traders have gathered in Fès, founded on a river at the crossroads of two trade routes. Soon there was an irrigation system, a university, resident craftsmen from Spain, and a diverse population of Muslims, Christians, and Jews. When France claimed Morocco in 1912, they made their capital in Rabat, and Fès fizzled. But the Fès marketplace is still Morocco's best.

▲▲▲**Marrakech**—Morocco's gateway to the south, this market city is a constant folk festival bustling with djellaba-clad Berber tribespeople and a colorful center where the desert, mountain, and coastal regions merge. The new city has the train station, and the main boulevard (Mohammed V) is lined with banks, airline offices, a post office, a tourist office, and comfortable hotels. The old city features the mazelike market and the huge Djemaa el-Fna, a square seething with people—a 43-ring Moroccan circus.

▲▲▲**Over the Atlas Mountains**—Extend your Moroccan trip several days by heading south over the Atlas Mountains. Take a bus from Marrakech to Ouarzazate (short stop) and then to Tinerhir (great oasis town, comfy hotel, overnight stop). The next day go to Er Rachidia and take the overnight bus to Fès.

By car, drive from Fès south, staying in the small mountain town of Ifrane, and then continue deep into the desert country past Er Rachidia and on to Rissani (market days: Sun, Tue, and Thu). Explore nearby mud-brick towns still living in the Middle Ages. Hire a guide to drive you past where the road stops, and head cross-country to an oasis village (Merzouga) where you can climb a sand dune and watch the sun rise over the vastness of Africa. Only a sea of sand separates you from Timbuktu.

APPENDIX

SPANISH HISTORY

In 1492, Columbus sailed the ocean blue—and Spain became a nation, too. Iberia's sunny weather, fertile soil, and Mediterranean ports made it a popular place to call home. The original "Iberians" were a Celtic people, who crossed the Pyrenees around 800 B.C. The Phoenicians established the city of Cádiz around 1100 B.C., and Carthaginians settled around 250 B.C.

Romans (c. 200 B.C.–A.D. 400)

The future Roman Emperor Augustus finally quelled the last Iberian resistance (19 B.C.), making the province of "Hispania" an agricultural breadbasket (olives, wine) to feed the vast Roman empire. The Romans brought the Latin language, a connection to the wider world, and (in the 4th century), Christianity. When the empire crumbled around A.D. 400, Spain made a peaceful transition, ruled by Christian Visigoths from Germany who had strong Roman ties. Roman influence remained for centuries after, in the Latin-based Spanish language, irrigation, and building materials and techniques. The Romans' large farming estates would change hands over the years, passing from Roman senators to Visigoth kings to Islamic caliphs to Christian nobles. And, of course, the Romans left wine.

Moors (711–1492)

In A.D. 711, 12,000 zealous members of the world's newest religion—Islam—landed on the Rock of Gibraltar and, in three short years, conquered the Iberian Peninsula. These North African Muslims—generically called "Moors"—dominated Spain for the next 700 years. Though powerful, they were surprisingly tolerant of the people they ruled, allowing native Jews and Christians to practice

Spaniards Throughout History

Hadrian (A.D. 76–138)—Roman Emperor, one of three born in Latin-speaking "Hispania" (along with Trajan, reigned 98–117, and Marcus Aurelius, reigned 161–180), who ruled Rome at its peak of power.

El Cid (1040?–1099)—A real soldier-for-hire who inspired fictional stories and Spain's oldest poem, El Cid ("the lord") fought for both Christians and Muslims during the wars of the Reconquista. He's best known for liberating Valencia from the Moors.

St. Teresa of Ávila (1515–1582)—Mystic nun whose holiness and writings led to convent reform and to her sainthood. Religiously-intense Spain produced other saints, too, including **Dominic** (1170–1221), who founded an order of wandering monks, and **Ignatius of Loyola (1491–1556),** who founded the Jesuits, an order of "intellectual warriors."

Ferdinand (1452–1516) and Isabel (1451–1504)—Their marriage united most of Spain, ushering in its Golden Age. The "Catholic Monarchs" drove out Moors and Jews and financed Columbus' lucrative voyages to the New World.

Hernán Cortés (1485–1547)—Conquered Mexico in 1521. Along with Vasco Núñez de Balboa, who discovered the Pacific, and Francisco Pizarro, who conquered Peru, Cortés and the Spaniards explored and exploited the New World.

El Greco (1541–1614)—The artist is known for his ethereal paintings of "flickering" saints.

Diego Velázquez (1599–1660)—Velázquez painted camera-eye realistic portraits of the royal court.

their faiths, so long as the infidels paid extra taxes.

The Moors were themselves an ethnically diverse culture, including both crude Berber tribesmen from Morocco and sophisticated rulers from old Arab families. From their capital in Córdoba, various rulers of the united Islamic state of "Al-Andalus" pledged allegiance to foreign caliphs in Syria, Baghdad, or Morocco.

With cultural ties that stretched from Spain to Africa to Arabia to Persia and beyond, the Moorish culture in Spain (especially around A.D. 800–1000) was perhaps Europe's most advanced, a beacon of learning in Europe's so-called "Dark" Ages. Mathematics, astronomy, literature and architecture flourished. Even wine-making was encouraged, though for religious reasons Muslims weren't allowed to drink alcohol. The Moorish legacy lives on today in architecture (horseshoe arches, ceramic tiles, fountains and gardens), language (e.g., Spanish el comes from Arabic al)…and wine.

Reconquista (711–1492)

The Moors ruled for more than 700 years, but throughout that time they were a minority ruling a largely Christian populace. Pockets of

Francisco de Goya (1746–1828)—The artist is best known for his expressionistic nightmares.

Francisco Franco (1892–1975)—General who led the military uprising against the elected Republic, sparking Spain's Civil War (1936–39). After victory, he ruled Spain for more than three decades as an absolute dictator, maintaining its Catholic, aristocratic heritage while slowly modernizing the country.

Salvador Dalí (1904–1989)—A flamboyant, waxed-mustachioed Surrealist painter, Dalí and a fellow Spaniard, filmmaker Luis Buñuel, made one of the first art films, *Andalusian Dog.*

Pablo Picasso (1881–1973)—Though he lived most of his adult life in France, the 20th century's greatest artist explored Spanish themes, particularly in his famous work *Guernica,* which depicts Civil War destruction.

Placido Domingo (b. 1941)—The son of zarzuela singers in Madrid (but raised in Mexico), this operatic tenor is just one of many classical musicians from Spain, including fellow "Three Tenors" singer José Carreras, composer Manuel de Falla, cellist Pablo Casals, and guitarist Andres Segovia.

Spaniards in the News Today—King Juan Carlos and his Greek-born wife, Queen Sofía, their daughter Cristina, socialist prime minister José Luis Rodríguez Zapatero, bicyclist Miguel Indurain, soccer star Raúl, golfers José María Olazábal, tennis player Arantxa Sanchez-Vicario, and pop singer Julio Iglesias (father of pop singer Enrique Iglesias).

independent Christians remained, particularly in the mountains in the peninsula's north. Local Christian kings fought against the Moors whenever they could, whittling away at the Muslim empire, "re-conquering" more and more land in what's known as the "Reconquista." The last Moorish stronghold, Granada, fell to the Christians in 1492.

The slow, piecemeal process of the Reconquista split the peninsula into many independent kingdoms and dukedoms, some Christian, some Moorish. The Reconquista picked up steam after A.D. 1000, when Al-Andalus splintered into smaller regional states—Granada, Sevilla, Valencia—ruled by local caliphs. Toledo fell to the Christians in 1085. By 1200 the Christian state of Portugal had the borders it does today, making it the oldest unchanged state in Europe. The rest of the peninsula was a battleground, a loosely-knit collection of small kingdoms, some Christian, some Muslim. Heavy stone "castles" dotted the interior region of "Castile," as lords and barons duked it out. Along the Mediterranean coast (from the Pyrenees to Barcelona to Valencia), three Christian states united into a sea-trading power, the kingdom of Aragon.

In 1469, Isabel of Castile married Ferdinand II of Aragon, uniting the peninsula's two largest kingdoms, and instantly making united Spain a European power. In 1492, while Columbus explored the seas under Ferdinand and Isabel's flag, the "Catholic Monarchs" drove the Moors out of Granada and expelled the country's Jews, creating a unified, Christian, sea-trading, militaristic nation-state, fueled by the religious zeal of the Reconquista.

The Golden Age (1500–1600)

Spain's bold sea explorers changed the economics of Europe, opening up a New World of riches and colonies. The Spanish flag soon flew over most of South and Central America. Gold, silver, and agricultural products (grown on large estates with cheap labor) poured into Spain. In return, the stoked Spaniards exported Christianity, converting the American natives with kind Jesuit priests and cruel conquistadors.

Ferdinand and Isabel's daughter (Juana the Mad) wed a German prince (Philip the Fair), and their son inherited both crowns. Charles V (1500–1558, called Carlos I in Spain) was the most powerful man in the world, ruling an empire that stretched from Holland to Sicily, from Bohemia to Bolivia. The aristocracy and the clergy were swimming in money. Art and courtly life flourished during this Golden Age, with Spain hosting the painter El Greco and the writer Miguel de Cervantes.

But Charles V's Holy Roman Empire was torn by different languages and ethnic groups, and by protesting Protestants. He spent much of the nation's energies at war with Protestants, encroaching Muslim Turks, and Europe's rising powers. When an exhausted Charles announced his abdication (1555) and retired to a monastery, his sprawling Empire was divvied up among family members, with Spain and its possessions going to his son, Philip II (1527–1598).

Philip conquered Portugal (1580, his only winning war), moved Spain's capital to Madrid, built El Escorial, and continued fighting losing battles across Europe (the Netherlands, France) that drained the treasury of its New World gold. In the summer of 1588, Spain's seemingly unbeatable royal fleet of 125 ships—the Invincible Armada—sailed off to conquer England, only to be unexpectedly routed in battle by bad weather and Sir Francis Drake's cunning. Just like that, Britannia ruled the waves, and Spain spiraled downward, becoming a debt-ridden, overextended, flabby nation.

Slow Decline (1600–1900)

The fast money from the colonies kept Spain from seeing the dangers at home. They stopped growing their own wheat and neglected their fields. Great Britain and the Netherlands were the rising sea-trading powers in the new global economy. During the centuries when science and technology developed as never before in other

European countries, Spain was preoccupied by its failed colonial politics. (Still, Spain in the 1600s produced the remarkable painter Diego Velázquez.)

By 1700, once-mighty Spain lay helpless while rising powers France, England, and Austria fought over the right to pick Spain's next king in the War of the Spanish Succession (1701–1714), which was fought partly on Spanish soil (e.g., Britain holding out against the French in the Siege of Gibraltar). The rightful next-in-line was Louis XIV's son, who was set to inherit both France and Spain. The rest of Europe didn't want powerful France to become even more stronger. The war ended in compromise, preventing Louis XIV from controlling both countries, but allowing his grandson to become King of Spain (Spain lost several possessions). The French-born, French-speaking Bourbon King Philip V (1683–1746) ruled Spain for 40 years. He and his heirs made themselves at home building the Versailles-like Royal Palace in Madrid and La Granja near Segovia.

The French Revolution spilled over into Spain, bringing French rule under Napoleon. In 1808, the Spaniards rose up (chronicled by Goya's paintings of the 2nd and 3rd of May, 1808), sparking the Peninsular War—called the War of Independence by Spaniards—that finally won Spain's independence from French rule.

Nineteenth-century Spain was a backward nation, with internal wars over which noble family should rule (the Carlist Wars), liberal revolutions put down brutally, and political assassinations. Spain gradually lost its global possessions to other European powers and to South American revolutionaries. Spain hit rock bottom in 1898, when the upstart United States picked a fight and thrashed them in the Spanish-American War, taking away Spain's last major possessions: Cuba, Puerto Rico, and the Philippines.

The 20th Century

A drained and disillusioned Spain was ill-prepared for modern technology and democratic government.

The old ruling class (the monarchy, church, and landowners) fought new economic powers (cities, businessmen, labor unions) in a series of coups, strikes, and sham elections. In the '20s, a military dictatorship under Miguel Primo de Rivera kept the old guard in power. In 1930, he was ousted and an open election brought a modern democratic Republic to power. But the right-wing regrouped under the Falange (fascist) party, fomenting unrest and sparking a military coup against the Republic in 1936, led by General Francisco Franco (1892–1975).

For three years (1936–1939), Spain fought a bloody Civil War between Franco's Nationalists (also called Falangists) and the Republic (also called Loyalists). Some 600,000 Spaniards died (due to all causes), and Franco won. (For more on the Civil War, see Valley of the Fallen, page 206.) For the next four decades, Spain was ruled by Franco, an authoritarian, church-blessed dictator who tried to modernize the backward country while shielding it from corrupting modern influences. Spain was neutral in World War II, and the country spent much of the postwar era as a world apart. (On my first visit to Spain in 1973, I came face-to-face with fellow teenagers—me in backpack and shorts, they in military uniforms, brandishing automatic weapons.)

Before Franco died, he handpicked his protégé, King Juan Carlos I, to succeed him. But to everyone's surprise, the young, conservative, mild-mannered king stepped aside, settled for a figurehead title, and guided the country quickly and peacefully toward democratic elections (1977).

Spain had a lot of catching up to do. Culturally, the once-conservative nation exploded and embraced new ideas, even plunging to wild extremes. In the 1980s, Spain flowered under the left-leaning Prime Minister Felipe González. Spain showed the world its new modern face in 1992, hosting both a World Exhibition at Sevilla and the Summer Olympics at Barcelona.

Spain Today

From 1996 to 2004, Spain was led by the centrist Prime Minister José María Aznar. He adopted moderate policies to minimize the stress on the country's young democracy, fighting problems such as unemployment and foreign debt with reasonable success. However, his support of George W. Bush's pre-emptive war in Iraq was extremely unpopular with the vast majority of Spaniards. In spring of 2004, the retiring Aznar supported a similarly centrist successor, Mariano Rajoy, who seemed poised to win the election. But during the morning rush hour on March 11, 2004, three Madrid train stations were bombed, killing 200 people. The terrorist group claiming responsibility denounced Spain's Iraq policy, and three days later, Aznar's party lost the election. The new prime minister, Socialist José Luis Rodríguez Zapatero, quickly began pulling Spain's troops out of Iraq, as well as enacting sweeping social changes in Spain.

Its political squabbles and heightened security aside, Spain is striding into the future. Though not considered wealthy or powerful, Spain is prospering, thanks in part to you and tourism.

SPANISH ART

El Greco (1541–1614) exemplifies the spiritual fervor of much Spanish art. The drama, the surreal colors, and the intentionally unnatural distortion have the intensity of a religious vision. (For more on El Greco, see Toledo chapter, page 232.)

Diego Velázquez (1599–1660) went to the opposite extreme. His masterful court portraits are studies in camera-eye realism and

Francisco de Goya
(1746–1828)

Goya's paintings evolved as his life did, showing different facets of this rough-cut man. As a struggling young painter, Goya captured the decadence of the 1700s and the naïveté of aristocrats at play while revolution simmered across the border in France.

Promoted to official court painter, Goya dutifully portrayed the king and queen in all their royal finery. But, as a budding political liberal, he subtly ridiculed the Spanish court for their arrogance and google-eyed stupidity.

In his personal life, Goya was a nonconformist. His *Nude Maja*—one of the first Spanish nudes in a hundred years—got Goya hauled before the Inquisition. The work was labeled obscene and locked away from the public eye until the 20th century. In 1808, the Spanish people rose up to overthrow French invaders. Goya, caught up in the action, was greatly disillusioned by all the senseless violence, seeing that common people were always the victims of war. His paintings threw a harsh light on the events for the whole world to see, becoming perhaps the first painter with a social conscience.

In his seventies, Goya—deaf, widowed, and bitter—retired from public life to a home outside Madrid. He painted the walls with his own unique—and dark—view of life...the Black Paintings. Black in color and in mood, with thick, smeared paint and bizarre images, these nightmarish works seem to foreshadow 20th-century Surrealism and Expressionism—works by a man unafraid of life's darker side.

cool detachment from his subjects. Velázquez was unmatched in using a few strokes of paint to suggest details.

Francisco de Goya (1746–1828) lacked Velázquez's detachment. He let his liberal tendencies shine through in unflattering portraits of royalty and in emotional scenes of abuse of power. He unleashed his inner passions in the eerie, nightmarish canvases of his last, "dark" stage. (For more on Goya, see sidebar above.)

Bartolomé Murillo (1617–1682) painted a dreamy world of religious visions. His pastel, soft-focus works of cute baby Jesuses and radiant Virgin Marys helped make Catholic doctrine palatable to the common folk at a time when many were defecting to Protestantism. (For more on Murillo, see page 296.)

You'll also find plenty of foreign art in Spain's museums. During its Golden Age, Spain's wealthy aristocrats bought wagonloads of the most popular art of the time—Italian Renaissance and Baroque works by Titian, Tintoretto, and others. They also loaded up on paintings by Peter Paul Rubens, Hieronymus Bosch, and Pieter Brueghel from the Low Countries, which were under Spanish rule.

In the 20th century, **Pablo Picasso** (see his inspirational antiwar *Guernica* mural in Madrid), **Joan Miró**, and surrealist **Salvador Dalí** made their marks. Great museums featuring all three are in or near Barcelona.

ARCHITECTURE

Spanish History Set in Stone

The two most fertile periods of architectural innovation in Spain were during the Moorish occupation and in the Golden Age. Otherwise, Spanish architects have marched obediently behind the rest of Europe.

Spain's history is dominated by 700 years of pushing the Muslim Moors back into Africa (711–1492). Throughout Spain, it seems every old church was built upon a mosque (Sevilla's immense cathedral, for one). Granada's Alhambra is the best example of the secular Moorish style. It's an Arabian Nights fairy-tale: finely etched domes, lacey arcades, keyhole arches, and lush gardens. At its heart lies an elegantly proportioned courtyard, where the designers created an ingenious microclimate: water, plants, pottery, thick walls, and darkness…all to be cool. The stuccoed walls are ornamented with a stylized Arabic script, creating a visual chant of Koranic verses.

As the Christians slowly reconquered Iberian turf, they turned their fervor into stone, building churches in the lighter, heaven-reaching, stained-glass Gothic style (Toledo and Sevilla). Gothic was an import from France, trickling into conservative Spain long after it had swept through Europe.

As Christians moved in, many Muslim artists and architects stayed, giving the new society the Mudejar style. (Mudejar means, literally, "those who stayed.") In Sevilla's Alcázar, the Arabic script on the walls relates not the Koran but New Testament verses and Christian propaganda, such as "Dedicated to the magnificent Sultan, King Pedro—thanks to God!" (The style of Christians living under Moorish rule is called Mozarabic.)

The money reaped and raped from Spain's colonies in the Golden Age spurred new construction. Churches and palaces borrowed from the Italian Renaissance and the more elaborate Baroque. Ornamentation reached unprecedented heights in Spain, culminating in the Plateresque style of stonework, so called because it resembles intricate silver *(plata)* filigree work (see, for example, the facade of the University of Salamanca).

The 1500s was also the era of religious wars. The monastery/palace of El Escorial, built in sober geometric style, symbolizes the austerity of a newly-reformed Catholic church ready to strike back. King Philip II ruled his empire and directed the Inquisition from here, surrounded by plain white walls, well-scrubbed floors and simple furnishings. Built at a time when Catholic Spain felt threatened by

Protestant heretics, its construction dominated the Spanish economy for a generation (1563–1584). Because of this bully in the national budget, Spain has almost nothing else to show from this most powerful period of her history.

For the next three centuries (1600–1900), backward-looking Spain recycled old art styles.

Much of Spain's 20th-century architecture feels like a rehash of its past, but Barcelona is a lively exception. As Europe leapt from the 19th century into the 20th, it celebrated a rising standard of living and nearly a century without a major war. Art Nouveau architects forced hard steel and concrete into softer organic shapes. Barcelona's answer to Art Nouveau was Modernisme, and its genius was Antoni Gaudí, with his asymmetrical, "cake-in-the-rain" buildings like Casa Milà and Sagrada Família.

BULLFIGHTING

A Legitimate Slice of Spain, or a Cruel Spectacle?

The Spanish bullfight is as much a ritual as it is a sport. Not to acknowledge the importance of the bullfight is to censor a venerable part of Spanish culture. But it also makes a spectacle out of the cruel killing of an animal. Should tourists boycott bullfights? I don't know.

Today bullfighting is less popular among locals. If this trend continues, bullfighting may survive more and more as a tourist event. When the day comes that bullfighting is kept alive by our tourist dollars rather than by the local culture, then I'll agree with those who say bullfighting is immoral and that tourists shouldn't encourage it by buying tickets. Consider the morality of supporting this gruesome aspect of Spanish culture before buying a ticket. If you do decide to attend a bullfight, here is what you'll see.

While no two bullfights are the same, they unfold along a strict pattern. The ceremony begins punctually with a parade of participants across the ring. Then the trumpet sounds, the "Gate of Fear" opens, and the leading player—el toro—thunders in. A ton of angry animal is an awesome sight, even from the cheap seats (with the sun in your eyes).

The fight is divided into three acts. Act I is designed to size up the bull and wear him down. With help from his assistants, the matador (literally "killer") attracts the bull with the shake of the cape, then directs the animal past his body, as close as his bravery allows. The bull sees only things in motion and (some think) in red. After a few passes the *picadores* enter, mounted on horseback, to spear the swollen lump of muscle at the back of the bull's neck. This tests the bull, while the matador watches studiously. It also lowers the bull's head and weakens the thrust of his horns. (Until 1927, horses had no protective pads and were often killed.)

In Act II, the matador's assistants *(banderilleros)* continue to enrage and weaken the bull. The *banderilleros* charge the charging bull and—leaping acrobatically across its path—plunge brightly-colored barbed sticks into the bull's vital neck muscle.

After a short intermission, during which the matador may, according to tradition, ask permission to kill the bull and dedicate the kill to someone in the crowd, the final and lethal Act III begins.

The matador tries to dominate and tire the bull with hypnotic cape work. A good pass is when the matador stands completely still while the bull charges past. Then the matador thrusts a sword between the animal's shoulder blades for the kill. A quick kill is not always easy, and the matador may have to make several bloody thrusts before the sword stays in and the bull finally dies. Mules drag the dead bull out, and his meat is in the market *mañana* (barring "mad cow" concerns—and if ever there were a mad cow...). *Rabo del toro* (bull-tail stew) is a delicacy.

Throughout the fight, the crowd shows its approval or impatience. Shouts of *"¡Olé!"* or *"¡Torero!"* mean they like what they see. Whistling or rhythmic hand-clapping greets cowardice and incompetence.

You're not likely to see much human blood spilled. In 200 years of bullfighting in Sevilla, only 30 fighters have died (and only three were actually matadors). If a bull does kill a fighter, the next matador comes in to kill him. Historically, even the bull's mother is killed, since the evil qualities are assumed to have come from the mother.

After an exceptional fight, the crowd may wave white handkerchiefs to ask that the matador be awarded the bull's ear or tail. A brave bull, though dead, gets a victory lap from the mule team on his way to the slaughterhouse. Then the trumpet sounds, and a new bull charges in to face a fresh matador.

Fights are held on most Sundays, Easter through October (at 18:30 or 19:30). Serious fights with adult matadors are called *corrida de toros*. These are often sold out in advance. Summer fights are often *novillada*, with teenage novices doing the killing. *Corrida de toros* seats range from €20 for high seats facing the sun to €100 for the first three rows in the shade under the royal box. *Novillada* seats are half that, and generally easy to get at the arena a few minutes before showtime. Many Spanish women consider bullfighting sexy. They swoon at the dashing matadors who are sure to wear tight pants (with their *partas nobles*—noble parts—in view, generally organized to one side, farthest from the bull).

A typical bullfight lasts about two hours and consists of six separate fights—three matadors (each with his own team of *picadors* and *banderilleros*) fighting two bulls each. For a closer look at bullfighting by an American aficionado, read Ernest Hemingway's classic, *Death in the Afternoon*.

TRAVELER'S TOOL KIT

Festivals and Public Holidays

Spain erupts with fiestas and celebrations throughout the year. Semana Santa (Holy Week) fills the week before Easter with processions and festivities all over Iberia, but especially in Sevilla. To run with the bulls, be in Pamplona—with medical insurance—the second week in July.

This is a partial list of holidays and festivals. For more information, contact the Spanish National Tourist Office (listed in this book's introduction) and check these Web sites: www.whatsonwhen .com and www.festivals.com.

Jan 1	New Year's Day
Jan 6	Epiphany
Early Feb	La Candelaria (religious festival), Madrid
Feb 28	Day of Andalucía (some closures), Andalucía
Holy Week	Week before Easter (March 20–27 in 2005)
Easter	March 27 in 2005
Early April	April Fair, Sevilla (April 12–17 in 2005)
May 1	Labor Day (closures)
May 2	Day of Autonomous Community, Madrid
Mid-May	Feria del Caballo (horse pageantry), Jerez
May 7–15	San Isidro (religious festival), Madrid
Mid-June	Corpus Christi
Late June	La Patum (Moorish battles), Barcelona
June 24	St. John the Baptist's Day
Late June– Early July	International Festival of Music and Dance, Granada
Mid-July	Running of the Bulls, Pamplona
Aug	Gràcia Festival, Barcelona
Mid-Aug	Verbena de la Paloma (folk festival), Madrid
Aug 15	Assumption (religious festival)
Mid-Sept– Mid-Oct	Autumn Festival (flamenco, bullfights), Jerez
Late Sept	La Mercé (parade), Barcelona
Oct 12	Spanish National Day
Nov 1	All Saints' Day
Nov 9	Virgen de la Almudena, Madrid
Mid-Nov	International Jazz Festival, Madrid
Dec 6	Constitution Day
Dec 8	Feast of the Immaculate Conception
Dec 13	Feast of Santa Lucía
Dec 25	Christmas
Dec 31	New Year's Eve

2005

JANUARY
S	M	T	W	T	F	S
						1
2	3	4	5	6	7	8
9	10	11	12	13	14	15
16	17	18	19	20	21	22
23/30	24/31	25	26	27	28	29

FEBRUARY
S	M	T	W	T	F	S
		1	2	3	4	5
6	7	8	9	10	11	12
13	14	15	16	17	18	19
20	21	22	23	24	25	26
27	28					

MARCH
S	M	T	W	T	F	S
		1	2	3	4	5
6	7	8	9	10	11	12
13	14	15	16	17	18	19
20	21	22	23	24	25	26
27	28	29	30	31		

APRIL
S	M	T	W	T	F	S
					1	2
3	4	5	6	7	8	9
10	11	12	13	14	15	16
17	18	19	20	21	22	23
24	25	26	27	28	29	30

MAY
S	M	T	W	T	F	S
1	2	3	4	5	6	7
8	9	10	11	12	13	14
15	16	17	18	19	20	21
22	23	24	25	26	27	28
29	30	31				

JUNE
S	M	T	W	T	F	S
			1	2	3	4
5	6	7	8	9	10	11
12	13	14	15	16	17	18
19	20	21	22	23	24	25
26	27	28	29	30		

JULY
S	M	T	W	T	F	S
					1	2
3	4	5	6	7	8	9
10	11	12	13	14	15	16
17	18	19	20	21	22	23
24/31	25	26	27	28	29	30

AUGUST
S	M	T	W	T	F	S
	1	2	3	4	5	6
7	8	9	10	11	12	13
14	15	16	17	18	19	20
21	22	23	24	25	26	27
28	29	30	31			

SEPTEMBER
S	M	T	W	T	F	S
				1	2	3
4	5	6	7	8	9	10
11	12	13	14	15	16	17
18	19	20	21	22	23	24
25	26	27	28	29	30	

OCTOBER
S	M	T	W	T	F	S
						1
2	3	4	5	6	7	8
9	10	11	12	13	14	15
16	17	18	19	20	21	22
23/30	24/31	25	26	27	28	29

NOVEMBER
S	M	T	W	T	F	S
		1	2	3	4	5
6	7	8	9	10	11	12
13	14	15	16	17	18	19
20	21	22	23	24	25	26
27	28	29	30			

DECEMBER
S	M	T	W	T	F	S
				1	2	3
4	5	6	7	8	9	10
11	12	13	14	15	16	17
18	19	20	21	22	23	24
25	26	27	28	29	30	31

Let's Talk Telephones

This is a primer on telephoning in Europe. For specifics on Spain, see "Telephones" in the introduction.

Dialing Direct

Making Calls within a European Country: What you dial depends on the phone system of the country you're in. About half of all European countries use area codes; the other half use a direct-dial system without area codes.

If you're calling within a country that uses a direct-dial system (Spain, Portugal, Belgium, the Czech Republic, France, Italy, Switzerland, Norway, and Denmark), you dial the same number whether you're calling within the city or across the country.

In countries that use area codes (such as Austria, Britain, Finland, Germany, Ireland, the Netherlands, and Sweden), you dial the local number when calling within a city, and you add the area code if calling long-distance within the country. Example: The phone number of a hotel in Munich is 089-264-349. To call it in Munich, dial 264-349; to call it from Frankfurt, dial 089-264-349.

Making International Calls: You always start with the international access code (011 if you're calling from the United States or Canada, 00 from Europe), then dial the country code of the country you're calling (see list below).

What you dial next depends on the particular phone system of the country you're calling. If the country uses area codes, you drop the initial zero of the area code, then dial the rest of the area code and the local number. Example: To call the Munich hotel from Spain, dial 00, 49 (Germany's country code), then 89-264-349.

Countries that use direct-dial systems (no area codes) differ in how they're accessed internationally by phone. For instance, if you're making an international call to Spain, Portugal, Italy, the Czech Republic, Norway, or Denmark, you simply dial the international access code, country code, and phone number. Example: The phone number of a hotel in Madrid is 915-212-900. To call it from Portugal, dial 00, 34 (Spain's country code), then 915-212-900. But if you're calling Belgium, France, or Switzerland, you drop the initial zero of the phone number. Example: The phone number of a Paris hotel is 01 47 05 49 15. To call it from Madrid, dial 00, 33 (France's country code), then 1 47 05 49 15 (the phone number without the initial zero).

Country Codes

After you dial the international access code (00 if you're calling from Europe, 011 if you're calling from America or Canada), dial the code of the country you're calling.

Austria—43	Ireland—353
Belgium—32	Italy—39
Britain—44	Morocco—212
Canada—1	Netherlands—31
Croatia—385	Norway—47
Czech Rep—420	Poland—48
Denmark—45	Portugal—351
Estonia—372	Slovenia—386
Finland—358	Spain—34
France—33	Sweden—46
Germany—49	Switzerland—41
Gibraltar—350	Turkey—90
Greece—30	U.S.A.—1

European Calling Chart

Just smile and dial, using this key:
AC = Area Code, LN = Local Number.

European Country	Calling long distance within ...	Calling from the U.S.A./ Canada to ...	Calling from a European country to ...
Austria	AC + LN	011 + 43 + AC (without the initial zero) + LN	00 + 43 + AC (without the initial zero) + LN
Belgium	LN	011 + 32 + LN (without initial zero)	00 + 32 + LN (without initial zero)
Britain	AC + LN	011 + 44 + AC (without initial zero) + LN	00 + 44 + AC (without initial zero) + LN
Czech Republic	LN	011 + 420 + LN	00 + 420 + LN
Denmark	LN	011 + 45 + LN	00 + 45 + LN
Estonia	LN	011 + 372 + LN	00 + 372 + LN
Finland	AC + LN	011 + 358 + AC (without initial zero) + LN	00 + 358 + AC (without initial zero) + LN
France	LN	011 + 33 + LN (without initial zero)	00 + 33 + LN (without initial zero)
Germany	AC + LN	011 + 49 + AC (without initial zero) + LN	00 + 49 + AC (without initial zero) + LN
Gibraltar	LN	011 + 350 + LN	00 + 350 + LN From Spain: 9567 + LN
Greece	LN	011 + 30 + LN	00 + 30 + LN

European Country	Calling long distance within...	Calling from the U.S.A./ Canada to...	Calling from a European country to...
Ireland	AC + LN	011 + 353 + AC (without initial zero) + LN	00 + 353 + AC (without initial zero) + LN
Italy	LN	011 + 39 + LN	00 + 39 + LN
Morocco	LN	011 + 212 + LN (without initial zero)	00 + 212 + LN (without initial zero)
Netherlands	AC + LN	011 + 31 + AC (without initial zero) + LN	00 + 31 + AC (without initial zero) + LN
Norway	LN	011 + 47 + LN	00 + 47 + LN
Portugal	LN	011 + 351 + LN	00 + 351 + LN
Spain	LN	011 + 34 + LN	00 + 34 + LN
Sweden	AC + LN	011 + 46 + AC (without initial zero) + LN	00 + 46 + AC (without initial zero) + LN
Switzerland	LN	011 + 41 + LN (without initial zero)	00 + 41 + LN (without initial zero)
Turkey	AC (if no initial zero is included, add one) + LN	011 + 90 + AC (without initial zero) + LN	00 + 90 + AC (without initial zero) + LN

- The instructions above apply whether you're calling a fixed phone or cell phone.

- The international access codes (the first numbers you dial when making an international call) are 011 if you're calling from the U.S.A./Canada, or 00 if you're calling from anywhere in Europe.

- To call the U.S.A. or Canada from Europe, dial 00, then 1 (the country code for the U.S.A. and Canada), then the area code and number. In short, 00 + 1 + AC + LN = Hi, Mom!

Directory Assistance

In Spain, dial 1003 for local numbers and 025 for international numbers (expensive). (Note: In Spain, a 608 or 609 area code indicates a mobile phone.)

U.S. Embassies and Consulates

Madrid, Spain: Serrano 75, tel. 915-872-240, or for emergencies after business hours, 915-872-200, www.embusa.es/cons/services.html
Gibraltar: Call embassy in Madrid (above).
Casablanca, Morocco: 8 Boulevard Moulay Youssef, tel. 22/26-45-50, www.usembassy.ma

Numbers and Stumblers

- Europeans write a few of their numbers differently than we do. 1 = 1 , 4 = 4 , 7 = 7 . Learn the difference, or miss your train.
- In Europe, dates appear as day/month/year, so Christmas is 25/12/05.
- Commas are decimal points and decimals commas. A dollar and a half is 1,50, and there are 5.280 feet in a mile.
- When pointing, use your whole hand, palm down.
- When counting with fingers, start with your thumb. If you hold up your first finger to request one item, you'll probably get two.
- What Americans call the second floor of a building is the first floor in Europe.
- Europeans keep the left "lane" open for passing on escalators and moving sidewalks. Keep to the right.

Metric Conversion (approximate)

1 inch = 25 millimeters	32 degrees F = 0 degrees C
1 foot = 0.3 meter	82 degrees F = about 28 degrees C
1 yard = 0.9 meter	1 ounce = 28 grams
1 mile = 1.6 kilometers	1 kilogram = 2.2 pounds
1 centimeter = 0.4 inch	1 quart = 0.95 liter
1 meter = 39.4 inches	1 square yard = 0.8 square meter
1 kilometer = 0.62 mile	1 acre = 0.4 hectare

Climate Chart

First line, average daily low; second line, average daily high; third line, days of no rain.

J	F	M	A	M	J	J	A	S	O	N	D

SPAIN
Madrid

J	F	M	A	M	J	J	A	S	O	N	D
35°	36°	41°	45°	50°	58°	63°	63°	57°	49°	42°	36°
47°	52°	59°	65°	70°	80°	87°	85°	77°	65°	55°	48°
23	21	21	21	21	25	29	28	24	23	21	21

	J	F	M	A	M	J	J	A	S	O	N	D

Barcelona

43° 45° 48° 52° 57° 65° 69° 69° 66° 58° 51° 46°
55° 57° 60° 65° 71° 78° 82° 82° 77° 69° 62° 56°
26 23 23 21 23 24 27 25 23 22 24 25

Almería (Costa del Sol)

46° 47° 51° 55° 59° 65° 70° 71° 68° 60° 54° 49°
60° 61° 64° 68° 72° 78° 83° 84° 81° 73° 67° 62°
25 24 26 25 28 29 31 30 27 26 26 26

MOROCCO

Marrakech

40° 43° 48° 52° 57° 62° 67° 68° 63° 57° 49° 42°
65° 68° 74° 79° 84° 92° 101°100°92° 83° 73° 66°
24 23 25 24 29 29 30 30 27 27 27 24

Converting Temperatures: Fahrenheit and Celsius

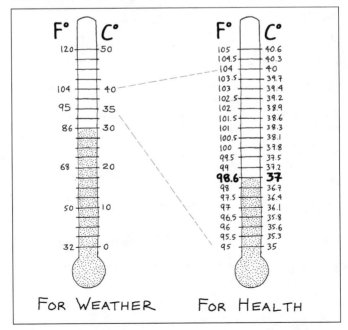

FOR WEATHER   FOR HEALTH

Making Your Hotel Reservation

Most hotel managers know basic "hotel English." Faxing or e-mailing are the preferred methods for reserving a room. They're more accurate than telephoning and much faster than writing a letter. Use this handy form for your fax or find it online at www.ricksteves.com/reservation. Photocopy and fax away.

One-Page Fax

To: _____ @ _____
              hotel   *fax*

From: _____ @ _____
              name   *fax*

Today's date: _____/_____ /_____
                   day   *month*   *year*

Dear Hotel _____ ,
Please make this reservation for me:

Name: _____

Total # of people:_____ # of rooms: _____ # of nights: _____

Arriving: _____ /____ /____   My time of arrival (24-hr clock): _____
              day *month* *year*   (I will telephone if I will be late)

Departing: ____ /____/____
              day *month* *year*

Room(s): Single _____ Double ___ Twin _____ Triple ___ Quad _____

With: Toilet _____ Shower _____ Bath _____ Sink only _____

Special needs: View ___ Quiet ___ Cheapest ___ Ground Floor ___

Please fax, mail, or e-mail confirmation of my reservation, along with the type of room reserved and the price. Please also inform me of your cancellation policy. After I hear from you, I will quickly send my credit-card information as a deposit to hold the room. Thank you.

_____
Signature

_____
Name

_____
Address

_____
City   *State*   *Zip Code*   *Country*

_____
E-mail Address

Spanish Survival Phrases

Spanish has a guttural sound similar to the J in Baja California. In the phonetics, the symbol for this clearing-your-throat sound is the italicized *h*.

Good day.	**Buenos días.**	**bway**-nohs **dee**-ahs
Do you speak English?	**¿Habla usted inglés?**	ah-blah oo-**stehd** een-**glays**
Yes. / No.	**Sí. / No.**	see / noh
I (don't) understand.	**(No) comprendo.**	(noh) kohm-**prehn**-doh
Please.	**Por favor.**	por fah-**bor**
Thank you.	**Gracias.**	**grah**-thee-ahs
I'm sorry.	**Lo siento.**	loh see-**ehn**-toh
Excuse me.	**Perdóneme.**	pehr-**doh**-nay-may
(No) problem.	**(No) problema.**	(noh) proh-**blay**-mah
Good.	**Bueno.**	**bway**-noh
Goodbye.	**Adiós.**	ah-dee-**ohs**
one / two	**uno / dos**	**oo**-noh / dohs
three / four	**tres / cuatro**	trays / **kwah**-troh
five / six	**cinco / seis**	**theen**-koh / says
seven / eight	**siete / ocho**	see-**eh**-tay / **oh**-choh
nine / ten	**nueve / diez**	**nway**-bay / dee-**ayth**
How much is it?	**¿Cuánto cuesta?**	**kwahn**-toh **kway**-stah
Write it?	**¿Me lo escribe?**	may loh ay-**skree**-bay
Is it free?	**¿Es gratis?**	ays **grah**-tees
Is it included?	**¿Está incluido?**	ay-**stah** een-kloo-**ee**-doh
Where can I buy / find...?	**¿Dónde puedo comprar / encontrar...?**	**dohn**-day **pway**-doh kohm-**prar** / ayn-kohn-**trar**
I'd like / We'd like...	**Quiero / Queremos...**	kee-**ehr**-oh / kehr-**ay**-mohs
...a room.	**...una habitación.**	**oo**-nah ah-bee-tah-thee-**ohn**
...a ticket to ___.	**...un billete para ___.**	oon bee-**yeh**-tay **pah**-rah
Is it possible?	**¿Es posible?**	ays poh-**see**-blay
Where is...?	**¿Dónde está...?**	**dohn**-day ay-**stah**
...the train station	**...la estación de trenes**	lah ay-stah-thee-**ohn** day **tray**-nays
...the bus station	**...la estación de autobuses**	lah ay-stah-thee-**ohn** day ow-toh-**boo**-says
...the tourist information office	**...la oficina de turismo**	lah oh-fee-**thee**-nah day too-**rees**-moh
Where are the toilets?	**¿Dónde están los servicios?**	**dohn**-day ay-**stahn** lohs sehr-**bee**-thee-ohs
men	**hombres, caballeros**	**ohm**-brays, kah-bah-**yay**-rohs
women	**mujeres, damas**	moo-**heh**-rays, **dah**-mahs
left / right	**izquierda / derecha**	eeth-kee-**ehr**-dah / day-**ray**-chah
straight	**derecho**	day-**ray**-choh
When do you open / close?	**¿A qué hora abren / cierran?**	ah kay **oh**-rah **ah**-brehn / thee-**ay**-rahn
At what time?	**¿A qué hora?**	ah kay **oh**-rah
Just a moment.	**Un momento.**	oon moh-**mehn**-toh
now / soon / later	**ahora / pronto / más tarde**	ah-**oh**-rah / **prohn**-toh / mahs **tar**-day
today / tomorrow	**hoy / mañana**	oy / mahn-**yah**-nah

In the Restaurant

I'd like / We'd like...	Quiero / Queremos...	kee-**ehr**-oh / kehr-**ay**-mohs
...to reserve...	...reservar...	ray-sehr-**bar**
...a table for one / two.	...una mesa para uno / dos.	**oo**-nah **may**-sah **pah**-rah **oo**-noh / dohs
Non-smoking.	No fumadores.	noh foo-mah-**doh**-rays
Is this table free?	¿Está esta mesa libre?	ay-**stah** ay-stah **may**-sah lee-bray
The menu (in English), please.	La carta (en inglés), por favor.	lah **kar**-tah (ayn een-**glays**) por fah-**bor**
service (not) included	servicio (no) incluido	sehr-**bee**-thee-oh (noh) een-kloo-**ee**-doh
cover charge	precio de entrada	**pray**-thee-oh day ayn-**trah**-dah
to go	para llevar	**pah**-rah yay-**bar**
with / without	con / sin	kohn / seen
and / or	y / o	ee / oh
menu (of the day)	menú (del día)	may-**noo** (dayl **dee**-ah)
specialty of the house	especialidad de la casa	ay-spay-thee-ah-lee-**dahd** day lah **kah**-sah
tourist menu	menú de turista	meh-**noo** day too-**ree**-stah
combination plate	plato combinado	**plah**-toh kohm-bee-**nah**-doh
appetizers	tapas	**tah**-pahs
bread	pan	pahn
cheese	queso	**kay**-soh
sandwich	bocadillo	boh-kah-**dee**-yoh
soup	sopa	**soh**-pah
salad	ensalada	ayn-sah-**lah**-dah
meat	carne	**kar**-nay
poultry	aves	**ah**-bays
fish	pescado	pay-**skah**-doh
seafood	marisco	mah-**ree**-skoh
fruit	fruta	**froo**-tah
vegetables	verduras	behr-**doo**-rahs
dessert	postres	**poh**-strays
tap water	agua del grifo	**ah**-gwah dayl **gree**-foh
mineral water	agua mineral	**ah**-gwah mee-nay-**rahl**
milk	leche	**lay**-chay
(orange) juice	zumo (de naranja)	**thoo**-moh (day nah-**rahn**-hah)
coffee	café	kah-**feh**
tea	té	tay
wine	vino	**bee**-noh
red / white	tinto / blanco	**teen**-toh / **blahn**-koh
glass / bottle	vaso / botella	**bah**-soh / boh-**tay**-yah
beer	cerveza	thehr-**bay**-thah
Cheers!	¡Salud!	sah-**lood**
More. / Another.	Más. / Otro.	mahs / **oh**-troh
The same.	El mismo.	ehl **mees**-moh
The bill, please.	La cuenta, por favor.	lah **kwayn**-tah por fah-**bor**
tip	propina	proh-**pee**-nah
Delicious!	¡Delicioso!	day-lee-thee-**oh**-soh

For hundreds more pages of survival phrases for your trip to Spain, check out *Rick Steves' Spanish Phrase Book.*

INDEX

Start your trip at
www.ricksteves.com

Rick Steves' website is packed with over 3,000 pages of timely travel information. It's also your gateway to getting FREE monthly travel news from Rick — and more!

Free Monthly European Travel News

Fresh articles on Europe's most interesting destinations and happenings. Rick will even send you an e-mail every month (often direct from Europe) with his latest discoveries!

Timely Travel Tips

Rick Steves' best money-and-stress-saving tips on trip planning, packing, transportation, hotels, health, safety, finances, hurdling the language barrier...and more.

Travelers' Graffiti Wall

Candid advice and opinions from thousands of travelers on everything listed above, plus whatever topics are hot at the moment (discount flights, packing tips, scams...you name it).

Rick's Annual Guide to European Railpasses

The clearest, most comprehensive guide to the confusing array of railpass options out there, and how to choo-choose the railpass that best fits your itinerary and budget. Then you can order your railpass (and get a bunch of great freebies) online from us!

Great Gear at the Rick Steves Travel Store

Enjoy bargains on Rick's guidebooks, planning maps and TV series DVDs—and on his custom-designed carry-on bags, wheeled bags, day bags and light-packing accessories.

Rick Steves Tours

Every year more than 5,000 lucky travelers explore Europe on a Rick Steves tour. Learn more about our 26 different one-to-three-week itineraries, read uncensored feedback from our tour alums, and sign up for your dream trip online!

Rick on TV

Read the scripts and see video clips from the popular Rick Steves' Europe TV series, and get an inside look at Rick's 13 newest shows.

Respect for Your Privacy

Ordering online from us is secure. When you buy something from us, join a tour, or subscribe to Rick's free monthly travel news e-mails, we promise to never share your name, information, or e-mail address with anyone else. You won't be spammed!

Have fun raising your Travel I.Q. at
www.ricksteves.com

Travel smart...carry on!

The latest generation of Rick Steves' carry-on travel bags is easily the best—benefiting from two decades of on-the-road attention to what really matters: maximum quality and strength; practical, flexible features; and no unnecessary frills. You won't find a better value anywhere!

Convertible, expandable, and carry-on-size:

Rick Steves' Back Door Bag $99

This is the same bag that Rick Steves lives out of for three months every summer. It's made of rugged water-resistant 1000 denier Cordura nylon, and best of all, it converts easily from a smart-looking suitcase to a handy backpack with comfortably-curved shoulder straps and a padded waistbelt.

This roomy, versatile 9" x 21" x 14" bag has a large 2600 cubic-inch main compartment, plus three outside pockets (small, medium and huge) that are perfect for often-used items. And the cinch-tight compression straps will keep your load compact and close to your back—not sagging like a sack of potatoes.

Wishing you had even more room to bring home souvenirs? Pull open the full-perimeter expando-zipper and its capacity jumps from 2600 to 3000 cubic inches. When you want to use it as a suitcase or check it as luggage (required when "expanded"), the straps and belt hide away in a zippered compartment in the back.

Attention travelers under 5'4" tall: This bag also comes in an inch-shorter version, for a compact-friendlier fit between the waistbelt and shoulder straps.

Convenient, durable, and carry-on-size:

Rick Steves' Wheeled Bag $119

At 9" x 21" x 14" our sturdy Rick Steves' Wheeled Bag is rucksack-soft in front, but the rest is lined with a hard ABS-lexan shell to give maximum protection to your belongings. We've spared no expense on moving parts, splurging on an extra-long button-release handle and big, tough inline skate wheels for easy rolling on rough surfaces.

This bag is not convertible! Our research tells us that travelers who've bought convertible wheeled bags never put them on their backs anyway, so we've eliminated the extra weight and expense.

Rick Steves' Wheeled Bag has exactly the same three-outside-pocket configuration as our Back Door Bag, plus a handy "add-a-bag" strap and full lining.

Our Back Door Bags and Wheeled Bags come in black, navy, blue spruce, evergreen and merlot.

For great deals on a wide selection of travel goodies, begin your next trip at the Rick Steves Travel Store!

Visit the Rick Steves Travel Store at
www.ricksteves.com

FREE-SPIRITED TOURS FROM

Rick Steves

Small Groups
Great Guides
Guaranteed Prices
No Grumps

**Best of Europe ▪ Eastern Europe
Italy ▪ Village Italy ▪ South Italy
France ▪ Britain ▪ Ireland
Heart of France ▪ South of France
Turkey ▪ Spain/Portugal
Germany/Austria/Switzerland
Scandinavia ▪ London ▪ Paris ▪ Rome
Venice ▪ Florence…and much more!**

Looking for a one, two, or three-week tour that's run in the Rick Steves style? Check out Rick Steves' educational, experiential tours of Europe.

Rick's tours are an excellent value compared to "mainstream" tours. Here's a taste of what you'll get…

- **Small groups:** With just 24-28 travelers, you'll go where typical groups of 40-50 can only dream.

- **Big buses:** You'll travel in a full-size 40-50 seat bus, with plenty of empty seats for you to spread out and be comfortable.

- **Great guides:** Our guides are hand-picked by Rick Steves for their wealth of knowledge and giddy enthusiasm for Europe.

- **No tips or kickbacks:** To keep your guide and driver 100% focused on giving you the best travel experience, we pay them good salaries—and prohibit them from taking tips and merchant kickbacks.

- **All sightseeing:** Your price includes all group sightseeing, with no hidden charges.

- **Central hotels:** You'll stay in Rick's favorite small, characteristic, locally-run hotels in the center of each city, within walking distance of the sights you came to see.

- **Peace of mind:** Your tour price is guaranteed for 2005; deposits are 100% refundable for two weeks; we include prorated trip interruption/cancellation coverage; single travelers don't need to pay an extra supplement; you can easily save a seat online at www.ricksteves.com.

Interested? Visit **www.ricksteves.com** or call (425) 771-8303 for a free copy of Rick Steves' 2005 Tour Catalog!

Rick Steves' Europe Through the Back Door
130 Fourth Avenue North, PO Box 2009, Edmonds, WA 98020 USA
Phone: (425) 771-8303 ▪ Fax: (425) 771-0833 ▪ www.ricksteves.com

Rick Steves

COUNTRY GUIDES 2005

France
Germany & Austria
Great Britain
Greece
Ireland
Italy
Portugal
Scandinavia
Spain
Switzerland

CITY GUIDES 2005

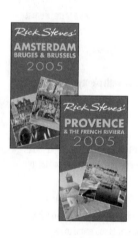

Amsterdam, Bruges & Brussels
Florence & Tuscany
London
Paris
Prague & The Czech Republic
Provence & The French Riviera
Rome
Venice

BEST OF GUIDES

Best European City Walks & Museums
Best of Eastern Europe
Best of Europe

More *Savvy.* More *Surprising.* More *Fun.*

PHRASE BOOKS & DICTIONARIES

French
French, Italian & German
German
Italian
Portuguese
Spanish

MORE EUROPE FROM RICK STEVES

Easy Access Europe
Europe 101
Europe Through the Back Door
Best European City Walks & Museums
Postcards from Europe

DVD RICK STEVES' EUROPE

Rick Steves' Europe All Thirty
    Shows 2000–2003
Britain & Ireland
Exotic Europe
Germany, The Swiss Alps
    & Travel Skills
Italy

For a complete list of Rick Steves' guidebooks, see page 7.

Avalon Travel Publishing
1400 65th Street, Suite 250, Emeryville, CA 94608

Avalon Travel Publishing
An Imprint of Avalon Publishing Group, Inc.

AVALON
publishing group incorporated

Distributed by Publishers Group West

For the latest on Rick Steves' lectures, guidebooks, tours, and public television series,
contact Europe Through the Back Door, Box 2009, Edmonds, WA 98020,
tel. 425/771-8303, fax 425/771-0833, www.ricksteves.com, rick@ricksteves.com.

ISBN 1-56691-884-7 • ISSN 1551-8388

Europe Through the Back Door Managing Editor: Risa Laib
Europe Through the Back Door Editors: Jennifer Hauseman, Lauren Mills
Avalon Travel Publishing Series Manager: Roxanna Font
Avalon Travel Publishing Project Editor: Patrick Collins
Copy Editor: Matthew Reed Baker
Research Assistance: Cameron Hewitt, Carlos Galvin, Debi Jo Michael
Production and Typesetting: Patrick David Barber
Production Coordinator: Amber Pirker
Cover Design: Kari Gim, Laura Mazer
Interior Design: Jane Musser, Laura Mazer, Amber Pirker
Maps and Graphics: David C. Hoerlein, Lauren Mills, Rhonda Pelikan, Zoey Platt, Mike
   Morgenfeld
Indexer: Greg Jewett
Front Matter Color Photos: p. i, Toledo, Spain © Getty Images/Photodisc Green; p. viii,
   Sagrada Família, Barcelona, Spain: © Digital Vision
Cover Photos: Back image: Nerja, Costa del Sol, Málaga, Spain: © Getty Images/Digital
   Vision; Front image: Gaudí's Batlló House, Barcelona, Spain © Jose Fuste
   Raga/CORBIS
Photography: David C. Hoerlein, Rick Steves, Cameron Hewitt, and Steve Smith
Avalon Travel Publishing Graphics Coordinator: Susan Snyder

Distributed to the book trade by Publishers Group West, Berkeley, California.